IN DEFENSE OF THE REPUBLIC
Readings in American Military History

IN DEFENSE OF THE REPUBLIC

Readings in American Military History

Edited by

DAVID CURTIS SKAGGS

Bowling Green State University

ROBERT S. BROWNING III

San Antonio Air Logistics Center

Wadsworth Publishing Company
Belmont, California
A Division of Wadsworth, Inc.

History Editor: Peggy Adams
Production Editor: Karen Garrison
Managing Designer: Cynthia Schultz
Print Buyer: Karen Hunt
Permissions Editor: Jeanne Bosschart
Text Designer: James Chadwick
Compositor: TCSystems, Inc.
Cover Designer: Harry Voigt
Cover Image: "Lobos Island, Mexico," drawing by David W. Haines.
From the Collections of the Dallas Historical Society

Printed in the United States of America   18
1 2 3 4 5 6 7 8 9 10—95 94 93 92 91

Library of Congress Cataloging in Publication Data

In defense of the Republic: readings in American military history/
  edited by David Curtis Skaggs, Robert S. Browning III.
      p.   cm.
   Includes bibliographical references and index.
   ISBN 0-534-14610-4
   1. United States—History, Military.   I. Skaggs, David Curtis.
II. Browning, Robert S.
E181.I49   1991
973—dc20
ISBN 0-534-14610-4   90-44308

CONTENTS

v

INTRODUCTION

Ever since the first English attempts at settlement along the coast of North America, Americans have been writing—and reading—military history. Military leaders have been celebrated in story and song. And more than one American has used military service, and his ensuing fame, as a springboard to a career in politics. The United States won its political independence on the battlefield and expanded westward behind an army that not only protected the frontier but also explored and mapped the routes followed later by thousands of settlers. Political issues involving the relationship between the states and the federal government, as well as the moral question of slavery, were settled ultimately in the ferociously contested Civil War, which left a legacy of bitterness diminished only by time. American soldiers and sailors spearheaded overseas expansion, and in the twentieth century Americans have fought and died in nearly every corner of the world. War and military affairs have loomed large in American history; indeed, military history cannot be separated from the larger story of the American experience.

Yet military history has never enjoyed complete acceptance as a legitimate specialty among academic historians. Wars and military affairs represented a darker side of the American character, a reminder of a violent aspect of our history rather than a part of national progress. As one of the humanities, "real" history involved the study of political, economic, intellectual, or social trends that illustrated the growth of American civilization. The study of war, on the other hand, seemed to emphasize destruction and violence, exactly what humanistic scholars abhorred the most. America, after all, stood for democracy and economic opportunity, for toleration and generosity, not for massed armies, fleets, and bombers. A reminder of past wars, military history also implied the potential of conflict in the future.

In part this situation was due to the emphasis within military history writing, which tended to concentrate on operational aspects of war—on tactics, strategy, and generalship. Military history served as a tool for training young officers and was thus often written by soldiers (or ex-soldiers) for other military men who could derive from its study appropriate lessons of the past to be applied in the future. Although a few historians explored other topics, military history rarely dealt with the interaction between the military establishment and the larger society. Given this context, it is not surprising that many academic historians believed that military history tended to needlessly glorify war and served to militarize society.

However, in the years after World War II this point of view slowly began to change. The armed services employed numerous professional historians to record the military operations of that massive conflict, and these scholars observed firsthand the complex and continuous interaction of politics, economics, and societal pressures with purely military operations and decision making. Moreover, the immense growth of the American military establishment following the war and the impact of that establishment upon American society was simply too large to ignore. Historians began increasingly to examine American military history as part of an ongoing process rather than as a series of isolated episodes.

Perhaps the leading example of this trend, and certainly one of the most important, was Walter Millis's landmark study of the American military, *Arms and Men*, first published in 1956. Millis argued persuasively that U.S. wars and military affairs had not taken place in a vacuum. "War," he wrote, "war preparations, military tactics and strategy, military manpower questions, military economics, are not problems arising only suddenly and sporadically in times of international emergency; they are continuous factors within the fabric of our society." In other words, the context of American military history was far broader and more complex than previously thought. The study of military history included the investigation of many topics beyond the traditional ones of battlefield tactics and generalship and encompassed the impact of technological change on military thought; the cultural, societal, and political forces that shaped the military establishment; the impact of military service upon the individual; and the ways military procurement practices influenced the national economy. While the importance of military events during wartime has always been clear, the current research concerning the American experience shows that the influence of military affairs does not stop with the conclusion of hostilities. Millis was right. Just as uniquely national needs and conditions shaped the development of the military establishment, America's growth and progress have been profoundly affected by its armed forces.

The selections that follow illustrate a variety of approaches now taken in the study of U.S. military history. Not all of them represent examples of the so-called new military history. Some reflect the continuing tradition of the more familiar "drum and bugle" history—the study of generals, tactics, and strategic thought. Yet even these more traditional studies are not, and cannot be, immune from the influence of the changes taking place in the investigation of the American military experience. For instance, in his analysis of Civil War infantry tactics, John K. Mahon forces us to realize the importance of technological change upon military operations and suggests some reasons why military institutions are—like all national institutions—sometimes reluctant or unable to change immediately in response to an altered environment. The face of battle and the troopers' motivations are made clearer in the essays of Robert Middlekauff and Rick Atkinson, which effectively remember the often forgotten human element in military operations.

Other selections provide a new perspective on the American military. Russell F. Weigley's conclusions regarding the development of military thought before World War II suggest some of the ways in which military institutions are shaped by historical forces of which they may not even be aware. John Shy's brilliant and innovative survey of the American military experience combines the basic concepts of learning theory with more familiar information to create an entirely new and thought-provoking way of looking at the forces that shaped the development of the American military.

Perhaps the most important aspect of the articles in this book is that they supply fresh ways of seeing familiar things. Together, they place the study of military, naval, and aerospace history in its larger context. It is simply one more way to study the American experience and one more way of helping us understand the world and nation in which we live.

We selected articles for a first course in American military history. Such introductory courses normally contain more students who are not history majors than do most upper-division history courses. For that reason we avoided discussions of historiographic issues and other topics mostly of interest to professional historians. At the same time we sought readings from some of the country's most distinguished scholars of America's military past. Military history concerns not just the clash of arms but also professionalization, strategic planning, technological change, and logistical support. Each article stands by itself. Yet there is a relatedness among many of them, as the introductions point out. We want the readers to see these essays not in isolation but rather in conjunction with one another.

In making these selections, we must acknowledge a debt of gratitude to friends and colleagues who offered advice and encouragement whenever asked and without stint. Professors Russell F. Weigley of Temple University and Allan R. Millett of Ohio State University were especially generous with their time, advice, and support. We followed many of their suggestions, and this anthology is better because of them. We thank the following individuals who reviewed the book in manuscript form: Edward K. Eckert, Saint Bonaventure University; Charles W. Johnson, University of Tennessee, Knoxville; Charles E. Kirkpatrick, U.S. Army Center of Military History; Major David Lamm, United States Military Academy, West Point; J. Gregory Oswald, University of Arizona; Richard Sadler, Weber State University; and Kenneth B. Shover, The University of Texas at El Paso. And we are very grateful to each of the authors whose work appears in this collection. Their efforts have created a generation of scholarship that we are able to sample here. Obviously, there are other writers and writings and other subjects we could have included. The limits of space forced us to narrow our selection list.

We appreciate the consent of the authors and publishers to print these pieces without the usual scholarly annotation. We decided to eliminate the footnotes in the interest of both brevity and readability. Those interested in the supporting evidence for an author's conclusions should consult the original books and journals in which these essays were published. As we noted, the selection process was not easy. That there are so many good, innovative, and intellectually stimulating articles now available testifies to the continuing and growing vitality of American military history scholarship. We encourage our readers to suggest additional or alternative selections for future editions of this anthology.

David Curtis Skaggs
Bowling Green State University
Bowling Green, Ohio

Robert S. Browning III
Kelly Air Force Base
San Antonio, Texas

ACKNOWLEDGMENTS

*T*he selections included are reprinted from the following sources.

John Mahon, "Anglo-American Methods of Indian Warfare, 1676–1794," *Mississippi Valley Historical Review*, 45 (September 1958): 254–275. Reprinted with permission.

R. Arthur Bowler, "Logistics and Operations in the American Revolution" in Don Higginbotham, ed., *Reconsiderations on the Revolutionary War: Selected Essays*, "Contributions in Military History, No. 14" (Westport, Conn.: Greenwood Press, 1978), 54–71. Copyright © 1978 by Don Higginbotham. Reprinted with permission.

David Syrett, "Defeat at Sea: The Impact of American Naval Operations upon the British, 1775–1778" in *Maritime Dimensions of the American Revolution* (Washington: Government Printing Office, 1977): 13–21.

Robert Middlekauff, "Why Men Fought in the American Revolution," *Huntington Library Quarterly*, 43 (Spring 1980): 135–148. Reprinted with permission.

Richard H. Kohn, "The Murder of the Militia System in the Aftermath of the American Revolution," *The Military History of the Revolution: Proceedings of the Sixth Military History Symposium, USAF Academy 1974* (Washington: Government Printing Office, 1976): 110–126. Reprinted with permission.

William B. Skelton, "Professionalization of the U.S. Army Officer Corps during the Age of Jackson," *Armed Forces and Society*, 1 (August 1975): 443–471. Copyright © 1975 by the Inter-University Seminar on Armed Forces & Society. Reprinted with permission of Transaction Publishers.

John K. Mahon, "Civil War Infantry Assault Tactics," *Military Affairs*, 25 (Summer 1961): 57–78. Reprinted with permission.

Edward K. Eckert, "The McClellans and the Grants: Generalship and Strategy in the Civil War," *Military Review*, 55 (June 1975): 58–67.

John D. Milligan, "From Theory to Application: The Emergence of the American Ironclad War Vessel," *Military Affairs*, 40 (July 1984): 126–132. Reprinted with permission.

Allan R. Millett, *Military Professionalism and Officership in America* (Columbus, Ohio: Mershon Center of Ohio State University, 1977): 12–22. Reprinted with permission.

John M. Gates, "Indians and Insurrectos: The U.S. Army's Experience with Insurgency," *Parameters*, 12 (March 1983): 59–68. Reprinted with permission.

John H. Maurer, "Fuel and the Battle Fleet: Coal, Oil, and American Naval Strategy, 1898–1925," *Naval War College Review*, 34 (November-December 1981): 60–77.

Edward M. Coffman, "American Command and Commanders in World War I" in Russell F. Weigley, ed., *New Dimensions in Military History* (Novato, Calif.: Presidio Press, 1976): 17–34. Reprinted with permission.

Donald Smythe, "St.-Mihiel: The Birth of an American Army," *Parameters*, 12 (June 1983): 47–57.

Dean C. Allard, "Anglo-American Naval Differences during World War I, *Military Affairs*, 44 (April 1980): 75–81. Reprinted with permission.

Russell F. Weigley, "To the Crossing of the Rhine: American Strategic Thought to World War II," *Armed Forces and Society*, 5 (February 1979): 302–320. Copyright © 1979 by the Inter-University Seminar on Armed Forces & Society. Reprinted with permission of Transaction Publishers.

Eugene Emme, "Air Power and Warfare, 1903–1941: The American Dimension," *Air Power and Warfare, Proceedings of the Eighth Military History Symposium, USAF Academy, 1979* (Washington: Government Printing Office, 1980): 56–82.

Martin Blumenson, "D-Day: Launching the 'Great Crusade,'" *Army*, 34 (June 1984): 22–37. Copyright 1984 by the Association of the U.S. Army and reproduced with permission.

Martin Van Crevald, *Supplying War: Logistics from Wallenstein to Patton* (Cambridge, Eng.: Cambridge University Press, 1977): 216–230. Reprinted with permission of the Cambridge University Press.

Louis Morton, "War Plan ORANGE Evolution of a Strategy," *World Politics*, 11 (January 1959): 221–250. Copyright © 1959 by Princeton University Press. Reprinted with permission of Princeton University Press.

John W. Mountcastle, "From Bayou to Beachhead: The Marines and Mr. Higgins," *Military Review*, 70 (March 1980): 20–29.

Robert Ross Smith, "Luzon Versus Formosa" in Kent Roberts Greenfield, ed., *Command Decisions* (Washington: Government Printing Office, 1960): 461–477.

Wayne P. Hughes, *Fleet Tactics: Theory and Practice* (Annapolis, Md.: U.S. Naval Institute Press, 1986): 85–110. Copyright © 1986, U.S. Naval Institute. Reprinted with permission.

Ronald Lewin, *The American Magic: Codes, Ciphers and the Defeat of Japan* (New York: Farrar, Straus & Giroux, 1982): 218–231. Copyright © 1982 by Ronald Lewin. Reprinted with permission of the publishers.

George H. Quester, "The Impact of Strategic Air Warfare," *Armed Forces and Society*, 4 (Winter 1978): 179–206. Copyright © 1978 by the Inter-University Seminar on Armed Forces & Society. Reprinted with permission of Transaction Publishers.

Harry L. Coles, "Strategic Studies Since 1945: The Era of Overthink," *Military Review*, 53 (April 1973): 3–16. Reprinted with permission.

George V. Herring, "American Strategy in Vietnam: The Postwar Debate," *Military Affairs*, 46 (April 1982): 57–63. Reprinted with permission.

Roy K. Flint, "The Relief of MacArthur" in Roy K. Flint, Peter W. Kozumplik, and Thomas J. Waraksa, *Selected Readings in Warfare since 1945* (West Point, N.Y.: Department of History, USMA, 1981): 152–156. Reprinted with permission.

Rick Atkinson, *The Long Gray Line* (Boston: Houghton Mifflin Company, 1989): 209–222, 227. Copyright © 1989 by Rick Atkinson. Reprinted with permission.

Daniel P. Bolger, *Americans at War: 1975–1986, An Era of Violent Peace* (Novato, Calif.: Presidio Press, 1988): 443–452. Reprinted with permission of Presidio Press. Copyright 1988.

John Shy, "The American Military Experience: History and Learning," *Journal of Interdisciplinary History,* 1 (1971): 205–228. © 1971 by The Massachusetts Institute of Technology and the editors of *The Journal of Interdisciplinary History.* Reprinted with permission of the editors of *The Journal of Interdisciplinary History* and MIT Press, Cambridge, Massachusetts.

THE COLONIAL ERA

JOHN K. MAHON

ANGLO-AMERICAN METHODS OF INDIAN WARFARE, 1676–1794

*F*rom *the beginning of the first English settlement at Roanoke, North Carolina, in 1587, until the battle of Wounded Knee, South Dakota, in 1890, the most consistent military foe facing the Anglo-Americans was the American Indian. Whether one is speaking of combat by colonial or territorial militias or by British or American regulars, frontier warfare remained a constant in military operations for over three hundred years. Each side had to adapt to the strategy and tactics of the other. But each side also maintained a consistency in tactics that persisted from the beginning until Wounded Knee. With very few exceptions, the central Indian tactics were surprise, ambush, and ruse. The Anglo-Americans invariably incorporated firepower, frontal assaults, fortifications, and destruction of Indian subsistence capabilities in their operations.*

Dr. John K. Mahon, professor emeritus of history at the University of Florida, is one of the leading authorities on early American military strategy and tactics. Best known for his studies of the Second Seminole War and the War of 1812, he is unusually adept at analyzing the impact of tactics upon military operations. The Anglo-Americans gradually learned the critical importance of discipline and security to the success of expeditions into the continental interior. Some of the whites' greatest defeats came when these lessons were ignored. For instance, in the defeats of General Edward Braddock on the banks of the Monongahela in 1755, of Colonel William Crawford in the Sandusky Valley in 1782, and of General Arthur St. Clair in the Old Northwest in 1791, a lack of discipline led to security lapses that resulted in major victories for the native Americans. But when security and discipline were maintained, success usually

3

accompanied the whites—as in General John Sullivan's Iroquois campaign of 1779 and General Anthony Wayne's Fallen Timbers campaign of 1794.

Long before the opening of King Philip's War with which Professor Mahon begins this article, British colonists learned that their most successful tactic was to destroy the enemy's villages and crops, thereby depriving the Indians of their sustenance. This remained a consistent military policy through the Seminole wars and in the campaigns on the Great Plains and in the Southwest. Such a policy often forced the natives to stand and fight from fortifications. As Mahon notes, the superior firepower and organization of white armies usually resulted in victory in these encounters, such as at Mystic, Connecticut, in 1637.

Continued woodlands fighting caused the whites to adopt several Indian tactics, such as the use of light infantry. The most famous of these units, Major Robert Rogers' rangers and Colonel Daniel Morgan's Virginia riflemen, were exceptionally valuable auxiliaries to the main armies to which they were attached.

At the same time, the Indians, particularly the southern ones and those on the Great Plains, incorporated the Europeans' imported horses into their operations, thereby increasing both their mobility and their logistical requirements. Beginning in the eighteenth century, the Indians were particularly adept in military cooperation with the white antagonists in the many wars for empire during the 1690–1815 era. Of significant note are the ways the Iroquois and the Creeks exploited European-American rivalries for their own benefit and survival. Thus, in such conflicts known in America as King William's War (1689–97), Queen Anne's War (1701–13), King George's War (1744–48), the French and Indian War (1754–63), the American Revolution (1775–83), and the War of 1812 (1812–15), Indian diplomats used their leverage with one side or the other to secure what they felt would be to their greatest advantage. The beginning of the long peace along the Canadian–United States border that followed the War of 1812, and the ending of Spanish outposts on the southern and western frontiers that followed the sale of Louisiana and Florida to the Americans, denied the Indians the allies they needed to continue to resist encroachments onto their lands.

Historical writing always reflects the contemporary environment in which it was written. Thus readers will note Professor Mahon's occasional references to the Native Americans as "savages" and to their methods of combat as "the ravages of the Indians." These loaded phrases in one of the most distinguished journals of American historical scholarship clearly indicate that Mahon was writing in the 1950s and they no longer reflect attitudes expressed in historical writings.

Readers should compare this article with the "Indians and Insurrectos" essay of John M. Gates, published later in this anthology. How do Gates's conclusions, relative to the trans-Mississippi Indian wars in the west, compare with the combat experienced in the eastern woodland wars and with subsequent guerrilla operations of the army? Do these experiences have any relevance to contemporary military operations?

The methods of Indian warfare developed in the English colonies in America by the late eighteenth century owed a great deal to trial and error techniques of earlier years. The first settlers, seldom effectively organized for warfare, were forced to fight as individuals or as part of local groups hastily and informally put together by the pressures of Indian raids or threats of war. Their exploits—and their captivities—have become part of our folklore. The more effective Indian warfare, however, was that carried on in a better organized fashion by groups supported by England or by a colonial governmental body. An analysis of colonial Indian warfare reveals a simple truth which our folklore has tended to obscure: that trained regular soldiery, first the redcoats and then their American counterparts, were more important than unorganized frontiersmen in breaking the power of the Indians.

The importance of organized soldiery became clear by the later years of the seventeenth century. King Philip's War in New England, which ended in 1676, though it was not a turning point in weapons or tactics, did mark a change in the scope of Indian-white warfare. Whereas prior to it the actions were mostly local affairs, afterwards they were nearly all linked with the great struggle for the control of North America. They remained so linked at least until the Battle of Fallen Timbers in 1794, when the fledgling United States won its first large-scale victory over the redskins. In that affair the United States Army, known then as the Legion, owed its triumph to methods which had been developed since 1676, forgotten in the meantime, and then revived once more.

Methods of Indian warfare were determined in part by the types of weapons available, and the weapons of Indians and whites were changing in the course of the colonial period. During the first forty years of the seventeenth century the Indians were shifting from bows and arrows to the firearms used by the colonists. There was a brisk business in Europe in the manufacture of muskets for the Indian trade, and by the middle of the century the French, the Dutch, and the English were carrying on an extensive exchange of guns and ammunition for furs in spite of official efforts to discourage such trade. The guns, known as "trade muskets," had the same fire power as those used by the whites, but they were usually more cheaply made, and were not fitted to mount a bayonet.

Adoption of the firearm by the Indians took longer in some areas than in others. As early as King Philip's War the warriors in New England had converted almost entirely to muskets, while forty years later in South Carolina (1715) the Yamassees still used many bows in their fight for survival. In any case, observers estimated that the change was virtually complete east of the Alleghenies by 1730; and in the opinion of some of the colonists it made the red men less formidable. William Byrd of Virginia, for example, noted in 1728 that the Indians had been able to shoot several arrows a minute, in silence, but could seldom get off more than one round of shot, and that with great noise, in the same time. He observed, too, that their adoption of firearms made them increasingly dependent on the English for weapons and ammunition. Time, however, tended to eliminate these advantages. Even so, the Indians never really mastered the white man's weapon. They were careless with their guns, yet did not learn to repair arms, much less to make them; and they rarely acquired the ability to make gunpowder. On the other hand, they were so valuable as allies to the European nations, struggling for control of the continent, that they usually had enough bargaining power to obtain the firearms and ammunition needed.

The firearm most common among the English colonists in the period (and most often used in trade with the Indians) was a smoothbore musket, caliber .69-.71, which fired a round lead ball weighing in the neighborhood of one ounce. The weapon itself, between nine and ten pounds in weight, was loaded at the muzzle and fired by means of a flint and steel mechanism. A very skillful musketeer could discharge three rounds a minute and could hit a man-sized target at one hundred yards perhaps four times in ten shots. Much better known, but less important in Indian warfare or as a trade gun, was the so-called Kentucky rifle, English North America's major contribution in the field of shoulder arms. Developed in Pennsylvania in the first quarter of the eighteenth century, the Kentucky was a true rifle with spiral grooves in the bore which imparted spin to the round bullet. Fired by flint and steel, and otherwise closely resembling the best of muskets in size and weight, it could be loaded faster than previous rifles. It was accuracy instead of speed, however, that gave it superiority. Whereas the musket was not expected to hit its target beyond one hundred yards, and did not even have a rear sight, the Kentucky was accurate up to three hundred yards. But it had serious disadvantages. Although it could be loaded faster than other rifles, it still took three times as long to load as a musket. More important, it was not made to mount a bayonet, and thus it was disqualified for effective use in the type of Indian fighting that depended upon shock action rather than weapons-fire to inflict destructive defeats. It came to be most widely employed, therefore, by frontiersmen acting singly or in small, loosely organized groups.

Unlike the rifle, the bayonet enhanced the power of the rank-and-file soldier. First devised in Europe around 1640, this weapon was introduced in the colonies before the end of the century. Samuel Sewall of Boston entered in his diary in 1687 that he had seen fifteen or twenty redcoats "with small guns and short lances in the tops of them." These were probably the first bayonets to reach this side of the Atlantic. They were part of the equipment of the regulars who had been sent with Sir Edmund Andros to establish the Dominion of New England. Although not used against Indians until some seventy years thereafter, bayonets at length became a decisive weapon in organized Indian fighting. Only disciplined bodies of soldiers could make effective use of them. The Indians, being virtually without discipline in their fighting methods, never adopted bayonets, but continued instead to rely on knife and tomahawk for infighting.

Another military weapon monopolized by the whites was artillery. The Indians never utilized even captured pieces. For example, when they inflicted a severe defeat on the army commanded by General Arthur St. Clair along the Miami River in 1791, they merely sank the captured cannon in a nearby swamp. Not only did they fail to use the big guns, they could rarely bring themselves to bear up long under artillery fire. There was nothing in the code of North American Indians which required warriors to endure a volume of fire they could not match. Instead, they would withdraw and return when the odds were more in their favor.

Closely related to the use of weapons as well as to warfare in a broader sense was the use of the horse in Indian warfare. In general, notwithstanding the heavy forest which blanketed eastern North America, horses, when used properly, added speed and mobility to military movements. So skillful an Indian fighter as Colonel Henry Bouquet thought light-horse troops essential in conjunction with light infantry. Anthony Wayne, too, used light-horse units with effect in the Fallen Timbers campaign in 1794. Although Wayne assigned his mounted troops to turn the Indian flanks in this battle, soldiers did not normally fight on horseback but used mounts simply to get them to the battle area. There were no clashes between men on horseback, with one exception—Colonel William Crawford's expedition into the Sandusky Plain region south of Lake Erie in 1782. Here some of the Indians had learned to fight on horseback, and in this particular case they were encouraged by a mounted detachment of Canadians from the famous British scouting unit known as Butler's Rangers.

Because the frontiersmen were usually unwilling to walk if there was any chance to ride, they frequently made the use of horses a condition of entering volunteer service. More often than not the result was to slow down, not to speed up, movement. One reason was that citizen soldiers would mercilessly overload their mounts. Another was that they usually selected their poorest old cobs for a campaign in order to save the good horses from injury. The typical result can be seen in Dunmore's War in 1774. The horses simply broke down and had to be rested. While the army was immobilized, in three columns too far apart to support each other, the Indians took advantage of the opportunity to open fire on one of the columns, and their action brought on the indecisive battle at Point Pleasant. Similarly, the determination of the volunteers to ride as far as possible into the zone of action before dismounting to assume a fighting formation helped to bring disaster to Crawford's command in 1782. At the moment when the soldiers were trying to form on foot to meet the Indian attack they were demoralized by a herd of overloaded, frightened horses milling about among them.

In general, the Indians of the forest region did not acquire horses in the seventeenth century, but after 1740 an Indian without a horse was rare, especially in the South. Yet these animals figured very little in their fighting techniques, and the use of horses in 1782 by the natives at Sandusky Plain was not at all typical. It is not surprising, therefore, that since they were used so sparingly the availability of horses did not measurably change the Indians' methods of warfare during the eighteenth century. Curiously, these methods were little more changed by the introduction of firearms, although the use of firearms had become common among the Indians.

Despite the fact that a change in weapons might have suggested a change in tactics, the method of warfare waged by the Indians followed a general pattern in the period between King Philip's War and the Battle of Fallen Timbers. The American Indians, normally the first to strike in warfare with the whites, in the main relied upon only one basic offensive tactic, surprise. They did not have the social organization needed to plan and execute operations of a more complicated nature, such as group maneuvers or frontal assault. Relying on surprise attack, their target was rarely an organized force of whites but rather isolated cabins and villages. Following the pattern of primitive warmakers in general, they usually sought to surround these and attack at dawn. Often during the eighteenth century their raids were under the direction of one or two white officers. Although this brought no remarkable alterations in pattern, it did produce forays in the dead of winter, something to which the Indians alone probably would not have resorted. Good examples are the assault on Deerfield, Massachusetts, in 1704 and Rale's War in 1723.

On several occasions the surprise attack was engineered with special skill. In 1711, for example, the Tuscaroras, in rare cooperation with four neighboring tribes, nearly wiped out a number of settlements in North Carolina. Surprise here sprang from an uncommon achievement—the preservation of perfect secrecy. No Indian woman betrayed the plot to white husband or lover, and the colonists suspected nothing to the last. So poorly was the Carolina militia system developed that Governor Edward Hyde could rally only 160 fighting men. These guarded the survivors, crowded into log forts, while the governor sent off frantic appeals to the neighboring colonies of Virginia and South Carolina for help.

A unique ruse achieved the desired surprise at Fort Michilimackinac at the start of Pontiac's War in June, 1763. Indians and white men there, at least so far as the latter knew, were on good terms, and on the day of the attack the small garrison was relaxed, anticipating no immediate danger. From time to time squaws entered the stockade, as was their custom, but on this day they were carrying weapons concealed in their clothes. Meanwhile, Indian warriors engaged in a game of lacrosse outside the fort, and most of the white soldiers went out to watch. When all was ready, one of the players lobbed the ball over the stockade, the teams rushed in after it, snatched the weapons from the squaws, and launched a fierce and barbarous slaughter of the whites.

In most cases where the attack was made upon a party of whites abroad in the forest, surprise was achieved by means of ambush. This was especially successful in attacking non-military groups such as exploring parties or moving settlers, but it was also used in those infrequent instances in which Indians made a sustained attack on an organized group of soldiers. For example, an engagement in Maine in 1725, known as Lovewell's Fight, began when a company of volunteers led by Captain John Lovewell advanced through the woods in pursuit of a single red man. This Indian, however, was acting as a decoy, and at an appointed moment a large body of Pequaket warriors rose from the brush on three sides and fired. In the ensuing fight the Indians deviated from the usual pattern by breaking cover and rushing in mass toward the whites. Then, after volleying at one another in the open, both sides closed in and grappled hand to hand. The soldiers could have expected the ambush, but they were not prepared to cope with this unexpected departure from the Indians' customary style of fighting.

Indian offensive tactics—aside from raids on isolated cabins and villages—were well summarized by Colonel Henry Bouquet, one of the most skillful professional soldiers who fought them during the eighteenth century. Bouquet, a Swiss serving as an officer in the British army, said there were three basic principles in the Indian's method of fighting: first, fight scattered; second, try to surround; and third, give ground when hard pressed and return when the pressure eased. He understood clearly that an Indian warrior had no intention of exposing himself if he could help it, and no determination to stand ground in the European style and fight to the last man. The war concept of the savages did not demand this sort of sacrifice.

In their defense against the Indians, white forces in the field could, and often successfully did, avoid ambush. On the other hand, there was no adequate defense, short of a twenty-four-hour watch every day of the year, against raids on habitations. Every settler's cabin was a vulnerable point, and the best that could be done was to reduce the degree of ever-present danger. To that end log forts were constructed in all the colonies; but in many instances they were not properly located for effective defense. For example, when the Yamassee tribe and allies attacked South Carolina settlements in 1715 it was found that the forts were too far apart to support each other, and the construction of ten new ones was authorized. Wherever there were groups of settlers, as in the New England frontier communities, blockhouses were built to serve as places of refuge for families in case of attack. Each exposed village contained at least one fortified structure, normally made of heavy logs cut to provide loopholes for musketry, and with the second story projected beyond the first to form an overhanging gallery which provided a protected platform from which defenders could beat off attempts to storm the building.

Besides blockhouses, there were many true forts built and maintained by colonial or federal and state governments. The cost of building was high, that of keeping a garrison higher still. Costs notwithstanding, by the time of the French and Indian War a chain of forts extended from New York to southern Virginia. The term "chain" sounds effective, but the chain itself displayed all the weaknesses of any passive defense system. The forts were never big enough to harbor all settlers who needed protection. Moreover, it was simple for the savages to pass between the strong points, raid the territory beyond, and slip away unharmed. The forts, like the Maginot Line in its time, tended to lull the apprehensions of settlers, but strategists saw the need for something to link them and at the same time seal the miles between them.

To fill this requirement all the colonies, and later the states, experimented with rangers. When weather and terrain permitted, rangers rode horseback, scouring the gaps between forts for signs of Indians. In New England horses were not practicable in winter time, and the scouts had to resort to snowshoes. On rare occasions rangers were full-time employees of colony, state, or nation; but more often, to save expense, they were qualified militiamen. Forts, and the rangers to scout between them, being forms of passive defense, required expenditures which tended to outrun the value received. Massachusetts utilized both forts and rangers during Queen Anne's War (1702–1713) and, according to Francis Parkman, spent about a thousand pounds for each Indian killed. If the taxpayers would bear such costs, a certain amount of protection resulted. In some instances, as is evident from a comparison of Pennsylvania and Virginia experience during the Pontiac uprising in 1763, protection on the frontier was proportionate to the enterprise of colonial governments. Virginia kept one thousand militiamen on duty at the frontier, and thus held depredations down. The Pennsylvania assembly, on the other hand, dominated by Quakers, authorized a smaller number of militia and confined their operations in such a manner as to leave the border settlers to their own devices, which meant leaving them to the ravages of the Indians. Whatever the defenses, casualties were high. George Croghan, one of the leading Indian traders and British agents, estimated that two thousand frontier folk were killed and thousands more ruined during the few months of Pontiac's War.

Since the Indians could strike wherever there was a frontier cabin or village, no satisfactory system of passive defense was ever devised. None was possible. As a result, in the year 1794 the federal government was still plagued with the same problem that had faced British commanders and colonial administrators. If the problem was the same, so were the recognized solutions. Henry Knox, the secretary of war, preferred rangers without forts, but for political reasons he was obliged to agree to a chain of blockhouses along the western border of Georgia, then the principal trouble spot. In the division of costs, which was arrived at more easily than in colonial times, it was agreed that Georgia would build the forts and provide the garrison, but the United States would pay the men.

Although the forts did not provide complete protection, their value was indicated in part by the fact that the Indians rarely attempted to storm a fortified place. Their first resort was to try to burn out the defenders. If fire failed they sometimes laid siege, but not in the formalized European style. A conspicuous exception occurred at Presqu'Isle in 1763 during Pontiac's War. There a war party, apparently coached by a white man who was with it, dug regular approach trenches, but unlike Europeans, it did not attempt an assault from the approaches. At Fort Pitt, on the other hand, Indians came close to assault when they gained the ditch just under the palisade. Once there, they brought upon themselves a time-tested siege weapon seldom used against red men. Soldiers tossed grenades over the stockade and dislodged them.

Much less frequently than white men, Indians themselves were sometimes defenders of fortified places. The Pequots had made their last stand in 1637, near the present town of Mystic, Connecticut, behind a log palisade. So had Philip's Narraganset and Wampanoag warriors in Rhode Island in 1675. Farther south about three decades later the Tuscaroras, in January, 1712, retired into a strong log stockade to repel the attack of South Carolinians and Yamassees. Their stockade had a trench, portholes that could be opened and closed, a rough abatis, and four round bastions. John Barnwell, the Carolina commander, believed that a runaway Negro had taught the tribe to fortify so well. In the Northwest, the Fox Indians, living on the shores of Lake Michigan, made a determined stand against the French in 1716 behind a strong palisade of three rows of heavy oak logs. Between rows they dug shallow pits from which to fire. Indian defenses behind log fortifications, however, were less effective than those of white men. There were two reasons: first, organized bodies of white men assaulted forts without delay and carried them, something rarely achieved by the natives; second, white attackers sometimes dragged cannon into position, and cannon spelled the doom of any Indian fort.

Whether the savages were in forts or out of them, white men, even before 1650, had found that the only sure way to defend themselves was to take the offensive. Some branch of government—if one existed which had the strength to raise and maintain troops—frequently organized punitive expeditions following Indian raids. Now and again the strength, but not the will, existed in government. The seaboard leaders, who usually controlled colonial and state governments, often were unwilling to help the backcountry people against the natives. The reasons for their unwillingness varied, sometimes being no more than the desire of private gain from the Indian trade.

When the whites took the offensive they resorted to a method of warfare which had been developed to cope with the unwillingness of the Indians to stand and fight in European fashion. They found that the most effective way to bring about a direct encounter with an Indian fighting force was to threaten the foundations upon which it stood—that is, the native fields and families. The technique was fairly simple and changed little throughout the colonial period. Adopting the Indian practice of surprise attack, the whites would surround a camp or village at night and attack it at dawn. This sort of surprise could be repeated again and again because of the failure of the Indians to post guards at night. Unable to use their favorite tactics of ambush and encirclement when thus attacked, and forced to defend their families and food supplies, the Indians had no alternative but to stand and fight, and when faced by trained soldiers usually to suffer defeat.

By the middle of the eighteenth century British regular troops were being sent to the colonies in larger numbers than before, and they were coming to play a much more significant role in Indian warfare than had been the case in the earlier colonial period. But they, along with some of the colonists, were still in the process of learning by experience how to meet an Indian ambush and encirclement. Although British soldiers had been in America in small numbers since 1664, their first major battle with the Indians took place in 1755 when General Edward Braddock led his troops on the disastrous expedition into western Pennsylvania. His defeat by the Indians forced British authorities to come to grips with the special problems of Indian fighting. Also, this battle is a good starting point from which to trace the major tactical developments in Indian warfare to the end of the century.

The first of these developments came about in an effort to devise greater security for an army operating against Indians in forest country. Braddock's column was surprised, and then enveloped, chiefly because it did not have the necessary complement of native scouts. This lack was a consequence of intertribal and intercolonial politics, and was not the General's fault. Wherever the fault lay, the outcome demonstrated very clearly to alert observers that a European army must try to develop a dependable substitute for Indian scouts.

The first attempt to provide a substitute was to enlist units of frontiersmen skilled in forest ways. The most famous, and perhaps the earliest, of these was Rogers' Rangers, commanded by Major Robert Rogers. It was composed of a varying number of companies, nominally, but never in practice, associated as a battalion. Rogers' Rangers performed good service as auxiliaries to the armies during part of the French and Indian War, but they also displayed serious drawbacks. First, their status as soldiers was halfway between regular and provincial which caused confusion and ill-feeling, especially among the provincials. Next, they were chronically unruly and consequently unreliable. Composed of some of the most rugged individuals from an individualistic frontier, no one but Rogers could control them, and he only part of the time. Finally, they drew high pay and were a costly expense. During 1758, for example, eight companies cost fifteen thousand pounds more than a full regiment of British regular troops. All in all, they were not worth that kind of premium.

The next step was to induce provincial frontiersmen to join special units which were unequivocally regular and so subject to military law. Colonel Thomas Gage—who had been with Braddock and who was to be commanding general during the tense decade before the Revolution—organized the first such regiment in 1758 and denominated it "light infantry." Other progressive officers inclined toward light troops. These troops were not only able to do part of their own scouting but were trained to serve in the battle line as well. They could impart some of their mobility to that line.

One of the most enterprising officers helping to establish and train light troops was Brigadier George Augustus, Lord Howe, who took instruction under Rogers himself. Howe saw that light troops must be more lightly clothed and armed than others. Accordingly, he ordered the tails cut off their coats and, to their dismay, the queues off their heads. He eliminated useless encumbrances, added such aids as leggings for protection in the brush, and ordered the shiny barrels of the muskets to be browned to give protective coloration in bright sunlight. Further to increase mobility Howe enjoined some of the camp followers who in those days habitually slowed down a British unit, and allowed no women with the column. The officers, however outraged, had now to do their own laundry. No one can say how far Howe might have carried the concept of light troops had he lived. He was killed at Ticonderoga on July 5, 1758.

Another important innovator with light troops was Colonel Henry Bouquet. He insisted that the frontiersmen who enlisted as regulars keep themselves clean and dress like soldiers. He trained them to run long distances and to perform evolutions on the run. He made them learn to disperse and rally at given signals. Practice in leaping logs and ditches and in carrying heavy loads rendered them tough. They had to be able to shoot kneeling and lying down, not an easy task with their muskets. Finally, he obliged them to master swimming and snowshoeing, as well as the European skills of making fascines, gabions, and digging trenches.

As an additional form of security, British officers also undertook to arrange their marches and camps to counteract an ambush. One plan was to place the men so that they could deploy at once into a defensive rectangle. Another was to move them in narrow columns with wide intervals between, but with each column in supporting distance of the others. Each column had its own advance guard, main body, and rear guard, with scouts protecting all from surprise. This arrangement made it extremely difficult for Indians to envelop all the columns or to get between them to encircle one. Colonel Bouquet took the lead in establishing the new order of march, and during the summer of 1764, when he led an expedition into western Pennsylvania to punish aggressive Indians, his advance was so perfect that the natives could not assail him. Overawed, they met in council and agreed to his terms. Thus, in that day as now, a show of real strength sometimes prevented a fight.

Tense as the following years were, and valuable as the light troops proved to be, by the time the colonies rebelled against England the training of such troops had virtually died out in the British army. But it remained vigorous among the Americans. "Come and help me fight the King's regular troops," Ethan Allen said to some of the Iroquois in May, 1775. "You know they stand all along close together, rank and file, and my men fight as Indians do." Some light corps were organized in the Revolutionary army for use against Indians, as in the previous conflict, as well as against the British. But the American development during the Revolution added a new type of unit, that is, light troops armed with Kentucky rifles. Ten such rifle companies, called into being by resolution of Congress on June 14, 1775, were the first units employed by Congress as purely continental troops. The most famous of these was Daniel Morgan's regiment of Virginia riflemen. When sent north to aid in stopping Burgoyne's column in 1777, Morgan's men brought eyes to General Gates's army, which theretofore had been virtually blind, and at the same time blurred the vision of the British by checkmating their Indian scouts.

Throughout the Revolution units of riflemen, usually small, served as auxiliaries to the main body of the American army. The core of the main body, whether against the British or against Indians, was an infantry line which moved as a block and which depended more upon volume of fire than upon individual firing. For that line, a musket, which could be loaded rapidly and to which a bayonet could be fixed, was a far more versatile weapon than a rifle. The task of the rifle units was to help advance the infantry line, usually by scouting forward with the Indian allies.

General John Sullivan's campaign against the Iroquois in 1779 illustrates well the use of light troops, both rifle and standard, to avoid ambush. To begin with, all of his men were intensively trained in brush fighting. When his army reached a point where ambush was threatened, every precaution was taken. For example, before exposing his column as it crossed the

Susquehanna River, Sullivan directed cannon fire along the forest on the far bank. Next, the light corps went into action. With the members of a platoon linked arm in arm because of the swift current, they waded the stream. When across they rapidly formed line of battle to protect the main army while it made the crossing. At the same time, the rifle company was moving ahead even of the rest of the light corps to scout the forest. Because of such precautions the Indians could not catch Sullivan unaware, and they were driven at last to make a stand, the thing they always sought to avoid.

Only disciplined troops were capable of carrying out good security measures of this kind. Undisciplined forces, on the other hand, brought security failures. Such failures were conspicuous in the expeditions, both state and federal, which were launched by the new nation after the Revolution. The most disastrous of all was the envelopment and destruction of the American army under General St. Clair in November, 1791. The Shawnees and allied tribes surrounded one portion of the sprawling camp in the early morning, attacked with the first light, and achieved perfect surprise.

It remained for General Anthony Wayne to re-establish sound practice. Appointed by President Washington in 1792 to replace St. Clair, Wayne trained his men during the next two years. When the General was ready the troops could be relied on to scout and to hold to a protective order of march. His disciplined force, designated the Legion of the United States, advanced in 1793 and 1794 into what is now Ohio without affording the natives any opportunity for an ambush. In the end, the enemy Indians, like Sullivan's foes fourteen years earlier, were obliged to make a stand, and also like them, suffered an irreparable defeat.

It is clear that in the years between the Braddock and the Wayne expeditions British and American military strategists had developed improved methods of tactical security in Indian warfare. The same period witnessed other changes and improvements. While it is true that surprise had weakened Braddock's army it need not have made defeat inevitable. The chief cause of disaster was the lack of a suitable technique by means of which the army could fight its way out of an encirclement. When firing began at the front, units farther back in the column pressed forward to join the action. Their zeal undid them, since the units did not re-form according to any plan, and their crowding together prevented deployment and formed dense targets for the concealed French and Indians. Those units that formed in line, the only tactic in which they were trained, had no visible target for their mass fire and were themselves vulnerable. They needed cover badly, but not cover from which to fire as individuals as the frontiersmen did; for had they sacrificed their group formation to fight as individuals they would almost certainly have fallen prey to the natives, who were more skillful than they in that style of fighting. What they needed as a counteroffensive was to combine an offensive movement with their massed fire. It is true that some groups did charge with fixed bayonets into the forest, but apparently they made no effort to create another front by assailing the enemy's flank or rear. In the main, the English tactics were purely defensive and did not give adequate protection against the destructive fire from a concealed enemy.

Braddock has been censured for not training his troops in Indian fighting; but the censure is only partially deserved. Since he was the first British commander to become engaged in a major battle with the Indians, he had only colonial precedents to guide him, and, like most other regular officers, he thought them irrelevant. Not until his undoing did enterprising officers begin to change. It seems likely, however, that even if Braddock had been willing to learn from the Americans they could not have taught the lesson he needed, because provincial troops seldom had the cohesion to execute the only kind of movements that could have saved his army.

It was Colonel Henry Bouquet who, eight years after Braddock's defeat, first resolved Braddock's problem. Bouquet's scouting was no better than Braddock's had been, and the Indians hemmed in his command about twenty miles east of Fort Pitt in August, 1763, in the vicinity of a rivulet called Bushy Run. Bouquet's regulars were not trained Indian fighters; in fact most of them were weakened from recent service in the West Indies. The Colonel does not seem to have had an advance plan, but to have matured one while under duress. As soon as the enemy envelopment commenced, he formed his men in a hollow rectangle just as he would have done to repel a cavalry charge in Europe, except that the soldiers took cover. He provided such protection as he could in the center by piling everything movable there. Thus far his defensive core was as sound as it could be; but the Indians greatly outnumbered him and had no intention of drawing off. As the hours passed Bouquet realized that he could not remain on the defensive and survive; he must create another front. Accordingly, he organized a picked party (perhaps more than one), and devised a counteroffensive. When the time was right he directed the soldiers manning the perimeter to show signs of weakening. The Indians edged closer for the kill, and while they did so Bouquet led out an attack party (or parties) from another sector. These men "sallied out from a part of the hill they [the Indians] could not observe and fell upon their right flank." Relying on the bayonet, they soon dispersed the besiegers.

Bouquet had not really added a new technique to warfare. He had simply used the old infantry square which all European troops were taught to form when beset by cavalry, and appended to it a counteroffensive movement that could not have been used against horse troops. He had reaffirmed a very old truth, which Braddock had disregarded, that it was necessary to move as well as fire. Such strategy had been neglected in America because it was impossible in the forest to see where the enemy was and where to move to threaten him.

American commanders, probably through their own discovery, later effectively combined fire and movement. General Sullivan did it in his skillful campaign of 1779 against the Iroquois. By destroying Indian crops and villages he at length forced the natives to make a stand. He had crossed the Susquehanna, having taken effective precautions against ambush. The Indians relied as usual on concealment, but Sullivan's rifle company located their position and reported it to the General. He ordered the light corps, screened by the forest, to form line in front of the stronghold, while the riflemen galled the foe from advanced firing points. Next, the artillery came forward to batter the position. Cannon fire was the decisive factor, but Sullivan made doubly sure of success by sending the rest of his force around the flank. They charged with bayonets without firing a shot. Present with the Indians were members of Butler's Rangers, but their support could not fend off defeat. In spite of the Rangers the Iroquois were dispersed and their power was badly crippled.

General Anthony Wayne used a variation of this technique at Fallen Timbers. Like Sullivan, having first destroyed Indian crops and villages, he forced the Miamis and their allies to make a stand. Next, when scouting elements reported the enemy position, Wayne sent light horsemen around the flanks while the main force charged the front with bayonets. "Rouse the Indians from their coverts at the point of the Bayonet," he ordered, "and when up . . . deliver a close and well directed fire on their backs, followed by a brisk charge so as not to give them time to load again."

Only trained troops showed themselves able to combine movement with fire. American militiamen, many of whom were practiced marksmen and few of whom knew how to handle a bayonet, naturally preferred to rely on marksmanship. As a result, local expeditions against Indians sometimes had indecisive results. Perhaps the most striking example was the Battle of Point Pleasant, in Lord Dunmore's War. This battle, which took place at the junction of the Ohio and Kanawha rivers in what is now West Virginia on October 10, 1774, was the one in which overloaded horses had broken down and had immobilized the expedition. The army itself had been split into three segments, too far apart to support each other. At sunrise the Indians began to shoot from cover upon the column commanded by Colonel Andrew Lewis. As the whites gradually formed a line, the warriors, and then the whites themselves, took cover. The line of whites extended for a mile and a quarter, much too far to control. Some of the militiamen lay behind logs in the rear and would not advance to the danger zone. Red and white lines banged away at each other from sunrise to sunset, but in all that time never undertook an assault. Chroniclers of Dunmore's War more often than not have called this action a great victory for the white men, but Englishmen who knew the Indian side took a different view. They have pointed out that although there were one thousand colonists against three hundred natives, the Indians escaped across the river at the end of the day with but slight loss.

The military operations described illustrate the fact that successful Indian fighting by organized bodies of men required, above all, cohesion within those bodies. Nothing affords better evidence of this than the numerous instances when cohesion was lacking. An outstanding and tragic example was the expedition commanded by Colonel William Crawford which set out against the Delawares, Wyandots, and Shawnees in what is now northern Ohio during the summer of 1782. Crawford had been with Braddock in 1755 and had had other broad experience as an Indian fighter. As a result, he began the march in a suitable order, like that devised by the British twenty years earlier, but because his men lacked the training to maintain it there was a good deal of straggling, as well as carelessness in scouting.

As in the case of Sullivan's defeat of the Iroquois in 1779, a detachment of Butler's Rangers supported the Indian action. The difference was that this time the Rangers were more numerous, seventy in all, and that some of them were able to serve on horseback. When the Indians opened fire from cover on part of the force, an indecisive exchange of fire developed like that at Point Pleasant eight years before. The cohesion necessary to launch any sort of assault did not exist. Meanwhile, more Indians continued to arrive, and from time to time knots of mounted Indians rode, cavalry fashion, against white parties—a form of warfare by Indians practically without parallel in the eastern forest region. When night came Crawford called a council of war. The leaders believed they were encircled, and the natives, by whooping from all quarters, took pains to reinforce this belief. The council decided upon withdrawal during the night, but some of the commanders refused to heed Crawford's plea that the force be withdrawn as a unit. Since he had no power to coerce them, scattered groups mounted and went separate ways; and most of them were ambushed and killed. Crawford himself was captured during the night and later burned to death.

Made bold by their success against Crawford, and at all times guided by Butler's Rangers, some of the northern Indians now initiated action farther to the south. About thirty Rangers and two hundred Wyandots and Lake Indians encountered a force of Kentucky militia at Blue Licks on August 18, 1782. Even though part of the Kentucky force was commanded by so redoubtable an individual Indian fighter as Daniel Boone it could not prevail. Indeed, a rare reversal of the usual sequence of events shattered the American effort. The British Rangers somehow got the natives to launch a charge, and the Kentuckians gave way before it with severe losses.

The engagements described have been chosen as best illustrative of methods of Indian warfare. They were but a few of the hundreds of encounters during the century in which lives were lost on both sides. Many of these encounters could not be called battles, using even the broadest definition of the word, and accordingly they have been excluded from the discussion. On the other hand, scores of battles have been omitted because analysis of them would serve only to illustrate further the conclusions already presented.

By way of recapitulation, the principal generalizations which this study warrants may be summed up as follows. First, Indians, as a rule, had but one offensive tactic, surprise. They were altogether incapable of strategic, as contrasted to tactical, operations. Second, the strategy of the white men was as simple as the tactics of the natives: by assailing Indian villages and crops to force the savages, contrary to their habits, to fight in bodies. Third, in the realm of tactics white men had to learn, at great cost, to apply a very old concept to warfare in dense forest: that it is vital to maneuver as well as fire. Fourth, it was evident that co-ordinated movement in wooded terrain required cohesion—internal tactical grouping—of a very high order, and this was attained only by those units which had been in service long enough to be well trained. For them, too, the bayonet proved an extremely effective weapon. Finally, the use of light troops subject to military law was an important development in Indian fighting, and one which carried over into European warfare after the eighteenth century. Light troops, in fact, combined Indian-style assets, such as extended order, mobility, and knowledge of woodcraft, with European-style cohesion and the use of the bayonet. Moreover, the American rifle companies represented a portentous variation of the light infantry unit.

United States folklore has enshrined the sharpshooting frontiersman as the conqueror of North America. Since the frontiersman rarely learned military co-operation, and since he fought mostly as a side line, his apotheosis has flattered two of our dearest traditions: that Americans are self-reliant, and that whether trained or untrained, together or as one, they are virtually invincible in a fight. Is the folklore accurate? Frontiersmen, it is true, kept up a constant attrition upon the Indians which counted heavily in the final triumph of the white man. But it does not appear that they could have annihilated native fighting power by themselves. There were some forgotten men in the background whose roles deserve greater notice in the national tradition. They were the soldiers in the ranks, British and American, often anything but heroic—indeed sometimes recruited from the outcasts of society—who carried not a rifle but a musket, and who knew how, in conjunction with their fellows, to handle a bayonet. Their careers were not individualistic like those of the civilian pioneers. On the contrary, often unwillingly, they trained to act together until they moved and fired, not as individuals, but as pieces of a machine. In so doing, when directed by perceptive commanders, they brought power to bear which the Indians were never able to match.

PART II

THE REVOLUTIONARY YEARS

R. ARTHUR BOWLER

LOGISTICS AND OPERATIONS IN THE AMERICAN REVOLUTION

"W*ars,*" *Field Marshal Erwin Rommel is reputed to have said, "are won by the quartermasters." His words are the ultimate tribute by a combat leader to the men who supply armies. Too often forgotten, seldom in the limelight of history, those who provide the money and gunpowder, the uniforms and tents, the wagons and mules, the food and forage, the rifles and bullets, the ships and sails, and the coal and gasoline are often the final arbitrators of modern warfare. It is they, more often than the combat commanders, who determine when and where, with how many, and for how long battles and campaigns will be fought.*

No better an illustration of this truth appears than in Professor Arthur Bowler's analysis of the logistical problems of the Americans and British during the War for American Independence. He dramatically illustrates how much of General George Washington's failure to capitalize on his advantages was the result of failures of logistics and public finance. Without an adequate overland transportation system and hampered by ineffective administrators, the Continental Army's supply system broke down early and was never fixed. Washington confided the level of his despair in a diary entry in early 1781:

> *Instead of having Magazines filled with provisions, we have a scanty pittance scattered here & there in the different States. Instead of having our Arsenals well supplied with Military Stores, they are poorly provided, &*

> *the Workmen all leaving them. . . . Instead of having a regular System of transportation established upon credit or funds in the Qr. Masters hands to defray the contingent Expences of it, we have neither the one nor the other and all that business, or a great part of it, being done by Military Impress, we are daily & hourly oppressing the people—souring their tempers and alienating their affection. . . . In a word—instead of having everything in readiness to take the Field, we have nothing—and instead of having the prospect of a glorious offensive campaign before us, we have a bewildered, and gloomy defensive one. . . .*

All this he wrote on the eve of the Yorktown campaign.

Washington's salvation was French finances, the heroic efforts of quartermasters, and the sacrifices of the common soldier. Even these might not have been enough had not the British faced formidable logistical obstacles themselves. The King's soldiers and sailors found themselves on the wrong side of the Atlantic without the logistical infrastructure that had previously supported them. As Bowler effectively illustrates and as David Syrett reaffirms in a later essay, one of the key reasons for the British failure was an inability to easily supply the Royal forces. The consequence was the diversion of too many men, too much time, and too many financial resources away from the effort to find and destroy the Continental Army and its French allies. The decisive campaign of the war—Yorktown—was won when the French navy severed General Charles Lord Cornwallis's logistical umbilical cord.

Readers should pay particular attention to how logistics affected other aspects of American military history, as illustrated in John Maurer's "Fuel and the Battle Fleet" and Robert Ross Smith's "Luzon versus Formosa." Logistical superiority alone will not win wars, as the Americans found in Vietnam, but comprehending the interconnection between logistics and operations often determines the successful from the unsuccessful campaign.

In the history of war, a tradition only now beginning to wither is that logistical problems are treated in the light of the old maxim "it is a poor workman who blames his tools." The traditional emphasis is on politics, strategy, and tactics; and even when the historian does consider logistical problems, they seldom enter into his final assessments in any serious way. There is, of course, often good reason for this—a lack of easily available information. Successful tacticians are great writers of memoirs and there seems to be a compulsion to reach for pen and paper that strikes eyewitnesses of battles. Commissaries and quartermasters, on the other hand, seldom write of their experiences, and the records of their work are often not considered worth keeping; their activities are prosaic and usually boring. Without records the full logistical story and the ways in which it is interwoven with the other aspects of a war are difficult to revive.

But if much of the history of logistics is irretrievable, the growth of bureaucratic government since the seventeenth century has meant that the records since that time at least are often remarkably complete. The price of overlooking the story they can tell is ignorance of factors just as significant as the tactical and strategic decisions of military commanders in deciding the course and final outcome of a war. For no war is this more true than the American Revolutionary War. When Sir Henry Clinton, commander of the British forces in America for most of the war, wrote to England that "I have no money, no provisions, nor indeed any account of the sailing of the Cork fleet, nor admiral that I can have the least dependence on, no army. In short I have nothing left but the hope for better times and a little more attention," and when Washington wrote to Congress that "with truth I can declare that no Man, in my opinion, ever had his measures more impeded than I have, by every department of the army," both were speaking to problems that took up a large part of their time and energy throughout the war. These problems could give reason to their actions with as much force as any other consideration.

That the American army faced enormous logistical problems is common knowledge to every school child who has read about Valley Forge. What is seldom realized, however, is that the difficulties experienced at Valley Forge were repeated at every winter encampment of the war except that of 1775–76 and were the result not of momentary failings but of fundamental problems arising, in part, from the immature structure of the American government, economy, and society. One of the most basic of these problems was that the economies of the thirteen colonies were primarily agricultural. Americans pro-duced very little not only of the wide variety of hardware demanded by an army but even of such fundamentals as cloth and canvas for uniforms and tents. The war enormously increased American capacity to supply these articles but never to the point that large and regular imports were not required. When they failed, the army suffered. And to pay for the imports there had to be exports. Although France was generous with loans and gifts, much that was imported could be paid for only by American exports. And in the reliance on imports and exports lay another problem. Throughout most of the war the British navy, abetted by loyalist privateers, controlled the seas, so imports were expensive and deliveries, in terms of both dates and place, uncertain.

British control of the sea had another serious effect. It threw the army, its logistical support, and, indeed, the whole economy of the colonies back on a totally inadequate land communications system. Before the Revolution, and for several generations after, communications between the colonies and even within individual colonies depended on water transport. Roads, where they existed, were often quagmires except in winter freezes and summer droughts. The best of them quickly broke down under the strain of an army on the march with all its equipment or even the regular passage of heavy supply wagons. The need to marshal and maintain the huge numbers of horses and wagons needed to move and supply the army, and to operate them over inadequate roads, was a persistent problem of nightmare proportions through much of the war. The innumerable unbridged rivers running into the sea made north-south land transport over any distance slow and outrageously expensive.

But without question, the most persistent and deadly problem of army logistical support was organization and administration. The process of building a logistical organization, like that of building the army and, indeed, the federal government itself, had to start from scratch in 1775. Inevitably, especially given the conditions of revolution and war under which the building was done, there were many mistakes, many poor decisions and false starts.

Throughout the war, Congress was a relatively small body of men, many of whom had experience in legislation but few in administration. Yet it was called on to be both a legislative and an administrative body and, to make matters worse, it had only slightly more real power than a debating society. It could recommend and even act, but its recommendations could be turned down or ignored and its actions repudiated by the states. If it had real power, it lay in the fact that it was the only body that could speak and act for the states as a whole; the state governments were usually well aware of the need for unity but often lacked the capacity to act decisively and effectively themselves.

Because of its unique position, Congress was flooded with work, of which establishing the army and its logistical support was only one part. In June 1775, it appointed George Washington as commander in chief and gave him a commissary general of stores and purchases and a quartermaster general, but nothing more. Not until a year later, in June 1776, was the Board of War and Ordnance created, charged with overseeing all military stores, superintending the raising, equipping, and dispatching of the land forces, and supervising the army generally. Even then, however, the board had no executive function; it was merely a standing committee that reported and recommended to Congress. None of its members had experience in military administration, and not until a year after its establishment did it even have any members who were not also burdened with regular congressional duties. Even at the best of times, however, the Board of War was seldom efficient, as Henry Laurens, president of Congress, had occasion to note: "I sent for Mr. Nourse Secretary pro tem, at the War Office," he wrote, "and between chiding for the repeated losses and miscarriages of public papers in that Office, and entreaties to search diligently . . . , I prevailed on him at an unseasonable hour, not any such in my four and twenty, to rummage, horrible idea to rummage, in an Office which ought to be accurate in all things." The ever changing makeup of the board over the years also meant that there was a dangerous lack of continuity in its policy and a continuous temptation to tinker with or even drastically alter basic administrative establishments. The latter was particularly evident in 1777, when an extensive reorganization was attempted in an effort to bring the army departments under closer congressional control. The result was such enormous confusion that Washington was led to complain that virtually his every plan for that year "was either frustrated or greatly impeded by the want of a regular supply of provisions." Not until late 1781 was a regular executive office, the War Office headed by the secretary at war, established.

The absence or slow growth of a stable, well-organized, experienced executive to look after army affairs had serious results. One was a lack of clear definitions of tasks. The original commissary general and quartermaster were given no instructions, no clear definitions of their functions, no limits to their authority. And despite their appointment, Congress went ahead and also com-missioned independent purchasing agents for army stores. Who had authority? Even after 1776, when Congress was able to turn its attention more fully to the army and undertake more systematic planning of the army services, areas of responsibility remained blurred. Throughout the war various agents of the army services regularly competed against each other, against agents of state govern-ments, and against civilians for scarce supplies, bidding up prices, to the detri-ment of everyone but the purchasing agents, who received a commission on all money that passed through their hands. The other end of the problem was those cases in which no one seemed to have authority. In 1779, for instance, when much of the army was in rags, 10,000 suits of clothing lay in storehouses in France and another large quantity in the West Indies because various agents of Congress could not decide whose business it was to ship them. At the lowest level, the army had to invent regulations 1777 to stem the enormous losses by theft or carelessness of common tools. Not until 1779 were regulations intro-duced to make soldiers strictly accountable for their weapons. Up to that time carelessness and the tendency of soldiers on short-term enlistments to take their issue weapons home with them had resulted in a requirement for 5,000–6,000 new muskets at the beginning of each campaign.

Such problems in organization meant that commissaries and quartermas-ters were frequently tempted to spend more time with Congress or the Board of War lobbying for workable systems and divisions of responsibility than with the army, often with unhappy results. Appointed commissary general of forage in mid-1777, Clement Biddle received virtually no direction from his superior, Quartermaster General Thomas Mifflin, because Mifflin was seldom with the army in the months before his resignation. Biddle's attempts to lay in stocks that fall and winter were regularly frustrated because he had no authority over the many other purchasers of forage.

It was in large part inexperience and new and inadequate organization—although incompetence cannot be discounted entirely—that produced the near-disastrous conditions under which the army had to exist at Valley Forge. By early 1777 the army service departments were just beginning to achieve a respectable degree of organization. Then disaster began to build. In August the commissary general of purchases, Joseph Trumbull, and a good part of his staff resigned as a result of changes in departmental organization and rates of pay instituted by Congress. The new appointee, William Buchanan, was probably not as incompetent as he has been pictured; but he was not particularly competent, and he was one of those who spent as much time attending Congress as the army. Buchanan resigned the following March; in the meantime departmental activity slackened and the vital process of laying in stores for the following winter was not well attended to.

Then in October 1777, Quartermaster General Mifflin, after largely neglecting his duties for some months, resigned. Because he was not replaced by Nathanael Greene until February 1778, his department was without adequate central direction for almost six months. Further, two newly created and vital offices in the quartermaster department, the Forage and Wagonmaster offices, were also weak. The Forage Office, responsible for organizing the feeding of all the army's horses, was established and put under the direction of Clement Biddle on July 1, 1777. Biddle was to prove to be a very competent administrator in time, but at this period he was new to office and lacked guidance from above and clear authority. The result was that the Forage Office was far less efficient than it could and should have been that fall and winter; the army's horses suffered accordingly.

More important than the forage problem, though, was the weakness in the wagon department. Congress had appointed a wagonmaster that spring and approved the purchases of several hundred wagons and teams for the army's use. Joseph Thornsbury, the first appointee, however, resigned his office in October without accomplishing anything significant and was not replaced until December. But more important than Thornsbury's inability to organize the army's own wagon train was the failure to deal with problems involving hired wagons. Throughout the war the army depended primarily on privately owned wagons. Whether the wagons were freely hired or impressed, this service had to be carefully organized if the army was to be adequately served. It was not. The low rates of hire set by Congress made impressment necessary, and poor organization meant that the burden of such service tended to fall most heavily on farmers near the army's encampments. Further, neither horses nor wagons fared well in the army service due to inadequate forage, poor maintenance facilities, and inexperienced wagoneers. Farmers took to hiding horses and wagons when army press parties were out and those who were impressed not infrequently deserted at the first opportunity, leaving their cargoes at the roadside.

The result of these many failures—this coordinated ill-fortune, if you wish—was privation in the midst of plenty. For there is no doubt that the fertile farms of the central states could easily have fed the small American army. Washington even had the power to confiscate supplies if necessary, although, wisely, he was extremely reluctant to use it. The problem was one of organizing the supply and getting it to the army. It was clear throughout the fall of 1777 that a crisis was approaching, but the army was powerless to prevent it. Only by the narrowest of margins did Washington's December prediction that the army would have to "dissolve or disperse in order to obtain subsistence" not come true.

By the spring of 1778, however, new leadership, better organization, and a substantial increase in the prices Congress authorized commissaries and quartermasters to pay for provisions and equipment began to have their effect. Supplies of all sorts, although never all that were desired, became better and more regular, and the development of a system of magazines along the main lines of communications from the Hudson to Virginia gave the army the mobility it needed to respond to British initiatives. The success of the logistical services at this period may be judged in part from army vital statistics for the winter of 1778–79: Washington was able to maintain the largest force-in-being of any winter of the war that season, and the sickness rate dropped to less than half of its level over the previous two winters.

But even while the logistical services were improving, a new disaster was building, largely the result of the precarious finances of the new nation. Congress, without taxing powers, financed the central administration of the war by issues of paper money—Continental bills. For the first two years of the war the Continentals maintained their value but that situation could have continued only if the state governments had retired the bills when they came in as payment for taxes. This was not done; indeed, most states even issued their own paper money. By late 1777 the inevitable depreciation had set in and ever larger issues of paper were required to purchase the same quantities of goods and services. In September of 1779, when Continental issues had reached the then frightening sum of $200 million, Congress called a halt.

The end of Continental issues, however badly depreciated they were, was disastrous for the army. The service departments, already handicapped by shortages of funds and a reluctance on the part of suppliers to accept Continental bills, virtually collapsed just when they should have been at their busiest, and the army had to live from hand to mouth through the harshest winter of the war. Of this period Baron de Kalb wrote, "Those who have only been in Valley Forge and Middlebrooke during the last two winters, but have not tested the cruelties of this one, know not what it is to suffer."

By early 1780 Congress devised and put into effect a new system for supplying the army, but it was a poor expedient. This was the system of specific supplies—requisitions upon each state for quantities of beef, pork, flour, and so on, with the promise that the value would be credited towards each state's part of Congress's debt. As a measure of economy, Congress also cut back and reorganized, somewhat, the army service departments.

The new system never worked well. The states had not imposed taxes to support congressional expenditures and were not much more enthusiastic about expenditures in kind. Appeals to forward quotas frequently went unanswered or, alternatively, resulted in more than could possibly be used before rot set in. But even when adequate supplies were forthcoming, the army still faced an overwhelming problem. The supplies were collected at central depots in each state, but it was then up to the army to move them to wherever they were needed. The problem was that transportation, which could not be by sea, was always difficult to obtain and often far more expensive than the supplies themselves. The result was severe and persistent shortages that virtually crippled the army.

Lafayette's attempts to halt Benedict Arnold's ravages in Virginia in March 1780 were completely frustrated by logistical problems, and in May, when news came from France that an army and fleet were being prepared to aid the American cause, Washington reported that his army was "pinched for provisions" and "reduced to the very edge of famine." Nathanael Greene, dispatched to take command of the southern army late in the year, took the precaution of asking the legislatures of several states for all the supplies he needed in the hope that they might, together, come up with his total requirement. Nevertheless, when he actually took command, his first move had to be to split the army and dispatch the parts to areas where it was hoped that adequate supplies of food and forage could be obtained.

The main army under Washington was in bad shape throughout the year. There were desperate and persistent shortages of food, clothing, and money for pay, and by early fall it was reduced to living on what it could borrow, impress, and confiscate. The near mutiny of two Connecticut regiments in May 1780 was a result of the dreadful conditions these problems produced; the Pennsylvania line needed only the addition of enlistment grievances to bring it to mutiny in January 1781. And all of these problems occurred despite the fact that the army was at a generally lower strength than it had been at any time since the first eight months of 1777. Indeed, Washington had to disband part of the army when he went into winter quarters in 1780 because "want of clothing rendered them unfit for duty, and want of

flour would have disbanded the whole army if I had not adopted this expedient."

The net result of the financial crisis and its logistical repercussions
was that the Continental army was handicapped almost to the point of im-
mobility for the best part of two years. Only heroic efforts, extensive reorganization, and French gold permitted the cooperation with Rochambeau
and de Grasse that brought Cornwallis's surrender and effectively ended
the war.

What comes out of a survey—even one as brief as this—of the logistical
position of the American army during the Revolutionary War is a clear
appreciation of the enormous hardships that dogged the life of the Continental soldier. But it also reveals the fundamental limitations that logistics placed
on the size and operational capacity of the Continental army. America in the
eighteenth century was a relatively rich and populous country. On the basis of
a simplistic computation, it should have been able to field a large army and,
indeed, at one stage Congress envisioned a force of 75,000 men. In fact,
Washington never commanded more than 19,000 regulars and on several
occasions had less than 10,000. The problem was that America in the
mid-eighteenth century was a country ill-suited to waging war, for reasons
made clear by the two crises that have been outlined here, those of 1777–78
and 1779–80. State governments were generally weak, and Congress was
even weaker; administration was rudimentary and often had to be invented as
the need arose; financial organization, at least of the kind necessary for war
finance, was almost nonexistent; transportation and communications were
appalling; and, by no means of least importance, the people were suspicious of
governments and armies, even their own.

The American army of the Revolution was small, far smaller than the
military situation demanded. It was kept small and was hamstrung in its
operation in very considerable measure by inadequate logistics and administration. For most of the war it remained, of necessity, on the defensive. When
it did undertake offensive operations, they were usually on a relatively small
scale and of short duration.

The obvious question arising from this analysis is why, if the Continental army was so weak, did not it and the Revolution fall easy victim to the
British army? The answer to that question, if it can ever be satisfactorily
answered, is at best highly complex. As others have pointed out, the quality
and sense of purpose of British generalship was a large factor, as was administrative and strategic confusion in Britain. What is suggested here, however, is
that Britain's military failure must be seen in part in terms of the logistical
problems that her army encountered when it attempted to function in Revolutionary America.

The British army had, of course, operated successfully in America before, during the Seven Years' War, and it is tempting to assume that the same logistical conditions existed during that war and the American Revolution. Such was not the case; logistically there were fundamental differences between the two situations. To understand the differences the British system of logistical administration must first be examined.

In the eighteenth century, British army logistics were the responsibility of a number of executive departments of the government. The Board of Ordnance, the War Office, and the Navy Board all had a part in it. But the largest responsibility rested with the Treasury. With it lay the burden of supplying all food, forage, wood, barrack supplies, cash, and land and coastal transport. For the most part, however, the Treasury carried out this responsibility by contracting. It either let contracts itself directly with London merchants or authorized its principal agent with the army, the commissary general, to let contracts himself or purchase directly through agents all that the army needed. This was the system by which the army in America during the Seven Years' War was supplied, and it was carried on for the forces that remained after that war. As it actually worked out, however, virtually all the supplies for which the Treasury was responsible came from America itself, for the London merchants who accepted the prime contracts turned to American subcontractors for the actual procurement and delivery.

With the coming of the Revolution this system broke down almost completely. One of the first actions of patriot committees throughout the thirteen colonies after news of Lexington and Concord had arrived was to cut off supplies destined for the army at Boston. By May 10, Gage had to write to the Treasury that "all the ports from whence our supplies usually came have refused suffering any provisions or necessary whatsoever to be shipped for the King's use . . . and all avenues for procuring provisions in this country are shut up."

Right from the beginning of the war, then, the army was forced back on Britain for supplies it had normally obtained in America. Nevertheless, this did not cause any great concern at first. On several occasions during the Seven Years' War it had also been necessary to procure some provisions in Britain. The contractors were notified, and before fall they had on its way a large flotilla filled with ample and, it has even been suggested, luxurious supplies for the troops. Even live sheep, pigs, and cattle were included in the cargo. But then disaster struck: the fleet, consisting of thirty-six ships, was caught in fierce autumnal storms that drove some back to England and others to the West Indies. A number of those that survived the storm fell easy prey to American privateers and the fledgling American navy. These same war vessels also picked up a number of other ships attempting to supply the army at Boston from Nova Scotia.

The results of this first disastrous supply attempt—besides short rations for the army—was a steep rise in rates of shipping hire and insurance. The contractors informed the Treasury that they could no longer take the responsibility for delivering provisions. The Treasury, never an active department in this way, promptly asked the Navy Board, which already looked after the transport of ordnance stores, to take on the task. When it refused, the Treasury had no choice. It remained directly responsible for provisions shipping until 1779, when the Navy Board, under due persuasion, finally relented.

But in early 1776 there was no thought that anything more than temporary supply from Britain would be necessary. Already in late 1775 it had been decided that the army would move its base from Boston to New York City. That would not only be a better base for operations, but, everyone expected, virtually all the supplies the army needed could be obtained locally. For the fall of 1776, these expectations were fully realized. As Washington was forced successively out of Long Island, lower New York, and New Jersey, the commissaries were able to procure huge quantities of supplies. By November, Commissary General Daniel Chamier was able to report that he was already putting up meat and flour for the next year's campaign and expected that the supplies from England could be substantially reduced in the near future.

As it turned out, he spoke too soon. On December 26, Washington proved that although he could not defeat the British army as a whole, he was quite capable of destroying it piecemeal. The annihilation of the Hessian brigade at Trenton and the mauling of Mawhood's brigade at Princeton that quickly followed sent the British army tumbling out of New Jersey. With them went the hope of supplying the army from America. Washington took up a position at Morristown and adopted a strategy that he was to follow throughout the war in the central colonies from such bases as Valley Forge, Middlebrook, and the Hudson highlands. Morristown was a strong natural position in which Washington's relatively weak force was reasonably secure and it was far enough from the British base to ensure against surprise attack. From that base he could launch offensives if the British were ever again so foolish as to divide their army up into isolated detachments in order to hold large areas. Although both the commissary general and Howe hoped that the move to Philadelphia might change the situation and Pennsylvania might become the breadbasket of the army, they were soon disappointed. After an initial period of abundance, the army was again locked into a tight perimeter and Howe found that he had to provide covering forces of several thousand men in order to obtain even the most meagre supplies from the countryside.

Thus, from the very beginning of the war, most of the army's basic food had to come from Britain. And the supply depended, first of all, on a department, the Treasury, which was neither prepared for nor wanted the job. It was to be five years before a consistent and adequate flow of supplies was organized: by that time the war was lost. This is not to say that the British army suffered horribly from want of provisions. Far from it. On only a few occasions did rations have to be cut, and the British soldier probably received his rations more fully and more regularly than did his American counterpart. The problem lay not with day-to-day supply but with reserves.

If the war was to be won, the army had to take the offensive, the rebel strongholds reduced, and Washington's army destroyed. But few eighteenth-century commanders, and Clinton least of all, would ever have even considered taking to the field without adequate supplies. The British supply route was 3,000 hazardous miles long, and both Howe and Clinton insisted on having provisions on hand before they began a campaign. An offensive that stalled for lack of supplies would be at best frustrating, at worst disastrous. Thus both generals in their turn recommended that shipments from Britain always be sufficient to keep a six-month reserve on hand in America. When France entered the war and her navy became a threat to the Atlantic supply line, Clinton sought a doubling of the reserve.

Even when no operations were in the offing, a reserve sufficient for at least two months was necessary if the army's position and, indeed, the army itself were not to be jeopardized. For when reserves fell to that level, the commander in chief had to think in terms of evacuation. To move the army with all its equipment and support personnel and with all the loyalists who depended on it for protection required shipping resources larger than the army ever had on hand. Even when Boston was evacuated in 1776, a move planned months in advance, many ships had to make two trips to Halifax. Only about 15,000 people were evacuated from Boston: there were seldom less than 50,000 who would have had to leave New York. Thus the decision to evacuate, if it were possible at all, had to be made while there were still provisions to feed the army during the time the move was organized and effected.

Thus, the need for reserves of provisions was vital, and the Treasury was regularly informed of that fact. Most certainly Britain was capable of supplying them, yet the army was seldom adequately supplied. The war in America lasted, effectively, for seventy-nine months—from the battles at Lexington and Concord in April 1775 to Cornwallis's surrender in October 1781—but for no more than twenty-three of those months did the army have the minimum six-month reserve that the commanders considered necessary for offensive operations. During twenty-eight months supplies were at the three- to five-month level and for eight months they were sufficient for no more than two to three months. During an additional eleven months, reserves fell to a paralyzing thirty to sixty days; and at least once in each year except 1777, for a total of five months, the army had less than thirty days' provisions on hand. Put another way, during only two summers of the war did the army have an adequate and consistent reserve on hand.

The reasons for these failures were many: bad provisions, inadequate accounting on both sides of the Atlantic, unexpected calls for rations, shipping shortages, and confused convoy schedules. But the basic problem lay in the Treasury itself. That department never seriously attempted to adapt to its new responsibility or even, it could be argued, clearly understood what it involved. Although it set standards of quality for provisions, it could never force contractors to live up to them; nor would it make allowances in the size of contracts for the fact that even under the best of conditions a proportion of the provisions shipped would be unusable on arrival in America. Year after year it received reports from the commissaries in America of the shortages caused by bad provisions. Yet when it was suggested that the problem could be eliminated by increasing the contracts by one-eighth, the Treasury responded that it could act only after a commissary had supplied evidence, attested to by a board of officers, that specific shipments were bad; then they would be replaced. Throughout the period of its responsibility, despite losses at sea and on land, despite reports of bad provisions, the Treasury never contracted for more than one ration per man per day on the basis of reported strengths and insisted on believing that every pound of food shipped became available to the army.

The list of Treasury failings could go on, but they are summed up in the fact that despite the repeated pleas of Howe and Clinton and its own assertions that it was planning such a move, the Treasury never seriously committed itself to building up and maintaining army provision reserves. When provisioning was being turned over to the Navy Board in 1780, Secretary of the Treasury John Robinson admitted, "This Board do not contract for greater quantities of provisions than may be ample supply for the troops on the respective service, and if possible to keep such a supply a few months ahead."

It would be difficult to attempt here to sort out all the other problems that beset the British army, including Clinton's very complex character, the particular effects of inadequate provisions reserves. Nevertheless, there is an interesting correlation between those reserves and offensive operations. In 1776 and 1777 reserves were consistently adequate and the army moved. From 1778 through mid-1781, reserves were high on only three occasions; on the first of those Clinton moved against Charleston. However viewed, though, provisions reserves were a fundamental problem for the British army.

But there was another aspect of the British logistical situation that was equally significant. For whatever the state of supplies from Britain, there were still commodities that the army needed that could be obtained only locally.

The most significant of these were forage for the army's horses, fresh food, and wood. Of these, forage, and particularly hay, was the most strategically important. Without hay the army could not feed the 3,000–4,000 horses it usually maintained; without horses it could not mount a sustained offensive. The problem was where to get hay. Early in the war the Treasury agreed, reluctantly, to supply from Britain the oats that the army required but absolutely refused, because of the cost of transportation and the scarcity of shipping, to provide hay. Instead, it sent several hay presses and told Howe to find his own supplies. The army had no choice but to look to America, and Howe planned the capture of Rhode Island in 1776 in part because he wanted its hay resources.

The requirements for livestock—horses, sheep, and cattle—fresh food of all kinds, and firewood were equally important. Horses were needed first to build up and then to replace the army's cavalry transport service. The wood, in quantities of up to 70,000 cords a year, was necessary to keep the army from freezing. The cattle and other items provided some variations from the monotonous and potentially deadly basic diet of salt meat and bread. On some occasions they were necessary simply to keep the army alive.

Because of these requirements no British army could remain completely within the tight cantonments that were established after 1776. Regular foraging expeditions had to be sent out into the countryside, and once out they became targets. Washington recognized immediately this weak spot in the British armor. A letter he wrote to General William Heath in February 1777 is well worth quoting at length since it lays out a policy he was to follow throughout the war:

> The securing the Forage in West Chester county, for our own use, or depriving the enemy from carrying it off for theirs, is an object of so much moment, that I desire some measures may yet be fallen upon to effect one or the other. Suppose a light body of troops, under an active officer, sufficient to repel any foraging parties of the enemy, except they come out in very large bodies, should be left behind, and stationed as near Kingsbridge as possible. While they kept a good look out they never could be surprised, for not being encumbered with any baggage, they could always move at a moment's warning, if the enemy came out with a superior force, and move back when they returned. This would oblige them to forage, with such large covering parties, that it would in a manner harass their troops to death. We have found the advantage of such practices with us, for by keeping four or five hundred men far advanced, we not only oblige them to forage with parties of 1500 and 2000 but every now and then give them a smart brush.

Those who picture the winters of the war as periods of idleness when the Americans sat around their campfires bewailing their lack of shoes and the British turned to dissipation, miss a neglected, but most fundamental, aspect of the war. The need for supplies drove the British with relentless regularity out into the countryside. There dispersed and encumbered by wagons, they were met and opposed by Washington's detachments, local militia, and the banditti who roamed the no-man's-land between the two armies.

In very short order, foraging parties became foraging expeditions involving as many as 5,000 troops. Howe had to employ that many to protect wagons bringing in 1,000 tons of hay from Darby to Philadelphia in December 1777, and an expedition to Salem, New Jersey, the following spring to bring in livestock and forage required the deployment of three regiments of regular troops, two provincial corps, and a navy frigate. The story of the previous winter is well told in the diaries of two British officers, John Peebles and James Robertson. Their regiments were engaged in as many as ten such expeditions a month. Sometimes the expeditions went without incident but more often they were a series of short, sharp clashes on the order of Lexington and Concord. And as in those battles, the British more often than not came out the losers. One officer felt that this sort of warfare was a positive advantage to the Americans: "The Rebel soldiers, from being accustomed to peril in the skirmishes, begin to have more confidence, and their officers seldom meet with foraging parties, but they try every ruse to entrap them, and tho' they do not always succeed, yet the following the people as they return, and the wounding and killing of our rearguards, gives them the notion of victory, and habituates them to the profession." The result of this kind of opposition to British foraging, he continued, was that it "kept the army the whole winter in a perpetual harassment, and upon a modest computation, lost us more men than the last campaign.

But the need to forage did more than open the British army to the kind of warfare at which Americans could win—guerrilla war, *la petite guerre*, or "a dirty kind of tiraillerie," as one British officer described it. As envisioned in the parlors of London in this age of limited war, foraging was an unfortunate necessity to be carried out, especially in areas where the population had to be assumed to be friendly, with as much discretion and as little disruption to the civil population as possible. Person and property were supposed to be respected, farmers paid for the things taken from them and always left enough for their own needs. That British commanders felt the same way is indicated by their repeated general orders and by the disgusted observation of one Hessian in a letter home that "at the King's express command the troops must treat these folk most handsomely—though we hear they are all rebels—and cannot demand even a grain of salt without paying for it."

The injunctions of the British commanders, however, seldom had any effect. The European regulars, British and German, usually drawn from the outcast orders of society and raised in the hard school, found it convenient, if they needed an excuse, to believe that every American was a rebel, his property fair game for looting and his female family for rape. Despite all the efforts of the commanders, this kind of conduct could never be curbed to any significant extent. Nowhere was this more true than in lower New York and New Jersey in 1776 and 1777. Congressional and other rebel accounts of the outrageous and brutal behavior of the British and Hessian troops toward the civilian population might well need to be discounted to some degree as propaganda, but not by much: they are supported by British and loyalist accounts. Lieutenant Colonel Stephen Kemble regularly deplored these depredations in his journal. Early in the campaign he noted that "the ravages committed by the Hessians and all Ranks of the Army, on the poor Inhabitants of the country make their case deplorable; the Hessians destroy all the fruits of the Earth without regard to Loyalists or Rebels, the property of both being equally a prey to them, in which our [the British] troops are too ready to follow their Example and are but too much licensed in it." The result was to drive Americans—neutral, apathetic, and even loyal—to the rebels for protection. "No wonder," Kemble noted a bit later, "if the country people refuse to join us." Foraging was the most persistent and continuous form of contact; and the more often the regulars of the British army came into contact with the civilian population, the more enemies they created. Even when they escaped the soldiers, the "country people" were still likely victims for the corrupt practices of British commissaries and quartermasters, a number of whom made fortunes by selling to the army supplies that were confiscated or purchased at ridiculously low prices from civilians.

What this all-too-brief survey of the logistics of the war in America has attempted to show is that, particularly from 1777 on, both the American and British armies were faced with enormous logistical problems that directly and indirectly had considerable effect on the course of the war. Most directly, they greatly reduced the offensive capacities of both armies. A historian once described the fighting in Burma in World War II between the British and the Japanese as a battle between giants who, because of the logistical problems created by climate and terrain, could do no more than tear at each other with their fingertips. The metaphor, with reservations, is not inappropriate to the War of the American Revolution. Each side possessed considerable military potential, but each could seldom bring more than a fraction of that power to bear and then use it only fitfully. The situation was what might be called a balance of weakness. In that balance, however, more advantage lay with the rebels than has traditionally been assumed. The greatest advantage came from the aggressive rebel organizations that gained control of every colony at the beginning of the war and were able to maintain or at least dispute that control except in the face of overwhelming British power. They denied the resources of the country to the British army except where it moved in force. Further, the American army, however weak it became, was never so weak that it was unable to challenge British attempts to pacify extensive areas of the countryside. To obtain the supplies it needed, the British army was forced throughout the war to engage in extensive foraging operations. This allowed the often untrained rebel forces to fight the kind of battles for which they were best suited, and the brutality of those operations drove more and more Americans to the rebel side.

DAVID SYRETT

DEFEAT AT SEA

The Impact of American Naval Operations upon the British, 1775–1778

Central to the thesis of naval theorists like Admiral Alfred Thayer Mahan is the necessity of proper fleet operations for achieving success in war at sea. Nothing is more deplored by the Mahanians than a naval strategy dependent on commerce raiding rather than gaining "command of the sea." Professor David Syrett of Queens College of the City University of New York explores Mahan's theory in a perceptive analysis of the impact of American cruisers and privateers upon British naval practices in the years before the French, Spanish, and Dutch navies opposed the Royal Navy in the latter years of the War for American Independence.

Lacking a battle fleet but having a substantial number of experienced commercial captains and crews, the Americans sought to fight a war with what they could muster. The naval resources of the young republic were incapable of conventional combat with the British, so they engaged in the anti-Mahanian strategy of pestering the British merchant marine and fleet. Even the Americans' small whaleboats could prompt the deployment of Royal Navy vessels to protect British bases from rebel raids. Individual British warships were vulnerable to capture by U.S. Navy vessels in single-ship actions.

In reality, the Americans built four navies, not just one. First was Washington's navy, a small set of privateers authorized by the commander-in-chief, which attacked the British supply system during the siege of Boston, 1775–76. A variant of this was the small force Benedict Arnold assembled to frustrate a British advance on Lake Champlain in the fall of 1776. The second was the state navies, consisting largely of barges, gunboats, and galleys which mostly protected harbors and inland waterways like the

Chesapeake Bay. Some of these forces, such as Pennsylvania's navy in the Delaware River in 1777, were engaged in serious actions. The third navy consisted of the privateers, over 2,000 commercial vessels operating under a letter of marque from various American governments. Such letters allowed them to engage in licensed piracy against British merchant vessels. This was potentially profitable to shipowners, officers, and crew. Their efforts eventually resulted in losses to the British of over $65,000,000. It also siphoned off British warships into convoy escort duty and related tasks. Finally, there was the Continental navy of approximately one hundred vessels. Authorized by the Continental Congress, this minuscule force mostly engaged in commerce raiding. This navy had only five ships in service in 1780.

Most critical, from the British standpoint, was the impact of American privateers and Continental navy cruisers upon unescorted supply ships supporting the King's troops in America. The situation became especially galling when these privateers and cruisers, embarking from French ports, began operating off the British Isles and in the Caribbean. As the weaker power, the Americans found tempting targets in the British merchant marine vessels. Caught in a strategic trap of not wanting to widen the civil war in America into a world war that would find them fighting from the Indian Ocean to the North Atlantic, the British allowed the subterfuge of French neutrality to continue despite the American inroads into their maritime supremacy. British losses in European and American waters were dramatic, 347 ships in 1776 and 350 in 1777. The American strategy frustrated the traditionalist tactics of the Royal Navy. To combat the United States' logistic strategy, the British needed to detail much of their fleet to the New World. But they could not concentrate their vessels in American waters because that made them vulnerable to an attack from the French, Spanish, or Dutch across the English Channel. Therefore, the British could not send the whole of British naval power into a blockade of the North American coastline.

Once the French, and later the Spanish and Dutch, entered the war, the entire character of the war changed. The British had to devote immense resources to protect their imperial possessions in the Caribbean, Africa, and India. An enormous British expedition to relieve Gibraltar allowed French Admiral François de Grasse to sail unmolested to the West Indies. Later de Grasse sailed north to the Chesapeake Capes where he isolated General Lord Cornwallis at Yorktown. De Grasse's subsequent victory over a British squadron is one of the decisive naval triumphs of history and helped guarantee the independence of the United States.

The unwillingness of the Americans to fight a conventional war for "command of the sea" has many implications for modern strategic policy. What would have happened if Germany had concentrated more than it did on its submarine fleet in World Wars I and II? What does such unwillingness to mirror the equipment, doctrine, and tactics of an enemy say about the need for unconventional ground warfare expertise in a world where small powers and revolutionary movements are unwilling and unable to contest American and Soviet nuclear and conventional firepower superiority on a traditional battlefield? Moreover, in what ways does one country's contempt for its opponent's *unconventional military capacity lead to strategic miscalculations? Was this a factor in the defeats of the French and the Americans in Indochina and the Soviets in Afghanistan?*

American naval operations in the Atlantic during the first years of the War for Independence were crucial to the success of the American effort. Navalists such as A. T. Mahan, however, have tended to ignore the American war at sea in the years 1775–1778. They have overlooked the fact that American blockade runners imported the munitions required to carry on the war and have failed to note that American naval forces disrupted British strategy, commerce, and diplomacy and forced the Royal Navy to fight a maritime guerrilla war for which it was ill prepared. Indeed, many historians have been no more perceptive regarding the importance and potential of American maritime strength than were the British in 1775.

Indicative of British ignorance of American military potential is the famous speech made by Lord Sandwich, the First Lord of the Admiralty, before the beginning of hostilities in which he put forth the remarkable theory that the more Americans who took up arms the easier would be the British victory. Clearly Sandwich, as was the case with most other British officials at the beginning of the American War, had gravely misjudged the Americans. Contemptuous of all things American, the rulers of Britain in 1775 did not see how the American rebels, without an army, navy, or even a national government could withstand the onslaught of the King's forces. In this atmosphere of ignorance and contempt, little thought was given to what war with America would involve.

To approach the strategic problems of a war with America so arrogantly, blindly, and simplistically was to invite disaster. Victory or defeat in the American War, as in all military conflicts, depended on a complex set of interactions and relationships between strategy, economics, and diplomacy. A failure, a setback, or even a stalemate in one area will affect all the others. At the beginning of the war the British for the most part thought of the problem of rebellion in America as one that could be solved simply by dispatching an army across the Atlantic to crush the revolt. It apparently did not enter anyone's head in Whitehall that the Americans could and would wage war at sea and that the American naval effort would adversely affect British arms, commerce, and diplomacy. Further, it was not perceived at the beginning of the war that the Royal Navy was not strong enough to fight the Americans and at the same time guard Britain against the possibility of French and Spanish attack.

The facts and figures were available to officials in London, but in the rush to hostilities in 1775 British naval strategic thinking apparently never went beyond the realization that Britain had the strongest navy in the world and the

Americans had no navy. What was not seen in London in 1775 was that America had a long maritime tradition and was capable of waging a large-scale maritime guerrilla war. A look at the lists in the Six Penny Receivers Office would have shown that in 1775, excluding men employed in such maritime occupations as fishing, there were at least ten thousand Americans serving in the British merchant service. A little additional research would have shown that America's shipbuilding industry was well developed, for at the beginning of the war at least one out of every four ships in the British merchant marine was American built. In discounting maritime opposition from America simply because she had no navy, it was forgotten that from the time of the first settlements large numbers of Americans had been engaged in the carrying trade, fishing, and shipbuilding; that in previous wars America had mounted large expeditions against the French settlements in North America and had sent forth cruisers to attack enemy shipping, with considerable success; and that by the beginning of the American War a large number of Americans had extensive experience as smugglers. In 1775 officials in London should have perceived that war with America would confront Britain and the Royal Navy with complicated and crippling strategic problems.

British officials may have been unaware of or unwilling to take into account the potential of American maritime and military strength, but they were very much aware of the power of the French. The French navy posed the greatest naval strategic problem for the British; and it was this threat which prevented the British from deploying the full force of the Royal Navy against the American rebels. Sloops-of-war, frigates, and 50 gun ships were sent to serve in American waters by the score, but the Admiralty thought that in the long run the greatest danger to the security of Britain lay not in America but in Paris. To guard against French, and possibly Spanish, intervention the vast majority of the ships-of-the-line of the Royal Navy were stationed in English waters. Admirals, generals, and other officials at various times demanded that the squadron in America be reinforced with ships drawn from the Channel Fleet; however, the Admiralty, with its eyes firmly fixed upon the French and Spanish fleets, refused to weaken the defenses of Britain by sending units of the Channel Fleet to serve in America. It was Sandwich's maxim that "England ought for her own security to have a superior force in readiness at home to anything that France and Spain united have in readiness on their side." Thus, the threat of possible French and Spanish intervention effectively placed a limit on the amount of naval power the British could deploy in American waters.

Limited by the need to maintain the strength of the Channel Fleet and overwhelmed by the length of the American coastline, the Royal Navy in America never had enough ships to simultaneously guard British bases from American raids, support the offensive operations of the British army, and effectively blockade the American coast. Operations in America simply ate up the strength of the Royal Navy. Ships of the Royal Navy, for instance, appeared to be almost helpless when confronted with one of the most effective of American weapons systems—the whaleboat. From the beginning of the siege of Boston until the end of the conflict, the Americans waged what one authority calls "whaleboat warfare" against the British. At Boston, Newport, New York, and Philadelphia the British were subjected to endless water-borne raids by Americans employing small craft such as whaleboats. Under the very eyes of the Royal Navy in Boston Harbor, American water-borne raiders destroyed the Boston Lighthouse and captured the party of marines who were guarding it. At Newport in 1777 the British garrison commander, Major General Richard Prescott, was surprised, captured, and brought back to the mainland by Americans in whaleboats. And in 1781 American small craft were capturing British vessels as far up in New York Bay as Governors Island. These are only a few of the more spectacular examples from among thousands of whaleboat raids carried out by the Americans. To counter such raids, warships were deployed to guard British bases. On March 1, 1777, for example, there were seventy-two ships of the Royal Navy deployed in North American waters, and of this force about two-thirds were involved in various ways protecting British bases from attack. Twenty-three ships were stationed in the New York area, seven vessels were in the St. Lawrence River, and twenty-three others were guarding Newport and Halifax and at the same time attempting to blockade the coast of New England. At any given time, the protection alone of British-held enclaves in America required a large number of the King's ships.

Another drain on the resources of the Royal Navy during the first three years of the war was the need to assist the operations of the army. Large numbers of warships were deployed in support of the British army as it conducted a series of indecisive amphibious campaigns at New York, Rhode Island, and Philadelphia. At the beginning of each campaigning season warships had to be assembled to aid the operations of the army by providing naval gunfire and the necessary manpower to man the flat-bottomed boats and other small craft required to conduct large-scale amphibious operations. During the summer and autumn of 1776, the British squadron in America averaged about seventy ships; and on August 13, 1776, twenty-seven of these warships (with an additional six expected to arrive) were deployed at New York in support of the army while another twelve were supporting land operations in Canada. In the middle of September 1776 there were thirty-three warships at New York and nine in the St. Lawrence supporting the army. On November 24, 1776, out of a force of seventy-four warships, fifty-four were deployed in support of the army. The situation 1777 was not any better, for twenty warships were needed to escort

General Howe's army from Sandy Hook to the head of the Chesapeake Bay for the invasion of Pennsylvania.

The need to maintain a two power standard in European waters, protect British enclaves in America, and support the army's amphibious operations made the maintenance of an effective blockade of the American coast impossible. At no time during the first three years of the war did the Royal Navy have the ships available to place the American coast under more than token blockade. In August of 1776, for example, there were only twenty-four warships on blockade duty, scattered along the North American coast from Prince Edward Island to St. Augustine. On November 24, 1776, there were only twenty ships on blockade duty. By the beginning of 1778, the effectiveness of the blockade had not improved for there were only twenty-three warships on blockade duty. With an average force of twenty ships it was impossible to effectively blockade a thousand miles of American coast. Admiral Lord Howe, the commander-in-chief of the squadron in American waters, was well aware that the blockade was not working but he also knew that no matter how he deployed his ships they were too few to be effective.

Tactically, the policy of scattering a force of about twenty mostly small warships in ones and twos up and down the American coast was a dangerous one, for it gave the Americans the opportunity to destroy the British squadron piecemeal. The tactical weakness of British naval deployments in America was revealed in the spring of 1776 when a force of eight American warships, commanded by Commodore Esek Hopkins, sailed from Cape Henlopen, which was not blockaded. On March 5, 1776, Hopkins' squadron seized New Providence in the Bahamas, stripped the island of munitions, and then left the Bahamas for America. Upon approaching the American coast, Hopkins captured an armed schooner, an armed brig, and off Block Island attacked and badly damaged the twenty-gun frigate H.M.S. *Glasgow*. In 1777 the tactical vulnerability of individual British warships on blockade duty was again shown when Captain John Manley of the Continental Navy escaped from Boston with two Continental frigates and nine privateers. When Manley captured the British frigate H.M.S. *Fox*, the blockade of New England had to be suspended while British warships hunted him down.

The tactical opportunities presented to the Americans for picking off the odd British warship on blockade duty were minor compared to the strategic advantages reaped by the Americans as a result of the weak blockade. The inability to blockade closely the American coast was one of the greatest British strategic failures in the first years of the war. If a blockade similar to the one instituted during the War of 1812 could have been set up in the first years of the American War, the rebellion would have been denied outside assistance and might have withered away. As it was, the weakness of the blockade allowed the

Americans to continue to export goods, such as tobacco, and to sustain their armies by munitions imported from Europe and the West Indies. When combined with the inability of the King's troops to decisively defeat Washington's army, the failure to prevent the importation of munitions by means of naval blockade in effect gave the Americans the means to continue waging war indefinitely.

The lack of an effective blockade also permitted the Americans to send forth cruisers to attack British ships, thereby extending the battlefield into the North Atlantic basin. The objectives of the American cruiser offensive were threefold: to capture British ships, especially those carrying military cargoes; to carry the war to the West Indies and European seas in order to tie up the Royal Navy in an endless search for American raiders; and lastly to create embarrassing incidents which would contribute to the breakdown of diplomatic relations between Britain and France and hasten French entry into the conflict. It was Britain's misfortune that the American cruiser offensive in the years 1775–1778 achieved, for the most part, its objectives.

The American cruiser offensive can be said to have begun on August 24, 1775, when Washington, using his authority as commander-in-chief of the Continental Army, commissioned the first of a series of vessels to be used to attack British storeships carrying supplies to the King's army at Boston. During the first year or so of the war the American seaborne assault on British supply ships produced some spectacular results, though the victories owed more to British mismanagement than to American skill and daring. During the autumn of 1775, out of thirty-five ships sent from England loaded with provisions for the army at Boston only eight arrived at that port. The rest were either captured or driven by the weather to the West Indies. On November 27, 1775, almost within sight of Boston, one of Washington's armed vessels captured the *Nancy*, an ordnance storeship loaded with, among other things, 2,000 muskets, 100,000 flints, 30,000 round shot, 30 tons of musket balls, and a large mortar. On May 17, 1776, another ordnance storeship, the *Hope*, was captured off Massachusetts and found to contain engineering equipment, 1,600 carbines, and 1,500 barrels of gunpowder. And on November 11, 1776, off Cape Breton, Captain John Paul Jones captured the transport *Mellish* which was carrying a year's supply of clothing for the British army in Canada. After the first months of confusion, the British began to institute measures to protect storeships from attack and windfalls of military equipment and munitions taken on the high seas became less and less frequent for the Americans.

Although the American cruiser offensive began as a modest effort to intercept ships in Massachusetts Bay carrying supplies to the British army at Boston, it quickly grew into a full-scale assault on all British shipping. British navy officers, merchants, and the authorities in London were caught unprepared by this attack on British seaborne trade; for American cruisers seemed able to range at will from the Caribbean Sea to the North Sea and from the Grand Banks to the Bay of Biscay. When the American cruiser offensive began, British naval forces appeared to be weak everywhere and strong nowhere. For example, the ten warships which were stationed in the West Indies at the beginning of hostilities in 1775 were woefully inadequate in number to protect British shipping throughout the whole region. And in Europe the situation was much the same, for most of the small warships suitable for hunting down cruisers and escorting convoys were serving in American waters and, according to Sandwich, there were at the beginning of 1777 only two frigates, eight sloops-of-war, and nine cutters in the British Isles to counter American cruisers.

Perhaps the first American cruiser to operate in European seas was the privateer *Rover* of Salem which was reported on August 31, 1776, by the British consul at Faro to have captured four British merchant ships off Cape St. Vincent. The *Rover* was quickly followed by other American warships and privateers; and the American commissioners in Paris began to issue naval and privateer commissions in European ports. The Americans intended to use French ports as sanctuaries from which to stage attacks on British shipping in order not only to capture enemy ships but also to aggravate relations between Britain and France. The British attempted to employ diplomatic pressure to deprive American cruisers of the use of French ports, for under articles XV, XVII, XIX, XXVI, and XXVII of the Treaty of Utrecht, France was not to allow the cruisers or prizes of Britain's enemies to enter her ports; nor was France to permit her territory to be used to fit out cruisers. These articles had been specifically renewed by the Anglo-French Treaty of 1763; however, the French government artfully violated these agreements.

It was soon evident to London that the French would give American cruisers all possible aid while ostensibly remaining neutral. American cruiser commanders found that it was generally possible to dispose of prizes and obtain refits, supplies, and seamen in French ports. The British authorities viewed the opening of French ports to American cruisers as an act of French duplicity which posed a grave threat to British seaborne commerce and as the probable prelude to French intervention in the American War. The arrival of the American cruisers in European water thrust a grim choice upon the British: if harsh measures were not taken, Britain's merchant marine would suffer greatly from American attack; yet the only firm action the British could take against the American cruisers in Europe would be to deny them use of French ports, and this could only be done by means of naval blockade and would precipitate a war with France.

Failing to deprive the Americans of the use of French ports by means of diplomacy and not desiring a war with France, the British were forced to attempt to confront the American cruisers in European waters with the Royal Navy. On the night of October 28, 1776, a general press was conducted in the Thames

River, and orders were issued during the next few days for readying thirty-four ships-of-the-line for Channel service. Great 64 and 74 gun ships-of-the-line drawn from the Channel Fleet were to be used to combat American cruisers. Units of the Channel Fleet were dispatched to cruise in the Bay of Biscay, the Western Approaches, and the Irish Sea in search of American commerce raiders. From the autumn of 1776 onward, a succession of ships from the Channel Fleet sailed between such points as Cape Clear, Ushant, and Cape Ortegal; others were stationed off commonly frequented landfalls, such as Cape Finisterre; and still others were dispatched far into the Atlantic to intercept and escort safely to Britain homeward-bound trade. Month in and month out the lumbering ships of the Channel Fleet sailed the Eastern Atlantic in search of a few small American armed vessels; but for the most part the ships suffered damage from the elements and the cruises were fruitless.

Losses at the hands of American cruisers prompted various groups of merchants, such as the London based West India Committee, to request that a system of convoys be set up to protect British shipping. The government acted on their request, and by mid-1777 almost every branch of British seaborne trade was conducted under convoy. The institution of a comprehensive system of convoys for merchant shipping, however, caused economic dislocations. British merchants were forced to operate under wartime conditions. Insurance rates shot up for merchant ships which sailed without convoys; yet demurrage bills piled up for those merchant vessels waiting in such places as the Downs for convoy. The convoy system also caused the British commodity markets to be subject to recurrent shortages and gluts. The difficulties of organizing convoys made delays common, and these delays were reflected in the commodity markets. When a convoy was months late arriving in Britain, prices would shoot up to artificial heights. Then, with the arrival in a single port of, for instance, a year's supply of sugar, prices would plummet. Despite the economic dislocations they caused, convoys were a necessary protection against American raiders. Nonetheless, the introduction of convoys and the dispatch of warships to hunt for American cruisers did not stop the American raiders, and the Admiralty was flooded with complaints about shipping lost to them.

From the West Indies to the Irish Sea, American cruisers appeared to be running amuck, capturing British merchant ships at will. Despite convoys, patrols, the blockade of America, and the capture of hundreds of American ships by the Royal Navy, there was no abatement in the American assault on British merchant shipping. Between March 10 and December 31, 1776, Howe's squadron in America recaptured twenty-six British vessels and took at least one hundred and forty American ships. The small squadron at Jamaica captured two hundred and thirty-six American ships between December 21, 1775, and February 26, 1778. Still, American cruisers using French and Dutch islands as bases continued to swarm over the Caribbean seizing British shipping and greatly alarming the British islands. In European waters American cruisers based in French ports roamed the seas around Britain. In June of 1777, for example, three Continental warships operating as a squadron captured fourteen British merchant ships in the Firth of Clyde. And during the summer of 1777, Lord George Germain exclaimed:

> We lately had so many privateers upon our coasts and such encouragement given them by the French, that I was apprehensive a few weeks ago that we should have been obliged to have declared war.

At least three hundred and forty-seven British ships were taken during 1776, and in 1777 some three hundred and fifty more fell victim to American cruisers; yet the Royal Navy managed to capture a mere handful of American raiders. The British were forced to suffer the humiliation of seeing the Royal Navy, the strongest in the world and a force with a tradition of victory, run ragged by a few American cruisers.

American naval operations produced for the British not only strategic problems, economic dislocations, and shipping losses, but also an endless series of unwelcome diplomatic incidents with the French. On March 8, 1776, for example, the French sent a diplomatic protest to London stating that British warships had repeatedly violated French territorial waters in the West Indies and that the Royal Navy had Martinique under blockade, with British warships hovering off the island stopping approaching ships, using gunfire if necessary. Then in 1777 the spectacular exploits of Captain Gustavus Conyngham of the Continental Navy alone produced a crisis between Britain and France which almost caused a break in diplomatic relations between the two countries. The operations of American cruisers, however, were not the only cause of diplomatic incidents. The British provoked a storm of protest in their efforts to prevent the Americans, who were aided by the French, from shipping munitions across the Atlantic. Most of the munitions appear to have been sent to the French West Indies on French flag vessels and then transshipped to America either on American ships or on nominal French ships. British warships in European waters had directions from the Admiralty not to seize French vessels "*without particular orders,*" for as Sandwich knew, "bringing in a French ship upon suspicions that appear not well grounded afterwards may draw us into a war, which in our present circumstances ought by all means be avoided." Nevertheless, French and other neutral ships were seized in European waters on suspicion of carrying munitions to the Americans, and Whitehall was flooded with diplomatic protests. Yet to seize French ships or American ships with French papers and flags, even if they were loaded with munitions bound for the Americans, was a dangerous practice; for if it was carried out on a scale large enough to effectively prevent arms from reaching America, war with France would be unavoidable.

By the beginning of 1778 the British were in a strategic trap. War with France was all but inevitable. One British army had been captured in the wilds of northern New York, and another was confined to several enclaves on the edge of the American continent. The Royal Navy had proved itself incapable of effectively blockading the American coast; and neither British diplomacy nor the Royal Navy could prevent the flow of munitions across the Atlantic to American armies or stop American cruisers from attacking British seaborne trade. Although the Royal Navy remained a force to be reckoned with and had inflicted heavy casualties on the Americans in a war as complex as the war in America victory is not necessarily measured by the number of ships taken. With the failure of British arms to produce decisive results in the campaigns of 1776 and 1777, the only possible way left to crush the rebellion in America was a truely effective blockade. The British, however, lacked the ships to carry out this measure, which in turn permitted the Americans to import the munitions necessary to continue the war, to send forth cruisers to attack British shipping, and to employ naval forces to facilitate the breakdown of diplomatic relations between Britain and France, thereby hastening the entry of the Bourbon powers into the conflict.

Although during the years 1775–1778 the Royal Navy never lost "command of the sea" in the Mahanian sense of the term, American naval operations resulted in defeat at sea for the British. The impact of this defeat went far beyond the fact that the strongest navy in the world appeared impotent in the face of the pigmy American naval forces. The ability of the Americans to take the war to the high seas was unforseen by the British, yet it played a major role in exploding the conflict in America into a worldwide naval war and in hastening Britain's ultimate defeat in America.

ROBERT MIDDLEKAUFF

WHY MEN FOUGHT IN THE AMERICAN REVOLUTION

F*ew things are more intriguing than just why men put their lives at risk in such dangerous occupations as soldiering or serving in a navy or air force. Certainly ideological causes, be they religious, political, or economic, have an enormous part to play. Undoubtedly some men fight for the prestige or the benefits from pensions or bounties that might be gained. Others look for adventure. Sometimes a great deal of social pressure is put on those who refuse to join in a noble cause.*

None of these is enough to keep most men in the line of battle once the carnage and confusion of war surrounds them. Rather, there is, wrote Stephen Crane, "a mysterious fraternity born out of smoke and danger of death." That mysterious fraternity is molded in an esprit de corps formed in the training, camp life, and combat that soldiers and sailors share with one another. As Robert Middlekauff so aptly illustrates, it is the unique combination of the social cohesion of the unit and the effectiveness of leadership that determines the steadiness of men under fire. The best British and American units of the War for American Independence exhibited that cohesion and leadership when facing the test of combat.

From the point of view of the regulars or at least the long-term volunteers like the Continental Army veterans, central to success on the battlefield was discipline. Discipline was the consequence of cohesion and determined leadership. Eighteenth-century weaponry, with its short-range, slow-firing, inaccurate musketry, demanded close order maneuvers which required long, effective training. Such tactics contributed to unit cohesion and to control over the great dread of all on the battlefield—fear. There is the fear of cowardice, the fear of death and mutilation, and the fear of disgracing friends and the unit's reputation. To succeed, military organizations have to bond their soldiers and sailors into the small groups that are the core of battle morale.

Most experts argue that well-supplied troops are more likely to have that cohesion necessary for success. Certainly most eighteenth-century officers felt adequate supplies were a necessary ingredient in maintaining unit morale. But it is not always the case. Hessian Captain Johann Ewald fought from 1776 to 1783 on behalf of the British crown. He was amazed that American soldiers stayed in the field. He could not comprehend how such ill-clad, ill-housed, and ill-paid troops would continue to resist. "With what soldiers in the world could one do what was done by these men, who go about nearly naked in the greatest privation?" he asked. "Deny the best-disciplined soldiers of Europe what is due them and they will run away in droves, and the general will soon be alone." Just before departing for a return to Europe, Captain Ewald visited the American garrison at West Point, New York. General Frederick von Steuben drew up his troops for inspection. "The men looked haggard and pallid and were poorly dressed. Indeed very many stood quite proudly under arms without shoes and stockings. Although I shuddered at the distress of these men, it filled me with awe for them, for I did not think there was an army in the world which could be maintained as cheaply as the American army." The Hessian captain concluded, "This . . . is a part of that 'Liberty and Independence' for which these poor fellows had to have their arms and legs smashed. —But to what cannot enthusiasm lead a people!"

Unit cohesion in the Revolutionary War came partially through close order formation. Such is not the mode of combat today. How does modern weaponry, which has forced men to fire from lumbering tanks, fast-moving ships, and speeding airplanes, affect the essential ingredients of cohesion and command that Middlekauff describes? Does modern warfare require those characteristics, which Washington both desired and epitomized? Or, do modern military forces require a different kind of leadership because the more lethal weaponry of modern combat requires them to separate from one another to survive? (For more on this subject, readers should consult Rick Atkinson's article on small unit actions in Vietnam.)

Moreover, is Middlekauff too harsh on the militia? If one looks at his examples, it is clear that, when effectively led, the militia contributed to some of the more significant victories of the American Revolution—witness Concord, Cowpens, and Kings Mountain. The militia made mighty (but usually ignored) contributions to the success of the American war effort. The militiamen kept Loyalists inactive or forced them to emigrate. They kept American farmers from selling supplies to the British, thus making the Royal quartermasters look elsewhere for food, forage, and fuel. They also insured that it was the Americans who controlled the instruments of local government under which most residents lived—the sheriffs, judges, tax collectors, and assemblymen.

*I*n the Battle of Eutaw Springs, South Carolina, the last major action of the Revolutionary War before Cornwallis surrendered at Yorktown, over 500 Americans were killed and wounded. Nathanael Greene had led some 2200 men into the Springs; his casualties thus equaled almost one fourth of his army. More men would die in battles in the next two years, and others would suffer terrible wounds. Although the statistics are notoriously unreliable, they show that the Revolution killed a higher percentage of those who served on the American side than any war in our history, always excepting the Civil War.

Why did these men—those who survived and those who died—fight? Why did they hold their ground, endure the strain of battle, with men dying about them and danger to themselves so obvious? Undoubtedly the reasons varied from battle to battle, but just as undoubtedly there was some experience common to all these battles—and fairly uniform reasons for the actions of the men who fought despite their deepest impulses, which must have been to run from the field in order to escape the danger.

Some men did run, throwing down their muskets and packs in order to speed their flight. American units broke in large actions and small, at Brooklyn, Kip's Bay, White Plains, Brandywine, Germantown, Camden, and Hobkirk's Hill, to cite the most important instances. Yet many men did not break and run even in the disasters to American arms. They held their ground until they were killed, and they fought tenaciously while pulling back.

In most actions the Continentals, the regulars, fought more bravely than the militia. We need to know why these men fought and why the American regulars performed better than the militia. The answers surely will help us to understand the Revolution, especially if we can discover whether what made men fight reflected what they believed—and felt—about the Revolution.

Several explanations of the willingness to fight and die, if necessary, may be dismissed at once. One is that soldiers on both sides fought out of fear of their officers, fearing them more than they did battle. Frederick the Great had described this condition as ideal, but it did not exist in ideal or practice in either the American or British army. The British soldier usually possessed a more professional spirit than the American, an attitude compounded from confidence in his skill and pride in belonging to an old established institution. British regiments carried proud names—the Royal Welsh Fusiliers, the Black Watch, the King's Own—whose officers usually behaved extraordinarily bravely in battle and expected their men to follow their examples. British officers disciplined their men more harshly than American officers did and generally trained them more effectively in the movements of battle. But neither they nor American officers instilled the fear that Frederick found so desirable. Spirit, bravery, a reliance on the bayonet were all expected of professional soldiers, but professionals acted out of pride—not fear of their officers.

Still, coercion and force were never absent from the life of either army. There were, however, limits on their use and their effectiveness. The fear of flogging might prevent a soldier from deserting from camp, but it could not guarantee that he would remain steady under fire. Fear of ridicule may have aided in keeping some troops in place, however. Eighteenth-century infantry went into combat in fairly close lines and officers could keep an eye on many of their men. If the formation was tight enough officers might strike laggards and even order "skulkers," Washington's term for those who turned tail, shot down. Just before the move to Dorchester Heights in March 1776, the word went out that any American who ran from the action would be "fired down upon the spot." The troops themselves approved of this threat, according to one of the chaplains.

Washington repeated the threat just before the Battle of Brooklyn later that year, though he seems not to have posted men behind the lines to carry it out. Daniel Morgan urged Nathanael Greene to place sharpshooters behind the militia, and Greene may have done so at Guilford Court House. No one thought that an entire army could be held in place against its will, and these threats to shoot soldiers who retired without orders were never widely issued.

A tactic that surely would have appealed to many soldiers would have been to send them into battle drunk. Undoubtedly some—on both sides—did enter combat with their senses deadened by rum. Both armies commonly issued an additional ration of rum on the eve of some extraordinary action—a long, difficult march, for example, or a battle, were two of the usual reasons. A common order on such occasions ran: "The troops should have an extraordinary allowance of rum," usually a gill, four ounces of unknown alcoholic content, which if taken down at the propitious moment might dull fears and summon courage. At Camden no supply of rum existed; Gates or his staff substituted molasses to no good effect, according to Otho Williams. The British fought brilliantly at Guilford Court House unaided by anything stronger than their own large spirits. In most actions soldiers went into battle with very little more than themselves and their comrades to lean upon.

Belief in the Holy Spirit surely sustained some in the American army, perhaps more than in the enemy's. There are a good many references to the divine or to Providence in the letters and diaries of ordinary soldiers. Often, however, these expressions are in the form of thanks to the Lord for permitting these soldiers to survive. There is little that suggests soldiers believed that faith rendered them invulnerable to the enemy's bullets. Many did consider the glorious cause to be sacred; their war, as the ministers who sent them off to kill never tired of reminding them, was just and providential.

Others clearly saw more immediate advantages in the fight: the plunder of the enemy's dead. At Monmouth Court House, where Clinton withdraw after dark leaving the field strewn with British corpses, the plundering carried American soldiers into the houses of civilians who had fled to save themselves. The soldiers' actions were so blatant and so unrestrained that Washington ordered their packs searched. And at Eutaw Springs, the Americans virtually gave up victory to the opportunity of ransacking British tents. Some died in their greed, shot down by an enemy given time to regroup while his camp was torn apart by men looking for something to carry off. But even these men probably fought for something besides plunder. When it beckoned they collapsed, but it had not drawn them to the field; nor had it kept them there in a savage struggle.

Inspired leadership helped soldiers face death, but they sometimes fought bravely even when their leaders let them down. Yet officers' courage and the example of officers throwing off wounds to remain in the fight undoubtedly helped their men stick. Charles Stedman remarked on Captain Maitland, who at Guilford Court House was hit, dropped behind for a few minutes to get his wound dressed, then returned to the battle. Cornwallis obviously filled Sergeant Lamb with pride, struggling forward to press into the struggle after his horse was killed. Washington's presence meant much at Princeton, though his exposure to enemy fire may also have made his troops uneasy. His quiet exhortation as he passed among the men who were about to assault Trenton—"Soldiers, keep by your officers"—remained in the mind of a Connecticut soldier until he died fifty years later. There was only one Washington, one Cornwallis, and their influence on men in battle, few of whom could have seen them, was of course slight. Junior and noncommissioned officers carried the burden of tactical direction; they had to show their troops what must be done and somehow persuade, cajole, or force them to do it. The praise ordinary soldiers lavished on sergeants and junior officers suggests that these leaders played important parts in their troops' willingness to fight. Still, important as it was, their part does not really explain why men fought.

In suggesting this conclusion about military leadership, I do not wish to be understood as agreeing with Tolstoy's scornful verdict on generals—that despite all their plans and orders they do not affect the results of battles at all. Tolstoy did not reserve all his scorn for generals—historians are also derided in *War and Peace* for finding a rational order in battles where only chaos existed. "The activity of a commander in chief does not at all resemble the activity we imagine to ourselves when we sit at ease in our studies examining some campaign on the map, with a certain number of troops on this and that side in a certain known locality, and begin our plans from some given moment. A commander in chief is never dealing with the beginning of any event—the position from which we always contemplate it. The commander in chief is always in the midst of a series of shifting events and so he never can at any moment consider the whole import of an event that is occurring."

The full import of battle will as surely escape historians as participants. But we have to begin somewhere in trying to explain why men fought rather than ran from revolutionary battlefields. The battlefield may indeed be the place to begin, since we have dismissed leadership, fear of officers, religious belief, the power of drink, and other possible explanations of why men fought and died.

The eighteenth-century battlefield was, compared to that of the twentieth, an intimate theater, especially intimate in the engagements of the Revolution, which were usually small even by the standards of the day. The killing range of the musket—eighty to one hundred yards—enforced intimacy, as did the reliance on the bayonet and the general ineffectiveness of artillery. Soldiers had to come to close quarters to kill; this fact reduced the mystery of battle, though perhaps not its terrors. But at least the battlefield lost some of its impersonality. In fact, in contrast to twentieth-century combat, in which the enemy usually remains unseen and the source of incoming fire unknown, in eighteenth-century battles the foe could be seen and sometimes even touched. Seeing one's enemy may have aroused a singular intensity of feeling uncommon in modern battles. The assault with the bayonet—the most desired objective of infantry tactics— seems indeed to have evoked an emotional climax. Before it occurred tension and anxiety built up as the troops marched from their column into a line of attack. The purpose of their movements was well understood by themselves and their enemies, who must have watched with feelings of dread and fascination. When the order came sending them forward, rage, even madness, replaced the attacker's anxiety, while terror and desperation sometimes filled those receiving the charge. Surely it is revealing that the Americans who ran from battle did so most often at the moment they understood that their enemy had started forward with the bayonet. This happened to several units at Brandywine and to the militia at Camden and Guilford Court House. The loneliness, the sense of isolation reported by modern soldiers, was probably missing at such moments. All was clear—especially that glittering line of advancing steel.

Whether this awful clarity was harder to bear than losing sight of the enemy is problematical. American troops ran at Germantown after grappling with the British and then finding the field of battle covered by fog. At that time groping blindly, they and their enemy struggled over ground resembling a scene of modern combat. The enemy was hidden at a critical moment, and American fears were generated by not knowing what was happening—or about to happen. They could not see the enemy, and they could not see one another, an especially important fact. For, as S. L. A. Marshall, the twentieth-century military historian, has suggested in his book *Men against Fire*, what sustains men in the extraordinary circumstances of battle may be their relationships with their comrades.

These men found that sustaining such relationships was possible in the intimacy of the American battlefield—and not just because the limited arena robbed battle of some of its mystery. More importantly it permitted the troops to give one another moral or psychological support. The enemy could be seen, but so could one's comrades; they could be seen and communicated with.

Eighteenth-century infantry tactics called for men to move and fire from tight formations which permitted them to talk and to give one another information—and reassurance and comfort. If properly done, marching and firing found infantrymen compressed into files in which their shoulders touched. In battle physical contact with one's comrades on either side must have helped men control their fears. Firing the musket from three compact lines, the English practice, also involved physical contact. The men of the front rank crouched on their right knees; the men of the center rank placed their left feet inside the right feet of the front; the rear rank did the same thing behind the center. This stance was called—in a revealing term—"locking." The very density of this formation sometimes aroused criticism from officers who complained that it led to inaccurate fire. The front rank, conscious of the closeness of the center, might fire too low; the rear rank tended to "throw" its shots into the air, as firing too high was called; only the center rank took careful aim, according to the critics. Whatever the truth of these charges about accuracy of fire, men in these dense formations compiled a fine record of holding their ground. And it is worth noting that the inaccuracy of men in the rear rank bespoke their concern for their fellows in front of them.

British and American soldiers in the Revolution often spoke of fighting with "spirit" and "behaving well" under fire. Sometimes these phrases referred to daring exploits under great danger, but more often they seem to have meant holding together, giving one another support, reforming the lines when they were broken or fell into disorder, disorder such as overtook the Americans at Greenspring, Virginia, early in July 1781 when Cornwallis lured Anthony Wayne into crossing the James with a heavily outnumbered force. Wayne saw his mistake and decided to make the best of it, not by a hasty retreat from the ambush, but by attacking. The odds against the Americans were formidable, but as an ordinary soldier who was there saw it, the inspired conduct of the infantry saved them—"our troops behaved well, fighting with great spirit and bravery. The infantry were oft broke; but just as oft rallied and formed at a word."

These troops had been spread out when the British surprised them, but they formed as quickly as possible. Here was a test of men's spirits, a test they passed in part because of their disciplined formation. In contrast at Camden, where the militia collapsed as soon as the battle began, an open alignment may have contributed to their fear. Gates placed the Virginians on the far left apparently expecting them to cover more ground than their numbers allowed. At any rate they went into the battle in a single line with at least five feet between each man and the next, a distance which intensified a feeling of isolation in the heat and noise of the firing. And to make such feelings worse, these men were especially exposed, stretched out at one end of the line with no supporters behind them.

Troops in tight lines consciously reassured one another in several ways. British troops usually talked and cheered—"huzzaing" whether standing their ground, running forward, or firing. The Americans may have done less talking and cheering, though there is evidence that they learned to imitate the enemy. Giving a cheer at the end of a successful engagement was standard practice. The British cheered at Lexington and then marched off to be shot down on the road running from Concord. The Americans shouted their joy at Harlem Heights, an understandable action and one which for most of 1776 they rarely had opportunity to perform.

★ ★ ★ ★ ★

The most deplorable failures to stand and fight usually occurred among the American militia. Yet there were militia companies that performed with great success, remaining whole units under the most deadly volleys. The New England companies at Bunker Hill held out under a fire that veteran British officers compared to the worst they had experienced in Europe. Lord Rawdon remarked on how unusual it was for defenders to stick to their posts even after the assaulting troops had entered the ditch around a redoubt. The New Englanders did it. They also held steady at Princeton—"They were the first who regularly formed" and stood up under the balls "which whistled their thousand different notes around our heads," according to Charles Willson Peale, whose Philadelphia militia also proved their steadiness.

What was different about these companies? Why did they fight when others around them ran? The answer may lie in the relationships among their men. Men in the New England companies, in the Philadelphia militia, and in the other units that held together, were neighbors. They knew one another; they had something to prove to one another; they had their "honor" to protect. Their active service in the Revolution may have been short, but they had been together in one way or another for a fairly long time—for several years, in most cases. Their companies, after all, had been formed from towns and villages. Some clearly had known one another all their lives.

Elsewhere, especially in the thinly settled southern colonies, companies were usually composed of men—farmers, farmers' sons, farm laborers, artisans, and new immigrants—who did not know one another. They were, to use a term much used in a later war, companies of "stragglers" without common attachments, with almost no knowledge of their fellows. For them, even bunched tightly in line, the battlefield was an empty, lonely place. Absence of personal bonds and their own parochialism, coupled to inadequate training and imperfect discipline, often led to disintegration under fire.

According to conventional wisdom, the nearer the American militia were to home the better they fought, fighting for their homes and no one else's. Proximity to home, however, may have been a distraction which weakened resolve; for the irony of going into battle and perhaps to their deaths when home and safety lay close down the road could not have escaped many. Almost every senior American general commented on the propensity of the militia to desert—and if they were not deserting they seemed perpetually in transit between home and camp, usually without authorization.

Paradoxically, of all the Americans who fought, the militiamen best exemplified in themselves and in their behavior the ideals and purposes of the Revolution. They had enjoyed independence, or at least personal liberty, long before it was proclaimed in the Declaration. They instinctively felt their equality with others and in many places insisted upon demonstrating it by choosing their own officers. Their sense of their liberty permitted, even compelled, them to serve only for short enlistments, to leave camp when they liked, to scorn the orders of others—and especially those orders to fight when they preferred to flee. Their integration into their society drove them to resist military discipline; and their ethos of personal freedom stimulated hatred of the machine that served as the model for the army. They were not pieces of machine, and they would serve it only reluctantly and skeptically. At their best—at Cowpens, for example—they fought well; at their worst, at Camden, they fought not at all. There they were, as Greene said, "ungovernable." What was lacking in the militia was a set of professional standards, requirements and rules which might regulate their conduct in battle. What was lacking was professional pride. Coming and going to camp as they liked, shooting their guns for the pleasure of the sound, the militia annoyed the Continentals, who soon learned that most of them could not be trusted.

The British regulars were at the opposite pole. They had been pulled out of society, carefully segregated from it, tightly disciplined, and highly trained. Their values were the values of the army, for the most part, no more and no less. The officers, to be sure, were in certain respects very different from the men. They embodied the style and standards of gentlemen who believed in service to their king and who fought for honor and glory.

With these ideals and a mission of service to the king defining their calling, British officers held themselves as aloof as possible from the peculiar horrors of war. Not that they did not fight; they sought combat and danger, but by the conventions which shaped their understanding of battle they insulated themselves as much as possible from the ghastly business of killing and dying. Thus the results of battle might be long lists of dead and wounded, but the results were also "honourable and glorious," as Charles Stedman described Guilford Court House, or reflected "dishonour upon British arms," as he described Cowpens. Actions and gunfire were "smart" and "brisk" and sometimes "hot," and occasionally a "difficult piece of work." They might also be described lightly—Harlem Heights was "this silly business" to Lord Rawdon. To their men, British officers spoke a clean, no-nonsense language. Howe's terse "look to your bayonets" summed up a tough professional's expectations.

For all the distance between British officers and men, they gave remarkable support to one another in battle. They usually deployed carefully, keeping up their spirits with drum and fife. They talked and shouted and cheered, and coming on with their bayonets at the ready "huzzaing," or coming on "firing and huzzaing" they must have sustained a sense of shared experience. Their ranks might be thinned by an American volley, but on they came, exhorting one another to "push on! push on!" as at Bunker Hill and the battles that followed. Although terrible losses naturally dispirited them, they almost always maintained the integrity of their regiments as fighting units, and when they were defeated, or nearly so as at Guilford Court House, they recovered their pride and fought well thereafter. And there was no hint at Yorktown that the ranks wanted to surrender, even though they had suffered dreadfully.

The Continentals, the American regulars, lacked the polish of their British counterparts but, at least from Monmouth on, they showed a steadiness under fire almost as impressive as their enemy's. And they demonstrated a brave endurance: defeated, they retired, pulled themselves together, and came back to try again.

These qualities—patience and endurance—endeared them to many. For example, John Laurens, on Washington's staff in 1778, wanted desperately to command them. In what amounted to a plea for command, Laurens wrote: "I would cherish those dear, ragged Continentals, whose patience will be the admiration of future ages, and glory in bleeding with them." This statement was all the more extraordinary coming from Laurens, a South Carolinian aristocrat. The soldiers he admired were anything but aristocratic. As the war dragged on, they came more and more from the poor and the propertyless. Most probably entered the army as substitutes for men who had rather pay than serve, or as the recipients of bounties and the promise of land. In time some, perhaps many, assimilated the ideals of the Revolution. As Baron Steuben observed in training them, they differed from European troops in at least one regard: they wanted to know why they were told to do certain things. Unlike European soldiers who did what they were told, the Continentals asked why.

Continental officers aped the style of their British counterparts. They aspired to gentility and often, failing to achieve it, betrayed their anxiety by an excessive concern for their honor. Not surprisingly, like their British peers, they also used the vocabularies of gentlemen in describing battle.

Their troops, innocent of such polish, spoke with words from their immediate experience of physical combat. They found few euphemisms for the horrors of battle. Thus Private David How, September 1776, in New York noted in his diary: "Isaac Fowls had his head shot off with a cannon ball this morning." And Sergeant Thomas McCarty reported an engagement between a British foraging party and American infantry near New Brunswick in February 1777: "We attacked the body, and bullets flew like hail. We stayed about 15 minutes and then retreated with loss." After the battle inspection of the field revealed that the British had killed the American wounded—"The men that was wounded in the thigh or leg, they dashed out their brains with their muskets and run them through with their bayonets, made them like sieves. This was barbarity to the utmost." They pain of seeing his comrades mutilated by shot and shell at White Plains remained with Elisha Bostwick, a Connecticut soldier, all his life: A cannon ball "cut down Lt. Youngs Platoon which was next to that of mine[;] the ball first took off the head of Smith, a Stout heavy man and dashed it open, then took Taylor across the Bowels, it then Struck Sergeant Garret of our Company on the hip [and] took off the point of the hip bone[.] Smith and Taylor were left on the spot. Sergeant Garret was carried but died the Same day now to think, oh! what a sight that was to see within a distance of six rods those men with their legs and arms and guns and packs all in a heap[.]"

The Continentals occupied the psychological and moral ground somewhere between the militia and the British professionals. From 1777 on their enlistments were for three years or the duration of the war. This long service allowed them to learn more of their craft and to become seasoned. That does not mean that on the battlefield they lost their fear. Experience in combat almost never leaves one indifferent to danger, unless after prolonged and extreme fatigue one comes to consider oneself already dead. Seasoned troops simply learn to deal with their fear more effectively than raw troops do, in part because they have come to realize that everyone feels it and that they can rely on their fellows.

★ ★ ★ ★ ★

By winter 1779–1780, the Continentals were beginning to believe that they had no one save themselves to lean on. Their soldierly qualifications so widely admired in America—their "habit of subordination," their patience under fatigue, their ability to stand sufferings and privations of every kind may in fact have led to a bitter resignation that saw them through a good deal of fighting. At Morristown during this winter, they felt abandoned in their cold and hunger. They knew that food and clothing existed in America to keep them healthy and comfortable, and yet little of either came to the army. Understandably their dissatisfaction increased as they realized that once again suffering had been left to them. Dissatisfaction in these months slowly turned into a feeling of martyrdom. They felt themselves to be martyrs to the "glorious cause." They would fulfill the ideals of the Revolution and see things through to independence because the civilian population would not.

Thus the Continentals in the last four years of the active war, though less articulate and less independent than the militia, assimilated one part of the "cause" more fully. They had advanced further in making American purposes in the Revolution their own. They had in their sense of isolation and neglect probably come to be more nationalistic than the militia—though surely no more American.

Although these sources of the Continentals' feeling seem curious, they served to reinforce the tough professional ethic these men also came to absorb. Set apart from the militia by the length of their service, by their officers' esteem for them, and by their own contempt for part-time soldiers, the Continentals slowly developed resilience and pride. Their country might ignore them in camp, might allow their bellies to shrivel and their backs to freeze, might allow them to wear rags, but in battle they would not be ignored. And in battle they would support one another in the knowledge that their own moral and professional resources remained sure.

The meaning of these complex attitudes is not what it seems to be. At first sight the performance of militia and Continentals seems to suggest that the great principles of the Revolution made little difference on the battlefield. Or if principles did make a difference, say especially to the militia saturated with natural rights and a deep and persistent distrust of standing armies, they served not to strengthen the will to combat but to disable it. And the Continentals, recruited increasingly from the poor and dispossessed, apparently fought better as they came to resemble their professional and apolitical enemy, the British infantry.

These conclusions are in part askew. To be sure, there is truth—and paradox—in the fact that some Americans' commitments to revolutionary principles made them unreliable on the battlefield. Still, their devotion to their principles helped bring them there. George Washington, their commander-in-chief, never tired of reminding them that their cause arrayed free men against mercenaries. They were fighting for the "blessings of liberty," he told them in 1776, and should they not acquit themselves like men, slavery would replace their freedom. The challenge to behave like men was not an empty one. Courage, honor, gallantry in the service of liberty, all those words calculated to bring a blush of embarrassment to jaded twentieth-century men, defined manhood for the eighteenth century. In battle those words gained an extraordinary resonance as they were embodied in the actions of brave men. Indeed it is likely that many Americans who developed a narrow professional spirit found battle broadly educative, forcing them to consider the purposes of their professional skill.

On one level those purposes had to be understood as having a remarkable importance if men were to fight—and die. For battle forced American soldiers into a situation which nothing in their usual experience had prepared them for. They were to kill other men in the expectation that even if they did they might be killed themselves. However defined, especially by a Revolution in the name of life, liberty, and the pursuit of happiness, this situation was unnatural.

On another level, one which, perhaps, made the strain of battle endurable, the situation of American soldiers, though unusual, was not really foreign to them. For what battle presented in stark form was one of the classic problems free men face: choosing between the rival claims of public responsibility and private wishes, or in eighteenth-century terms choosing between virtue—devotion to the public trust—and personal liberty. In battle, virtue demanded that men give up their liberties and perhaps even their lives for others. Each time they fought they had in effect to weigh the claims of society and liberty. Should they fight or run? They knew that the choice might mean life or death. For those American soldiers who were servants, apprentices, poor men substituting for men with money to hire them, the choice might not have seemed to involve moral decision. After all they had never enjoyed much personal liberty. But not even in that contrivance of eighteenth-century authoritarianism in which they now found themselves, the professional army, could they avoid a moral decision. Compressed into dense formations, they were reminded by their nearness to their comrades that they too had an opportunity to uphold virtue. By standing firm they served their fellows and honor; by running, they served only themselves.

Thus battle tested the inner qualities of men, tried their souls, as Thomas Paine said. Many men died in the test that battle made of their spirits. Some soldiers called this trial cruel; others called it "glorious." Perhaps this difference in perception suggests how difficult it was in the Revolution to be both a soldier and an American. Nor has it ever been easy since.

PART III

THE MILITARY OF THE YOUNG REPUBLIC

RICHARD H. KOHN

THE MURDER OF THE MILITIA SYSTEM IN THE AFTERMATH OF THE AMERICAN REVOLUTION

O*ne of the consequences of the American Revolution, wrote historian Walter Millis, was that it "democratized war." "If this freed [the Americans] from the arrogance and exactions of 'royal hirelings,' " he continued, "it laid upon them, whether they liked it or not, an obligation which they could not refuse." Citizenship in the young republic implied an obligation of military service when the political system demanded such duty. Much of that obligation was assumed by proxy through the regular army and navy, which protected the frontiers, coastal cities, and sea-lanes from Indians, surprise attack, and pirates. But what if there should be a major conflict? What sort of mobilization system would the citizens use? Who would organize the effort and how would they do so? Critical to the policymakers was a deep distrust of "standing armies" that permeated the national psyche. At the same time, among the veterans of the Continental Army and in the national political leadership there was a deep disdain for the ability of the militia system to serve as an effective, reliable military force. Moreover, there was a decided lack of financial capacity to support an effective militia system no matter how much the public believed the citizen-soldier to be critical to maintaining national security.*

No problem so beset early American military planners as providing for a backup force for the regular army. Two basic issues emerged from the beginning. First, should every adult male be required to perform some sort of military service as an obligation of citizenship? Second, what level of government, state or national, should be responsible for organizing, paying, officering, equipping, and training the citizen-soldiers?

Exacerbating the problem was the question of military needs. The new nation (or, for that matter, the present one) had no security requirement for universal military training and could not justify the expense of providing such a system. Moreover, one of the more important colonial legacies was a distrust of standing armies. The concept of the citizen-soldier was so ingrained in the American psyche that it could not be dismissed even by those, such as Gouverneur Morris and Alexander Hamilton, who advocated a large regular establishment. Secretary of War Henry Knox in 1790 proposed a large, nationalized militia, a plan that offended those who were economically frugal, as well as the states-rights advocates.

The net result, as Chief of Air Force History Dr. Richard H. Kohn describes, was the "murder" of any effective militia system. What is not discussed is whether there was a compromise position between the nationalized, universal militia on the one hand and the ill-funded, localized militia on the other. Given the lack of an aggressive neighbor threatening national survival, did the United States need the large militia advocated by Knox? Given the need for governors to have some military force at hand to provide local defense against Indians and dissidents, did there not need to be some state authority over the militia? Should there not have been a distinction made between an organized, volunteer peacetime militia and a volunteer or conscripted armed force for wartime purposes? To some degree, these problems remain unresolved today in a country that has a national guard (the organized state militia), army, navy, marine corps, and air force reserves (the organized national reserve), and, if needed, a draft (conscripted young men). The problem confronting the nation in the 1990s will be whether we should "murder" the reserve components in the name of more efficient active duty forces or possibly "murder" the active component by relying excessively on the reserve components. Thus the issues raised in the 1790s still plague decision makers today.

More than a quarter century after the Constitution was adopted, Gouverneur Morris, chairman of the committee of style and author of much of the Constitution's final language, explained that in shaping the militia provision the framers "meant chiefly to provide against . . . the hazarding of the national safety by a reliance on that expensive and inefficient force. An overweening vanity leads the fond many, each man against the conviction of his own heart, to believe or affect to believe, that militia can beat veteran troops in the open field and even play of battle. This idle notion, fed by vaunting demagogues, alarmed us for our country," Morris remembered. "[To] rely on undisciplined, ill-officered men, though each were individually as brave as Caesar, . . . is to act in defiance of reason and experience." "Those, who, during the Revolutionary storm, had confidential acquaintance with the conduct of affairs, knew that to rely on militia was to lean on a broken reed."

In spite of their own doubts the framers of the Constitution understood the tremendous popular affection for the militia, how greatly Americans looked to militia for the nation's protection, how deeply ingrained was the concept and tradition of the citizen soldier in American defense. Some of the most politically conscious of the nation's military leaders after the Revolution, although not champions of militia prowess, felt compelled to acknowledge its primacy: "The first principle of the Security of the United States," conceded Henry Knox; "the only palladium of a free people," intoned Timothy Pickering; "this Great Bulwark of our Liberties and independence," echoed George Washington. In numerous debates after the war, in the Congress and outside, the militia was defended and glorified in the same sacrosanct terms. When Alexander Hamilton publicly denigrated "small fugitive bodies of volunteer militia" as the "mimicry of soldiership" in a July 4, 1789, New York City speech attended by some of the nation's top leadership, it was interpreted as a general attack on the militia. Nearly a year later in the House of Representatives, South Carolina's Aedanus Burke rose to the defense. "I now declare, that the assertion was false," Burke declared heatedly, and then, turning to the crowded gallery where he thought Hamilton sat, "I throw the lie in Colonel Hamilton's face." Burke later apologized, but not before he extracted from Hamilton an explicit denial of any intention to slur the effectiveness of militia in general. Endorsement of the militia's importance went beyond public displays for popular consumption. As John Adams travelled through Europe in the 1780s, he repeatedly cited the militia, along with the "Towns, . . . Schools and Churches as the four Causes of the Growth and Defence of N[ew] England" and the source of "the Virtues and talents of the People"—"Temperance, Patience, Fortitude, Prudence, . . . Justice, . . . Sagacity, Knowledge, Judgment, Taste, Skill, Ingenuity, Dexterity, and Industry."

American trust in their local forces reflected more than a century's political and military development. From the first years of settlement colonists had relied on the citizenry organized in local units for defense against Indians. The militia was used in nearly every major conflict involving European foes up until the Revolution. By the middle of the eighteenth century, however, colonists were relying more heavily on British forces for protection, while serving as volunteers in specially organized expeditions or in Crown units. But provincial regulars were a rarity except for patrols or garrisons in frontier or seacoast forts, and the men usually were drafted or volunteered out of local militia organizations. Even while the militia system was deteriorating markedly during the generation before the Revolution and falling into disuse in older settled areas, American faith remained unshaken. On the surface the system seemed to work and to be flexible. It permitted different colonies to adapt their forces to special local conditions or, if performance dropped, to modify fines, training, organization, and the conditions of service.

More important still, Americans depended on the militia for political reasons, because they feared and distrusted standing armies, and because they knew of no other institutional alternatives. Throughout most of the colonial era their experience with the British military establishment was one of friction and antagonism, or arrogant, snobbish, or dictatorial officers and officials, of harsh and brutal discipline in the army, of shady enlistment practices—all calculated to fortify the warnings in the anti-standing army literature which made its way across the Atlantic in the early 18th century. In their writings radical Whig opponents of standing armies presented militia as the safe, proper forces for peaceful people who valued liberty. As John Trenchard put it in 1697, "There can be no danger where the Nobility and chief Gentry . . . are the Commanders, and the Body [is] made up of the Freeholders, . . . unless we can conceive that the Nobility and Gentry will join in an unnatural Design to make void their own Titles to their Estates and Liberties: and if they could entertain so ridiculous a Proposition, they would never be obeyed by the Souldiers."

The Revolution, as historians always have known, strengthened the militia tradition immeasurably. The emplacement of a substantial British force in the colonies, its gradual transfer to urban areas, the resulting conflict, and the explosion of the Boston Massacre in 1770 emblazoned the hatred of standing armies upon the Revolutionary experience. As the British Army, and standing armies generally, became fixed as the symbols of monarchy, of European corruption, of tyranny, and of the ministry's conspiracy against liberty, so too did the militia become identified with America, freedom, republicanism, and colonial virtue. Battles like Bunker Hill, in the outpouring of self-congratulations after the war, enshrined the militia in popular mythology. The central element in the militia tradition, the concept of the citizen soldier, became basic to the language and history of independence and nationhood. As recently as 1940 the Chairman of the Senate Military Affairs Committee publicly proclaimed that the American "people . . . are different from the peoples of virtually every other country . . . from the standpoint of natural, inherited national defense." Announced the Senator, "I am not . . . 'afear'd' of Hitler coming over here because our boys have been trained to shoot." Yet, in spite of the Senator's extravagance, one of the little remembered results of the Revolution was that it set in motion forces that ultimately destroyed the colonial militia as an institution, and prevented it from becoming the primary institution for the defense of the United States.

★ ★ ★ ★ ★

One of the oldest controversies in the history of warfare, already by 1776 the subject of a century's debate in England and America, was the superiority of regulars as compared to militia in battle. The Revolution, for all its reinforcement of the political popularity of militia, provided no definitive military answers. The war was too complex and the fighting too varied to make possible a comparative assessment. The struggle was for national independence and it all too often made a mockery of orthodox strategy and tactics. For one group, however, the lessons were anything but ambiguous. Washington and most of the leaders of the Continental Army, working desperately to maintain in the field a stable force capable of defeating the British in open eighteenth-century battle, saw the militia as undisciplined, ill-organized, and unreliable. They concluded early in the war that militia were inferior, and they never changed their minds. Militia "come in you cannot tell how, go, you cannot tell when; and act, you cannot tell where," Washington wrote in dismay, "consume your Provisions, exhaust your Stores, and leave you at last in a critical moment."

Recent scholarship, of course, indicates that the militia was central to the winning of independence: screening the Continental Army, preventing the British from maneuvering, foraging, raiding, or pursuing an "oil slick" strategy without mounting major expeditions, and helping to pen up British forces in urban areas until by the end they depended on overseas transport for nearly all their supplies—an unbelievable financial, administrative, and logistical burden for the government in London. The militia also operated as a political force, intimidating individuals into declaring their allegiance, enforcing loyalty, retaliating against Tories, and drawing the indifferent and the lukewarm into the maelstrom of revolution. Many British officers learned a grudging respect for American troops, no matter what their origin. As Lord Cornwallis lamented in mid-1781, "I will not say much in praise of the Militia of the Southern Colonies, but the list of British Officers & Soldiers killed & wounded by them since last June, proves but too fatally that they are not wholly contemptible."

What counted most after the war, when Washington questioned his staff and the department heads of the Continental Army in response to a congressional request for ideas on a permanent system of national defense, was the perception of what had occurred and what was needed for the future. From their perspective Washington and his advisors saw militia as difficult and unpredictable in nearly every military situation. They believed that the United States had to have a national army in order to guard the country's natural invasion routes and physically to possess the West where state jurisdiction did not extend. A peacetime force was needed to keep alive military knowledge, to prepare for future conflicts, and to act as the nucleus for wartime armies. To Washington and his officers, warfare demanded practice and expertise. Officers must be professional and, if possible, be trained at military academies. Washington and the officers of the Continental Army, who had fought for *all* the states and who by the end of the war supported efforts to strengthen the central government, also recognized in the militia some very disturbing political implications. Should the new nation decide to rely solely on local institutions for defense, the states and not the Confederation would possess the power of the sword, an essential power of government and one that along with the power of the purse defined the ultimate sovereignty in society.

In 1783 the nationalists faced a difficult dilemma: how to defend a republic which rejected standing armies when they themselves rejected militia for political and military reasons. The solution appeared to be reform and nationalization of state forces. Washington and others in the army believed that three essential changes were necessary, none wholly susceptible to action by the states individually. First, all the militias must become uniform in equipment, organization, and doctrine so that they could fight together effectively in the field. Second, training should be increased dramatically with annual bivouacs and stiffer fines regularly enforced for absence from muster or failure to possess the stipulated arms or accoutrements. Some of Washington's advisors wanted the appointment of federal inspectors to harden training and to monitor the reforms. Third, because adequate training and preparation of the entire male population seemed impractical and wasteful, Washington and the officers advocated classing: singling out the young men (in Washington's words the "Van and flower . . . ever ready for Action and zealous to be employed") for special units, extra training, greater readiness, and additional obligations in military emergencies. All of these reforms, endorsed by Washington and adopted eventually by the nationalists and later the Federalists, required central coordination and management. In short, reform demanded the assumption of some degree of national control over what always had been purely state institutions.

For the next 10 years the arguments for creating a national military establishment and for reforming the militia were inextricably linked together, pushed by nationalists and by their Federalist successors in the belief that the United States had to maintain some system for protection in peacetime and for possible war, and that defense was the responsibility of the central government. Because of the prejudice against standing armies, because of disagreements over the relative merit of regulars and citizen soldiers, and most importantly because of the delicate issue of state versus national power, both of these programs met stiff opposition. Many Americans, unable to distinguish between a national military establishment and the classic standing army of European history, undoubtedly opposed a regular army. But few could disapprove of reforming the militia. After the war, several states moved to revise statutes and to improve their forces. Logic dictated that any future war would require integrated plans and leadership from the central government. Not even opponents of nationalizing the militia disputed the advantages of increased training, standardization of organization and equipment (although some questions arose later in Congress), or providing realistic procedures for enforcement. It is true that the plans advanced in public in the 1780s by Friedrich Steuben and by Henry Knox were extreme. Steuben advocated abolition of all state authority and reduction of the forces to 25,000 continentally enlisted volunteers. Knox called for classing, with enough training to make the total annual expense unbearably large. But for the future the nation needed armies that could fight outside state boundaries, garrison the frontiers, and defeat the Indian or European adversaries. Clearly the old colonial militias, a patchwork hodgepodge of indifferently prepared and haphazardly armed units, were unsuitable legally and militarily. Their future in the defense system of the United States rested upon reform.

The first obstacles to reform that the nationalists faced in the 1780s were the ambiguity in the Articles of Confederation about Congress's ability to raise peacetime armies and the unmistakably clear absence of any congressional authority over the militias. In the constitutional convention nationalists moved resolutely to overcome those barriers. On the question of army power, opposition was negligible except for Elbridge Gerry, who almost singlehandedly had blocked the creation of a national establishment in 1784. The militia question sparked a fierce exchange. When Virginian George Mason moved to allow Congress "to regulate the militia," a power included in several plans of union before the convention, several delegates pointed out that the states would never assent to their own disarmament. "They would pine away to nothing after such a sacrifice of power," objected Oliver Ellsworth. Gerry was adamant. "[T]his [was] the last point remaining to be surrendered"; if adopted, "the plan will have as black a mark as was set on Cain."

As so often happened in the convention, the delegates quickly put together a compromise that allowed state and national governments to share authority over the militia, just as they jointly exercised the taxing power. The Committee of Eleven offered a clause permitting Congress "[t]o make laws for organizing, arming, and disciplining the militia, and for governing such part of them as may be employed in the service of the United States, reserving to the States . . . the appointing of the Officers, and . . . training . . . according to the discipline prescribed" by the central government. Again a bitter fight erupted over the extent of national control. According to Rufus King of the committee, "organizing" meant specifying the size and composition of units, "arming" meant stipulating the weapons, and "disciplining" meant "prescribing the manual[,] exercise[,] evolutions, etc." Gerry saw through that interpretation immediately: "[A] system of Despotism," he charged, "making the States drill-sergeants." Yet neither Gerry nor other dissenters could block nationalists who demanded uniformity and reform or Southerners who wanted a strengthened militia for internal purposes and to protect their open frontiers. At one point James Madison suggested that the states be limited to the appointment of officers below the rank of general, but that went too far even for many nationalists. In the end the convention adopted the committee's recommendation and, along with provisions for federalizing the militia under the President as commander in chief, gave the federal government substantial new military power.

What appeared on the surface to be a nationalist victory (and was on the military sections generally) was in reality the first step toward the eventual demise of the militia reform movement. As bitter fights in Congress for the next decade would testify, the convention never defined adequately the powers of the states and of Congress. New Hampshire's John Langdon had warned his fellow delegates about "the confusion of the different authorities on this subject," but most in the convention, wanting to nationalize the militia but apprehensive about the reaction in the coming fight over ratification, evidently preferred to leave the government's powers open to interpretation. For the next 10 years at least, a conflicting welter of local interests, personal views, and partisan disagreements, all played out against a background of strife over national and state jurisdiction, was destined to stymie legislation which could strengthen the militia system. The Constitution was merely the first step, as Gouverneur Morris knew when he pressed Washington to accept the presidency. "No Constitution is the same on Paper and in Life."

★ ★ ★ ★ ★

President Washington first began to press Congress about militia reorganization a few months after taking office, but other business prevented the congressional committee from drafting legislation. Before the next session started, the President studied various European and American systems and forwarded his ideas to Secretary of War Knox, who then worked them into a revision of his 1786 plan and submitted the final product to Congress. The Knox plan of 1790 was the culmination of nationalist thinking on ways to transform state forces into "powerful" and "energetic" armies. The central ideas were classing and nationalization. An "advanced corps" of 18- to 20-year-olds would attend 30-day "camps of discipline" (the 20-year-olds would attend 10 days only), where, "remote from . . . the vices of populous places," they would learn the trade of war. Afterwards they would pass into a "main corps" (21- to 45-year-olds) to form a reserve pool from which armies would be drawn for war and which, while mustered only four times yearly, would maintain its efficiency by the "constant accession" of well trained youth. (The oldest group would muster twice yearly and would act as a home guard against invasion.) Furthermore, Knox proposed division of all companies into 12-man sections so that federal authorities could draft individuals for as long as 3 years if enough volunteers did not come forward in an emergency. Naturally the federal government specified a single, uniform organization and would oversee all training. And in a major reversal designed to insure military readiness, all arms, equipment, and clothing would come from federal supplies—even pay for the men on bivouac. To deal with the problems of enforcement and exemptions Knox proposed to do away with fines and to make graduation from the advanced corps a prerequisite to "exercising any of the rights of a free citizen." While he accepted exemptions in principle, "measures of national importance never should be frustrated for accommodation of Individuals."

Congress and the public greeted the administration's plan with shock and disbelief. It is "so palpably absurd and impolitic," reacted DeWitt Clinton, "that I take it for granted it will meet with no success." Obviously Knox wanted complete nationalization of the militias with the states left merely to appoint officers and arrange exemptions. Even state inspectors, quartermasters, and adjutant generals would be required to report to federal officials. The administration probably phrased its recommendations in extreme terms in hopes that after debate and compromise Congress still would accept major changes in the system. But nearly every aspect of Knox's plan brought heavy criticism: the expense, estimated at 400,000 dollars yearly; classing, which would take apprentices and young laborers away from employment for a month every year; the bivouacs, which some felt would militarize the nation and corrupt youth; the stingy exemption policy that was so blatantly anti-Quaker that one congressman refused to send the plan to the printer lest Quakers desert the Federalist party. "There are a number of opinions," Knox learned from a Massachusetts friend, "all tend[ing] to damn it."

For the next 2 years Congress struggled to produce a national law and in the process stripped away every meaningful proposal for reform. In the wake of the hostile reaction to Knox's plan a congressional committee weakened classing, reinstituted the old fine system, and changed the arming provision back to individual militiamen supplying their own equipment. The only tough sections remaining in the draft legislation were administrative: the addition of state adjutants, commissaries of military stores, and presidentially appointed inspectors to attend regimental musters and direct training. In July, 1790, the House cautiously had the bill printed in order to test public reaction. Like nearly all the proposals for change, the new bill pleased few, including some of its authors. "I do not look upon it [as] a very perfect system," admitted George Thatcher, a member of the committee. "[E]very time I run it over, I think I can point out imperfections."

In truth, the idea of a national system made most congressmen very uncomfortable. Any law, no matter what the benefit to the country as a whole, might tread severely on local interests and very likely would preclude needed local variations in organization or equipment. In towns classing hurt tradesmen who employed apprentices. In the South a uniform tactical structure might make impossible extra cavalry units for slave patrol. The expense of a national system, especially federal arming and training, seemed huge. Quakers mounted a potent lobby against a strong system fearing that any law out of Philadelphia, which was then the capital city, might prevent exemptions for reason of conscience. As Rhode Island's senators openly admitted, every voter would feel the effect of more training and stiffer fines or would view the schedule of exemptions with jealousy. Many senators and representatives, themselves veterans or active in the militia, had pet theories as to changes needed or desired. Lurking in the background lay the explosive question of just how far federal authority actually extended over the state forces.

The first extensive debate in December, 1790, in part the product of General Josiah Harmar's defeat at the hands of the Indians in Ohio and the President's continual prodding, reflected the jumble of interests and opinions. Every provision in the bill was dissected and disputed—"too much into the minutiae of the business," complained one congressman; "puerile," snapped Jonathan Trumbull of Connecticut. Gradually, inexorably, every strong provision was stripped away to satisfy the chorus of conflicting views. Erased was classing, opposed by several Federalists because it discriminated against tradesmen and by others because young men might live so scattered about the countryside as to make their mustering impossible. Federal inspectors were transferred to state control in order to avoid expense and because the Constitution seemed to mandate that all militia appointments be made by the states exclusively. After 10 days the bill was, in Trumbull's words, "so mutilated, maimed, & murdered" that the House appointed a committee to prepare another draft, but the new version solved little. Quakers in Philadelphia and in Rhode Island intensified their opposition to any specification of exemptions. Knowledgeable observers predicted that Congress would not produce any legislation in the foreseeable future.

In December, 1791, news of General Arthur St. Clair's defeat in Ohio rocked the capital. With the regular army annihilated and the President without authority to mobilize the militia or to reimburse militiamen called out by state officials, the frontiers were all but naked. To meet the threat the administration proposed a 5,000 man army, the third request for more regulars in 3 years. Never was the tradeoff between reform of the militia and a national military establishment more clearcut, nor was the need for a militia law more desperate. As the President told Senator Benjamin Hawkins, who opposed the administration's western military program, "No man wishes less that the P_____ to see a stand[in]g army established; but if Congress will not Exact a proper Militia law (Not such a milk and water thing as I expect to see if I ever see any) Defence and the Garrisons will always require some Troops." Republican James Monroe agreed. "Anything is preferable to nothing as it takes away one of the arguments for a standing army." In February, 1792, discussion began anew on the weakened congressional bill. This time debate hinged on the extent of national control, the most divisive issue and one increasingly central to the emerging party struggle. Opponents attempted to block every assertion of national authority; at one point they moved to abandon the requirement of uniform caliber muskets. Finally, in order to achieve any agreement at all, Congress struck out every controversial provision, heeding the reasoning of Elias Boudinot (who pleaded at the outset that "a plan of conciliation alone would every procure . . . a militia bill") to make "the law . . . very simple in its construction, and refer to as few objects as possible."

In the end the Uniform Militia Act passed in 1792 (and signed by the President at the last possible moment, undoubtedly to register his disgust) was so weak that many Federalists could not bear to support it. Gone was every vestige of the reforms that nationalists and Federalists had advocated for a decade: classing, increased training, and guarantees of uniformity. The law contained no fines, no officials specially charged with upgrading standards or reporting to the federal government, and no procedures for insuring a national system. Militiamen (all men aged 18 to 45) were to arm and to equip themselves; states were to adopt the tactical organization prescribed if "convenient"; and training was to conform to Steuben's wartime manual unless "unavoidable circumstances" dictated otherwise. If the states or individuals ignored the law, the government was powerless to intercede.

Almost universally, contemporaries viewed the act as unsound and inadequate. State laws passed to implement it contained tremendous variations in unit structure, fines, and numbers of musters. After his legislature had wrestled with the statute, Federalist Senator Charles Carroll of Carrollton concluded that, "Never . . . did a body of wise men pass so mischievous an act." Every Congress for the next 30 years attempted to strengthen it, but even in the aftermath of the Whiskey Rebellion, when Secretary Knox reported that the War Department had been forced to furnish two-thirds of the men mobilized with arms and Congressman Samuel Smith, who had commanded the Maryland contingent in the march to Pittsburgh, berated his colleagues with tales of the troops' dismal performance (in response to one order to load, fifty men had "put down the ball before the charge of powder"), Congress could not agree on another law.* Because of the pressure of Harmar's and St. Clair's defeats, Congress had been forced to fulfill its duty to implement the militia provision of the Constitution.** True reform could have cost tens of thousands annually, forced changes that the states did not want, worked hardships on special groups, and increased the burden on individual voters. No one could agree on fines, exemptions, whether training camps would school youth to defend the country or debauch their morals, or whether nationalization would revitalize or destroy the system. As the party struggle hardened, the disagreement over the extent of congressional author-ity grew more heated and partisan. Federalist military theoreticians might want classing, but party stalwarts from seaboard constituencies saw difficulties for their towns. Some Federalists undoubtedly realized that a weak militia would enhance the need for a strong military establishment. Republican Senator William Maclay accused Knox of proposing a purposely extreme plan in 1790, knowing that it could never pass and thus forcing Congress to accept a standing army. Republicans might wish to improve the militia in order to avert a military establishment, but too many in the party wanted to keep federal budgets small and federal authority over the states at a minimum. As Dwight Foster explained in 1795 after a long and fruitless debate over revising the law, "this is a subject which affects the various Interests of Individuals in every part of the United States and consequently many great and various are the Sentiments and opinions which are formed by different persons on Questions of this Nature."

★ ★ ★ ★ ★

With the passage of the 1792 act and the failure of the reform move-ment, the colonial militia system continued to decline as a viable military force until it finally passed into oblivion, in ridicule and disorganization, before the Civil War. Ironically, those who had opposed increasing federal

---

* Knox also estimated that three-quarters of the nation's militiamen lacked arms.

** A good example of the way this pressure worked was North Carolinian William Barry Grove's comment that the law "is not altogether what I could wish, but the necessity in my opinion of having some general principles for the States to act on induced me to give in my assent. I am persuaded if We had had a Militia Law in existence so many Regular Troops would not have been needed to defend the frontier from a Set of Naked *Indians.*" To Governor Alexander Martin, March 17, 1792, in the Governors's Papers, North Carolina Division of Archives and History, Raleigh, North Carolina.

military powers were in part responsible for the ultimate triumph of the national government in military affairs. But it was also true that once the mantle of the British Army had been removed by independence, the old militia system of universal service and state control could not provide alone for America's military security. The new nation needed coordinated, trained armies commanded by skilled officers and equipped with standard arms and equipment—forces that would respond to the will of a central government, fight outside a particular state or overseas, and stay abreast of changes in warfare and technology. The leaders of the Continental Army and many nationalists recognized the problem as early as 1783, and as would happen often after American wars, military programs were proposed that proved unacceptable for essentially political reasons.

And yet by 1800, after a decade of Indian conflict, rebellion in Pennsylvania, a war scare with Britain and a Quasi-war with France, and the smashing triumph of France's new legions across the face of Europe, some of the militia's most fervent champions began to realize that even citizen soldiers must be well trained and that the defense of the Republic must be managed with efficiency by a single authority. "We are all Republicans, we are all Federalists," declared Thomas Jefferson in his inaugural address. Nowhere did Jefferson prove the point more clearly than in a statement which, because it revealed a consensus on the role of militia, marked the true epitaph for those institutions in the American defense system "a well disciplined militia," proclaimed the new President, "our best reliance in peace and for the first moments of war, *till regulars may relieve them.*" ***

*** Emphasis added.

W I L L I A M   B .   S K E L T O N

PROFESSIONALIZATION IN THE U.S. ARMY OFFICER CORPS DURING THE AGE OF JACKSON

The United States fought two significant wars and several Indian conflicts in the first half of the nineteenth century. One of the most important military developments in the early nineteenth century was the emergence of a professional officer corps in the aftermath of the War of 1812. That war marks a turning point between leadership by political generals with little military training (best represented by William Henry Harrison and Andrew Jackson, but more often incompetent officers such as Stephen van Rensselaer and Wade Hampton) and a new corps of career officers like Winfield Scott and Edmund P. Gaines. According to William B. Skelton, professor of history at the University of Wisconsin–Stevens Point, this second group remolded the U.S. Army officer corps with a standard of professionalism that exceeded anything before their time.

They achieved this professionalism not in isolation from the contemporary world but rather by duplicating the emerging standards of civilian professions such as lawyers and physicians. Despite their personal quarrels, members of the generation of 1812 inculcated a sense of common purpose into their long careers that affected the entire officer corps. Several officers visited Europe, especially France, where the magnet of Napoleonic genius attracted such young officers as William J. Hardee, Philip St. George Cooke, Winfield Scott, Robert Anderson, and Henry Heth. Dennis Hart Mahan and his star pupil at West Point, Henry W. Halleck, were among the most important military intellectuals of the era. After studying at the Artillery and Engineering School at Metz, Mahan returned to West Point where from 1830 to 1871 he taught military art and engineering. The growing percentage of U.S. Military Academy graduates that *dominated the lower and middle grades of the officer corps and which, by the time of the Civil War, controlled over three-quarters of the officerships, reinforced the professionalism of the generation of 1812.*

But West Point alone was not going to professionalize the officer corps. Far more critical was the self-education and group study that occurred at outposts throughout the country. Despite the inertia and stifling idleness at many posts, a few officers with exceptional dedication and self-discipline sought to enhance their professional capabilities. For instance, Lieutenants Braxton Bragg, Alfred Mordecai, and James Duncan worked diligently to provide modern, mobile light artillery units for the army. A number of officers became voracious readers of everything from the latest Charles Dickens novels to military treatises. A few, like Hardee, Halleck, and Mahan, published professional commentaries.

Given the relatively low prestige of military service in the young republic and given the relatively few chances of rapid promotion in the small military establishment created by Congress, the degree of professionalism in the U.S. Army was remarkable. In the Mexican War, these young army professionals achieved considerable distinction and demonstrated a capacity for leadership unequalled in previous American campaigns. General Scott's march from Vera Cruz to Mexico City is one of the more sophisticated operations in American military history and could not have been accomplished without a cadre of competent, professional subordinates.

Yet, as the Civil War would demonstrate, this professionalism was largely at the regimental level. Few officers studied larger military operations and there was little formal instruction beyond the undergraduate training at West Point. As the subsequent reading by Allan Millett demonstrates, the U.S. military had one more phase to achieve in the development of professional standards before it approached the expectations of contemporary European officer corps.

A seeming paradox of American history in the first half of the nineteenth century was the appearance of a distinct military profession in a society generally considered to be fragmented, fluid, undisciplined, and egalitarian. While military historians have recognized this development—dramatically revealed in the comparative performances of the Regular Army in the War of 1812 and in the Mexican War—few have placed it in a broad historical context. Those who have done so have attributed it to one of two basic causes: the unique military interests of the Southern plantation aristocracy, or an ambiguity in American character which at once distrusted a military elite and tolerated it as a reflection of a popular martial spirit. In either case, the Regular Army emerges as a historical aberration—an isolated pocket of authority and discipline in an otherwise amorphous, egalitarian social order.

Attention has focused on the efforts of the officer corps to preserve professional cohesion in the face of democratic hostility rather than inquiring about the process that produced such cohesion in the first place. Was military professionalism an isolated phenomenon, explicable solely by internal factors, by the unique character of military service? Or was it part of a more general tendency, the product of general social forces at work in nineteenth-century America? An examination of these questions may lead to a greater understanding of the military profession as an institution. It may also shed light on broader social changes occurring in the Jacksonian Era.

The several characteristics of an occupational group form its "professionalism," and among these is expertise: a systematic body of specialized knowledge transmitted to group members by a formal educational process. Another is social responsibility: a commitment to use professional knowledge to perform functions important to the well-being of society as a whole. A third component is corporateness: a feeling among group members that they constitute a subculture distinct from the rest of society; a high degree of self-government within that subculture, sanctioned by the larger community; and institutions that uphold codes of group behavior, educate aspiring practitioners, and add to the body of professional knowledge. The history of the professions may best be approached in terms of "professionalization"—the process by which professional standards and procedures are applied in fields formerly handled by intuitive or empirical means—rather than in terms of professionalism as an achieved state. Few occupational groups in the nineteenth century would fully incorporate professional characteristics, but the tendency toward such characteristics in various callings has been one of the most important social developments of recent history.

Here I shall try to show that the professionalization of the army officer corps between the War of 1812 and the Mexican War was in large measure self-induced, the product of a reforming elite of young officers who rose to positions of power during the War of 1812. As a result of their wartime experiences and their career aspirations, these men developed a common ideology, centering on the need for a well-organized, educated, and professionalized officer corps capable of directing a future mobilization. The American social environment reinforced their efforts. First, they faced no entrenched feudal aristocracy clinging to traditional, nonprofessional practices as a sign of class privilege. Second, military professionalization coincided with more basic changes in the social order, especially the erosion of the personalized, community-oriented social patterns of the Colonial Era and the transition toward impersonal, centralized, and bureaucratic institutions. Thus military reformers rationalized military administration, instilled regularity into the officer selection process, attained a considerable degree of security in the pursuit of their careers, and cultivated—through West Point and a variety of other institutions—an intellectual, scientific approach to military problems. Ironically, the popular suspicion which the Regular Army attracted in an egalitarian era intensified group awareness and diffused professional attitudes through the officer corps as a whole. A significant outgrowth of these influences was the self-image of the officer corps as an apolitical instrument of public policy.

ROOTS PREDATING THE WAR OF 1812

Before the late eighteenth century, the scarcity of labor in the American colonies, the diffuse, rural patterns of settlement, and the absence of internal transportation facilities checked the growth of professionalism. Colonial society produced local elitism—informal hierarchies dominated by the "better sort" of the community and cemented by kinship ties and deference patterns—but it did not support professional consolidation. The latter required a high degree of occupational specialization and a network of communication which would allow practitioners to exchange ideas, to exercise discipline over one another, and, in general, to develop a corporate identity. The dominant social type of colonial America was the pragmatic, nonspecialized individual: the planter who divided his time among agriculture, the law, and scientific observations; the clergyman who treated the sick as well as preached the Gospel; the merchant and part-time magistrate who appeared on infrequent muster days as a militia officer. Aside from the Puritan clergy, professional training was nonexistent or confined to informal apprenticeships.

After 1750, the growing complexity of provincial society produced a limited professional development. Aspiring lawyers and physicians traveled to Great Britain for training. In 1765, graduates of the University of Edinburgh founded the first American medical school at the University of Pennsylvania. A scientific community emerged, centering in the Royal Society and the American Philosophical Society, and bound by a network of correspondence among amateur scientists on both sides of the Atlantic. Professional organization accelerated after the Revolution. During the first four decades of American independence, numerous professional associations and schools appeared, and several states adopted formal licensing procedures for law and medicine, controlled by professionals themselves. Nonetheless, it would be easy to exaggerate the importance of these developments. Professional consolidation was an urban phenomenon in an overwhelmingly rural society. Professional institutions were local in scope, closely intertwined with family and communal patterns. When professional men looked beyond their localities, traditional lines of commerce and communication tied them to a trans-Atlantic intellectual community rather than to the majority of isolated, unorganized practitioners in the hinterland. Licensing procedures were often ignored in practice. Daniel H. Calhoun is undoubtedly correct in describing the professional institutions of the early republic as "a brittle crust concealing much popular indifference to such forms."

The nature of military organization gave military men particular potential advantages over other callings. By the late eighteenth century, the major states of Europe had adopted the standing army as a permanent extension of the governmental structure. The rudiments of modern military administration had been worked out: the officer's commission; a hierarchy of ranks; distinctions between staff and line; and central offices to coordinate civil-military relations and to supervise supply and personnel services. Although popular rhetoric opposed standing armies, the Revolutionary government had adopted these principles in the Continental Army. Congress reluctantly revived them in the 1780s, when troops were called up to extend federal control into the Old Northwest. Under the Federalist administrations of the next decade, a small Regular Army became an accepted feature of the central government. The overlapping of formal bureaucracy with a group of specialists in arms provided a potential framework for professionalization.

In practice, however, the officer corps of the early republic reflected the same diffuseness, the same close connection with local power centers that typified other professions. One factor was the general state of the military calling in the Western world. Officers of eighteenth-century European armies, particularly those of cavalry and infantry, derived overwhelmingly from the landed aristocracy. For most, military service was but one aspect of a larger social position. Political influence, wealth, and family ties interacted with military life, binding officers to a civilian social milieu.

American officers derived from no particular social level. During the Revolution and for several decades afterward, military service offered a channel of upward mobility for many young men from obscure middle-class origins. Indeed, the absence of a titled nobility freed the American army from one of the principal barriers to professionalization in Europe. During the early national period, however, Americans modeled their behavior on their European counterparts—or rather on what seemed to them accepted conduct for army officers. Military attitudes tended to be aristocratic attitudes: an obsession with personal honor; the pursuit of individual glory in battle; the cultivation, where possible, of a luxurious life style. Military leadership was seen as an "art" to be grasped intuitively by men of genius or, more commonly, as a trade to be acquired through practical experience. Rarely was it defined as a learned science. Nothing reveals the individualistic, preprofessional character of the officer corps as well as the widespread reliance on dueling to settle personal differences, a practice tacitly condoned by the highest authorities.

Even if strong European models had existed, the decentralized nature of American society in the early national period would have retarded professional integration. For most Americans, traditional loyalties to family, community, and state outweighed a national orientation. The size and organization of the army fluctuated greatly, the result of popular distrust, faith in the declining militia system, and the generally unsettled condition of national administration. Aside from the thoughts of individual Federalist leaders, there was no well-defined military role to give focus to the officer corps. The army's principal functions were the immediate, practical problems of frontier defense and Indian control. Troops were scattered in small garrisons along thousands of miles of frontier and coastline. The absence of adequate communication and administrative precedents made it impossible for high commanders, had they been so inclined, to impose uniform standards of conduct on the officer corps.

In this unstructured situation, few officers made a full commitment to a military career. They remained rooted in social elites at home or cultivated civilian ties in the regions where they were stationed. Politics blended with military life as officers took partisan stands and appealed to political friends for redress in professional matters. During the 1790s, for example, Brigadier General James Wilkinson actively lobbied in Congress for the removal of his commanding officer. When Major John Fuller felt wronged by a superior, he made clear that he had "as many friends in my Native state as any other man," and threatened publication of the matter in the newspapers. A number of officers were implicated in Aaron Burr's Western conspiracy. The government itself seems to have used military commissions as a form of patronage: the officer corps of the 1790s was largely Federalist in sympathy while the expansions of 1808 and 1812 brought a majority of Jeffersonians into service, many of them former officeholders and journalists. Officers engaged freely in a wide range of economic activities—land speculation, the fur trade, transportation enterprises, agriculture—which often absorbed more of their time than military duties did. In other words, the social environment encouraged the survival of the nonspecialist, even among supposed experts in arms.

As in other fields during this period, there were occasional signs of professional consciousness. In particular, individual artillery and engineer officers responded to a trend among their European counterparts toward formal military education and expertise. One result was the founding of the U.S. Military Academy in 1802, originally intended as a school for engineers. A second was the appearance of the U.S. Military Philosophical Society, established by officers at West Point to encourage both military and scientific study. The program of coastal fortifications begun in the 1790s, and the attempt during Jefferson's second administration to develop units of light artillery, encouraged professionally oriented officers. But these activities formed only tiny pockets of professionalism among an indifferent mass of practitioners. The Military Academy and the fortification program barely survived their early years. The Military Philosophical Society drew its energy from its principal founder, Colonel Jonathan Williams, and disappeared when Williams left the service. The artillery experiment fell victim to governmental thrift. Whatever cohesion among officers had developed during the 1790s and early nineteenth century evaporated with the expansion of 1808, which more than tripled the number of officers and brought an influx of citizen appointees directly into the higher ranks.

A PROFESSIONAL IDEOLOGY

The War of 1812 marked a major transition in the history of the military profession. The war effort dramatically revealed the basic characteristics of both the society and the military establishment: localism, lack of coordination, and reliance on spontaneity rather than centralized planning. The result was near disaster, as American armies tried ineffectively to invade Canada and British forces descended at will on the exposed coastline. Repeated failure had another effect, however. By discrediting established commanders, in some cases superannuated veterans of the Revolution, it opened channels of upward mobility for young, reform-minded officers. At the end of the war, Generals Jacob Brown, Edmund P. Gaines, Winfield Scott, and Alexander Macomb were still under forty, but had experienced the responsibility of high command. Scores of others had entered the army in the expansions of 1808 and 1812, and had reached the middle levels of the officer corps.

This War of 1812 "generation" hardly constituted a unified professional cadre. Its members feuded among themselves and dabbled continually in politics and business. Few had received formal military education. But they carried out of the conflict a pride in their wartime accomplishments, primarily their respectable showing in the Northern campaigns of 1814 and an enthusiasm for things military. In the opinion of most, the republic could no longer rely for defense on a spontaneous mobilization of the citizenry. Preparation for war must be a continual function of the federal government, and the peacetime army must concentrate on that task. Such a policy would require long-term training and a more permanent bureaucratic structure than the prewar system. With many young officers, the desire for an adequate defense system undoubtedly coincided with personal factors. They lacked firm roots in local elites and identified with military service as the main source of their status. Their career aspirations could best be realized through a strong and well-organized army.

These views were not entirely new. Veterans of the Continental Army and certain Federalist leaders had expressed them during the 1780s and 1790s. Now, however, they coincided momentarily with civilian opinions— the tide of postwar nationalism and the neo-mercantilist turn of the Democratic-Republican party. Officers found a valuable ally in John C. Calhoun, secretary of war in the Monroe administration, who shared their conception of the army's role and drew heavily on their advice. There resulted a period of unprecedented reform: army administrators strengthened the Military Academy, set in motion an integrated system of coastal fortifications, and incorporated European methods into many aspects of the service. Perhaps the most important step was a reorganization of army bureaucracy. In place of the prewar practice by which supply and support functions were left to civilians or to officers scattered among the various commands, the government established centralized bureaus in Washington, headed by officers, to coordinate such operations for the army as a whole. In part, this "General Staff" was an economy measure, designed to reduce the waste and confusion left from the war. But it also represented an effort to regularize military administration and to place it on a permanent basis.

Ironically, the postwar reform movement reached a climax in 1821, when Congress reduced the army from its postwar strength of twelve thousand officers and men to six thousand. Acting on the advice of high regular officers, Calhoun proposed that the military establishment be organized on a cadre basis, retaining a proportionately large number of officers to enlisted men. Such a plan would preserve a pool of experienced leaders. In a crisis, the government could systematically expand the army by filling out the "skeletonized" units with recruits. Inherent in this program was a reorientation of American military policy. Where the peacetime army had served as a frontier police force, and the militia had been defined as the first line of defense "for great and sudden emergencies," Calhoun's plan reversed the relationship: the Regular Army must replace the militia as the central institution of land defense; spontaneity and improvisation must give way to continual planning; the cultivation of expertise rather than of frontier service should be the central concern of the officer corps.

Because of congressional suspicions, the bill reducing the army made no mention of the cadre principle. Implicit in its provisions, however, was a diluted version of the plan. Moreover, the reduction made little structural change in the General Staff bureaus. In fact it indirectly expanded the central military bureaucracy by retaining a single major general, who became a permanent, though controversial, commanding general of the army. While unclear at the time, the reorganization of 1821 fixed the new position of the army as the nucleus of the land-defense system. In the future, practically every president and secretary of war would define the army's main function as preparation for a future war. According to Andrew Jackson in 1835, the army "contains within itself the power of extension to any useful limit, while at the same time it preserves that knowledge, both theoretical and practical, which education and experience alone can give, and which, if not acquired and preserved in time of peace, must be sought under great disadvantage in time of war."

Of course, preparedness was not the only occupation of the officer corps. The typical line commander remained as before, absorbed in routine, practical tasks such as road-building, Indian control, exploration, and fortification duty. For an articulate minority, however, the cadre plan provided an ideological stimulus for professionalization. First, it charged the army with a clear and permanent responsibility—defense of the nation from outside threat. Second, it implied an approach which was essentially intellectual. In its preparedness functions, at least, the army was to be an educational institution as well as a force-in-being, a repository of specialized knowledge for use in a future war.

RATIONALIZATION OF THE MILITARY BUREAUCRACY

The pace of structural change slackened after 1821. But reform-minded officers remained in service and continued in quiet ways the transformation of the army. In large measure, the impulse was ideological—key men identified with the army's new role and sought to fulfill its implications. Increasingly, however, their personal efforts interacted with more general changes in American society. These stemmed from the great economic boom which gained momentum after 1815 and continued, with temporary setbacks, through the century. The construction of an internal transportation network, combined with the rise of early industry, the increasing tempo of immigration, and agrarian expansion into the trans-Appalachian West, undermined the relatively stable social order of the late colonial and early national periods. Traditional institutions—a political system still reflecting family and deference, neo-mercantilist economic policies, rigid church organizations—came under attack as "aristocratic" barriers to the fulfillment of individual aspirations. The dominant characteristics of the time were mobility and social fragmentization, as the American people wrenched loose from localistic and communal patterns.

Egalitarian rhetoric in its extreme form made little distinction among institutions, denouncing organizational restraints generally and urging the total liberation of the individual. In practice, however, the era produced a profusion of institutional forms, created either to perform new functions arising from economic expansion and political democratization or to preserve traditional values of community and social order threatened by the same disruptive forces. Lynn L. Marshall has described the appearance of the modern bureaucratic political party in the 1830s, with its emphasis on rational organization and direct appeal to the voters. Other emerging institutions were the business corporation, the urban public school system, the secular reform group, and the asylum to handle poverty and deviance. The impact on the professions was two-sided. The egalitarian impulse, combined with the force of individual aspiration within the professions themselves, caused the reduction of formal licensing procedures in law and medicine and attacks on the supposedly monopolistic practices of local professional groups. But the development of internal communications eroded the parochialism which had long isolated professional men and encouraged occupational specialization within society as a whole. In all professions, journals, schools, and voluntary associations proliferated, and in several the first steps were taken toward national organization. The trend toward social atomization often identified with the Age of Jackson signaled both the dissolution of traditional social patterns and the early stages of "modern" ones.

The army shared in this general trend toward specialization and organizational efficiency. Changes were subtle and largely imperceptible to outsiders, but their cumulative effect contributed greatly to professional consciousness. One example was the proliferation of army manuals. Before the War of 1812, the rules governing the army had appeared erratically and had followed no uniform pattern. The only officially authorized works on military administration had been the Articles of War, establishing the code of military discipline, and a short guide by Baron von Steuben, basically a drill manual, but including a few regulations on organization, property accountability, and similar matters. Although individual officers had adopted European manuals for their commands, the government had made little effort to update procedure or to codify the mass of standing orders into a coherent system.

The chaotic practices of the War of 1812 demonstrated the need for standardization. During the conflict, the War Department published the first official set of general regulations in the army's history. Revisions of this work appeared at intervals, and in 1820, Brigadier General Winfield Scott compiled a more comprehensive and integrated system, including separate sets of regulations for the General Staff bureaus. Simultaneously, army administrators replaced Steuben's manual with a more advanced code of infantry drill, or "tactics," based on French precedent. Both went through several revisions before the Civil War. In 1818, the army began a long-term project to standardize ordnance and other types of equipment on the basis of European developments and changing technology. The reintroduction of mounted troops in the 1830s and the growing importance of field artillery caused the adoption of tactical manuals for those branches. In 1825, Captain Trueman Cross published the mass of congressional legislation concerning the army as a single compendium, the first of several such collections to appear in the nineteenth century. Perhaps the best-known attempt to rationalize procedure occurred at West Point after 1817, where Superintendent Sylvanus Thayer standardized the curriculum and the regulations governing the Military Academy.

Closely related to the appearance of uniform regulations was a trend toward centralization and efficiency in the army's administrative structure. As they evolved through the 1820s and 1830s, the General Staff bureaus differed greatly from the support services of the Revolutionary and Federalist eras. While the government had attempted to coordinate supply and personnel matters in the late eighteenth century, offices had overlapped in function and lacked permanent, systematic procedural patterns. In the absence of formal structure, they had relied for their energy on individual incumbents, often civilians. Military administration at the center had been a reflection of the army as a whole—a continually shifting conglomeration of personal fiefdoms, only loosely coordinated by the secretaries of war and the treasury. The Jefferson administration had reduced even this limited bureaucracy.

Dominant personalities played a role in shaping the postwar bureaus: Daniel Parker and Roger James in the Adjutant General's Office, Thomas S. Jesup in the Quartermaster Department, George Gibson in the Commissariat of Subsistence, Joseph Lovell in the Medical Department, and others. But the drive to reduce expenses and the impact of the new defense ideology, with its emphasis on a well-managed army, led them to work out rational patterns of procedure which remained in operation despite changes in personnel. They attached to their bureaus relatively permanent cadres of officers who spent most of their careers in managerial duties. They compiled codes of regulations for their departments which grew longer and more specific as time passed. During the 1820s, the executive branch institutionalized the relationship between the bureaus and the War Department through the introduction of periodic reports, providing a means of surveillance and control. Although the General Staff departments retained much autonomy within the military establishment as a whole, they evolved into relatively rationalized, efficient miniature bureaucracies. When the generation of founders passed, they continued to operate according to formalized procedures, having assumed institutional lives of their own.

Because of its size and its scattered nature, the line—the "combat" branches of the service—posed greater difficulties to military reformers. Nevertheless, the trend toward centralization and standardization affected this area as well. High army administrators continually denounced the dispersion of officers and men in small, isolated garrisons. This policing of the frontier distracted the army from its newly defined role—the development of expertise in preparation for a future war. During the 1820s, the army experimented with systematic transfers of units, designed to weaken local and sectional ties. It also established "schools of practice" for the artillery and infantry. Based on French precedent, these institutions allowed the concentration of relatively large numbers of troops and instruction for officers in professional subjects. Units served at the schools on a rotation basis, and West Point graduates usually drew them as their first assignments. The artillery school developed a special set of regulations and an ambitious curriculum. Lack of congressional support and the conflicting requirements of frontier service obstructed the schools' operations and caused their discontinuance in the 1830s. But army reformers continued to warn of the professional dangers of diffusion. From time to time, the War Department organized temporary concentrations for educational purposes, such as the "camp of instruction" at Trenton, New Jersey, in the summer of 1839. The artillery school underwent a revival before the Civil War.

Military administrators made more lasting progress in the matter of personnel. In the Articles of War and the system of military justice, the officer corps had always had the rough equivalent of a professional code of conduct and the potential apparatus to enforce it, advantages unavailable to other professions in this period. After 1815, the expansion of military bureaucracy in Washington provided central direction to personnel administration. The key figure was the commanding general. An accidental by-product of the reduction of 1821, this office occupied an ambiguous position in the military hierarchy and would remain a source of controversy through the century. Its incumbents, however, conceived of it as the administrative center of the entire army and attacked the individualism and local attachments long characteristic of the officer corps. For example, commanding generals tried to rationalize lines of command and communication between Washington and outlying posts. In a series of obscure bureaucratic struggles, they checked the tendency of officers to by-pass prescribed channels and to correspond directly with the secretary of war and the president. They clashed with powerful frontier commanders, firmly rooted in their remote domains and long accustomed to virtual autonomy, over the right to order troop movements and to make independent calls for state militia. While a degree of local responsibility necessarily continued, the flamboyant individualism of a James Wilkinson or an Andrew Jackson became less common. Commanding generals also resisted the intervention of congressmen and other influential citizens on behalf of officers seeking favors and tried, with limited success, to bring the General Staff bureaus under their control.

A major preoccupation of military administrators was the bitter personal quarrels which traditionally divided the officer corps. While hardly above such affairs themselves, high authorities repeatedly denounced controversies among their subordinates and tried to keep them out of the public eye. The most dramatic accomplishment in this area was the decline of dueling. The Articles of War had prohibited dueling at least since 1806, but the practice had continued unabated through the war years. In 1814, the War Department issued the restriction on dueling as a general order and later incorporated it into the General Regulations. By 1821, the threat of enforcement had apparently taken effect. Although officers continually talked of resorting to the field of honor, actual encounters became rare. Personal differences were settled by bureaucratic means or channeled into courts-martial and courts of inquiry. Officers remained a contentious lot, sensitive about personal honor and obsessed with a desire for recognition, but they learned to demonstrate these qualities in a restrictive institutional context.

It would be misleading to portray military administration in the antebellum period as an efficient, mature bureaucracy, comparable to the complex structures of modern industrial society. Attempts at centralized controls and rational patterns of procedure met with only partial success. Many officers, especially older and high-ranking commanders, continued to cultivate local ties, to pursue their economic interests, and to resist organizational pressures on their independence. Nevertheless, the subtle bureaucratic changes of this period established a trend toward system and uniformity within the army. Responding to their newly defined professional role, army administrators constructed a rudimentary bureaucratic framework over the officer corps. Interacting with broader developments in the social milieu—particularly the spread of internal communication—this framework grew gradually stronger and eroded older, nonprofessional commitments. By the 1840s, military administration had evolved into the most extensive and sophisticated organizational structure to appear up to that point in American history.

A PROFESSIONAL ETHOS

It is one thing to trace the growth of military bureaucracy, but something else to describe the emergence of professional consciousness. The first is the work of an elite, imposing standards from above; the second involves common attitudes and loyalties among the mass of group members. The two trends were nonetheless closely related in the Jacksonian army. The attempt to infuse discipline and regularity into military administration merged with the evolution of a professional ethos.

This relationship appeared clearly in the officer selection process. Before 1821, no formal standards had existed for officers' appointments aside from an attempt to maintain geographical balance. A West Point education implied a degree of competence, of course, but graduates had comprised only a small percentage of the officer corps and had concentrated in the engineers and artillery. For 11 years after the reduction of 1821, however, with the exception of semi-military branches such as the Pay and Medical departments, the government reserved all new officers' commissions for West Point graduates. The rationale behind this practice is not entirely clear; it may have reflected the patronage functions of Military Academy appointments. But it meshed with the postwar conception of the army as an educational institution, a repository of expertise. The number of West Pointers in the officer corps rose steadily: 82 of 553 (14.8%) in 1817; 183 of 465 (39.7%) in 1823; 333 of 522 (63.8%) in 1830. This temporary monopoly allowed military men, by determining the academy curriculum, to set standards for granting commissions—in effect, to control professional licensing.

As with other professions, the egalitarian surge of the 1830s weakened these controls. Reacting to pressure from Congress and the public, the executive branch appointed citizens directly to the army, especially when new units were added. A small number of enlisted men received commissions. This tendency was partially counterbalanced, however, by more rigid admissions procedures for civilian applicants. In 1832, for example, the Medical Department established a system of examinations for all candidates for appointment or promotion. Beginning in 1837, citizen appointees to other positions were also subjected to examinations, though these necessarily focused on the candidate's "character" and general knowledge rather than on professional expertise. At any rate, West Pointers continued to receive most commissions and by 1860 constituted 75.8% of the officer corps. The overall effect of the tightening of admission standards was to increase the uniformity and degree of self-government within the military profession.

A related development was the rise of the long-term military career. The reduction of 1821 introduced a period of unprecedented stability for the military establishment. There were no drastic cutbacks in the decades that followed, no violent fluctuations of army organization. In fact, the size of the officer corps gradually increased—from 530 in 1821 to 1,108 in 1860. Officers found it possible to pursue their careers in a relatively secure institutional context. At certain times, the mid-1830s in particular, the unpleasant prospects of frontier duty, the absence of promotion opportunities, and the lures of civilian life caused many young officers to resign. In comparison with the past, however, the outstanding characteristic of officer corps at the time was the continuity of its membership. The turnover in the highest grades was exceedingly slow: as late as 1860, 20 of the 32 men at or above the rank of full colonel had held commissions in the War of 1812, 10 of them as field-grade officers. The trend was similar among their subordinates. A comparative analysis of the army registers of 1797 and 1830 demonstrates that the median career length for officers under the rank of captain on those lists increased from 6 to 17 years. The proportion of such officers who would serve 10 or more years expanded from 35.2% of the total in 1797 to 78.1% in 1830. Those who would serve 20 or more years rose from 6.6% to 44%. In other words, a military career became for an increasing proportion of the officer corps a lifelong commitment. Although difficult to gauge, the fact that officers served together over a prolonged period of time, sharing common experiences and developing institutional loyalties, was probably the most important single factor in creating a corporate identity.

Another aspect of emerging professionalism was the rise of an intellectual tradition within the officer corps. As described above, an intellectual approach to military matters was implied in the cadre system adopted in 1821. If officers were to prepare for a future war, they must devote their energy to the development and diffusion of professional knowledge. Military leadership must become scientific rather than intuitive, based on formal study rather than derived from practical experience. While traces of this approach had appeared as early as the 1790s, they had been limited to isolated individuals, mainly in the technical branches. By the 1830s and 1840s, however, the intellectual aspects of officership were affecting directly or indirectly all branches of the officer corps and were becoming an important element of a collective self-image among military men.

The central intellectual institution of the army was of course West Point. There is no need to examine in detail the curriculum of the Military Academy; that subject has already received considerable attention. In common with military education in much of Europe, the emphasis was on mathematics, engineering, and tactics rather than on strategy, high administration, or the social implications of warfare. Thus military expertise partially overlapped with nonmilitary fields such as science and civil engineering. Nevertheless, the academy instilled in its more intelligent cadets a respect for professional study, however narrowly defined, which continued through their careers. Of special importance was the influence of Dennis Hart Mahan, professor of military and civil engineering and the science of war from 1830 to 1871. He stressed military history and the flexible application of theory to warfare, and apparently deeply influenced his students. The assignment of young officers as assistant professors at West Point provided the equivalent of postgraduate study to a small but significant group. During the 1850s, for example, Mahan was the central figure in the Napoleon Club, composed of West Point officers who examined Napoleon's campaigns in search of strategic lessons.

West Point was not an isolated phenomenon. As time passed, it was surrounded by a web of institutions and activities which reinforced officers' professional inclinations and related theoretical knowledge more closely to specific military subjects. While they lasted, the schools of practice served this function. Of more permanent significance were the military boards which convened continually to consider professional problems. In particular, a long series of ordnance boards acquainted officers with the relationship between changing technology and the evolution of warfare. The coastal fortification program, gradually implemented through the antebellum period, led military men to reflect on broad strategic questions. A common practice was the assignment of officers, either as individuals or members of boards, to translate and adapt foreign works for the American service or to revise existing manuals.

Another important stimulus was contact with Europe. The nineteenth-century trend toward noninvolvement in the political affairs of the Old World did not affect cultural ties. In common with Americans in other fields—science, medicine, literature, reform—military men formed part of a loosely defined trans-Atlantic community which grew stronger as communications improved. European influence had been extensive during the Revolution and had continued in the early national period through the employment of foreign officers. After the Peace of Ghent, these contacts increased. Many officers visited Europe at that time, where they examined military installations and observed the forces occupying France. An official mission toured the Continent from 1815 to 1817, collecting works for the West Point library. The War Department used former Napoleonic officers in advisory and instructional positions. Beginning in the 1820s, the army sent young officers to Europe to obtain technical information and to study at military schools. Scores of others took extended leaves abroad, combining the grand tour with professional improvement. Perhaps the best-known mission occurred in 1855 and 1856, when Major Richard Delafield, Major Alfred Mordecai, and Captain George B. McClellan observed the closing stages of the Crimean War and investigated military developments across the Continent.

It is possible to view these contacts as a retarding influence, stifling independent speculation by American officers. For a number of intelligent men, however, they produced an exhilarating sense of participation in an international professional community. As with officers of developing nations in the twentieth century, Americans drew from their European contacts models for professionalization—not only in the form of manuals, equipment, and organization, but also, more subtly, in the form of attitudes and styles of behavior. Significantly, Americans were drawn most often to France, with its strong emphasis on military science and education.

A final aspect of the emerging intellectual tradition within the army was the appearance of the first military journals. In 1833, the monthly *Military and Naval Magazine of the United States* began publication, though it failed three years later. The *Army and Navy Chronicle,* a weekly, proved somewhat more successful, surviving from 1835 to 1842. It was superseded briefly by the *Army and Navy Chronicle and Scientific Repository.* Hardly professional organs in the modern sense, these periodicals focused on service news, travel accounts, congressional proceedings on military and naval matters, and excerpts from foreign military journals. Their most interesting function was to publish letters from officers, usually signed with pseudonyms, which aired army and navy problems and occasionally reflected on the role of the military profession in society. To some extent at least, they provided outlets for professionally oriented officers and focused attention on group concerns. The temporary eclipse of military journalism in the 1840s and 1850s should not be taken as a sign of the army's indifference. During the antebellum period, the mortality rate for specialized journals was generally high. The military services posed particular circulation problems because of their remoteness and the tendency of officers at a single post or aboard a single ship to subscribe as a group. After the Mexican War, the dispersion of the army into the Far West increased these difficulties. When the specialized journals failed, officers continued to express their opinions in more general publications.

The intellectual orientation of the Jacksonian army may be easily exaggerated. Through the antebellum period, officers' educational activities competed with their frontier role. Older commanders frequently shared the distaste of Brigadier General Edmund P. Gaines for "officers who have never seen the flash of an Enemy's Cannon—who have acquired distinction only in the mazes of French Books, with only that imperfect knowledge of the French Language which is better adapted to the Quackery of Charlatans, than the common-sense science of war." The individualistic, "heroic" view of officership, emphasizing personal honor and physical courage, continued to occupy a central position in the military world view. But the quest for professional knowledge was gradually institutionalized and incorporated into the officer corps' evolving sense of social responsibility. This trend accelerated as West Point graduates moved up the military hierarchy into high command positions.

Thus professional attitudes arose originally from the internal dynamics of the military establishment—the conscious efforts of War of 1812 veterans to stabilize military procedure and to prepare for a future war. The relationship between the army and the larger society contributed to the trend. In a basic way, of course, the transportation revolution facilitated the exchange of ideas and eroded, if it did not destroy, officers' feeling of isolation. More direct was the attack on the army during the 1830s and 1840s. As historians have often shown, the numerous attempts to abolish West Point or to reduce the army were a reflection of the egalitarian impulse of the time. Undoubtedly the threat was more apparent than real. The army performed functions considered desirable by large segments of the population. The representation of prominent families in the officer corps deflected the practical impact of the criticism. Through this period, however, officers were subjected to a continuous volley of speeches, pamphlets, resolutions, and editorials denouncing their profession as both undemocratic and useless and extolling the virtues of the military version of the "natural man"—the citizen volunteer or militiaman.

Officers' responses to this assault varied. Some considered resigning rather than continuing to serve a profession for which "there is no longer a feeling of respect entertained by the country." Except for brief periods, however, relatively few took this step. Instead, the main effect of egalitarian criticism was to intensify group awareness. Officers drew together in an effort to define their collective role and to justify the existence of a standing army and a system of military education in the midst of a democratic nation. On one side, they universally denounced the militia and volunteers. Citizen soldiers were politically motivated, undisciplined, ineffective in combat, extravagantly expensive, and given to committing atrocities. There was a basis to these charges, of course, as Indian campaigns and the Mexican War demonstrated. But the frequency and bitterness of the counterattack indicate that regulars used citizen soldiers as a foil for their growing group consciousness, a counterimage representing the reverse of the qualities they prized most highly.

In contrast, officers stressed the advantages of military professionalism, defining it in the context of the cadre system. Quartermaster General Thomas S. Jesup thought that the purposes of the army were "to acquire and preserve military knowledge and perfect military discipline; to construct the permanent defences, and organize the matériel necessary in war; to form the stock on which an army competent to the defence of the country may be engrafted." "The rank and file of an army can be obtained at any time," wrote Inspector General John E. Wool, "but not officers, for it requires years of study and reflection to qualify them for command." A correspondent of the *Military and Naval Magazine* echoed these arguments, but noted an additional advantage: "that nationality of feeling which pervades the officers of the army, who, having no interest but in their country's glory and union, are entirely devoid of all sectional partiality and prejudice." A collective image emerged in reports and military journals of a devoted band of brothers, motivated by selfless patriotism, cultivating specialized knowledge for the welfare of an uncaring public. However exaggerated, this image provided an ideological "lowest common denominator" for officers from diverse backgrounds and educational levels. It diffused through the army views confined earlier to a reforming elite. Even the most unreflective Indian fighter had a stake in professional institutions and military science—if nothing else, they distinguished him from citizen soldiers.

Another unlikely factor contributing to the coalescence of professional attitudes was the army's experience with Indian removal. From the 1820s to the early 1840s, the army was involved in this unpleasant business; the "war" in Florida against the Seminoles was the principal military operation between the War of 1812 and the Mexican War. Officers generally disliked Indian removal, as it offered few chances for distinction, detracted from preparedness, and embroiled the army in complex civil-military controversies. While assuming removal to be inevitable, many officers had sincere moral doubts about the exploitation of the red man, especially their role as agents of that exploitation.

Officers never fully incorporated Indian relations into their professional self-image. One of the ironies of the army's early history—and an indication of its commitment to the preparedness doctrine—was its failure to develop a body of thought concerning the most important practical task. In coming to grips with this problem, however, officers increasingly portrayed themselves as detached instruments of the public will, dedicated to the principle of objective service. Such an approach compensated them for the absence of glory and distinction; it also lessened the guilt that many vaguely felt. Captain John T. Sprague, the chronicler of the Florida War, expressed this tension clearly in describing the forced emigration of a Seminole band:

> To those who are not engaged, and are removed from the immediate participations in incidents of this kind, there is much to create a high degree of enthusiasm, even triumph. But to the officer of the government who perfects the policy so unavoidably adhered to towards the Indian, there are humiliations and embarrassments almost sufficient to deter him from the execution of the orders enjoined, or what to many appear the reasonable expectations of citizens. He has to observe stern and inflexible justice on one side, and forbearance and humanity on the other; and whether the administration of justice be in consonance with the rights and feelings of the Indians, is a subject not to be descanted upon or discussed. . . . Even that which the officer seeks in his profession, distinction, is narrowed down to so small a compass, and attended with so much "unworthy of his blade," that he becomes indifferent to it, content with the conscientious conviction that to his country he performs his duty.

Or as Lieutenant William Wall put it more simply: "I feel that I cannot bear so much glory as is about to be obtained from this Florida concern. However as Uncle Sam wills it I shall try to bear up." The conception of the officer corps as a neutral agent of public policy, though still poorly defined, meshed with the emphasis on group unity and social responsibility emerging as a consequence of other causes. In this sense, of course, "responsibility" meant unquestioning service to the government rather than adherence to a higher moral code.

A final aspect of professionalization remains to be examined—the relationship of the officer corps to politics. Until at least the Civil War, the interaction between the army and the political arena was both intense and complicated. Officers of all grades cultivated political sponsors and used them to seek appointments, transfers, and similar favors. The nature of frontier service made close contact between military and civil leaders inevitable; post and department commanders often exercised considerable political authority, on occasion serving as Indian agents or even territorial governors. The commanding general and the General Staff officers in Washington mingled in the highest political circles.

Nevertheless, a gradual change occurred in the way that officers viewed politics. In the early nineteenth century, political and military life had formed a continuum. Not all officers were absorbed in political affairs, but there was little effort to distinguish the two fields, to define them as separate realms of endeavor. This relationship, of course, reflected the undifferentiated leadership patterns of early American society. By the 1830s and 1840s, however, officers were becoming more circumspect in their political activities. In part, the stimulus came from above. High administrators tried to weaken officers' political ties in order to promote bureaucratic efficiency. Another factor was the practice, adopted unofficially after the War of 1812, by which congressmen made appointments to West Point. This system did not nullify political interference, but it ensured that the officer corps would not be dominated by a particular party, as had been the case earlier. The principal impetus, however, was the growing self-image of the officer corps as a specialized elite, devoted to the national interest rather than to a faction. Too close an identification with politics would undermine this image; it might also confirm popular fears of military influence.

A sampling of officers' opinion reveals these changing attitudes. "Without questioning the right of any citizen in civil life, and in a state of peace, to act upon party principles," wrote Brigadier General Edmund P. Gaines in 1838, "I contend that whenever we assume the attitude of soldiers, in the national defence, we must take leave of the spirit of party." When approached regarding the vice presidency in 1843, Quartermaster General

Thomas S. Jesup disavowed any interest in the office: "So long as I hold a military commission, I cannot consistently with my obligations to the country, and the opinions I entertain of what is due to its institutions, allow my name to be used in connection with that or any other elective office." Lieutenant William T. Sherman considered himself a Whig by family tradition, but stated that it was his "intention and duty to abstain from any active part in political matters and discussions, and for that reason I never permit myself to become interested in the success of either party." While Major General Zachary Taylor reluctantly agreed to stand for the presidency in 1848, he insisted repeatedly that, if elected, he would be "the president of a nation & not of a party." Expressions of this kind frequently included an undercurrent of contempt for the give-and-take world of party politics, especially among young West Point graduates. Few went as far in print as Lieutenant Daniel H. Hill who, in reference to the secretary of war, bemoaned the "melancholy fact, that the *soldier*, who has devoted himself to the science of war from his childhood, can never rise above an inferior grade, whilst the command of the Army is entrusted to a *politician*, who has gained distinction by courting the mob." Such comments were common in private correspondence, however, and officers tended to use the term "demagogue" interchangeably with "politician."

Given the extent of officers' political involvements, their professions of neutrality might be interpreted as hypocritical attempts to allay public suspicion. Although some evidence supports this view, a subtle shift did occur in the nature of these connections. Early in the century, individual officers had intervened freely in civilian matters. They had been especially active in president-making during the Era of Good Feelings. By the 1830s, however, their political actions focused mainly on issues within the service—appointments, promotions, favorable stations—rather than support for civilian candidates or nonmilitary issues. Interest-group tactics became popular. Military men petitioned Congress for higher pay and a retirement system; line officers attempted to limit staff privileges. One of the most politically oriented of the West Point graduates, Lieutenant Isaac I. Stevens, organized a lobbying effort during the early 1850s to push army bills. "It is time for officers having a common purpose to act together, and do something for their profession . . . ," he wrote to a friend. "If we act in concert, compare views in a fraternal and generous spirit, merging the *arm* in the *army*, and taking views as large as our country, and occupying the whole ground of the public defense, and thus come to conclusions, we shall be right, and Congress will act accordingly, I care not what opposition be made in interested quarters."

Thus regulars increasingly viewed politics from a professional perspective. No issue drew the officer corps into the political arena as a body; its members knew that such an event would arouse public reaction and threaten their careers. But the trend was toward the exclusive use of political influence to attain professional goals, either personal advancement or the improvement of particular branches of the service. Accompanying this change was the articulation of the opinion that politics and military service formed separate fields of endeavor, each guided by its own set of values, and that the army should remain politically neutral. This view naturally contributed to the image of the officer corps as an objective army of national policy.

Although parallels are by no means exact, the consolidation of the military profession resembled developments in other professions during the Age of Jackson. While egalitarian criticism caused the decline of formal licensing procedures and other corporate privileges, the result was not the disappearance of professional attitudes. Reacting to public distrust, lawyers used law magazines as a vehicle to develop a collective self-image which distinguished law from politics and stressed the objectivity and social utility of their calling. The conflict between regulars and citizen soldiers had its counterpart in the struggle of the orthodox medical profession against such irregular practices as Thomsonianism and homeopathy. Among physicians as well as officers, the emphasis was on professional education, internal standards, and an experimental, scientific approach as rationale for their collective existence. Historians of the scientific and civil engineering professions have found growing self-awareness in these fields as well. Perhaps the group most resembling the army was the naval officer corps. Although evidence for the Jacksonian Era is not fully available, naval men by the 1850s were developing a consensus on their professional role resembling that of their army colleagues. It seems clear, therefore, that the professional consolidation of the officer corps was not an isolated phenomenon, but part of a broader trend toward specialization and group consciousness in the antebellum social order. Where military officers differed from civilian callings was in their ability to retain and even to extend their formal structure, including the practical control of licensing, in a time of institutional flux.

The Mexican War had an important, albeit ambivalent, effect on military professionalism. On one side, it opened opportunities for advancement and distinction, thus stimulating the "heroic" aspects of officership. Each campaign produced bitter quarrels which reinforced the traditional individualism of the officer corps, eroded but never destroyed by the growth of corporate identities. In a more basic way, however, the war provided a test for the preparedness functions of the Regular Army, thus deepening officers' professional consciousness. Captain Philip N. Barbour spoke for the officer corps as a whole when he expressed hope, in April 1846, that Taylor's army would push the enemy back. "This *must* be done before the arrival of volunteers, or the Army is *disgraced.*" Almost without exception, officers' correspondence dwelled on the superiority of regulars to citizen soldiers in discipline and expertise. The war seemed to the officer corps undeniable proof of the value of formal military education and the cadre system. Out of the spectacular victories in Mexico emerged a body of tradition, exaggerated but nonetheless effective, which would fire future generations of officers with institutional pride. In the opinion of one lieutenant, the siege of Vera Cruz was "the most complete victory of science in modern warfare." Another considered the clashes at Contreras and Churubusco "unquestionably the greatest battle that has ever been fought on this continent and the most brilliant."

CONCLUSION

By the end of the Mexican War, the officer corps was well along in the process of professionalization. The principal stimulus had been the emergence of an elite of young officers during the closing stages of the War of 1812 which shared a common view of the army's role, emphasizing the cadre plan, preparation for a future war, and formal military education. In contrast to the experience of European armies, these men faced little resistance from an aristocratic tradition within the officer corps which would retard professional consolidation. Rather, professionalization meshed with the personal aspirations of American officers—their quest for career security and for public recognition of their superiority to the militia. This emerging professional spirit found institutional expression in the rise of West Point influence, the experiments with schools of practice and military journalism, the interaction with European affairs, and the general tightening of administrative procedure. Egalitarian criticism of the army deepened group awareness and encouraged the gradual separation of the officer corps from party politics. It would be inaccurate, of course, to portray the majority of officers as articulate and fully committed professionals. Only a small portion of them served on military boards, translated European works, wrote professional articles, or otherwise contributed directly to the development of professional knowledge. Their concept of leadership continued to prize such traditional qualities as physical courage, military bearing, and intuitive brilliance. But the inclusion of professional values had begun and would be carried further after the Civil War.

While the emergence of a distinct military profession is obviously important in the history of the U.S. Army, it is also a significant part of the broader evolution of American institutions in the nineteenth century. Military developments of the period must be viewed in the context of massive dislocations brought on by the transportation revolution and rapid economic growth. These changes undermined traditional relationships based on kinship, community, personality, and social deference. At the same time, they opened the way for the development of more "modern" institutions, oriented toward functional specialization, national organization, and impersonal, bureaucratic relationships. For most groups, the Age of Jackson was a time of flux, the disrupting stage of the modernization process. For certain institutions, of which the military profession is a prime example, it was a period of early consolidation. While the officer corps of the 1850s retained elements of its individualistic, unstructured past, it was moving quietly but inexorably in the direction of centralization, uniformity, and efficient management.

An interesting comparison may be made between the role of the American officer corps and that of military elites in the emerging nations of the twentieth century. Because of their discipline, their administrative skills, and their responsiveness to Western technology, military officers often play a role in the transition of "underdeveloped" countries toward industrialism and national unity. As bureaucracies organized along relatively rational lines, armies contribute to overriding the parochialism and cultural conservatism of traditional societies. The American army, of course, did not set the direction of national development. Officers contributed to economic development through engineering, road-building, suppression of the Indians, and exploration, but they did so as agents of a stable government rather than as determiners of national policy. The importance of the officer corps was more representative than causal. As one of the first major institutions to consolidate along functional, bureaucratic lines, it anticipated the course followed by other institutions—professional, governmental, economic, educational—in later years.

BLUE AND GRAY

JOHN K. MAHON

CIVIL WAR INFANTRY
ASSAULT TACTICS

When the American Civil War broke out in 1861, the Industrial Revolution was beginning to alter a weapons technology which essentially had not changed over the previous century and a half. The smoothbore, flintlock musket with an attached bayonet had been the primary infantry weapon since the end of the seventeenth century. Two of its characteristics as a weapon dictated much of the shape of infantry tactics on the battlefield. First, the musket was a wildly inaccurate weapon at much beyond fifty or sixty yards, although the large caliber musket ball could inflict crippling and fatal wounds at longer ranges. Moreover, even the best trained soldiers could not sustain a rate of fire much over three shots per minute. Battlefield tactics, increasingly based on firepower instead of physical shock, emphasized volume of firepower rather than accuracy. Formations became increasingly linear, allowing more men to fire. At the same time, the inherent inaccuracy of the musket and its slow rate of fire meant that fighting took place at relatively short distances which advancing enemy forces could cover in a few moments. Individual soldiers might be able to fire only one or two shots during the period a rapidly advancing foe was within effective musket range. To counter this threat, it was necessary to place men essentially shoulder-to-shoulder in formation. Although massing troops in this way made them a better target for both musket and artillery fire, it had two significant benefits. It generated a high volume of fire in a given space, and it allowed the men in the formation to protect each other with their bayonets during the time they were reloading and their relatively thin formation was most vulnerable to a physical attack.

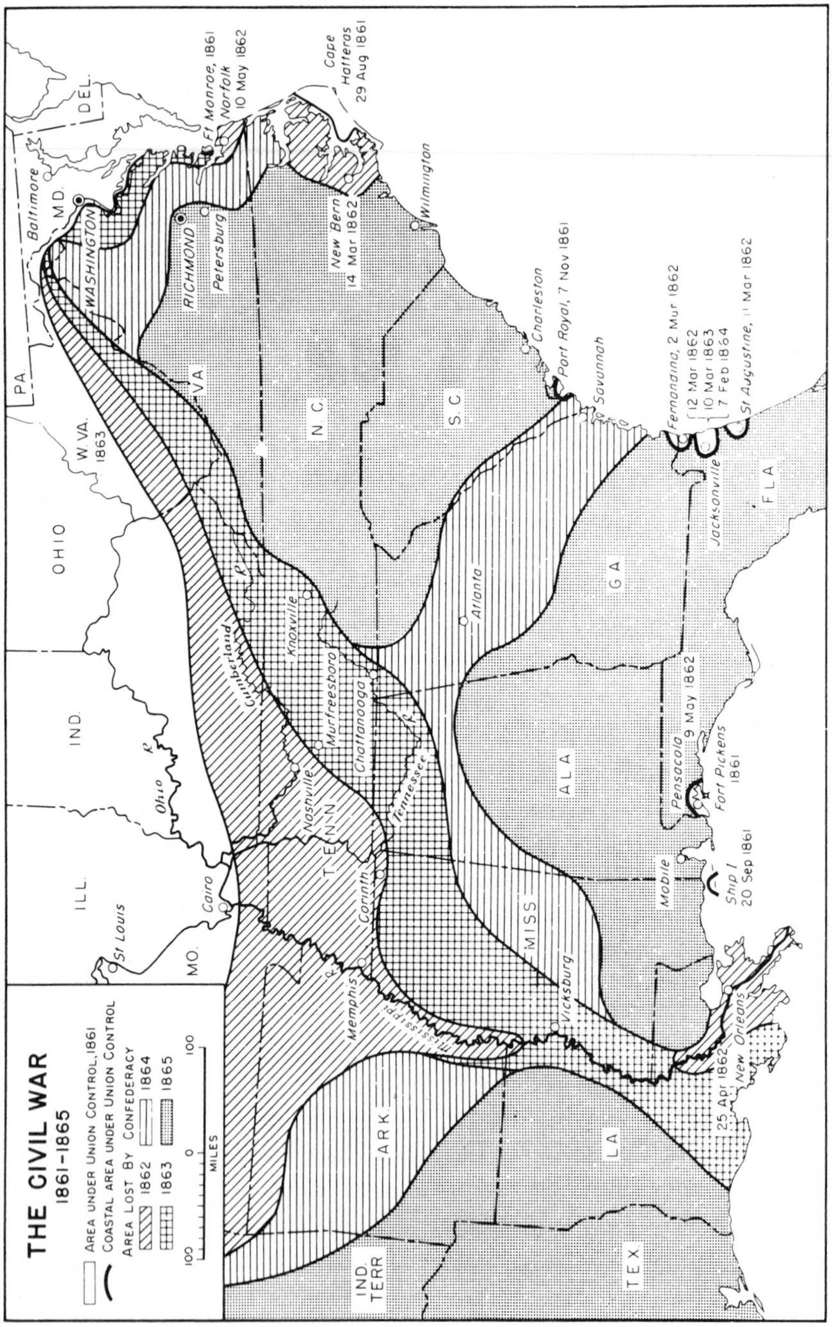

THE CIVIL WAR
1861–1865

Area under Union Control, 1861

Coastal area under Union Control

Area lost by Confederacy
1862   1864
1863   1865

MILES
100   0   100

Ft Monroe, 1861
Norfolk
10 May 1862

Cape Hatteras
29 Aug 1861

Baltimore

DEL.

MD.

PA.

WASHINGTON

W.VA.
1863

VA.

RICHMOND

Petersburg

Wilmington

New Bern
14 Mar 1862

N.C.

S.C.

Charleston

Port Royal, 7 Nov 1861

Savannah

Fernandina, 2 Mar 1862
12 Mar 1862
10 Mar 1863
7 Feb 1864
St Augustine, 11 Mar 1862

Jacksonville

FLA.

GA.

OHIO

IND.

ILL.

Ohio R.

St Louis

MO.

Cairo

Memphis

Mississippi R.

ARK.

IND.
TERR.

TEX.

LA.

New Orleans
25 Apr 1862

Vicksburg

MISS.

Mobile

Ship I.
20 Sep 1861

Pensacola, 9 May 1862

Fort Pickens
1861

ALA.

Cumberland R.

Knoxville

Nashville

Murfreesboro

Chattanooga

Tennessee R.

Corinth

TENN.

Atlanta

110

MAP 28

With the predominate battlefield weapons unchanging, tactics evolved into a well-understood series of actions. Maneuvering the long lines characteristic of musket period warfare was a complex and time-consuming task, but the skilled and intelligent commander could rely with confidence on both his own experience and the communicated experience of his predecessors. Manuals and tactical treatises remained valid guides for decades.

American military manuals reflected this situation as fully as their European counterparts. William J. Hardee's manual Rifle and Light Infantry Tactics, published in 1855 by the War Department, largely echoed earlier manuals, such as Winfield Scott's three-volume Infantry Tactics of 1835, which was essentially a translation of the French infantry manual of 1831, itself mainly a revision of the earlier French ordinance of 1791. Although the American manuals placed slightly more emphasis on rapid movement and aimed fire than the French manuals, the shift was only one of degree, not kind. Through the 1830s, infantry relied on mass formations and a high volume of fire during battle. So long as the primary infantry weapon remained the smoothbore musket, however, this continuity of tactical thought was entirely appropriate. The French manuals that inspired their American counterparts represented the best synthesis of European experience through the Napoleonic Wars, and the tactics they encouraged were demonstrably successful on the battlefield. In the Mexican War, from 1846 to 1848, American troops trained according to Scott's manual won a series of impressive victories, validating in action the traditional tactical emphasis on mass formations.

The Mexican War, however, was the last American war in which both sides relied primarily on the smoothbore flintlock musket. By the mid-1850s a number of developments were fundamentally altering the character of infantry weapons. During the first decades of the nineteenth century, experiments with various priming compounds culminated in the development of the percussion cap, a sandwich of thin copper around a fulminate of mercury core. Unlike the flintlock mechanism, the percussion primer worked even in wet weather and was far less susceptible to misfire. At the same time, British Captain John Norton and French Captain Claude-Etienne Minié developed a conoidal bullet with a hollow base. The hollow base expanded upon firing, forming a tight seal with a rifled gun barrel. The first rifle-muskets were issued to British troops in 1851, and in 1855 Secretary of War Jefferson Davis approved production of an American version. These rifle-muskets were still muzzle-loaders, and their rate of fire did not differ significantly from that of the smoothbore musket. But accuracy was dramatically different; aimed shots became possible at four or five times the effective range of the smoothbore. As the introduction of the rifle-musket began in both America and Europe, other inventors were hard at work in efforts to use the technology of the percussion primer in the creation of breechloading weapons using self-contained cartridges, and refinements in metalworking and machine making had allowed inventors such as Samuel Colt to begin selling successful revolving pistols and rifles. The result was a "firepower revolution" that fundamentally changed the centuries-old balance between weapons and tactics.

Professor John K. Mahon's following article on infantry tactics examines the impact these changes had on the conduct of Civil War battles. The Civil War was the first major war in which both sides were armed with the new rifle-musket, and in which the rapidly evolving breechloading weapons, many of them repeating weapons of one design or another, played an important role. As Professor Mahon's analysis makes clear, military commanders on both sides were slow to recognize the implications of these new weapons. Both Confederate and Union commanders persisted in using traditional tactical methods and manuals no longer appropriate. In many cases, the soldiers on both sides developed means of coping with the new weapons before their commanders did. One result of this was the development of new tactics, featuring field entrenchments. Another was the enormous casualty lists generated during Civil War engagements.

Although Professor Mahon's article overtly deals with the tactics of the Civil War, during a period when rapid change in weapons technology overwhelmed an outdated tactical system, his analysis also has important implications for military leaders today. Since the mid-nineteenth century the pace of technological change has continued at an ever-faster rate, with even more rapid changes in weapons technology than those experienced by Civil War commanders. Were Civil War leaders unusually slow in adapting to a new technological environment? How much of their initial reluctance to change tactical methods was due to their training and the heritage of the previous 160 years, and how much was simply due to the psychological difficulties always associated with adapting to unknown situations? Is it really possible to predict the kinds of tactics that will be successful under changing conditions, or will battlefield methods inevitably be developed by trial and error in times of change? A number of other essays in this collection examine technological innovation and its impact on military thought. Readers might examine Wayne P. Hughes' study of naval weaponry, for example, to see how a later generation of military leaders tried to adapt to change. It is well worth asking what similarities existed between the 1860s and the 1940s, and even more worth asking what military leaders must do today to adapt to a technological environment in almost constant flux.

In 1848 Claude Etienne Minié, a captain in the French Army, perfected a bullet which revolutionized warfare. Napoleon III, recognizing his accomplishment, conferred on the Captain both money and honor. Minié's new bullet was conoidal and hollow at the base instead of round. When fired from a gun it acquired horizontal spin because the explosion of the propellant expanded the hollow base so as to engage the rifling of the barrel. In consequence a soldier could drop the Minié ball down the muzzle of his shoulder arm almost as easily as if it had been round, yet fire it in the opposite direction with horizontal spin imparted to it. Such spin, unobtainable with a round ball in a musket (all muskets were smoothbores, hence without rifling) meant additional range, velocity and accuracy. Indeed, because of it infantry tactics may be labeled "before Minié" (BM) and "after Minié" (AM). BM infantrymen had had to carry muskets because such rifles as existed were too slow to load; AM they could graduate to rifles. BM the footsoldier could reach out about 100 yards to injure his foe with some degree of accuracy, AM he could be accurate at two or two and one-half times that distance.

The United States Army adopted the Minié principle in 1855 and the government arsenals soon began to manufacture weapons incorporating it. By 1861 the arsenals had standardized a muzzleloading shoulder arm with a rifled barrel known as a "rifle musket." Four feet, eight inches in length, nine pounds one ounce in weight, .58 caliber in bore, it was fired by means of a percussion cap. Because of the conoidal bullet with the hollow base, loading was simple, at least compared to earlier muskets. The soldier took in his hand a paper cartridge in which powder and ball were wrapped together, bit the end off it, poured the contents into the barrel via the muzzle, stroked a couple of times with his ramrod, then fitted a small copper cap loaded with fulminate onto a nipple outside the barrel. Now he was ready to fire. A trained soldier could get off two or three rounds a minute. The greatest disadvantage was that none but a contortionist could load the weapon lying down. You had to roll over on your back and virtually wrestle with it. But once loaded this weapon was able to stop an attack at 200 to 250 yards, and kill up to 1,000 yards.

The story of infantry assaults in the American Civil War must begin with Captain Minié; for it was his improvement of shoulder arms which conditioned tactics. Because of Minié's innovation bullets dominated the battlefields where Johnny Reb fought Billy Yank.

By no means did every infantryman have so fine a weapon as the standard product of the government arsenals. No less than eighty-one different types of shoulder arms were used by the Union forces, generous numbers of them obsolete. Agents of both sides scoured Europe for guns and picked up the castoffs of every army. Consequently all sorts of firing mechanisms were represented in the American armies from flintlock to rimfire; all sorts of loading systems from muzzleloading singleshot to breechloading repeater. Calibers were legion; small wonder that ammunition supply was tangled.

Better shoulder weapons existed than the best muzzleloaders issued to the bulk of the infantry. Among them were good breechloaders, Sharp's, Henry's, and Spencer's; and good repeaters, notably the Henry and the Spencer. The former carried sixteen charges, the latter seven. Men fortunate enough to be armed with repeaters naturally had a great advantage over others armed with singleshot muzzleloaders. Troops who had once used them were never thereafter satisfied with the old style. But only a few on either side had a chance to try the new ones. Around six and one-third muzzleloaders were issued to Union soldiers for every breechloader. Most of the latter went to the cavalry, becoming for that branch the standard arm in 1864.

Responsible latter day students, and some contemporaries, have claimed that the Union could have armed enough of its men with repeaters to have ended the war in 1862. What stood in the way was a conservative point of view in certain high places. Brigadier General James W. Ripley, Chief of Ordnance, who occupied the key position, disapproved both Spencer and Henry in December 1861. They were too heavy, he said, required special ammunition which had not been proved, were constructed of untested parts that might malfunction, and were far too high priced (roughly $36.00 as compared to $20.00 for the standard Springfield muzzleloader). Only when President Lincoln himself overruled the Chief of Ordnance were repeaters put into production. It ought to be added in defense of Ripley that he was in distinguished company. Robert E. Lee himself did not favor repeaters because he thought they encouraged poor fire discipline.

To place American weapons-conservatism in context one must remember that no important nation had unqualifiedly adopted a breechloader. Prussia came closest with her needle-gun (loaded at the breech), but she issued it only to one battalion in each regiment and to one or two elite corps. Neither had any nation adopted a repeating shoulder arm. Now, when one remembers that America had always leaned heavily upon Europe in military matters, it is not at all surprising to find the nation entering the war virtually without breechloaders and repeaters. Three years of war, and a change of chiefs of ordnance, reversed this initial position, but it was too late then to supply the improved rifles to more than a few infantrymen.

Even granting that the rifle musket was not the best shoulder weapon available, it was good enough to alter tactics. It enforced the following vital changes: (1) Stretched battle lines, (2) obliged armies to form for combat much farther apart, (3) reduced the density of men in the battle zone, and (4) made battles into firefights with shock action decidedly subordinate. Still more important it caused battles to be at once much longer in time and less decisive in outcome. There were to be no more Waterloos. Finally, it made defense a good deal stronger than offense. For this last result there were two principal reasons: the new firepower literally drove men to throw up temporary earthworks; and behind these they could gather in greater density and be better supplied with ammunition than their attackers. Nowhere was the superior power of the defense better illustrated than at the Battle of Fredericksburg. Here, at the foot of Marye's Hill Confederate infantry, protected by a stone wall, stood four ranks deep to blast their assailants. Inasmuch as the front rank stepped to the rear to load after firing, the fusillade never slackened. This spelled carnage for the Federals, relatively minor losses for their foes.

General J. F. C. Fuller contends that the bullet and the trench, due to heightened firepower, dominated the battlefields of the Civil War, and continued to do so at least through World War I. Their power deprived the combat arms of true mobility. It does not detract from his thesis to point out that excessive numbers of bullets were required to achieve this domination. One scholar has estimated that 900 pounds of lead propelled by 240 pounds of powder were required to drop every Confederate who was killed. This was a somewhat worse record than Napoleon's soldiers had scored. But it was a better record than the bayonet made. Throughout the bloody struggles in the wilderness north of Richmond during May, June, and July of 1864—where there was more hand to hand fighting than usual—33,292 Union men received treatment for bullet wounds, only thirty-seven for bayonet thrusts. Nor are there any grounds to suppose that most of the bayonet casualties were lying dead on the battlefield. Heros von Borcke, a German soldier of fortune serving with the South, took the trouble to ride over battlefields examining corpses, and he reported finding very few that displayed thrust wounds. Generally speaking the physical damage done by bayonet attacks was inflicted by bullets, and the issue decided before the two fighting lines closed with each other. In short, it was the threat of being run through, coupled with firepower, not the act itself that made attacks with the bayonet effective.

There is no intent to contend here that bayonet attacks were invariably ineffective. On the contrary, to pick some notable examples, they were significant at Malvern Hill, Seven Pines, and Mill Springs (all in 1862), and at Missionary Ridge in 1863. But more critical than their occasional effective use was the impact which the tradition of bayonet assaults had on tactics. Civil War attack formations were arranged with the idea that the bayonet would decide the outcome. This is one of the reasons why assault formations were so dreadfully at the mercy of defending troops. General Fuller, by the way, claims that the same mistaken theory underlay tactics as late as World War I.

Bullets worked their greatest execution against bodies of men advancing to the assault. The fact is that the firepower of the rifle musket was relatively modern whereas the formations used in attacks were obsolete. One reason for this has just been presented: attack formations were based upon the outmoded theory that bayonets would win. In the second place, shoulder arms had outpaced artillery in rate of development. Because of the drawing apart of armies, enforced by heightened firepower, attacking infantry was obliged to pass across extended areas scourged by fire, in the case of Pickett's charge about 1,400 yards. Supporting cannon had not the capability either to do the defenders great harm or to follow the attacking lines and aid them efficiently. After all, the zone of attack was sprayed by three times as many bullets as had been the case during the American Revolution only eighty-five years before. In contrast, defending artillery was at its deadliest just in the zones where supporting artillery fire could not go. At 400 yards the defenders opened with grapeshot, at 200 they switched to canister. Both, being scattershot, wreaked havoc.

What were the human blocks of which assaulting formations were composed. In general they were divisions of four brigades, brigades of four regiments, and regiments of ten companies. The authorized number of officers and men in a full-strength regiment totaled 1,046. Of course the number actually on the field varied widely from this norm, witness the average figures for six important battles:

Shiloh	6 and 7 April, 1862	560
Fair Oaks	31 May to 1 June 1862	650
Chancellorsville	1–5 May, 1863	530
Gettysburg	1–3 July 1863	375
Chickamauga	19 and 20 September, 1863	440
Wilderness	5–7 May 1864	440

General Lee wasted fewer men in obsolete assault formations than Grant. This may have been because his strategic problem was fundamentally a defensive one. He could afford to hold his ground and let the Federals try to dislodge him. According to General Augur, a perceptive French observer writing in the 1880's, Lee had a typical tactic which reflected the defensive character of his strategy. He habitually sought a vital plot of ground where the enemy could not afford to leave him, threw up earthworks, taking care to open avenues through which to take the offensive, and awaited the attack. Once it came he blasted it with devastating fire, and at the proper moment issued from his works upon its flanks, or, if possible, its rear. When he could not do this, but stumbled into battle instead, as at Gettysburg, the result was unhappy for the Confederacy.

Obsolete though they were in the 1860's, attack formations had changed many times during the hundred years since Frederick II. Density of men on a battlefield had shrunk from eight per unit of ground to one, while the rising firepower had followed about the same ratio in reverse, that is from one to eight. Within the decade just passed the Crimean War had demonstrated the terrible effect of gunfire on great masses of men such as Russia had employed. But it also had revealed weaknesses in the thin line. The latter, two ranks deep, was the basic line formation for American troops. When in drillbook formation men stood side by side with an interval of twenty-one to twenty-four inches between them while the distance from the back of a man to the face of the one behind him was no more than thirty-two inches. Before the war, American drill manuals had given promise of the increasing use of extended order, that is of increased distance and interval between men in a battle line. This promise was not fulfilled. Neither was the wider use of platoons, sections, and squads implied in the drill manuals of the 1850's. Whence came these lapses? For one thing, it was easier to instruct green recruits to fight in close order than otherwise. And drill masters of the Civil War were forced to work with little else, especially at the beginning.

In general it may be said that attack formations were more apt to be irregular in the early years of the war than at the end. For instance at the Battle of Belmont, 7 November 1861, Grant's initial combat command (not counting the earlier war with Mexico), the First Illinois Infantry advanced from tree to tree Indian fashion. Likewise, formal battle formations rarely developed during the Peninsular Campaign in the spring of 1862; rather the men took advantage of cover and advanced in short rushes. In contrast, there are examples of line actions in the first two years as formal as if directed by Frederick the Great himself. For instance, in the opening engagements of Second Bull Run, August 1862, two lines which happened upon each other stood in close order and blazed away in the style of half a century earlier. At Corinth, 3 October 1862, the Confederate line advanced at a slow step which could not be maintained without the strictest discipline and training. Finding the delay hard to bear the Federals lay down. At thirty yards they rose and fired point blank; then when Confederates were a musket length away, they fired again. So quick a refire indicates that part of the line did not join the first volley.

Even if men started in good formation, withering fire drove them to seek cover. There is the case of the Ninth New York charging Confederates behind a stone wall at Antietam. Forced to lie down, the soldiers reformed by crawling into place. Still the fire sought them out and killed so many that they were glad to get to their feet and resume the assault.

A skirmish line in advance of the main force was by no means new with the Civil War. It had been developed, at least in modern form, in the time of Frederick II and perfected during the American Revolution. The armies of the Napoleonic Wars had also made extensive use of skirmishers. But until close to the middle of the nineteenth century skirmishing had been the special mission of light troops who took little part in line fighting. Thereafter improvements in firearms (and other changes) had increased the importance of skirmishing so much that by the time of the Civil War all soldiers, Union and Confederate, were given light as well as line training.

Skirmishers assaulted in an irregular line of one rank, taking advantage of the terrain. They also invariably fired at will. Nevertheless they were subject to the control of the officer commanding their line, and when well trained could display impressive cohesion. Their purpose was to prepare the way for the main battle line by throwing the enemy off balance and by drawing his fire. After the war there was a brisk argument among students as to the relative efficiency of line and skirmish line. Statistics showed that aimed fire delivered by the latter made twice as many hits as the volley fire of the line. On the other hand it was claimed that skirmishers had retreated upon suffering two percent losses while lines had held even with forty percent of their men down. Naturally, a skirmish line suffered fewer casualties than a battle line because the interval between the men was much wider and because it had no depth. At Antietam the battle line of the Sixth Wisconsin lost fifty-four percent while one of its companies acting as skirmishers lost only five percent. With the benefit of perspective it may be said that the skirmish line was the assault formation of the future. If anyone saw this at the time it was General Sherman, who in some cases used a line or lines of skirmishers instead of the battle line of two ranks. Obviously skirmish formations thrust added responsibility upon junior officers.

G. F. R. Henderson, one of the most perceptive students of the War, credits Americans with having devised two assault techniques to meet the threat of annihilative firepower. One of these became the typical assault formation, if any can be said to have been typical. This was a succession of lines, containing two ranks each, with a prescribed distance of thirty-two inches separating ranks. The lines varied greatly in width and in the distance at which they followed one another. Some were as wide as a whole brigade lined up in two ranks, others only as wide as a company. If there was a usual width it was that of a brigade, and the resulting formation, although in reality it was a succession of lines, was called a division in column of brigades. When a division attacked in this formation it had as many lines as there were brigades in it, with each brigade forming a line of two ranks. Distance between lines ranged up to 300 yards and down to 50, but the commonest was 150. If the lines were three hundred yards apart they were likely to be beaten in detail. The intervals between men and the distance between ranks and lines were almost identical with those Napoleon had used. Unfortunately the rifles which played upon attackers were by no means comparable to the muskets of Napoleon's time.

When a company of volunteers was at full strength it occupied about twenty-seven yards in the line of battle. Thus, a regiment of ten full companies, with an interval of three yards between the companies, took up three hundred yards, and a brigade of four regiments close to 1,300 yards. This meant that a division attacking in a column of brigades advanced on a front nearly three-quarters of a mile wide.

If the successive lines were under good control they stopped in the midst of the assault to fire. On rare occasions the fire was by volley, that is the whole company, or some large subdivision of it, fired together at a command. If the fire was by file, the right file, being the two men at the right end of each rank, shot first; then the fire passed down the line by file from right to left. Most of the time, however, individual soldiers fired when they were ready. But it was customary for the two soldiers of a file to work together, one of them loading while the other fired.

Officers on foot led a charge while mounted officers were supposed to follow the line. Whether before or behind, their lives were precarious, for sharpshooters among the defenders preferred them as targets.

As might be expected, the successive lines ran together and approached the defenders bunched into vulnerable crowds. Yet if they held a semblance of their formation they could keep the enemy reeling by striking him with recurring waves of fire and shock. The best officers understood this advantage and sought to have the benefit of it. For example General George H. Thomas trained his troops so well that they even climbed Kenesaw Mountain in formal lines which did not bunch. In contrast, though equally well trained, General James McPherson's Army of the Tennessee went up more or less Indian style. Brigadier General Emory Upton undertook to prevent bunching, by giving detailed orders. At Spottsylvania on 10 May 1864 he required the first line of his brigade to break to the flanks when within the enemy position to try for envelopment. The second line was ordered to halt at the enemy works and fire straight to the front, while the third lay down farther to the rear. The fourth was directed to remain at the edge of a wood two hundred yards distant until sent forward.

Pickett's charge at Gettysburg was a succession of lines with a front about 500 yards wide. It had to cross 1,400 yards under severe fire, in the course of which it became bunched, and was then vulnerable to the cannon fire raking it from Little Round Top. General Longstreet said he watched one shell time and again knock over five or six of Pickett's men.

The second innovation which G. F. R. Henderson credited to the Americans of the Civil War was the attack by a succession of rushes. This type of assault doubtless occurred many times by chance, but Arthur Lockwood Wagner contends that it was first used formally at the Battle of Ft. Donelson, 15 February 1862. General Morgan L. Smith's brigade of two regiments was advancing in a succession of lines. Under heavy fire the two lines lay down, the second forming on the left of the first. All the while the skirmishers plied the enemy with an effective fire. When the foe's fire abated, the brigade rose again, rushed forward, absorbed its skirmishers, and again lay down and opened fire. Taking cover when the enemy's fusillade was hottest and dashing forward in slack periods, the brigade at length reached and carried the hostile position with but slight loss. Such tactics were far in advance of the time. Indeed, concerning the tactics of the war as a whole, Henderson claims that they were more modern than those of the Austro-Prussian War which began after the Civil War ended and was waged by two of the great military powers of Europe.

The basic dilemma which commanders had to resolve in assault tactics was whether to use a column or a line. Both formations had shown strengths and weaknesses during the recent Crimean War. The advantage of the column was that it had great penetrating power. Furthermore, it was sanctified by the fact that Napoleon had used it (heavy versions of it) during his later campaigns. His most frequent attack formation had been a line of battalions in close column by division at deploying distance. Roughly explained this was a group of battalions side by side with an interval of one hundred or one hundred and fifty yards between them. Each battalion was massed nine or twelve ranks deep. The line of battalion masses advanced abreast, striking the enemy every hundred yards or so along his entire front. It was the mission of the skirmishers to protect the gaps between battalions and to shake the aim of the enemy at the easy targets the masses presented. Usually lines of battalions followed each other in succession, and the masses of the second struck the places in the enemy line missed by the first. This formation, or something approximating it, was later adopted by nearly every European power.

The weaknesses of mass formations sprang from firepower, or the lack of it. Only the first rank or two of a column could shoot; the rest were neutralized. But when it came to receiving the enemy's fire, all ranks were nakedly vulnerable, particularly to scattershot from cannon. Lines in contrast had been developed to allow every soldier to shoot, but possessed of course much less penetrating power than columns. The American succession of lines was in reality an unconscious attempt to avoid the two horns of the dilemma. It allowed full expression of firepower, yet also was capable of some of the shock impact of a column.

But the succession-of-lines technique did not eliminate heavy columns from the Civil War tactical repertory. It was during Grant's hammering north of Richmond in the spring of 1864 that the tendency to use masses reached its peak. This stemmed partly from the thickly wooded nature of the country and partly from Grant's determination to break the Army of Northern Virginia at whatever cost. The heaviest mass formation of all appears to have been used by Winfield Scott Hancock's Second Corps at Spottsylvania on 12 May 1864. Here 20,000 Union infantrymen in close order formed almost a solid rectangle. The Federals knew that the Confederate artillery had been shifted away from the point they meant to attack, and this influenced the formation. The huge body advanced through thicket and in fog. It was made up, as were most Civil War mass formations, of regiments (synonymous with the battalions of Napoleon's time) in Napoleonic masses, that is in close column by division. (The term division as here used designated two companies.) In it the two companies of a division were in line side by side, but in two ranks instead of the three still used in Europe. The regiment, then, was in five lines of two ranks each (unless a company or two had been detached as skirmishers) with thirty-two inches' distance between the ranks and a distance of three yards between the lines. The interval between the men in the ranks was one foot. In summary, if the regiment was full strength, its attacking mass was eighty-two men wide and ten deep. When the regiments of a brigade were side by side in close column by division, the interval between them was usually sixty yards.

But Hancock's divisions at Spottsylvania were not all formed in column. David Birney's Third Division was arranged in two deployed lines. Francis Barlow's First Division, in contrast, was solid, forty ranks deep. The men under Barlow were ordered to uncap their guns and rely on shock action. Nelson Miles serving in the massed division recorded that he saw bayonets crossed for the first time in the war, although he had been in it since the beginning. Whatever the cause, Barlow's Division suffered more than the others. For the two weeks 8–21 May it lost 2,393 casualties while Birney suffered 1,015. As for the defending Confederates, they were able to pour three volleys into the Corps before it struck them. So intense was their fire that it cut down big trees. The Corps' casualty list from 8–21 May totalled 6,642, probably about twenty-five per cent of those present for duty.

Apparently General Barlow had had enough of mass formations, for at Cold Harbor on 3 June he formed his division into two deployed lines, two brigades per line. But this time John Gibbons commanding the Second Division assumed a mixed formation. His first wave comprised two brigades in two lines of two ranks each, but his second line was in close columns.

The use of mixed formations was not confined to Grant's army struggling through the Wilderness. General Thomas in his successful assault on Hood at Nashville, 15 and 16 December 1864, used a deployed front line and a second in close column by division. It may be asserted that his was the more hazardous use of this vulnerable formation, for in Grant's 1864 campaign the terrain prevented the full effect of artillery while in Thomas's that destructive arm was uninhibited.

It took seventeen months of war for the deadly firepower of the rifle musket to oblige men defending a position regularly to dig like badgers. But after Antietam in September 1862 nearly every force which defended against an assault usually protected itself with temporary earthworks. Hereafter the armies seldom came together without digging entrenchments. Foreign observers were amazed at the speed and completeness of their burrowing. For example, a brigade in the spring of 1865 was observed to have erected a breastwork across its entire front in forty minutes. Reverting to Barlow's division at Cold Harbor, when it had advanced as far as possible, it quickly switched to the defensive and erected earthworks, in some places no more than thirty yards from the enemy lines. There it stayed. Such habitual use of hasty field fortifications was one of the innovations in the craft of war contributed by Americans during the Civil War. Thus was achieved the use of the trench which shared with the bullet the domination of the battlefield, and which, General Fuller contended, had not changed when the First World War broke out half a century later.

If only indirectly, the soldiers' load affected assaults. The Confederate infantrymen began the war lightly loaded and remained so. Stonewall Jackson exploited their lightness so well that he set records in the swift movement of foot troops. In contrast the Union forces had to achieve lightness by discard. Very early they began to throw away the issue knapsack and, as the Confederates did, roll their extra things up in their blankets and sling these in a horseshoe over the shoulder. The custom was to pile the bedrolls in a heap before an action, but since there was not time, the bedrolls often went into battle too. Weapons were not exempt from discard; indeed there are many records of men throwing away their bayonets, especially in the western armies.

Hardly anyone will deny that infantry was "queen of battles" during this war. But naturally she relied heavily on the other combat arms, for example the artillery. That arm had not advanced apace, and as a result its fire was very little more destructive than during the Mexican War fifteen years before. This was because no such revolution had touched cannon as had transformed the infantryman's shoulder weapon from musket to rifle in the interlude. It is true there were rifled artillery pieces with twice the range and accuracy of any employed against Mexico, but they did not become the chief reliance during the Civil War. Instead the twelve pounder Napoleon, a smoothbore, was preponderant. Firing shells at 1,200 yards, grapeshot at 400, and canister at 200, this piece decimated attacking infantry. Yet, marvellous to tell, it was not equal to the infantrymen's rifle as a killer. For example the Medical Director of the Army of the Potomac reported for the two weeks from 8 May to 21 May 1864 that 749 wounds from artillery projectiles were treated as compared to 8,218 from bullets, that is one-tenth as many. To complete the figures only 14 bayonet cuts and one from a sword entered the report.

Like the artillery of World War I (carrying out General Fuller's parallel), the artillery of the Civil War could not solve its problems. As previously noted it had not the range, precision or elevation to give assaulting infantry the supporting fires needed in the critical area just in front of the enemy's lines. In other words it could not deliver what are now called effective preparations. For example, although 150 guns pounded the Union lines to prepare the way for Pickett's charge, they did little damage. The defenders calmly lay down until the preparation had spent itself. Nor could the cannon successfully aid assaulting troops by following closely after them. Fifteen or sixteen pieces followed Pickett's charge, but were not able to distract the defenders. The latter ignored them and poured destruction upon the infantry. All in all artillery was useful primarily as a defensive weapon, one which added materially to the superiority of the defense over the offense.

In defense, artillery was sometimes decisive. One factor that made it so was in increasing tendency to use it in masses. At Malvern Hill during the Peninsular Campaign in the spring of 1862 the Federals massed many cannon (Henderson said 300) in a commanding position and repulsed what could have been a fatal Confederate thrust. Half the Southern casualties in this engagement were from artillery fire, a very rare circumstance. Again, twenty-five cannon along Plum Run at Gettysburg held the Federal line without infantry support. Later at Atlanta General O. O. Howard united sixteen batteries behind his threatened right wing and thus prevented almost certain envelopment. On the morning of 18 May 1864 twenty-nine of his cannon, firing spherical and case shot, held 12,000 infantry at bay. He here demonstrated the technique which had developed for defensive use; namely to concentrate pieces behind the portion of the line which had been penetrated and with them drive the invaders out. At Pea Ridge, Arkansas, in March 1862 General Franz Sigel even made good use of artillery to cover his retreat.

Of course there were unusual uses of artillery. For example it sometimes moved forward with the skirmishers. Also, General Thomas at Nashville, not being able to rely on green infantry to hold the enemy in position, pinned them by means of cannon fire.

In contrast to artillery, cavalry, since it had greater mobility than the other arms, played an offensive role, albeit a different one than had been traditional in Europe. On the battlefield it rarely made mounted charges against coherent infantry. Indeed to do so was a last desperate resort. Nevertheless there are some notable instances of this use. For instance Union Major General John Buford led a mounted attack at Gettysburg which the Confederate infantry repulsed by forming the square just as Wellington's troops would have done fifty years earlier. Again, when it was necessary to delay Stonewall Jackson's infantry column at all cost in May 1863, Alfred Pleasanton's cavalry struck it at right angles to its front. The price in lives was high, but the vital delay was achieved. Later at Winchester on 19 September 1864, a mounted charge was successful against Confederate infantry.

Neither side in the American war supported heavy cavalry of the sort Napoleon had used to clinch his victories. When that great captain had seen that a portion of the enemy's line was wavering he had often ordered his heavy horse to hurl themselves at it and by the power of shock break the position and win the day. In contrast when American cavalrymen assailed the enemy's line they usually did so as infantry. They were in reality dragoons, the forerunners of armored infantry. They used their horses to reach the scene of an action with speed, then dismounted and fought on foot. In spite of their lack of infantry training they gave a good account of themselves, and when they were armed with Spencer repeaters, as most of the Union cavalry was by mid-1864, they were as good as the best infantry.

The habit of fighting on foot was reflected in armament. At the start a horse soldier had sword or sabre, pistol, and carbine. As time passed many discarded the cutting weapon and relied more heavily on firepower. At least one unit of Union cavalry started the war armed with lances, but in its earliest actions the lances slowed down a precipitate retreat. After that they were soon discarded.

In summary, if cavalry affected infantry assaults—which by the way were the principal assaults of the war—it did so, except in rare cases, acting as infantry.

The study of Civil War tactics is a dwarf compared to strategy, and probably justly so. There is doubtless little of a practical nature to be learned in the thermonuclear-missile age from the way men advanced against fire one hundred years ago. Antiquarian though the pursuit be, perhaps some readers will feel enriched by a more perfect knowledge of how their forbears assaulted their enemies. The one clear lesson that emerges—and it seems to have modern application—is that Civil War assault formations were obsolete in comparison to the fire against which they were launched.

EDWARD K. ECKERT

THE MCCLELLANS AND THE GRANTS
Generalship and Strategy in the Civil War

*T*he assessment of military leadership has long fascinated historians, and the Civil War has proven a fertile field for this form of analysis. Traditionally, Confederate generals have garnered most of the accolades. In the late-nineteenth century, British students studied "Stonewall" Jackson's 1862 campaign in the Shenandoah Valley, while Robert E. Lee is still seen by many historians as epitomizing Civil War generalship.

On the Union side, the two men most often examined over the years have been General George B. McClellan and General Ulysses S. Grant. Traditionally, McClellan is viewed as a cautious general, whose hesitation, consistent overestimation of enemy strength, and lack of effective control negated the fine qualities of his army. More recently, however, historians such as Warren Hassler and Rowena Reed have tried to alter this perception of McClellan by arguing that his strategic insights and ability to organize and train his army contributed more to Union victory than was previously recognized. Grant, on the other hand, has been both lionized and villainized over the years, with his detractors pointing to the enormous casualties he sustained during his 1864 campaign in Virginia and his supporters emphasizing his enormously successful campaign against Vicksburg, Mississippi, in 1863. While McClellan is most often portrayed as a man whose frame of reference was the past, Grant is usually presented as a general whose methods of warfare foreshadowed those of the twentieth century.

In the following essay, Professor Edward Eckert attempts to analyze northern generals in the Civil War by dividing commanders into two categories: "McClellans" and "Grants." The former type, he argues, tended to avoid risk, overemphasize pomp and ceremony in their headquarters, and relied too much on formal theories acquired during their training. Their campaigns, he suggests, were marked by slow and hesitant movement, and were usually indecisive. In contrast, the "Grants" were less impressed with themselves and paid little attention to ceremony and style. They were more inclined to take risks, and generally relied on their own insights rather than theories or formal education. Eckert argues in addition that the "Grants" recognized the political and economic natures of the Civil War more readily than the "McClellans." Their success was based, in large part, on their ability to act in harmony with the national policies established by President Lincoln.

Eckert suggests that one reason for the failure of the "McClellans" was their overdependence on the theories they learned during their formal training—particularly the strategic concepts of the Swiss-born theorist Baron Antoine Henri Jomini, widely regarded during the early nineteenth century as the foremost interpreter of Napoleonic warfare. Jomini, born in 1779, first rose to prominence as a French staff officer whose earliest writings on strategy received praise from Napoleon himself. Jomini is generally seen more as a theorist of the eighteenth century rather than of Napoleon, largely because of his consistent search for a rational and logical "system" of warfare. His writings were a blend of analysis from the wars of Frederick the Great and Napoleon, and he is often criticized by modern historians for presenting his strategic ideas as a series of almost mathematical models. It must be noted, however, that Jomini, unlike the Prussian theorist Carl von Clausewitz, was not a philosopher of war. His analysis was an effort to provide a systematic guide to military operations, and in this regard his theories were more appropriate to their time than many current writers are willing to admit. More important, from an American standpoint, is the fact that Jomini's writings were not widely available in English; his works, along with those of a number of other French theorists, were presented to American military students through the filter of Dennis Hart Mahan, an instructor at West Point from 1830 to 1871.

Widely read in French military theory, and a firm believer in the value of theory and education, Mahan wrote a series of treatises, derived from several French sources, which were adopted as texts at the United States Military Academy. Mahan modified many of the arguments in the original sources to fit what he saw as American needs. Recognizing that in any major war the American armies would consist of citizen-soldiers rather than full-time professionals, he placed great emphasis on the use of field entrenchments, fighting from the defensive whenever possible, and maneuvering to avoid frontal assaults. Almost all the major Civil War commanders, with the exception of Robert E. Lee, who graduated before Mahan began teaching at the academy, had some knowledge of these ideas at some point in their professional training. However, few had more than brief exposure to the ideas of either Jomini or Mahan. Prior to the Civil War, the West Point curriculum contained no permanent course on the theory of war; the school's primary emphasis was on the training of engineers. Mahan, in fact, taught the senior level course in military engineering. While he did include some of his theoretical principles in that course, he could devote only a small proportion of his classroom time to them. Only for the brief period from 1858 to 1861 was Mahan able to get a small course on the theory of war into the curriculum, making it hard to calculate how much impact such ideas had on most Civil War commanders.

Thus most of the senior commanders on both sides during the Civil War were confronted by situations that neither training nor experience had prepared them to face. True, most had attended West Point. Others had combat experience from the Mexican War, or from Indian fighting on the frontier. None, however, had ever handled more than a few hundred men at a time, and most had command experience over only a company or less. Of necessity, Civil War commanders used what knowledge they retained from their formal training, but relied primarily on what they could teach themselves and on their intuition and instinct, as they literally learned the art of generalship in the field.

In terms of Eckert's analysis, it is worth noting that George B. McClellan was unusual in his exposure to European ideas and theories. In 1856 he was one of three officers sent to observe the Crimean War. Nevertheless, he was still very young when he emerged as the army's general-in-chief in 1862. Eckert suggests that McClellan, and others like him, relied too much on theory as a guide. Is it possible to be too well versed in theory, so knowledgeable that various theories begin to form contradictions and paralyze both thought and action? Considering that even McClellan's severest critics acknowledge his great skill at organization and training, was his formal training a handicap, or were his difficulties and failures due to other factors, such as age or personality? Labeled as relative failures in Eckert's classification, theoretically trained Northern generals such as Henry B. Halleck did succeed in creating a relatively modern command system for the Union armies by 1864. In contrast, Lee is now often criticized for his failure to develop an effective and efficient staff system in the Army of Northern Virginia. Lee was one of a handful of West Point graduates never exposed to Mahan's teachings. It is worth asking if their theoretical foundation helped Northern generals establish a better system of command, and what contribution the development of that command system made to the final Union victory. Is Eckert accurate in evaluating the "McClellans" as failures? Under what circumstances could the boldness and risk taking of the "Grants" lead to disaster? Is there really a spectrum of leadership styles, ranging from the cautious and doctrinaire to the bold and creative, rather than the dichotomy of styles presented by Professor Eckert? Finally, it is an interesting exercise to apply categorizations similar to Eckert's to Confederate commanders, too. Is it possible to divide them along similar lines? If so, what does this suggest about the inherent difficulties of generalship, both in the Civil War and beyond?

*D*uring the four years of the Civil War, there were almost 600 men who made general in the Union Army. Of course, not all were successful, and some were admitted failures. Yet, out of that number, only three men were cashiered and another 110 resigned. A number of others were relieved of their commands and allowed to sit out the remainder of the war in an obscure post or on permanent leave.

Two peculiar types of general officers appeared during the war: "the McClellans" and "the Grants." The former achieved important commands first because their former military or civilian life marked them for future success. Such men as George B. McClellan, Joseph Hooker, Ambrose Burnside, Henry W. Halleck and George G. Meade were individuals who tended to view the entire Civil War in the light of their commands alone. They continually overemphasized their personal importance as well as the size of the enemy force they faced. The chief similarity among these men and others with like characteristics was that they were unwilling to fight unless all odds appeared to be in their favor. Armies were continually being reorganized, troops were perpetually in need of further training, and all feared to follow up a battle with an aggressive pursuit because their overly organized minds could not face the certain confusion which any pursuit must entail. A pursuit also would mean that chance had become a concomitant element in their tactics—a heresy which these men trained in the Jominian tradition at West Point never would commit.

Henri Jomini was a 19th-Century commentator on warfare as fought by Napoleon. He had prepared a handbook on military tactics and strategy which he called *The Precise Art of War.* To Jomini, the emphasis was on the second word. In this book Jomini attempted to provide solutions for every possible military puzzle as solved by Napoleon. Jomini cautioned future military readers never to deviate from his advice. His chief admonition was to use as large a mass as possible against the enemy's critical points. At West Point, strategy and tactics were taught from Jomini as interpreted by Dennis Hart Mahan. The two best examples of Jominian strategy in the Civil War are McClellan's Peninsula Campaign and Halleck's drive on Corinth, Mississippi.

When asked what he thought of Jomini's work, Ulysses S. Grant, who at times could be embarrassingly candid, was reputed to have admitted that he had never heard of the man or his work. The Grants, including Grant himself, William T. Sherman and Philip H. Sheridan were reckless to an extreme in the opinions of their more conservative contemporaries. Grant had been a failure at almost everything he had attempted before the war; Sherman's banking ventures in California were a disaster; and Sheridan first flunked the entrance exams and then later was expelled for quarreling before finally being permitted to graduate from West Point in 1853 close to the bottom of his class. Yet this trio gained invaluable experience from their failures to become the greatest successes of the war. Never fully appreciating the need to avoid committing an anti-Jomini heresy—indeed, one wonders if they would recognize one—these men rose to become the three great Union commanders and, in the view of some writers, the three greatest generals in the war.

McClellan, after receiving notification of his appointment to come east and lead the defeated and demoralized Army of the Potomac following the First Battle of Bull Run, envisaged himself a Cincinnatus, a Washington, a military dictator if necessary, but one who, unlike Cromwell, would never govern his country after the war. Instead, he would lay down his life cheerfully for the cause. Shortly after arriving in Washington, he wrote his most intimate thoughts to his wife:

> The people call on me to save the country. I must save it, and cannot respect anything that is in the way. . . . I would cheerfully take the dictatorship and agree to lay down my life when the country is saved.

Even a stronger man would have been weakened by McClellan's ideas of grandeur. Contemptuous of all others, most especially the Republican administration which he had opposed politically, he went so far on one occasion to insult the President purposely. History records that the greater of the two wearily returned to the White House with malice toward none. McClellan was convinced that his ideas alone were correct, and he refused to accept counsel or guidance from anyone. Ironically, the tyranny which he feared might come from the Republican administration was more clearly envisaged in his own contempt for civilian control over the military. No matter how benign a military dictator might be, he would be clearly outside of, and a danger to, American democracy.

McClellan either was unwilling or unable to accept the right of civilian officeholders duly elected by the people of the United States to provide necessary direction to the military. No clearer case of this conflict presented itself during the war than the often misunderstood "President's General War Order No. 1" of January 1862. President Lincoln had come to recognize early that a civil war, almost by definition, is as much a political contest as a military one. Consequently, at times political needs must take precedence over military ones. Lincoln's problem was that inaction appeared to most Americans and Europeans as acceptance of the *fait accompli* of Southern independence. After almost a year of war, there was really only one major battle and that was a disastrous routing of the Union Army. Time is always an ally for the revolutionaries. Permanent inaction would mean ultimate Confederate success. Lincoln's concern was not so much for a major military victory but for at least a few smaller ones to demonstrate to the world that his administration was serious about quelling the rebellion.

McClellan, on the other hand, approached the entire war, and most especially his own campaigns, as elaborate engineering problems. Well-immersed in Jomini as taught by Mahan at West Point, both of whom envisioned military tactics as civil engineering problems and encouraged the study of past wars for answers to future situations, McClellan was fighting today's war with the tactics and strategy of the last generation. McClellan had had a firsthand view of European warfare and was appalled at the losses which occurred in the Crimea from foolhardy decisions. America's own "Little Napoleon" would never permit his reputation to suffer for politics. Consequently, while Lincoln was pleading for some sort of minor, successful action to convince the world of his administration's intentions, McClellan was creating an American Austerlitz by which the entire resistance would collapse and the Union restored with a minimal amount of human or property loss. Then, as the victorious general, he would retire, at least temporarily, amid the accolades and gifts of a grateful nation. McClellan's answer to Lincoln's call for immediate action was the Peninsula Campaign, as elaborate a quadrille as any battle planned by a Caesar, Marlborough or Napoleon.

Similar, though admittedly less elaborate, campaigns, were offered the administration by McClellan's brothers-in-arms. Halleck, the only living American general to write a major study of warfare, envisaged equally elaborate and well-planned moves down the Mississippi and Ohio Rivers. Burnside, the humblest of the lot, and Hooker, misnamed "Fighting Joe," offered equally elaborate campaigns to outflank the enemy in northern Virginia only to find out that Lee had outflanked them and had them whipped before they had started to move. Book strategy could only be successful when the opponent agreed to adhere to the same book. Unfortunately, their principal adversary was Lee who had not only read their book, but had prepared his own, and he could check every move they planned almost before they had begun to march.

The second common characteristic of the McClellans was, to use the President's own words, a case of "the slows." This deadly disease's symptoms first appeared during the planning of a campaign, gradually increased during the fighting and would prove fatal at the end when the army would be put to bed allowing the enemy to move along his own chosen course at a leisurely pace. In the planning stage, "the slows" meant that manpower, training and equipment would have to be quantitatively and qualitatively superior before the army would commence any operations. During the movement to the battlefield, all chance would have to be eliminated. While the battle raged, reserves would be held back uselessly when they were obviously needed on the field, and, following the conflict, their armies would need time to regroup, reequip and readjust before pursuing the wounded enemy.

No one denies that Hooker's training and reorganization paid dividends at a later time. Few would argue that McClellan's cautious moves up the Virginia Peninsula or Halleck's slow march on Corinth, Mississippi, reduced

Union casualties. And most military historians agree that some reorganization is necessary, especially after a difficult battle such as Gettysburg or Antietam. Yet the combination of all three during the same campaign is deadly. The entire Peninsula Campaign was fraught with "the slows." Cumbersome since almost all the manpower and equipment had to be moved to the Peninsula via water, the strategy had become well-advertised to the enemy. Supercaution became the watchword as a great army became bogged down fighting logs painted as cannons, mysterious infantry and a theatrical enemy between Yorktown and Richmond. McClellan's large army took almost two weeks to move 50 miles only to fall apart when they actually met the real enemy for whom they had prepared so cautiously.

"The slows" would reappear even after a successful engagement such as Antietam. Too cautious to deliver the *coup de grâce* during the battle, McClellan permitted the enemy to retreat. Historians too long have accepted McClellan's and Meade's excuses following two of the greatest battles of the war. These men were not interested in destroying a revolution; they only sought to fight the perfect textbook battle, and indeed, in their eyes, they had done so. Of course, the enemy was preparing himself for a counterattack at Gettysburg, but he also prepared for one during the Wilderness Campaign, and he was driven back. True, the Union forces were tired after having fought a major, day-long battle along the Antietam Creek, but so, too, were Union men tired after the first day at Shiloh. And, certainly, the enemy would be on the defensive during the spring of 1863 around Chancellorsville as he would also be on the defensive outside of Atlanta in the summer of 1864, on the mountains around Chattanooga in the fall of 1863, and in the Shenandoah Valley during the last year of the war.

The McClellans were hazardous to the Union's health during the Civil War. These men never seemed to realize the political nature of a civil war. Their battles should have been fought on a great plain in Europe where massive armies could meet and fight the way they were supposed to. Small bits of property would change hands, future generations could discuss the brilliant strategy of the generals, and preparations would be made for the next inevitable war based on the lessons learned from the past. What is ironic is that the McClellans interpreted their role as inherent in the great American military tradition and were unable to understand how their refusal to cooperate fully with the Lincoln administration could threaten that very heritage. To McClellan, Hooker and Halleck as demonstrated by their actions in Virginia, on the road to Gettysburg and in the Mississippi Valley, they were making their decisions in light of their needs rather than those of the nation. They cared little about current political problems plaguing the administration. Like future militarists in Europe, they argued that, when the politicians had taken the nation into a war, only the generals could make the extraction. In their eyes, professional military men, left to themselves, would be the best cure for the disease of war.

Lincoln was never impressed by their argument. Like the future French political leader, Clemenceau, Lincoln believed that wars were too important to be left to the generals. Indeed, to a great extent, the story of the ultimate Union success in the war can be told accurately as Lincoln's ultimate success in finding generals. Above all else, Lincoln understood that the nation was fighting a rebellion, a civil war, a revolution. He also knew the long history of antagonism between the sections. Lincoln understood better than most men the Southern mind and pride since he had been born in a slave state and married a Southern woman. He was never convinced that one magnificent campaign or battle would end the war, be it Winfield Scott's great "Anaconda" plan, McClellan's Peninsular Campaign, or McDowell's drive on Richmond. The President saw the war as a whole. He not only had to supervise the military actions, but he had to conduct political, economic and diplomatic strategy as well. The President was attempting to orchestrate all into a symphony that would come to a crashing crescendo as many individual pieces played their parts in one harmonious effort under the watchful eye of Lincoln as the conductor. The President never really cared for McClellan's plans for the Peninsula because it subordinated political, diplomatic and economic efforts to the one great military action. He was willing to allow the general a chance to prove himself primarily because he had no other viable alternative at the time. What Lincoln wanted was a general who would fight with the men, equipment and money which the administration could provide him and not keep demanding more. He sought generals who would win military battles while he won the political, ambassadors the diplomatic and bankers the financial. He did not want commanders to tell him to forget politics, diplomacy and finance, for he well understood that this war could be won only by triumphing in all four areas. Consequently, the President sought generals who would fight hard with what they had, accept direction from him, and ultimately destroy a revolution. Lincoln found these characteristics in Grant, Sherman and Sheridan.

Ironically, none of these three men were as dramatically successful early in the war as McClellan had been in western Virginia. They made mistakes, but they grew from them. None of the three was impressed with his own abilities. Indeed, by most objective standards, all three could be considered failures in their previous lives. Apparently, none had learned textbook tactics very well, for all three disregarded most of the accepted admonitions except the most important one of all—victory. Consequently, these men who concentrated on victory rather than maneuver, who refused to accept defeat, and who would not be tied down by rules created to fight a war a generation before would achieve a standard of success unmatched by any of their more bookish colleagues. It is difficult for historians observing the interesting panorama of their lives to say exactly what the secret of their success was during the war. After more than a century, no one has provided a better insight than Henry Adams who saw the key to their success as their vast human energy. This scion of two Presidents observed in his autobiography, *The Education of Henry Adams*, that:

> In time one came to recognize the type in other men, with differences and variations, as normal; men whose energies were the greater, the less they wasted on thought; men who sprang from the soil to power; apt to be distrustful of themselves and of others; shy; jealous; sometimes vindictive; more or less dull in outward appearance; always needing stimulants; but for whom action was the highest stimulant—the instinct of fight. Such men were forces of nature, energies of the prime, like the Pteraspis, but they made short work of scholars. They had commanded thousands of such and saw no more in them than in others. The fact was certain; it crushed argument and intellect at once.

It must be admitted that, by the time all three had achieved independent command, their armies had been forged into a fighting machine unequaled elsewhere in the world. Yet, unlike McClellan and Hooker and Halleck, none of the Grants demanded an opportunity to sit down and reorganize or to stop and retrain the army they had received. They either accepted what they had inherited or reorganized and retrained while on the march. Furthermore, perhaps as indicated by their previous failures, they rarely planned a campaign much beyond the initial drive toward the objective. Relying on chance as an ally, they accepted battle in situations which would have frightened off the McClellans. Finally, none of them could ever be accused of having "the slows." Before, during and after battle, they pushed relentlessly toward victory, scarcely giving the enemy time to recover before pushing him once again. Note, too, that it was the enemy himself—not a city, state or river valley—on which the Grants marched. They aimed for the jugular with its living blood.

The loss of manpower caused by Grant's relentless pursuit of Lee in northern Virginia created for him the epithet of "butcher." Sheridan's success in the Shenandoah Valley was so total that it was said a crow would have to carry his own provisions across it. And Sherman's "march to the sea" is legendary in the destruction it caused. Yet all three were personally just as concerned with human and materiel loss as was any other individual in the war. At times, Grant would retire into his tent at night and drink heavily to avoid thinking of the destruction. It was Sherman who provided such generous terms of surrender to his opponent Joseph E. Johnston that the pro-Southern administration of Andrew Johnson rejected it. It was Sherman—not any of the McClellans—who later exclaimed, "There is many a boy to-day who looks on war as all glory, but, boys, it is all hell."

The Grants were fighting something larger than a mere battle and vaster than a war. Grant, Sherman and Sheridan each realized that they were subduing a revolution. They were convincing the Southern people that their peculiar way of life would suffer more from continued independence and warfare than from a reunion of the nation. No state, no county, no city or town could be permitted to maintain the fiction that secession had been a success there. Not only the ability to fight but the will as well must be conquered. The Southern will had to be destroyed as completely as Lee's army. The interconnection between a war waged against civilians and the political nature of the Civil War was obvious to all three. Since none were brutal men, they could only justify the destruction they caused by seeking a transcendent goal—the goal of a reunited nation.

Southerners always wondered why Northerners fought so hard in the war. The Southern leaders recognized that the North as a whole did not favor abolition and, in most ways, was equally as racist as the South. The Northerners fought for the same reason as Southerners—the romance of the nation, only their nation included the South as well as the North. Sentiments such as these played their part in the formation of the character of the Grants. Early in the war, Grant demanded that his former classmate Simon Buckner surrender Fort Donelson unconditionally. Yet, after three more years of conflict when the war was obviously at an end and the nation close to reunion, he could be magnanimous to the man who kept the war going more than any other single individual.

Southerners too had a fondness for the united nation that even a civil war could not entirely shake. Pickett's salute of the US flag after crossing into Pennsylvania, the continuing observance of the Fourth of July and Washington's Birthday as holidays, and a slavish plagiarism of the US Constitution and flag for their own were only a few of the ways by which Southerners remembered and honored the nation of which they once were a part. These underlying feelings made eventual reunion and reconciliation possible. The Grants—like the President, at least through their actions—demonstrated a sensitivity to these sentiments.

The political connection was the reason for the war, and Grant, Sherman and Sheridan were willing to allow politicians to provide them with direction in that area. By rarely challenging and never disobeying the administration, this trio acted in the best tradition of the American military heritage. They accepted the President's legitimate role in the military hierarchy via his office as Commander in Chief. Life and property were destroyed in the Civil War to a degree unknown in all other domestic American wars combined, yet this destruction only occurred during legitimate campaign actions. Indeed, when Grant had no place to keep his prisoners adequately following the fall of Vicksburg, he simply paroled almost all of them. The vast destruction of the South was purposely undertaken to extinguish all flickering hope for a separate Southern nation—the political as well as the military goal of the war.

The second characteristic of all three was their daring or what some contemporary and later critics have called their recklessness. Grant's pushing had left him vulnerable at Shiloh, and Sherman violated all accepted textbook strategy by stretching his supply line across all of northern Georgia before Atlanta. Because they accepted the total nature of the war, none would ever boast that the forthcoming battle would end the conflict dramatically. All three intuitively realized that the war would only be won by pushing the enemy armies until they had broken over all of the Confederacy. The surrender of Richmond alone, as traumatic as that might be, would not win the war. Thus, while Grant spent the best part of a year sparring with Lee between Richmond and Petersburg, he was aware that Sheridan was aiding him by fighting his way up the Shenandoah Valley, and Sherman would be marching through the heartland of the Confederacy. By the time the Southern capital actually fell, the revolution would have been destroyed too. Unlike other rebellions, there was no guerrilla resistance following the loss of the capital and the government. The South had been thoroughly defeated. Richmond's demise was the climax rather than the beginning of the war. One is forced to reflect upon what would have happened had Richmond fallen in the spring of 1862 to McClellan. The war would not have ended as McClellan had boasted. The Jefferson Davis administration would have become a peripatetic government and, like the rebel civilian leadership during the American Revolution, would have tired out their opponent by traveling over the countryside.

The final element of success possessed by this Union trio was the ability to accept chance as a necessary element in war. Jomini had never really understood the genius of Napoleon. Tactical reorganization, adequate planning and battlefield leadership do not add up to genius. The American Army teaches that leaders are made not born. Perhaps so, but they obviously had not been made at West Point before the Civil War. The place where the Grants learned leadership was on the very battlefields of that war. But, moreover, they possessed intuitively what no school can teach, the visceral ability to exploit that unknown element in all wars—chance. Chance had played too great a part in their own careers for them to deny its importance.

As little more than failures, the chance of war gave them the opportunity to display the genius which they had within them. Something had favored them from the start of this conflict, and they were not about to deny it. They did not brag about their luck; they accepted it and, because they knew it was there, they fought with a confidence never possessed by the McClellans. McClellan and his intellectual colleagues had tried to factor out that most fickle part of human experience—the unknown—by planning their campaigns down to the last horseshoe. So precise was their preparation that, when the enemy behaved unpredictably, as he almost inevitably did, their plans fell apart like the weakest building of all—a house of cards.

Grant planned little for his campaigns at Chattanooga or against Lee later in the war. Acting instinctively and unable to do anything about it at the time anyway, he accepted and exploited the unexpected charge of George H. Thomas' troops to the top of Missionary Ridge, or he kept pushing to the left even after he had been defeated in the Wilderness. Sherman and Grant accepted chance completely, dispensing entirely with a line of supplies—the former in Georgia and the latter in Mississippi. Sheridan refused to give his enemy a chance to relax, and he moved his columns up the Shenandoah Valley exploiting opportunities wherever they existed. He removed men like William W. Averell who retired to his camp with the cavalry after a battle and allowed Sheridan and the infantry to chase the enemy.

Generals Grant, Sherman and Sheridan all possessed the attributes which the President had sought from the beginning of the war. Accepting political direction without opposition and with every sentiment that it was right, they allowed Lincoln to conduct the national policy and strategy. Never impressed by their own importance, they listened to suggestions and accepted political guidance. They well recognized that their military efforts were only a part of the national endeavor to quell a revolution which had political, diplomatic and financial repercussions as well as military. They could see and accept the overall goal for which the war was being fought—the goal of a reunited nation—and they designed their battlefield strategy to meet that demand. One can only wonder what would have happened to the United States if the President had fully accepted the ideas of the McClellans.

JOHN D. MILLIGAN

FROM THEORY TO APPLICATION
The Emergence of the Ironclad War Vessel

From the end of the sixteenth to the middle of the nineteenth centuries, changes in the methods and weapons of naval warfare represented little more than refinements to existing methods. A sailor from one of the English galleons that stood off the Spanish Armada in 1588 would, with relative ease, have been able to serve effectively aboard any of the British, Spanish, or French vessels at the Battle of Trafalgar in 1805. Indeed, British Admiral Horatio Nelson's flagship at Trafalgar, HMS Victory, was already forty years old, yet was not at all outdated. Armed with over ninety smoothbore cannon, the largest firing a thirty-two-pound solid roundshot, HMS Victory carried her guns in a series of three main gundecks. Fleet tactics might evolve, and Nelson's victory at Trafalgar in fact signaled a major shift in the way a fleet might be used in battle, but for the individual ship, the goal changed very little. Once the gun became the dominant weapon at sea, the objective was simply to get to close range and pound the enemy as rapidly as possible.

In less than two decades following Trafalgar, however, a number of changes, spurred by the Industrial Revolution, would begin to fundamentally alter the shape of naval warfare that had evolved over the previous three centuries. By the middle of the nineteenth century a sailor from Nelson's fleet would have had increasing difficulty in serving aboard a warship; by the end of the 1870s he would find himself in a totally unfamiliar environment.

The first major change to occur was in naval armament. From the first introduction of guns to ships, war vessels relied on the heaviest smoothbore artillery the ship could

137

carry. The only major innovation in naval weaponry prior to the early nineteenth century was the development of the so-called "carronade," a gun allegedly invented at Scotland's Carron Foundry in the eighteenth century. The carronade had a shorter barrel than usual and could fire a heavier shot than a traditional gun of the same weight—at some cost in range. In 1824, however, seeking some method of overcoming British naval superiority, a French artilleryman named Henri Paixhans demonstrated a shell-firing gun of his own design by destroying an anchored wooden hulk in a well-publicized test. Although Paixhan's gun did not end British naval superiority, it effectively made all wooden-hulled warships obsolescent, if not obsolete. This was made particularly clear when a Russian squadron armed with shell-firing guns totally annihilated a Turkish squadron at Sinope in 1853.

The natural counter to the shell gun was armor. Initially this consisted of thin plates bolted to a wooden hull, but as the power of naval guns began to grow it was clear that the thickness—and thus the weight—of the armor would have to grow. Moving such increasingly heavy vessels would have been impossible for ships using only sails, but by that time the Industrial Revolution had provided an alternative to sails in the form of steam power.

The first successful steam-powered vessels appeared shortly after the beginning of the nineteenth century. In Britain, the Charlotte Dundas was launched in 1802, and in 1807 American inventor Robert Fulton's steamship, Clermont, traveled 150 miles up the Hudson River. By 1837 the successful Atlantic Ocean crossing of the British-built steamship Sirius demonstrated that steamers were not limited to coastal or inland waters. Naval officers in most countries resisted the development of steam-powered warships for a variety of reasons, one being that early steamships used paddle wheels, which were vulnerable to gunfire and took up a large proportion of the area where guns could be mounted. In the 1840s, however, American navy Captain Robert F. Stockton designed and built the first successful warship using a screw propeller, the USS Princeton. The screw propeller was not only more efficient than paddle wheels, its use allowed the full deck space to be utilized for armament, and it allowed designers to place the engine machinery lower in the ship's hull. Within a few years almost all warships built had steam power, although the vast majority continued to have sails and rigging as well. By 1857 the sailing line-of-battle ship had vanished from the Royal Navy.

Acceptance of steam power accelerated the use of iron and steel in warship design, first simply as armor plating and later as the basic material in hull construction. In 1859 the French launched La Gloire, a wooden-hulled frigate with four and a half inches of armor. A year later, the Royal Navy countered with HMS Warrior, the first armored warship with a hull built of iron. The U.S. Navy also had steam-driven warships. Commodore Matthew Perry's expedition to Japan in the 1850s included the steam frigates USS Mississippi and USS Missouri, and many of its ships were armed with versions of a powerful shell-firing gun developed by Admiral John Dahlgren. However, when the Civil War broke out in 1861, none of these vessels had been used in combat.

In the following selection, Professor John D. Milligan examines the use of armored, steam-driven vessels during the early campaigns in the West during the Civil War. Although these first American ironclad warships were river gunboats rather than oceangoing warships, they reflected the emerging technology and their use forced naval officers and designers to develop the best ways to make use of untested theories and untried weapons. Milligan's essay can be read simply as a narrative description of the river campaigns of the Civil War, but underlying his story is a theme much like that explored by John K. Mahon two selections earlier. Naval commanders, like their army counterparts, were often confronted with situations in which their training and experience did not offer a sure guide to their actions. Their efforts to integrate new technologies into their operations, and the difficulties they sometimes had in doing so, suggest that even when military leaders want to adapt to new technology there are inherent problems they must face. Resistance to a new technology may not always be simple stubbornness, or reflect blindness to the potential benefits of a particular development; it may be an honest result of the difficulty of using a new technology most effectively.

Traditionally, the process of military adaptation to changing technology has been viewed in simple terms. Military resistance to technological innovation was most often described in terms of conservative military leaders attempting to preserve a familiar and psychologically comfortable status quo in terms of equipment, doctrine, or influence within a military system. More recent commentators are, however, less willing to accept this traditional frame of reference. One example is the Israeli military historian Martin van Creveld, who argues that changes in technology not only have profound psychological consequences for individuals, but also influence all aspects of doctrine, training, and even the organization of military forces. When change in all these areas is rapid, the possibility exists that a military system will suffer a loss of cohesion, and may be disrupted to the point it can no longer fulfill its basic mission. Like many other recent examiners of the impact of technology on the military, van Creveld suggests that there are costs to technological change. These costs may be very high and are not just monetary. Readers should ask themselves what costs were associated with the changes described by Professor Milligan, and whether the process of adaptation Civil War naval leaders went through was in fact a typical reaction to change. Readers might also compare this selection to others in this collection that examine the effect of new weapons or new ideas on the American military, particularly Eugene Emme's study of the evolution of American ideas on air power. Clearly there are many factors that must be considered as military systems react to technological change. Some of these are psychological, and some are simply a result of trying to force a new technology into a doctrinal approach better suited to an older technology. To understand the effect of technological change requires an understanding of all the adjustments—mental and emotional—military leaders must make as they struggle to adjust to an unfamiliar environment.

*R*ecent events in the South Atlantic have again affirmed an old truth: the only genuine test for new military and naval technology is the test of battle itself. The historian, however, does not always seem to appreciate this fact. Already knowing the outcome of the introduction of a new weapon, he may as it were read history backwards by forgetting that there was a time when the weapon's developers could not know whether it would succeed or fail. Such a time occurred before the first American ironclad naval vessels underwent their trial by fire. These craft, for the first time in this hemisphere, combined in addition to iron armor three more of the five naval revolutions of the 19th century—steam propulsion, rifled ordnance, and the shell gun.

The present article will attempt two things: to reconstruct the period when the innovators of these ironclads, albeit seeking to anticipate all contingencies, could really only speculate about what the eventual battle results would be; and to describe what success the vessels actually achieved in combat.

Contrary to the popular impression, the first American craft to be designed and built as ironclads did not include the USS *Monitor* of Civil War fame. True, they were constructed by the North during that conflict; but they were rather seven river gunboats designed to operate on the inland waters. Conceived early in the war, they were meant to implement General Winfield Scott's "Anaconda" policy of completing the blockade of the Eastern Confederacy by seizing control of the Mississippi River and its tributaries. Although their construction and operations were initially administered and financed by the War Department, personnel from the Navy Department contributed substantially to their design, supervised their construction, and, once they were commissioned, took command of them. Appropriately, in September, 1862, the Mississippi Squadron was transferred to Navy Department jurisdiction.

The ironclad program, nevertheless, would never have floated had not the Army and Navy been able to tap the expertise of Western boat designers and builders who already had experience with steam-driven, shallow-water craft. And yet, none of the latter group and few of the naval group could claim experience with all of the innovations concerned; and none of either group could claim experience with *fresh-water* war vessels of the type contemplated. The consequence, as will be seen, was a continual evolution of what initially was only a vaguely articulated scheme, an evolution which included plenty of extemporary improvisations and which was further confused by the time constraint imposed by war.

Once the War Department's wishes were known, the architectural imaginations of a number of people gave genesis to the gunboats it requested. The first to try his hand was John Lenthall. Chief of the Washington Naval Bureau of Construction and Repair, Lenthall seems to have felt little commitment to the concept. Having previously devoted himself to blue-water ships, he felt slight optimism that armed vessels adequate to fresh-water conditions in the West could be devised. He drew up only a sketchy outline of a hull and steam machinery. If he lacked commitment, his doubts were also occasioned by a conviction that certain intrinsic factors would render a river gunboat too vulnerable. First, screw propellors being likely ruled out by shallow waters, the craft would needs depend on side-mounted paddle wheels that would present ample targets. Second, the hold of a light-draft vessel being shallow, much if not all of its steam machinery would have to be exposed above deck. The bureau chief's experience with steam engines was sufficient to impress on him that, unlike a vessel which relied on wind for propulsion, one that relied on steam could be rendered *hors de combat* by a single shot to a vital spot.

His doubts notwithstanding, Lenthall provided Scott's chief engineer with a brief description of the gunboat he had in mind. Measuring 170 feet by 28 feet and drawing five feet of water, the level-bottomed hull should be constructed entirely of wood. Two high-pressure steam engines, one to a paddle wheel, would supply motive power, and four eight-inch shell guns, firepower. The completed craft would displace 436 tons and cost $20,000. Thus, while calling for steam engines and shell guns, the design at this stage still did not contemplate iron armor or rifled ordnance.

The next individual to put his mind to the project was John Lenthall's subordinate, Naval Constructor Samuel Pook. Lenthall may have held out little hope for the gunboat program, but on his recommendation, Pook was assigned to carry on. The result was a radically changed conception which included both armor and rifles.

Some of the ideas which Pook introduced were the outcome of his already being in the West, consulting with knowledgeable boat builders and helping to supervise for the Army the conversion of three commercial steamers into unarmored, wooden gunboats, themselves the first naval product of Scott's Anaconda. For example, where the narrow hull of the vessel projected by Lenthall had reflected deep-water thinking, Pook, recognizing that navigable rivers were virtually always calm, broadened the beam by 22 feet. This modification allowed him to add another five feet to the length and still provide a more stable gun platform, and one better able to bear the additional weight he planned for it. The wide, flat-bottomed hull as designed by Pook was to draw six feet of water and measure 175 feet from stem to stern and 50 feet on the beam.

Above the hull, completely covering the deck excepting the blunt bow and extreme stern, Pook planned a rectangular, wooden casement with 8-inch-thick oak planking on its forward face and 2½-inch oak planking on its other surfaces. The four sides of this structure, which were to rise at inward angles of about 35 degrees to the hurricane deck, later inspired onlookers to liken the gunboat's appearance to a turtle's. Inside the carapace would be sheltered the boat's vitals—its gundeck, its steam machinery, and its single paddle wheel. This last item meant that Pook was replacing Lenthall's two exposed side wheels with one laterally-centered wheel located between twin sterns. Unfortunately, the trade-off would mean less maneuverability in confined and flowing waters.

To arm his vessel, Pook went well beyond Lenthall's four shell guns. He recommended that the total number of cannon be increased to 20 and that they include an assortment of shell, rifled, and smoothbore guns. Pook also went to considerable lengths to make his creation proof against enemy fire. To keep it afloat should it be hulled, he directed that the hull be divided into water-tight sections. To protect the delicate steam machinery, he recommended what was to be the gunboat's most innovative feature—cast iron plates bolted to the exterior wood surfaces. Probably believing that decisions respecting the armor's optimum placement could better be made once construction was underway, Pook did no more than suggest that 75 tons of it be procured for each vessel and that the individual iron slabs be 2½ inches thick.

While he laid down most of the data for the architecture of the gunboats, Pook did not attempt to provide the particulars for the design of the steam engines. To develop these, the services of a specialist were required; and the Navy called in A. Thomas Merritt, an experienced steam engineer from Cincinnati. Although Pook had reduced John Lenthall's two paddle wheels to one, Merritt still agreed with Lenthall that each ironclad should mount two steam engines. Unlike Lenthall, however, the engineer was convinced he could stuff all of the steam machinery—engines, boilers, and steam drums—into the shallow hold, leaving nothing exposed on deck. More precisely, Merritt planned his engines to have cylinders with 22-inch bores and pistons with six-foot strokes. Set transversely to the hull, each engine, sharing a common shaft with its mate, would sit directly forward of one end of the wheel with its aft-canted, cast-iron piston driving that end through a wrought-iron connecting rod. The engineer would squeeze five high-pressure boilers with their steam drums into whatever space remained ahead of the engines. In common with other river steamers, exhaust and smoke from the fire box would be discharged above deck through two tall chimneys.

With Pook's and Merritt's instructions in hand, the War Department invited western boat builders to submit bids. The one it accepted came from the well-known civil engineer, James B. Eads of St. Louis. On 7 August 1861, Eads signed with the Department an agreement to build seven ironclad gunboats at $89,600 the boat, or over four times the sum anticipated by Lenthall. Eads began work on the vessels in boatyards at Carondelet, Missouri, on the Mississippi, and at Mound City, Illinois, on the Ohio. Samuel Pook having by then returned east, the job of general superintendent of the building program fell to naval Commander John Rodgers.

The experience that Rodgers had already acquired in fresh-water matters was identical to that which Samuel Pook had brought to the ironclad program, because, along with Pook, Rodgers had been involved in the conversion of these three river steamers into wooden gunboats. Now it was left largely to him to address problems which Pook had not resolved; these problems mainly concerned pilot houses and iron armor. Rodgers' directives for pilot houses asked that on each gunboat, atop the casemate and forward of the twin smoke stacks, Eads erect an octagonal, wooden structure, low in profile with sloping sides. The slope of the sides, like that of the sides of the casemate, was, of course, to deflect hostile shot.

More difficult of solution were the problems of deciding the proper dimensions and location of the iron armor, problems exacerbated by the possibility that armor sufficient for adequate protection might constitute a burden too great for the boats to bear. The Chief of the Bureau of Naval Ordnance, John A. Dahlgren, put his finger on the nub of the dilemma: "The ship builder finds himself compelled to changes of the most radical nature, in order that the ship may carry the ponderous armor intended for it." Rodgers sought to solve the problem in three ways. Respecting the configuration of the iron plates, he firstly added other dimensions to the $2\frac{1}{2}$-inch thickness set by Pook. Each plate would be cast with a width of 13 inches and "with a projection or lip on each side two inches wide and half the thickness of the plate." The lips would allow the plates to be laid in an overlapping fashion. The lengths of the plates would depend on the respective areas they were to cover.

Secondly, Rodgers sought to secure the plates in a way that enemy shot would be less likely to "start" or knock off. All of the plates would be attached to the outer side of the wood surfaces by $1\frac{1}{2}$-inch bolts, which, piercing the plates at their centers and at their sides where they overlapped, would be secured on the inner sides of the vessels either by nuts and washers or by drift bolts.

Thirdly, Rodgers made what was perhaps his most crucial decision: where to place the iron slabs so that they would afford the best protection. To shield the steam machinery, he concluded that on each vessel Eads should lay plates along the sides of the hull and casemate "from 2 feet forward of the boilers to abreast the piston rod guides," a length of perhaps 32 feet. The plates were to be set vertically so that those on the sides of the hull would extend up "from 1 foot below the water line . . . to the upper plates" on the sides of the casemate, and those on the sides of the casemate would extend down "from the edge of the upper deck [i.e. the top of the casemate] to $2\frac{1}{2}$-inches below the angle of the boat's side so as to cover the ends of the lower plates." Further, Rodgers asked Eads to sheath completely both the forward side of the casemate and all sides of the pilot house with $2\frac{1}{2}$-inch plate, and to overlay the main deck ahead of the casemate with thinner $\frac{3}{4}$-inch plate. The commander was obviously seeking to provide adequate protection while also staying within the weight tolerances that buoyancy could support and steam engines propel. The result was 122 tons of armor per vessel, or about half again the tonnage projected by Pook. This amount would serve to cover many of the critical areas of each vessel, but unfortunately would still leave the casemate bare of iron on its quarter and aft surfaces and the whole of its roof or hurricane deck.

Beyond resolving questions that Samuel Pook had left hanging fire, Rodgers modified some of the arrangements that the naval constructor had seemingly settled. Thus he increased the thickness of the casemates' wooden walls by adding 5½ inches of wood to the 2½ that Pook had defined for the side and aft surfaces and a significant 16 inches to the eight that Pook had defined for the forward surfaces. This meant that these latter surfaces would be the gunboats' strongest. Rodgers manifestly assumed that in narrow, moving waters these craft would usually be attacking bows on.

Though surviving sources document the contributions of Samuel Pook and John Rodgers to the design of the gunboats, they do not provide much evidence about the contribution of engineer-contractor James Eads. Eads, to be sure, did fulfill his contract to build the vessels, but anyone at all familiar with his quick mind and assertive personality would know that the man doubtless contributed ideas to the project as well.

Be that as it may, before the ironclads went into service their detailing underwent some additional mutations. Because the documents do not reveal who instigated certain of these changes and refinements, indeed because they do not describe the changes themselves, modern chroniclers did not learn about them until the 1960s. In that decade a salvaging expedition raised the wreckage of one of the ironclads, the *Cairo,* from the floor of the Yazoo River where it had lain since being sunk by a Confederate mine some 100 years before. The primary evidence provided a few revelations. For example, the armor on the sides of the hull was found to extend further below the water line than the one foot originally requested by John Rodgers' instructions. Secondly, the armor on the sides of the pilot house was found to have a thickness of 1¼ and not the 2½ inches which Rodgers had ordered. Thirdly, Rodgers' call for the side walls of the wooden casemate to be 8 inches thick had been modified. On the salvaged *Cairo* these walls were about the same 24-inch thickness as the casemate's forward wall. Finally, an examination of the raised gunboat revealed that the wood backing for the armor on the three forward sides of the eight-sided pilot house was 19½ inches thick while that of the other five sides was merely 12 inches.

If the documents are unhelpful in revealing whether or not James Eads was responsible for some or all of these changes, they do attest that he was responsible for one significant modification. To offset the burdens of armor and thick wooden walls, he reduced the 20 guns that Pook had advised for each vessel to 13. As armed, the individual ironclad, of almost 900 tons displacement when fully loaded, carried six traditional smoothbore 32-pounders, four recently rifled, old smoothborers, throwing 42-pound solid shot, and three Dahlgren-designed shell guns with bores of eight-inch diameter. Gunports pierced the casemate to allow three of the cannon to fire over the bow, four to each side and two over the stern. The rifled guns were usually set in the bow, but since all of the guns were mounted on carriages, they could be moved from gunport to gunport to provide shell, rifled, and smoothbore fire in various combinations.

The armament of the ironclads, then, included both types of the new class of cannon, but a point should be emphasized regarding each. Given the combination of weakness in primitive gun metal and internal pressure generated by less windage, even the best of rifles in those days were liable on occasion to burst when fired. The rifles on the ironclads were unhappily even more fragile; as noted, they were simply old, surplus army smoothbores, the bores of which at the suggestion of the War Department had been further weakened by rifling. In the eventuality, they sometimes proved more lethal to their crews than to the enemy. If the shell guns were less apt to burst, their ability to wreak destruction was inhibited by another factor. Because the early shell relied on a wick-type fuse to ignite its explosive contents, accurately estimating the length of the fuse before loading the shell into the cannon was an all-important determinant of whether or not the projectile would explode at the proper instant.

An examination of the characteristics of the first American ironclads may be completed by describing one additional change which is revealed in the documents. Steam engineer Thomas Merritt had been wrong in believing that he could crowd the engines and all the appurtenances into the gunboats' shallow holds. On the very first runs that the craft made, the low elevation of the steam drums caused water as well as steam to pass into the engines. On orders from naval Captain Andrew H. Foote, who by then had replaced John Rodgers as chief of the project, Eads shifted the drums to sit atop the boilers. Their new position solved the immediate problem but placed them where they would be more vulnerable under fire.

In addition to the seven sister-boats which the Union had built as ironclads, it had also converted into ironclads two river steamers, one a double-hulled snag boat which became the *Benton,* the other a ferryboat which became the *Essex.* Though larger and more heavily armed and armored than the seven turtles, they were similar in conception and configuration and embodied the same technical features.

Having, then, considered the impromptu manner in which the creators of these gunboats had gone about working the new technology into their design, it remains to examine how well these vessels stood to the test. "The test" in this case could not mean shake-down trials or subjecting the respective technical techniques to complete review under simulated conditions. The exigencies of war simply did not permit time. The only comprehensive testing the new ironclads would receive would be at the mouths of the enemy's cannon.

Going into commission in early 1862, the seven sister-boats—and the two larger vessels which had been converted into ironclads from commercial craft—were assigned the role of implementing the Union policy of seizing control of the navigable rivers flowing through the Western Confederacy. To determine with what effectiveness the vessels met the combat conditions of that role, this writer will consider three of the early engagements—at Fort Henry, Fort Donelson, and Island No. 10—in which these first American ironclads fought. Taken together, the three engagements offered environments and conditions generally representative of the river campaigns of the Civil War, because, though the Confederacy did manage to put a few ironclads on the interior waters, its industrial weakness forced it by and large to rely on fixed, riverbank works to contest the Federal objective of establishing river supremacy in the West.

In late 1861, the Confederacy had constructed Forts Henry and Donelson just south of "neutral" Kentucky's border. The former, on the east bank of the Tennessee River, and the latter, twelve miles to the east on the west bank of the Cumberland River, were meant to prevent Federal waterborne forces from steaming up those waterways into the heart of the western Confederacy.

Although the attack on Fort Henry was supposed to be a joint Army-Navy venture, recent heavy rains, which had turned local roads into mud and streams into impassable torrents, kept the troops of General Ulysses S. Grant out of action. The attack, consequently, was solely the Navy's show. In truth, the Union commanders seem already to have concluded that the Navy's ironclads would be sufficient. After reconnoitering the enemy's position, one of Grant's generals predicted "that two iron-clad gunboats would make short work of Fort Henry"; and his chief seemed of similar mind. At the same time, Andrew Foote, now the flag officer commanding the gunboats, apparently also had complete trust both in his new craft and in God to support them; he later wrote that before the battle he had spent considerable time on his knees. Perhaps the expectations fostered by such confidence help explain why these Northern officers so completely misinterpreted the outcome of the Navy's strike against Fort Henry.

True, the four ironclads, which on February 6 Foote ordered upstream line abreast to attack the fort with direct fire, and the three wooden gunboats, which lobbed shells into the fort from a distance, had indeed made short work of the Confederate position. But what the Federals do not seem to have appreciated were the overwhelming advantages that played into the Navy's hands and would only infrequently be repeated in future engagements. First off, advancing against the current directly on the fort, the ironclads generally presented to the enemy their strongest feature—the thickly wooded, completely armored forward faces of their casemates. Secondly, Fort Henry sat on an atrociously chosen site. It was virtually at river level which meant (a) that the same rains which prevented Grant's army from marching had partially flooded the work, and (b) that its low-sited guns would be sending their shot through a horizontal trajectory most apt to be deflected by the sloping sides of the gunboat casemates. Thirdly, although the gunboat crews could not know this, Lloyd Tilghman, the Confederate general commanding Forts Henry and Donelson, believed Henry's position so unpromising that before the Federal attack he sent most of its troops to Donelson. Having in mind nothing more than a delaying action, only he and one artillery company stayed at Henry to man its 17 guns.

Finally, during the fight, of the 12 guns in the fort which bore on the river, the two most effective pieces were disabled, not by fire from the gunboats but by accidents. Not long after the ironclads had opened fire, the Confederates' only riverside rifle gun exploded, killing or wounding its whole crew. Virtually the next instant a priming wire became jammed in the vent of the Confederates' largest gun, a 10-inch columbiad. These losses left the Confederates to meet the attack with no more than eight 32-pounder and two 42-pounder smoothbores, and one of the latter also soon blew up.

Notwithstanding that the gunboats enjoyed these considerable advantages, Confederate fire still developed their weaknesses. If their armor resisted shot, the unarmored oak quarters of the casemates did not. Several shot penetrated two of the gunboats, killing or injuring 11 men. Even more significantly, the larger *Essex* took the most destructive shot of the battle. Cutting through the port casemate and piercing the center boiler, it filled the vessel with scalding steam. Her executive reported 32 casualties.

Still, given its feeble nature, the Confederate position succumbed. Whatever their limitations, the rifles, shell guns and smoothbores of the ironclads and the shell guns of the supporting vessels were effective against the vulnerable fort. By the time General Tilghman surrendered, only four of his cannon were still serviceable, and 21 of his garrison were casualties. He and the rest of his men were taken prisoner.

The Yankee sailors were ecstatic; their ironclads, supported by wooden gunboats, had won their first battle without military assistance. When Foote was not attributing the victory to Heaven—"Bless the Lord who has given me this victory"—he gave full credit, indeed too much credit, to his ironclads.

And the conviction that the Federal ironclads were fearsome weapons was not confined to Navy personnel or to the Northern side. The next time the Navy went into action, at Fort Donelson, Grant and his army would purposely refrain from attacking, while it endeavored to duplicate its triumph at Henry. Further, the Confederate Generals A. S. Johnston, P. G. T. Beauregard and W. J. Hardee, at a conference held immediately subsequent to the fall of Henry, decided that Bowling Green, Kentucky had to be evacuated because, reported Johnston, "the slight resistance of Fort Henry indicates [that] the best open earthworks are not reliable to meet successfully a vigorous attack of ironclad gunboats, and . . . [the latter] will probably take Fort Donelson without the necessity of employing their land force in cooperation."

One who had been present in Fort Henry, however, perceived the ironclad's effectiveness quite differently. Understanding perfectly their "weak points," Lloyd Tilghman in his official report wrote that the considerable damage done by his guns to the Federal vessels had been wrought "principally [by] no heavier metal than the ordinary 32-pounder, using solid shot." At the time of his capture Tilghman had assured Flag Officer Foote that "he would have cut [the ironclads] . . . all to pieces, had his best rifle not burst and his 128-pounder been stopped in the vent." Finally, he predicted in his report that Confederate batteries, sited on higher ground, could with devastating effect pour down plunging fire on "the immense area, forming what might be called the roof" of the ironclads.

Certainly, the riverside guns of Fort Donelson seemed ideally positioned to exploit the weaknesses which Tilghman spied in the Federal craft. Cut into a bluff 40 feet above the Cumberland, the two batteries which bore on the river numbered eight 32-pounder smoothbores, one 10-inch columbiad, one rifle firing a 128-pound projectile, and two small cannonades. No matter, then, that the combined weight of fire of these Confederate guns was less than that of the water battery at Henry; no matter, even, that the Confederates' rifled gun soon suffered the same accident as had befallen the columbiad at Henry; no matter, either, that Andrew Foote sent in his vessels in the same order as he had at Henry. It was no contest. The Confederate commander, Gideon Pillow, might complain of the serious execution done to his parapets by the gunboat fire; Flag Officer Foote might insist that victory was within his grasp when two of his ironclads were disabled. There is little evidence to support either contention. On that afternoon of 14 February, not one Confederate gun was dismounted, not one Confederate soldier even wounded, by over an hour's gunboat fire at ranges down to 400 yards.

The ironclads, by contrast, were sorely battered. The rain of Confederate balls and shells crushed armor, cut through pilot houses, entered gun ports, and pierced unarmored casemates and decking and started fires and serious leaking. Two of the ironclads were compelled to leave the fight, when one had her tiller ropes cut and the other had her tiller smashed and her pilot killed. Five more minutes under fire were sufficient to force the other two also to withdraw, badly mauled. Casualties among their crews numbered 52. Included were Foote himself, with what at first seemed only a slight wound, and those killed and injured by the explosion of one of the Federals' own weakened rifled guns. Although the ironclads later made a "feint" toward Fort Donelson, the subsequent capture of that work was owed solely to the action of Grant's army. The Navy at that time was simply in no condition to undertake additional operations.

The formidable reputation of the ironclads among the Confederates, however, seemed undiminished. Federal and Confederate reports suggest that the threat these vessels seemed to pose had earlier thrown into panic the countryside along the Tennessee up to Florence, Alabama, and now the countryside along the Cumberland up to Nashville. And, in fact, the fall of Forts Henry and Donelson had opened the two rivers to incursions by the river navy, as well as outflanked Confederate positions on the Mississippi down to Columbus. The results were the evacuations of Bowling Green, Nashville, and Columbus. Having made those withdrawals, the Confederates prepared to defend a new line, stretching from Chattanooga on the upper Tennessee to Memphis on the Mississippi, with an outpost of the latter river at Island No. 10. It was at this island in March that the Federal Navy next tested its strength.

Whatever liabilities the ironclads had revealed when fighting up the Tennessee and Cumberland, they had enjoyed one advantage. When disabled by hostile fire, they had been swept by the current away from the point of danger. Now moving *down* the Mississippi, they lost this advantage. Moreover, downriver operations revealed other weaknesses intrinsic to their design. For example, the gunboats were so weighed down with armor and armament that they were unable, even with full heads of steam, to hold position against the current, much less back against it. Thus, a sally too close to the enemy and they could be swept under his guns anyway. Should, on the other hand, they seek to come about to head back up the river, their single, stern paddle wheels guaranteed slow, agonizing turns under fire and, if they succeeded in completing the maneuver, their unarmored sterns, vulnerable targets, as they crept away against the current.

Already made cautious by the drubbing his vessels had taken at Donelson and perhaps, too, by his wound which refused to heal, Flag Officer Foote looked for ways at Island No. 10 to overcome these additional handicaps. The Confederate position, defended by 52 guns on the Tennessee bank, the island itself, and a floating battery, did indeed look formidable. Foote first tried tying his gunboats to the banks above the island and letting them play their bow rifles on the enemy from long range. When this fire, augmented by that of a number of 13″ mortars on rafts, had no visible effect, Foote on 17 March tried a second expedient. He lashed three of his ironclads together side by side, and on the theory that their combined power would enable them to maneuver in the current, sent them down to engage the Confederates' shore batteries.

Still playing it cautiously, the three ironclads only closed the range slightly and then, holding position, opened fire. The sailors were convinced that before they withdrew they had done considerable execution among their opponents. One Yankee officer wrote these words: "When . . . our shell entered the fort, a tremendous explosion was seen—supposed to be a magazine"; and another officer these: "That they suffered by the attack . . . it is impossible to doubt; . . . the shell were literally tearing up the breastworks at every discharge, cutting off trees which fell whole length into the battery." As at Fort Donelson, however, seeing apparently should not have led to believing. Confederate reports listed only one gun dismounted and one man killed and seven wounded. The gunboats had taken six or seven hits in return, but the most serious damage and the only Federal casualties resulted when again one of these weakened rifled guns burst.

Foote spent the next 18 days ineffectually bombarding the foe from long distance. Meanwhile Federal General John Pope and his army had occupied New Madrid, Missouri, downriver from Island No. 10, as well as the right river bank further to the south. The General immediately began urging Foote to send several ironclads down to him. He wanted them to knock out the Confederate batteries on the opposite bank and thereby allow his army to cross over and cut the enemy's communications to Island No. 10. To that time, no one had tried to run an ironclad past heavy riverside batteries, and Foote demurred. His caution held, until, urged by superiors, he accepted Commander Henry Walke's offer to make the attempt with the ironclad *Carondelet*. To enhance Walke's chances, on the night of 1 April, a small Federal landing party spiked the guns of the uppermost Confederate battery on the Tennessee shore; and the next morning, the mortar boats and gunboats, by concentrating their fire on the Confederate floating battery, forced it to shift its mooring further down the island.

At the same time Walke, a seasoned veteran of Henry, Donelson and the Mexican War, was preparing the *Carondelet* for its passage. After lashing a loaded coal barge to the port beam, which would be exposed to the enemy, and packing his boat with an additional "armor" of iron cables, lumber, sacks of coal and cotton bales, he waited until nightfall of 4 April to start down. Just as the *Carondelet* got underway, a violent storm broke. A Federal observer on shore later remembered how a particularly brilliant bolt of lightning clearly revealed the ironclad. Immediately, the upper Confederate batteries opened fire; and, as the silently moving craft came into range, every Confederate gun on the shore, the island and the floating battery, which could bear, got off at least one round. All of the missives but two overshot, and those two did no damage. Unscathed, Walke, his crew, and his craft arrived at New Madrid to the cheers of Pope's men. On 6 April, the ironclad *Pittsburg* repeated the feat, again under a raging storm.

Conditions had been propitious for the Navy on both occasions. One Confederate on the island reported that "the intense darkness intervening the lightning" made it impossible to strike the *Carondelet,* and another that the darkness meant that "nothing could be seen of the [*Pittsburg*]." A Federal officer, having inspected the Confederate position after its surrender, wrote to his fiancee that, by keeping "so close to shore," the gunboats had escaped loss, because "the embankments [of the enemy's batteries] do not allow them sufficient depression."

Though these explanations may have pointed up factors unique to the particular situation, other more general factors also help explain the inaccuracy of the Confederate fire. The primitive sighting devices common to all cannon of that day, when added to the unpredictable trajectory which the more numerous smoothbores gave to their projectiles, made it difficult to hit even a stationary target at any distance. When the target itself was underway, training a gun on it became well-nigh impossible; and, furthermore, awkward, contemporary loading techniques could preclude getting off more than one shot at it. Such deterrents to accurate gunnery were to have profound significance for future naval operations; and Commander Walke and his crew and the *Carondelet* had shown the way. Because of them, the running of Federal ironclads past shore-based, Confederate batteries became virtually common practice.

Almost immediately, in fact, Walke not only gave a second demonstration of the technique but combined it with another innovative tactic which on first examination also seemed promising for future naval operations on the Mississippi. When he attacked those Confederate batteries below New Madrid which were preventing Pope from getting his army across the river, Walke eschewed hitting them from above with the current at his back. Instead, he took the *Carondelet* and *Pittsburg* right past them, came about, and, with the advantage of heading upstream, proceeded to silence the opposing guns one after the other, until suitably impressed, the Confederates abandoned the rest. Though grand in its daring, in truth, this particular tactic did not really lend itself to frequent repetition. Hastily put in position to oppose Pope's army, some of the guns that Walke had silenced were light of weight, and all of them seem to have been sited on low ground and probably without adequate breastworks. In short, their plight was reminiscent of that of the guns at Fort Henry. And, apparently, the Navy took care to avoid again drawing overly optimistic conclusions. In the future, when it ran its gunboats past Confederate batteries, it was usually in the expectation that the latter would fall to other forces or that the vessels could be supplied from other directions.

Of more significance was the fact that Walke and his two ironclads were engaged with Pope's army in a combined operation. No sooner had the Navy silenced the Confederate guns than transports, which had come by way of a shallow canal hastily dug to by-pass Island No. 10, disembarked Pope's army on the Tennessee bank under cover, naturally, of the ironclads. The landing was unopposed. The Confederate general commanding the forces on and about Island No. 10 had gathered most of his men on the peninsula west of the island. Initially intending to beat off any Federal attempt to put troops ashore, he had changed his mind when he saw the covering ironclads, and instead, ordered his men to retire on Tiptonville to the South. This movement also failed; the gunboats held it up on one riverside road long enough for Pope's troops to pass it on a second parallel road. When the Confederates finally arrived in Tiptonville, the Federals were there, waiting to capture them. A regiment left behind on Island No. 10 surrendered to Flag Officer Foote.

What all this meant was that those operations in which both services joined were proving more effective under riverine conditions than lone performances. The crucible of battle had again provided the ultimate test. Those people who, even before the ironclads had seen action, had been so confident that the new technology would gain the triumph, had been in some measure wrong. To be sure, Fort Henry had submitted to waterborne attack only, and that atypical action had for a time apparently deceived practically everybody. Fort Donelson set the record straight: if the enemy occupied a strong position with well-sited, shore-based guns, the Navy alone probably could not subdue it. The Army too was learning the lesson. True, it alone was finally able to subdue Donelson, but the fact did not, as General Pope discovered at Island No. 10, invalidate the premise that combined operations were often the only solution. Once Andrew Foote agreed to Pope's request and sent two of his ironclads to cooperate with the Army, the joint effort hurried to a successful conclusion.

The example should have set the precedent for future combined operations, but it was not always observed. Still, whenever these first ironclads, or even those more advanced armored craft that were soon joining them, ignored the lesson, as in attacks up the Yazoo River on Drumgould's Bluff or down the Mississippi River on Grand Gulf, they did so at their peril. On the other hand, the optimistic predictions of the advocates of the new naval technology had not been entirely wrong. When the ironclads joined with military partners in combined actions, as in the attack up the Arkansas River on Fort Hindman or in the final campaign against Vicksburg, they were usually successful. If their technology was frequently not sufficient for solo feats, it was without question a notable asset to successful joint endeavors.

PART V

PROFESSIONALIZATION, REFORM, AND EMPIRE

ALLAN R. MILLETT

MILITARY PROFESSIONALISM AND OFFICERSHIP IN AMERICA

One of the more important aspects of the evolution of officer corps in the nineteenth century was the development of professionalism in European and American armies and navies. Members of the corps saw military officership involving the same characteristics and dedication as membership in other professions like medicine, law, and education. Although after the Civil War there was a higher percentage of non-West Pointers than just before that conflict, the war tended to reinforce the need for career leadership of men in combat. It was also obvious that West Point provided only an introduction to the management of large modern armies. Its curriculum was an undergraduate one, devoted to military engineering and company-level tactics, not strategy. The same could be said of the Naval Academy at Annapolis, Maryland. The navy became the first service to develop a serious school for the sophisticated study of military strategy and support—the Naval War College (1884). The army began slowly with its School of the Line and Staff College (which would eventually become the Command and General Staff College at Fort Leavenworth) and the Army War College (1901).

It was at the Naval War College that the United States developed its first strategist of international repute—Alfred Thayer Mahan. Son of West Point's famous instructor Dennis Hart Mahan and named for the "father of the Military Academy," Sylvanus Thayer, Captain (later Rear Admiral) Mahan became one of the world's foremost authorities on naval history and strategy. His lectures at the Naval War College were later collected and clarified in a series of volumes titled The Influence of Sea Power upon History, published in the late nineteenth and early twentieth centuries. This apostle of sea power urged the United States to create a fleet of capital ships that would allow it to gain command of the sea and to strangle the commercial seaborne lifelines of an enemy state. Whatever the weakness of Mahan's strategic thinking (in particular it was both geographically sensitive, in that its effect mostly came at the expense of island powers like Great Britain and Japan, and technologically sensitive, in that it was more suited to an age of wood and sail than steam, steel, and submarines), Mahan's thoughts were the first significant contribution by an American to international strategic thought and he had an immense impact on the development of the United States Navy in the quarter century before the outbreak of World War I.

But professionalism was more than education and strategic thought. It also involved more sophisticated organization. The efforts of the line (combat) officers to gain control over administration were strengthened throughout the late nineteenth and early twentieth centuries. The navy, with a tradition of regular officers dominating policy decisions and with a need for a fleet-in-being at the start of any military effort, moved first in this direction with the creation of the general board and the chief of naval operations. In the army, the slow evolution of the general staff and of the chief of staff position after the administrative debacle of the Spanish-American War did not see its final evolution until after World War I.

As Professor Allan Millett of Ohio State University makes clear in this essay, "World War I provided the critical opportunity to demonstrate that American military professionalism could coexist with and indeed strengthen civilian control." This had to be done within the context of foreign organizational models and American political realities. Some might argue that the military professionalism was not fully achieved until the relief of General of the Army Douglas MacArthur in the Korean War, as General Flint's article points out. The administrative skills demonstrated by men such as General James G. Harbord proved useful not only in the logistical support of the American Expeditionary Force, but also transferable to the leadership of corporations such as the Radio Corporation of America after the war. Harbord's dual career may constitute the best example of how military professionals became part of the national leadership elite of the postwar United States.

The development of a professional officer corps was not conducive to the romanticism of battle and strategy so strong in the nineteenth century. Nonetheless, professionalism was an absolute necessity for success in modern military operations. The emergence in the critical half century between Appomattox and the Marne of the attributes of professionalism described by Professor Millett marks one of the great turning points in the American military tradition. But there are those who argue that professionalism can become careerism and management rather than leadership. See for instance the issues raised in Edward M. Coffman's article on World War I commanders.

W hether one considers military officership a profession or not depends to a large degree on one's views on the morality of war as human activity and the legitimacy of the national government that employs military officers. In the European intellectual tradition, denying officers professional status may be a normative exercise of civilian control of civil-military relations. Since much Western writing on military affairs pivots on the issue of military subordination within a nation's political life, it is not surprising that the subject of profes- sionalism is generally regarded as a sub-issue, relevant only as a weapon in arguments about theories and practices of civil-military relations. If one has serious intellectual reservations about a society's need for armed forces or the degree of power military men wield, it follows that one will not admit military officers to professional status, for to do so would sanction their function and presumably increase their political autonomy.

If, on the other hand, one recognizes a continuing need for expertly-led armed forces and believes that ascribing professional status to officers will pro- duce a proper balance of skill and political control, then officership will be judged a profession. Given the occupational values of contemporary Western society, it is, of course, too much to expect officers themselves to deny that they are professionals. It is equally unjust to assume that this self-assignment is entirely selfish. Since wars and armies antedate the occupation of full-time officership in Western culture, since there is scant historical evidence that the status of officership makes much difference to the incidence of wars and coups, there is merit to military officers' pleas that their status be determined not as part of some argument about civil-military relations or "militarism," but by a non- prescriptive assessment of their skill, their degree of collegial corporateness, and their sense of responsibility to the society they serve, ideally to the point of sacrifice of life.

Without becoming mired in the theoretical debate of social science profes- sionals and military officers on the character of officership, there is considerable evidence that the officer corps in Europe and in the United States developed professional attributes in increasing measure in the nineteenth century. Military officers sought professional status and worked assiduously to justify their occupa- tion as a skill-oriented, theoretically based, socially useful, and culturally unique career. Although the process of professionalization differed in speed and degree from nation to nation, military professionalism was a common development in all the advanced industrial states of Europe and in the United States.

The general cultural conditions that stimulated the growth of military professionalism were several and of varying importance. The most important factors, however, were probably the differentiation of political leadership from military management and the subordination of the latter to the former; the institutional reforms of European armies in the Napoleonic and post-Napoleonic era; the adoption on the Continent of the cadre-conscript mass army; the growing body of specialized literature that emphasized the possibility of scientific military leadership; the increased popular sense of national identity and the transference of patriotism to the agencies of the nation-state, including the standing armed forces; and the increasing technological complexity of weapons themselves.

The thrust of professionalization produced a reasonably coherent rationale for professional status by World War I. The fundamental assumption was that nation-states would continue to settle some of their disputes by war and that they would maintain or create armies and navies for this purpose. The goals of military action and the character of the armed forces that a nation might use would undoubtedly vary, but the training of military forces in peacetime and their effective direction upon the land and sea battlefields of any war required men who had made officership a career. The development of large and complex military organizations, the adoption of progressively sophisticated weapons, and the increased ability of national governments to produce the resources for such armed forces provided strong arguments for specialized officership. Wartime mobilization had not yet become so total as to blur the lines between "civilian" and "military" in war-waging. Wars were to be decided on the battlefield by armed forces, and battlefield leadership was too important to be left to men who had not trained for such a role on a continuous basis.

The most impressive argument for military professionalism, an argument created by officers and eventually accepted by most civilians, was that direction of armed forces was a learned skill, not a matter of innate genius that could be found even in civilians. The organizational corollary to this assault on the idea of the "Great Captain" or "inspired amateur" concept of leadership was that military command was a collective effort that required a high degree of mutual trust and understanding between officers. Unless an officer had accepted the norms of his military organization and passed through its formal and informal educational system, he would not be accepted by his colleagues as a fully competent peer. Unless he voluntarily adhered to the prevailing concepts of his officer corps on matters of strategy, tactics, discipline, organization, and training, he could not work effectively as a commander or a member of a commander's staff. The attribute that separated a military officer from other practitioners was his understanding of the theoretical constants in the waging of war, pretentiously labeled "military science." Although officers wrote on the recurring problems of command before the Napoleonic Wars, the "lessons" of nearly twenty years of European war produced a revolution in military theorizing by career officers, theorizing which was then used as the basis of formal military education. Very little of this "military science" had anything to do with science and technology, but focused instead on strategic decision-making and the nature of war. Predictably, the search for principles of war created a special language of command even if it did not produce immutable laws for battlefield victory. As important as the strategic theories themselves was the fact that the language of strategic discourse was monopolized by military officers and served as the intellectual basis for professionalization.

To what degree the process of professionalization created a unique philosophical outlook for officers ("the military mind") or "alienated" them from civil society is unanswerable with any precision. Obviously officers might stress the permanence of the nation and war, the priorities of the organization over individual needs, the value of stable institutions and traditions, the need for discipline, and the virtues of duty, honor, and country. If there was anything approaching a "military mind" that all career officers shared, it was probably a product of the priorities of a particular military organization and the officer's role in some part of that organization. Since the armed forces in which professionalism grew were complex and required varied roles in many specialties, an officer could hardly avoid the dilemmas posed by changing roles as he changed rank and assignments. Officers closest to the "military ethic" in their attitudes were likely to be those whose careers were limited to regimental duty. They were not the professional leaders of their armies. The professional elite of late nineteenth century armies, especially in Germany, exhibited qualities of mind common to any manager of large-scale enterprise: loyalty to the organization and its mission, a commitment to rational planning, a continuing search for the most efficient use of available resources, and as much control as possible over an unstable and unpredictable external environment. Although the prerequisites of combat leadership (physical and moral courage, physical stamina, and competence in inspiring men and using weapons) did differentiate the officer from the civilian bureaucrat, it is at least debatable that even long-term professional socialization produced a coherent philosophical point of view that was uniquely military.

Of all the nineteenth century European officer corps, the British were the least given to strategic speculation and professional study, presumably because they saw little need for it after Waterloo. The life of the British army officer revolved around sport, the regimental mess, parades, and haphazard field training. Officers who took soldiering as a serious full-time job gravitated to the technical branches (the Royal Engineers and the Royal Artillery) or went to India. The concept of scientific, highly-organized, and educated officership struck the British officer as Continental pretentiousness. The British officer felt no social compulsion to seek professional status since he was likely to come from the same social elite that managed the government, the economy, and the national institutions. Gentlemen officers of a nation enjoying geographic security and a strong navy saw little need to insist upon individual or collective privileges connected solely with officership. They much preferred retaining their inherited social status to creating a new professional identity by studying books and attending staff colleges. Had British officers militantly sought professional status (as did the Prussians) they would have been "alienated" from their portion of English society, which they certainly were not. The serious students of strategy and battlefield command made scant headway in the nineteenth century British Army, and military reform was more a product of sporadic ministerial interest than a grass-roots development from within the officer corps. Despite three generations of military fiascos scattered around the Empire from Afghanistan to the Crimea to the Transvaal, the British officer corps ended the century with its gallant amateurism intact.

If it had not been for the Civil War, the same condition would have been true for their American cousins. Although the United States Military Academy served as a conduit for the French version of military science and European concepts of officership, the officer corps of the small standing United States Army was not even led by West Pointers until after the Civil War, and even then Academy graduates were not a numerical majority. Officership as an occupation was defined by American civil society, and the roots of its culture were in England, not France or Prussia. Military professionalism was retarded by traditional prejudices against career officers who deviated from the casual British stereotype. The American officer was not necessarily an evil influence, but his popular acceptance depended on his ability to play a socially defined role that had little to do with his competence as a battlefield commander. He was expected to be a military gentleman whose value was measured by his commitment to literary education, outdoor sport, republicanism, personal honor, and American egalitarianism. The ideal Army officer was a man of few specialties and many general aptitudes: explorer, surveyor, canal-builder, Indian agent, diplomat, author (but not of military works), and artist. The American officer was certainly expected to be a heroic and successful leader in war, but the peacetime roles most related to wartime command were those roles civilians found most "militaristic" and hence alien and scorned. Americans preferred officers whose image combined the attributes of George Washington, Audubon, and the Deerslayer, not Napoleon or Clausewitz.

The barriers facing the professionalization of the officer corps of the United States Navy were not quite so acute. Most importantly, the Navy had important peacetime clients who required its services: the merchant marine and the State Department. Between wars the Navy was the visible hand-maiden of international commerce and American diplomacy, and even if Congress would not fund a fleet of ships-of-the-line to protect the United States from European navies, it funded frigates and sloops suited for protecting American merchantmen from pirates and capable of landing marines and sailors to protect American diplomats and business agents. Secondly, a naval officer had to be first and foremost a mariner, which required skills and experience in seamanship and navigation clearly denied landsmen. With the introduction of steam engines, naval officers had to learn something about marine engineering, a development that brought at least some officers into the engineering profession. As the Navy shifted to more complex vessels with steampower, heavy breech-loading naval guns, and steel construction, the naval officer corps could claim a scientific expertise not generally associated with Army officers except in the Corps of Engineers. Even before the Navy realized that the essence of professionalism meant war-readiness and expertise in fleet operations, it manifested more professional autonomy than the Army.

The Civil War killed some six hundred thousand American military amateurs and the concept of amateurism, at least in part of the officer corps of the postwar United States Army. Between the Civil War and World War I, the Army officer corps became an institutionalized profession. Its teachers, writers, and thinkers, influenced by both Continental developments and their own experience, created an educational system for career-long formal training in the techniques of contingency planning and the management of large troop formations in war. At least two of the Army's commanding generals, William Tecumseh Sherman and John M. Schofield, encouraged more rigorous evaluation of officer performance and attempted to curb active political partisanship. Unlike the officer corps of the United States Navy, Army officers were not confronted with a new philosophy of national development, naval strategy, and war ("Sea Power"), or bewildering disputes about technology and ship design. The "technological revolution" in land warfare was to come only with World War I; the changes in Army ordnance and mobility came slowly and were absorbed without crisis.

The Army's concern was managerial: who would direct the nation's wartime armies on the battlefield and how would these generals be selected? The professionalist Army reformers had an obvious answer: career officers with both practical field experience and theoretical training on the European model. To use any other criteria, particularly political influence, was nonprofessional. Unlike other professions (including the Navy's officers), Army officers did not claim that generalship was a "scientific" matter that could be reduced to predictable formulas for human behavior. At the risk of being called romantic irrationals and of accepting "inspired" amateurs to their ranks like Theodore Roosevelt, Army officers insisted that their fundamental expertise was in the moral inspiration of fighting men. The professional officer was most capable of understanding and integrating both the rational and irrational characteristics of combat leadership. An army trained and organized by such officers would be the most efficient in war. The professionals recognized the value of the "scientific management" movement in business and other organizations; they recognized that technology would change the weapons of war; they appreciated the value of European military practices. But they insisted that the social environment of America and the unpredictable nature of war demanded that the professional officer be hero, gentleman, student of human psychology, and manager. He could not, however, learn or balance this set of occupational roles without long experience and formal education. This was the professionals' argument, and by 1918 they had won it with the American people.

By the time the United States entered World War I, the professionalization of American naval and army officers had taken observable form in the organizational sense. The sum of professionalism's institutional expression hinged on the key values of the modern military officer: the function of the officer is to prepare for and wage war in the name of the nation. The "management of violence," moreover, required life-long education, collective planning, and corporative officer responsibility to the service and society. Despite uneven acceptance by both the federal government and many officers, the structural changes in the Army and Navy clearly reflected the growing consensus on the basic tenets of military professionalism. Both services provided Line officers with mid-career training in fleet and army operations at the Naval War College (1884), the Army School of the Line and Staff College (started as the Infantry and Cavalry School in 1881), and the Army War College (1901). By holding colloquia and publishing journals, new officer associations pressed for more emphasis on education, organizational reform related to war readiness, Line officer primacy in making military policy, and greater public sympathy for the military. Duplicating British associations, regular officers formed the U.S. Naval Institute (1874) and the Military Service Institution (1879), complemented by the National Guard Association of the United States (1879).

Although civilian control was never seriously challenged, Line officers found increased opportunity (largely because of their own lobbying for reform) to express their professional opinions in institutionalized form. Ad hoc advisory groups like the War Department's Endicott Board (1885), which analyzed coast defense, and the Navy Department's Policy Board (1890), which recommended an ambitious fleet building program, gave way to formal, continuing planning agencies. Line officer influence in the Navy Department spread upward from the Bureau of Navigation (1862) and the Office of Naval Intelligence (1882) through the General Board (1900) and the Secretary of the Navy's aid system (1909) to the final creation of the Office of the Chief of Naval Operations (1915). Although the CNO still shared substantial power with the fleet commanders and the bureau chiefs, the Office of the Chief of Naval Operations and the General Board assured Line officers that their preparedness priorities would receive serious consideration in the Navy Department and Congress. Capitalizing on the crisis created by the War Department's temporary mismanagement of the mobilization of 1898, Army reformers persuaded Congress to create a War Department General Staff in 1903 and then fought to give the Line control of this planning agency. This change, however, built upon an earlier organizational innova-tion that reflected preparedness concerns, the Military Intelligence Division of The Adjutant General's Office (1885). In the Joint Board (1903) Navy and Army planners found a formal way to link their collective advice to the service secretaries and, through them, to the President.

World War I provided the critical opportunity to demonstrate that American military professionalism could coexist with and indeed strengthen civilian control, a critical problem for the American officer corps. The war also fused the general trend of professionalization in civilian occupations with officership and set the rules for a pattern of civilian-military wartime collabo-ration that lasted until the nuclear age. The tacit division of responsibility for the war's management was in retrospect sensible and obvious. Within the war aims established by President Woodrow Wilson, Army and Navy Line officers conducted active operations against the Germans while civilian officers and military administrators collaboratively handled the enormous problems of manpower and industrial mobilization on the Home Front. The great con-troversies within the military over operational questions were no longer civilian-military conflicts or even Staff-Line conflicts. The friction was, instead, between central and theater commanders, backed by their formida-ble staffs. For the Navy, operational policy hinged on the disputes between Admiral William S. Sims, the Navy's commander in European waters, and Admiral William S. Benson, the Chief of Naval Operations. For the Army, the central clash was the set of controversies created by General John J. Pershing and his General Headquarters American Expeditionary Force and General Peyton C. March, chief of the General Staff. When the senior officers could not settle their disagreements by negotiation, their civilian superiors, Secretary of War Newton D. Baker and Secretary of the Navy Josephus Daniels, adjudicated the disputes, a pattern of decision that satisfied civilian control. What is often overlooked, however, is that the Sims-Benson and Pershing-March conflicts centered on essential questions about the orga-nization and deployment of combat units. All the parties argued the issues on professional (operational) grounds and seldom on any other.

The nearly complete operational autonomy that professional high com-manders enjoyed in World War I rested in part on the reciprocated respect between military officers and the civilian professionals and businessmen who contributed so much to Home Front mobilization. Operational commanders and the mobilization leadership shared one challenge—responding to Allied pressures for quick, effective American participation. The Home Front leaders faced an additional domestic responsibility—to demonstrate their mastery of professionalized, scientific management. This new concept had grown during the Progressive era (roughly 1890 through 1917) to include most major public and private institutions, including major corporations. Although the mobilization managers' actual wartime performance was uneven, the war brought civilian professionals directly into the War and Navy Departments in a way that did not menace the professional officers' essential concern for autonomy in operational command. At the same time, Home Front collaboration satisfied the concern about civilian control. With World War I the American officer corps cemented its alliance with a new generation of civilian "national defense" managers, whose own professional standing enhanced the status of the military without seriously endangering the officer corps' sense of functional uniqueness and self-importance. In a sense, the war was an unparalleled victory for all American professionals and gave the military the same public esteem formerly enjoyed only by civilian professionals.

As illuminated by the theoretical literature on professionalism, the development of other American professions, and by the experience of the officer corps of other industrial nations, the history of the development of military professionalism in America illustrates the interrelationship of unique national characteristics and more general cultural values. One key issue is that of the identity of the client. Since the officer corps serves the nation, it cannot gain a public acceptance until the people (or at least the political elite) of a democratic republic come to value nationalism above other conflicting political loyalties. The only alternative for the officer corps is to see the Army or Navy as the "client," but such organizational loyalty in a pluralistic, amilitary (or even anti-military) society is unlikely to survive either Congressional budget authority in peacetime or a strategy of popular mobilization in wartime. The history of professions in America suggests that occupational autonomy in a democracy based on the limited, decentralized powers of government is fragile for any profession and particularly for public service professions. The countervailing influence against aprofessionalism, especially for diplomats and military officers, is an activist foreign policy. In the American case the extra-continental thrust of American interest after the 1880's gave military professionalism a legitimacy it had not previously enjoyed, and World War I provided the last impetus by thrusting the United States into a military conflict shaped for better or for worse by military professionals on a global scale.

In terms of models, officership in America after the Civil War drew its central concepts from both foreign and domestic models. Given their dramatic influence on European affairs, the Royal Navy and Imperial German Army served as obvious models for American officers, but it may be closer to the truth to recognize that the U.S. Navy was *sui generis* and that the Army, because of its smallness and frontier constabulary missions, was more comparable to the regular British Army than to the German Army. Of equal importance is the fact that military professionalism in America flourished during the Progressive era, a period of fundamental reform for most American institutions. Significantly, civilian professionals filled the front ranks of Progressive reformers, and the linkage of professional people with organizational reform probably made Line officer reformers more acceptable to the political elite. The increased size of the Army and the Navy and the expanded strategic responsibilities of the armed forces after 1898 also gave military officers more policy relevance than they had previously enjoyed in peacetime. The new complexity of both the Army and Navy (stimulated both by growth and new technology) mirrored the increasing complexity of American society. Yet the very dependence of the United States upon professionals in the Progressive era suggests that military officers benefited from the general respect for organizational expertise in Progressive America. The most appropriate paragons for civilians and soldiers alike were corporation managers and public service professionals, not the German *Grossergeneralstab*. In an era of ardent nationalism, the crucial accomplishment of the American military profession was its ability to draw its technical inspiration from foreign military models while it drew its political strength from the nation's emerging civilian professional elite. Legitimized by World War I, military professionalism in America reached a new plateau of public esteem. Major General James G. Harbord, chief of staff of the American Expeditionary Force and later president of the Radio Corporation of America, described General John J. Pershing in terms that can be applied to the whole American officer corps: "An organizer and a leader, a negotiator, and a diplomat of the kind our country needs, we owe him as much for building an integral American army as we do for the high quality of leadership he gave it after it was created. Not of the era of our Civil War or that of 1870 in Europe, he was a pioneer in directing the management and administration of the tremendous agencies of mechanized modern warfare. Not the last of the Old, he is one of the first of the New." Such qualities placed the American officer corps within the ranks of the nation's leadership elite. They also met American society's criteria for public service professionalism.

J O H N   M.   G A T E S

INDIANS AND INSURRECTOS

The U.S. Army's Experience with Insurgency

One of the more popular views of history is that the study of the past will reveal "lessons" which can be used as a guide to current and future decision making. Military history, in particular, is often studied for this reason, and the favorite device in such an effort is the analogy—an event in the past whose broad outline resembles a current situation. Unfortunately, this technique is more often misused than used correctly. Many authors and speechmakers are more concerned about convincing their readers and listeners than in fully examining the analogies they choose. In fact, while there are "lessons" in the past, they are often hard to discover. And the deeper study of most analogies reveals that past situations are less like current ones than it first seems.

As Professor John Gates indicates at the beginning of the following selection, one very popular argument during the 1970s and early 1980s was that the American army had forgotten its own experience with limited war when it began to fight in Vietnam. Several analogies were used in framing this argument, among them the army's experiences in Mexico, in fighting guerrillas during the Civil War, and the Indian campaigns waged by the frontier army of the nineteenth century. As Gates demonstrates, none of these is a true analogy. The Mexican War involved the actual invasion of Mexico by the U.S. Army. Guerrilla opposition to it ended when the war ended and the army returned to the United States. During the Civil War, guerrilla activity, while sometimes a source of trouble, was largely harassment. Again, with the surrender of the main Confederate armies, such activity ceased. In the case of the Indian Wars, Gates argues that the

Indians could not practice true guerrilla warfare since they lacked both a population in which to hide and a regular army.

The strongest analogy, and one which Gates admits he supported at one point himself, used the army's experience in the Philippine insurrection as the basis for a comparison with the situation confronted by the army in Southeast Asia sixty-five years later. Yet, while the army's struggle against the Philippine insurgents has many parallels with the later fighting in Vietnam, it too is not a complete analogy.

However, Gates does point to a number of "lessons" that might be drawn from an examination of the army's experiences with guerrilla wars in the nineteenth century, and, in doing so, raises a number of important questions. For example, Gates points out that the army's response to the threat posed by guerrillas was strikingly similar in each case. Although he does not delve deeply into the issue, the reader must ask why this was so. Is it a reaction rooted in basic human nature? Or is it a function of the army as an institution? Also, in many cases the army attempted to deal justly with their enemies, following conciliatory policies aimed at winning over the population. Gates argues that this was because the soldiers of the nineteenth century recognized the need to preserve as much of their best values as they could during what could become brutal situations. Gates, in fact, downplays the reports of atrocities that surfaced during the Philippine campaign, arguing that these were exceptions to the army's usual conduct. The reader is left to ask if indeed these were exceptions, or if they represented a darker aspect of all such guerrilla wars. He also implies that twentieth-century American soldiers are perhaps less restrained than their nineteenth-century counterparts, forcing the reader to ask if this is actually the case or not.

For Gates, the key lessons from these past campaigns do not involve themes that can easily be translated into a doctrine prescribing the best way to fight a guerrilla war. Instead of a series of simple prescriptions, Gates sees the record of the past suggesting the need for soldiers to act responsibly and morally under conditions of great stress, and especially when the urge to retaliate is strongest. This is an important argument, but the question remains: can such behavior be expected during guerrilla campaigns? Readers might also look at the later essay by Eugene Emme on the development of American airpower doctrine. Where, if at all, can the line be drawn between severity and humanity in modern warfare?

Both during the Vietnam War and after, students of 19th-century American military history frequently claimed to see important similarities between whatever campaign they happened to be surveying and the conflict in Indochina. In his 1976 Harmon Memorial lecture, Robert M. Utley, a distinguished historian of the Indian-fighting Army, drew attention to the "parallels with frontier warfare" in the so-called "limited wars" of the nuclear age. Jack Bauer, in his study of the Mexican War, implied much the same thing in a reference to

General Scott's operation to secure his line of supply from attack by Mexican guerrillas. Scott's problems, wrote Bauer, were "as complex and difficult as any faced by modern American soldiers who think the problem unique to mainland Asia." I concluded my own book with the observation that a study of the Army's Philippine campaign might provide insight into the solution of similar problems in the 20th century. Underlying all such observations seems to be a belief that the Army had failed to learn as much as it could or should have from its 19th-century counterinsurgency experience.

Utley blamed the leaders of "the Indian-fighting generations," civilian and military alike, for the failure of 20th-century counterinsurgency doctrine to "reflect the lessons" of the 19th-century experience. As he observed in his lecture, "Military leaders looked upon Indian warfare as a fleeting bother. Today's conflict or tomorrow's would be the last, and to develop a special system for it seemed hardly worthwhile." Alternatively, one might argue that 19th-century experience was absent from 20th-century doctrine because of a lack of attention on the Army's part to its own history of counterguerrilla operations. Only nine lines are devoted to the guerrilla war in the Philippines in the *American Military History* volume of the Army Historical Series, for example.

Probably both interpretations are correct. In the 19th and 20th centuries alike, the Army's leaders do appear to have given insufficient attention to the problems of fighting unconventional wars, but there may be a third and even more important reason why no doctrine of counterinsurgency emerged from the campaigns of the 19th century to serve the purposes of those of the 20th. The Army's efforts against such diverse enemies as the Mexicans, Confederates, Indians, and Filipinos took place in such different contexts and over such a long span of time that whatever common elements might have been present were either too obvious to merit discussion by the officers involved at the time or too hidden from their view to be discerned.

In the Mexican War, American soldiers faced guerrillas in the context of an international war fought between two governments, each of which acknowledged the existence and legitimacy of the other. Although the contest was quite one-sided and the Mexican government weak and frequently in disarray, the war was a conventional one in which the uniformed forces of each party, fighting in regular formations and pitched battles, carried the major burden of effort on each side. Mexican guerrillas were never more than an annoyance to US forces. The Americans could not ignore them, but the outcome of the war was not dependent on their actions. The Army did an excellent job of keeping Mexican guerrillas under control and preventing them from interdicting American supply lines. It also managed to convince the Mexican population at large that a people's war against the American Army was both unwise and unnecessary. For the United States, however, success in the war came, as one would expect, from the repeated defeat of Mexico's regular forces and the deep penetration of an American Army into the interior of Mexico, seizing the nation's capital as well as its principal port.

As in Mexico, guerrilla activity during the American Civil War drew troops away from front-line units to guard supply lines and garrison posts to the rear, but the war itself was decided by the fortunes of the uniformed forces locked in mortal combat on such battlefields as Shiloh, Antietam, and Gettysburg. Even more important was the wearing down of the Confederacy by the North's overwhelming superiority in both human and material resources, particularly when Sherman projected those resources into the heart of the Confederacy or when Grant threw them relentlessly against Lee's hard-pressed forces in Virginia. As it evolved in the context of the Civil War, guerrilla activity never amounted to more than harassment. Although Virgil Carrington Jones has argued persuasively that "gray ghosts and rebel raiders" operating in northern and western Virginia prevented Grant from implementing his plans for an attack against Richmond for the better part of a year, thus prolonging the war, Jones made no case whatever that such guerrilla activity was in any way decisive. In the end, Grant defeated Lee, and the South surrendered. Only a full-scale people's war, something as abhorrent to many Southern leaders as it was to the Northerners opposing them, might have had a truly significant effect on events, but that did not happen. The Army's operations against Civil War guerrillas remained, as in Mexico, a sideshow to the real war fought by regular units on the battlefield.

One important difference between the war in Mexico and that in the United States did exist. In Mexico, the United States government did not seek to conquer the entire country, only to make the Mexican government acquiesce in its demands regarding westward expansion into a sparsely populated Mexican territory hundreds of miles from the Mexican heartland. Not threatened by permanent conquest, Mexicans had little incentive to embark on a war of national liberation comparable to that which they launched a decade later against the forces of Maximilian. When the Mexican government admitted defeat, the American Army quickly withdrew, leaving the two belligerents at peace, at least with each other.

The Civil War, however, was not an international conflict between two sovereign states, despite Southern claims to the contrary. Instead, as a war of secession (or rebellion), it raised, for Army officers, significant problems that had not existed in Mexico. Union commanders, for example, were unsure of the treatment to be accorded to prisoners who, under civilian laws, might well be guilty of treason. A more important, though related, problem stemmed from the necessity to fight the war in such a way that reunion could be accomplished. If a people's war of resistance comparable to that faced by Napoleon in Spain had emerged in the South, a lasting peace might never have been achieved. Thus, the political problems presented by Confederate guerrillas were much more complex than those facing the Army in the Mexican War.

The Indian Wars present the greatest problem for anyone seeking to generalize about the Army's guerrilla war experience. Although the Indians of North America used guerrilla tactics, they were not really engaged in a guerrilla war. Unlike the guerrillas of Mexico or the Confederacy, they were not part-time soldiers hidden by a friendly but sedentary population. Nor did they act in support of an existing regular army. Instead, they were a primitive people under attack by a host of forces, many of which they only partially understood, and they responded with violence in a sporadic fashion, with no strategic concept to guide their actions. Often they resisted because they had no other acceptable choice, but they fought as nomads or from insecure bases and not, as the Mexicans and Confederates, hidden in the arms of a larger population living behind the lines of their enemies. In the terms of Mao's analogy, the Indian warriors were fish without a sea, easily identified as enemies, if not so readily hunted down.

★ ★ ★ ★ ★

In his well-known survey of primitive war, anthropologist H. H. Turney-High listed five attributes of what he called "true war": the presence of "tactical operations," "definite command and control," the "ability to conduct a campaign for the reduction of enemy resistance if the first battle fails," a clear motive that is the motive of the group rather than that of an individual member, and "an adequate supply." Applying his criteria to the Indians of North America, one sees that they rarely engaged in "true war." Although most Indian groups possessed a rudimentary knowledge of tactics, they usually lacked discipline and commanders able to exert military control over warriors in the heat of battle. In some tribes, such as the Osage, battle had evolved as a religious ritual in which, according to ethnographer Francis Lee Flesche, the pre-battle ceremonies and songs could take longer than the battle itself. In most tribes, participation in battle was usually voluntary, making either total mobilization or total war impossible. Similarly inhibiting were the lack of a clear objective, which distinguishes the more complex and longer phenomenon of "true war" from simply a successful battle, and the absence of the ability to sustain a campaign with adequate supplies. Although Indian scouting and intelligence gathering was often superb by Army standards, Indians also relied upon magic to divine enemy intentions or make plans, and the absence of methodical planning was yet another negative feature of the Indian approach to battle. The Indians, widely known for their stealth and ferocity, demonstrated those characteristics in a context that was significantly different from that of a guerrilla war so often attributed to them.

When Indians fought against the Army they fought as warriors. Although tactically they fought as guerrillas, and often displayed tremendous skill in the process, strategically they were not guerrillas. They were not attempting to wear down the enemy by harassment, nor were they in a position to create secure base areas or win over the civilian population living in the heartland of the Army they confronted. They fought as they did because it was the only way they knew to fight, and their success in keeping in the field as long as they did resulted as much from the Army's meager size as from the Indians' prowess as warriors.

Much of the Army's work on the frontier was that of a constabulary. It served eviction notices on Indians and then forcibly removed them when required. If "imprisoned" Indians "broke out" of the reservations, the Army found them and coerced them back. Failing in the latter, it would attempt the equivalent of an arrest, an armed attack to force the Indians to surrender. Indians who raided white settlers, Army posts, or peaceful reservation-Indians engaged in criminal activity, in white eyes at least; and the Army's task was that of the police officer, to track down the guilty parties and bring them back for punishment. Because of the numbers involved those activities sometimes looked like war, and in a few instances, when entire tribes rose up in arms to fight against the intrusion of the white, it was. Most of the time, however, it was routine though difficult police work.

As the US Army's only military activity between the 19th century's infrequent real wars, the so-called Indian Wars have received far more attention than they deserve. At best, except for a few significant successes, such as that against Custer at the Little Big Horn, the Indians were little more than a nuisance. In the final analysis, one must agree with Robert Utley that the Army was only

> one of many groups that pushed the frontier westward and doomed the Indian. Other frontiersmen—trappers, traders, miners, stockmen, farmers, railroad builders, merchants—share largely in the process. They, rather than the soldiers, deprived the Indian of the land and the sustenance that left him no alternative but to submit.

The pressure of an expanding white civilization, not the campaigns of the Army, was the primary reason for the end of Indian resistance. The Indian Wars are both the most extensive and also the least relevant of the Army's 19th-century experiences fighting "guerrillas."

The Army's confrontation with guerrillas in the Philippines differed markedly from all its previous experiences, being much more comparable to the guerrilla wars of national liberation waged after World War II than to any of the

Army's earlier campaigns. Unlike the Mexican or the Civil War, the war's outcome would not be decided by the clash of regular forces, and the outcome was not, as in the Indian conflicts, certain from the start. In the Philippines, the United States was engaged in a war of conquest, although Americans both at the time and later have seen fit to hide their actions by referring to the enemy as insurgents, or worse. There could be no insurrection, however, because the United States did not control the Islands when the Philippine-American War began in 1899. The fighting that ensued took place between two organized forces, one representing the government of the United States and the other representing the revolutionary government of the Philippine Republic under the leadership of Emilio Aguinaldo. The conflict began as a conventional war, pitting American regulars and volunteers against the Philippine army that had seized control of the Islands from Spain. Although beginning as a guerrilla force, the army surrounding the Americans in Manila had adopted conventional organization and tactics, planning to engage the American forces in regular combat and hoping to gain international recognition for the Philippine Republic as a result.

When their attempts at regular warfare ended in disaster, the Filipinos shifted to a guerrilla strategy aimed at making an occupation of the Philippines too costly for the Americans and achieving by a political solution what they had failed to achieve through a more conventional military approach. The problems presented by the Filipino strategy were greater than any faced by the Army in its previous confrontations with Indians or true guerrillas. Bent on conquest of the entire Philippines, the United States could not achieve peace and accomplish withdrawal by arranging a partial cession of territory as it had done in Mexico. And because the value of the Islands as a colony resided, at least in part, in the population, policies of removal or extermination were also inappropriate, even had they been acceptable on moral grounds—and, of course, they were not. Filipino numbers and the colonial nature of the conflict thus precluded a solution based on the experience of the Indian Wars. Finally, the Filipino leadership, unlike that of the South in the Civil War, had no reservations about calling their followers into the field in a people's war of prolonged guerrilla struggle. From the Army's point of view, however, the Philippine situation, like that of the Civil War, demanded that the war be fought and ended in a way that would help create a lasting peace.

★ ★ ★ ★ ★

The tremendous differences in the contexts of the Army's guerrilla war experiences make generalizations difficult, but not impossible. Some uniformities can be discerned, although frequently they are not nearly so important as the differences, a point to be doubly emphasized when one attempts to compare any of the Army's guerrilla war experiences with the war in Vietnam.

The most obvious uniformity is that of guerrilla technique; General George Crook's observation that Apaches "only fight with regular soldiers when they choose and when the advantages are all on their side" might just as easily have been made about Mexican, Confederate, or Philippine guerrillas. And a Confederate guerrilla leader spoke in terms readily understandable to the other guerrillas confronting the Army during the century when he described his mission against the Yankees as

> to hang about their camps and shoot down every sentinel, picket, courier and wagon driver we can find; to watch opportunities for attacking convoys and forage trains, and thus render the country so unsafe that they will not dare to move except in large bodies.

Whether in Mexico, the Shenandoah Valley, the Great Plains, or the Philippines, guerrillas behaved much the same: fleeing from strength, attacking weakness, preying upon small isolated garrisons and poorly defended supply trains, killing the lone sentry or the unwary patrol, living off the land with the aid of their people—and terrorizing those who refused to cooperate or joined with the enemy.

A second uniformity, only slightly less obvious than the first, can be seen in the Army's response to the threat posed by Indian and guerrilla bands. The actions taken to counter them were remarkably similar from place to place over time. Whether the enemy was Mexican, Confederate, Indian, or Filipino, the Army responded eventually with many of the same general techniques of counterguerrilla warfare. To protect supply lines, commanders increased the size of the guard assigned to supply trains and strengthened garrisons along their routes of march. To facilitate operations against marauding bands and to provide security to populated areas, commanders garrisoned towns and built forts. To hunt down enemy units and force them to disband or be destroyed, the Army sent highly mobile, self-contained units into the field to pursue them relentlessly. Often at a disadvantage because of their unfamiliarity with the terrain or the local population, Army officers enlisted the support of indigenous inhabitants whenever possible. In Mexico, for example, Lieutenant Colonel Ethan Hitchcock obtained the aid of robber Manuel Dominguez and his band, and in the American southwest General George Crook formed units of friendly Apaches to help him find and fight renegades such as Geronimo. In perhaps the most celebrated use of indigenous collaborators, Frederick Funston used a force of Filipino scouts to capture Aguinaldo in his own headquarters in 1901.

The Army was relatively successful in developing methods to deal with the problems presented by hostile Indians and guerrilla bands in the field. A more difficult set of problems emerged, however, regarding the treatment to be accorded guerrilla combatants who had been captured, particularly part-time guerrillas, and the noncombatant population from which the guerrillas derived support. Throughout the 19th century one sees tension between two general policies, one rooted in severity and the other more humane. The frustrations of guerrilla warfare, the ease with which guerrilla bands eluded regular troops when aided by a friendly population, the atrocities committed by irregulars, and a common assumption that guerrillas were not legitimate combatants all worked to push commanders in the field toward a policy of reprisal. But recognition by these officers that their enemies were frequently doing nothing that they themselves would not do in a similar situation, the need to fight and terminate conflicts in a fashion that would bring a lasting peace, and the desire to keep one's humanity even in the midst of barbarous war all supported policies of conciliation aimed at winning over the opposition by good works rather than fear.

Nineteenth-century customs and laws of war reflected, rather than resolved, these tensions. Although the United States had yet to promulgate any official statement on the laws of war to guide officers during the Mexican War and the early years of the Civil War, by February 1863 Professor Francis Lieber, a noted authority on international law, had drafted a code that was summarized and distributed to the Army on 24 April of that year as General Order No. 100, "Instructions for the Government of Armies of the United States in the Field." It became the cornerstone of the growing body of international law upon which current practices rest, and by the time of the Philippine-American War it had become the final word for American Army officers on the laws of war.

General Order 100 manifested the tension between the two different approaches to pacification. On the assumption that "sharp wars are brief," the order asserted that "the more vigorously wars are pursued the better it is for humanity." In an 1862 commentary written for General Halleck on the status of guerrilla parties in the laws and customs of war, Lieber concluded that "armed bands" rising "in a district fairly occupied by military force, or in the rear of an army," were "universally considered" to be "brigands, and not prisoners of war" when captured. He also observed that such groups were "particularly dangerous because they could easily evade pursuit, and by laying down their arms become insidious enemies." His negative view of guerrillas was carried over into General Order 100. Although item 81 of the order stated that properly uniformed "partisans" were entitled to be treated as true prisoners of war, item 82 stated that guerrillas who fought without commissions or on a part-time basis, returning intermittently to their homes to hide among the civilian population, were to be treated "summarily as highway robbers or pirates." Similarly, so-called "armed prowlers" were also denied the privileges of prisoners of war, and all who rose up against a conquering army were "war rebels," subject to death if captured. As item 4 noted, "To save the country is paramount to all other considerations."

At the same time that it condemned the guerrilla and sanctioned reprisals, however, General Order 100 also recognized that the conduct of officers administering martial law should "be strictly guided by the principles of justice, honor, and humanity." Although military necessity might justify destruction, even of innocent civilians, it did not sanction "cruelty . . . revenge . . . [or] torture." General Order 100 reminded officers that men who took up arms did not cease "to be moral beings, responsible to one another and to God." Unarmed citizens were "to be spared in person, property, and honor as much as the exigencies of war will admit." Retaliation, deemed "the sternest feature of war," was to be used with care, "only as a means of protective retribution" and "never . . . as a measure of mere revenge." As item 28 observed:

> Unjust or inconsiderate retaliation removes the belligerents farther and farther from the mitigating rules of regular war, and by rapid steps leads them nearer to the internecine wars of savages.

Lieber knew that in war the barrier between civilization and barbarism was exceedingly thin, and he provided few opportunities for conscientious soldiers to breach it.

★ ★ ★ ★ ★

Even before the development of the guidelines set forth in General Order 100, the Army's campaigns against guerrillas had demonstrated both the severity and the humanity evident in Lieber's work. In Mexico, for example, captured guerrillas had been treated as criminals, either killed upon capture or after trial by military commissions. The Army also resorted to more general and collective punishments, including the destruction of villages suspected of harboring irregulars and the assessment of fines against municipalities and their officials to compensate for the destruction done by Mexican guerrilla bands. At the same time, General Scott and other commanders attempted to convince Mexicans that if they remained at peace, the United States would neither interfere with their customs and religion nor subject them to exploitation.

Civil War soldiers appear to have been guided by the experience of the Mexican War, and many Union officers began the war with the hope that by treating the Confederates leniently they could achieve a swift peace. In the first months of the war, the Army attempted to enforce a conciliatory policy aimed at protecting both the private property and constitutional rights of Confederate civilians. In the winter of 1861, for example, Sherman complained that his men suffered from exposure and short rations while the slaveholders of Kentucky ate fresh food in the warmth of their homes, and Grant said of his march to Missouri that "the same number of men never marched through a thickly settled country like this committing fewer depredations."

The frustrations of trying to counter Southern guerrillas, however, soon led many officers to treat Southerners more severely. In Virginia, for example, General John Pope levied contributions on communities to compensate for damage done by guerrillas. He also decreed that male civilians within his lines take an oath of allegiance or be expelled, threatening them with death if they returned. When Confederate irregulars fired upon Union boats from the banks of the Mississippi, Sherman retaliated by burning a nearby town, and he told Grant that he had

given public notice that a repetition will justify any measures of retaliation such as loading the boats with their captive guerrillas as targets . . . and expelling families from the comforts of Memphis, whose husbands and brothers go to make up those guerrillas.

In Missouri, following the 1863 raid on Lawrence, Kansas, by the band of William Quantrill, General Thomas J. Ewing ordered the population removed from four counties and their crops and property destroyed or confiscated. Endorsing his actions, his commanding officer, General John Schofield, observed that "nothing short of total devastation of the districts which are made the haunts of guerrillas will be sufficient to put a stop to the evil." The following year, in Virginia, Grant demonstrated his agreement. Frustrated by Mosby's guerrillas, he ordered Sheridan to send a division "through Loudoun County to destroy and carry off the crops, animals, Negroes, and all men under fifty years of age capable of bearing arms" in an attempt to destroy Mosby's band. "Where any of Mosby's men are caught," Grant told Sheridan, "hang them without trial." Only Mosby's retaliatory execution of some Union soldiers prevented Sheridan from carrying out Grant's order to the letter.

A special case, clearly different from the wars already described, the campaigns against the Indians displayed the same tension between severity and humanity, although in a different context. Officers were frequently appalled by Indian outrages such as those described by Sheridan in an 1870 report to Sherman:

> Men, women, and children . . . murdered . . . in the most fiendish manner; the men usually scalped and mutilated, their [ ] cut off and placed in their mouth [Sheridan's omission]; women ravished sometimes fifty and sixty times in succession, then killed and scalped, sticks stuck in their persons, before and after death.

At times, however, the officers bent on the destruction of a people they saw as brutal savages also expressed a degree of understanding and even admiration. Colonel Henry B. Carrington, who viewed the mutilated bodies of the soldiers killed in the 1866 Fetterman massacre, could still say that had he been a red man, he "should have fought as bitterly, if not as brutally, as the Indian fought." And General Nelson Miles praised the Indians' "courage, skill, sagacity, endurance, fortitude, and self sacrifice," as well as their "dignity, hospitality, and gentleness."

Historian Richard Ellis has concluded that commanders such as O. O. Howard, George Crook, and John Pope were "sincere and benevolent men performing a difficult job." Pope observed in 1875 that only "with painful reluctance" did the Army

> take the field against Indians who only leave their reservations because they are starved there, and who must hunt food for themselves and their families or see them perish with hunger.

Many officers recognized, as did Crook, that hostilities could be prevented if only the Indians were treated with "justice, truth, honesty, and common sense." But such a humane policy was impossible for the American nation of the 19th century, bent on expansion and development. Soldiers recognized that they had little control over the fate of the Indians; instead, they believed the Indian to be doomed to "extinction" by forces "silently at work beyond all human control." Given such assumptions, Sherman's remark in 1868 that "the more we can kill this year, the less will have to be killed the next war" takes on the quality of statement of fact, rather than that of a cruel, unfeeling comment by a soldier committed to waging total war.

The pattern in the Philippines at the century's end had much in common with events both in Mexico and in the Civil War. Many of the officers in the islands—such as General Elwell S. Otis, in command when the war began, and General Arthur MacArthur, his successor—were convinced that the swiftest way to end the war and pacify the population was to demonstrate the benefits of American colonial government; and the Army put considerable effort into establishing municipal governments, schools, and public works projects. Rejecting the concept of total war implied in Sherman's March to the Sea, most officers in the Philippines, at least initially, seemed to accept the idea put forth by Captain John Bigelow, Jr., in his *Principles of Strategy* that "the maintenance of a military despotism in the rear of an invading army must generally prove a waste of power."

As the frustrations of the guerrilla war increased, however, officers began to either urge upon their superiors in Manila a policy of greater severity or engage in harsh reprisals without waiting for official sanction. As Colonel Robert L. Bullard wrote in his diary in August 1900:

> It seems that ultimately we shall be driven to the Spanish method of dreadful general punishments on a whole community for the acts of its outlaws which the community systematically shields and hides.

A few months later General Lloyd Wheaton urged "swift methods of destruction" to bring a "speedy termination to all resistance," claiming it was "no use going with a sword in one hand, a pacifist pamphlet in the other hand and trailing the model of a schoolhouse after." Fortunately, General MacArthur recognized the value of the reform programs being implemented by the Army as well as the efforts being made to prevent excesses in the campaign against the guerrillas. Even he was frustrated, however, and, by the end of 1900, sanctioned the enforcement of the most severe sections of General Order 100. In areas where guerrillas and their supporters proved most intransigent, such as Batangas Province, the Army even resorted to population relocation and a scorched-earth policy comparable to that of General Ewing in western Missouri. On the island of Samar the line between retaliation and revenge became blurred beyond recognition for some soldiers.

Atrocities have taken place in virtually all wars, but the frustrations of guerrilla warfare, in which the enemy's acts of terror and brutality often add to the anger generated by the difficulty of campaigning, create an environment particularly conducive to the commission of war crimes. In almost all such wars one can discover numerous incidents in which counterinsurgents resorted to acts of counterterror, punishment, or revenge that fell clearly outside the relatively severe actions sanctioned by 19th-century laws of war.

During the Civil War, reprisals sometimes went well beyond those sanctioned by the laws of warfare. Robert Gould Shaw, for example, witnessed the "wanton destruction" of Darien, Georgia, in 1863, an act that made him ashamed to be an officer of the Union force that committed the act. According to Shaw, the city was destroyed for no apparent reason other than his commander's desire to subject the Southerners to the hardships of war. As described by Shaw, it was an act of pure revenge and a war crime. In other instances, when the enemy was perceived as savage, the Army's actions could be even more severe, as exemplified by Custer's 1868 attack of Black Kettle's Cheyenne camp on the bank of the Washita. The men of the 7th Cavalry destroyed numerous Indians (including women and children), the camp's tepees (thus denying the survivors food and winter robes), and 875 Indian ponies.

Stories of atrocities would become the hallmark of the Philippine campaign. No history of that war is complete without a description of the "water cure," in which unwilling suspects were seized and their stomachs forcibly filled with water until they revealed the hiding place of guerrillas, of supplies, or of arms—or, as happened on occasion, until they died. The more frustrating the campaign became, the more frequently the Americans crossed the line separating the harsh reprisals sanctioned by General Order 100 from such crimes of war as torture and wanton destruction.

Although often quite harsh, the Army's 19th-century response to problems of guerrilla warfare was, in general, based upon the existing laws of war. Widely publicized, of course, have been the deviations from those laws that took place. In virtually every conflict, officers and men alike committed atrocities, such as shooting prisoners or noncombatants, or torturing people suspected of withholding information. Significantly, despite the tendency of those committing such acts and of their supporters to plead the extenuating circumstances of barbarous guerrilla war as a defense, few people accepted their argument that no crime or breach of the laws of war had been committed.

★ ★ ★ ★ ★

The conclusion that American soldiers in the 19th century made an effort to fight guerrillas within the context of a set of legal and moral restraints would not be particularly significant were it not for the tremendous contrast presented by current counterinsurgency campaigns. In places as remote from each other as El Salvador and Afghanistan, one sees an acceptance of widespread and seemingly indiscriminate terror against civilians as a primary technique for dealing not only with insurgents and their supporters, but with the uncommitted as well. At present, the laws of war are frequently ignored, and war against potential as well as actual insurgents is fought with a barbarity associated more with the likes of Attila the Hun than the soldiers of supposedly civilized nations.

For American soldiers not yet directly involved in this wholesale assault on the laws of war and humanity, the contrast between the attitude of many American officers in the 19th century and that evident in a number of foreign armies at present, particularly in Latin America, highlights a moral problem of immense proportions. That American officers are not unaware of the problem has been demonstrated by events such as the 1980 West Point symposium on "War and Morality." At that gathering, Professor Michael Walzer spoke of "two kinds of military responsibility," and his approach to the subject had much more in common with the views held by most 19th-century military officers than those exhibited by many of the world's soldiers currently engaged in counterguerrilla warfare. In language that Francis Lieber would have readily endorsed, Walzer observed that the military officer "as a moral agent" has a responsibility beyond that upward to the officers over him and downward to the soldiers under him. He also has a responsibility "outward—to all those people whose lives his activities affect." In the 19th century, Walzer's second kind of military responsibility was accepted by American officers as they attempted to defeat guerrillas without sinking to the level of barbarity that is now deemed "indispensable."

Today, if US Army officers fail to give careful attention to the moral problems inherent in warfare against determined guerrilla forces, they may find themselves drawn more into the inhumane form of contemporary counterinsurgency practiced by communists and capitalists alike. To avoid such a fate, they must continue to ask themselves what at first glance seems to be a very 19th-century question. In countering insurgents, they must ask—in the moral sense of these words (a sense not commonly brought to bear in gauging the potential effectiveness of military operations)—what response is *right, good,* and *proper.* To do less is to risk the loss of their humanity as well as any claim to be defending a government based upon the rule of law.

J O H N   H.   M A U R E R

FUEL AND THE BATTLE FLEET
Coal, Oil, and American Naval Strategy, 1898–1925

*L*ogistics—literally, the science of providing the materiel with which military forces operate and fight—is the least understood, and least studied, of the forces that dictate the shape of national military policy. Yet, it may be the most important.

Over time, changes in weaponry and transportation have made the task of supplying military forces more difficult. The primary worry for ancient armies was obtaining enough food and water. Insuring this could, and did, strain both the agricultural and transportation systems of the time. By the eighteenth century, however, along with the basic necessities, armies required steady supplies of ammunition, uniforms, and other equipment, much of which could not be obtained by foraging the countryside. The Industrial Revolution, which provided the means for dramatically increasing agricultural yields (freeing an increasing percentage of the male population for military service) and more powerful weapons, added still further to the logistical burdens of commanders. Not only did more men have to be fed, clothed, housed, and equipped, the machinery they used to fight required maintenance and repair. All the items needed to keep the weapons working had to be stockpiled, recorded, and shipped to the proper destination. Modern armies, dependent upon the internal combustion engine to transport both soldiers and weapons, must not only be able to provide food, shelter, spare parts, and new equipment on a steady basis, but also must have regular supplies of fuel or they will be unable to move or fight. Any military policy that does not take these logistical needs into account is doomed.

The Industrial Revolution had a similar effect upon navies. For centuries naval power resided in wooden sailing vessels. Although the hulls of these vessels might suffer from worms or rot, sailors effectively could go anywhere the wind blew and expect to replace food, water, rigging, and sails almost anywhere. The only items not easily found might be guns, gunpowder, and ammunition. But even these might be purchased in many parts of the world, or seized from an enemy if the chance appeared. In contrast, the steam-powered, iron and steel warships developed during the late nineteenth century were both immensely more powerful and more limited in their ability to operate. No matter how large a ship's guns, steam-driven vessels required fuel, increasingly oil rather than coal, and without that fuel the most powerful fleet was almost helpless.

American naval strategists during the first two decades of the twentieth century were well aware of the way the need for a steady supply of oil influenced the way a fleet could operate. They were especially aware of the impact this would have in the Pacific. The need to develop secure sources of coal in strategic locations had been a factor in naval thinking as early as the 1870s, and the navy supported American efforts to gain control of Hawaii, Samoa, and the Philippines. Many naval officers supported the notion of American colonies because it was clear that the navy could not effectively protect American commerce in the Pacific without refueling stations at important locations.

In the following essay John Maurer examines the navy's search for a strategic policy that would allow it to effectively protect American interests and American territory in the Pacific in the face of increasing Japanese antagonism. Although the basic problems confronting the navy in the Pacific were obvious, particularly the vast distances between the areas the navy had to protect and its major bases on the West Coast, Maurer makes clear that there was still plenty of room for debate on how the navy might best achieve its goals. One step was the substitution of oil for coal. Oil burned more efficiently, extended a warship's range, and was more easily transported. But as Maurer also makes clear, this change merely alleviated the navy's strategic dilemma, it did not eliminate it.

If American naval planners were not able to completely solve all the problems they faced, it is nevertheless instructive to reexamine the arguments they raised as they tried to reconcile ends with means, and balance desired goals with logistical reality. Today's military planners must deal with strikingly similar problems, in an environment of increasingly complex weapons which pose ever-increasing logistical burdens on the services that use them. Interested readers might recall R. Arthur Bowler's study of British logistical efforts during the American Revolution to see the ways logistical problems changed from the eighteenth to the twentieth century—and some of the ways those problems remained the same. The reader might also examine Professor Louis Morton's essay on the development of War Plan ORANGE later in this collection to see how the same dilemmas faced by naval planners from 1898 to 1925 shaped the *large-scale planing for a possible Pacific war during the 1930s. What effect, one must ask, do logistical limits on military action have in our own time? Should not logistical issues be among the first items debated by military planners?*

To the generation of Mahan and Tirpitz the battle fleet represented the "Queen" on the diplomatic and strategic chessboard of imperial rivalries. The battle fleet, formed around the capital ship, was the decisive weapon in the battle at sea. Battleships acted as "yesterday's deterrent" in the competition between the Great Powers. Because of their importance in the balance of power, a decision concerning the movement of battleships from one station to another inevitably aroused a serious debate on strategy and foreign policy. In the decade before 1914, this type of far-reaching debate on the proper disposition of the fleet engaged the attention of policymakers in both the United States and Great Britain. In the United States this debate centered on whether the fleet should be concentrated in the Atlantic or the Pacific before the completion of the Panama Canal, and in Britain it was caused by the underlying tension between worldwide imperial commitments and the Admiralty's policy of massing battleships in home waters to meet the German threat. Yet the disposition of the battle fleet often depended on logistics considerations as much as strategic dogma or a government's foreign policy. This essay is an examination of the relationship between the logistics problem of securing access to fuel supplies and American naval strategy during the first quarter of this century.

Probably the single most important logistics requirement of a navy at the turn of the century was a supply of coal. Capt. Asa Walker, who served on the General Board of the U.S. Navy, clearly states this fundamental importance of coal:

> The modern man of war presents no canvas to the winds; within her bowels is an insatiable monster whose demand is ever for *coal* and still more *coal*. Every cubic inch of available space is filled with fuel, and when this is consumed the vast machine becomes an inert mass. Coal then may be considered as the lifeblood of the man of war, and upon its supply depends her existence as a living factor in the battle equation.

In addition to coal, a modern navy required, of course, other logistics support: supplies of food and water, ammunition, repair facilities equipped with machine tools capable of refurbishing a ship's machinery and weapons, and drydocks capable of handling the largest warships; all were needed to ensure the operational readiness of the fleet. While it is impossible to ignore these elements, providing the fleet with its "lifeblood" of coal was the biggest logistics headache facing naval planners in this period.

The strategic axioms guiding naval policymakers of that age—concentration of the fleet and the closely related short war dogma—accentuated the Navy's appetite for coal. Although its fuel requirements could vary depending on its size and activity, a battle fleet consumed large quantities of coal even in port. One logistics study in 1912 estimated that the mobilization and concentration of the battle fleet in the Caribbean would require almost 300,000 tons of coal and the fleet would continue to need at least 150,000 tons of coal a month thereafter to conduct operations. Because fuel "is the largest single item to be supplied as to both weight and volume," this operation would have required all the colliers in the U.S. merchant marine in addition to those possessed by the Navy. Of course, the mobilization, concentration, and operations of the battle fleet in the vast distances of the Pacific would need much greater logistics support. As the 1912 Summer Conference of the Naval War College reported, modern naval operations demanded "coal, coal, and more coal."

An appreciation of the logistics constraints on a fleet's operations in this era can be readily gained by examining the process of coaling a ship. Coaling was the bane of every crew's existence: it was dirty, back-breaking work. One commentator went so far as to say: "Coaling causes more desertions from the Navy than any other feature of the service." To take on coal, a battleship would return to a base where a stockpile had been established, or tie up alongside a collier in a calm sea sheltered by land. Coaling at sea was dangerous as collisions frequently occurred when the warship came alongside. Once alongside, relays of men entered the collier's hold, working a maximum of half-hour shifts, shoveling coal into bags. When it was filled, a bag would be hoisted by crane from the collier to the battleship. The coal would then be dumped down the battleship's coal chutes into its bunkers where it was leveled and packed into place. To keep up morale, the ship's band would play popular music while the men shoveled. Once started, this process would be continued nonstop until the bunkers were full. To get the ship ready for action in the shortest period of time, officers tried to hasten this onerous chore by timing the crew and attempting to set record speeds for coaling. A good crew could transfer over 100 tons of coal an hour but coaling a fleet could last several days. In 1899 and 1900 the Navy conducted experiments aboard the collier *Marcellus* and the battleship *Maine* to develop means to speed this process and permit coaling at sea. As a result of these tests the Navy began building in 1904 specially designed colliers capable of trolleying 800-pound bags of coal on cables rigged between the ships. Until these ships were ready, Admiral Dewey told the Secretary of the Navy, there were no colliers "suitable for accompanying the fleet and keeping it supplied with coal."

Even with their arrival, however, coaling remained a painfully slow process and proved impractical for ships while underway at sea; the operations of a fleet consequently remained circumscribed by the location of coaling stations.

This constraint worked to the advantage of Great Britain. During the 19th century Britain produced and exported more coal than any other country. Coal was one of Britain's two major export commodities; it was calculated that nine-tenths of the tonnage of British exports consisted of coal. This coal helped to pay for the vast quantities of imported raw materials and food that Britain consumed. As an outcome of this export business, British firms acquired a virtual monopoly on the world's coal trade and established coaling stations stretching around the globe. One reason for this commanding position was the unsurpassed quality of coal from Newcastle, South Wales, the Clyde, and the Mersey. Welsh coal out of Cardiff, considered the best marine coal in the world, was sought after by all navies. Nor were British governments above using this dominance of the seaborne coal trade as a weapon in its foreign policy. Without access to her coaling stations, Britain's rivals found that problems of fuel supply could drastically limit the range of their naval operations, especially in distant waters. In a perceptive (and comical) remark to Chancellor Bülow, Kaiser Wilhelm best described the dilemma facing the other Great Powers when trying to supply overseas naval deployments without British cooperation: "Aber wie der Chinese sagt, in pigeon English: 'If not have got coal, how can do?'"

The dependence on British bases and good will is well illustrated by the logistics problems of supporting Dewey's campaign in the Philippines during the Spanish-American War. In a now legendary telegram of 25 February 1898, Assistant Secretary of the Navy Theodore Roosevelt ordered Dewey to concentrate his scattered Asiatic Station at the British colony of Hong Kong to await the anticipated outbreak of war with Spain. The telegram warned Dewey to pay particular attention to his fuel supplies: "Keep full of coal." Dewey's squadron was desperately short of all supplies: provisions, ammunition, and fuel. When he arrived at Hong Kong, Dewey received the rude shock of finding that he could not buy enough coal to meet his needs for a protracted campaign. The naval commanders of other countries also at Hong Kong had brought up all the existing supplies of Welsh coal to prepare their squadrons in case that war erupted from the Great Power rivalry in China. Dewey also learned that Japan, the other important source of supply in the Far East, intended to enforce strictly its neutrality in the event of war, thereby denying the American squadron coaling facilities. Dewey eventually found the coal needed, but only at the price of buying the collier *Nanshan* then en route from England. To carry provisions for his squadron, Dewey also purchased the steamer *Zafiro*. On 22 April, only a day before being ordered to quit Hong Kong by its Governor, Dewey's logistics preparations were completed when the cruiser *Baltimore* arrived with a badly needed supply of ammunition. While the destruction of the Spanish squadron in Manila Bay on 1 May relieved Dewey of that naval threat, it did not end his logistics difficulties. That supply problems were never far from Dewey's mind can be seen in his handling of the battle, when he ordered the squadron to retire because of a report (subsequently proven to be untrue) showing his ammunition supplies practically exhausted. At Manila Dewey had no means to communicate news of his victory because the Spanish Governor refused to let him use the Manila-Hong Kong telegraph cable. Dewey retaliated by dredging up the underwater line and severing Manila's link with the outside world. Only by sending the revenue cutter *McCulloch* to Hong Kong with two brief telegrams, requesting ammunition and troops to occupy Manila, could Dewey announce the victory over the Spanish squadron. Fortunately for Dewey, the British authorities in Hong Kong did not interfere with these communications. There can be little doubt that without British cooperation, Dewey could not have mounted his successful campaign against the Spanish squadron in the Philippines.

With the collapse of Spain's empire in 1898, the United States was burdened with the formidable strategic task of defending its newly acquired overseas territories. In the Far East, where the continuing unrest in China seemed to presage a Great Power confrontation, American military planners faced an especially difficult problem because of the great distances from the centers of production and command on the eastern seaboard of the United States. The isolation of any American forces in this region had been clearly demonstrated during the final stages of the war with Spain. At that time, it looked as if the Spanish Government would dispatch a squadron more powerful than Dewey's force to recapture the Philippines. This force, commanded by Admiral Camara, would be sent from Cadiz to the Philippines via the Suez Canal. To the members of the Naval War Board set up to guide American strategy during the war, there appeared to be little that could be done to reinforce and resupply Dewey to prevent defeat by Camara's squadron. Fortunately for the United States, the Spanish Government decided on peace before Camara's force passed through the Suez Canal. The intervention in China, 2 years after the close of the war with Spain, confirmed the immense logistics difficulties in supporting American forces in the Far East. "To show the difficulty that is experienced in getting coal to our ships at Taku," Secretary of the Navy John D. Long wrote, "it is sufficient to state that it is shipped by our own colliers from Hampton Roads and from Cardiff, involving voyages of 12,000 to 14,000 miles." Without adequate bases, the United States could not expect to repeat the triumph of Manila Bay against a better prepared foe.

America's "New Empire" would need to copy the British model and develop a system of bases and cable lines, with an isthmian canal as "lifeline," to support the movements of the fleet. Moreover, strategic concerns, and not congressional politics, should dictate the location of these naval bases. In a report to the Secretary of the Navy, Alfred Thayer Mahan tried to show this relationship between strategy, bases, and fuel supplies:

> Fuel stands first in importance of the resources necessary to a Fleet. Without ammunition, a ship may run away, hoping to fight another day, but without fuel she can neither run, nor reach her station, nor remain on it, if remote, nor fight.
>
> The distribution and storage of fuel is, therefore, eminently a strategic question . . . the positions for storing, and . . . the quantity to be stored at each position, are amenable to strategic considerations.

Three principal requirements should govern the choice of location for a base: ready access for the fleet and proximity to the theater of operations, security from an enemy seizure or attack, and ease of transporting coal to the place of storage. Mahan called these three elements: "Position, Strength, and Resources." Thus,

> a place suited for a strategic centre of operations for a fleet should equally be a position for a coaling station; because (1) there it will be near the fleet; (2) it will be under the shelter of the fortifications established for the position as a naval base; and (3) at the base should be accumulated all the resources of every kind, fuel included.

As can be seen from this report, considerations of fuel supplies should predominate in the location of the Navy's bases.

During the first two decades of this century the General Board devised guidelines on the Navy's base requirements that agreed with the tenets on logistics and strategy contained in Mahan's report. At times, however, one base project might be the focus of attention rather than any comprehensive plan. An example of this occurred during the turmoil in China at the turn of the century when the Navy tried to win approval for the establishment of a coaling station in the Chusan Islands to counterbalance German, Russian, and British bases at Kiaochow, Port Arthur, and Weihaiwei. Despite such anomalies, there did exist an underlying pattern of base development guiding the Board's proposals. Central to this pattern was the development of bases in the Caribbean to turn it into the "American Mediterranean" (to borrow RADM Henry Taylor's phrase). Guantanamo would be the most important base in this scheme, with a more advanced fleet anchorage at Culebra. These positions, unlike the major facilities along the east coast of the United States, stood directly in the path of any European power that might want to upset the Monroe Doctrine by seizing territory in the Western Hemisphere or attack the proposed isthmian canal. Not surprisingly, the Board also wanted the fortification and construction of coal storage facilities along the canal to protect and expedite the movement of the fleet from one ocean to the other. In the Pacific, the Board wanted as a minimum major fleet facilities in the San Francisco area and at Puget Sound. The Board also wanted a fortified advanced base in the Pacific: Pearl Harbor, Guam, and Subic Bay all were considered at one time or another. As can be readily grasped, the Board wanted bases to carry out two strategic tasks: defense of the Western Hemisphere and support for a transpacific advance of the battle fleet to the waters around Japan.

The arguments and recommendations put forward by the General Board, the Naval War College, and navalists like Mahan on the need for a comprehensive base policy derived from strategic considerations, received little support from the Government. The more rousing index of national power, construction of battleships, evoked more widespread interest than the development of coaling facilities. In 1916 RADM Austin Knight, President of the Naval War College, testified before Congress that for the price of only one battleship ($15 million) all of America's possessions in the Pacific could be safeguarded by the construction of a major base at Guam. Yet in that same year, when Congress approved appropriations to build a "Navy Second to None," it continued to pass over proposals on base construction. Moreover, it would not be unfair to argue that the development of Pearl Harbor as America's premier advanced base in the Pacific owed more to congressional politics than strategic considerations. Administrative quarrels within the Navy between the General Board and the Bureau of Equipment on the location and number of bases certainly did not help the chances for an improvement in the logistic support of the fleet. The policy of the General Board remained consistent in wanting to concentrate on developing a few key positions required to carry out war plans. This view often clashed with the recommendations of the Chief of the Bureau of Equipment, who was nominally in charge of all matters relating to the Navy's coaling stations and coaling supplies. The more famous fight, between the General Board and the Army over the location of the Philippine base, is another instance of how the Navy's vision of creating a string of bases could remain incomplete because of interservice rivalry. The General Board nonetheless continued to press for a comprehensive program of bases tailored to perceived strategic needs, despite the dismal prospects of it ever being adopted, because such a "policy should be prepared and available for those concerned, as the ideal to be sought."

After the San Francisco School Board ordered the segregation of the city's Asia school children from its other students on 11 October 1906, the problem of developing bases in the Pacific acquired an immediacy because of the threat of war with Japan. The defeat of Russia only a year before showed Japan to possess the naval and military prowess to seize American possessions in the Pacific. Some even thought, like the novelist Homer Lea in *The Valor of Ignorance,* that the Japanese had the capability to invade and conquer the United States west of the Rockies. In this paper it is not necessary to show the genesis, evolution, and context of the various Orange Plans as this has been the subject of many fine studies; however, the logistics arrangements for the advance of the battle fleet to the Far East were staggering, and deserve special consideration.

In the late autumn of 1906, the General Board drew up an operational plan, based on the previous summer's conference at the Naval War College, to serve as a guide for the movement of a battle fleet from the Atlantic coast to the Far East. Once again, American dependence on British coal supplies is apparent by the route the fleet would follow to get to the Pacific. Starting from Hampton Roads, the fleet would steam across the Atlantic to the Zafarin Islands off the coast of Morocco, where 5 days would be spent coaling. The next leg of the fleet's voyage would be through the Mediterranean Sea and Suez Canal to Aden and another 5 days of coaling. The fleet would then cross the Indian Ocean, coaling en route in the Seychelles Islands and once again in the Straits of Sunda, before setting out for Philippine waters. Once in the Philippines the first task of the fleet would be the seizure of a base, as it was expected that the Japanese would overrun the American facilities at Manila Bay during the opening stages of any conflict. Because the Navy did not possess enough colliers to support this fleet movement, agents were to be sent abroad to purchase 197,000 tons of coal to be positioned in the Zafarin Islands, Aden, the Seychelles Islands, and Lampung Bay. This route, which is the approach a European navy would use to get to the Far East, shows the undeveloped state of American support facilities in the Pacific. It also raises the important question of how much would a British government hinder the movements of the American battle fleet in a war against Japan after the conclusion of the Anglo-Japanese Alliance of 1902.

Subsequent war plans against "Orange," though adopting a transpacific advance of the battle fleet to the Philippines in place of the path around the belly of the Eurasian land mass, continued to be plagued by grossly inadequate logistics support. In the Administrative Section of the Orange War Plan of

1911, the General Board set out the importance of logistics preparations to a successful outcome of a campaign against Japan. "The logical development of the strategy of war with Orange demonstrates how absolutely all operations depend upon the logistics of war." The development of a plan of war against Japan would not have much meaning if it were not accompanied by improvements in the logistic support needed to maintain the fleet in the Pacific.

> If the logistic means are lacking to insure the arrival of the full naval strength of a country in the area where the decisive battles of the war must be fought, and to keep it adequately supplied in that area, it is as overpowering a national calamity as a decided inferiority in the equality of the personnel and in the number and character of the fighting ships.

Just as the fleet in this era was considered "unbalanced" in the number of battleships to smaller fighting vessels, the Navy in the Pacific was logistically unbalanced because it lacked support facilities and auxiliaries to carry out its operational plans.

To support its Pacific advance, the General Board wanted to establish coal piles with 200,000 tons capacity at five points: Puget Sound, San Francisco, Pearl Harbor, Panama, and Corregidor. This coal would have to be shipped from England or the east coast of the United States because the coal of the western states was not considered of high enough quality for efficient steaming. Because it did not possess enough colliers to meet even its peacetime requirements, the Navy was forced to depend on foreign companies to move coal to its Pacific bases inasmuch as American firms had failed to bid for the Government's business. The cost of transporting coal in 1910 was $4.50 per ton to Honolulu and $2.75 per ton to Manila. This General Board plan never came to fruition: in 1910 the Navy had no coal at Pearl Harbor, Panama, or Corregidor, and only 20,000 tons at San Francisco and 74,000 tons at Puget Sound. The gravity of the fuel situation was brought home once again in 1913 when the California state legislature passed the Webb bill limiting the amount of land that aliens could own. The Bureau of Supplies and Accounts reported that the United States had barely a quarter of the 175 colliers required to support the battle fleet on a voyage to the Far East. Assistant Secretary of the Navy Franklin D. Roosevelt ordered coal shipments bound for the Philippines be diverted to San Francisco and all Navy colliers on the west coast be made ready for service. The Navy also acquired operations on British colliers to accompany the fleet. Despite these efforts, the Navy lacked the resources to keep the battle fleet supplied with the

200,000 to 250,000 tons of coal it would need every month to carry out its operations.

Yet many American officers, like Capt. Sydney Staunton and Cdr. Clarence Williams of the General Board and the influential Gen. Leonard Wood, had come to view Japan as the most likely, and dangerous, antagonist the United States would have to face in a future war. They believed that the best way to deter Japanese military expansion was to move the battle fleet, or at least a sizable portion of it, to the Pacific. While acknowledging the logistics difficulties of such a move, they argued that only by shifting the battle fleet to the Pacific would an acceleration occur in base development. These strategic recommendations were not only "heresies" to the majority of the General Board swayed by the Germanophobic Dewey, but were logistically infeasible because of the high cost of supporting coal-burning battleships in the Pacific. One estimate placed the cost of marine coal in the Pacific as five to eight dollars more expensive per ton than in the Atlantic. Overall, the maintenance of a battle fleet in the Pacific would raise Navy estimates by at least $4 million. The dollar sign, as much as contending strategic assessments, determined the location of the battle fleet.

In the Atlantic the logistics requirements of coal-burning battle fleets can be seen underlying the evolution of American plans for war with Germany. The technological constraints of refueling in this era provided limits on the capability of the German battle fleet. American naval planners correctly reasoned that a German battle fleet, attempting to strike at the east coast of the United States from German home ports, would need to stop to coal in the Azores before crossing the Atlantic. Once this transatlantic voyage had been completed, the German Fleet would need to find a location, sheltered by land, where it could coal once again. Depending on the season, whether it was winter or summer, the German battle fleet would coal either in the Caribbean or along the New England coast before seeking out the American Fleet for combat. Naval War College studies estimated the German battle fleet would require 97 colliers and "would tax to the utmost Black's (Germany) ability to transport coal at sea." American naval planners believed that their best chance for defeating such a scheme would occur after the German battle fleet had completed the leg of its journey from the Azores, but before it had a chance to coal in the Western Hemisphere. This required that a scouting force discover the German approach from the Azores, and that the fleet's battleships be concentrated to intercept and bring to battle the German Fleet.

One operational study of how this battle should develop bears a remarkable resemblance to Japanese plans of the interwar period to destroy the U.S.

battle fleet as it advanced across the Pacific and before it could establish a secure base in the Far East. In case the German Fleet managed to elude detection, American naval planners developed a wide range of plans to occupy, in conjunction with the Army, prospective locations in the Caribbean where the German Fleet could establish a coaling depot.

The need to deny Germany a coaling station in the Western Hemisphere thus played an important part in the diplomacy of the United States in the period before the First World War. In a lecture at the Naval War College, Assistant Secretary of State Francis B. Loomis warned naval officers that a "certain government" meant to gain a "foot-hold in South America. . . . This is a contingency which offers one of the most intricate and delicate problems that can be suggested by our future relations in Latin America. The ultimate fate, declaration, scope and interpretation of the Monroe Doctrine is indissolubly connected with it." President Roosevelt was constantly on guard to prevent Germany from acquiring a naval station in the Western Hemisphere. In a letter to Senator Henry Cabot Lodge, Roosevelt maintained that Germany might "hanker" after a coaling station in the West Indies under the guise of "commercial purposes."

> It is the thin end of the wedge and I do not like the move at all. A coaling station is what Germany most lacks in our waters and the Kaiser could use this commercial station for warships. He is restless and tricky and this ought to be looked after. It is and always has been a danger point.

As long as Germany did not possess a coaling station in the Western Hemisphere, its chances of defeating the American battle fleet would be greatly reduced.

In the spring of 1912 the German Government dispatched the most modern addition to their fleet, the battle cruiser S.M.S. *Moltke,* on a good will tour of American ports on the Atlantic seaboard. Instead of producing amity, however, *Moltke* created a sensation in the press that almost amounted to a "naval panic." The *Washington Post* ran an editorial on 1 June 1912 entitled, "Pride of Our Navy Outclassed." In the press *Moltke* was depicted as a warship that could rapidly strike across the Atlantic and attack the defenses of the soon to be completed Panama Canal before the slower American battle fleet could respond. The officers from the Office of Naval Intelligence who inspected *Moltke* paid special attention to discovering its steaming radius. In making the journey from Germany to Hampton Roads at the relatively fast speed of 15 knots, *Moltke* could steam about 3,000 miles; or in other words, it could make a voyage from Germany to the Western Atlantic. The intelligence officers discovered, however, that *Moltke* had made the voyage direct from Germany only by storing coal in "various bins about the gun deck and apparently all the broadside gun compartments were filled with coal." The speed and efficiency of the German crew in coaling their ship further impressed the American intelligence officers. With *Moltke*, Germany possessed a capital ship with a transatlantic steaming capability that seemed to upset previous estimates of the time needed for a German Fleet to attack American possessions in the Western Hemisphere.

Of course, no German armada crossed the Atlantic to seize territory in the Western Hemisphere, and the most impressive demonstration of long-distance steaming by coal-burning battleships involved the Battle Fleet of the U.S. Navy—the voyage of the Great White Fleet. This celebrated 14-month cruise around the world by 16 American battleships, without any major mechanical mishaps, was an amazing engineering feat for a fleet of pre-dreadnought battleships. It is possible to gain an even greater appreciation of the magnitude of this undertaking when the voyage of the Great White Fleet is compared to the long-distance naval movements of the other Great Powers in this period. The largest comparable movement of German battleships away from European waters took place in 1900, when the Second Division of the First Battle Squadron, a total of four battleships and thus only a quarter of the size of the American Fleet, was dispatched to help reduce the Taku forts guarding the approaches to Peking. Perhaps the best known example of a fleet movement of this era is the ill-fated voyage of Admiral Rozhdestvenski's Baltic Fleet to the Far East during the Russo-Japanese War. Yet this fleet numbered only eleven battleships: five less than the number in the Great White Fleet. Even Britain's Royal Navy, with its worldwide security interests, never deployed more than seven battleships to the Far East in this period. In the words of one thrilled Congressman: "No other power, not even England, whose drumbeat is heard around the world, ever sent such an enormous fleet around the world."

Behind the fine fighting facade presented by the fleet and the success of its diplomatic mission, the voyage of the Great White Fleet showed once again how completely dependent the United States was on the good will of Great Britain for its fleet movements. Without British supplies of coal, colliers, and bases, the voyage would not have been possible. In the decade after the Spanish-American War none of the General Board's recommendations for the establishment of coaling stations had been met, and the Navy's eight colliers were woefully inadequate to meet the logistics needs of supporting the battle fleet across the Pacific. In order to supply the fleet with the 430,000 tons of coal it consumed during the round-the-world cruise, the Government hired one Austro-Hungarian, seven Norwegian, and forty-one

British ships to deliver coal to various ports along its route. Despite these arrangements, the fleet frequently found itself short of coal because scheduled deliveries failed to arrive on time. In Australia and New Zealand the failure of British colliers in meeting their contracts caused Admiral Sperry "great embarrassment." At Auckland only three of the expected six colliers arrived; and at Albany, only four of the scheduled six colliers appeared. In a letter to his son, Sperry complained that Britain could make the American Fleet the "laughing stock" of the world by stranding it in Australia without coal to move. Only by inducing local coal dealers to cancel their contracts did Sperry find the coal he needed to complete the next leg of his voyage to Manila. This episode in Australia only too clearly shows the inadequacy of the logistics resources available to the United States in this period. As Senator Hale correctly observed, "the greatest fleet of formidable ships the whole world has ever seen" must depend "on the indulgence of foreign powers."

The world cruise did benefit American naval planners by giving them important practical experience to serve as a guide in the fashioning of naval policy and war planning. One particularly useful exercise occurred when the battle fleet steamed 3,850 miles from Honolulu straight across the South Pacific to Auckland, New Zealand, the longest single leg of its voyage. Bags of coal stowed on deck supplemented what was held in the fleet's fully laden bunkers. This run showed that American battleships possessed the capability of steaming directly from Hawaii to the Philippines without coaling en route and still remain in good mechanical condition. The importance of Hawaii, as the location of the Navy's principal strategic outpost in the Pacific, was thereby heightened at the expense of Philippine base projects. The inability of the Army and Navy to agree on a site for a base in the Philippines certainly served to strengthen this contention, and on 8 November 1909 the Joint Army and Navy Board recommended that no major naval base should be established further west in the Pacific than Pearl Harbor. A fleet based on Pearl Harbor would "control the Pacific and provide strategic defense" of the Philippines and the west coast of the United States. In the Philippines there need only be established a stock of coal and a naval magazine that could be protected by the Army's guns on Corregidor. The Navy also learned that the time needed to move the battle fleet from the east coast to the Pacific was 75 days, rather than the earlier projection of 120 days. This time would be cut even further once the Panama Canal was completed. Armed with this experience, the Navy could anticipate an earlier move across the Pacific in case of war with Japan.

The vast distances to be overcome in a war against Japan in the Pacific ran contrary to the constraints imposed on operations by coaling and the short war dogmas of the age. Coal tied a fleet to its base; but the United States possessed no secure, well-stocked bases in the Pacific. Only by the dangerous expedient of establishing advanced bases as it moved could the battle fleet be supported in the Western Pacific. The logistics problems of coaling thus prohibited a knockout blow being delivered early in the war by the big guns of the battleline: a war with Japan instead would entail a protracted conflict centered on the bases set up along the fleet's line of advance. Mahan feared that this slow advance would enable Japan to "hold out till the American people weary of the war." Yet his operational plans to speed the tempo of an advance to the Japanese home waters were rejected by Naval War College planners primarily because of the limitations in steaming distance of coal-driven battleships. As has been shown, American planners considered these limitations a distinct advantage in any coming conflict with Germany in the Atlantic; but in the situation of war with Japan, the problem of coaling in conjunction with the vast distances to be traversed in the Pacific would weigh heavily against the chances for success.

The dimensions of this logistics nightmare could be somewhat reduced, however, by the use of oil fuel in warships instead of coal. As a naval fuel, oil possessed many advantages over coal. Oil has roughly twice the thermal content of coal, which means that for any given weight of fuel and machinery a ship can steam twice as far. Moreover, oil can be stored throughout the ship and pumped to the furnace; thereby eliminating the need for stokers and reducing by half the personnel required to tend the engines. Oil also had the great operational advantage of permitting a fleet to refuel at sea from tankers.

Beginning in 1897, the U.S. Navy experimented with oil fuel for marine engines, and by 1904 there existed an impressive amount of evidence showing its great potential in warship construction. Despite this evidence, the Navy moved very slowly in shifting to oil and lagged behind Britain in building oil-burning warships. Perhaps the most important reason for this caution was the fear that domestic supply would not be sufficient to meet the Navy's needs. In a letter to Secretary George von L. Meyer, the Chief of the Bureau of Steam Engineering expressed this fear:

A deterrent affecting the use of oil to even our present limited extent has been the fear of a failure of the supply. With the general use of oil by all navies, which now seems inevitable, and the probable considerable increase in its use for commercial purposes, this uncertainty of supply might develop into a condition menacing the mobility of the fleet and safety of the nation.

One way to ensure the Navy's supply of oil was to set aside rich oil lands in the western states and create a strategic petroleum reserve. On 27 September

1909 the Taft administration began the project by withdrawing lands in California at Elk Hills and Buena Vista Hills, that were subsequently organized 3 years later into Naval Petroleum Reserves 1 and 2. The Wilson administration added to these California sites the famous Teapot Dome reserve in Wyoming in 1915. Even with the creation of these reserves, many in the Navy Department continued to fear the depletion of domestic oil sources and dependence on foreign markets.

In conjunction with the creation of oil reserves, the Navy began to adopt oil fuel for its battleships. Oil was first used in battleships in the "mixed firing" technique where it is sprayed on burning coal to increase furnace efficiency by reducing ash. Not until the *Nevada* class, authorized by Congress in 1911, did the Navy decide to rely entirely on oil fuel for its battleships. With this step, not only battleships, but the entire fleet was committed to oil. Secretary Daniels correctly observed that the "recent tests of the *Nevada*, the first dreadnoughts equipped for the exclusive use of oil as motive power, emphasize the growing need of a large supply of oil for the Navy." To shift to oil had important strategic consequences as well with regard to the disposition of the fleet. Oil fuel would be especially useful for warships operating in the Pacific. In 1907 one oil industry journal stridently called on the Navy to start construction of oil-burning ships for the Pacific:

> With fuel regarded as the pivot upon which victory or defeat would swing in case of hostilities on the Pacific, inaction on the part of the navy department in equipping a Pacific squadron with oil-burning apparatus, can be characterized as nothing short of criminal negligence. It is [a] question of highest efficiency. If "full preparedness" is the watchword of the navy department, then it does not live up to it, if there is further delay in actively recognizing crude oil as fuel on board warships.

Four years later, Chief Engineer Hutch I. Cone echoed these sentiments when he told a gathering of the Navy League that the construction of oil-burning battleships would greatly ease the fuel problem in the Pacific. Because oil fuel was cheaper than coal in the Pacific, and the proximity of the oil reserves to the coast ensured supply in a crisis, the earlier financial and transportation problems that kept the battleships concentrated in the Atlantic no longer mattered in deciding where to concentrate the fleet.

By 1913, the General Board anticipated the gradual decline of coal consumption by the Navy as oil-driven ships entered the service. As a guide to policy, the Board moreover gave priority to the construction of fuel stations in the Pacific over those in the Atlantic. In the Pacific, where coal piles had not been established anyway in the quantity desired by the Board, the advantages of increased radius of operations of oil-burning ships would be more useful. Within little more than a decade of this recommendation, the Navy consumed the insignificant amount of 15,000 tons of coal annually in the Pacific even though the number of warships based on the west coast had increased dramatically.

With the conclusion of the First World War and the surrender of the Kaiser's *Hochseeflotte*, Secretary Daniels ordered the creation of a powerful Pacific Fleet, commanded by Adm. Hugh Rodman, in the spring of 1919. The core of Rodman's fleet, eight new oil-burning battleships, passed through the Panama Canal and steamed north to a Presidential fleet review at Seattle on 13 September 1919. It is difficult to disagree with Braisted's conclusion that the movement of Rodman's fleet to the Pacific, in conjunction with the opening of a modern drydock at Pearl Harbor in August 1919, "epitomized the reappearance of the United States as a great naval power in the Pacific." American naval strength in the Pacific was further augmented by the Navy Department's decision to replace four coal-burning battleships with four oil burners in the spring of 1921. While the Navy continued to lack adequate shore support in the Pacific to dock this fleet, this movement of battleships, and the shift in American strategic focus that it represented, ensured the gradual development of west coast naval facilities. The adoption of oil fuel greatly aided this shift. The advantages of oil fuel were dramatically shown by a cruise of the Pacific Fleet to Hawaii in the fall of 1920. On the voyage out the fleet speed was held down to 12 knots by the coal-burning battleships. This exercise convinced Rodman, and most other naval officers, that the ability to operate in the Pacific depended on oil. It also demonstrated the difficulties of operating coal- and oil-burning battleships together. No commander afloat would want to steam into battle with the flag-hoist signal: "Coal burners to the rear." If the fleet was not encumbered by coal-burning ships its speed and tactical efficiency would be much higher. The lessons of these exercises can be seen in the recommendations of the Navy Department of the interwar period that the six coal-burning battleships be converted to oil. With this conversion the range of these battleships would almost double. The most impressive demonstration of the endurance and range of oil-burning warships in this period occurred, however, in 1925 when the American battle fleet steamed 13,000 miles to New Zealand and Australia after the conclusion of joint Army-Navy maneuvers in Hawaiian waters. Commanded by the former Chief of Naval Operations, Adm. Robert E. Coontz, this force, numbering 46 ships (11 of them battleships) and 23,000 men, was supplied during this cruise by the 13 auxiliaries of its own service support.

In Australia and New Zealand the battle fleet received a warm welcome, one paper called it the "mightiest armada ever seen in New Zealand waters." Coontz' force certainly dwarfed the British "Special Service Squadron," consisting of the two battle cruisers *Hood* and *Repulse*, that had visited Australasian waters 2 years earlier. Thus even before the tragic "Andrianople" of the British Empire in 1941, when the battleships *Prince of Wales* and *Repulse* went down, politicians and popular opinion in Australia and New Zealand recognized that their security depended on an American naval "umbrella" rather than the Royal Navy.

This shift to oil fuel had the added advantage that rival Great Powers were not as fortuitously endowed as the United States in domestic oil production. Oil industry bulletins estimated that Germany depended on the United States for 80 percent of its oil supplies in 1914. Because it did not possess domestic sources of oil, Germany continued to depend upon coal-fired machinery for its battleships through the First World War. This restricted the radius of operations of German capital ships and made virtually impossible the notion of raiding Allied sealanes in the Atlantic. The Japanese Empire, the other feared antagonist of the General Board before 1914, also lacked oil resources for its navy and depended on American and British firms for supplies. Japanese leaders knew that any naval competition with the United States would need to take into account the question of oil and not just comparisons of capital ship strength. Japan's vulnerable strategic position was graphically demonstrated in the use the United States made of the "oil weapon" during the diplomatic crisis before Pearl Harbor, and the stationing of their battle fleet in Southeast Asia, where it would be closer to the sources of oil production, instead of in the home islands before the great naval battles of 1944.

Even Great Britain's naval supremacy, that had heavily depended on coal, was called into question by the shift to oil fuel for warship machinery. Despite the heroic efforts of Winston Churchill and Jackie Fisher, the earlier advantage of dominating the world's coal trade was rapidly being eroded. To the doubters that questioned Churchill's oil policy, the First World War convincingly demonstrated the necessity of oil in modern war. Lord Curzon said at the time that the Allies "Floated to victory on a sea of oil." The bulk of this oil, perhaps over 80 percent, came from the United States. A startling transformation had taken place during the course of the war, with the Royal Navy becoming dependent on American sources of oil. Moreover, the submarine peril demonstrated the precarious nature of this oil lifeline. During several months of 1917 the Royal Navy experienced a critical shortage of oil fuel: stockpiles were down to 3 weeks' supply as a whole and to 6 days' supply at some bases; limitations had to be imposed on fleet movements to conserve fuel. The British Government was forced to send what one recent writer has termed, "urgent and humiliating" telegrams to the United States "warning that the Royal Navy would be immobilized unless the American government made available . . . the necessary supplies of naval fuel to Britain." In September 1917 the Admiralty director of stores reported that "without the aid of oil fuel from America our modern oil-burning fleet cannot keep the seas." The American dispatch of four coal-burning battleships in November 1917 (with one more being sent later) to form the Sixth Battle Squadron of the Grand Fleet, rather than the more modern oil-fired battleships, shows how the problem of oil supply could affect naval deployments. Reflecting on this wartime experience, Secretary Daniels wrote: "The war on sea and in the air as well as on land has depended so much on transportation that it can be laid down as a basic principle that no nation that does not control an adequate oil supply can successfully maintain its forces in the field."

With the conclusion of the war, oil emerged as a major irritant in Anglo-American relations. The oil crisis of 1917 had graphically demonstrated to British leaders their country's critical dependence on American oil. As a way to decrease this dependence, the British Government tried to gain control of Middle East oilfields and exclude American companies from participation. In a speech in March 1920 by the First Lord of the Admiralty Walter Long said that "if we secure the supplies of oil now available in the world we can do what we like," and that "the nation must take care to occupy the house, or others will take it, and with it the key to all future success." The subsequent San Remo agreement between Britain and France a month later served to further fuel the antagonism between the United States and Great Britain. One commentator, writing in The Fortnightly Review, compared this antagonism to the imperial rivalries in the Far East: "The world is in danger of drifting into much the same sort of struggle over oil concessions as was waged twenty odd years ago over China; and the chief protagonists in the struggle threaten to be Great Britain and the United States."

The U.S. Navy clearly recognized the political and strategic advantages of America's commanding position in world oil production. In a memorandum to the Secretary of the Navy dated 5 May 1911, the Chief of the Bureau of Steam Engineering drew attention to the "probability of an eventual demand for petroleum greatly exceeding the supply, together with the fact that we produce the greater part of the world's supply, should give us a distinct advantage over other nations. The control of our exports of oil might limit the extent of the adoption of the oil engine by our possible enemies." Two years later in a report to the Secretary of the Navy entitled "Supply of Oil Fuel at a Reasonable Price," Admiral Dewey strongly endorsed the adoption of oil fuel for the fleet: "The military advantages of burning oil, the advantage to the United States in being the greatest oil producing country, and the added advantage that the Navy has its own oil-bearing lands, are all so great that the return to coal burning could only be viewed as a calamity." Oil would be the foundation of American overseas expansion much as coal served to underpin British imperial policy.

Of course, the advantage possessed by the United States because of its oil production did not necessarily translate into improved readiness for the Navy. The compromise at the Washington Conference, whereby the Japanese accepted an inferior tonnage ratio for their capital ships of 60 percent of the American strength in return for the nonfortification Article XIX of the naval treaty, prohibited base development in the most likely theater of operations. Given the tight-fisted policies of the Congress and Republican administrations during the interwar period, when it proved difficult to find funding for fuel to conduct large-scale maneuvers, perhaps the United States did not surrender much in Article XIX. Moreover, the Navy managed to offset partially its lack of bases by retaining the 35,000-ton limitation on battleships when both the British and the Japanese Governments wanted to establish an even smaller tonnage for capital ships.

It must also be remembered that the other great naval powers found the problems of finding fuel supplies even more daunting. The establishment of oil stocks at British bases proved to be a favorite item for reduction by Treasury officials during the interwar period, and the development of the Singapore base, lynchpin of the Empire's security in the Pacific, progressed only haltingly. During the Second World War, fuel problems frequently hindered British naval operations. One glaring instance occurred during the hunting of the German battleship *Bismarck*. On the run to the French ports, the pursuing British battleships almost had to call off the chase because they were critically short of fuel, and no tankers existed to refuel them at sea. Nothing better shows the startling reversal of British naval fortunes. The U.S. Navy meanwhile overcame the sizable logistics problems of moving the fleet across the Pacific to the Japanese home islands during the Second World War. It is difficult to imagine this hazardous undertaking succeeding without the benefits of oil fuel. The foundation for America's naval supremacy after 1945 was laid over two decades earlier with the shift to oil fuel for the fleet. America's global military deployments continue to depend on this vital commodity.

PART VI

GOING OVER THERE

EDWARD M. COFFMAN

AMERICAN COMMAND AND COMMANDERS IN WORLD WAR I

The American army that went to war in April 1917 was still, in many respects, a nineteenth-century force. It had few machine guns and little modern artillery. Its small air arm had no combat-worthy aircraft. Some of its senior officers were veterans of the Indian Wars. While the other belligerents fielded armies numbering in the millions, the American army had fewer than 128,000 regular soldiers, backed by fewer than 100,000 men in the National Guard. By November 11, 1918, however, the army had more than four million men, half of them overseas, and the American Expeditionary Force was a vital part of the Allied drives that finally broke the back of the German army. In just over nineteen months the army had literally transformed itself. It was an impressive achievement, possible mainly through the professional skill of its leaders. Officers accustomed to the slow-paced life of the prewar army had to cope with vastly increased responsibility and unheard of amounts of materiel and men, and do it all in a chaotic, confusing, and fast-changing environment. Some found the demands on their skills or physical stamina too great; others, however, emerged from relative anonymity with glittering reputations.

Of all the intangibles in war, that of leadership may be the most mysterious and impenetrable, and the most important. The following essay by Professor Edward M. Coffman is an attempt to examine the high command of the American army in World War I, both in terms of the military environment most of the officers shared in the prewar years and in terms of their relative success or failure as commanders during the brief six months the American Expeditionary Force was in combat. Although the public perception of American commanders was based primarily on their images as heroic warriors, Professor Coffman suggests that the most effective American commanders were those who successfully mastered the skills of effective military managers, able to maneuver, supply, and motivate modern mass armies.

As Professor Coffman notes, it was difficult for the public to reconcile this reality of twentieth-century warfare with the traditional image of the general as a heroic figure, literally leading his troops forward into battle. Indeed, it was also undoubtedly difficult for many military commanders to accept such a new definition of leadership. They, too, saw themselves in heroic terms, even when this image did not reflect the new circumstances they faced. Even though Professor Coffman suggests in his conclusion that more sophisticated soldiers and civilians in later generations would more easily understand the changed role of a military commander, that has not always occurred. An image of heroic leadership is still often expected, even from modern and sophisticated audiences, and balancing this need to be perceived as heroic against the real need for managerial skills has created problems the American military is currently struggling to solve.

In a recent study of leadership entitled The Mask of Command, the British military historian John Keegan argues that in the modern age the traditional mechanisms and imagery of leadership are no longer valid. For centuries, suggests Keegan, military commanders persuaded their men to follow their orders by establishing an emotional bond with them (which Keegan calls "kinship"), communicating their personalities in clear and direct terms, enforcing discipline and rewarding valor, setting an example of courage and self-sacrifice, and taking direct, decisive action whenever necessary. Now, Keegan writes, such traditional mechanisms of command "all fail." The heroic ethic, he suggests, is utterly inappropriate to today's world.

Keegan's argument ranges far beyond the limits of military combat leadership, in an attempt to also in some way define the proper limits for national leadership. But his argument on behalf of the "post-heroic" modern leader runs counter to much of the thinking in the army, which since the late 1970s has been deeply concerned about arguments that its officers were managers rather than warriors. This allegation was given its widest circulation in Richard Gabriel and Paul Savage's book Crisis in Command, published in 1978. Although army supporters argued that Gabriel and Savage were wrong, other critics echoed their complaints: army officers were steeped in managerial technique, but had forgotten how to command. By the mid-1980s, the army had quietly accepted at least part of this argument, and was firmly stressing the need to "lead" instead of "manage." Army manuals stressed the need to set an example, to communicate clearly and directly, and to take decisive action whenever the situation demanded it, to act, in other words, within the traditional framework of heroic leadership, while continuing to practice effective management at the same time. Clearly, the image of the heroic commander continues to be a part of the general image of military leadership.

The issues raised by Professor Coffman's analysis of the American high command in World War I have a continuing relevance to current dilemmas. Military commanders must have tactical and strategic abilities; they must, in our modern world, have managerial skills akin to those of successful businessmen; and, apparently, they must also have the proper image as heroic leaders. But can one man, or woman, balance all these characteristics? Readers might return to Edward Eckert's study of Civil War generalship earlier in this collection, and re-examine the categories he uses to divide his Union commanders. Can similar categories be used today? It is worth noting that one of the commanders studied by Keegan was none other than Grant, whose leadership style Keegan called "unheroic leadership." Since McClellan adopted many of the techniques Keegan argues were the traditional validators of command, what made Grant more successful? What factors brought success to some American commanders in World War I, and failure to others? Can those factors be identified beforehand, prior to the onset of fighting? Or, is the weeding out of unsuccessful commanders, such as that experienced by the American Expeditionary Force in World War I, inevitable? Such questions do not lend themselves to easy answers. But they need to be asked and answered nonetheless, for in an uncertain world we depend upon our military leaders and the answers we give to such questions will determine, in part, the kind of leaders we will have.

September 13 is a most appropriate day to talk about American commanders in the First World War. It was the official birthday of the one American general of that war of whom most people have heard—John J. Pershing. The terms "was" and "official" may be useful because Pershing's most recent biographer, Donald Smythe, has discovered that the date is false. Apparently the future General of the Armies lied about his age, changing it probably from January 13 to September 13 in order to be within the maximum age limit for entering cadets at the Military Academy.

The American Regular Army numbered only some 127,500 (including 5,791 officers) at the time the United States intervened in World War I in April 1917. It was a small army in comparison with the large armies of the belligerents, and it had neither conscription nor a comprehensive reserve system to enable it to expand rapidly in an emergency. At that, this 1917 army was five times larger than the tiny 25,000-man army that virtually all of the senior American officers of World War I had entered as lieutenants during the last quarter of the nineteenth century.

The Civil War dominated the thought and the life of the Army throughout the early careers of the World War I commanders. Those who attended West Point in the seventies and eighties were personally exposed to the great names. The superintendents from 1876 to 1889 were famed Union commanders—John M. Schofield, Oliver O. Howard, Wesley Merritt, and John G. Parke—and the visitors were even more impressive.

George B. Duncan, a member of Pershing's Class of 1886 and a division commander in 1918, recalled:

> We often saw at West Point Generals Grant, Sherman and Sheridan, back to visit friends and to imbibe the atmosphere of their Alma Mater. To see these great soldiers was an inspiration to all of us. They were all present at the unveiling of the Thayer Monument [during Duncan's plebe year in the spring of 1883], seated side by side. After the ceremonies, the crowd formed in line to shake hands with General Grant; he just dropped his hand over the side of the rail, and continued his smoke and conversation with the other two generals. The procession came by, shaking the inert hand of a dangling arm. The General paid not the slightest attention to any individual who shook that hand.

Among the seventy-seven graduates in this class were, in addition the General of the Armies, fifteen generals and ten brigadier generals of World War I vintage. Smythe also points out that more than a quarter of the World War I generals were at West Point during Pershing's years there.

During their first-class year, Grant died and Pershing as First Captain commanded the Corps of Cadets when it presented arms at the station as the funeral train passed through. He recalled this as "the greatest thrill of my life." Then and later, he regarded Grant "as the greatest general our country has produced."

The Army was so small that there were not enough vacancies for all of the seventy-seven of the Class of '86. Congress, however, did give a special dispensation and commissioned those without vacancies as additional second lieutenants to be promoted to second lieutenant whenever vacancies occurred. What they found when they reported to their first posts might well have caused doubts as to their wisdom in choosing a military career. Duncan was one of those:

> Fort Wingate, New Mexico, when I joined the 9th Infantry was the home station of several troops of the 6th Cavalry and 13th Infantry; other companies were in camp waiting assignments to permanent stations. All had just been paid. The post trader's store was in full blast. The part reserved as the officers' club was filled night and day and there were card games galore with stakes from drinks to twenty dollar gold pieces. The bar for enlisted men was lined up until taps.

Intoxication was evident on all sides. Of course there were exceptions but with all there was tolerant acceptance of conditions. No military duties were attempted beyond guard mounting and required roll calls.

To my unsophisticated mind this introduction to an army post made a deeply unfavorable impression and a regret that I had not resigned after graduation and taken a job which had been offered me on the New York Central Railroad. After five or six days the Commanding Officer called a halt by placing some officers in arrest and threatening court-martial.

The Army was stagnant. Civil War veterans—overage in grade and who had often held much higher rank in their youth during the war—held virtually all positions of responsibility. In 1888, when Peyton March joined the Third Artillery at Washington Barracks, he had a Mexican War veteran as his regimental commander and more than half of his fellow officers were Civil War veterans. As late as 1900, all regimental commanders in the infantry, cavalry, and artillery and some captains were veterans of that war. Old men dominated the Army down to and including company level.

Then too, there simply was not much to do. T. Bentley Mott, another of Pershing's classmates, remembered that during his first two years in an artillery battery in the garrisons around San Francisco Bay—"our whole military work consisted of dress parade and one hour of drill each day. . . ." Another artillery officer, who was commissioned from the ranks in 1898, Richard McMaster, recalled that one officer of this era when asked what his duties were answered "mostly social." McMaster added: ". . . that was about it. As a result many took up fads. I remember one who wove rugs—another carved wooden figures and so on." Mott summed up life in this period: "Nobody who has not seen it can picture the desolate narrowness of life in army garrisons during the 'eighties and 'nineties, or imagine the intellectual rigidity of almost all the men who, with an iron hand, commanded them."

The Spanish War, followed closely by the Philippine Insurrection, livened things up. Congress increased the strength in the Regular Army, and many of the officers and men had to act as governmental administrators as well as combat leaders. And in Mindanao there would be active service virtually up to World War I. William H. Simpson, who commanded the Ninth Army in World War II, recalled recently that he spent three-fourths of his tour in Company E, 6th Infantry, at Camp Keithley on Lake Lanao, 1910–1911, in the field chasing Moro outlaws. And General Pershing fought a full scale battle against the Moros at Bud Bagsak on Jolo in June, 1913. In reminiscing about the Army he served in from 1909 to 1917, General Simpson pointed out that it was "almost a Civil War

Army." Infantry relied on rifles and pistols. As he recalled, there were only two machine guns in his regiment (Benet-Mercier), and neither would operate. In those days, "the soldiering was kind of simple. . . ."

One of the most striking things about garrison life of this era is that officers did not seem to have much to do; indeed, neither did enlisted men. Close-order drill, perhaps a class or two, or a tactical exercise on the parade ground—not in the field—in the morning; then the rest of the day was free. Experienced noncoms were expected to handle routine problems. Officers retired to the club for lunch, followed by an afternoon of bridge or perhaps polo if in the cavalry or artillery.

Mott had pursued an interesting career as a military attaché in Europe, but in 1913 he went to Camp Stotsenberg in the Philippines as a lieutenant colonel in a field artillery regiment. "I had absolutely no work to do from morning until night. . . ." The regimental commander symphathized with him about this predicament; but "as he put it, he couldn't give me anything to do without taking it away from the battalion commander or himself, and he had promised the job of building a golf course to an 'extra' cavalry colonel having no more to do than myself." Faced with this dull life, Mott retired—only to return to active duty during the war when he served as Pershing's liaison with Marshal Ferdinand Foch. It was, as William A. Taft's Secretary of War, Henry L. Stimson, put it, "a profoundly peaceful army."

There were some intellectual stirrings. At Fort Wright, Washington, a battalion post of the 14th Infantry in 1915–1916, Omar Bradley, just out of West Point, joined a group of other second lieutenants, led by Forrest Harding, who met in each other's quarters to discuss tactical problems. Incidentally, Harding, a West Point graduate of 1909, did not make first lieutenant until July, 1916. And this was not unusual. A check of his class in G. W. Cullum's *Register* shows that while coast artillerymen and engineers were promoted in two or three years respectively, field artillery, cavalry, and infantry officers had to wait six or seven years. The latter group included, George S. Patton, who made first lieutenant on May 23, 1916; Jacob L. Devers, April 1, 1916; Robert L. Eichelberger, July 22, 1916; and William Hood Simpson, July 1, 1916.

There were also the schools where the Army attempted to formalize the intellectual proclivities of selected officers. At Forts Leavenworth, Monroe, and Riley and at the Army War College, these officers devoted full time to study of the military art. Leavenworth, in particular, had undergone an exciting renaissance after the turn of the century. The young officers—George C. Marshall, Hugh Drum, and others—who occupied the key staff positions in the AEF profited greatly from this training.

Apparently there was little thought that the United States might intervene when war broke out in Europe in 1914. The European military experts assumed that it would be a short war anyway. As it progressed without any decision, military and some civilian groups began to support preparedness. These advocates did not propose intervention but rather defense in case of invasion. Pervading the movement was the belief that military training would make a better and healthier citizen of the average American youth.

War, if it came, seemed more likely to be with Mexico, where political upheaval had brought about almost continuous friction since 1911. In the spring of 1914, President Wilson sent an expedition into Veracruz and kept it there for several months. Again, in March, 1916 he dispatched a force (consisting of four cavalry and two infantry regiments and two batteries of field artillery initially) into northern Mexico and followed this up by mobilizing the National Guard and ordering it to the border. These operations proved to be valuable rehearsals. John J. Pershing, the commander of the Punitive Expedition, was thus tested by his superiors. He, in turn, tested his subordinates and was able to form opinions as to the fitness for command and staff assignments of these men. This was in addition to the value of the field service and training for both Regulars and Guardsmen.

The German gamble on unrestricted submarine warfare in the winter of 1916–1917 precipitated the chain of events leading to President Wilson's appeal to Congress for a declaration of war on April 2, 1917. At that time, neither Wilson, who was never very much interested in the military, nor Congress fully realized what this meant. The general assumption was that the United States would extend financial and material aid to the Allies and perhaps some naval reinforcement. Within weeks, visiting Allied missions spelled out the situation and made their wants known. While they did not at that time press for men, they indicated that they would welcome a "show-the-flag" token force.

The government began to mobilize the economy and to expand the armed forces. Congress enacted conscription, and workers hastily built camps for the hundreds of thousands of draftees. The Army gave priority to officers' training camps, which turned out their first ninety-day graduates in the summer of 1917.

At the senior level, Secretary of War Newton D. Baker had to decide which officers he would recommend for stars. He described his method in a letter to President Wilson on May 30, 1917, in which he sent the names of three brigadier generals and nineteen colonels to be promoted. Secretary Baker pointed out that customarily the War Department apportioned the brigadier-general appointments to the various arms. Then he continued:

> I began by taking a confidential vote among the general officers of
> the Army and after tabulating this vote went over the record of each
> man with a view to eliminating any whose records seemed to indi-
> cate they ought to be passed over. I then made my final selections on

the basis of a conference with General [Tasker H.] Bliss, General [Ernest A.] Garlington and General [Henry P.] McCain [these were the Acting Chief of Staff, Inspector General, and the Adjutant General respectively] and this list is the outcome.

Baker concluded that although he had not adhered strictly to seniority, he had taken it in consideration, but he had emphasized the mental and physical vigor of the officers in question and the opinions of their superiors. Hugh L. Scott, the Chief of Staff at this time, wrote another major general, J. Franklin Bell, on September 5, 1916 in regard to an earlier promotion list. He said then that "in most cases" Baker went along with the majority vote of the generals.

A great personality threatened to disrupt the process of selection of commanders early in the war. Theodore Roosevelt had been planning for some time a Rough Rider-like volunteer division with himself as commander and outstanding Regular officers in key positions. He proposed this to the Secretary of War shortly after the United States entered the war. On the strong advice of the Chief of Staff, Hugh Scott, who argued that granting this request would thwart plans for the systematic raising and officering of the Army, Baker and Wilson flatly rejected the former President's urgent pleas. This meant that unlike the past, there would be no political generals.

Baker's most critical decision as to commanders came when he chose John J. Pershing as the commanding general of the expedition to France. Pershing's handling of the Punitive Expedition made him the obvious choice for this assignment. No other officer had had the opportunity to demonstrate his abilities in such a command during Baker's tenure in the War Department. Once he selected Pershing, Baker backed him completely.

As Commander in Chief of the American Expeditionary Force, Pershing occupied a semi-autonomous position. This led to subsequent problems in relations with the War Department, since Pershing considered his requests as orders. As long as the Chief of Staff subordinated himself to Pershing this system worked after a fashion, although at times Pershing's lack of knowledge and understanding of the home front situation created difficulties. Tasker H. Bliss, who actually carried the load as Chief of Staff throughout most of the first seven months of the war, later said that he considered his position as Chief of Staff in reality to be that of Assistant Chief of Staff to the Chief of Staff of the AEF. When a strong man—Peyton C. March, came to the office in the spring of 1918—became Chief of Staff of the Army, friction developed between the War Department and Pershing's headquarters.

Pershing was a hard, tough soldier, whose service in Mindanao had won him a jump from captain to brigadier general during the Roosevelt administration. General Ben Lear, who was a lieutenant in Pershing's troop in the 15th

Cavalry during the Moro War, told a story that reveals one side of the Pershing personality.

> One day I was in the outpost area and was fired on by one of our outposts. I happened to mention it to the adjutant. I was not complaining. Pershing who overhead the conversation said: "He should have killed you." I thrust out my chest . . . and said: "I disagree with you, sir." Wasn't that a harsh thing to say to a kid lieutenant? I never heard him praise anyone. The Army was harsher in those days than it was in World War II.

General of the Army Omar N. Bradley confirmed Lear's comparison of the World War I and II approach to leadership. He recalled an incident that took place when he was with the Veterans Administration after the war. As he was returning from Atlanta, he filled up his plane with servicemen hitching rides to Washington. As soon as the plane took off, soldiers crowded around him, some talked about the war, and others asked him for his autograph. After a while they settled down and one of Bradley's staff remarked, "times had certainly changed." This veteran of World War I remembered on one occasion that he had walked a mile out of his way to avoid General Pershing. Bradley concluded that he didn't know whether or not his and Eisenhower's approach was better than Pershing's. Of course the men were different from their fathers and expected a different relationship with their officers. Ironically, Ben Lear, who had the reputation of being a martinet, found that out in the summer of 1941 when he disciplined some Guardsmen for yelling at girls on a golf course. The resulting furor in the press indicated the great change since 1918.

There was more to Pershing than this hardness. He had a phenomenal memory. His classmate Duncan remarked on another valuable trait, that he "had the quickest eye and most accurate estimate of a body of troops as to their defects or to their efficiency of any officer that I have ever known." He also had presence, which served him in good stead when he went to Europe. There, as a mere major general without experience in this war, he had to deal on equal terms with field marshals and premiers—all of whom were very experienced. James G. Harbord commented on this during their first month in France: "General Pershing certainly looks his part since he came here. He is a fine figure of a man; carries himself well, holds himself on every occasion with proper dignity; is easy in manner, knows how to enter a crowded room, and is fast developing into a world figure." For his great work in the AEF, Pershing relied heavily upon his ability to pick able subordinates and to inspire their intense loyalty. Finally, in the words of Douglas MacArthur: "His greatest point was his strength and firmness of character." MacArthur added that Pershing was not a strategist or tactician and that he was not as smart as March.

On May 28, 1917, within a month after the notification of his momentous assignment, Pershing sailed from New York with a small staff. His closest confidant and Chief of Staff, Harbord, a newly promoted lieutenant colonel, was perceptive about the challenge facing him and his fellow officers. He wrote after he had been at sea three days: "Officers whose lives have been spent in trying to avoid spending fifteen cents of government money now confront the necessity of expending fifteen millions of dollars,—and on their intellectual and professional expansion depends their avoidance of the scrapheap." At that time neither Pershing, Harbord, nor anyone else foresaw the great expansion that did take place in the next seventeen months. The Army's strength would reach about 3.7 million, and it would take more than 200,000 to officer this huge force. In turn some two million officers and men would serve under Pershing's command in the AEF before the Armistice in November, 1918. What this meant was that many middle-aged field grade officers suddenly found themselves rapidly going up the promotion ladder. After a career of lockstep promotion by seniority within their branch (prior to 1890 it had been within the regiment), they welcomed the opportunity that selection on the basis of merit brought.

Harbord's career is an example of the good fortune enjoyed by some. Commissioned in 1891 after two years in the ranks, he had served as a major of volunteers in 1898. When the Spanish War came to a close, he reverted back to his first lieutenancy. In 1917, he was fifty-one, a student at the Army War College and a major with date of rank of December 10, 1914. In May, he became a lieutenant colonel; in August, a colonel; and in October he put on a star. After he left Pershing's staff in the spring of 1918, he commanded a brigade, and after he became a major general in July, 1918, a division.

A similar advance took place on John L. Hines' promotion record. A West Pointer in the Class of 1891, Major Hines had accompanied Pershing into Mexico as his adjutant. As in the case of Harbord, he also received promotion to lieutenant colonel in May, 1917 (he outranked Harbord as a major by more than two years). He went with the Pershing party to France as the assistant adjutant general and also received a promotion to colonel in August. That fall, "Birdie" Hines left the staff and began one of the most remarkable careers as a combat commander in the AEF. He led with outstanding success a regiment, brigade, division, and corps in the last year of the war. Commensurate with these commands, he wore a star in April, 1918 and became a major general in August.

Harbord and Hines had exceptional careers in the AEF but theirs were not so dissimilar from other Regulars' promotions. In the late summer and fall of 1918, the Army promoted to brigadier general several officers who had been captains when the war began. Some thought that a disproportionate number were field artillery officers (among them, William Bryden and Robert M. Danford), which provoked some suspicion that the Chief of Staff, a former field artilleryman, was partial to his branch. The Chief of Staff pointed out that his rationale was to give field artillery officers command of field artillery brigades. At that, one officer outstripped the artillerymen in promotion. The commander of the first aero squadron in the Army, Benjamin D. Foulois, was a thirty-seven-year-old captain with less than a year in grade when the war came. Because of his specialty, he found himself a major in June and then enjoyed a spectacular leap to brigadier general in September, 1917. The irony of these promotions was that with the end of the war and the reduction in strength of the Army, most of these men who had advanced rapidly went down almost as far—faster.

In the summer of 1917, while Pershing and his staff were laying the foundation for the AEF, the War Department organized the bulk of the divisions that would see combat. During the early days of training, Secretary Baker thought that it would be a beneficial experience if he sent the division commanders and their chiefs of staff to France. This would serve two purposes. For them, it would be an introduction to the war and, presumably, they could pick up all sorts of valuable information in their conversations with Allied division commanders and staffs. At the same time, the visits would give Pershing the opportunity to judge their fitness for command. On their return, Baker himself would interview each general individually and form an opinion as to "their vigor and alertness both of mind and body."

Aside from the fact that this would take the commander and the chiefs of staff away from their divisions in the critical early period, the plan did have merit. Many of these generals who made the two-month sightseeing trip did not meet Pershing's standards. His subordinates, as well as the British and the French, commented on the physical debilities and the seeming lack of grasp various of these generals showed on their tours. In a personal and confidential memorandum Pershing frankly spelled out each man's deficiency, as a few examples indicate:

> *General Thomas H. Barry.* General Barry is past 62 and, although comparatively vigorous, is, I fear, too far along in years to undertake to learn the handling of a division or to stand the arduous work very long. He has never had a large tactical command.
>
> *General Harry F. Hodges.* This officer has not had any practical experience in commanding troops, as all his life has been spent as a constructing engineer. He is 58 years of age and it is too late for him to begin to learn to be a soldier. It will simply be a waste of time, with no result except failure.

> *General Henry A. Greene.* General Greene is in his 62nd year. He
> never has been an active man and he is very fleshy. I would recom-
> mend that he be not sent back as a division commander.

Pershing concluded this memo with the general comment: ". . . many of
these officers will do perhaps to take the administrative control of training
camps, but some of them are so old and infirm in appearance that they should
not be allowed to have a command, where their infirmities will react upon
younger and more capable men." In this last category, Pershing placed a former
Chief of Staff, America's most famed soldier, Leonard Wood.

Doing so led to a controversy with political overtones, since Wood was a
close friend of TR's and had been considered a possible opponent of Wilson in
the 1916 Presidential election. March, Baker, and Wilson, however, backed
Pershing and were criticized. A postwar cartoon in the *North American Review's
War Weekly* called up memories of Wilson's campaign slogan of 1916 when it
showed Wood saying to Roosevelt: "Well, he kept *us* out of the war."

During the war—particularly in the winter of 1917–1918 and the following spring—there raged the greatest controversy between the Allies and the
Americans. This touched significantly on the quality of the American officer
corps. After a series of disasters in late 1917, the grinding to an inconclusive halt
of the British offensive on the Western Front, and the German action at
Caporetto, and the Russian Revolution which meant the withdrawal of Russia
from the war, the Allies began to think seriously of the need for a great
reinforcement of manpower by the Americans. Logically, fewer men would be
needed and they could all be combat troops if they served as replacements in
British and French units. This method would obviate the necessity for garrison
commanders and staff officers as well as American logistical troops. It seemed a
dangerous gamble to await the transportation of the larger number of officers and
men required for an independent army, to say nothing of the lengthy time it
would take for commanders and staffs to gain experience. But Pershing stood
firmly against amalgamation, again with the support of the War Department and
the White House.

Meantime, Pershing went about the business of building an independent
force. Throughout 1917, the AEF increased slowly; it was not until the spring of
1918 that the transports began to speed up. Although Pershing was determined
to have an independent army (indeed his orders so stated), he was willing to
have the French and British play a large role in training his army. His program,
in brief, was to divide training into three phases. He assumed, correctly, that the
troops would get little training in the States. (In fact, the War Department took
large drafts from the divisions in the training camps in order to bring other
divisions up to strength at the ports. This meant a constant, large-scale turnover

in the divisions, with the obvious damage to training.) French and British instructors either gave or supervised instruction in the first phase of weapons training and tactical exercises up to division level. Since the automatic weapons and field artillery were of Allied make, the need for their help in weapons training was evident. They also showed how to construct trench systems and demonstrated techniques of trench warfare. In the second phase, the Americans went to the front, where they served as subordinate units within and under French or British command. Frederick Palmer, the noted war correspondent, commented on how carefully the French treated the first American units to reach the front: "We were nursed into the trenches with all the care of father teaching son to swim." The final phase consisted of division maneuvers, concluding with the division going to the front as part of a French corps.

Allied tutelage became burdensome, and so did the close supervision of Pershing's staff. The Chief of Staff of the 2nd Division, who later commanded the 3rd Division in the fall of 1918, Preston Brown, indicated his problems in both regards in this story: "Shortly before the jump off at St. Mihiel, a young lieutenant, 24 or so, came to his headquarters from GHQ. He asked, 'Is there anything I can do for you?' P. Brown answered, 'Since we've been here, we've had to fight the British, French, Italians and Belgians before we could fight the Germans. You can get the hell out of here.' "

Pershing did not want the Allies to have too much control or influence over his troops. He also wanted to keep a firm hand, through his staff, on his army. This is one reason why it is difficult to evaluate the abilities of the commanders who served under him. First under the Allies then under Pershing, they were given little discretion. Hunter Liggett as a field army commander in the last month of the war evidently did gain a good deal of independence from this close supervision, but his army and the various corps staffs were keeping the divisions under a rather tight rein. The type of warfare contributed to this. As the Americans began to get out of the trenches and go on the offensive the tight control continued, but it is doubtful if it would have over a long period of open warfare.

Time, itself, is a key problem in evaluating division commanders. Most had little opportunity to show their abilities because the Americans were not heavily engaged until the last six months of the war. The first regimental assault took place on May 28. And more than 1.3 million of the two million men in the AEF arrived in the five months between that action at Cantigny and the Armistice. The First Army did not go into battle until September 12 at St. Mihiel, two months before the end of the war.

Then, just as there were great turnovers in personnel in the divisions, there was a large turnover in division commanders. Of the twenty-nine divisions that saw combat, three had four different commanders; eleven had three; nine, two;

and only six kept the same commander. This does not include *ad interim* commanders. Since twenty-one of these divisions were formed in the summer of 1917 and the other eight in the following fall or winter, it is evident that few generals had very much time in command, let alone leading the division in combat.

Good commanders surfaced as well as did some bad ones. Pershing was ruthless in relieving those who failed. In the midst of the Meuse-Argonne campaign in October, 1918, he replaced a corps commander, three division commanders, and several brigade commanders. He even had the objectivity to see that he was trying to do too much as C-in-C, AEF and Commanding General, First Army. He called on Liggett to take over the second job. This was a wise move. The new commanding general rested the First Army and prepared it for its last battle, which turned into a breakthrough in the first week of November.

In assessing American commanders in the war, one must return to that point about time. The United States was in the war nineteen months and, of that period, the AEF participated on a large scale in combat for less than six months. In that brief period, Liggett, Hines, Charles P. Summerall, and a few others did demonstrate clearly their skill as commanders. Others—such as Harbord, who had a reputation as a successful brigade and division commander—do not appear so favorably after a study of the records. This is not to say Pershing was not a great commander; but Pershing himself did not show any particular skill as a strategist or tactician. For his leadership in developing the AEF from less than a hundred thousand to more than two million he deserves the highest tributes. He was a superb military manager and he was always the commander—every doughboy knew that.

Just as Pershing built the AEF, Peyton C. March invigorated the War Department General Staff and spurred it to a high level of efficiency in the last eight months of the war. Unlike Pershing, March came to power after his organization had weathered severe shocks and great changes. He had to break established patterns and bring powerful and reluctant bureaus into line for the war effort. Lear also knew March in the pre-World War I period, and he thought him as harsh and as abrupt with subordinates as Pershing. He was, if anything, more so. He set the tone of his ruthless but efficient and effective administration as Chief of Staff when he turned on an officer who was presenting papers to him. When this man gave him a document concerning relief of a general, March asked him why he was showing him this. The officer replied it was because he understood that the general in question was a friend of the new Chief of Staff. March exploded: "Don't ever bring in another paper to me because you consider that it concerns some[one] who you think is a personal friend of mine. I want it distinctly understood by you and by everyone else in the office that as Chief of Staff I have no friends." Douglas MacArthur pointed out another of March's attributes: "He was a man of principle. When he said—'No'—he said 'No'— without making black seem whitish or white seem blackish. . . . When you left March's office, you knew exactly what he wanted."

There was a good deal of friction between the two strong men—March and Pershing—whose perspectives were naturally different as Chief of Staff and as the C-in-C, AEF. One of the most irritating problems that came up was the handling of the promotions to brigadier and major general. The first confrontation came within a month after March, who had served in France as Pershing's Chief of Artillery, had returned—a major general—to be Acting Chief of Staff. He asked Pershing for recommendations for the generals' list. When the nominations appeared, only three of the ten officers Pershing had recommended for promotion to major general and less than half of those names he had sent in to be new brigadier generals were on it. To make matters worse, one artillery colonel—a friend of March's then serving in the AEF—was on the list even though Pershing had not recommended him. Pershing, a four-star officer, complained to March—still a major general. March's response was that he had to think of the Army as a whole and that he valued Pershing's recommendations no more and no less than those of other commanders.

Again in the summer and fall of 1918, this same issue arose. The fact that March was by then no longer merely Acting Chief of Staff and had become a full general did not help matters. Pershing was accustomed to having his recommendations complied with. Beyond that, he found it intolerable when March continued to promote an occasional AEF officer without his recommendation, including Douglas MacArthur in particular.

While March was right in considering the Army as a whole, he should have shown more tact and awareness of Pershing's special position. The issue was never resolved. Promotions stopped on Armistice Day. And in the months following the war, AEF generals were bitter toward March when he promptly reduced them to their regular ranks as their units returned to the United States to be demobilized. At the same time officers in the War Department who still held emergency slots kept their temporary rank.

Both March and Pershing were military managers, but the public showed more interest in the heroic-leader image—to borrow terms from Morris Janowitz. As commander of the AEF, Pershing projected the image the public wanted. Congress responded by honoring him with the rank of General of the Armies. March, in turn, was available as a scapegoat for complaints against the wartime Army (most of which ironically concerned the AEF) which were ventilated after the war. Congress reflected this in its refusal to promote March to permanent four-star or even three-star rank. Thus he reverted to his regular major general's rank in June, 1920, and left office and retired a year later to oblivion as far as the public was concerned.

The role of American command and commanders changed in 1917–1918. The leading generals showed their skills as organizers and managers. There simply was not enough time for commanders to lead their divisions, corps, or armies long enough to evaluate them as long-term combat commanders. Yet it was difficult for both soldiers and civilians to accept that the outstanding American generals were what could be called desk officers. Indicative of this lack of understanding is that one Congressman in the spring of 1918 suggested that staff officers on duty in Washington be required to wear a white band on their sleeves. By the same token Harbord, who commanded the 2nd Division less than two weeks, including a total of two days in combat, was considered by Pershing and others a top-notch division commander—even though what happened to that division at Soissons under Harbord's command indicates that his talents were much better used as the logistical manager of the Services of Supply.

In World War II both soldiers and civilians were more sophisticated, so there was not the same lack of understanding of the role of a military commander. Then the war lasted long enough for a real testing of combat commanders. For these officers, that time of great transition from a Civil War army to a modern army—World War I—was a valuable training ground.

DONALD SMYTHE

ST.-MIHIEL

The Birth of
an American Army

*T*he United States entered World War I on April 6, 1917, but had no combat forces in the field until October. Indeed, the American contribution in terms of troops at the front remained limited until the middle of 1918. During June and July some American forces operated at divisional strength, but only as a part of even larger British and French organizations. Some of the battles during this period were critical; the American Second and Third Divisions played important roles in stopping the German offensive along the Marne River. The Second Division's attack on Belleau Wood as a part of an allied counterattack earned its units, particularly the marines, richly deserved praise.

Despite the honors won by American units in these actions, the goal of American political and military leaders remained the creation of an independent American army, operating in its own section of the front under its own commanders. Both President Woodrow Wilson and General John J. Pershing, commander of the American Expeditionary Force, were completely committed to achieving this. Pershing's stubborn insistence on it infuriated many British and French leaders, who hoped to use the fresh American units as replacements in their own armies. Pershing allowed American units to serve under foreign commanders in the summer of 1918 only when the threat of a German breakthrough posed an obvious danger to the entire front. When that German drive was stopped, in large part due to the efforts of American troops, Pershing renewed his demands for a totally American sector of the front. In August 1918 he finally got his wish when the First U.S. Army came into existence. Its first task would be the *elimination of the St.-Mihiel salient, a 200-square-mile bulge in the German trench lines southeast of Verdun.*

The following selection by the late Father Donald Smythe describes the First Army's preparations and assault on the St.-Mihiel salient. As Father Smythe points out, this attack was the first real test of the American army and of the American high command. The St.-Mihiel area had been a quiet sector for some time; the German forces within the salient were not thought to be high-caliber troops. Should the Americans fail to overcome the salient, or even suffer inordinately heavy losses, the British and French were immediately ready to renew their demands that American units be placed under their commanders. Such an outcome would not only be a shocking indictment of American military leadership, it would, as President Wilson knew, effectively deny the United States a voice during any later peace talks. Both politically and militarily, Pershing and the American high command had a lot riding on the outcome of their attack.

The Americans did not fail, as Father Smythe describes. Although it is true that the Germans, aware of the impending attack, had already begun withdrawing from the salient, it is also true that American troops moved far faster than either their allies or the enemy expected. The attack was a triumph. And, as Father Smythe suggests by the title of his essay, it marked a "birth" of sorts for the American army. Even though the attack on the salient did not always go smoothly—traffic jams held up movement of men and supplies, orders went astray or unread, some units did not perform up to Pershing's exacting standards—the final outcome ended British and French attempts to reduce the independent role of the American army, and gave the inexperienced American officers new self-confidence. From that time on, the American army had to be taken seriously. By extension, so did the United States.

Although Father Smythe's essay can be read simply as a narrative description of a World War I battle, it is better viewed as a study of a pivotal moment in the institutional history of the American military. Here, for the first time, American troops under American commanders faced, and defeated, the troops of a European enemy, and did so on European soil. The reader must ask what impact this had, both personally and professionally, upon American officers whose images and ideas about professional soldiering had long come from Europe. Consider, too, the leaders of this American army as described by Professor Coffman in the preceding essay. How well had their professional training prepared American officers for the demands of leading a large army in overseas operations?

Readers should also examine Professor Russell Weigley's essay on American strategic thought up through World War II, which appears later in this collection. Professor Weigley's arguments suggest that many American views about warmaking predate World War I, but experience in World War I helped bring some ideas into greater favor than ever before. How much did the success of St.-Mihiel contribute to these ideas, or to other American notions of war in the twentieth century? What lessons from World War I did the army carry into the remainder of the century? Was the Battle of St.-Mihiel truly, as Father Smythe suggests, the "birth" of an American army?

The year 1918 was in its final months. The United States had been at war for a year and a half, but until now efforts by the American Expeditionary Forces had been of limited significance on the western front. Not until October 1917 had its troops gone on line, and then only at the battalion level, in a quiet sector, as part of a French division. Not until January 1918 had one of its own divisions taken over a section of the front, again in a quiet sector. And not until May 1918 had it engaged in an offensive operation, and then on a limited scale—some 4000 men, a reinforced regiment, at Cantigny.

During the summer of 1918, American contributions to the Allied effort increased. The 2d and 3d Divisions helped block the German advance at Belleau Wood and Château-Thierry in June. The 3d Division earned the sobriquet "The Rock of the Marne" for its heroic stand at that river in July. The 1st and 2d Divisions helped spearhead the Allied counteroffensive in July against the Marne salient near Soissons, while other US divisions subsequently helped collapse the salient completely in July and August. But almost without exception, these divisions operated as part of Allied corps. No US army yet existed.

All that changed on 10 August when the American First Army, under the command of General John J. Pershing, became operational. Its first assignment was to reduce the St. Mihiel salient, a huge triangle jutting into Allied lines on the southern part of the front. The salient cut the Paris-Nancy railway and served as a possible jump-off point for a German flanking attack against Verdun to the west or Nancy to the east. It also served as an effective German bulwark against any Allied advance toward Metz or the vital Briey iron mines.

Reducing the salient had long been an American dream. Pershing had spoken of it to General Henri Philippe Pétain, head of the French Army, on first meeting him in June 1917. And then, in the fall of that year, a strategic study by GHQ staff officers recommended that it be the first US operation. Colonel Fox Conner, AEF Chief of Operations, confirmed this view in February 1918. Finally, on 24 June 1918, when General Ferdinand Foch, Allied generalissimo, met Pershing, Pétain, and Sir Douglas Haig, the British commander, to plan future offensives, Foch assigned reduction of the salient to the Americans.

At the end of August, however, just two weeks before the St. Mihiel attack was to take place, Foch suddenly proposed that the main American effort be directed not east against the salient, but north in the direction of Mezieres and Sedan, in an attack that eventually would become known as the Meuse-Argonne Operation.

A reluctant Pershing agreed to this proposal and thus committed himself to what was really too large an undertaking. An untested, and in many ways untrained, American Army was to engage in a great battle (St. Mihiel), disengage itself, and move 60 miles to another great battle (Meuse-Argonne)—all within the space of about two weeks, under a First Army staff that Pershing admitted was not perfect and, as of 2 September, had no inkling that the Meuse-Argonne Operation was even being contemplated. Army staffs normally required two to three months to produce a fully articulated battle plan with all its technical annexes. This staff—and again it must be emphasized that the staff was new, inexperienced, and untested—would have about three weeks. It was a formidable commitment, if not an impossible one, and it is not clear that Pershing should have undertaken it. Two of his four army corps had just been organized, while the army staff had no experience yet working as a team.

The alternative, however, was to leave the St. Mihiel salient bulging in the Allied lines, menacing the flank and rear of any army operating west of the Meuse River. Its reduction would eliminate the last German salient on the western front. Besides—and perhaps this was the major consideration—the Americans were all set to go.

★ ★ ★ ★ ★

The St. Mihiel salient was approximately 25 miles across and 16 miles deep, with its apex at St. Mihiel and its base anchored at Haudiomont and Pont-à-Mousson. It had been a quiet zone for most of four years. The Germans had settled down, planted vegetable gardens, and fathered children by local women.

They had also had time to construct some formidable defensive works: four or five zones with elaborately constructed trenches, shelters, barbed-wire entanglements, machine-gun nests, and artillery emplacements. The barbed wire seemed endless; in one place it ran 13 rows, some as deep as a room. A measure of the salient's strength, perhaps, was that after two strong but futile attacks in 1915 the French had been content to then leave it alone. Pershing called it "a great field fortress."

To be sure, it had some weaknesses. Like all salients, it was vulnerable to converging attacks from the sides. Perhaps because the salient had been quiet for so long, the Germans manned it with second- or third-class troops. Of the eight and one-half divisions assigned to its defense, one had recently arrived from Russia and was, by the Germans' own admission, "not reliable." Another was "completely worn out." A German noncom wrote home, "The men are so embittered that they have no interest in anything and they only want the war to end, no matter how."

Despite these German shortcomings, considerable pessimism existed in the Allied high command concerning the coming US attack. Sir Henry Wilson, Chief of the Imperial General Staff, told Lloyd Griscom, Pershing's liaison officer with the British, that he viewed the "premature" formation of the American Army with "great concern." Although the doughboys themselves were brave, American staff officers suffered from "incapacity and inexperience." One of two things would surely happen: the Americans would encounter heavy resistance and be stopped with "cruel losses," as the French had been; or, encountering light resistance, they would pursue and fall into a trap. Since the Americans were sure to make a mess of it, jeopardizing the cause, Wilson sent a special messenger to Foch to persuade him to cancel the operation. Foch refused to, although he did admit that the American Army was "inexperienced and immature."

Planning for the St. Mihiel operation, which was scheduled for 12 September 1918, went forward, both at First Army headquarters and at AEF GHQ. Because Pershing was busy as commander of both headquarters, he delegated considerable responsibility to the First Army Chief of Staff, Lieutenant Colonel Hugh Drum, a brilliant 38-year-old officer of wide staff experience who had been on Pershing's staff at Fort Sam Houston before the war. Fox Conner, AEF Operations Chief, loaned the First Army Lieutenant Colonel George C. Marshall, Jr., who had a reputation for working hard, being on top of things, and doing well whatever he was assigned to do. Marshall, then 37 years old, was a graduate of the Command and General Staff School at Fort Leavenworth, as were Conner and Drum. They understood the same language and worked well together.

The materiel buildup for the St. Mihiel operation had begun in August and was formidable: 3010 guns; 40,000 tons of ammunition; 65 evacuation trains; 21,000 beds for the sick and wounded; 15 miles of reconstructed roads using 100,000 tons of crushed stone; 45 miles of standard-gauge and 250 miles of light railway; 19 railhead depots for distributing food, clothing, and equipment; 120 water points that furnished 1,200,000 gallons a day; and a 38-circuit central switchboard with separate nets for command, supply, artillery, air service, utilities, and other functional areas. Maps alone for the operation weighed 15 tons.

Much of what was furnished had to be borrowed from the French and British, since priority shipments of infantry and machine gunners during the spring and summer from the United States had thrown the American Army thoroughly out of balance in matters of artillery, transportation, and needed services. Not one of the 3010 guns was of American manufacture, nor were any

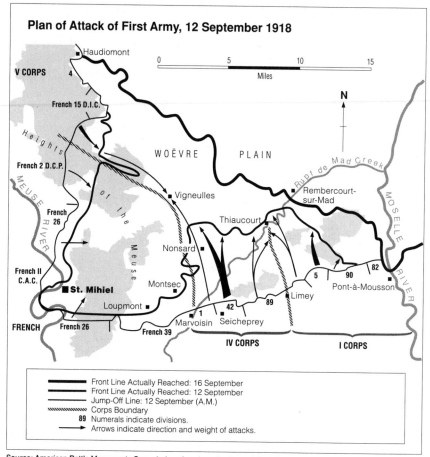

Plan of Attack of First Army, 12 September 1918

Front Line Actually Reached: 16 September
Front Line Actually Reached: 12 September
Jump-Off Line: 12 September (A.M.)
Corps Boundary
89 Numerals indicate divisions.
Arrows indicate direction and weight of attacks.

Source: American Battle Monuments Commission, *American Armies and Battlefields in Europe* (Washington, 1938), p. 109.

of the 267 tanks. The French provided virtually all the transportation and nearly half the artillerymen, tank crews, and airplanes. The air force, under Colonel Billy Mitchell, had 1400 planes—the largest air armada ever assembled to that time—but not one was American-built.

To use this mass of materiel, some two thirds of a million men—550,000 Americans and 110,000 Frenchmen—moved into position around the salient. The Americans gathered from all parts of the front: from the British Expeditionary Force, from the Château-Thierry area, from the Vosges—all joining Americans who had been stationed near the salient. Finally, 18 months after the nation had declared war, and more than a year after beginning its training and service with various other Allied units, the American Army was coming into being as a living, working organism.

★ ★ ★ ★ ★

Massing the subordinate elements of this new army for battle was difficult, for movement had to take place secretly and at night. In the dark, the roads swarmed with men, animals, trucks, guns, caissons, tanks, and every kind of impedimenta. During the day, the men hid in woods or billets and tried to catch what sleep they could. At night, they were on the road again, without lights, struggling forward in the direction of the salient. The American Army was moving up.

Or, rather, slogging up. The mud was incredible, and the continuing rain kept making more of it. Elmer Sherwood, a 42d (Rainbow) Division veteran, speculated that the only vehicles making their usual speed were the airplanes. Another soldier suggested that the American high command ought to substitute "submarines for tanks, ducks for carrier-pigeons, and alligators for soldiers." Grimy, slimy, wet, and cold, the troops cursed the mud; it got into clothes, hair, food, drink, and equipment. It was one of the agonies long remembered—sunny France!

The Order of Battle, from right to left, was as follows: the US I Corps (Hunter Liggett) with the 82d, 90th, 5th, and 2d Divisions. Then came the US IV Corps (Joseph T. Dickman) with the 89th, 42d, and 1st Divisions. The two corps lined up on the south face of the salient.

At the apex was the French II Colonial Corps with three French divisions (39th, 26th, and 2d Dismounted Cavalry).

On the west face of the salient was the US V Corps (George H. Cameron) with the 26th Division, part of the 4th, and the French 15th Colonial.

Against the German salient, then, Pershing was sending four corps, composed of four French and eight and one-half US divisions.

Strategically, the most important corps were those of Dickman and Cameron. Entrusted with the veteran 1st and 42d Divisions, Dickman was to hit from the south face and drive hard for Vigneulles, where he was to be met by Cameron driving in with the veteran 26th Division from the west face. The juncture of the two US forces would close the salient and bag the Germans inside it.

The attack on the south face by the IV Corps (Dickman) was designated as the primary attack, and that on the west face by the V Corps (Cameron) three hours later was to be the secondary attack. Supporting attacks would be delivered on the right shoulder by the I Corps (Liggett) and at the apex by the French corps.

Pershing was gambling not only on the new and untried First Army staff, but on two new corps commanders and four untested divisions. The new corps commanders were Dickman and Cameron, both promoted from divisional command after the Aisne-Marne campaign in July; they had been given less than a month to organize their headquarters and prepare for battle.

The four new divisions were the 5th, 82d, 89th, and 90th. Two of them, the 5th and 89th, were commanded by West Point classmates of Pershing, John E. McMahon and William M. Wright, while the 90th was headed by Henry T. Allen, who had been with Pershing in the Punitive Expedition in Mexico in 1916. These three divisions had received front-line training, either in the Vosges or near the salient. William P. Burnham's 82d, however, which had trained in the rear with the British, had no front-line experience. And none of the four, of course, had seen active combat operations yet.

The other five divisions were workhorses that Pershing knew he could depend upon. The 1st and 2d had spearheaded the Soissons counteroffensive on 18 July, as mentioned, and were ranked "excellent" with regard to training, equipment, and morale. The 4th, 26th, and 42d had seen hard fighting in the drive from Château-Thierry to the Vesle River. They too ranked high.

The 1st Division was under the capable Charles P. Summerall, a commander without peer; the 2d was under John A. Lejeune, former commander of its Marine Brigade; the 4th was under John L. Hines, Pershing's adjutant during the Punitive Expedition, who had come with him to Europe on the Baltic; the 42d was under Charles T. Menoher, another of Pershing's West Point classmates, and the 26th was under Clarence R. Edwards. Although Edwards was beloved by his men, many officers on Pershing's staff had serious doubts about his competence. Lejeune and Hines were new commanders, replacing James G. Harbord, who had gone to head the Services of Supply, and Cameron, who had moved up to command the V Corps.

In using the 1st, 2d, 4th, 26th, and 42d Divisions, Pershing was calling upon the best he had. Hoping to ensure the success of the St. Mihiel operation, he was leaving the cupboard quite bare of experienced front-line troops for the Meuse-Argonne operation, scheduled for two weeks later. He knew the risk, but there was little he could do about it. The decision to employ these experienced divisions had been made before Foch had suddenly sprung the Meuse-Argonne operation on him on 30 August. By that time all five divisions were so thoroughly committed to St. Mihiel that they could not be withdrawn from the operation.

In planning the attack, the First Army had counted on borrowing 300 heavy tanks from the British and 500 light tanks from the French, but when the time came the British could not spare the "heavies" and the French could furnish only 267 "lights," about which they were pessimistic. The muddy terrain, they said, would probably bog down the machines, which were none too reliable, and the deepest German trenches were eight feet across, a distance two feet wider than the tanks were able to span.

Brigadier General Samuel D. Rockenbach, AEF Chief of Tank Corps, and Lieutenant Colonel George S. Patton, Jr., a tank brigade commander, were nevertheless convinced that the tanks could advance, provided that the mud didn't get worse. Even though the small Renaults could not cross the deepest German trenches, they could effect initial surprise, crush the wire, and lead the infantry up to the first line of trenches. Then, if the trenches were too wide, the tanks could cross with the aid of pioneers. "You are going to have a walkover," Rockenbach assured Pershing.

★ ★ ★ ★ ★

On 10 September, two days before the attack, Pershing held a conference with his corps commanders and key members of their staffs concerning the preliminary artillery bombardment. Liggett and Dickman, hopeful of achieving tactical surprise, wanted no artillery preparation, unless continued rain inhibited the use of tanks. Cameron wanted a four-hour barrage. Major General Edward F. McGlachlin, Jr., First Army Chief of Artillery, was undecided, but inclined toward a 22-hour barrage. Lieutenant Colonels George C. Marshall, Jr., and Walter S. Grant, both on loan to First Army from AEF GHQ, urged an 18-hour preparation.

Pershing postponed a decision. It had been raining off and on all day, sometimes quite hard. That night he decided on no artillery preparation, then reversed himself the next morning, 11 September, and ordered a four-hour preparation on the southern face and a seven-hour bombardment on the western. The preparation fire would disconcert the enemy, give a psychological boost to the attackers, and insure that the wire was damaged if the tanks weren't able to get to it.

It kept raining on 11 September. Pershing wrote in his diary, "Luck seems to be against us." He worked at his headquarters all day, waiting for the attack; all his corps commanders said they were ready and confident of success.

The night of 11 September was jet black with steady rain. The artillery was in position, in some cases almost hub to hub, ominously silent. The troops were moved into the front lines at the last possible minute to achieve surprise. Sergeant William L. Langer, carrying ammunition in the trenches, found them practically empty at 2000 hours, but a short time later they were crowded with infantrymen, waiting apprehensively for the dawn.

Precisely at 0100 hours on 12 September, thousands of cannon fired simultaneously. Light belched from their muzzles, flaming out so frequently up and down the line that one soldier read the *Stars and Stripes* newspaper by the glare. Sergeant Langer compared the noise "to what one hears beneath a wooden bridge when a heavy vehicle passes overhead."

Watching the preliminary bombardment, Pershing found the scene both "picturesque and terrible." He exulted that now, at last, after 18 months of effort, an American army was a living reality, "fighting under its own flag." Yet how many men would die on that day—American, French, German.

In the trenches, cold, wet, and miserable men huddled over their rifles, shocked by the thunder of cannon, gazing with frightened fascination at the weirdly illuminated landscape, lit up as they had never seen it before. "Will I still be alive a few hours from now?" each must have wondered.

The artillery fire was directed at German command posts, rail lines and junctions, trenches, and wire. It was not terribly effective, but it did, as Pershing had hoped, give a psychological boost to the waiting infantrymen, especially those who had not heard so much artillery before.

At 0500 hours the whistles blew. All along the front, men took a tight grip on their rifles, clambered up the wood ladders out of the trenches, and went "over the top."

Watching from a commanding height at old Fort Gironville, Pershing could not see clearly because of the drizzling rain and mist, but he followed the advance by watching the explosions of the rolling barrage. He hoped that the infantry was right behind.

The first thing they encountered was the barbed wire. The artillery had taken out some of it, but not much, because of the shortness of the preliminary bombardment. But trained teams of pioneers and engineers were in the lead, armed with axes, wire cutters, and bangalore torpedoes (long tin or sheet-iron tubes containing TNT). Fortunately, German counterbarrage fire was weak, giving them time to cut holes in the wire.

The infantry rushed through the gaps or, where there were none, used American ingenuity to pass. Leading platoons carried chickenwire, which, thrown across the top of the German wire, formed a bridge. Where chickenwire was lacking and the German wire was thick and low, the doughboys simply vaulted up on top of it and ran across, somewhat like a kid crossing a stream by jumping from rock to rock.

The advance went well, especially on the south face, paced by the veteran 1st, 2d, and 42d Divisions, to which Pershing had assigned the open terrain so they could flank the wooded areas, which had been assigned to the four new divisions.

"Get forward, there," Wild Bill Donovan yelled to his Rainbow Division men; "what the hell do you think this is, a wake?"

It was almost exactly that for Terry de la Mesa Allen of the 90th Division. Shot in the mouth, teeth missing, blood running down his face, he helped wipe out a machine-gun nest before loss of blood sent him to a first-aid station. In World War II Allen would command the 1st Division in North Africa and Sicily.

Some incidents were bizarre. Sergeant Harry J. Adams of the 89th Division saw a German run into a dugout at Bouillonville. The American had only two shots left in his pistol, so he fired them both through the door and called for the man to surrender. The door opened, and the German came out, followed by another, and another, and another, and another, and another—some 300 in all! Amazed, Adams marched the whole contingent back toward the rear, covering them with his empty pistol. Americans who saw them coming thought at first it was a German counterattack.

Other incidents seemed equally unbelievable. The 2d Division captured prisoners from 57 different German units—an impossible melange. It was found that they were from all over the western front, sent to Thiaucourt to attend a machine-gun school there.

★ ★ ★ ★ ★

Much of the ease with which the Americans advanced was due to an earlier German decision to evacuate the salient, orders having been given to that effect on 10 September. Some materiel had already been withdrawn, and more was in the process of moving when the Americans struck.

The attack thus caught the Germans embarrassingly *in via*. There were units that had practically no artillery in position, and those that did were almost out of ammunition. The German defenders were certainly not of a diehard type, as Sergeant Adams discovered when he marched in his 300 prisoners with an empty pistol. Thus it was Pershing's luck to attack a salient that the Germans were just about to hand over to him anyway, capturing without heavy losses positions which if stoutly defended would have heaped up American corpses. A wag described St. Mihiel as the battle "where the Americans relieved the Germans."

By the afternoon, troops on the southern face of the salient had reached their objectives; by evening, they were one day ahead of schedule. On the west face, progress was slower, the 26th Division being delayed by the failure of the French 15th Colonial to keep up on its left. Some of its own units on the right of the line, however, had projected a long finger into the German lines pointing toward Vigneulles; through that town ran the main road of escape out of the salient. Pershing picked up the phone and ordered Cameron and Dickman to move toward Vigneulles "with all possible speed."

Pushing hard under "Hiking Hiram" Bearss, a regiment of the 26th Division reached Vigneulles at 0215 hours; some four hours later a regiment of the 1st Division closed from the east. The main road out of the salient was now cut; the mouth of the bag was squeezed shut.

On 13 September the advance continued from the south and west, wiping out the salient and stopping at the line agreed upon by Pershing at his 2 September conference with Foch. Local operations continued until the 16th, consolidating positions for defense, while the First Army prepared to pull out and head for the Meuse-Argonne operation. It had captured 450 guns and 16,000 prisoners, at a cost of only 7000 casualties.

The operation reduced the salient, restored 200 square miles of French territory, freed the Paris-Nancy railroad, opened water transportation on the Meuse, and secured the right flank of the First Army for its coming operation in the Meuse-Argonne. It also paved the way for a possible future attack against Metz, the Briey-Longwy industrial complex, and a crucial railroad supplying the Germans to the northwest.

Finally, and perhaps most important, it demonstrated that the American Army was able to successfully handle an operation of some magnitude. As the British *Manchester Guardian* put it:

> It is as swift and neat an operation as any in the war, and perhaps the most heartening of all its features is the proof it gives that the precision, skill, and imagination of American leadership is not inferior to the spirit of the troops.

Actually, American success came a bit too easily at St. Mihiel, engendering perhaps an unwarranted optimism and confidence similar to that which afflicted the South after the first Battle of Bull Run. Knowing that the salient was to be evacuated anyway, German soldiers abandoned their positions more readily than they might otherwise have done. Even as it was, they delayed the First Army long enough to allow most of the defenders to escape before the jaws of the pincers closed.

On the afternoon of 13 September, Pétain came to Pershing's headquarters and together they visited the town of St. Mihiel. Ecstatic at their deliverance after four years of German occupation, the people—mostly women, children, and old men—crowded around them waving little French flags. Graciously, Pétain explained to the people that although the French had taken the city, they served as part of the American First Army, whose soldiers had made victory possible by their attacks on the shoulders of the salient.

Tremendously elated by the victory, Pershing felt that it vindicated his insistence on building a separate American army. "We gave 'em a damn good licking, didn't we?" he remarked. On the evening of 13 September, when receiving the congratulations of Dennis Nolan, AEF Chief of Intelligence, Pershing rose from his desk and, pacing the floor, gave the most eloquent tribute to the American soldier that Nolan had ever heard. Going back into history, Pershing remarked

> how wave after wave of Europeans, dissatisfied with conditions in Europe, came to [America] to seek liberty; how . . . those who came had the willpower and the spirit to seek opportunity in a new world rather than put up with unbearable conditions in the old; that those who came for that reason were superior in initiative to those,

their relatives, who had remained and submitted to the conditions; that in addition to this initial superiority in initiative they had developed, and their children had developed, under a form of government and in a land of great opportunity where individual initiative was protected and rewarded . . . .

As a consequence,

we had developed a type of manhood superior in initiative to that existing abroad, which given approximately equal training and discipline, developed a superior soldier to that existing abroad.

Flushed with success, with an American army in being and growing daily more important, Pershing faced the future not only with confidence but with higher aspirations. With American soldiers flooding into France, the day would not be far off when the American Army would be larger than either the French or the British. "And when that time comes," he told George Van Horn Moseley, AEF Supply Chief, "an American should command the Allied Army."

The St. Mihiel victory left Pershing in a jaunty mood. When the British Prime Minister, David Lloyd George, telegraphed his congratulations from a sickbed, saying that the news was better than any physic, Pershing answered: "It shall be the endeavor of the American Army to supply you with occasional doses of the same sort of medicine as needed."

The witty Harbord, who had once commanded the 2d Division, pointed out in his congratulatory message that nearly 300 years before on the same date, 13 September, Oliver Cromwell had led his Ironsides into battle quoting Psalm 68. It seemed remarkably apropos to Pershing's recent success: "Let God arise and let His enemies be scattered; let them also that hate Him. Like as the smoke vanishes so shalt thou drive them away." Pershing answered: "Your old division might well be termed The Ironsides, though I doubt whether they went to battle quoting Psalm 68."

Public German reaction to the American victory was of the sour-grapes variety. Newspapers and the official German communique pointed out that Germany had planned to evacuate the salient anyway, and that the troops had retired in good order to previously prepared positions. Privately, however, the German High Command was considerably upset. Though intending to evacuate, they had not wished to do so until absolutely necessary. And although most of the defenders had gotten out, considerable stores had been either captured or destroyed in place to preclude seizure. General Max von Gallwitz, the Army Group Commander, had warned Lieutenant General Fuchs, commanding Army Detachment C opposite Pershing, "not to concede an easy success, particularly since we are dealing with Americans." Despite that warning, in 48 hours the Americans had wiped out a four-year salient twice unsuccessfully attacked by the French.

Eric von Ludendorff, who functioned as the supreme German commander, was terribly disturbed. A German officer who visited him the night of 12 September found him "so overcome by the events of the day as to be unable to carry on a clear and comprehensive discussion." Field Marshal Paul von Hindenburg, the titular German Commander in Chief, called 12 September a "severe defeat," which rendered Gallwitz's situation "critical."

★ ★ ★ ★ ★

In later years a number of people believed that the Americans might have achieved an even greater victory had the First Army been allowed to keep moving east. Douglas MacArthur was among them. On the night of 13–14 September, MacArthur, a brigade commander in the 42d Division, stole through the enemy lines in the direction of Mars-la-Tour and, ten miles to the east, studied the key German fortress at Metz through binoculars. From this reconnaissance and from interrogation of prisoners, he concluded that Metz was "practically defenseless," its garrison having been temporarily withdrawn to fight on other fronts. MacArthur immediately requested that he be permitted to attack Metz with his brigade, promising to be in the city hall "by nightfall."

The request was denied. The St. Mihiel offensive was a limited operation and had already achieved its objective. Further advance ran the risk of overinvolving the American Army, already committed to a new and even greater operation on a different front some two weeks hence.

MacArthur believed that this failure to push on toward Metz was "one of the great mistakes of the war." Although at the time Pershing believed that he had no choice other than to keep St. Mihiel a limited operation in order to be on schedule for the Meuse-Argonne attack, he would come to share MacArthur's view.

Hunter Liggett, however, put the matter in a different light. Liggett claimed that taking Metz was possible "only on the supposition that our army was a well-oiled, fully coordinated machine, which it was not as yet." Even doing its damnedest, the First Army "had an excellent chance of spending the greater part of the winter mired in the mud of the Woëvre, flanked both to the east and the west."

Liggett, the I Corps commander in this operation, and later First Army commander, knew what he was talking about when he said that the Army was not well oiled and coordinated. American infantry fired at their own planes. Further, when encountering machine-gun nests, many seemed to have no sense of how to take cover. Instead of hugging the ground and crawling forward, they charged recklessly across open spaces or fell back walking bolt upright.

Artillery fire was delayed and slow to adjust during the rolling barrages, holding up the infantry, and then the artillery was slow in displacing cannon forward, so that the infantry outstripped it during the advance. Despite the fact that the terrain furnished excellent observation posts, the artillery fired by map rather than by direct observation, using ammunition extravagantly and inefficiently.

Discipline was lax. When halted, men tended to get out of ranks and disperse, becoming stragglers. Pilfering of prisoners was almost universal. Animals were misused, abused, or not used at all. During traffic jams, instead of dismounting and resting both horses and men, the riders slouched in their saddles for hours. Animal-drawn ambulances, vitally needed at the front for transportation over muddy roads that were impassable for motor transport, were used in one division for evacuating field hospitals in the rear. And when telephone lines went dead, instead of using a horse relay system that would have provided quick, practical service over roads impassable to vehicles, commanders simply remained out of touch.

Command headquarters were too far to the rear and inadequately marked. One staff officer carrying an important message wandered for hours before he could find either one of a division's two brigade headquarters, although he was not far from either.

Divisions issued wordy orders, full of contingent clauses and appendices, repeating information available in standard manuals and prescribing detailed formations, even down to battalion level. Most subordinate commanders and their staffs probably never even read them.

The traffic jams were monumental. Patton's gas trucks took 32 hours to cover nine miles on 13 September. Two days later Georges Clemenceau, the French Premier, was caught in a jam so huge that it confirmed all his fears about US incapacity to handle large forces. "I had warned them beforehand," he wrote in his memoirs.

> They wanted an American Army. They had it. Any one who saw, as
> I saw, the hopeless congestion at Thiaucourt will bear witness that
> they may congratulate themselves on not having had it sooner.

Indeed, the very day MacArthur recommended a further advance, his division's Chief of Staff was complaining that because of logistical problems the men were not being adequately fed and clothed.

Far from being impressed by the American effort, many felt that it revealed serious deficiencies that boded ill for the future. "The Americans have not yet had sufficient experience," said a German intelligence report, "and are accordingly not to be feared in a great offensive. Up to this time our men have had too high an opinion of the Americans."

The decision to terminate the St. Mihiel offensive as planned was undoubtedly sound. Apart from the fact that striking out toward Metz might have enmeshed the First Army in a fight from which it could not readily disentangle itself in time to meet its Meuse-Argonne commitment, and apart from the fact that Pershing had already, with Pétain's permission, pushed beyond Foch's original boundaries for a "limited offensive," the American Army was as yet new and largely untested. It was better to take one sure step with success than to attempt to run before one was ready, and stumble.

DEAN C. ALLARD

ANGLO-AMERICAN NAVAL DIFFERENCES DURING WORLD WAR I

British military writer Sir John Slessor once remarked that "war without allies is bad enough—with allies it is pure hell!" Slessor was being witty, but he was expressing a sentiment that staff officers might easily agree with. It is never easy to settle on strategic goals and plans; interservice rivalries alone can create many points of contention, and conflicts are compounded when discussions begin with allies. They will not only have all their own inter- and intraservice conflicts, but differences of philosophy and national interest will inevitably create further conflicts over strategic plans.

In this regard it may be fortunate that the United States was not directly involved in coalition warfare until the twentieth century. From the end of the American Revolution to American entry into World War I, we went our own way and fought our own wars. For well over a century, American military and political leaders could frame policies and goals without the need to accommodate foreign interests and war aims.

Beginning with American entry into World War I, however, that isolation changed. Ever since 1917, American military leaders have had to take allied interests, aims, abilities, and perspectives into account. Many times, this has been a difficult task.

In the following essay, Dr. Dean Allard of the U.S. Naval Historical Center examines some of the most important issues that faced the American navy during World War I as naval officials attempted to cooperate with our British allies. As Allard points out, some American naval officers, especially Admiral William Sims, were eager to cooperate and shared many ideas with their British counterparts. Others, however, including several of Admiral Sims' superiors in Washington, did not accept the British perspective quite so easily. The result was a serious dispute over the proper role for the U.S. Navy, carried out within the navy as well as between the Royal Navy and our own people. Although the term "allies" suggests a commonality of purpose and a sharing of responsibilities, Allard makes clear that in the Anglo-American naval effort these were often conspicuous by their absence.

The American navy of 1917 was, in relative terms, a newcomer. A large and powerful force by any measure in 1865, the Navy declined sharply in size and strength during the next fifteen years. In 1889 the American navy ranked twelfth in the world in number of warships behind not only Britain, Germany, Russia, France, and Italy, but also Holland, Turkey, China, Norway, and the Austro-Hungarian Empire. In later years, naval historians blamed this humbling situation solely on a penny-pinching Congress, but there were mitigating circumstances. For one thing, naval technology changed at an incredible rate during the last years of the nineteenth century. It was widely known that steam would replace sails, and navies were moving rapidly toward new types of engines; armor plate was changing rapidly, too, partly in response to changes in gun manufacture that made large, breech-loading rifled guns of unparalleled hitting power a reality. The truth was, for much of the period prior to 1900, naval architecture was in a constant state of change, and many warships were obsolete before they were even finished. Thus, for all its apparent lack of progress, the U.S. Navy was far less "behind" than it seemed when Congress began authorizing the construction of steel-and-steam warships. Modern studies of the navy during the last quarter of the nineteenth century suggest, in fact, that the navy was far more appropriate to its role during those years than was noted either by historians of the early twentieth century, or by many naval officers of the time.

For the American navy, things began to change in the 1880s with congressional authorization of the first steel vessels and the founding, by Admiral Stephen B. Luce, of the Naval War College at Newport, Rhode Island, in 1884. Luce gathered a number of bright, young, and articulate officers at the school—including Captain Alfred Thayer Mahan, who became the second president of the college and the world's chief theorist of seapower. In 1890 Mahan, the son of West Point's Dennis H. Mahan, published his lectures on the history of naval warfare as The Influence of Seapower Upon History, 1660–1783. It was a worldwide bestseller, and it convinced many Americans, both in and out of the navy, that the United States needed a large fleet that could help project American power overseas.

The first test for the still-small "modern" American navy was the Spanish-American War of 1898. The result was apparent vindication of the theories of the articulate supporters of Mahan; in the Philippines an American squadron under Commodore George Dewey destroyed the Spanish flotilla in Manila Bay, and a few weeks later the American fleet commanded by William Sampson utterly annihilated a Spanish fleet along the coast of Cuba. In the words of Professor Ronald Spector, these stunning victories were the culmination of a decade of "ideological triumph," and this was reflected in the continued growth of the American fleet between 1900 and 1917.

One of the young officers brought to prominence in the aftermath of the Spanish-American War was Captain William Sims. Graduated from the Naval Academy at Annapolis in 1880, Sims was a reform-minded officer who came into conflict with the established bureaus of the navy in the 1890s when he criticized the designs of American warships. In 1902, angered at the opposition of his superiors to a new, more accurate method of gun-aiming, he wrote directly to President Theodore Roosevelt. As a result, Captain Sims became inspector of target practice. Sims' actions were not atypical of the younger officers who shared his views. Some joined Sims in writing directly to the president, while others simply leaked information to the press. On occasion they won the ensuing dispute. Sometimes they did not. In either case, they demonstrated both a refusal to accept tradition and a willingness to make enemies.

In March 1917 Sims went to London to coordinate American naval efforts with those of the Royal Navy and other potential allies. Told by the British that the German submarine offensive was rapidly driving them to ruin, Sims urgently demanded that the U.S. Navy take a larger and more active role in the war than planners had originally foreseen. Sims' ideas reflected British thinking, but they did not reflect the priorities of the American building program. In the ensuing debate, President Woodrow Wilson sided with Sims. As a result the United States sent only one squadron of battleships to European waters, concentrating instead on destroyers and submarine chasers. As Professor Allard notes, the British anticipated using these vessels solely as auxiliaries to their fleet and Sims was willing to allow this. His superiors in Washington, however, had different ideas.

On one level, Professor Allard's essay might be read simply as an example of the kinds of disagreements that often occur between allies as they attempt to reconcile conflicting doctrines in the search for a common course of action against the foe. However, the episode he describes has other, and perhaps more important implications. During World War I, and afterward, American naval officers not only argued with their British allies, they argued among themselves. On one hand were Admiral Benson and his supporters, mostly part of the existing bureaucracy; on the other was Admiral Sims, a man already demonstrably impatient with superiors who did not agree with him. Where should the line be drawn? Was Sims correct in continuing to argue with his superiors, in support of the British position? Were Benson and the other members of the Naval Board the reactionaries they are sometimes labeled? When armies and navies fight as part of allied groups, they face problems they do not have to face when acting independently. Readers might compare, for example, General John J. Pershing's attitude about allied control over his troops with Admiral Sims' approach. What made their attitudes so different? What factors made the situations different for each man?

Finally, the reader might look at Martin Van Creveld and Martin Blumenson's essays later in this collection. Both men write about the Allied invasion of France during World War II, and both describe the many compromises that had to be made to carry out the D-Day operation. Professor Allard, too, makes clear that compromises are often necessary, and they may be necessary within one's own military as often as they are with *the military of an ally. But can such compromises also alter the political or economic goals a nation seeks in war? When, and upon what premises, should national leaders refuse to compromise what they see as the national interest?*

Anglo-American military cooperation in World War I has been the subject of a number of historical works. Scholars such as David Trask have demonstrated, for example, that the United States accepted the grand strategy of the Allies in which the focus of the land campaign was on the Western Front while the all-important naval mission was the Royal Navy's blockade of the continent. Other writers have described the high level of tactical cooperation achieved in the war zone between American and Allied forces, including the notably harmonious joint United States-British destroyer patrol operating from Queenstown, Ireland.

But while cooperation was evident, there also were significant differences between the Allies and the United States that influenced the shape of America's military contributions and reflected the nation's outlook toward the conflict as a whole. This article will discuss several areas of tension that particularly involved American and British naval efforts. In developing this theme, the contrasting views of Washington officials and Admiral William S. Sims also will be explored. This is necessary since Sims, the well-known, popular, and effective American naval commander in Europe, substantially shared the perspective of Great Britain. In fact, the admiral based his entire approach to the war on his long-held belief that American and British security interests were identical. Sims also recognized the unequaled Royal Navy as the dominant naval factor in the conflict and the leader of all other Allied maritime forces. As a consequence, it was his opinion that the task of the United States fleet should be to augment British operations and most particularly to aid in defeating the German submarine counter-blockade of the British Isles.

Although Sims' outlook has sometimes been seen as typifying the American Navy's approach to the war, his concepts were not shared by officials in Washington who framed the nation's naval policy. These leaders included Rear Admiral Charles J. Badger, chairman of the influential advisory body known as the General Board; Secretary of the Navy Josephus Daniels; and President Woodrow Wilson himself. The central figure, however, was Admiral William S. Benson, the Chief of Naval Operations, who under the direction of Secretary Daniels was responsible for the "operations of the fleet" and the preparation of "plans for its use in war."

Benson has sometimes been viewed as an Anglophobe, but he might more accurately be described as a nationalist who trusted no state's benevolent intentions. This austere and relatively little-known naval officer was noted for integrity, loyalty to political superiors, and his sympathy for Wilsonian idealism. Although lacking the popular reputation of Sims, Benson obviously shared with the European commander the objective of military victory. Where Benson differed was in refusing to set aside other considerations in responding to the needs of the Royal Navy or any other ally. He once described his attitude in these words: "My first thought in the beginning, during, and always, was to see first that our coasts and our own vessels and our own interests were safeguarded. Then . . . to give everything we had . . . for the common cause. . . ." At another point, the Chief of Naval Operations revealed his feelings of Wilsonian independence by commenting that, "It is difficult and really impossible for me to state [when] I felt that we must be involved with the Allies. . . . In fact, I do not know that I ever fully came to that conclusion."

As indicated by Benson, the defense needs of the United States received priority consideration. Upon America's entry into the war, the Admiral's conviction that German submarines would launch operations in the Western Hemisphere—an estimate based on U-boat activities off the East Coast earlier in the conflict—led him to establish a patrol force of destroyers and other light craft to safeguard the American continent. To the British and Admiral Sims, however, these steps seemed almost entirely unnecessary since they saw submarine operations in American waters as unlikely and, if they occurred, as diversions of little military consequence. At the same time, Sims, deeply concerned that the U-boats would force the United Kingdom to her knees, was calling for the urgent dispatch of American patrol forces to Europe.

When the German submarine threat in American waters did not materialize during the Spring of 1917, the General Board and planning officers in Benson's office supported Sims' position that the United States should assign all possible anti-submarine ships to support the defense of Great Britain. As a result, over the next two months, about 70 percent of America's small force of modern destroyers was deployed to Queenstown, Ireland. Here, Sims assigned the ships to the operational control of the Royal Navy which primarily employed them in protecting Allied merchant vessels in the danger zone surrounding the British Isles.

This early deployment appeared to indicate that the American Navy's anti-submarine forces would serve as an auxiliary to the British Fleet, a development that was entirely consistent with the thinking of Admiral Sims. But Sims soon was to be disappointed. Throughout the Summer of 1917, and indeed until the end of the war, the admiral was critical of the Navy Department for retaining a relatively small number of destroyers and other light craft in American waters for coastal defense. But, of more fundamental importance, Washington naval authorities soon began to stress the use of their anti-submarine units for a basically different mission than the protection of mercantile convoys supplying Great Britain.

This shift in emphasis began as early as the Summer of 1917 when the Navy Department became convinced that England would survive despite the enemy's submarine attacks. The German U-boat offensive had become less effective by that time, but American planners also concluded that the crisis depicted by Sims and the British earlier in 1917 had been exaggerated. If a national collapse actually had been imminent, they noted that the far superior Royal Navy had upwards of 300 destroyers, including more than a hundred with its Grand Fleet that were not directly committed to the anti-submarine campaign. In contrast, the American Navy entered the war with 51 modern destroyers and, even after a major building program, could claim a total of only 107 by November 1918.

★ ★ ★ ★ ★

It was also in the middle months of 1917 that American leaders recognized the feasibility and need of a national army in Europe. As a result, the United States Navy became responsible for the massive task of transporting the American troops and munitions that would allow America's land power to be exerted on the Western Front. As early as May 1917, the President indicated his personal concern with this effort by cautioning the Navy to reserve enough destroyers from Queenstown to protect troop movements to the ports of western France. In the same month, Wilson took the unusual step of personally reviewing and approving a technical military plan for the safeguarding of such convoys. When it appeared that neither British officials nor Sims recognized the urgency of establishing a sizable American land force on the continent, Washington officials sent repeated instructions to Sims to assign American ships based in the United Kingdom to the primary task of protecting the lines of communication to France, as opposed to their original mission of guarding cargo convoys supporting the British Isles. Sims, however, was not personally convinced of that priority until the Summer of 1918.

In April 1918, as it became evident that the Allies faced a grave crisis on the Western Front, Great Britain at last recognized the importance of American ground reinforcements. At that time and throughout the remaining months of the war, the British finally made available from their unmatched inventory of passenger liners a significant volume of shipping for the transportation of the U.S. Army. As a consequence, and ironically considering the nationalistic outlook of the Navy Department, a slightly larger number of American troops eventually was carried to Europe in English bottoms than in American vessels. Nevertheless, the American Navy was responsible for delivering without a single casualty more than 900,000, or 46 percent, of the two million Army personnel sent to the Continent.

These operations in support of the land campaign involved a large fleet that was based largely in the United States. Forty-one troop transports, operated by the Navy, formed the core of this force. Protecting the liners on their Atlantic passage were some 30 destroyers—which Sims would have preferred to have had under his command in Europe—the majority of America's 31 cruisers, and late in the war a number of older battleships. In addition, approximately 350 cargo ships operated by the Naval Overseas Transportation Service were used primarily to carry military supplies to the Continent. A notable supplement to the more than 450 trans-Atlantic escort and transport vessels was a group of 85 ships homeported in Brest, France, under the command of an American flag officer, that protected American ships on the final leg of their passage to Western Europe. Setting aside the force at Brest, no more than approximately 275 of the Navy's other 1500 units and fewer than 15 percent of the Navy's personnel were in eastern Atlantic and Mediterranean waters at the time of the Armistice.

The organization of the ships committed to the projection of American land power to the Continent indicated that the Navy Department was as sensitive to the amalgamation of its units into European formations as General Pershing was in regard to American ground forces. The Queenstown destroyers and a squadron of battleships that eventually operated with the Grand Fleet were under British operational control. However, the escort units based outside the British danger zone, including those operating from the French coast, were exclusively in an American chain of command. In contrast to the mercantile convoys proceeding from the United States to the United Kingdom, which were under British strategic direction, the troop convoys that sailed to the Continent also were entirely American operations.

Following the war, in reviewing the American Navy's overall contributions, Admiral Benson concluded that the "major part" played was in "getting our troops and munitions and supplies over there." He differentiated these operations from the general defeat of the German submarine, stating that even if the U-boat campaign had been maintained at its "maximum," the American Army would have been established successfully in France due to the exceptional measures taken by the United States in protecting the troop convoys. Captain William Veazie Pratt, Benson's capable assistant in Washington, also felt that the service's key mission had been to support the land component of Allied grand strategy, focusing on the Western Front, rather than augmenting the naval campaign undertaken primarily by the Royal Navy. He asserted that "our great naval contribution to the war lay not in the fighting ships we could throw to the front, but in our ability to mobilize and transport America's great reserve power quickly to the European war front. . . ." Pratt, with his usual astuteness, contrasted this effort with the perspective of the Royal Navy and Admiral Sims by pointing out that "The impelling reason of the British was protection to food and war supplies in transit. Our basic reason was protection to our own military forces in crossing the seas."

★ ★ ★ ★ ★

During 1917, the Navy Department was concerned with another aspect of American security that was tangential to the British maritime campaign in Europe. Upon its entry into the war, the United States became associated with Japan, Britain's long-time ally. But, despite the fact that the United States and Japan were now co-belligerents, President Wilson remained suspicious of the Pacific power. There was even greater apprehension by American strategists who bore in mind, for example, the Japanese seizure during 1914 of positions in the Marshall, Caroline, and Mariana Islands, a development which obviously endangered American lines of communication to the Far East. The two-ocean challenge perceived by U.S. planners was revealed in a proposal made by Admiral Benson's office in February 1917 to deploy American capital ships to the Pacific where their "potential as a fleet in being might be used to the best political advantage." This deployment was not made, especially due to the department's assessment early in the war that Britain might well collapse, a contingency that could lead to a German surface fleet assault in the Western Hemisphere. The threat was connected with Japan in an April 1917 study by Admiral Badger's General Board which noted that, in addition to the short-term danger in the Pacific, consideration had to be given to a hostile alliance between Japan and Germany in a "war resulting from the present one." In the following month, the advisory body recommended to the Secretary of the Navy that every effort be made to embroil Japan in combat on the Eastern Front since the prospects of German-Japanese cooperation"will be minimized on account of the resulting antagonism." During the Summer of 1917, attention also was given to reports that the British were planning to transfer capital ships to bolster Japan's already formidable fleet. These rumors were particularly alarming since the United States had elected to defer battleship construction for the balance of the war in order to concentrate on building anti-submarine and merchant vessels.

The various aspects of the Japanese problem received concentrated attention in October 1917 when the General Board held hearings on a British request that a squadron of battleships join the Grand Fleet. The Board's witnesses indicated that American confidence in short-term Japanese intentions was a precondition to the commitment to European waters of any part of the battle fleet which, up to that point, had been carefully reserved in home waters. Captain Pratt noted, for example, that the initial decision to hold the battleships on the east coast had resulted from the "unsettled state" of the "far Eastern Question." The captain added, however, that he now had been reassured by Viscount Ishii's mission to Washington. Therefore, Pratt urged that the requested dreadnoughts be sent to Europe, especially since he hoped that Japan would imitate America's example by sending her own reinforcements to the war zone.

Another witness at the hearings, Captain Frank H. Schofield, also saw the dispatch of American battleships to European waters in the context of American-Japanese relations. In his view, this move would indicate the good will of the United States to Japan. It also would place Great Britain in America's debt, thus deflecting the British from transferring ships or offering other assistance to Japan that might threaten American interests.

Benson did not immediately agree with Pratt's and Schofield's position, since he continued to feel that the battle fleet should be kept together to meet the anticipated postwar challenge of Japan and Germany, a belief fueled by his pessimism that the Allies could achieve a decisive victory over the Central Powers. But later that Fall, as the Lansing-Ishii Agreement was signed which appeared to commit Japan to the *status quo* in China, Japanese-American tensions declined in the Pacific. Most U.S. ships were moved to the Atlantic, and apparently congenial relations developed as the remaining American units cooperated with the Japanese and British in patrolling that vast ocean area. In November 1917, Benson also departed for Europe as a member of the House Mission for the purpose of discussing the war effort with the Allies. While there he at last concluded that Japan's immediate intentions and—as will be discussed later—his desire to promote an offensive campaign against German submarines, indicated that the American battleships could be assigned to the Grand Fleet. In the following month these four dreadnoughts, later joined by a fifth unit, crossed the Atlantic and reported to the British command. They represented about a fourth of America's modern battleships.

Thus, after eight months of American participation in the European war, American fleet deployments were no longer constrained by the immediate threat of Japan and her potential allies. Yet Washington officials, who along with their Allied counterparts were deeply concerned with national interests in the postwar era, continued to fear aggression by Japan at a later date. These apprehensions were reinforced by the limited naval and military forces actually sent to Europe by Japan and the distinct possibility until the latter part of 1918 that Germany could emerge from the conflict with her fleet intact. Very late in the war, as it became evident that the Central Powers were on the verge of collapse, the specter of a Japanese-German combination was replaced by a possible hostile alliance between the fleets of Great Britain and Japan, a situation that influenced Wilson and his naval leaders in opposing the distribution of German warships to the Allies. All of these considerations obviously prevented American naval leaders from riveting exclusive attention on the Royal Navy's campaign in Europe.

★ ★ ★ ★ ★

In the light of this sometimes detached perspective, it is paradoxical that another fundamental difference between Anglo-American naval policies involved United States efforts to initiate a vigorous offensive in European waters.

From the earliest days of American participation in the war, Admiral Benson and Josephus Daniels expressed profound disapproval of British anti-submarine efforts, which they considered to be lethargic and essentially defensive. Although eventually accepting such measures as convoying, Washington officials emphasized the critical importance of attacking enemy submarines in their home ports, or otherwise preventing them from reaching the high seas where the tasks of detection and destruction were greatly compounded. By the Summer of 1917, Washington proposed to British authorities that a massive mine barrier be placed across the North Sea as the first element of this campaign. In August, Admiral Henry T. Mayo, Commander-in-Chief of the U.S. Atlantic Fleet, was dispatched to Britain to discuss this scheme as well as further measures to prevent the U-boats from proceeding to their attack areas.

Woodrow Wilson personally spurred these efforts to impress the American way of war on the campaign against the German submarine. In July he forwarded a well-known message to Sims demanding the formulation of bold plans supplementing British methods, which the President noted "do not seem to us effective." Nevertheless, Sims' response indicated that he shared the Royal Navy's pessimism regarding the feasibility of offensive schemes. A month later, Wilson delivered his famous "Hornet's Nest" speech to officers of the Atlantic Fleet calling for an attack on the nests, or bases, from which the submarines operated. Prior to Mayo's departure on his European mission, the President reiterated this position to the admiral and added the important requirement that the United States take the "lead" and "be the senior partner in a successful naval campaign."

Mayo's discussion with the British came at a time when pressures for a more aggressive approach were growing within British circles. This combination of factors led the First Sea Lord, Admiral Sir John Jellicoe, to present a daring proposal for the capture of the islands of Heligoland and Wangerooge guarding the approaches to the German North Sea coast, followed by the sinking of 83 old battleships and cruisers to block the adjacent river mouths used by the U-boats. The British offered to provide 31 of these block ships, but they expected the balance to come from America, Japan, and the other Allies.

Despite the President's stated desire to "do something audacious in the line of offense," the North Sea scheme was entirely unacceptable both to Woodrow Wilson and his naval advisors. One member of Admiral Mayo's staff, who was none other than Ernest J. King, the famed naval leader of a later world war, summarized the naval reaction by terming the plan a "straw man" developed by the British to demonstrate the enormous dangers and costs of a maritime offensive. The President was openly disgusted with the proposal since he felt the Germans could easily blast new channels through the North Sea ship obstructions.

However, at the last moment during Mayo's mission, the British took a step that was more consistent with American views by assenting to a mine barrage across the North Sea between Scotland and Norway on the understanding that it would be undertaken largely by the United States. During November and December 1917, this proposal and the entire strategy of an offensive campaign were taken up personally by Admiral Benson when he accompanied Colonel House's mission to Europe. Upon his return to Washington, Benson, perhaps for the first time, was enthusiastic in his desire to employ American naval power on the maritime front lines of Europe since he now was convinced that the British had accepted American naval thinking.

Benson's optimism resulted in part from the decisions reached during his visit to establish two bodies—the Allied Naval Council and the American Naval Planning Section in London—that were designed to improve inter-Allied cooperation. But, perhaps of equal importance, these organizations were viewed by the admiral and Colonel House as establishing American leadership in shaping future operations in Europe. This opinion, which soon proved to be in error, may serve as a remarkable example of American innocence, considering the nation's recent entry in the war and Britain's historic status as the world's great naval power. But it was consistent with Wilson's instruction that the House Mission take the "whip hand" in establishing an effective maritime campaign.

In the case of the Allied Naval Council, British leadership appeared to Benson to have been effectively replaced by the United States since, in his view, the Allies were "anxious that we should dominate the entire allied situation." The same principle can be discerned in Benson's agreement to establish the London Planning Section. That step complied with a standing request of the Admiralty and Admiral Sims, but the proposal was modified by the nationalistic Benson. Specifically, he assured that the London planning section was created as a separate entity which would work closely with the British naval staff but not be amalgamated into it. Further, the Chief of Naval Operations directed that the assigned American officers be "imbued with our national and naval policy and ideas." Benson clearly saw the London staff as a tool to persuade the British to develop the type of aggressive measures that, in Washington's estimation, had long been lacking.

So far as specific operations were concerned, Benson "insisted" that American agreement to undertake the North Sea mine barrage be coupled with a vigorous British mining and naval patrol campaign to close the alternate submarine transit route through the Dover Straits. In making this proposal, however, the admiral and other Navy Department officials recognized that the bulk of the British battle fleet needed to be conserved for the critically important task of blockading the Continent and maintaining readiness for another Jutland-type fleet engagement, which conceivably could determine the entire outcome of the war. Thus, in order to allow a supplemental offensive campaign to be undertaken, the United States expressed her willingness to send capital ships to Europe. The battleship division that Benson dispatched late in 1917 represented the first increment of these forces. As has been noted, the decision to send this force was associated with declining Japanese-American tensions. But the deployment also was linked with the Wilsonian offensive since the addition of American dreadnoughts to the Grand Fleet allowed the British to decommission an equal number of battleships. The crews of these units then were reassigned to anti-submarine ships, including those essential for the Dover Straits barrage.

Besides the distant blockade of the submarine nests represented by the Dover and North Sea barriers, Benson was convinced in December 1917 that he had won British assent to a close-in surface ship assault against German seaports. And, once again, the admiral accepted the obligation to provide additional units from the American battle fleet in order to make these operations possible. At the conclusion of the House Mission, Benson reported agreement on a "definite plan of offensive operations [probably a reference to an attack by older battleships on the German submarine bases in Belgium] in which our forces will participate in the near future." Benson further noted that a "tentative agreement" had been reached to send the "entire Atlantic Fleet to European waters in the Spring provided conditions warrant such action."

Benson's naive optimism was soon dampened. To be sure, the North Sea mine barrage, which was the most tangible realization of the American naval offensive, was begun in the Spring of 1918. Nevertheless, this ambitious project was not entirely completed by the Armistice, even though some 57,000 American and 16,000 British mines were planted by that time. American encouragement may have been partially responsible for the British revitalization of the Dover Straits barrage. Yet, despite the operation's increased effectiveness, Admiral Badger concluded that the British never fully met their part of the bargain to close this submarine transit zone.

The close-in attack on the German U-boat bases was almost entirely abandoned and, as a result, the large American fleet offered by Benson late in 1917 was not deployed. Although a number of the American battleships that would have been committed to this operation later proved useful in protecting troop convoys, Benson continued to regret that a seaport offensive was not undertaken. The most essential explanation for its absence was the fact that the Admiralty—no doubt recalling its experiences at Gallipoli in 1915—could not accept the feasibility of attacking fortified shore positions, despite Benson's hopes in December 1917. The Royal Navy continued the strategic blockade of Europe and its containment of the German fleet, but for these essential missions there was little need for additional capital ships. This was especially the case since an American force would have demanded logistical support by Allied shipping which was always in critically short supply. Admiral Badger of the General Board also suggested one additional factor. Apparently referring to Benson's offer of the entire Atlantic Fleet, he stated that the British "never wanted" such a force "over there under American command. They wanted the American aid to be in the way of reenforcements to their own fleet."

★   ★   ★   ★   ★

A prominent theme in all of these issues was the isolation of American policy based on national self-interest and distinctive strategic concepts. In contrast to the model developed by the British and Admiral Sims, Washington officials—often reflecting the personal views of President Wilson—did not believe that America's primary role was to provide unqualified assistance to the Royal Navy. Instead, the United States fleet gave priority to establishing and supporting an independent American Army in France, an effort that was entirely separate from the defense of the mercantile convoys serving Great Britain or of the general defeat of the German U-boat. Naval officials were concerned to varying degrees with the defense of the continental United States, preparedness to counter Japan in the Pacific, and an expected challenge from Japan, Germany, or even Great Britain in a conflict following the World War. There was basic disagreement on an offensive against the submarine bases and an attempt, that was only partially successful, to shape an aggressive campaign against these targets in accordance with American concepts.

These unresolved differences offer at least a partial explanation for the pattern of American naval deployments which saw only a small percentage of the American Navy committed to the Allied maritime campaign in European waters. But, of more fundamental importance, Anglo-American naval tensions demonstrate once again the continuing independence of American policy in World War I despite the fact that, in her own way, the United States was committed to the defeat of Germany and the other central powers.

PART VII

STRATEGIES OF GLOBAL WAR: EUROPE

RUSSELL F. WEIGLEY

TO THE CROSSING
OF THE RHINE

*American Strategic Thought
to World War II*

T he evolution of American strategic thought has long fascinated military historians. Until the mid-twentieth century it was common for American military historians to argue that American ideas about war and warmaking had emerged almost entirely out of American experience. Although some historians still suggest this, the general consensus now is that much early American thought about the conduct of war was based on European ideas, imported both before and after the American Revolution. Formal training at the United States Military Academy, for example, was dominated by ideas derived from French sources. Dennis Hart Mahan, a teacher at West Point from the 1830s to 1871, was an avid student of Napoleon, translated many French manuals for use as texts, and for a time led a Napoleonic club whose members studied and discussed his campaigns. Although Mahan always attempted to restructure the theories he taught to meet what he saw as uniquely American needs, there is little question that through most of the nineteenth century many of the theories of war and warmaking expressed in the United States were based, to some degree, on European models.

By the end of the nineteenth century, however, that situation began to change with the emergence of arguments on strategy based more and more on American experience—particularly the operations of the Civil War. In the thought-provoking article that follows, Professor Russell Weigley argues that one result of this shift was that American strategic thinkers either forgot or ignored examples from American conflicts before the Civil War as they formulated their ideas on the conduct of war. Instead, he suggests, Americans increasingly emphasized the apparent lessons from the victorious campaigns of Grant and Sherman, stressing the need for the destruction of the enemy army in combat above all other considerations. The result, argues Weigley, was a strategic approach that eschewed subtlety in favor of the direct application of military power; an approach that sought total victory through the complete annihilation of the enemy, including the social and economic foundations of the enemy society.

Professor Weigley is perhaps the foremost scholar of American strategic thought. To a large extent, the argument presented in his essay summarizes the arguments of his much larger study The American Way of War, originally published in 1973. In examining the development of American ideas on war, Weigley argues that during the American Revolution, both George Washington and the lesser-known American General Nathanael Greene, fought a war of attrition in the sense that both men sought to wear away the British army without risking their own smaller armies. It was, suggests Weigley, a strategy that reflected the relative weakness of American forces, and took maximum advantage of American resources.

Later, during the Mexican War, American General Winfield Scott waged a brilliant campaign for limited goals. Since the American aim in the war was simply to acquire land, including California, Scott was required to defeat the Mexican army, not necessarily destroy it, nor totally conquer Mexico. In addition, Weigley argues that Scott avoided battles when he could, preferring to fight a war of maneuver that cost fewer casualties and still achieved his objectives. His goal throughout the war was to win the limited objectives of the United States, not utterly crush his enemy.

In contrast, the Civil War campaigns of Grant and Sherman sought the total annihilation of the enemy. Their approach was shared, argues Weigley, by their most famous opponent, Robert E. Lee, but unlike Lee the Union commanders did not believe in the possibility of achieving this complete triumph as the result of a single climactic battle. Instead, Grant in particular sought the complete destruction of the Confederate army by fighting continually, confident that ultimately his superior numbers and resources would prevail. Sherman's marches through the South, and the associated destruction of Confederate resources, was a reflection of the same basic approach. The objective was not only the destruction of the Confederate armies, but the destruction of the system that kept them fighting. For both Grant and Sherman, Weigley argues, the war was as much against the people of the Confederacy as against the enemy armies.

This strategic approach, the seeking of what Weigley argues is a victory of annihilation, was, he contends, adopted by both the American army and navy in the years after the Civil War, and American experience in World War I seemed to confirm it. During the 1930s American manuals and the writings of American military thinkers stressed the idea that war involved a bloody but conclusive struggle. This view, which led most senior American officers to argue for an early cross-channel assault on German-held France during World War II, contributed to the sometimes acrimonious disputes between British and American military leaders on the proper joint strategy to follow during the war. Even while admitting that ultimately it was a successful strategic approach in World War II, Weigley argues that American preference for a direct confrontation produced "victory belatedly and at an unnecessarily high cost."

The cost of victory was also high because, as Weigley suggests, the equipment and tactical doctrine of the American army were not appropriate to a strategy of direct confrontation with a determined and well-equipped enemy. Our tanks and anti-tank weapons, as well as our small-unit tactical doctrine, were simply not as good as the equipment and doctrine of the Germans. The result was that American commanders had to rely on weight of numbers, overwhelming the enemy with brute force rather than skill. In Weigley's view the United States thus fought World War II with a strategic approach that was unimaginative, inflexible, and utterly inappropriate for the wars the country would fight later in the twentieth century.

Weigley's is a provocative and challenging argument. There is no doubt that Americans have a dearly held belief in the total domination of the enemy as the objective of war. "There is," General Douglas MacArthur is quoted as saying, "no substitute for victory." Doubtless most Americans would agree, and some historians have argued that such a point of view was exhibited by our colonial ancestors in their wars with the Indians long before it was practiced by Grant and Sherman. Yet, Weigley raises a serious issue that demands a thoughtful response. Is total victory always the proper national goal in wartime? Indeed, in an age of nuclear weapons, is total victory even possible? On the other hand, the reader must ask, What alternative strategic approaches existed for American military leaders? Did American military thought follow a direct path from Grant to the Second World War, or was the development of American ideas about the waging of war a more complicated process? Few of the other essays in this collection will offer help in answering these questions; the history of American thought about the means and ends of war is an area that few historians have investigated in depth. The reader might, however, look back at Professor John K. Mahon's essay on Anglo-American–Indian warfare which opened this collection for an indirect look at the way the first Americans conducted military operations. It is worthwhile, too, to look forward at Professor John Shy's essay on the American military experience which concludes this collection, and ask what geographic and cultural factors have shaped American ideas about war. There are no easy answers to such questions, but they must be asked, for upon the strategic policies our military chooses to follow rests the military future of the United States.

THE PRE-1914 BACKGROUND

The history of American strategic thought, through the second world war, may be regarded as illustrating yet another of the varieties of the nemesis of power. The greater has been the potential military power of the United States at any period in the nation's history, the less have those creating American strategic thought felt obliged to contemplate a military strategy more subtle than that of a play which overwhelms adversaries with the sheer weight of American military resources. By World War II, American strategists were willing to fight a war of massive application of resources, overwhelming the enemy with a weight of armaments great enough to permit American strategy to be reduced to performing the obvious and the expected. During that war American resources overmatched those of the country's enemies to the point that such a strategy sufficed to achieve the desired objectives at even a tolerable cost. However, so unsubtle a strategy may have prolonged and possibly increased the overall costs of the war. An era of scarcity in resources, especially of the relative weight of American resources against potential military adversaries, raises the question whether American strategic thought has become so wedded to past habits and attitudes that it may be incapable of adjusting flexibly and rapidly enough to new circumstances.

In the early years of the republic, when we were barely able to consolidate an army in the field and even less able to supply it, American strategists were more creative and subtle than in any subsequent era. Amidst the extreme weakness of the Continental Army and the revolutionary state militias, George Washington became preeminently a strategist of the indirect approach, contrary to the "direct application of power" approach later favored. In the battle around New York in the summer and autumn of 1776, Washington learned that he could match neither the discipline and skill of the British army qualitatively nor count on Congress and the states to recruit the numbers of soldiers he needed to even approach numerical parity. He then decided that he should not risk the main revolutionary military forces in battle against the main British forces, lest British superiority in combat totally destroy the Continental Army and, consequently, the revolutionary cause. After 1776, through five more years of active campaigning, there was only one battle in which Washington directly confronted the main rival armies: along the Brandywine Creek in September 1777, when he concluded that the dangers of yielding the Continental capital of Philadelphia without a show of resistance were even more severe than the dangers of a battle.

Otherwise, throughout the war, Washington sought to break the might of the British army—or rather, the political will of the British government to persist in the war—by striking indirectly, at the British army's weaker outposts and at its morale. The hallmark of his offensive activity became the Trenton, Princeton, Stony Point, or Paulus Hook attack, that is, the hit-and-run raid on a vulnerable detachment. By a series of such small victories he hoped to erode British patience while sustaining American. If Washington could maintain the army's revolutionary morale enough to nourish perseverance, while still avoiding major battle, then at least the Revolution was not lost.

Persistent avoidance of major battle demanded extreme wariness on Washington's part, and to impose damage on enemy outposts in the meantime demanded an exceptionally alert intelligence service able to perceive the opportunities for surprise against vulnerable detachments. Yet the strategic ingenuity, dexterity, and flexibility thus encouraged by American military weakness were destined not to survive long once that very weakness was overcome. Reviewing the history of American strategy for an Army War College audience in 1939, the assistant commandant of the college remarked deprecatingly, but correctly, "I have not found that we Americans have been especially prone to [effecting] surprise, although Washington surprised the Hessians at Trenton in 1776."

When the United States was militarily weak, it also produced its one approximation of a strategist of guerrilla war, Major General Nathanael Greene—to say nothing of such nontheoretical practitioners of this style of war such as Francis Marion, Thomas Sumter, and Andrew Pickens. While the nation's military power remained relatively limited, the United States also produced in Lieutenant General Winfield Scott another strategist of indirection. Scott's campaign from Veracruz to the City of Mexico was built upon the avoidance of battle whenever possible, in favor of a series of turning movements to maneuver the enemy army out of one position after another, with the territorial and political objective of capturing the Mexican capital and thereby the hope of compelling the Mexicans to negotiate peace on terms favorable to the United States. Only twice on the long march to Mexico City did Scott depart from this evasive strategy; once the departure was not of his will: success at Contreras fired his subordinates to lead their divisions to a frontal assault against the Mexican army along the Rio Churubusco. On the other occasion, a mistaken report of an active Mexican cannon foundry at the Molino del Rey pursuaded Scott that he had to attack the place.

Winfield Scott was a general who so deplored battle that with every evidence of sincerity, he wrote to his adversary General Antonio López de Santa Anna in hopes of ending the fighting: "Too much blood has already been shed in this unnatural war." Regarding bloodshed as an impediment to a satisfactory peace, Winfield Scott pursued a military strategy of maneuver and indirection to serve both wartime goals and longer-range policy goals.

In the evolution of American strategy, Scott was quite different from his successors, the triumphant Union generals of the Civil War. Up to the Civil War, the United States passed the take-off stage of industrial development, and by the 1860s the country was able to apply its burgeoning economic and population resources to military mobilization on an unprecedented scale. Leading lavishly-well-equipped armies of a million men, Lieutenant General Ulysses S. Grant sought victory in the Civil War not by a strategy of indirection, but by the most direct means possible. He exploited the Union's manpower and material superiority to directly confront, overwhelm, and utterly destroy the rival armies of the Confederacy. Grant professed admiration for Winfield Scott as a strategic mentor, but there was no Scott-like eschewing of bloodshed or war of maneuver without confrontation in battle for Grant in the climactic campaigns of 1864–65. Furthermore, after the war, Grant wrote skillfully and persuasively on behalf of his strategy, the better to fix its influence upon subsequent American soldiers:

> Soon after midnight, May 3d–4th [1864], the Army of the Potomac moved out from its position north of the Rapidan, to start upon that memorable campaign, destined to result in the capture of the Confederate capital and the army defending it. This was not to be accomplished, however, without as desperate fighting as the world has ever witnessed; not to be consummated in a day, a week, a month, or a single season. The losses inflicted, and endured, were destined to be severe; but the armies now confronting each other had already been in deadly conflict for a period of over three years, with immense losses in killed, by death from sickness, captured and wounded; and neither had made any real progress toward accomplishing the final end. . . . The campaign now begun was destined to result in heavier losses, to both armies, in a given time, than any previously suffered; but the carnage was to be limited to a single year, and to accomplish all that had been anticipated or desired at the beginning of that time. We had to have hard fighting to achieve this.

While Grant thus relied on hard fighting, accepting heavy losses for his own army in "bleeding to death" the enemy army, his principal lieutenants, Major General William Tecumseh Sherman and Philip H. Sheridan, carried his direct strategy a step further. They visited destruction not only upon the enemy but upon its enemy's economy as well, as evidenced in Sherman's marches through Georgia and the Carolinas and Sheridan's devastation of the Shenandoah Valley. With such destruction, they also carried terror to the hearts of the enemy civilians. Like Grant, Sherman also penned his memoirs for future generations of soldiers.

When the American navy came of age in the 1890s, Rear Admiral Alfred Thayer Mahan, led the way for American naval strategists, following the lead of Civil War soldiers. The material wealth of the United States permitted the construction of a fleet powerful enough to apply Mahan's strategic precepts which emphasized confrontation as the means to destroy of the enemy battle fleet, and attain command of the sea, and with it all the advantages Mahan believed inherent in sea power. Mahan's naval strategy was built on the model of U.S. Grant, not Winfield Scott.

Early in the twentieth century, with the emergence of the United States as a world power, American military writers sometimes called for the formation of a distinctively American doctrine of war, appropriate to American political and military circumstances. In 1912, for example, Major George H. Shelton, editor of the *Infantry Journal*, wrote that the French and Germans already had their distinctive national conceptions of war, "infusing with life the whole body" of their armies:

> No other nation can hope to take either [the French or the German] doctrine and apply it in the same way and with equal success to its own problems. The regulations which every nation finds essential, and which most nations steal liberally from others better prepared, are, even when stolen, necessarily revamped and rewritten in an attempt to adapt them to the national characteristics of the country of adoption. But without a native doctrine, however well the translation and adaptation may have been made, "the most admirable texts and precepts enshrined in regulations are but dead bones and dry dust." Therefore, though we take not merely the text of our regulations from abroad, but the fundamental facts of a doctrine also, we must still attempt to formulate the latter to fit the facts of our national development just as we try with our regulations to adapt them to our national characteristics. Until we do this anything like an American conception of war is impossible.

In fact, the American conception of war was already further developed than Major Shelton recognized; in the Civil War—and, for that matter, the Indian wars—military power was directed not only at the enemy and the complete destruction of his armed forces, but, whenever possible, at the destruction of the economic and social foundations of his warmaking ability as well. It was the articulation of this concept, not the fixing of its assumptions and attitudes upon the American military mind, that remained incomplete when Shelton wrote in 1912.

THE FUTILITY OF STRATEGIC SUBTLETY

Additional calls for the articulation of an American concept of war followed in the years immediately after the *Infantry Journal*'s plea. The inability of military strategy to avoid or to break the deadlock of World War I, however, exerted a much more potent stimulus toward defining the American conception of war. The apparent failures of strategy in this war were not those of the United States; this nation entered the war too late and found Allied strategy already too firmly set to contribute much, positively or negatively. But observation of and experience in the war did stimulate American military writers to an appraisal of European strategy that helped them articulate their strategic assumptions and, in turn, to find reinforcement for those assumptions.

The Americans did not allow the narrowness of their own role to inhibit their criticism of the first-world-war strategy of the other powers. As General Tasker H. Bliss, Army Chief of Staff early in the war and then American military member of the Allied Supreme War Council put it: "The paucity of scientific strategical combinations in the military operations of the World War has often been commented upon." But American commanders came to believe that this "paucity of scientific strategical combinations" was inherent in the circumstances of twentieth-century war, and that nothing could be done to render strategy more effective and innovative—a conclusion that confirmed the national predisposition. General Bliss developed this view by emphasizing in particular

> the limitation imposed by the great size of modern armies. The essential element of strategy is surprise. Under modern conditions this element is most likely to be found, on a strategical as distinguished from a tactical scale, in the initial war plans. . . . If both [rival] initial plans fail in their object these huge masses cannot be readily manoeuvred into new strategical combinations. The tendency then is for the two sides to take offensive-defensive positions which from the magnitude of the forces engaged, may extend across the entire theatre of war. This theatre, which is the field for strategy, then becomes one great battle-ground, which is the field for grand tactics . . .
>
> [The pattern of the World War then automatically follows.]. . . . And thus the remaining struggle for four years became rather a test of the courage and endurance of the soldier and of the suffering civil population behind him than of the strategical skill of the general.

If there was an American strategic thinker of the inter-war period capable of attaining international influence, it was Commander H. H. Frost of the Navy. Frost's study of *The Battle of Jutland* remains one of the most provocative analyses of the battle, and he contributed stimulating and innovative critiques to the body of American strategic thought until his untimely death in 1935 at age forty-five. In 1925, Frost offered conclusions much like Bliss's about "National Strategy." He believed the era of strategic creativity and flexibility was passing: "While it might have been possible for the Germans to have gained a decisive military success in the French campaign of 1914, this is now beginning to appear more and more doubtful. Two great armies, when their morale is unbroken, tend to reach a state of equilibrium." "It was only where a lesser power, Belgium, Serbia, or Rumania, was attacked that a purely military decision could be won, although even here brilliant leadership was usually necessary to supplement superior resources." The only promising option left to the strategist was to strike with superior force, and to do it quickly,

> it would appear to be the correct policy to strike first with full force in the attempt to win a rapid military decision before the fronts are stabilized. Failing to accomplish this, we should then endeavor to form our battle lines as far to the front as possible in order to secure, to use a naval term, the control of the greatest possible amount of enemy territory and to confine the operations of the enemy field armies to as restricted areas as possible, denying him, insofar as possible, areas of industrial and economic impor-tance. . . . We should then carry out such offensive operations as may be possible in order to wear down the enemy by constant pressure and limited offensives, but only in such tactical situations that the relative losses, both moral and material, will be to our advantage. We must always be ready to seize the opportunity for an attack in full force whenever the opposing field armies have been so reduced in physical and moral strength that there is good prospect of decisive success.

Speaking to the Army War College class of 1923–1924, another fre-quent contributor to strategic commentary, navy Commander G. J. Meyers, offered a similarly pessimistic appraisal of the bankruptcy, of strategy, unless overwhelming force permitted swift defeat of the enemy at the outset of war:

> Not only should we prepare [before war comes] forces adequate to attain the object in view, but when war comes, we should have these forces in such condition of material readiness and personnel training as to be able "to overthrow the enemy's main strength by bringing to bear upon it the utmost accumulation of weight and energy withour our [sic] means." (Foch) This action should be swift and bold so that our enemy may not perfect his preparation,

nor be able, because of the immensity of the shock and its sudden-
ness, to gain breathing space in which to take the initiative in war
preparations.

If strategy had to be simplistic, at least it fitted one of the oldest clichés
of the American conception of war:

> One contribution of note [said Colonel Ned B. Rehkopf to the
> Army War College in 1939] that the United States has made to
> strategy is the definition, commonly attributed to [Nathan B.]
> Forrest: "Git the mostest men thar firstest." Whether or not
> Forrest ever said it is immaterial. Whoever did originate it has
> reason to be proud of a phrase that expresses the primary elements
> of strategy most clearly and concisely. To have the strongest
> force, a head start and the choice of ground; what further advan-
> tages could one ask?

THE PRINCIPLE OF THE OBJECTIVE

If modern strategy consisted of the rapid accumulation of superior force with
the purpose of simply overwhelming the enemy, then any diversion of force
away from the main theater of war, any subtraction from the ability to
overwhelm, became an anathema to American strategists, especially if more
subtle strategies had gone bankrupt. There must be no side shows.

The period immediately after World War I was the time when American military men followed the lead of J. F. C. Fuller, who began lists of the
"principles of war." The first American codification of the principles was
published in War Department Training Regulation 10-5 of December 23,
1921. In American formulations, the principle of the objective not only came
numerically first; it consistently received special emphasis as the principle
that enjoins against side shows, to assure that superiority of force mustered
against the correct objective, the main body of the enemy armed forces,
would always receive proper recognition as the remaining recourse of strategy.

In one of the earliest exegetical dissections of the principles of war,
a month after the publication of the initial American list of them, Colonel
W. K. Naylor told the Army War College on January 5, 1922:

> The real objective in every war is the destruction of the *enemy's*
> *main forces*. And every operation, no matter how insignificant,
> should be carried out with that end in view. . . .
>
> The fact that at present many German writers, in their desire to
> show that their army was not really defeated, are attributing their

failure to economic breakdown, introduction of Bolshevistic ideas, and other causes not directly connected with the army, may create the budding idea that the thing to do in modern war is to seek to bring about the overthrow of the enemy by some other means than merely fighting his main armies. Don't allow yourselves to be beguiled by any such idea. My own observation, drawn from the writings of those Germans who have no defense to plead, is that the war was won by taking the fighting spirit out of the German army. What did economic breakdown or Bolshevistic propaganda have to do with the retreat from the Somme in 1916, called by some of these writers the "Bath of Blood"? What did economic breakdown, etc., have to do with the fiasco at Verdun, or finally, with the failure of the German drive in 1918?

The real answer is that the fighting spirit had been taken out of the German soldiers and they were cured of their desire to prolong the war by defeats on the battlefield, and these other mentioned reasons were merely contributory, but would not have been sufficient had the German army remained undefeated in the field.

. . . .

Great Britain [with such operations as the Gallipoli campaign] has been the greatest offender in regard to divergent operations.

Lieutenant Colonel Oliver Prescott Robinson put the matter more succinctly in this 1928 elaboration of *The Principles of Military Strategy* as he had taught them at the Command and General Staff School: "the first objective should be the hostile main forces."

Especially with the example of Gallipoli before them, American strategists harshly criticized enterprises that drew forces away from the first objective in the main theater of war. In retrospective debates about the strategy of the First World War, they squarely favored the "Westerners," the champions of the Western Front, over the "Easterners" who had urged peripheral strategies. Of Great Britain's peripheral operations, General Bliss wrote critically: "With success on the western front all these [peripheral objectives such as the Dardanelles, Mesopotamia, and Palestine] would have fallen like ripe apples from the trees." (Though Bliss acknowledged, with an eye to Britain's political as distinguished from military interests, "Only, in that event, it was uncertain into which ally's hands they would fall.") Nevertheless, Britain "had not the ships for [such] expeditions on a large scale, to even enough to make the Gallipoli campaign successful."

American naval strategists continued to emphasize the same essentials as the Army strategists. Faithful to Admiral Mahan's precepts, they persisted in targeting the rival main forces in the form of the enemy's battle fleet as their own first objective. Lieutenant Commander C. T. Gladden stated a standard dictum when he wrote in the Naval Institute *Proceedings* in 1929: "Lord Grey of Falloden said: 'The errors of strategy in past wars may be expressed in two words—"Side Shows."'' They must be avoided in the choice of the objective."

NOT MANEUVER BUT HARD FIGHTING

So singleminded was the focus of standard American strategy upon the destruction of the enemy's armed forces as the first and overriding objective in war, so decidedly did American strategists reject any hint of a side show, that even strategic maneuver came to be regarded as a dubious enterprise. In tactics, American doctrine after the first world war, like the tactical doctrine of all the armies responding to the 1914–18 demonstrations of modern firepower, came to revolve around conjoined fire and maneuver: one part of an assaulting force must always be suppressing the defenses with fire while another part maneuvers for a position of tactical advantage. But strategic maneuver, as distinguished from tactical, might too readily connote diversions. If the principle of the objective demanded the destruction of the enemy's main forces, then army, navy, and air force must confront those forces and grapple with them directly. The American reading of the history of the Great War indicated that strategic maneuver was no longer a genuine alternative anyway.

Thus Colonel Naylor stated in his pioneering analysis of the principles of war:

> I wish to stress this point: that warfare means fighting and that war is never won by maneuvering; not unless that maneuvering is carried out with the idea of culminating in battle.
>
> . . .
>
> Disabuse your mind of the idea that you can place an army in a district so vital to the enemy [t]hat he will say "What's the use" and sue for peace. History shows that the surest way to take the fighting spirit out of a country is to defeat its main army. All other means calculated to bring the enemy to his knees are contributory to the main proposition, which is now, as it ever has been, namely; the defeat of his main forces.

George J. Meyers, by now a navy captain, argued similarly in his 1928 book on *Strategy:* "Maneuvering in itself will not gain victories, but is valuable only in so far as it gives us advantages in achieving our ends. Its greatest value is in the making of dispositions [for the battle] in time." The battle is the true means to victory in war: "The combat is the scene of the greatest violence in war. As it is the only act in war from which victory flows, we should be prepared to achieve victory at a cost no less than the price of blood. All preparation for war and in war must aim at victory in battle."

Clearly, this line of American strategic thought rejected a major theme of contemporary British strategic thought, Captain B. H. Liddell Hart's strategy of the indirect approach. Both reacting to the bloodshed of the Somme and Passchendaele and seeking to reassert what he believed to be the true British way in war, Liddell Hart preached avoidance of direct confrontation with the enemy's main forces in favor of an indirect approach which sought to topple that main strength by action against vulnerable rear areas, thus crippling the enemy's communications, headquarters, and ultimately, by weakening his will to fight. Liddell Hart claimed an example of this indirect approach was William Tecumseh Sherman, one of the greatest generals of American history. He praised Sherman for allegedly winning victory by marches, not battles; but in praising his version of Sherman, Liddell Hart disdainfully rejected the credentials of U. S. Grant as a strategist, even while the Americans preferred to remain the strategic heirs of Grant—and of Sherman who, in his own memoirs, proclaimed his strategy to be identical to Grant's. So, as for Liddell Hart, the staff reviewer for the American General Service Schools' *Review of Current Military Writings* pronounced Liddell Hart's *Paris, Or the Future of War* a work "of negative value to the instructors in these schools."

Liddell Hart believed war could be won by maneuver, without hard and costly fighting; the Americans believed rather that "War means fighting; it has only one aim, to crush the enemy and destroy his will to resist." In his disquisition on strategy, Colonel Robinson illustrated his argument by drawing on one of the Americans' favorite negative examples, the consequences of Admiral Sir John Jellicoe's reliance on maneuver, instead of pressing insistently to a conclusion in battle at Jutland in 1916:

> Without entering into the controversy as to Lord Jellicoe's actions in the battle of Jutland in 1916, the fact remains that, had he destroyed the German fleet, it might have ended the war. At least, it would have prevented the unrestricted submarine campaign. As it was, Jellicoe saved his fleet and the Germans *all but won the war* in 1918.
>
> The objective for military forces is the defeat or destruction of the hostile main forces, and all the operations of war are indirectly, or directly, directed to that end.

So let it be understood that, when war comes, there should be only one question that will ever be asked of a commander as to a battle, and that one is, not what flank did he attack, not how did he use his reserves, not how did he protect his flanks, but did he fight?

Commenting of Jutland, Robinson was an Army officer evaluating a naval battle, but his judgments echo the customary American naval view of the matter. As Commander Frost wrote of Jellicoe's and, in his estimation, the whole British Admiralty's policies that shaped Jutland:

There was the choice: to fight or not to fight. Ours in the place of the Admiralty, would have been to fight. Theirs was not to fight. That decision fastened upon the British navy an incubus of which it will not rid itself for many a year. Every British commander with an instinctive willingness to assume risks, which is the very foundation of naval and military greatness, will be confronted with a formidable library purporting to prove by every form of skillful plea and clever argument that Jellicoe won the World War without "leaving anything to chance."

Frost conceded that Jutland and the entire naval experience of the world war indicated the difficulty of forcing battle upon a reluctant enemy fleet and of then forcing the issue to its conclusion. All the more, then, he argued

despite these difficulties, the importance of decisively defeating the enemy battle fleet is so great that every opportunity for action should be seized; in addition, we must endeavor in every possible way to bring about and force such opportunities, which must not be missed just because all the conditions are not in our favor. These opportunities occur so seldom to a superior fleet that they should be regarded as absolutely priceless and distinctly unfavorable battle conditions should be accepted if necessary.

This emphasis on battle in American strategy penetrated even the American conception of air power, though the assumptions of the prophets of air power were not especially hospitable to the idea that "War means fighting." The principal European strategist of air power, Giulio Douhet, believed that the attack airplane represented so revolutionary a form of war that it could destroy an enemy's vital centers without first fighting against the rival air fleet for control of the air. Admiral Mahan had believed that for sea power to do this work, the battle fleet must first destroy the enemy battle fleet in combat. Douhet conceded no necessity for an aerial equivalent of the Mahanian naval battle for control of the seas. No matter what the condition of the enemy's air fleet, the attack planes would always get through. Many American champions of air power, however, were not so sure.

Billy Mitchell was much interested in the development of pursuit planes and interceptors, implying the possibility of a successful defensive battle against attacking aircraft—implying that the bombers would not always get through. Contrary to some legend, the Army Air Corps was not altogether indifferent in the 1930s to escort fighters to accompany its strategic bombers and contend for command of the air; but Air Corps funds were limited, restricted resources went to strategic bombers first, and no promising design for an escort fighter came along. The B-17 Flying Fortress itself was thought to be designed and armed to be capable of fighting its own battle for supremacy against enemy interceptors.

In 1926, navy Lieutenant Forrest Sherman, a future carrier admiral as well as Chief of Naval Operations, recognized and emphasized the potential of air power in undercutting the enemy armed forces' capacity to fight, by "reducing the resources, in material, personnel, and morale upon which . . . [those armed forces] depend." But Sherman also believed that before air power could strike the enemy's vital centers, "The destruction or neutralization of enemy air forces is the *primary military aim* of air power."

THE DIRECT STRATEGY OF THE SECOND WORLD WAR

On the eve of the second world war, the American strategists' near-rejection of strategic maneuver, of regarding confrontation in battle as the means of destroying the enemy armed forces and thus achieving victory in war, received its summation in a new revision of the basic army field manual FM 100-5 and in an authoritative commentary upon the new manual in *Military Review*. The field manual restated that "The *ultimate objective* of all military operations is the destruction of the enemy's armed forces in battle. Decisive defeat breaks the enemy's will to war and forces him to sue for peace which is the national aim." "An objective," said the manual, "may sometimes be attained through maneuver alone; ordinarily, it must be gained through battle." To leave no doubt about where the emphasis lay, the commentary added: "It should be remembered that the price of victory is hard fighting and that no matter what maneuver is employed, ultimately the fighting is frontal. . . . Blood is the price of victory. One must accept the formula or not wage war."

This formula was emphatically accepted by American strategists of the coming war. Their acceptance of it, their embrace of a strategy of direct confrontation with the enemy's main armed forces in order to destroy them, shaped the prolonged Anglo-American strategic debates about how to conduct World War II. The American conception of war that had matured since World War I permeated the Victory Program of 1941, with its succinct statement: "we must prepare to fight Germany by actually coming to grips with and defeating her ground forces and definitely breaking her will to combat." Dwight D. Eisenhower, as a member of the War Plans Division of the General Staff stated just after Pearl Harbor the basic idea yet more concisely: "We've got to go to Europe and fight." Beyond strategic debate, in strategy applied in action, the matured American conception of war expressed itself in the American strategists' eventual accomplishment of the cross-Channel invasion of France on June 6, 1944, to go to Europe to fight. It expressed itself also in the series of naval battles in the Pacific from Midway to Leyte Gulf, in which American naval strategists fulfilled the Mahanian strategic goal of the destruction of the enemy battle fleet as the necessary preliminary to the complete application of sea power.

In the second world war, the characteristic American strategy of confronting the enemy's main force to destroy it by overwhelming it in direct collision was an ultimately effective strategy; but the strategy was also unimaginative and inflexible. On occasion, it was pursued inflexibly beyond reason and good sense, as in Admiral William F. Halsey's chase of the Japanese decoy fleet in October 1944, endangering the invasion forces in Leyte Gulf. In Europe, the emphasis on a strategy of direct confrontation with the main German armies in the West was pressed almost to the point of sacrificing tactical as well as strategic maneuver, for the sake of grasping and grappling with the enemy. There is some merit in Chester Wilmot's complaint that the costs of Omaha Beach were as high as they were because "The plan for OMAHA was a tactical application of the head-on strategy which [General George C.] Marshall had so consistently advocated in pressing the case for cross-Channel invasion."

Furthermore, the American strategic preference for enemy confrontation often caused them to sacrifice some of their most promising opportunities of destroying the enemy's armed forces. German strategic doctrine at least equalled American in its will to destroy the enemy forces; but German doctrine relied on maneuver as well as superior power to accomplish this objective, particularly on strategic envelopment. Only occasionally had American strategic writers made note of a principle that was central to the thinking of the German General Staff after Helmuth von Moltke: "The only strategic maneuver which lends itself to producing a battle of annihilation is the wide envelopment." When, in the European campaign of 1944, then, Hitler's strategic errors favored the Anglo-American armies with a series of opportunities to surround and annihilate German armies the opportunities were not completely grasped and large German forces escaped from both the Falaise pocket and the wider envelopment at the Seine.

Americans have become fond of berating Field Marshall Montgomery for these failures, especially the incomplete closing of the Argentan-Falaise gap until it was too late. But the American generals contributed much to this failure as well; with his premature shift of the XV Corps eastward away from the Argentan jaw of the trap Lieutenant General Omar N. Bradley was especially at fault. The significance of that shift is its indication that, if the means to annihilation had to be a maneuver of envelopment, then, despite all the American emphasis on the demand of the principle of the objective for destroying the enemy forces, the American command was less intent on destruction than on uninterrupted straightforward territorial advance.

The Americans' preference for thrusting overwhelming power forward and their aversion to strategic maneuver, contributed much to the broad-front approach to Germany and the Rhine in 1944. The Americans were still rejecting Liddell Hart, who was to write of this period of the war, "The war could easily have been ended in September 1944," and to elaborate:

> Eisenhower's "broad front" plan of advance on the Rhine, de-signed before the invasion of Normandy, would have been a good way to strain and crack the resistance of a strong and still un-beaten enemy. But it was far less suited to the actual situation, where the enemy had already collapsed, and the issue depended on exploiting their collapse so deeply and rapidly that they would have no chance to rally. That called for a pursuit without pause.
>
> In these circumstances, Montgomery's argument for a single and concentrated thrust was far better in principle.

That is, in Liddell Hart's judgment, the Americans had become so completely committed to a single strategic approach that they adhered to it inflexibly, even when changing circumstances called for a different kind of strategy. American military strategy had grown inflexibly monolithic.

It ought quickly to be noted, too, that Liddell Hart did not argue that Montgomery should have been the commander to make the single concentrated thrust; unlike Montgomery's own arguments, Liddell Hart's were not self-servingly and nationalistically in favor of British direction of the war. On the contrary, Liddell Hart believed that George S. Patton would have executed the Montgomery strategy better than Montgomery himself.

Nevertheless, admitting the logistical bind that cramped the Allies in September 1944, it was the inflexibility—the ponderousness, indeed—of American strategic doctrine more than any other factor that frustrated imaginative efforts to seize the opportunity to win the European war with a bold, pre-winter thrust into Germany.

The American strategic thinkers, for all their emphasis on the principle of the objective, and despite their abhorrence of strategic side shows, had paid surprisingly little attention to another of the principles of war, that of concentration. Instead, an Army War College committee in 1926–1927 analysing the implications of World War I for the strategy of future wars, frankly discounted concentration: "A superior combatant operating on exterior lines can by a coordinated offensive on all fronts prevent his enemy from using interior lines to gain superiority on one front, and can thus break down the enemy and win victory."

The combination of a military past favoring the direct application of America's huge resources to overwhelm and annihilate inferior enemy forces (best exemplified in the strategy of U. S. Grant during his 1864–1865 of the Civil War) with a reading of the World War I experience, concludes that subtle strategic maneuver and even concentration had become futile: war means simple, straightforward fighting. This combination of the basic elements of American strategic thought culminated in General Eisenhower's broad-front strategy of 1944. In the second world war, this American strategy of direct application of superior power produced the complete destruction of the enemy's warmaking capacities and the unconditional surrender toward which it was aimed. Even in this war, however, when American military power, together with that of the Allies, remained indisputably superior to the power of the enemy coalition, a strategy of direct confrontation may well have produced victory belatedly and at an unnecessarily high cost.

TOWARDS THE FUTURE

Clearly, in the late twentieth century the United States can no longer rely on superior economic and manpower resources to overwhelm military adversaries. The American armed forces, therefore, can no longer count on an inflexible military strategy of direct confrontation with enemy power. The latest edition of the basic Army field manual FM 100-5 *Operations* acknowledges these circumstances. "We must assume," it says at the outset, "the enemy we face will possess weapons generally as effective as our own. And we must calculate that he will have them in greater number than we will be able to deploy, at least in the opening stages of a conflict."

Whether this recognition of strategic, as well as tactical, circumstances greatly different from those of American wars of the past 150 years has yet consistently reshaped the whole of the American conception of war is not so evident from a careful reading of the rest of the current FM 100-5. There, the recognition seems less than completely sustained. For armed forces to abandon strategic conceptions that have served them satisfactorily for so long and that are so deeply rooted in their history, without the shock of a major defeat as a stimulus, is a feat rarely accomplished. Yet the military future of the United States demands a repudiation of the deepest currents of strategic thought flowing from the American past.

EUGENE M. EMME

AIR POWER AND WARFARE, 1903–1941

The American Dimension

In December 1903, at Kitty Hawk, North Carolina, Wilbur and Orville Wright realized the centuries-old dream of human flight. Although the American army did not establish specifications for a military aircraft until 1907, or purchase a plane until 1909, visionaries both within and without the military sensed almost at once the immensity of changes the advent of powered flight would impose on the conduct of war. More than a technological innovation that modified existing tactical practices, the coming of the airplane literally created a new dimension in military thought.

However, as the following selection by Dr. Eugene Emme, former historian for the National Aeronautics and Space Administration, suggests, the development of American air power in the decades prior to the outbreak of World War II was neither smooth nor rapid. Senior officers of both the army and the navy were reluctant to make the sweeping changes demanded by proponents of air power. Those proponents, often young officers excited more by the airplane's potential as a weapon than by its current capabilities, regarded much of their seniors' hesitation as deliberate obstructionism. Arguments were heated on both sides, and the divisions and tensions these arguments aroused lingered within both the army and the navy for years to come.

Public enthusiasm for airplanes and the men who flew them was fed by stories of the exploits of World War I aces, daredevil young men who seemed to embody a spirit of chivalry and individual courage which the carnage of trench warfare had seemingly eradicated from war on the ground. Among the flyers, men such as General Hugh Trenchard, commander of the Royal Air Force, Guilio Douhet of Italy, and General

275

William "Billy" Mitchell of the American Air Service, saw the airplane as a weapon that could reach over the battlefield, bypassing in one move the grinding deadlock on the ground, and strike directly at an enemy's homeland. As commander of the British Independent Air Force in 1918, Trenchard had attempted to orchestrate a strategic bombing campaign against Germany in the last months of the war. A firm believer in the offensive, his views helped shape those of Mitchell. Douhet, on the other hand, was primarily a theorist. He served briefly as director of the Italian Aviation Section in 1913–14, and again briefly in 1918, but it is likely that he never learned to fly. Nevertheless, in 1921 he published Command of the Air, which offered the first comprehensive strategy of air power. In this book, and other writings which followed, Douhet argued that the single most important aspect of military air power was the ability to strike at enemy centers of production and population, a concept known as "strategic bombardment." A full-scale aerial offensive would be terrifying, he readily admitted, but it would also be both unstoppable and decisive.

The direct impact of Douhet's theories on Billy Mitchell, or the other American proponents of air power, can be debated. Some historians argue, in fact, that Douhet had almost no influence on American air power theorists. However, his views do represent, in an extreme form, the views held by most outspoken supporters of military air power in the United States prior to World War II. During the 1920s and early 1930s, these men argued that the revolutionary nature of the airplane demanded a new, independent service and that strategic bombardment was the true role of such an independent air force. Indeed, the two arguments depended on each other, for, as historian Walter Millis observed, institutional independence required a doctrine that established an entirely independent role for an independent arm.

As American airmen argued their case for an independent air force, they also emphasized that strategic bombardment did not necessarily mean the indiscriminate bombing of noncombatants. By the early 1930s, theorists at the Air Corps Tactical School had developed the doctrine of precision strategic bombing. In their view, attacks on a few key industries, even just a few key factories or power plants, could cripple a modern enemy's ability to wage war. Moreover, the doctrine of precision bombing satisfied a number of other political and bureaucratic needs. It promised victory without the need to commit large ground forces; it suggested that bombing could be done with an almost surgical exactitude; and it implied that bombing was as much, or more, a defensive strategy as an offensive one.

One major problem all air power supporters had during the years after World War I was the fact that existing aircraft were incapable of carrying out the kinds of attacks air power advocates argued were required. American airmen were no exception; until the 1930s their weapons were small, underpowered biplanes with short ranges and small bombload capacities. However, in 1935 the Boeing Company demonstrated its Model 299 four-engine bomber. The Air Corps was immediately enthusiastic, despite the crash of the prototype, and ordered the plane, to be known as the B-17. Rapidly labeled the "Flying Fortress," the B-17, equipped with the top-secret Norden bombsight developed at the beginning of the 1930s, was exactly the weapon the Air Corps needed. When Army Air Force planners formulated Air War Plan 1 in 1941, they were confident in both their doctrine and in the aircraft that would carry it out.

The story of the development of American air power doctrine, as traced by Dr. Emme, is a fascinating illustration of the way entrenched bureaucracies react to the introduction of a radically different weapon. It is more than simply the saga of a handful of insightful pioneers successfully overcoming obstacles; in developing their doctrine, American airmen deliberately ignored or slighted other potential uses of air power. They did so for what they saw as sound military reasons, but good arguments existed for other alternatives. The senior officers of the army and navy were not simply obstructionists; in formulating their objections to the strident claims of the airmen, they too used what they considered sound military logic, albeit with different conclusions. As illustrated by other selections in this collection, particularly the essay by Professor Mahon on Civil War infantry tactics, John D. Milligan's discussion of the first use of ironclad warships, and W. P. Hughes' analysis of naval tactics in World War II, military organizations face difficult adjustments, both psychologically and doctrinally, with the introduction of any new weapon or technology. In the disputes over air power's military role, emotions often ran high—and they still do. Although the predictions made by American air power enthusiasts during the 1930s were farsighted in many respects, it is worthwhile to avoid using hindsight and instead attempt to evaluate the arguments on both sides within the context of the information available to all the participants at the time. Indeed, it is worthwhile to critically examine any claims that the air power advocates were proven entirely correct in their predictions. Did they ignore important issues or arguments in framing their doctrine even before a suitable aircraft existed to carry it out? What role did bureaucratic interests play in the struggle over the role of air power prior to World War II? In today's era of constantly changing technology and bitter struggles over the allocation of resources, what lessons, if any, does the story of American air power between the wars have for us?

The United States had only just acquired some measures of world influence at the turn of the century. It had inherited new responsibilities in the Philippines and Cuba from Spain, and soon completed the Panama Canal. As historian [A. T.] Mahan had argued, and the Naval War College understood, the "New Navy" was still the "first line of defense." The "dreadnaught," or battleship, was now the capital ship. The submarine was just coming out of its experimental stage. Coastal artillery still remained in place as the key to a second line of defense. The Army had begun a major reorganization featuring a general staff and a war college which studied the classic principles of war derived from the great battles of the past. The validity of that experience and, ultimately, all American defense arrangements would be called into question by the arrival of the airplane and the powered balloon called the airship.

THE BEGINNING: 1903–1917

Military aviation received its decisive impetus in December 1903 from Orville and Wilbur Wright, whom we commemorate here. In world military history, balloons such as the American vehicle flown in action at San Juan, Cuba, in 1898, had made a mark, but never as lasting as that to be made by the successor vehicles of the Wright invention.

While perfecting their flying machine at Dayton, Ohio, in 1905, the Wrights twice offered their airplane, or exclusive use of their pending patents, to the U.S. Army. They explained that they considered their Flyer practical for scouting and communications, but that any potential commercial use must await further development beyond their present resources. The Army's Board of Ordnance and Fortifications brusquely turned down each offer of the Wrights because it still smarted from the bad press over the failure of the aerodrome built by Dr. Samuel P. Langley with an unpublicized federal grant of $50,000. Rebuffed by their government, the Wrights stopped flying, fearful that further exposure would invite the theft of their hard-earned innovations.

A New York congressman and some Ohioans stirred the interest of Theodore Roosevelt and his administration in both the Wright Flyer and its implications. A miniscule Aeronautics Section of the Signal Corps, organized on 1 August 1907, became the government's instrument for staying in touch with aeronautical advances. The Signal Corps soon was advertising for "a practical means of dirigible aerial navigation" and set up a balloon facility at Fort Omaha, Nebraska. By December 1907, the Signal Corps was seeking bids for one flying machine. On 8 February 1908, the Wrights agreed to deliver one Flyer within 200 days.

In July 1908, Lt. Benjamin Foulois, who always had one eye cocked to the future, submitted his thesis to the Signal Corps School at Ft. Leavenworth on the "tactical and strategical value of balloons and aerodynamic flying machines." In a future war, Foulois wrote, an air battle would influence "the strategic movement of hostile forces before they have actually gained contact." As Foulois explained later, he had mainly elaborated upon the doctrine in the Infantry Manual by inserting aviation whenever tactical employment of the cavalry or artillery had been called for. The first fruit of the thesis was his assignment to aeronautical duty.

In August, Wilbur Wright began his spectacular flights in France, from which he would go on to make over a hundred more in Europe, all demonstrating the superior flight control of the Flyer over any European aircraft. But the first demonstration at Fort Myer, Virginia, also in August, was that of the impressive non-rigid airship of Thomas Scott Baldwin of California. His flight engineer was Glenn Curtiss, a builder of motorcycles and of the airship's 20 hp engine. The

Army bought the airship, designated it "Signal Corps 1," and later shipped it to Fort Omaha, where it was used to check out a few airship pilots and to provide demonstrations at Fort Leavenworth and at air shows and state fairs. In 1912 it was sold for scrap. (Also in 1908, German Army accepted its first large rigid Zeppelin, and Kaiser Wilhelm was to declare Count von Zeppelin the "greatest German of the century." Later, in Nazi days, a German history of flight was to publish a picture of the Wright Brothers' "German grandfather.")

On 9 September 1908 Orville Wright made two spectacular flights at Fort Myer, one of fifty-seven minutes, the other of over an hour, to be followed by other demonstrations before Washington officials and thousands of onlookers. The most qualified Army officer was Lt. Thomas Selfridge, who had worked with Alexander Graham Bell and associates and had already flown an aircraft. When he flew with Orville, the Flyer crashed from a height of seventy-five feet, killing Selfridge. Orville Wright was seriously injured, thus postponing completion of the Army acceptance flights until 1909. It was little wonder, given the fragile state of the flying art and its barely organized sponsorship in the Signal Corps, that the Congress rejected a budget request of the Secretary of War in 1908 for $500,000 for Army aeronautics.

Already increasingly evident in the public arena were the non-military speculations about the potentialities of military power to be served by an air weapon not tethered to surface forces. In 1908, H. G. Wells published *The War in the Air*, which, even before Louis Bleriot's hop across the English Channel, depicted "The Battle of the North Atlantic" and "How War Came to New York" in Italian-style airships. In Wells' account, the United States was attacked because:

> It was known that America possessed a flying machine of consider-
> able practical value, developed out of the Wright model; but it was
> not supposed that the Washington War Office [sic] had made any
> wholesale attempts to create an aerial navy. It was necessary to strike
> before they could do so.

Orville Wright completed the trials of the Flyer at Fort Myer in July 1909 in the presence of President Taft and the Secretaries of the War and Navy Departments. The rebuilt Wright Flyer exceeded all Signal Corps specifications, remaining aloft seventy-two minutes and averaging forty-two mph with a passenger. The U.S. Army soon had the first and only military airplane in the world, a short-lived and singular technological lead never again enjoyed by the United States until the appearance of the B–17 and the later atomic bomb. As agreed in the contract with the Army, Wilbur Wright proceeded to check out Lts. Lahm and Humphreys at College Park, Maryland. Although both officers were then transferred back to their respective non-flying line organizations, others, including Henry H. Arnold, were later given instruction at locations such as Dayton, Ohio; College Park, Maryland; and Augusta, Georgia.

After the International Air Meet in Rheims, France, in 1909, the flying machines of dedicated mechanics and sportsmen generated a flying boom around the world. In September of that year, Orville Wright flew a record altitude flight of 1,600 feet above Berlin, Germany, while, on the same day, Wilbur flew around the Statue of Liberty in New York. Soon many airplanes were built in the United States, and, even if they did not fly very well, they replaced balloons at county fairs.

The first congressional appropriation of $125,000 in 1911 for Army aviation ended the Wright Flyer era. Five new aircraft were ordered, and a permanent flying school was soon established at North Island, San Diego. A few experiments, beyond those involving only higher and further flights, had long term significance but were not immediately pursued by the Army. The low-recoil machine gun developed by Colonel Isaac Lewis and fired from an aircraft by Captain Chandler, chief of the Aeronautical Section, was to become a standard air weapon in Europe. A bomb sight was tested, bombs dropped, and airborne photography and radio tests made. Twelve of the first forty-eight officers assigned to Army aviation were killed in accidents. Pusher aircraft of the Wrights and Curtiss were dropped in favor of tractor aircraft (with the propeller in front of rather than behind the crew) such as the Curtiss JN–1 or "Jenny." This tractor evolved after 1914 into the basic trainer used throughout the war to come, and later was used as a bomber by Marine aviators and as a plaything by hundreds of civilians.

On 18 July 1914, Congress authorized the Aviation Section of the Signal Corps, with a strength of 60 officers and 260 enlisted men. After the outbreak of war in Europe in August, the First Aero Squadron was created on 1 September 1914, under Captain Foulois. In his "History of Rockwell Field," Major Henry H. Arnold later wrote about the First Aero Squadron:

> This was the first operating unit of any kind ever organized. . . .
>
> The question now arose for the first time as to whether a flying officer of limited administrative experience or non-flying officers of considerable administrative experience in the Army should not be placed in command of such a squadron. It is also to be noted, however, that this question had not been satisfactorily solved even several years later [1916].

The First Aero Squadron was always provisional until 1917, in the sense that it did not have a full complement of planes, even when three other squadrons were organized on paper. Also apparent was the need for greater understanding of the potential of combat aircraft, beyond the obvious reconnaissance mission. Lt. Thomas D. Milling summarized very well the relationship between doctrine and equipment at that time when he observed, "Our doctrine has been consistent since 1913 within the limits of our equipment."

On the day before the founding of the First Aero Squadron, a British Royal Flying Corps reconnaissance plane spotted the armies of German General von Kluck's "inward wheel" heading southeast to Paris. This intelligence, soon confirmed, led to a series of battles called the "miracle of the Marne." The halt of the German offensive and the eventual "race to the sea" created the trenches of the Western Front. Within a few months, the Army Signal Corps issued its first specification for a reconnaissance two-place biplane with a speed of 70 mph. Twelve bids were received, but the lack of a reliable engine thwarted procurement of the desired airplane.

At first, few Americans, including military leaders in Washington, seriously believed that the war in Europe would involve the United States. With the sinking of the *Lusitania* in May 1915, unrestricted German U-boat operations greatly increased military concern despite President Woodrow Wilson's strict neutrality posture. Hindering American understanding of the war, especially its evolving air operations, was the inability of neutral observers to penetrate the cloak of secrecy laid down by both sides.

The U.S. Navy knew about Dr. Langley and the Wright brothers, Navy Lt. George Reed having almost flown in the tests at Fort Myer. Later he flew with Army Lt. Frank Lahm at College Park. To handle the queries about aviation being directed at the Navy Secretary's office, Captain W. I. Chambers was made its air coordinator. Along with Glenn Curtiss, the developer of the first practical seaplane, Chambers brought the airplane into the Navy, which had expressed no interest in aviation until convinced it could help the fleet.

Chambers arranged the first ship-to-shore flight by Eugene Ely, a pilot employed by Curtiss in one of his firm's pushers, from a plank platform on the cruiser USS *Birmingham* at Hampton Roads on 10 November 1910. Two weeks later, Glenn Curtiss informed the Secretary of the Navy that he would provide free flight training for an officer at his winter camp on North Island, San Diego. Lt. T. G. Ellyson was detailed and became the first naval aviator. In early January 1911, Ely landed on a platform on the USS *Pennsylvania* at anchor in San Francisco Bay and soon took off again. Later in the month, Glenn Curtiss made the first successful hydro-airplane flight with his "Silver Fish" off North Island, Lt. Ellyson assisting in the preparations. In February, Curtiss taxied his seaplane out to the *Pennsylvania*, was hoisted aboard and then returned to the water to taxi back to North Island. It was a persuasive demonstration, and in March, Congress appropriated $25,000 for naval aviation. The Wright Company now offered to train one Navy pilot, contingent upon the purchase of one airplane for $5,000. Lt. John Rodgers was sent to Dayton, to become Naval Aviator No. 2. By 8 May 1911, the U.S. Navy had purchased three airplanes: the Curtiss "Triad," a "hydra-terra-airplane" to whose float Curtiss had added wheels for both land and water landings, a Curtiss pusher, and a Wright Flyer.

Captain Chambers was directed to set up an experimental station at Annapolis, where Lt. John Towers and others were training. There and on exercises, experiments went on in the application of the airplane to Navy needs. Off Cuba, Lt. Towers confirmed that submerged submarines could be seen from the air; other experiments went on with radio telegraphy, photography, and water-based operations to include the testing of catapults. At the Washington Navy Yard, Naval Constructor Holden C. Richardson worked on hull designs for seaplanes, a wind tunnel for aircraft design, and flight testing. From 1912 on, year-round flight training and operations were located at the first Naval Aeronautics Station, Pensacola, Florida.

In 1912, a Marine, Lt. A. A. Cunningham, began flight training at the Burgess and Curtiss factory at Marblehead, Massachusetts, and became Naval Aviator No. 5. Later called the "Father of Marine Corps Aviation," Cunningham and his associates soon were engaged in exercises in Cuba with an Advance Base Brigade.

One of the earliest steps taken by the United States after the "guns of August" began firing in Europe, was to create in March 1915 the first federal agency responsible for coordinating and stimulating aeronautical research. A rider to the Naval Appropriations Act of 1915 created the National Advisory Committee for Aeronautics, "N.A.C.A.," which could never live down its Navy birthright in the eyes of some Army airmen. Modelled after a British body founded in 1910, the NACA was to examine and make recommendations "on the problems of flight, with a view to their practical solution," a general and unwarlike charter in keeping with the neutral position of the United States. The twelve man membership of NACA included the chiefs of the Army Signal Corps and its Aviation Section, the director of Naval Aviation and its Constructor, the chiefs of the Weather Bureau and the Bureau of Standards, and professors interested in aerodynamics as it grew out of fluid mechanics.

At the first meeting of NACA in the office of the Secretary of War, chaired by Brig. General George Scriven, Chief Signal Officer, on 23 April 1915, the membership considered his previously submitted position that the problem "most requiring attention involved military aviation and national defense." "Nothing," he said, "will so readily bring order from chaos as the carefully considered decisions [sic] of this Advisory Committee." But the NACA was to become concerned with the technical problems of civilian as well as military aviation. Its recommendations bound none of its members, and, in unmilitary fashion, it elected its own chairman.

A month after NACA's first meeting, the first German Zeppelin attacks on London highlighted a capability unavailable in the United States. The Committee, for its part, modestly surveyed research capabilities nation-wide, gathered what basic knowledge it could in Europe, and began to issue its widely-used bibliographies. In 1916, the NACA undertook some policy initiatives by inviting aircraft engine manufacturers to discuss the problems of attaining more powerful and more reliable aircraft engines, by recommending a government air mail service, and by seeking the creation of a laboratory at an Army-Navy aircraft proving field, which became Langley Field at Hampton, Virginia, in 1917. The dozen or so employees of NACA at Langley, however, did no research in its wind tunnels until after the war.

Another scientific initiative, this time by the National Academy of Sciences in 1916, prompted President Wilson to establish a National Research Council (NRC) to engage scientists on defense problems, particularly submarine detection. Once the United States entered the war, some scientists put on uniforms. Among them was Major Robert Millikan of the California Institute of Technology, the head of the Signal Corps Science Research Division.

In November 1915, Major William Mitchell, then a General Staff officer, apparently prepared a survey of national defense needs in aviation. He claimed that aviation would be particularly useful as "a second line of defense," by acting as a backstop to the Navy when attached to harbor and coastal defenses, by carrying on reconnaissance and spotting for artillery, and by destroying attacking aircraft and submarines. Army aviation should be increased, said Mitchell, to 46 officers, 243 enlisted men, and 23 aircraft of various capabilities. By 1916, and at his own expense, Mitchell began taking flying lessons during his off-duty time.

In early 1916, Congressional support for aerial rearmament greatly accelerated when the First Aero Squadron quickly wore itself out in supporting General John Pershing's Punitive Expedition against Pancho Villa. An emergency appropriation for the Aviation Section of $500,000 was followed by the enormous sum of $13 million, a figure nine times the total of all funds which had been received by Army aviation to date. (Incidentally, Captain Foulois must have had a typing pool larger than the Aviation Section, since so many original and carbons of his report on the demise of the First Aero Squadron are scattered through the files in the National Archives.)

In April 1917, when the United States entered the war in Europe, its Army's aviation had 131 officers (mostly pilots), 1,087 enlisted men, and no aircraft capable of combat. Naval aviation had forty-five float seaplanes, six flying boats, three land planes, and one blimp, none ready to operate with the fleet. Almost ten years had passed since the Army accepted its Wright Flyer, but American air power was almost non-existent, with a handicraft industry, no organized planning or research and development, and very little knowledge of aviation progress in Europe.

WORLD WAR I: 1917–1918

American air power in the Great War was scarcely born when it was demobilized. A nightmare for that air power ensued from the utterly rash promises by industrial, military and political leaders in 1917 that thousands of American planes would gain perpetual air superiority, darken the skies over Berlin, and end the war. The first American-built but British-designed DH–4s reached France in May 1918, unready for operations and often damaged in transit. The American model had a reputation as a "flaming coffin" until the gas tank between the pilot and observer was re-positioned after the war. To the hundreds of airmen arriving for flight training in France, it appeared that their presence was designed more to raise that country's morale rather than to get on with the air war. When promised first-line European aircraft were not delivered, the American airmen who eventually qualified in Allied flight schools had to take whatever aircraft were offered them. Those American airmen who got to the front did a great job with what they had. James Lea Cate's assessment seems sound: "Had the war dragged on into 1919, the boasts might have been made good."

German Field Marshal Hindenburg and General John J. Pershing credited the Allied victory to the waves of fresh American infantrymen whose assaults cracked the Western Front. But it was also true that those ground forces were protected by air actions that denied superiority to the Germans over the battlefront. In the rear areas, by the fall of 1918, British bomber crews attempted to strike at the center of cities in the Reich. The resulting panic caused the German government to ask for an immediate halt to the bombing raids as part of its armistice proposals.

Perhaps it was indeed inopportune, as Raymond Fredette has observed, that General Pershing just missed witnessing the first bombing raid by German Gotha bombers on London on 13 June 1917. A vivid demonstration of air power's potential might have been most persuasive. The Gotha bomber raids on England, for example, helped to spur the creation of the independent Royal Air Force in the midst of the decisive phase of the war on the Western Front.

Professor-General Bill Holley has treated very well the incredible history of the American aircraft production program in his *Ideas and Weapons*. The haste and waste in the program offered lessons that were well learned in time for the World War II buildup. Hampering the World War I American air effort as well were the requirements to mobilize and train tens of thousands of raw recruits after the United States had entered the war, not to mention the problems of organizing and staffing the higher direction of the air effort.

A few highlights from the American experience in the Great War may be suggestive. The splendid biography of Billy Mitchell by Colonel-Professor Al Hurley provides a clear understanding of Mitchell's early air power role. Mitchell got himself to Spain and then to Paris four days after the American declaration of war. Fluent in French, he wrangled his way to that nation's share of the front, absorbing briefings on air employment and taking lessons in flying its latest aircraft. Mitchell seemed more influenced by his three-day visit early in May with British airmen, principally Major General Hugh Trenchard. Trenchard impressed on Mitchell the concepts of "forward action" and the "relentless offensive." For various reasons, Mitchell's reports to Washington about all this had little impact.

Mitchell also had contributed to the preparation of French Premier Ribot's request for American resources that became the bottom line for the take-off of the ambitious U.S. aircraft construction program. Ribot asked for an American "flying corps" of 4,500 planes, 5,000 pilots, and 50,000 mechanics to be sent to France in 1918. American acceptance of this goal led to sending the Bolling Mission to Europe to determine what kinds of airplanes should be built. Its prompt recommendations included ideas on the strategic bombing of enemy industries. Top priority was given to the production in the United States of the British DH–4 reconnaissance bomber and the American all-purpose Liberty engine, with the second priority, pursuit planes, to be purchased in France and England. In the meantime, Pershing made Lt. Colonel Mitchell the Aviation Officer of the AEF. Soon, however, Mitchell was subordinated to Brigadier General Benjamin Foulois. Eventually, the leadership and talent Mitchell showed as Chief of the Army Air Service, First Brigade, on the American sector of the front won him fame. General Trenchard's early impression of Mitchell was noteworthy: "If only he [Mitchell] can break the habit of trying to convert opponents by killing them, he'll go far."

Those few American squadrons which reached France by late 1917 served with French and British units after they had been organized and trained. General Pershing refused to flesh out depleted and tired Allied air units with Americans. After April 1918, a few American squadrons began to operate in support of their own forces. While news from the trenches was drab and bloody, the individualism of air combat made heroes of Eddie Rickenbacker, Frank Luke, and others. Contrary to Hollywood's later dramatization, however, aerial combat involved a lot more than glamorous dawn patrols and was fully subject to the vagaries of the weather and the fragility of the flying machines themselves.

Pershing made Brigadier General Mason Patrick, a West Pointer, his Chief of Air Service, A.E.F., in May 1918. Eventually Patrick assigned Mitchell the leadership of all American air units with the First Army. The struggle for the St.-Mihiel salient offered the best example of air power's potential on a battlefield. Mitchell's plan to gain air superiority required 1,500 planes, only 609 of them piloted by Americans, the rest being drawn from Trenchard's Independent Force, along with a French Air Division, and other Allied squadrons. Only a third of the force directly supported the First Army; the rest, in two brigades, struck at the flanks of the salient and at the German air force facilities in the rear of the salient. Pershing praised the action's success, and all airmen saw it as a model for the effective concentration of air forces.

In the remaining Allied offensives, Mitchell usually had only American squadrons at his disposal and used them mainly in close support and counterair roles. German air opposition persisted to the end. Meanwhile, Trenchard's Independent Force bombed German targets in an effort that gained momentum from September onward. The Armistice aborted planning for a much larger bombing campaign by the Inter-Allied Independent Air Force under Trenchard, who would have been responsible to Marshal Foch, the Supreme Commander.

How is one to evaluate the limited American effort? Statistics are one measure. The U.S. Army Air Service in France constituted 10 percent of the Allied air forces, dropped 139 tons of bombs, and reached as far as 160 miles behind the German lines. Some 237 American airmen were killed in battle; no figures for greater operational, training, and other losses are available. There were 58,000 Army airmen in France, 20,000 in training in England, and some in Italy. A total of 10,000 Army aviators completed flight training, but one must also note that 27,000 officers and men of the Air Service had been assigned to obtaining the spruce used in the manufacture of aircraft.

Over 3,000 DH–4s and 7,800 training planes had been produced, a total of some 11,000 aircraft against the 27,000 planned. Of the 1,005 aircraft in American air units at the front, only 325 were American made. There was no lack of doctrine, or leadership, or courage for the employment of American air power in France, only the absence of the equipment and the manpower at the right time and place.

For its part, U.S. Navy aviation concentrated on the development of the HS series of flying boats. The Royal Naval Air Service had used some of those flying boats, two-engine long-range Curtiss "Large America" flying boats, to score a unique success by shooting down, at sea, two German naval dirigibles in May and June 1917. American naval aviation operated out of twenty-seven bases in Ireland, England, France, and Italy. On anti-U-boat patrol, the Navy reported attacks on twenty-five U-boats, sinking or damaging a dozen. Operating with the Northern Bombing Group in France, the mission of the naval airmen was expanded to bomb German submarine and dirigible installations with DH–4s. Round-the-clock bombing was being discussed when the Armistice intervened. In the Italian theater of war, Navy, Marine, and some Army pilots flew Caproni bombers in Allied air units against Austrian targets.

The U.S. Navy's air force had grown to a total of 6,716 officers and 30,693 men in Navy units, and 282 officers and 30,000 men in Marine Corps units. Of these, 18,000 had been sent abroad.

Despite the employment of air power and its rapid development during the war, for many observers, air power had yet to prove itself in warfare as a military and naval instrument. As America demobilized her military forces after the Armistice, the contrast between reality and vision would set the tone for its military aviation during the next twenty years.

NASCENT AIR POWER: 1919–1937

With the conclusion of "the war to end wars," "the long armistice" began. From its position of isolation, the United States tried to secure peace through the Washington Naval Treaties of 1921–1922 and the Kellogg-Briand Peace Treaty six years later. In preparation for a presidential election during a deepening depression in 1932, the Hoover Administration, supported by Army Chief of Staff Douglas MacArthur, considered a ban on all submarines and aircraft carriers for submittal to the World Disarmament Conference in Geneva. In an increasingly nationalistic world, fantasies about disarmament abounded while Congress investigated "merchants of death" and the impact of the airplane on national defense. Congress tried to perpetuate peace by passing the Neutrality Acts prohibiting the sale of armaments to any belligerent while Adolf Hitler tore up the Treaty of Versailles by announcing the existence of the Luftwaffe and universal military service in Nazi Germany.

In the United States, the postwar demobilization was chaotic. American airmen returned from France to help answer Congressional inquiries about the failure of the billion dollar aircraft construction program. Of the 200,000 men in the wartime Army Air Service, only 10,000 officers and enlisted men remained on duty by June 1920. A year later, the aircraft inventory was 1,100 DH–4s, 1,500 Jenny trainers, 179 SE–5 pursuits, and 12 Martin MB–2 bombers. There were fewer than 900 active Army pilots and observers. Sixty-nine of these were killed in 330 flying accidents in 1921 alone. Ninety percent of the aircraft industry was bankrupt. The Army

Reorganization Act of 1920 was a crushing blow to Army Air Service expectations. Although authorized strength was set at 1,516 officers, 2,500 flying cadets, and 16,000 enlisted men out of a total postwar Army of 280,000, there was no money to recruit to these levels or to purchase many new airplanes. The airmen would have to make do with Liberty engines until late in the 1920s.

Most frustrating to Army airmen who were usually junior in rank and rarely West Pointers, was the prevailing dim view of the future of military aviation held by those who managed the purse strings and the promotion lists. Frustration soon turned into a struggle not only with the General Staff and the Secretary of War, but also at the summit on Capitol Hill, where the fate of the post-war services was being deliberated. The fundamental issues then, as now, inevitably involved the White House.

The first postwar Congressional dialogue on aviation centered on whether all Federal aviation activities should be centralized in a cabinet-level Department of Aeronautics. Foulois and Mitchell at least agreed on this possible step. But it proved impossible to achieve unified command of "air power" whether it operated over land or over the sea, despite the precedent in the creation of the Royal Air Force in England. Billy Mitchell soon directly challenged the Navy's long-standing claim to be "the first line of defense," by asserting that his bombers could sink any battleship. The celebrated and highly publicized sinking of the unsinkable German battleship *Ostfriesland,* seemed to justify Mitchell's claim, but his oral "bombs" led President Harding to note that Mitchell gave the admirals "apoplexy"; and later President Coolidge was provoked into calling him a "God-damned disturbing liar."

After 1923, a single Department of Defense with an independent air force became the central issue in the American air power story. Mitchell, after cooling-off trips to Europe in 1922 and to the Far East in the first half of 1924, launched even more inflammatory attacks upon the Navy's admirals and the Army's General Staff. Having succeeded in alienating every responsible person with authority to help him, he was transferred into "exile" at San Antonio. The crash of the Navy dirigible, the *Shenandoah,* gave Mitchell the occasion he wanted to assure his court martial. He accused the Navy and War departments of "incompetency, criminal negligence, and almost treasonable administration of aviation." To undercut the airman's charges, President Coolidge created the Morrow Board, which met, heard all of the familiar witnesses, and reported out before Mitchell's trial. The framers of the Army Air Corps Act of 1926 would attempt to remove some complaints on flight pay and promotions and gave the Air Corps a spokesman by authorizing an Assistant Secretary of War for Air. In the meantime, Mitchell resigned and continued to express his views.

Billy Mitchell's legacy was permanently ingrained in the Army Air Corps. Not the least of his marks was made by the corpus of his many papers on the role of airplanes in national defense. Defining "air power" as "the ability to do something in the air," Mitchell's central idea was that air forces rendered armies and navies obsolete because they could achieve a decision in war by directly attacking "vital centers" of an enemy nation. After he resigned, he continued to spread the gospel, wherever possible, that "the airplane is the arbiter of our nation's destiny." Colonel Hurley's biography and Dr. Frank Futrell's monumental work on the history of Air Force thought permit me little opportunity to say more.

The beliefs of Mitchell, however, made it absolutely unnecessary for him to quote Hugh Trenchard or, if he knew them, the theories of Giulio Douhet, later collected in *The Command of the Air*. Mitchell met and talked with Douhet, although where and when he did remains not fully clear. It would be interesting to know if there is more on the Mitchell-Douhet connection. We have more evidence about the views of Douhet's associate, Count Caproni, which were communicated to Americans in 1917. At any rate, General "Hap" Arnold's later judgment on Billy Mitchell seems fair enough: despite his political failings, no one should ever forget that Mitchell was ahead of his time in his ideas on the employment of air power.

Demobilization proved equally as disruptive to Naval Aviation. During the war, that aviation had been loosely organized and was mothered by various bureaus of the Navy. Most of its pilots were reservists, and few remained on active duty after demobilization. The Navy had only 319 active naval aviators in June 1920, with 3,296 inactive, including reservists.

The Chief of Naval Operations, Admiral William Benson, vehemently opposed the proposal in 1919 to combine Army and Navy aviation. Billy Mitchell lashed out directly at Benson, decrying his shabby outlook on the "ugly duckling" of the Navy. More air-minded admirals on the Navy's General Board advised the Secretary of the Navy in June 1919 that "a naval air service must be established, capable of accompanying and operating with the fleet in all waters of the globe." The president of the Naval War College, Admiral William S. Sims, gave Congressional friends studies which argued that a superior fleet of aircraft carriers, similar to those developed by the Royal Navy, "would sweep the enemy fleet clean of its airplanes, and proceed to bomb the battleships, and torpedo them with torpedo planes. It is all a question of whether the airplane carrier, equipped with eighty planes, is not the capital ship of the future."

Naval aviation got another boost when the National Advisory Committee on Aeronautics (NACA) recommended that the War, Navy, Post Office, and Commerce Departments have separate bureaus of aeronautics, to be coordinated by a top-level board of civilians. This NACA proposal, which smacked of retaining for NACA a post-war policy role in all aviation, was rejected by the Joint Army and Navy Board. The Secretaries of War and Navy successfully refused any connections with the NACA by creating an Aeronautical Board to consider policy questions regarding the roles and missions of aviation in both services. In February 1920, CNO Benson agreed to give bureau status to naval aviation. The new status was not to be public knowledge, however, until 10 August 1921, after the sinking of *Ostfriesland* by Mitchell's bombers in July.

Admiral William Moffett, chief of the Navy Bureau of Aeronautics until he was killed in the crash of the dirigible *Akron* in 1933, was a different personality from Mitchell. Moffett, an Academy graduate, worked within the system to put aviation into the corpus of the Navy. With the help of airmen executives who were all Annapolis products after 1922, the Navy learned to operate aircraft carriers, which evolved from surface auxiliaries into capital ships in a task force. With the commissioning of the first make-shift aircraft carrier, *Langley*, the Bureau of Aeronautics (BuAer) was underway. Moffett, who now bore the brunt of Billy Mitchell's attacks on the Navy, came to regard him, he said, as a man "of unsound mind and suffering delusions of grandeur." One wonders what Moffett and Major General Mason Patrick, again Chief of the Army Air Service, said to one another about Mitchell at meetings of the NACA.

The Navy steadily advanced its sea-air capabilities after an NC–4, one of the three flying boats built during the war, completed in May 1919 the first trans-Atlantic flight from Newfoundland to Plymouth, England, by way of the Azores and Lisbon. The Naval Appropriation Act for FY 1920 had already funded conversion of a collier into the *Langley*, which used aircraft landing hooks and deck cables developed by the British and catapult launchings. Also authorized in 1920 was the procurement of two merchant ships as seaplane tenders, the construction of one rigid dirigible (later the *Shenandoah*), and the purchase abroad of another (the ill-fated British R–38). A third dirigible, the *Los Angeles*, was acquired from Germany as part of the reparations settlement. By 1923, flights from the *Langley* had begun, and the fleet exercises in Panama used patrol squadrons. The next year, while he was flying mail to the Canal Zone, Army Lt. Moon, bombed the *Langley* with ripe tomatoes and delayed a fleet exercise for a day.

"BuAer's" greatest achievement in the 1920s was the development of the aircraft carrier as a part of the Navy's capital ship construction program. Two battle cruiser hulls, permitted under the Washington Naval Treaties of 1922, became the aircraft carriers *Saratoga* and *Lexington*, commissioned in 1928. The completely new carrier *Ranger* appeared in 1934, followed by *Enterprise* and *Yorktown* in 1936, and the promise of another carrier, *Wasp*.

All major Navy ships had catapult scout planes, and flying boats were not neglected. The "flying aircraft carriers," the *Akron* and *Macon*, however, were expensive disasters. C. G. Grey, editor of the English journal, *The Aeroplane*, once quipped: "The airships breed like elephants and aeroplanes like rabbits." The Navy could afford no more of the airships, which most Army airmen always considered unworthy combat vehicles.

Since the Washington Naval Treaties forbade the United States to build a major naval installation in the Philippines, Pearl Harbor became the major port for the Pacific Sea Frontier. Fleet exercises after 1931 included the *Saratoga* and *Lexington*, although the cost of fuel was a major constraint. In the 1932 exercises, aircraft from the "Sara" and the "Lex" successfully "bombed" Pearl Harbor. Supplemented by the three new carriers, the carrier force was generally divided by 1936 between the Atlantic and the Pacific Sea Frontiers. Only the *Langley*, converted to a seaplane tender, was ever on station in Asiatic waters.

After the Japanese Army, supported by carrier aircraft, invaded China in 1937, the U.S. Navy's efforts to equip its sea-based air power with up-to-date aircraft, to lay keels for more aircraft carriers, and to train manpower became most urgent. In the fleet exercises of 1939, Naval Aviation was deemed to be "fast reaching a high state of readiness." Still, in 1940, the Japanese carrier force had grown to ten.

When the MacArthur-Pratt agreement of 1931 affirmed that the Army Air Corps was to be responsible for the land-based air defense of the United States and its possessions, Marine Corps aviators were required to become qualified on aircraft carriers. By 1934, sixty of the hundred-odd regular Marine Corps aviators had served on aircraft carriers and had gained experience on more up-to-date aircraft. In 1933, however, the creation of the Fleet Marine Force to seize shore bases for naval operations basically altered the mission of the Marine Corps aviation to one of close air support for amphibious operations. By 1939, the number of active Marine Corps aviators had grown to 245, plus reservists, but those numbers would soon double again and again.

Meanwhile, the Army Air Corps got its first veteran flyer and non-Academy-graduate as its chief in the person of Major General James E. Fechet in 1927. In the post-Mitchell period, every Army airman was still a rebel, but he maintained a low profile. One of Fechet's aides, later General Ira Eaker, has said that Fechet approved "more special projects to keep the air effort in the headlines than any of his predecessors." The Pan-American Goodwill Flight and the in-flight refueling endurance flight of the *Question Mark* occurred during Fechet's regime.

Fechet's successor, Benjamin Foulois, sounded a theme that rapidly would become more than a theory, telling an Army War College class that air power was "the strength of a nation in its ability to strike offensively in the air. . . . The real effective air defense will consist of our ability to attack and destroy the hostile aviation on the ground before it takes to the air." Four years before, when defending fighters had failed to intercept a bomber attack during maneuvers in Ohio, Major Walter Frank concluded that "a well planned air force attack is going to be successful most of the time." In the classrooms at the Air Corps Tactical School, Lt. Kenneth Walker was credited by his students with originating the theorem that: "A well organized, well planned, and well flown attack will constitute an offensive that cannot be stopped." A similar emphasis on the power of the air offensive prevailed in Europe, and Douhet was not its sole author. The most famous acknowledgment of the power of the air offensive came from Prime Minister Stanley Baldwin of England who, enroute to the World Disarmament Conference in Geneva in 1932, stated: "The bomber will always get through."

Without a doubt, President Roosevelt's assignment to the Army Air Corps of the task of flying the air mail proved a turning point in 1934. General Foulois took up the assignment with a "can do" attitude. Beginning in the depths of a severe winter across the nation in late February, nine Army airmen were killed within three weeks while flying the mail. The press deemed the Army Air Corps to be incompetent or ill-equipped. Roosevelt's Postmaster General eventually renegotiated air mail contracts with the same airlines, which had merely changed their names. But there were at least two important consequences for Army aviation. First, a War Department board under Newton Baker reviewed once again the status of aviation in the Army. It re-stated that the Air Corps should remain in the Army and recommended that the War Department buy aircraft directly from industry through bid contracts or design competitions. Secondly, the White House set up a Federal Aviation Commission under Clark Howell, a publisher, to consider once more the idea of a separate air force.

Before the Howell Commission reported out, the Army chose a solution recommended earlier by two of its own boards and gave the Air Corps a mission not tethered to other Army forces by establishing a provisional General Headquarters Air Force (GHQAF). Brig. General Frank Andrews became head of the GHQAF on 1 March, 1935. The GHQAF was headquartered at Langley Field, Virginia, with other wings at Barksdale Field, Louisiana, and March Field, California, to support the "tactical mission" of coastal defense. In the meantime, Lt. Colonel Henry H. Arnold had led a flight of ten Martin B–10 bombers to Alaska, returning to Seattle non-stop over water on a 8,290-mile round trip. The B–10, the first prototype of the modern bomber, had closed cockpits, retractable landing gear, and a speed faster than that of contemporary fighters.

Sustaining the continued struggle of the Army Air Corps to develop and procure heavy bomber forces was the dynamism of the revolution in flight technology in the early 1930s. It suffices to stress here the appearance of the Boeing 229, designated the XB–17, which flew non-stop from Seattle to Wright Field in August 1935—2,100 miles at 232 mph with four modest-sized engines in flush wing-mounts. To Army airmen from Generals Oscar Westover and Andrews on down, the XB–17 "was a vision of the promised land." Earlier, in May 1934, Air Corps arguments with the Army General Staff had prevailed and had secured the mission of "the destruction by bombs of distant land and naval targets." The Boeing Aircraft Company had then begun "Project A," a more advanced bomber with a range of 5,000 miles, and a speed of 200 mph with a 2000-lb bomb load. The resultant X–15, contracted for in June 1935, flew in 1937. It was underpowered but contributed to the ultimate B–17 and the B–29. In October 1935, the War Department contracted for the XB–19, a forerunner of the wartime B–29 and post-war B–36.

In testimony before the Howell Commission, most of the senior Air Corps representatives had supported the idea of giving the GHQAF a fair trial before seeking a further reorganization. But some of the heady thoughts on the primacy of air power in modern war as taught by the majority of the instructors at the Air Corps Tactical School were freely expressed by Major Donald Wilson, Captains Harold George and Robert Olds, Lts. Kenneth Walker and Laurence Kuter, and others. To George, air power was "the immediate ability of a nation to engage effectively in air warfare." To Walker, "An Air Force is an arm which, without the necessity of defeating the armed forces of the enemy, can strike directly and destroy those industrial and communications facilities, without which no nation can wage modern war."

It is generally conceded that between 1933 and 1937 the Army and the Navy had not been ungenerous in funding their respective air arms within the fiscal constraints imposed by the state of the national economy and inevitably slim budgets. The Army Air Corps justified its infant heavy bombers in terms of coastal defense rather than by trying to sell a concept of a strategic air offensive against some specific enemy. From a budget of $6 million for FY 1936, the Army Air Corps only received $3.5 million for aircraft procurement for FY 1938, the year the German Luftwaffe rose like a phoenix to dominate the diplomatic balance of power in Europe. A numbers game also may have come into vogue in the selection of aircraft in this period. In 1936, the Air Corps was directed to order more airplanes for the dollar, or more two-engined Douglas B–18s rather than fewer B–17s. The interregnum came to an end for the Army Air Corps in September 1938, however, thanks to ex-Corporal Adolf Hitler. He remembered trench warfare.

TAKE-OFF: 1938–1941

Erosion of the "long armistice" had been underway in Europe ever since Nazi Germany falsely claimed in 1935 that its new Luftwaffe already had "air parity" with the Royal Air Force. Nazi Germany's aggrandizement was transparent in 1936 with the reoccupation of the demilitarized Rhineland and the commitment of the Condor Legion to the Spanish Civil War. In the United States, the interregnum persisted despite President Roosevelt's attempt to alert public opinion concerning the stark portents for the future of peace reported by his ambassadors and attaches in London, Paris, Berlin, and Tokyo. In September 1937, President Roosevelt tested the public's readiness for a policy change by calling for an active "quarantine of aggressors," a thought that was not well received nationwide. "FDR" was branded a "war monger" by the isolationists; Congress responded by extending the Neutrality Act. But a series of international crises were to prompt small changes in American military policy, if only to prepare adequate defenses for the continental United States.

In December 1937, Japanese bombers intentionally sank the USS *Panay* and machinegunned its lifeboats in Chinese waters. The United States only protested, and the undeclared war by Japan continued. However, American rearmament began when Roosevelt soon called for augmenting American defenses because of the threats "to world peace and security." U.S. Navy aviation got the first boost with the passage of the Naval Expansion Act in May 1938, which marked a significant step toward a "two-ocean navy" and which provided for a 3,000-plane program to move carrier aircraft beyond the biplane era. From this legislation came the Navy's first modern production fighter, the Brewster Buffalo, the precursors of the Grumman F4F and TBF, and the Douglas SBD, the dive bomber which would win the battle of Midway four years later.

For the Army Air Corps, the thrust to expand its initial force of B–17s continued to fare poorly under a President who had once been Assistant Secretary of the Navy. At Langley Field, the GHQAF under General Andrews was developing heavy bomber operations with thirteen B–17s. In May 1938, three of these bombers departed Langley Field and intercepted the Italian liner *Rex*, 725 miles out of the port of New York. It was a good navigation job by Lt. Curtis LeMay. The next day, pictures of a B–17 at mast-height alongside the *Rex* appeared on the front pages of the New York *Times* and other eastern newspapers. The Navy blew a fuse. The primary mission of the B–17 in national strategy was scrubbed when the word was passed down from on high that Army Air Corps planes were limited to operational flights not to exceed 100 miles from shore. Secretary of War

Harry Woodring laid it on the line when he directed that no production B–17s be procured in FY 1940. Deputy Chief of Army Staff General Stanley Embick stated simply: "Our national policy contemplates preparation for defense, not offense . . . Defense of sea areas other than within the Continental Zone, is a function of the Navy." It was little wonder that General Andrews told the National Aeronautical Association convention in St. Louis that the United States was no better than a fifth or sixth rate air power in the world.

The so-called "Munich Crisis" of September 1938 was the turning point in American air power policy before World War II. England and France appeased Hitler because of their fantastic belief that, in the event of war, the German air force was more powerful than all of the Western air forces combined, plus that of the Soviet Union. Everyone forgot that air operations from German bases could barely reach England, but the collective action required of both England and France proved impossible. It was a triple tragedy: Hitler's bloodless victory gave him the Czech "Little Maginot Line"; it put him in command of the German Army General Staff which had been prepared to depose him; and, it encouraged more adventures by Hitler, who believed that those "worms of Munich will not fight."

It is difficult to recreate the climate of Munich. Douhet virtually became a household word in France and England. There had not been enough gas masks, air-raid shelters, or hospital beds in Paris or London during the crisis. "Peace in our time" was the scrap of paper which British Prime Minister Neville Chamberlain brought back from the Munich conference, for which the mobilization of the English fleet and the activation of the Maginot Line had been to no avail. There were only four armed Spitfires, and the relative weakness of the Royal Air Force and the French Air Force presented grim alternatives. Hitler was correct. Neither Britain nor France really fought until they were attacked, which was also true of the Soviet Union and the United States. But that is another subject.

Two days before the Munich outcome, President Roosevelt dispatched Harry Hopkins, the director of the Works Progress Administration, on his first secret fact-finding mission to survey the capacity of the American aircraft industry. Hopkins, with the Deputy Chief of the Army Air Corps, General Arnold, reported that American production was almost 2,600 planes of all types per year. After Munich, Roosevelt confided to Hopkins that he was "sure then that we were going to get into the war and he believed that airpower [sic] would win it."

On 14 November 1938, Roosevelt outlined the "Magna Carta" of American air power, as Arnold termed it, at a top level White House conference. The President wanted at least an Army air arm of 20,000 planes and an annual production of 24,000 aircraft. Only this would influence Hitler. Congress, Roosevelt opined, might only approve 10,000 aircraft, of which 3,370 would be combat effective types and 3,750 combat reserve. Seven aircraft factories should also be built, only two of which would be activated. And, he said, the United States had to defend the Western hemisphere "from the North Pole to the South Pole."

Support of the White House was now the pacing factor in the rise of American air power, although other events also proved fortuitous. With the death of General Westover in a crash, Brig. General H. H. Arnold became Chief of the Air Corps in September 1938. He recruited officers to staff the air portions of the President's budget and message for the Congress in January 1939 (Colonels Carl Spaatz and McNarney, Majors Ira Eaker and Muir Fairchild, and Captains George Kenney and Lawrence Kuter). In November 1938, the Army's new Assistant Chief of Staff was Brig. General George C. Marshall, who proved to be the point man in getting Arnold into the Combined Chiefs of Staff. By late 1938, as Dr. Joseph Ames, Chairman of the NACA, wrote Charles A. Lindbergh in France, a new atmosphere pervaded Washington. It was a state of "peacetime war." Lindbergh had urged NACA to aim for the development of a 500mph airplane, and Ames, in reply, invited him to help NACA obtain additional laboratories for its aerodynamic and engine research and flight cleanup work on all new Navy and Army aircraft.

The take-off of American air power began on 12 January 1939, in President Roosevelt's State of the Union Message to the Congress. Responding to Munich, he declared that "our existing forces are so utterly inadequate that they must be immediately strengthened," and he sought $300 million (less than he had said he wanted) for Army Air Corps aircraft procurement. Within three months, Congress authorized upwards of a three-fold expansion of the Air Corps to 5,500 planes, 3,203 officers, and 45,000 enlisted men. This was a sharp contrast to the existing "utterly inadequate strength" of 1,700 tactical and training planes, 1,600 officers, and 18,000 enlisted men. As events would show, this was only the first expanded blueprint for the Army Air Corps. Planners had first to program for twenty tactical combat groups in the spring of 1939, and then re-program for forty-one groups by May 1940, fifty-four groups by July 1940, and eighty-four groups by the fall of 1941. These goals could not be instantly attained, and many growing pains would be experienced.

A major early problem soon stemmed from the purchase of first-line aircraft by Britain and France at the cost of the build-up of the American forces. By the end of 1939, the two countries had ordered 2,500 aircraft of all kinds and by April 1940, 2,500 combat aircraft. Obsolete planes such as the P-36 and its water-cooled offspring, the P-40, had to be produced until the more advanced P–38s and P–39s could be built. B–25s and B–26s were ordered to replace B–18s and A–20s, and the P–47 design was pushed. For FY 1940, seventy B–17s were ordered as well as sixteen four-engine Consolidated B–24s on a second production line. Contract civilian flying schools expanded pilot training to 7,000 per year in 1940. Bases for air defense and training had to be built "boom-style" in many places, including Alaska, Puerto Rico, and Panama. In March 1939, the GHQAF became a responsibility of the Chief of Air Corps, not the General Staff of the Army.

In May 1939, Colonel Lindbergh returned from Europe to attend meetings of the NACA. He met with General Arnold at West Point, briefing him on European aviation, particularly the German Air Force. Lindbergh agreed to serve on the Kilner Board, with Colonels Spaatz and Naiden, to determine the technical characteristics of all military aircraft. The Kilner Board also recommended that first-line aircraft sold to England and France carry with them a responsibility on the part of the purchasers to report on their combat effectiveness. With the help of Lindbergh, Arnold, and BuAer chief Admiral John Towers, the NACA put together its requirements for an additional laboratory. In July 1939, production models of the B–17 arrived at GHQAF at Langley Field. Seven made a "goodwill flight" to Argentina, at an average speed of 260 mph.

On 1 September 1939, the day the German *Wehrmacht* lunged into isolated Poland and World War II began, George C. Marshall became Acting Chief of Staff of the U.S. Army and Roosevelt declared the neutrality of the United States. U.S. Navy ships and PBY flying-boats began a Neutrality Patrol over the Carribbean and Atlantic sea approaches. Roosevelt also promptly dispatched an appeal to Germany, Italy, France, Britain, and Poland to refrain from "ruthless bombing from the air of civilians in unfortified centers of population." Herr Hitler replied that FDR's request "corresponds completely with my own point of view." American airmen noted that the German air force seized command of the air by destroying in one day the Polish air force on its airfields. The bombing of Warsaw to end the final resistance was the largest such bombardment of a city to date. The Polish campaign ended quickly and demonstrated a new word for the textbooks— *Blitzkrieg*. Screaming Stuka Ju-87 dive-bombers were shown in newsreels around the world and shocked Americans. The "phony war" began in Western Europe, but there was no air war yet.

American airmen also noted that Polish opposition to the Luftwaffe in the air had been virtually nil, although the Stuka, however stable a bombing platform, was indeed vulnerable without air superiority or greater defensive firepower. There was some soul searching. Major Harold George, commanding the 94th Bombardment Squadron, advised the GHQAF commander that "today American bombardment groups could not truly defend themselves against American pursuit groups." Early outcomes of the continuing bomber versus fighter debate were an increase in the defensive armament of the war-improved B–17s and arguments for "pursuit escorts," even before the effectiveness of radar was fully appreciated.

General Arnold dispatched hand-picked observers to the "phony war." Lt. Colonel George Kenney reported from Paris that observation balloons were worthless and most reconnaissance planes were slow and vulnerable. Just before the German attack in the west, General Delos Emmons and Colonel Spaatz were sent to Europe. From May to September 1940, Spaatz observed the fall of Belgium, Holland, and France, and the Battle of Britain. Once the British Fighter Command's system of integrated radar-fighter sector control was appreciated, even General Arnold began to think that night operations might be essential for B–17 forces. Spaatz's diary and his reports consistently maintained that England, fighting alone, would survive. The Luftwaffe, he argued, would not win daylight air superiority over England or otherwise achieve a decision during the ill-coordinated bombing campaign against the city of London. The German bombers could not defend themselves from the Hurricanes and the Spitfires, and Spaatz clearly agreed with Winston Churchill, who most persuasively stated what has been quoted only partially ever since—that Bomber Command was a part of the Battle of Britain. On 20 August 1940, Churchill said, lest anyone continue to ignore it:

> Never in the field of human conflict was so much owed by so many to so few. All hearts go out to the fighter pilots, whose brilliant actions we see with our own eyes day after day, but we must never forget that all the time, night after night, month after month, our bomber squadrons travel far into Germany, find their targets in the darkness by the highest navigational skill, aim their attacks, often under the heaviest fire with serious loss, with deliberate, careful discrimination, and inflict shattering blows upon the whole of the technical and war-making structure of the Nazi power. On no part of the Royal Air Force does the weight of the war fall more heavily than on the daylight bombers who will play an invaluable part in the case of the invasion and whose unflinching zeal it has been necessary in the meanwhile on numerous occasions to restrain.

Bomber Command's first raid on Berlin, a modest one, caused Hitler to alter the outcome of the entire Battle of Britain, the first turning point for the Allies in World War II.

While the German *Blitzkrieg* raced through Belgium and Holland and poured over France, President Roosevelt began his secret correspondence with the other former naval person, Winston Churchill, now just made Prime Minister. This tie led to the Atlantic Charter and coalition planning for the defeat of the Axis. On 16 May 1940, before Dunkirk and the Battle of Britain, President Roosevelt called upon the Congress for a further expansion of annual American aircraft production to 50,000 airplanes. He emphasized the importance of the Army and Navy air arms in hemispheric defense, but also planned to make available to the Royal Air Force new bombers from among the 50,000. Months before Roosevelt's request, General Marshall had approved the "First Aviation Objective" of the Air Corps, a force of 12,835 planes by April 1942. But by July 1941, the Army and the Navy had authorization for 50,000 airplanes. Arnold and Marshall also agreed that the buildup of the Army air forces did not mean their complete independence; they still depended on the Army's supporting services. In the process, however, the Army Air Corps became the Army Air Forces (AAF).

The tragedy of France in May 1940 masked other decisions by President Roosevelt which influenced the future history of air power, including his unpublicized decision to develop an atomic bomb before the Germans could. In June 1940 he created the National Defense Research Committee, later called the Office of Scientific Research and Development (SRD), in response to a proposal by Vannevar Bush of M.I.T., Chairman of the NACA and the first director of the SRD. The new office established working committees, similar to NACA's technical committees, to develop high technology armaments such as the proximity fuse, computers, radars, and rockets, all without putting scientists into uniform. NACA retained responsibility for aerodynamic research, though most of its work in the war would focus on solving the problems of existing equipment.

One of the remarkable documents in the history of American air power was the first product of the new War Plans Division of the Air Staff of the Army Air Forces. "AWPD–1" appeared just before Pearl Harbor in response to a White House request through the Secretaries of War and of Navy on 8 July 1941 for an estimate of the "overall production requirements required [sic] to defeat our potential enemies." Arnold placed Colonel Harold George in charge of an Air War Plans Division, to which was assigned a bevy of non-Ph.D.'s who were products of the Air Corps Tactical School. The plan was drafted, approved by Marshall and the Secretary of War, and submitted to the President on 11 September 1941 as the "Air Annex" to the estimate of overall production requirements.

AWPD–1 became the blue print for the procurement and deployment of the rapidly expanding Army Air Forces, particularly for the European theater. In concept, it was a "synthesis" of the doctrine of strategic air power as it had evolved at the Air Corps Tactical School and as it related to a global war outlined in the joint Rainbow 5 Plan modified by the Anglo-American Combined Chiefs of Staff. AWPD–1 proposed "Possible Lines of Action" which called for the defeat of the Luftwaffe and the support of an invasion of Nazi-held Europe by targeting bombing on electric power, oil, and transportation systems, in that order of priority. These priorities were remarkable forecasts, confirmed by events and the post-war testimony of the members of the U.S. Strategic Bombing Survey, Albert Speer, and scholars. The only post-war complaint would come from the airmen authors who yet believe that AWPD–1 could have been carried out much sooner at less cost in blood and energy. But that document's projection that strategic air power could not be built up in England to conduct decisive operations until mid-1944 proved right on the mark.

The major contribution of the AAF, according to AWPD–1, was for simultaneous war against Germany and Japan by strategic bombing. The AAF would need 239 combat groups and 108 support squadrons, 63,467 planes of all types, and 2,164,916 men. By April 1944, if the concerted effort was instituted immediately, the air offensive against Germany would reach effective strength. This forecast by anonymous staff officers ranks among the most valid in modern military history, since the Army Air Forces eventually had a peak strength of 2,400,000 men, 243 combat groups, and nearly 80,000 aircraft.

In the fall of 1941, the Navy air arm, like the Army Air Forces, was not yet prepared or deployed for a global war in Europe or Asia. The Navy could muster eight aircraft carriers, seven large and one small, five patrol wings and Marine aircraft wings, 5,900 pilots, and 21,678 enlisted men. The naval battles to come in the Pacific would be fought most often in the air where surface fleets never saw one another. For openers, Japanese naval air forces struck Pearl Harbor on 7 December 1941.

MARTIN BLUMENSON

D-DAY: LAUNCHING THE "GREAT CRUSADE"

*T*he most impressive event in American military history is the campaign for Normandy in 1944. Here came together the elements of naval, air, and ground power in a dramatic battle to reclaim western Europe from Nazi tyranny. Martin Blumenson, one of the country's foremost historians of the Second World War, argues that this event was more than a tactical maneuver, it marked the climactic strategic moment for both the Western Allies and Nazi Germany. If a successful lodgement could be made on the French coast, the doom of Adolf Hitler's Third Reich seemed obvious. Should the invasion fail, all the Allied victories in North Africa, Sicily, and Italy would become part of a great strategic economy of force effort by the Axis powers. The Normandy campaign was the climax of American strategic thought as outlined in the earlier article by Russell Weigley. Intellectual exercises were now put to the test of battle.

For six weeks the two sides fought bitterly contested battles for small gains. When Field Marshal Sir Bernard Montgomery's British-Canadian forces could not advance into the good tank country south of Caen, General Omar Bradley's First American Army secured the Cotentin Peninsula and advanced to a jumping-off site in the midst of the difficult hedgerow country around St.-Lô. With most of the German forces concentrated opposite the British-Canadian army, Bradley developed Operation Cobra, which grew from a limited breakout into a pursuit across open country in central and northern France. One of the critical consequences of this period was the failure to capture the German forces nearly entrapped between the advancing troops of Montgomery and Bradley at the town of Falaise. The missed opportunity in closing the Falaise pocket is one of the most hotly debated postwar controversies. Was it Montgomery's or Bradley's fault? Or, as Blumenson argues, was it a consequence of "a deficiency in doctrine" which focused more on terrain objectives than the enemy's armed forces? In this argument he emphasizes the lack of creative imagination among Allied senior commanders which Russell Weigley discussed in his article.

Moreover, the decision to deploy forces in a broad front movement across France and Belgium led to the next major strategic controversy of the war. Could the war have been ended in 1944 with a single stroke across the lowlands into the north German plain rather than with a broad front which confronted the Germans from the Alps to the North Sea? This is the issue confronted by Martin Van Creveld in the next article.

None of this should denigrate the magnitude of the Allied achievement. By the autumn of 1944 the Allies were on the German border far ahead of their schedule. Most of France and Belgium was liberated and the German army, not yet defeated but certainly badly mauled, was licking its wounds while preparing for one last, desperate strategic gamble. That gamble, known as the Battle of the Bulge, effectively eliminated the offensive capacity of the Germans.

For all the postwar controversy, one must not diminish another, often forgotten, element of this campaign. It marks the apex of joint and combined operations in American military history. Joint operations—involving the integration of combat and support elements of two or more services from the same country—were epitomized by the way in which the U.S. Navy both tactically and logistically supported the massive movement of men and supplies from North America to the French coast. Another example of joint operations came with General Dwight Eisenhower's integration of Army Air Force elements with the ground maneuver plan. Operation Cobra required a massive aerial bombardment which disrupted German troops and command and control apparatus to such an extent that the Allied ground troops could break through the defenses in the hedgerows. The aerial interdiction of the battlefield frustrated German reinforcement efforts throughout the campaign. Finally, during the breakout, close air support of the fast-moving troops of the First and Third U.S. Armies allowed greater operational flexibility on the part of ground forces than at any time previous in army history. In effect, the U.S. Army taught the Germans lessons on how to wage a blitzkrieg.

Successful combined operations, involving the services of military forces from several nations, required a tact which few military men possessed in greater abundance than General Eisenhower. In addition to being a military commander, Eisenhower needed the skills of a diplomat to soothe the ruffled feathers of nationalism and personality best epitomized by the careers of General George S. Patton and Field Marshal Montgomery. With a combined force utilizing the services of the British,

Americans, Canadians, Belgians, Dutch, Poles, and Frenchmen, Eisenhower navigated the treacherous shoals of international military cooperation with the skill of a master mariner.

D-Day, 6 June, 1944, had thrilled much of the world—those whose military forces precipitated the battle, as well as those who waited in bondage for their freedom. A psychological stroke of great impact, the invasion fulfilled an Allied promise to return to the Continent and to liberate the people occupied and oppressed by the Third Reich. It challenged the German territorial and political domination over much of Europe and signified the probable final act of the war.

The Allied endeavor was impressive by its very immensity. Fleets of aircraft, armadas of ships, armies of soldiers came across the English Channel and struck the German defenses. On that day, Allied planes flew a seemingly never-ending total of 14,000 sorties, dropped bombs on the area and brought three airborne divisions, more than 20,000 paratroopers and glidermen, to Normandy. Almost 200,000 men working more than 5,000 ships of all kinds shelled the beaches and transported five divisions to designated landing sites.

At the end of the day, 156,000 Allied combatants were on French soil. In the process of coming ashore, they turned Ste.-Mère Église, Pointe-du-Hoc, Vierville-sur-Mer, Arromanches, Benouville and other localities into sacred places.

The mighty undertaking was the climax of years of hope and preparation. From the summer of 1940, after their expulsion from the Continent, their necessary departure from Dunkirk and other ports, the British resolved to reenter the mainland and dislodge the Germans from their control. After Pearl Harbor, in the spring of 1942 the Americans joined in common aspiration to close with and defeat the main German forces in western Europe.

The Allied campaigns in the Mediterranean—in North Africa, Sicily and southern Italy–in 1943 delayed the cross-Channel attack. Finally, at the beginning of 1944, the Allies were firmly determined to confront the enemy and to destroy him. Breaking the crust of the German defenses on D-Day was the opening stage of a struggle that was bound to continue. Both sides had the opportunity to inflict or to suffer a strategic victory or defeat.

If the Germans turned back the invaders in the next few days or weeks and forced the Allies to retire from the contested shore, the European war, begun in 1939, would go on indefinitely; and the Allies would have to concede the prolongation of German power in Europe.

If the Allies remained in France, expanded their beachhead and gained a firm lodgment, the Germans would have to recognize the fact that they had lost the war.

Warfare is a political act and military action is undertaken in pursuit of political ends. In northwest Europe in World War II, the basic political Allied goal was the removal of Adolf Hitler's government. This was to be accomplished by a German admission of unconditional surrender, a political decision. And this was to be achieved by a military victory, by soundly defeating the enemy forces.

A strategic victory is achieved when a defeat of the enemy military forces compels the enemy government to modify its political aims. In other words, a tactical victory, defeating the enemy on the field of battle, is different from a strategic success. The victory is strategic when it has repercussions on the enemy's political desires and prompts a change in the enemy's political objectives.

For example, Field Marshal Erwin Rommel's outstanding success at Kasserine Pass in Tunisia, although a severe Allied setback and disaster, was nothing more than a tactical triumph, for it stopped short of inflicting a strategic reverse on the Allies, that is, of affecting Allied long-range political designs. The Allied conquest of Sicily, on the other hand, was strategic in its consequences, for it prompted both the overthrow of Benito Mussolini and, shortly thereafter, Italian capitulation—political actions.

The Allied landings on D-Day had the makings of a strategic success. If the Allies succeeded, they would trigger an adverse effect on the enemy government. But their failure would compel the Allied governments to rethink their political wishes. Thus, throughout the final three weeks of June, 1944, the adversaries fought for strategic advantage.

Very generally, the immediate mission of the Allied troops coming ashore on D-Day and shortly thereafter was to push inland, to get away from the sea, to stake out a toehold, then to carve out a substantial beachhead where additional men, equipment and supplies could be placed and committed; finally, to secure a lodgment area, that portion of France bounded by the Seine and Loire rivers and including Brittany and about half of Normandy.

Possession of the lodgment area, it was hoped by D plus 90, early in September, would signify completion of the "Overlord" operational invasion plan. Only then, according to pre-invasion thinking, after building up resources in manpower and weapons, would the Allies launch their final and climactic—strategic—battle to overcome the German forces on the approaches to Germany.

In June, the Americans of Lt. Gen. Omar N. Bradley's First U.S. Army found themselves for the most part in water-logged meadows, land barely above sea level, flooded plains crossed by causeways, which rigidly canalized routes of advance easily blocked by small numbers of German troops. In that region the hedgerows are particularly thick and ubiquitous; they presented natural obstacles to forward movement, as well as fortresses for defenders. American progress, it was obvious to everyone, was bound to be slow on that highly defensible ground.

In contrast, the British and Canadians of Lt. Gen. Sir Miles C. Dempsey's Second British Army were on dry ground excellent for mechanized offensive warfare. Just beyond Caen, which Field Marshal Sir Bernard L. Montgomery, the army group commander, had designated a D-Day objective but had failed to take, was the Falaise plain, exactly right for maneuvering armored forces offensively and for building airfields to support the ground units. Driving from Caen to Falaise and beyond was also the shortest route to Paris, an important objective for many reasons. A push from the beaches in the British and Canadian zone was obviously the promising avenue of advance.

As a consequence, the British-Canadian force brought amphibiously to France for the D-Day assault was initially larger than the American contingent, about 75,000 to 55,000. The British and Canadians also had more tanks and artillery, and the buildup at first favored the British and Canadians over the Americans. This made sense, not only for immediate offensive operations in suitable terrain, but also for defense.

The differences of the terrain were apparent to the Germans, too. They could tell clearly where the advantageous ground was located for their purpose—and their reaction was to get off an immediate counterattack. Their traditional doctrine was the lightning strike, *blitzkrieg*. They had planned and executed quick and overwhelming offensives against Austria in 1866 and against France in 1870. They had mounted a lightning attack in 1914 to carry out the Schlieffen plan. Their *blitzkrieg* in Poland in 1939, in western Europe in 1940, in the Soviet Union in 1941 and 1942 was masterful.

In 1944, the Germans set about to launch a decisive—strategic—counterattack to throw the Allies back into the sea. Where could they do this? In terrain favorable for offensive operations, on the ground where the British and Canadians stood. They mounted two serious thrusts in June. Both failed against stout British and Canadian resistance bolstered by Allied air power and naval shelling. But in the process, the Germans blunted Allied progress.

The situation at the end of June resembled a standoff. The Allied beachhead was relatively small and congested. Very few airfields had been constructed. The flow of supplies was behind schedule. Yet, on balance, the Allies had won the opening round. They had joined and consolidated their initial footholds on the shore and held a sizable beachhead. They were no longer seriously troubled by the danger of being expelled from the Continent.

They had brought a million soldiers to France. They had captured the major port of Cherbourg. If the Germans had obstructed their attempts to expand their beachhead further, they had failed to eject the invaders or even to cripple seriously their efforts to come to the Continent in strength.

Was the invasion then a strategic success? The top German military commanders reading the signs believed so. Field Marshal Gerd von Rundstedt, commander in chief in the West, advised Hitler's headquarters over the telephone to "make peace, you fools." And Field Marshal Rommel, commander of Army Group B, asked Hitler, in a daring impertinence, how he still expected to win the war.

Hitler refused to accept the Allied victory as a triumph with strategic dimensions. Believing mystically in a miracle, convinced emotionally that he would eventually win the war, he was incapable of acknowledging the meaning of the events. He was, as a matter of fact, blindly irrational.

Because Gen. von Rundstedt was too prominent a figure to reprimand or to punish, Hitler immediately relieved him from his command on the ostensible basis of his old age and poor health and placed him on the retired list. After dressing down Gen. Rommel for what he called his defeatism, Hitler allowed him to remain at his post.

It was then, apparently, that Gen. Rommel joined the conspirators who plotted to do away with Hitler, not because of his internal policies and concentration camps but rather because he had lost the war and could not face the reality. In their eyes, the Allies had gained a strategic triumph. Continuing the conflict was senseless.

On 20 July, 1944, they tried to assassinate the *Führer*. They came close to doing so, but he survived the bomb planted under the table in his conference room. Had they succeeded in killing him, they would have replaced him and formed a new government in order to negotiate for peace.

Thus, the success of the Overlord operation was a strategic victory because it had an impact on Germany's political aims. Hitler's stubborn refusal to alter his political position, even after the attempt on his life, compelled the Allies to drive the truth home to him and to his followers. Having produced no strategic results of an overt nature, the Allies set about to conquer the ground of their defined lodgment area in July.

Now Gen. Montgomery changed the plan. If the primary factor in ground operations is the terrain, then both Allies and Germans had reacted to this condition. The Germans were massed in strength facing the British and Canadians because of the dictates of the ground. And during the first three weeks of the invasion, Allied progress into the interior of France had been slow and difficult. The Allies seemed to be bogged down, and visions of stalemate and of World War I-type static war haunted the Allied camp.

Gen. Montgomery had failed to capture Caen, the gateway to the Falaise ground. With the Germans concentrated against the British and Canadian part of the front, a costly battle was required to break through their defenses. And British manpower resources were declining to such an extent that the British were already disbanding divisions and using the troops as replacements in active formations. Gen. Montgomery had to be careful, prudent, even cautious, for he lacked the manpower to be bold.

Instead of pursuing a major offensive on the Falaise plain, he looked elsewhere. He stated that he would attract and hold the bulk of the German forces to the British and Canadian side, where the Germans were already in position, so that the Americans could make the main Allied effort in the water-logged region on the right.

This fell to Gen. Bradley, who accepted the role without qualm. Although he certainly understood the difficulties of driving ahead in the area, he agreed either because he was a good soldier or because he saw no alternative. In little more than two weeks in July, Gen. Bradley's First Army pushed through the flooded meadows and the hedgerows to dry ground—but at a frightful cost. The Americans took 40,000 casualties to move about seven miles forward. In terms of the troops on hand, this figure is the highest casualty rate for the entire European campaign, worse than the Hürtgen Forest, worse than that for the Battle of the Bulge.

The point is that the Germans massed their forces in front of Gen. Montgomery not because he drew them there and held them but because that was where the logic of ground warfare attracted them. They had relatively few units facing the Americans, but that was all they needed. Gen. Montgomery's failure to get onto the Falaise plain had made it necessary for Gen. Bradley to engineer the Allied main effort on ground distinctly disadvantageous for offensive warfare.

At last on dry ground favorable for mechanized operations, Gen. Bradley planned an attack to break through the German defenses. He would use strategic bombers to saturate a target immediately ahead of the ground troops and open a hole for mobile exploitation. Gen. Bradley's plan, code-named "Cobra," employed two corps, the VII and VIII under Maj. Gens. J. Lawton Collins and Troy Middleton, respectively. Several infantry divisions in Gen. Collins's corps would hold the sides of the hole opened by the bombers and enable two armored divisions and a motorized infantry division to rush through. The goal was Coutances, a relatively limited objective about seven miles ahead of Gen. Middleton's front. The idea was for Gen. Collins to cut off the Germans facing Gen. Middleton.

When Gen. Bradley informed Field Marshal Montgomery of his plan, Gen. Dempsey was present. Gen. Montgomery approved the Bradley concept. After Gen. Bradley departed, Gen. Dempsey suggested to Gen. Montgomery that he try a similar operation. Gen. Montgomery told Gen. Dempsey to go ahead and draw up a plan. In compliance, Gen. Dempsey formulated "Goodwood," an attack much like Cobra. The major difference was the vagueness of the objective. Whether the endeavor was to get troops all the way to Falaise, whether it was to get armored forces, as Gen. Montgomery said, "cracking about" in the Falaise area or whether it was designed to draw the attention of the Germans away from Cobra has since been in dispute.

The two operations were supposed to go relatively quickly together, Cobra soon after Goodwood, like a one-two punch. But bad weather interfered, prompting postponements. Eventually Goodwood started on 18 July, Cobra a week later.

Goodwood was a difficult attack for several reasons. The approaches to the battleground were extremely constricted. What was more important, the Germans had by then built a solid defensive line in depth across the Falaise plain. Savage fighting took place for 3½ days, and the Allies were unable to penetrate the German defenses. Gen. Montgomery brought the battle to an end on a note of Allied disappointment and gloom.

Cobra, in contrast, was successful beyond all expectation. It started an extraordinary series of events that fashioned another strategic triumph in embryo, one that again brought the Allies hope for a quick end to the war. Cobra broke the German defenses near St.-Lô, and on the third day of the battle, Gen. Bradley extended his objective from Coutances to Avranches, 30 miles ahead. By the end of July, American troops had opened a huge hole in the German line and had taken Avranches, a decisive objective that gave access to Brittany on the south and west, and to LeMans, Chartres and Paris on the east.

As the long and wearing positional warfare in the hedgerows gave way to mobile operations of a most fluid nature, Lt. Gen. George S. Patton Jr.'s Third U.S. Army became operational. Lt. Gen. Courtney H. Hodges replaced Gen. Bradley at the head of the First Army, and Gen. Bradley stepped up to command the 12th U.S. Army Group. Although Gen. Bradley was now coequal in status with Gen. Montgomery, who directed the 21st Army Group, with Gen. Dempsey's British and Lt. Gen. Henry D. G. Crerar's Canadian armies under his command, Gen. Montgomery remained the Allied ground forces commander.

Gen. Patton's army was supposed to enter into and conquer Brittany in order to secure the ports of Brest, Lorient and other harbors. But because the German left had been crushed, Gen. Dwight D. Eisenhower on 2 August decided to send only one corps of Gen. Patton's troops to the west into Brittany. The rest went to the east. In the lead was Maj. Gen. Wade H. Haislip's XV Corps coming through Avranches. Gen. Haislip began a headlong rush, and after a week his men were 75 miles east of Avranches, at LeMans.

At that time, three things happened. Gen. Patton, with Gen. Bradley's permission and Field Marshal Montgomery's approval, turned Gen. Haislip north toward Argentan. Gen. Crerar's Canadian forces attacked from the Caen area south toward Falaise. And Hitler, trying to reestablish a solid left flank in Normandy in order to restore the conditions that had hemmed in the Allies during June and most of July, launched an attack to the west through Mortain toward Avranches.

If the Germans reached and regained Avranches, they would cut off Gen. Patton's army. Once again, they would have a strong and relatively short defensive line in Normandy. That would reimpose the static fighting that had marked the combat before Cobra. Jumping off toward Avranches, the Germans were stopped cold in Mortain.

As Gen. Haislip raced north toward Argentan, as the Canadians advanced south toward Falaise, as the Germans struggled for several days to move westward to Avranches, the Falaise pocket was in the process of being formed. With the Canadians at Falaise and the Americans at Argentan, 15 miles would separate the two Allied forces. This was the Argentan-Falaise gap, sometimes known simply as the Falaise gap. If the Canadians and Americans continued beyond those towns to junction, they would completely encircle the German Fifth Panzer and Seventh armies in Normandy. Thus surrounded, the German forces were doomed to be swept from the field.

Here was a classic opportunity for a battle of annihilation, another Cannae, another Tannenberg, another Stalingrad—and it never came to a satisfactory conclusion. On 13 August, as Gen. Haislip approached Argentan, as the Canadians fought toward Falaise, Hitler finally and with great reluctance gave the German troops permission to turn back from Mortain and to cut their way out of their potential encirclement. At that decisive moment, the Allied direction of the battle fell apart. During the next three days of critical importance, there was apparently no communication between Gens. Montgomery and Bradley.

No doubt aware through Ultra Secret intercepts of German messages of a German plan to stampede out of the closing pocket, fearing that Gen. Haislip's corps was overextended and vulnerable, Gen. Bradley instructed Gen. Patton to halt Gen. Haislip at Argentan. Gen. Montgomery, believing that the Canadians coming down from the north would reach not only Falaise but also Argentan before the Americans, remained silent. On the following day, without informing Gen. Montgomery, Gen. Bradley gave Gen. Patton permission to keep two divisions at Argentan and to send the corps headquarters and two divisions to the east, to the Seine River, there to trap the Germans escaping the pocket through the Falaise gap.

When the Canadians finally took Falaise on 16 August, Gen. Montgomery asked Gen. Bradley to push north through Argentan in order to meet the Canadians moving south from Falaise. The two forces were to meet at a place called Trun. To comply with the request, both Gens. Bradley and Patton improvised a corps headquarters at Argentan, each misunderstood the other, both fumbled, and the result was slippage and delay.

The pocket was finally closed—but not very firmly—three days later. By then, most of the Germans had escaped. Another strategic opportunity on the part of the Allies had slipped away.

How can this be explained? It is always difficult to ensure close cooperation and coordination in coalition warfare, particularly at vital moments. At Waterloo, for example, the Duke of Wellington did not know until the last minute whether Field Marshal Gebhard von Blücher would arrive on the battlefield in time to defeat Napoleon Bonaparte. So it was, too, at Argentan and Falaise 150 years later. What is now called "interoperability" is terribly difficult to carry out, and Gens. Montgomery and Bradley failed to grasp a marvelous opportunity to attain a decisive—strategic—victory that would undoubtedly have brought the end of the war within close reach.

Another reason for the Allied failure to close the pocket firmly in time to trap and destroy the bulk of the German forces probably stemmed from a deficiency in doctrine. The Allied objective was confusing instead of clear-cut. There were conflicting notions of the proper Allied course of action. Part of the lack of focus came from a legacy of World War I, when the thoughts of all commanders were concentrated grimly on the need to gain ground.

Furthermore, the overall objective of operation Overlord was to secure the defined lodgment area. Having gained all this ground, all this room, the Allies were supposed to halt at the Seine and regroup and reorganize for the subsequent battle to get to Germany.

Field Marshal Montgomery had had his eyes fixed on obtaining the Overlord lodgment area when Gen. Bradley, spurred by Gen. Patton, had pointed out the marvelous opportunity to create the Falaise pocket. Gen. Montgomery agreed, but he no doubt regarded the larger perspective as being more important. If so, he betrayed an inflexible conformance with previously established plans, an inability to seize advantage of unpredicted breaks.

Beyond the lodgment area, the ultimate objective of the Continental operations was Germany, and specifically the Ruhr. Before the cross-Channel attack, the Combined Chiefs of Staff had instructed Gen. Eisenhower to strike to the heart of Germany and to destroy the German armed forces. With this as the directing idea, the Allies were looking to Germany and to the Ruhr, the industrial heart, which they believed the Germans would have to defend with the major part of their forces.

That, the Allied commanders had long believed, was where they would destroy the German military might. They had the glittering opportunity to do so at Argentan and Falaise.

Although the pre-invasion planning had contemplated a pause at the Seine, the chance to pursue the Germans fleeing from the pocket was too good to overlook. Gen. Eisenhower ordered his armies to cross the Seine at once and to race toward the German frontier and the heart of Germany.

There was one possible exception among the high Allied commanders. Gen. Patton had been the first to grasp the idea of encirclement at Argentan and Falaise. Halted at Argentan, he persuaded Gen. Bradley to send half of the XV Corps to trap the Germans at the Seine. Still later, he talked of a third great outflanking maneuver to catch the Germans at the Somme. This was consistent with Gen. Patton's thought. In December, when he learned of the German Ardennes counteroffensive, his initial reaction was to let the Germans go as far as they wished in order to increase the Allied chances of cutting them all off at the base of the Belgian Bulge.

But his concept did not prevail, and in August, after Gen. Bradley reoriented the Third Army to go eastward across the Seine River below Paris, Gen. Patton had no option but, like everyone, to drive as far and as fast as he could toward Germany. That was the magnet, and its pull obscured an edict central to Karl von Clausewitz's theory. According to Clausewitz, the main objective of an army at war is to defeat the opposing army. The legitimate target is the enemy armed forces—unless, of course, the Allied commanders thought that they had already crushed and destroyed the German armed forces at Argentan and Falaise. For there was much evidence that they had inflicted a catastrophic defeat on the Germans. They could see, immediately afterward, the horrendous conditions. According to one report:

> The carnage wrought . . . as the artillery of two Allied armies and the massed air forces pounded the ever-shrinking pocket was perhaps the greatest of the war. The roads and fields were littered with thousands of enemy dead and wounded, wrecked and burning vehicles, smashed artillery pieces, carts laden with the loot of France overturned and smoldering, dead horses and cattle swelling in the summer's heat.

It looked as though the Allies had smashed two German field armies. The remnants who escaped had lost and abandoned much equipment and many weapons. They then had to run another gauntlet of fire as they crossed the Seine River. As they streamed across France toward the German border, into Belgium and Holland, harassed by air power and by pursuing Allied ground units, they were obviously disorganized and disheartened.

What remained of the formidable German combat units in Normandy, the Allies believed, was a weak and insignificant force. The end of the war seemed to be around the corner. The Combined Chiefs of Staff meeting in Quebec turned their attention to the Pacific. It was all over in Europe but the shouting.

The problem was, no one could tell, then and now, exactly how many Germans escaped. The Allies counted and buried approximately 10,000 German bodies inside the pocket. They estimated, for they did not know for sure, 50,000 prisoners taken. If there had been 300,000 troops engaged, the rest—or most of them—reached safety, and probably in better condition than originally believed. Only one corps headquarters was captured inside the pocket; the other important headquarters managed to get out more or less intact.

The failure to close the pocket earlier and to eliminate the two German field armies in Normandy made it possible for the Germans to live to fight another day. Despite their apparent disorganization and weakness, they erected a cohesive defensive line on the approaches to their homeland, an achievement they later called the "Miracle in the West."

And then the whole exhilarating pursuit across and beyond the Seine reached a dead end as gasoline supplies dwindled and dried. The pursuit ran out and winter approached, and the two opponents settled down and resumed the struggle in a static manner. The war, it was plain to see, was far from over. Hitler had yet to be strategically defeated. He took Gen. von Rundstedt out of retirement and gave him back his old job early in September. Perhaps Gen. von Rundstedt was not so pessimistic as he had been at the beginning of July.

At this point, another strategic opportunity for the Allies arose, "Market-Garden." An airborne operation to seize important bridges at Eindhoven, Nijmegen and Arnhem in Holland, together with a ground offensive driving up that corridor to reinforce the airborne troops, Market-Garden was the result of several motivations—among them, to outflank the German West Wall, to get onto the north German plain, to threaten the Ruhr, to liberate Holland, to overrun the V1 and V2 rocket missile sites. But Gen. Eisenhower, it seems more than probable, approved the attack both to provide impetus to the dying pursuit and to gain a dramatic victory to win the war.

Success in Market-Garden meant capturing the bridge at Arnhem. That would get the Allies across the lower Rhine River. The special feature of this accomplishment was the hope of breaking the German will to resist. There was something mystical about the Rhine to the German people; it was their legendary protection. To cross that obstacle would show the Germans as nothing else that further opposition was hopeless, useless. The situation again was one posing a strategic opportunity.

Market-Garden, as it turned out, was almost successful—according to Gen. Montgomery, 80-percent successful. But the bridge at Arnhem eluded the Allies. And if crossing the Rhine had strategic validity, that sealed the fate of ending the war in 1944. No further possibility existed of bringing the war to a conclusion that year. Allied forces had to wait until March, 1945, to cross the Rhine River and only then did the German forces begin to collapse. Canadian troops entered Arnhem on 15 April. Three weeks later, Germany surrendered unconditionally.

Three strategic opportunities existed during the course of the European war. The Allies succeeded the first time by coming ashore in Normandy in strength, only to be balked by the implacable and insane resolve of the *Führer*. At Falaise and at Arnhem, the Allies were on the verge of attaining strategic victories, and both times the possibility slipped away.

Perhaps in view of Hitler's lack of logic, his unwillingness to face the facts and accept reality, no strategic coup was feasible. If so, what was left was only a campaign of attrition. In that case, the Normandy invasion was the glorious commencement of all that followed, the beginning that made the rest possible.

"BROAD FRONT" OR "KNIFELIKE THRUST"?

N*o single factor more affects operational decisions than logistics. The capacity to develop, acquire, provide, move, distribute, maintain, and dispose of military materiel and to acquire, train, move, and replace personnel is central to success in combat. Resource limits constrain operational options. In the summer of 1944 this became painfully obvious as the Allied armies broke out of Normandy and moved across France and Belgium toward the German frontier. Logisticians are notoriously cautious, whereas field commanders can be exceptional risk takers, men who disregard the limits that supply places upon their daring plans. These are the problems that faced General Dwight Eisenhower and the Supreme Headquarters Allied Expeditionary Force staff. The laborious planning that went into Operation Overlord predicted slow progress across France, based on the assumption that the Germans would defend along each major river line. Logistically this could be supported since plans called for reaching the Seine River by the end of August and the Rhine River by June 1945. Suddenly such caution seemed outrageous as the army groups commanded by General Omar Bradley and Field Marshal Sir Bernard Montgomery moved across France and Belgium to the German border by early September 1944.*

What General Clausewitz called "the friction of war" inhibited operations in Normandy. This dissipated somewhat after Operation Cobra and the Anglo-American armies found themselves facing limited resistance as the German generals moved their troops back in the face of the Allied onslaught. Instead of an enemy, the Allies found their operations constrained by a limit on supplies. Three basic factors caused this situation.

First, a long-term planning decision was made by General of the Army George C. Marshall early in the war to limit the ground forces of the U.S. Army to ninety divisions and to expend greater resources on Army Air Force procurement, training, supply, and operations. This "ninety-division gamble" was one of the greatest calculated risks of General Marshall's career. In hindsight we know that the strategic bombing campaign against Germany was not nearly as successful as War Department planners expected. It took from the ground forces combat and supply troops and materiel, especially gasoline, which were necessary to support any exploitation of the Normandy breakout. Dr. Maurice Matloff of the army's Center of Military History concluded:

> *The 90-division troop basis represented . . . [the War Department plan-*
> *ners'] attempt to provide a realistic meeting ground of three fundamentals*
> *of modern warfare—strategy, production, and manpower. It represented*
> *the relatively small, if compact, ground combat force that the country that*
> *was also served as the "arsenal of democracy" found it could provide for a*
> *global coalition war without unduly straining the war economy and stan-*
> *dard of living of the American people.*

The second cause of the logistical shortfall were the limits imposed by the lack of adequate port facilities to receive the vast array of supplies available and by a transporta- tion system across western Europe that was disrupted by a combination of Allied bombardment and German demolition. As Martin Van Creveld of the Hebrew University, Jerusalem, makes clear in this excerpt from his Supplying War: Logistics from Wallenstein to Patton, *the capacity to support Montgomery's and Bradley's armies at a distance of several hundred miles from the coast was limited. This problem could have been alleviated had British forces seized the islands in the Scheldt estuary, which would have allowed the use of the port of Antwerp. Clearly Montgomery and his staff failed to recognize the critical importance of this port to the logistical support of any operational plan.*

These two factors then affected the final, strategic difficulty: How should the campaign against Germany proceed? Should there be a broad front attack across a line running from the Alps to the Channel? Or should there be a narrow thrust deep into Germany through the Lowlands and across the Rhine near the center of German industrial output in the Ruhr valley? Advocates of the broad front strategy contended it was logistically more supportable and would compel the Germans to disperse their limited forces across a wide front. Proponents of the narrow thrust, led by Field Marshal Montgomery, felt that such an attack would end the war in 1944 and forego the bloody battles of the winter of 1944–45 and the dramatic loss of life in the concentration camps and from aerial bombardment that would continue until the following April.

They felt the broad front strategy dispersed Allied forces and violated the principle of concentration of effort. Eisenhower decided to proceed with the broad front strategy.

No study of this decision can exclude the nationalistic and personality clashes that were at the center of the controversy. Montgomery's contentious personality and British arrogance made him highly suspect in the American camp. To this day most of the vigorous advocates of the narrow front strategy are British. Nigel Hamilton, Montgomery's biographer, argues: "By attempting simultaneously to seize the Ruhr and Frankfurt and the Saar [the broad front strategy], the Allies risked failing to achieve any of these—thus surrendering the chance of a concentrated drive upon Berlin." Clay Blair, who helped General Bradley write A General's Life, concludes: "Events would soon prove Bradley correct on all counts" relative to the necessity of a broad front strategy and Montgomery's inability to develop his vaunted thrust in the abortive Operation Market Garden, known in film lore as A Bridge Too Far. Professor Van Creveld tries to avoid these arguments and to concentrate on the logistical constraints.

For readers unfamiliar with the cast of characters and units in this discussion and Van Creveld's use of British forms to designate units, a glossary of units and commanders is included here.

> SHAEF—*Supreme Headquarters Allied Expeditionary Force, General of the Army Dwight D. Eisenhower.*
>
> 21. Army Group—*Twenty-First Army Group, Field Marshal Sir Bernard L. Montgomery, containing two armies:*
>
> 1. Canadian Army—*First Canadian Army, Lieutenant General H. D. G. Crerar.*
>
> 2. British Army—*Second British Army, Lieutenant General Sir Miles Dempsey.*
>
> 12. Army Group—*Twelfth Army Group, General Omar N. Bradley, containing two armies:*
>
> 1. U.S. Army—*First U.S. Army, Lieutenant General Courtney H. Hodges.*
>
> 3. U.S. Army—*Third U.S. Army, Lieutenant General George S. Patton, Jr.*
>
> COMZ—*Communications Zone, Lieutenant General John C. H. Lee, supply headquarters and troops for U.S. forces in Europe.*

Of all the problems raised by the Allied campaign in northwestern Europe in 1944–5, the question whether it would have been possible to put an early end to the war by means of a quick thrust from Belgium to the Ruhr is perhaps the most important. The literature on this subject is vast and still growing. Here we shall only attempt a brief summary of the main views. These appear to be as follows:

(a) The one put forward by Chester Wilmot and, above all, Field Marshal Montgomery himself. These two have argued that the strategic opportunity presented itself in September 1944. Given a clear-cut decision and a willingness to stake out a meaningful order of priorities on the part of the supreme commander, 2. British and 1. American Armies could have captured the Ruhr—and perhaps Berlin as well. Eisenhower, however, refused to concentrate his logistic resources behind Dempsey and Hodges. In particular, he did not want to halt Patton's 3. Army. Consequently, the opportunity to end the war in 1944 was lost.

(b) To counter Montgomery's accusations, Eisenhower has defended his decision on strategic grounds, claiming that a thrust by part of his forces into 'the heart of Germany' was too risky and would have led to 'nothing but certain destruction'. Subsequent writers have produced more arguments to justify his decision, including the need to avoid offending Allied (that is, American) public opinion by halting Patton, differences over the structure of the chain of command in France, and—last though not least—logistics.

(c) Finally, Basil Liddell Hart has suggested that, while the opportunity to go for the Ruhr did exist, failure to utilize it lay not so much with Eisenhower as with Montgomery himself. In particular, the discovery at the critical moment that 1,400 British-built lorries had defective engines was decisive. Given this, there was little that Eisenhower could do to help, for Patton's 3. Army was receiving so few supplies that not even by stopping it could enough transport have been made available to enable Montgomery to occupy the Ruhr.

Although the accounts of the situation that faced the Allies early in September 1944 differ in conclusion and even in detail, there is little doubt that operations in the period just preceding had been among the most spectacular in history. Having sent its advance formations across the Seine on 20 August, Patton's 3. Army covered almost 200 miles in twelve days until it stopped in front of Metz. Hodges' 1. Army on his left advanced even further, reaching the Albert Canal in eastern Belgium on 6 September. Montgomery's 21. Army Group, whose rate of progress had hitherto been markedly slower than that of the American forces, now surpassed itself by surging forward across northern France and Belgium, capturing Antwerp—its port virtually intact—on 5 September and only coming to a halt on the Meuse–Escaut Canal four days later. It was a performance of which the originators of the *Blitzkrieg* would have been proud, and one which the Allies themselves had not foreseen.

As might have been expected in the light of previous events, all these operations were carried out against the advice of the SHAEF logisticians, who declared them to be utterly impossible. Compelled to revise their cautious estimates of July, they completed a new feasibility-study on 11 August. This showed that *if* a whole series of conditions was met it *might* be possible to support a tentative offensive by four U.S. divisions across the Seine on 7 September. Even this conclusion, however, was qualified by the suggestion that operations south of the Seine should be halted in favour of an attack on the Channel ports, and that the liberation of Paris should be postponed until late October when railways from the Normandy area would hopefully be available to carry relief supplies. As it was, Paris was liberated on 25 August. By the target date of 7 September both Patton and Hodges had already gone 200 miles behind the Seine. A week later 16 U.S. divisions were being supported, albeit inadequately, on or near the German frontier on both sides of the Ardennes while several more were engaged on active combat operations in Brittany. All this was achieved in spite of the fact that the conditions laid down in the paper of 11 August had been only partly met. Seldom can calculations by staff officers have proved so utterly wrong.

Supply over the rapidly expanding lines of communication—those in the American sector grew from 200 or 250 miles to over 400, and those in the British one from 80 to nearly 300—could not, of course, be effected without abandoning all orderly procedures and employing emergency measures. With petrol in their tanks and rations in their pockets, combat units, faced with very little organized opposition, could accelerate their progress almost at will. Not so COMZ, however, which found it impossible to make depôts keep pace with the rapidly advancing front. No sooner had a site been selected than it was left behind, and after several attempts (each costly in terms of transport) COMZ gave up in despair and concentrated on bringing up the most essential items from bases that were sometimes as much as 300 miles in the rear. The transport to carry the supplies across these distances came from hundreds of units considered less essential—heavy and anti-aircraft artillery, engineers, chemical warfare, and the like—which were stripped of their vehicles and left immobilized, sometimes on reduced rations, as were three divisions newly arriving in France, whose organic trucks were taken away and formed into improvised GTR companies. While rations, POL and ammunition were being rushed forward, the supply of everything else, including, in particular, clothing and engineering stores, had to be deferred. Air transport was used on a grand scale but failed to deliver more than an average of 1,000 tons a day because of the lack of airfields near the front line and, even worse, because aircraft were withdrawn to take part in a series of would-be airborne operations that never materialized. The most famous of all these expedients to supply the front was the Red Ball Express, a loop

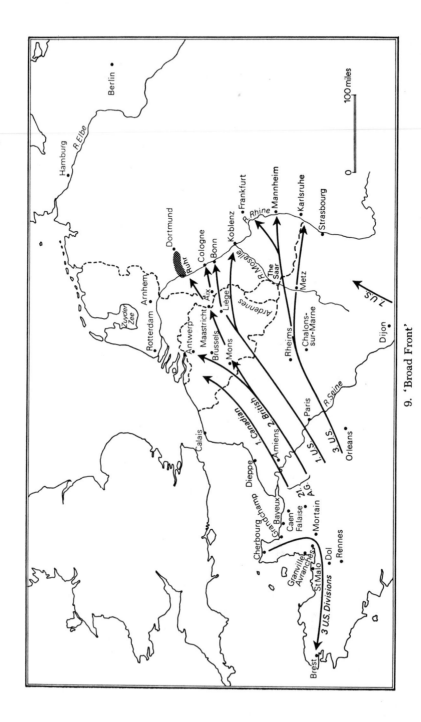

9. 'Broad Front'

320

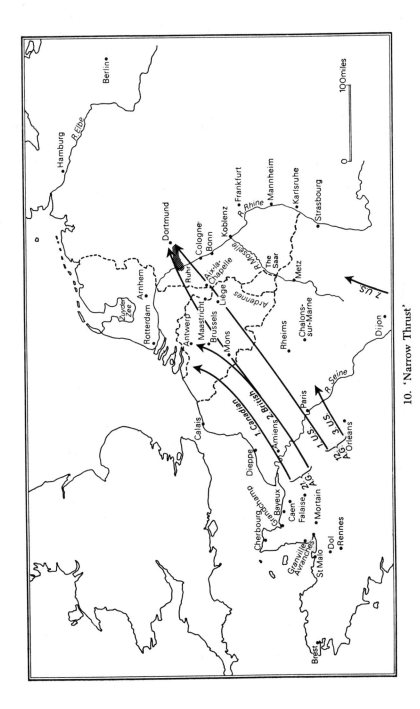

10. 'Narrow Thrust'

system of one-way highways reserved exclusively for the supply service over which thousands of trucks rumbled night and day.

These emergency measures notwithstanding, the flow of supplies reaching the front gradually diminished until, on 2 September 3. Army's advance was brought to a halt. 1. Army struggled on for a few more days before it too came to a standstill. Compared with deliveries to both Armies of over 19,000 tons a day during the second week of August, COMZ could only promise 7,000 at the end of the month, and it is doubtful whether even this figure was in fact met. Stocks in the hands of the front-line units dwindled at an alarming rate, e.g. from 10.5 days of POL supply at 1. Army on 5 August to 0.3 days on 2 September and zero one week later. Meanwhile, reserves available in Normandy actually rose as they could not be transported forward. Though consumption of ammunition had fallen off by thirty to ninety per cent since July, deliveries fell so short of demands that a single corps (the XX) could request supplies in excess of all the tonnage allocated to 3. Army, to which it belonged, put together. Since whatever ammunition dumps that could be established were quickly left behind, both 1. and 3. Armies resorted to the creation of rolling magazines, a procedure which, though effective in ensuring that at least some supplies would always be available, wasted transport.

As always happens when supplies are short, friction and even tension arose between the front-line troops and the supporting services in their rear. 3. Army in particular was notorious for the unorthodox means it employed in order to obtain what it needed. Roving foraging parties impersonated members of other units, trains and convoys were diverted or hijacked, transportation companies were robbed of the fuel they needed for the return journey, and spotter planes were sent hundreds of miles to the rear in order to discover fuel-shipments. Inside the zone of communications itself, the strain on men and material working around the clock led to fatigue, accidents, malingering and occasional sabotage. Vehicles went without maintenance until they broke down and the number of major repairs needed rose rapidly. Recordkeeping of the movement of supplies, which had always been a weak point in the Allies' organization, became even worse during the rapid advance of August, with the result that some of the limited transport available was wasted on items which the Armies had not requisitioned and did not need. Occasionally, instances of a worse kind of waste occurred. Thus, out of 22,000,000 jerrycans more than half had been lost by the end of August, with the result that this humble item limited the entire POL supply system. Supply discipline, especially at 3. Army, was poor and led to enormous quantities of equipment, particularly clothing, being left behind, so that the salvage companies were swamped with work. Instead of trying to capture French locomotives and rolling-stock, Patton's men deliberately shot them up—finding them, as one author puts it, 'a rewarding target in more senses than one'.

Though the logistic situation of the British forces operating in Belgium was also strained, it was not as difficult as that of the two American Armies. Distances here were smaller—21. Army Group was operating on the 'inside track' along the coast—and roads were more numerous than in Lorraine. On 30 August, when Hodges and Patton had run out of fuel, Dempsey informed SHAEF that his supply situation was 'very favourable'. Though the length of their communications increased to almost 300 miles during the subsequent week, the British coped by reducing unloading at the ports from 17,000 to 6,000 tons per day—thus freeing truck companies—and immobilizing many units, including one complete corps (the VIII). So rapid was the advance that the Belgian railroad network, the world's best, was captured intact, though its utilization was delayed because the Americans did not hand over rolling-stock as scheduled. Above all, Montgomery's advance did not take him away from the ports, as did that of Bradley's forces. On the contrary, it put him in a position to clear up a whole series of ports along the Channel—including Le Havre, Dieppe, Boulogne, Calais and Dunkirk—so that their situation regarding un-loading capacity promised to become much better than had been expected even a month earlier.

Meanwhile, what of the German enemy? Since D day, the Wehrmacht's casualties in the west had been staggering: 400,000 men, 1,800 tanks and assault guns, 1,500 other guns and 20,000 vehicles of all kinds had been lost. The units that still remained had been battered beyond recognition by Allied air and land forces, had been compelled to withdraw from a series of pockets such as those at Falaise and Mons and had lost all resemblance to organized fighting formations. Thus, for example, 1. SS division escaped over the Seine with only 40 tanks and 1,000 fighting men left. 84. infantry division had 3,000 men whereas 2. armoured division had only 2,000 men and 5 tanks; 2. parachute corps, despite its name, numbered only some 4,000 men—hardly more than a strong brigade—with all but light weapons lost. According to its own estimates, the Wehrmacht was outnumbered along the entire front by ten to one in tanks, three to one in artillery (this particular imbalance was regarded as 'not too serious' in itself, but the Germans suffered from a shortage of ammunition) and to an 'almost unlim-ited' extent in the air. Hitler, moreover, concentrated most of his forces on the Moselle in order to stop Patton, with the result that, according to Eisenhower, he only had the equivalent of two 'weak' armoured and nine infantry divisions available north of the Ardennes, all of which were said to be 'disorganized, in full retreat and unlikely to offer any appreciable resistance'. Indeed, such was their state that a member of Eisenhower's staff (probably COS [Chief of Staff] Bedell

Smith himself) considered it 'possible to reduce the strength of the Allies' forces in this area by 3 divisions and, far from prejudice the advance, aid it'. In short, the route to the Ruhr—Germany's industrial heart, where more than half of her coal and steel were produced—lay wide open. As Liddell Hart has written, rarely in any war had there been such an opportunity.

In order to understand why this opportunity was missed, it is necessary to return to the spring of 1944 when the Allies' basic strategy for the coming Continental campaign was laid down. In a memorandum of 3 May—signed, incidentally, by British officers—it was laid down that Berlin, while forming the Allies' ultimate objective, was too far away and that their first goal in Germany should therefore be the Ruhr. While it was recognized that the easiest and most direct route to this area led north of the Ardennes through Liège and Aix-la-Chapelle, it was decided that there should be a second thrust through the Saar in order to compel the Wehrmacht to stretch its resources and keep it guessing as to the Allies' intentions. On 27 May, the principles formulated in this memorandum were embodied in a directive issued over Eisenhower's signature.

Whether the best way to utilize an overwhelming numerical superiority such as the Allies possessed is to split it up so as to enable the enemy to operate on internal lines will not be discussed here. Suffice it to say that the battle for Normandy had, as we saw, developed in a manner very different from what had been expected. While progress had initially been slow, the breakthrough when it came proved much more decisive than anyone had hoped. In view of this, Field Marshal Montgomery began to entertain second thoughts as to the wisdom of the Allies' strategy and—so it seems—first voiced them to his American colleagues on 14 August. Three days later, his ideas had crystallized sufficiently for him to tell Bradley that 'after crossing the Seine, 12. and 21. Army Groups should keep together as a solid mass of forty divisions which . . . should advance northwards . . . with their right flank on the Ardennes'. Montgomery, however, did not see Eisenhower until 23 August, and by then had modified his argument. Instead of demanding that the whole of 12. American Army Group be deployed to protect his right flank in Belgium, he now considered that this task would have to be carried out by the nine divisions of Hodges' 1. Army alone. The rest of 12. Army Group— that is, Patton's 3. Army—was to be kept in its place, for the Allies did not possess enough logistic resources to support a simultaneous advance by all their forces and, in trying to be strong everywhere, would end up by being too weak to gain a decisive victory at any one point. While Eisenhower refused to halt Patton—instead, he authorized him to continue eastward at least as far as Rheims and Châlons-sur-Marne—Montgomery gained his point in that Hodges' entire Army was ordered to advance north of the Ardennes in conjunction with 21. Army Group. However, Eisenhower intended that the main objective of the northward thrust would not be the Liège–Aix-la-Chapelle gap, but the port of Antwerp, without which he believed no further advance into Germany could be sustained.

With that, the first round of the great argument came to an end. It took place at a time when Montgomery was only just completing his eighty-mile approach to the Seine, whereas Patton, who had far longer distances to go, was already across the river and advancing fast. Apart from all considerations of national prestige and public opinion, it is not surprising that Eisenhower did not want to stop his most dashing commander in favour of one who, up to that point, had scarcely proved himself a master of pursuit operations. Ten days later, however, 21. Army Group had pushed forward 200 miles and was closing on the German border. With his position thus immensely strengthened, Montgomery wrote Eisenhower that:

1. I consider that we have now reached a stage where one really powerful and full-blooded thrust towards Berlin is likely to get there and thus end the German war.
2. We have not enough maintenance resources for two full-blooded thrusts.
3. The selected thrust must have all the maintenance resources it needs without any qualification and any other operation must do the best it can with what is left over.
4. There are only two possible thrusts: one via the Ruhr and the other via the Saar.
5. In my opinion the thrust likely to give the best and quickest results is the northern one via the Ruhr.

The wording of this message was extremely unfortunate, for the objective mentioned—Berlin—was still over 400 miles away and, as we shall see, definitely beyond the reach of the Allied forces at this time. Nor did Montgomery aid his cause by sending, a few days later, an 'amplification' in which he spoke of a 'knifelike thrust . . . into the centre of Germany'. These exaggerations subsequently enabled Eisenhower to claim, with some justification, that the British Field Marshal's proposals were reckless and ill-considered.

The confusion as to the nature and direction of the proposed offensive in the north increased still further when, on 8 September, the first V 2 landed on London and caused the British government to demand that 21. Army Group overrun the launching sites in Holland. This led to Montgomery modifying his ideas once more, and instead of striking east at the Ruhr he now decided to move north to the Zuider Zee. In so far as he authorized the

Arnhem operation, Eisenhower supported him. However, he remained adamant throughout that no advance into Germany was possible unless Antwerp was first opened up.

Thus, Montgomery's own ideas as to just what he wanted to do were much less clear than he would have us believe. His original 'solid mass' had been whittled down to a 'knifelike thrust', and his mention of Berlin as the objective continued to bedevil all discussion. The confusion surrounding the issue, however, should not be allowed to obscure the main question, namely whether it was logistically possible, in September 1944, to capture the Ruhr *without first opening Antwerp*. The argument as to whether or not Germany was at that time on the point of collapse is not directly relevant to this question, for there is no doubt that, whatever forces Hitler was or was not able to mobilize 'in the centre of Germany', the way to the Ruhr lay wide open in the early days of September. The only question, therefore, is whether the logistic means at the Allies' disposal were sufficient to support a drive for the Ruhr.

First, a few definitions must be made. For the purpose of our inquiries, a 'drive to the Ruhr' is taken to mean an advance by 2. British and 1. American Armies, with a combined total of 18 divisions, to Dortmund, a move which would have left the Ruhr encircled. The starting point of the British forces would have been the Meuse–Escaut Canal (that is, if the Arnhem operation had not been launched), whereas the Americans would have set out from the Maastricht–Liège area. The distance from these starting points to the objective of Dortmund is almost equal and amounts to some 130 miles. It is assumed that all railway transportation facilities in Germany would have been put out of action and that no supply by air to the forward troops would have been possible owing to the non-availability of airfields. All calculations are made in terms of 200-ton American GTR companies, which was the practice of the SHAEF logisticians themselves. The target date for the start of the attack is taken as 15 September.

If a consumption of 650 tons per division per day is assumed (as an average for both American and British units, this may be somewhat too high) overall supplies required for the operation would have amounted to $18 \times 650 = 11,700$ tons a day. Of this, the British with their 9 divisions would have accounted for 5,850 tons. This quantity would have been brought forward to the starting bases in Belgium by rail (2,800 tons); by air, in planes diverted from the Arnhem operations, to Brussels (1,000 tons), and by road, in American trucks taken from three divisions immobilized in Normandy (500 tons), making a total of 4,300 tons. The remaining 1,550 tons Montgomery would have had to bring up from the Caen–Bayeux area by means of his own motor transport. Assuming that each truck company was capable of no more than the regulation 100 miles per day, forty-six such companies would have been required for the purpose. The operation itself, assuming a turning time of two days for the distance of 260 miles to Dortmund and back, would have required $(5,850 \times 2):200 = 58$ GTR companies in support. Since the British at that time possessed a grand total of 140 such companies, thirty-six would have been left to supply the six divisions of 1. Canadian Army and for port clearance. It could be done—though only just.

By contrast, the situation of Hodges' 1. Army was considerably more difficult. His nine divisions consumed 5,850 tons per day, but his allocation at this time amounted to 3,500 only—and COMZ found it difficult to deliver even this. To bring up the difference from the railways south of the Seine, 200 miles away, approximately thirty-five additional GTR companies would have been required. The advance on Dortmund itself would have necessitated fifty-eight such companies, so that the total deficit amounted to 93.

The question, then, is how many lorries could have been freed if 3. Army, instead of being allowed to continue to the Moselle, had been halted on the general line Paris–Orleans. No detailed figures as to the amount of transport supporting Patton are available, but a rough estimate can be made. On 15 September, 3. Army was receiving at least 3,500 tons per day—possibly somewhat more, for Patton used his own trucks for hauling the line of communication, instead of confining them to the zone of operations. To move this quantity over the 180 miles between the above-mentioned line and his front, the equivalent—in one form or another—of fifty-two GTR companies must have been employed.

In the middle of September, a U.S. corps—the VIII—was operating against Brest. Originally meant to secure adequate port capacity, this operation had by now become out of date. If it was nevertheless carried out, the reason was simply prestige. Though detailed figures of consumption and transport for this operation are, as usual, not available, a rough guess can be made. At that time, the Allied-operated railway in Normandy reached from Cherbourg to the Dol–Rennes area. To bring up supplies for three divisions over the 80 miles from there to Brest, some fifteen GTR companies must have been kept busy.

In addition, there were the organic trucks of all these units. Though no detailed figures are available, there is reason to think that, if formed into provisional transportation companies, the vehicles of the nine divisions involved could have increased the quantity of supplies reaching Hodges in Belgium by another 1,500 tons. His overall requirements would thereby have been cut by twenty-two GTR companies, and of the seventy-one such companies needed to carry out the drive on Dortmund $52+15=65$ would have been available. Our conclusion, though necessarily tentative, must therefore be that it could have been done, though only just.

CONCLUSIONS

On the basis of the best information available, we have calculated that, in September 1944, enough transport could have been found to carry Dempsey and Hodges to the Ruhr. The number of truck companies at hand, however, is only one factor among the many involved. To complete our investigation, these must now be briefly considered.

Had Eisenhower accepted Montgomery's proposals and concentrated all his logistic resources behind the thrust by 2. British and 1. American Armies, twelve out of the forty-three Allied divisions in France would have been completely immobilized and their truck complements taken away. In addition, seven divisions coming up from the Mediterranean in operation 'Dragoon' were irrelevant to the main effort, so that only twenty-four would have been left over. Of these, six belonging to 1. Canadian Army would have been operating against the Channel ports. For the advance on the Ruhr proper, only eighteen divisions would have been available—a fairly small number, admittedly, but one which would in all probability have sufficed to break through the weak German opposition at this time.

Since distances to be covered inside Germany were relatively small, providing air support for the exposed flanks should not have been unduly difficult—as it would no doubt have been in an advance on Berlin. Instead of having to cross four rivers, which was what the Allies tried to do during the Arnhem operation, they would have found their way barred by two only. The road network leading eastward to the Ruhr was excellent and superior to that leading north into Holland.

Since transport to set up substantial forward dumps in Belgium, in addition to daily consumption, was not available, the drive on the Ruhr would have to be launched with the Allies' main supply base still hundreds of miles in the rear. This would no doubt have entailed long delays between the requisitioning of supplies and their arrival at the front, a fact that could have serious consequences in case of a sudden emergency. However, an allocation of 650 tons per day was generous almost to a fault, and Allied communications in France and Belgium—especially rail transportation facilities—were being rapidly and daily improved. In view of this, the risk of operating at such distances from base could have been accepted, especially as the Luftwaffe was powerless to interfere with the line of communications.

Against this, it has been argued that the Allies, having already twice preferred strategic to logistic considerations during their advance across France, could not have done so a third time without stretching their communications to the breaking point. This view, however, ignores the fact that the distance from Bayeux to Dortmund is no longer than that which Patton covered from Cherbourg to Metz. In other words, the Allies *did* succeed in supporting their forces over 450 miles—but did so in the wrong direction.

An interesting aspect of the problem is the fact that, contrary to what is generally believed, acceptance of the plan for a drive to the Ruhr would *not* have entailed the transfer of transport from American to British units, with all its consequent complications. Rather, it was a question of switching vehicles from one American Army to another. Of the three Allied commanders in Belgium—Crerar, Dempsey, and Hodges—it was Hodges whose supply difficulties did most to prejudice Montgomery's plans. Had Patton been stopped, it was to his 1. Army that the transport thereby freed would have gone. By refusing to halt 3. Army Eisenhower made his prophecy come true that no advance into Germany would be possible without Antwerp, for it was only when that port was opened in late November that distances behind Hodges were cut from over 400 miles to seventy. The British did not need Antwerp, as they were by that time living comfortably from the Seine and Channel ports.

If Eisenhower must therefore be held responsible for failing to realize where the centre of gravity lay and adjusting his priorities accordingly, it cannot be denied that to have done so would have required almost superhuman foresight. At the time when the idea of a change in the Allies' fundamental strategy was first voiced, Patton was marching at full steam whereas Montgomery—even though the distances he had to cover were much smaller—was merely inching his way forward towards the Seine. By no stretch of the imagination was it possible to foresee that, during the next two weeks, this normally so cautious commander would suddenly surpass himself and advance 200 miles to the German border. Nor, it will be remembered, did Montgomery at first even ask that Patton be halted. On the contrary, he wanted him to protect the flank of his own offensive, and for that purpose demanded that the direction of Patton's advance be altered from east into Lorraine to northeast into Belgium. By the time he realized that forty divisions carrying out 'the Schlieffen Plan in reverse' could not be supported logistically it was already too late, as he himself admitted.

Montgomery did even more to prejudice acceptance of his plan by engaging in loose talk, first of an advance on Berlin and then of a 'knifelike thrust' into the heart of Germany. While there is good reason to believe that a drive by eighteen divisions against the Ruhr would probably have succeeded, there could be no question of occupying the greater part of Germany with such a small force. As for knifelike thrusts, they may be successful if conducted over a distance of a mere 130 miles but become distinctly risky and even reckless when launched in search of objectives 400 miles away—and with the nearest base another 300 miles to the rear. Nor could such a thrust by even eighteen divisions have been supported logistically. Rather, Montgomery's staff were thinking in terms of twelve only. The latter's maintenance would have to be reduced to 400 (in some cases, 300) tons per day and even this was more than 21. Army Group could manage with its own resources. As Eisenhower has rightly said, nothing but certain destruction could have resulted from such a move.

In the final account, the question as to whether Montgomery's plan presented a real alternative to Eisenhower's strategy must be answered in the negative. Though our computations seem to show that the means required for a drive to the Ruhr could, in theory, have been made available, it is not at all certain that, even if strategic developments could have been foreseen in time, the supply apparatus could have adapted itself with sufficient speed or displayed the necessary determination. Given the excessive conservatism and even pusillanimity that characterized the logistic planning for 'Overlord' from beginning to end, there is good reason to believe that this would not have been the case. It is impossible to imagine the prudent accountants, who considered the advance to the Seine impracticable even while it was being carried out, suddenly declaring themselves willing to take the risk of supporting an 'unscheduled' operation across the German border. That the SHAEF logisticians were not cast in the heroic mould it seems impossible to deny. Yet it is hardly for us, who have seen so many great campaigns come to grief owing to a lack of logistic support, to condemn one which did after all terminate in an undisputed—if possibly belated—success.

STRATEGIES OF GLOBAL WAR: PACIFIC

L O U I S   M O R T O N

WAR PLAN ORANGE
Evolution of a Strategy

Although General Helmuth von Moltke of the Prussian General Staff is quoted as saying "No plan survives contact with the enemy," military leaders have long recognized that war planning, however much it might be based on intuitive speculation, is fundamental to success. It is certainly critical that military leaders understand the geographical, technological, and political problems they might face in wartime, and recognize the various limits that might be placed upon their actions. Perhaps above all else, military leaders must know the objectives of any military campaign, and develop a clear sense of how those objectives can best be achieved.

For American military leaders in the twentieth century, only the ongoing development of plans for the defense of Western Europe since World War II has dominated their thinking as much as planning for a possible war in the Pacific did from 1901 to 1941. American acquisition of the Philippines, Guam, and Hawaii during the Spanish-American War focused attention on the Pacific region as early as 1898. Following the Russo-Japanese War of 1904–05, it was clear to American planners that Japan represented the most likely foe in any Pacific conflict, and within a few years both the army and the navy staffs were hard at work attempting to develop plans for defense of American possessions. By 1913 these planners had created a series of color-coded plans, covering a multitude of possible contingencies.

In this sequence of plans, each potential enemy was identified by a specific color. Germany, for example, was black while Britain was known as red. Japan's color identifier was orange, so the plan for a possible war with Japan was known as Plan

ORANGE. Although it would undergo any number of changes over the years, it remained the basic blueprint for a Pacific war until American entry into World War II.

In the following selection, the late Professor Louis B. Morton traces the changes made in Plan ORANGE over the years, and describes the geographic, political, and technological problems American planners had to confront—particularly the problems of geography.

In broad outline the ORANGE plan envisioned a prolonged army defense of the Philippines, seen as the most likely Japanese objective should war erupt, until the navy could reach them. American planners expected the Japanese fleet to confront the U.S. Navy as it approached the Philippines, and the plan suggested that the war would be decided in a massive naval battle near the islands. However, as Professor Morton points out, despite clinging to one or another version of the ORANGE plan for over two decades, naval planners were never entirely confident in the navy's ability to carry it out, and army planners doubted the Philippines could be held in any case.

From the navy's perspective the problem was one of geography. An American fleet attempting to operate in Asian waters would be several thousand miles from its nearest base of supply. Without a base nearby, navy planners did not see how the fleet could both transport a relief force and fight the Japanese. The only American base in the Western Pacific was in the Philippines themselves. If that base could not be held by the army, the navy would have to establish a series of bases as it moved slowly westward. This process would inevitably delay any relief of the islands. On the other hand, army planners estimated that the Japanese could attack the islands with a force of over 300,000 men within thirty days, and 100,000 men within two weeks. Since the American garrison in the islands until the late 1930s was fewer than 11,000 men, 3,000 of which were American regulars, it was likely that the islands would be overrun long before the fleet arrived. Thus, American planners boxed themselves into an impossible situation. They tacitly acknowledged that the islands could not be held, but for reasons of national prestige the garrison must remain and American leaders continued to argue that they could be defended. The result, suggests Professor Morton, was a fundamental contradiction between American commitments and American ability to meet those commitments.

Professor Morton's argument can be taken as an indictment of American planners in the prewar years, and can also be viewed as a criticism of American political leaders who failed to provide the funds and forces necessary to make the plan work. Indeed, the reader must wonder what led American planners to persist in sponsoring a plan which, given the inherent problems of geography and the limitations of American military power in the 1930s, was apparently foredoomed to failure. Although it can be argued that the constant effort to deal with the problems of a Pacific war led the navy to a greater appreciation of carrier aviation than is generally realized, led the navy to convert more rapidly from coal to oil as fuel, and hastened the development of capability to resupply the fleet while at sea, it remains true that by early 1941 the navy had abandoned its plans to defend the Philippines. Under joint war plan RAINBOW 5, approved in May 1941, the navy would undertake to do no more than assist the British in defending Malaya, and defend Midway and Hawaii. The Asiatic fleet would assist the army in defending the Philippines as long as possible, but then it would retreat south. It would not be reinforced, and the navy had no timetable for attempting to relieve the army garrison.

The issues raised by Professor Morton, however, go beyond the story of American military planning in the interwar years. Underlying his argument is the larger question of how military planners can balance military means with national objectives as they formulate their plans. Certainly the 1920s and 1930s were a time of small budgets and too little equipment, but the lessons of this period are still valid, for will the military always have unlimited funds and abundant materiel? Should not political leaders also recognize the limits of military power as they frame national goals? Readers should examine the debates of more current military planners as they are reflected in the essays by Professors Harry Coles and George C. Herring later in this collection. How do the problems of today's military planners, including global commitments and a shortage of funds for expensive systems, compare with those faced by the planners of the interwar years?

"It is impossible," once wrote British Prime Minister Winston Churchill, "to draw any precise line between military and non-military problems." How then, in light of the issues raised by Professor Morton, do military and political leaders reach agreement on the goals of national policies?

I

The emergence of the United States as a world power at the opening of the twentieth century found the nation ill-prepared to assume the burdens imposed by its new status. For American military and naval leaders, possession of an island empire stretching across 7,000 miles of ocean from San Francisco to the Philippines and almost to the mainland of Asia created new and serious problems. Slowly, during the first years of the century, the Army and Navy evolved a military strategy which would ensure the defense of these islands while supporting the foreign policy shaped by the nation's civilian leaders.

The basic components of this military strategy were sea power and naval bases. Without these, argued Captain A. T. Mahan and his influential followers, the island empire so recently acquired would fall to the first determined enemy. Only naval supremacy could ensure the defense of an insular position.

But there were other requirements for defense of an island—an Army garrison, coastal fortifications, and mobile forces to meet any invader who might land on its shores. And perhaps more important than any of these was close co-operation between the Army and Navy. In a sense, this was the vital element that would blend the ingredients into a strategic formula for victory.

The mechanism devised for Army-Navy co-operation was the Joint Army-Navy Board, organized in 1903 and consisting of eight members, four from the Army's General Staff and four from the General Board of the Navy. The Joint Board's task initially was a modest one. It was to discuss all matters requiring the co-operation of the two services in an effort to reach agreement on a program acceptable to both. Admiral of the Navy George Dewey, the senior member, acted as President while continuing to preside over the General Board of the Navy.

Though the Joint Board concerned itself from the start with the defense of American interests in the Pacific and Far East, it was not until Japan's attack on Russia in February 1904 threatened to destroy the balance of power in that part of the world that the Board began seriously to develop war plans. The impetus was provided by Lt. Gen. Adna R. Chaffee, Army Chief of Staff, who proposed in April 1904 that the Joint Board prepare a series of plans for joint action in an emergency requiring the co-operation of the services. These plans, he suggested, should be based upon studies developed by the Army General Staff and the General Board of the Navy.

From General Chaffee's proposal stemmed a series of war plans known as the "color plans." Each was designed to meet a specific emergency designated by a color, which usually corresponded to the code name of the nation involved. Thus, ORANGE denoted Japan and the ORANGE plan provided the strategic concept and missions to be followed in the event of war with that nation. On the basis of the joint color plans, each of the services developed its own plan to guide its operations in an emergency, and field and fleet commanders drew up the plans to carry out these operations. In many cases, these early war plans were little more than abstract exercises and bore small relation to actual events, but in the case of the ORANGE series they were kept under constant review and revised frequently to accord with changes in the international scene.

The first ORANGE plan consisted chiefly of a statement of principles which, it was piously hoped, could be followed in the event of war. By 1913, the strategic principles of the plan had been exhaustively studied and were well understood. If war with Japan occurred, it was assumed that the Philippines would be the enemy's first objective. Defense of the Islands was dependent upon the Battle Fleet, which on the outbreak of war would have to make its way from the Caribbean area around the Horn—the Panama Canal was not yet completed—and then across the wide Pacific. On the way the Fleet would have to secure its line of communication, using the incomplete base at Pearl Harbor and Guam, which was still undeveloped. Once the Fleet was established in the Philippines, it could relieve the defenders, who presumably would have held on during this period, optimistically estimated at from three to four months. Thereafter the Army forces, reinforced by a steady stream of men and supplies, could take the offensive on the ground while the Navy contested for control of the Western Pacific.

The key to this strategy was a naval base in the Western Pacific and it was this problem that ultimately proved to be the downfall of the Joint Board. The Army, which had responsibility for defense of the Philippines, wanted the Fleet base in Manila Bay, whose narrow entrance was protected by Corregidor and its neighboring islands. The Navy opposed this view. First it held out for Subic Bay, outside the entrance to Manila Bay, and when it lost that argument it chose Pearl Harbor as the site for a major naval base. Later, when the choice was between Guam and the Philippines, the Navy came out strongly for Guam as the site for base development.

The inability of the Joint Board to agree on the fundamental question of a naval base led in 1908 to an open break with President Roosevelt and the suspension of Board meetings for more than a year. Under Taft the influence of the Board continued to decline, and in 1913 President Wilson, as a result of its activities during the Japanese crisis of that year, suspended the Board a second time. So unimportant had the Board become by 1917 that it met only twice during the First World War. To all intents and purposes, joint planning for the Army and Navy had come to an end with the outbreak of war.

II

At the conclusion of the First World War, the Army and the Navy were faced with the necessity of redefining the military requirements for national defense, but the strategic problems in the Pacific and Far East had altered greatly since the early years of the century. Military aviation had proved itself and though its potentialities for naval warfare were not yet fully appreciated, air power was recognized as a factor to be considered.

Of more immediate importance was the transfer to Japan of the German islands in the Central Pacific. President Wilson had opposed this move at Versailles, arguing that it would place Japan astride the U.S. Fleet's line of communication and make the defense of the Philippines virtually impossible. But Wilson had been overruled by the other Allied leaders and Japan had acquired the islands under a mandate from the League of Nations which pro-hibited their fortification. "At one time," wrote Capt. H. E. Yarnell (USN), "it was the plan of the Navy Department to send a fleet to the Philippines on the outbreak of war. I am sure that this would not be done at the present time. . . . it seems certain that in the course of time the Philippines and whatever forces we may have there will be captured."

Japan's position in the Western Pacific was further strengthened during these years by the agreements reached at the Washington Conference of 1921–1922. In the Five Power Naval Treaty concluded in February 1922, Japan accepted the short end of the 5 : 5 : 3 ratio in capital ships in return for a promise from the other powers that they would preserve the *status quo* with regard to their bases in the Western Pacific. This meant, in effect, that the United States would refrain from further fortifying its bases in the Philippines, Guam, the Aleutians, and other islands west of Hawaii, and that Great Britain would do the same in the case of its possessions. The net result of this bargain was to give Japan a strong advantage over the Western powers in the Pacific, for the agreement virtually removed the threat to Japan posed by the Philippines, Guam, and Hong Kong. The British still had Singapore, but the United States had lost the opportunity to develop adequate base facilities in the far Pacific. With that loss, wrote Capt. Dudley W. Knox (USN), went all chance of defending the Philippines and providing a military sanction for American policy.

The effect of the Five Power Naval Treaty can be observed in the War Department's immediate suspension of all measures for the defense of the Philippines that might be construed as a violation of the letter or spirit of the agreement. Even the fourteen 3-inch anti-aircraft guns and other matériel en route to the Philippines in February 1922 were diverted to Hawaii. "The maintenance of the *Status quo*," one officer advised the Army Chief of Staff, ". . . implies that no new fortifications or naval bases shall be established in the territories and possessions specified; that no measures shall be taken to increase the existing naval facilities . . . ; and that no increase shall be made in the coast defenses. . . ." Only such repair and replacement of weapons and equipment as were customary in time of peace were to be permitted.

If the problems of defending American interests in the Pacific had become difficult, those that had beset the early efforts to co-ordinate Army and Navy planning had been at least partially solved by the reorganization of the Joint Board in 1919. Though it had ceased to meet and was practically defunct when the war ended, the Joint Board remained the only body established to co-ordinate the planning activities of the two services. In May 1919, the Army planners of the General Staff's War Plans Division had recommended that the Board be reconstituted, reorganized, given a working committee of planners from the two services, and be empowered to originate studies on its own initiative, a power it had never had. It was not to have any executive functions or command authority. These recommendations were quickly accepted by the two Secretaries, and the reconstituted Joint Board held its first meeting that summer.

Though the range of the strengthened Joint Board's activities from 1919 to 1942 was broad, the development of joint war plans remained its major task, with most attention being given to War Plan ORANGE. Almost the first question that came before the Board dealt with this plan. How could such plans be made, asked Captain Yarnell, one of the naval members of the planning committee, without a definition of national policy? What were America's interests in the Far East? Did they require, in the event of war with Japan, that operations should be directed toward the decisive defeat of the enemy? Or would national interests be best served by a limited war? Would the cost of an all-out effort to hold the Philippines and support American policy and trade in the Far East be prohibitive? "These questions," concluded Yarnell, "are not for the War and Navy Departments to answer, but for the State Department."

The uncertainty about national policy with regard to the Pacific islands was not confined to the military and naval planners. On the one hand, Congress in 1916 had promised the Philippines their independence as soon as a stable government was established and, on the other, it expected the Army and Navy to defend the Islands although it refused to grant funds for military installations that would pass to the Filipinos on independence. Nor was there agreement as to what would constitute a stable government or when it would be achieved. Finally, there were many who thought the Islands could not be successfully defended in any case without the expenditure of "hundreds of millions of dollars." Even then, it would take perhaps half a century to make the Philippines safe from a determined enemy attack.

It is not surprising, therefore, that Captain Yarnell received no answer to his questions, though efforts were made from time to time to secure a more active partnership between strategy and policy. In the absence of such an arrangement, the military planners did their best to anticipate political action. Thus, in March 1920 Col. Stanley D. Embick pointed out that naval plans for war in the Pacific which were based on the assumption of war between the United States and Japan alone would be obsolete if the League of Nations became an effective agency. "Either the United States will face a coalition of the member states of the League," Embick reasoned, "or it will be aided by a coalition." In the latter case, the United States would be free to use British bases in the Far East and would have no need for Guam and the Philippines. And if the League members supported Japan, Embick pointed out, the United States would have to concentrate its forces in the North Atlantic against possible attack from Europe and, again, would not need bases in the Far East. His advice, therefore, was that the planners accept the inevitability of delay in seeking a decision on the fortification of Guam and concentrate on plans for the defense of Hawaii and Panama.

As in the period before the First World War, Pacific strategy in the postwar era was viewed largely in terms of naval base requirements. Japan was still considered the most probable foe, and the war as one which would be decided ultimately by naval action in the far Pacific. In such a war, the Navy would require a string of strongly held bases across the Pacific to enable the Fleet to operate against the enemy with a secure line of communication. In order of priority, these bases were Hawaii, Guam, and the Philippines.

Hawaii, with its facilities at Pearl Harbor, was the strongest of the Pacific bases in 1920; Guam, with its garrison of 172 Marines, was the weakest. The Philippines had only minor naval facilities but an Army garrison capable of holding Manila Bay for a limited time. Whether its defenses were strong enough to resist a determined effort by a major naval power like Japan was a moot question. The General Board of the Navy believed the garrison could hold out long enough for reinforcements to arrive, but the Army War Plans Division and officers at the Naval War College disagreed. "This college has long held," wrote Admiral Sims, President of the War College, "that the retention of Manila Bay cannot be counted upon and that any plans based on its retention are in error."

The Washington Conference altered the theoretical priority of Pacific bases radically and brought the Philippines to the fore in a way apparently neither intended nor foreseen. Of the bases available for operations in the Western Pacific, it alone had facilities capable of supporting a naval force large enough to challenge Japanese supremacy in that region. Guam, which up to this time had been regarded as a more desirable base site than the Philippines but which had not yet been developed, now became of secondary importance. The Aleutians and Samoa were too remote to serve the purpose. The Philippines were, therefore, in the view of the joint planners, "our most valuable strategic possession in the Western Pacific." So long as the Five Power Naval Treaty remained in effect, they argued, the Islands' fleet facilities and coastal defenses should be maintained to the extent permitted. At the same time, the Philippines garrison should be so strengthened, urged the planners, as to make the capture of the Islands by any enemy "a costly major operation."

On the basis of this estimate, it was not surprising that less than a year after the conclusion of the Washington Conference the U.S. Navy reorganized its surface forces and created a separate Battle Fleet for the Pacific. To this fleet were assigned twelve modern battleships, thus making it the main striking force of the Navy. There was no mistaking the significance of the move. It was a clear reflection of the Navy's estimate of the Japanese threat and its concern with Pacific affairs.

By now the situation in the Pacific had so invalidated the assumptions of earlier planning for a war with Japan as to require a complete review of strategy and the preparation of new plans. This need was emphasized by the Army planners when they submitted to the Joint Planning Committee in December 1921 a "Preliminary Estimate of the Situation," together with a recommendation for a new joint Army-Navy ORANGE plan. "It may safely be assumed," they declared, "that Japan is the most probable enemy." That nation's policy of expansion and its evident intention to secure a dominant position in the Far East, argued the Army planners, were bound to come into conflict sooner or later with American interests and policy in the region. Unless either or both countries showed some disposition to give way, a contingency the planners regarded as unlikely, this conflict of interests would lead ultimately to a situation that could be resolved only by force.

The Army's request seems to have had the effect of channeling various strategic studies dealing with the Pacific into specific planning for a possible war with Japan. Thus, the joint planners, in a study of base development, emphasized the danger in the Pacific and asserted that "without discussion it may be admitted our most probable enemy is ORANGE." Previous studies, they observed, had demonstrated that in a war with Japan the issue would be decided in the Western Pacific. This meant that the United States would have to fight an offensive war, advancing across the ocean "by progressive steps." Such a strategy, because of its dependence upon naval bases in the far Pacific, made the Philippines and Guam "invaluable," the planners now pointed out, even though the latter, "in its present state, can be easily captured by ORANGE." They could have said the same of the Philippines without serious contradiction.

The Navy planners had by this time virtually completed their own estimate of the situation in the Pacific. Their conclusion, submitted at the end of July 1922, was that the Japanese could, if they wished, take both the Philippines and Guam before the U.S. Fleet could reach the Western Pacific. The role of the Philippines garrison, as the Navy planners saw it, would be to hold out as long as possible and to make the operation as costly as possible to the enemy. What would happen to the garrison thereafter the planners did not specify, but they hoped that the sacrifice of the American forces would be justified by the damage done to the enemy. This pious hope would have been cold comfort indeed for the defenders had they known of the plans then being made for their future.

But Leonard Wood, Governor-General of the Philippines, did know of these plans. A former Chief of Staff of the U.S. Army and commander of the Philippine Department with influential friends in Washington, he was a man whose word carried considerable weight. In his view, the "assumption on the part of the Navy that in case of war with Japan the Philippine Islands could not be defended, must be abandoned, and a long war waged to take them back and reestablish ourselves in the Far East" was a fatal error. Such a course, he told the Secretary of War with feeling, would damage the prestige of the United States in the eyes of the world, would have a "disintegrating and demoralizing effect upon our people," and could end only in national dishonor. "I feel sure," General Wood wrote to the Secretary, "that when you and the President realize the effect of this on our future . . . , steps will be taken at once to see that the Army assume that the Philippine Islands must not only be absolutely defended but succored by the Fleet." The American people, he warned, would not stand for a policy that required "abandonment of American posts, American soldiers, an American fleet, American citizens in the Far East. . . ."

Just how the Fleet would come to the rescue of the Philippines in the event of war Governor Wood did not specify, but he felt sure the planners in Washington could solve the problem. They had undoubtedly reached their conclusions when faced by seemingly impossible tasks, he observed sympathetically. But American ingenuity was equal to any task, declared General Wood, and the planners "should be directed to keep alive that problem and work it out to show just what could be done to make it possible." And, as a starting point, he recommended that the Navy take for its mission: "First, the relief of the Philippines and the establishment of its base in Manila as an essential preliminary to the accomplishment of our main objective. . . . Second, the destruction of the Japanese fleet." That the Navy would agree to so flagrant a violation of the first canon of naval strategy—that the primary mission of a fleet was always to destroy the enemy—was, to say the least, doubtful.

Whether as a result of General Wood's intervention or for other reasons, the final estimate presented to the Joint Board as a basis for the preparation of a war plan carefully skirted the question of the abandonment of the Philippines. A war with Japan, the joint planners now declared, would be primarily naval in character and would require offensive sea and air operations against Japanese naval forces and vital sea communications. The first concern of the Army and Navy in such a war, therefore, would be "to establish at the earliest date American sea power in the Western Pacific in strength superior to that of Japan." To accomplish this, the United States would require a base in that area capable of serving the entire U.S. Fleet. Since the only base west of Pearl Harbor large enough for this purpose was in Manila Bay, it would be essential, said the planners, to hold the bay in case of war and be ready to rush reinforcements, under naval protection, to the islands in time to prevent their capture. An additional mission recommended by the planners was the early capture of bases in the Japanese mandated islands along the line of communication to the Philippines.

Within two weeks the Joint Board had taken action. On 7 July 1923, General of the Armies John J. Pershing, senior member of the Board, noted the Board's agreement with the study made by the planners and recommended to the two service Secretaries that it be approved as the basis for the preparation of a war plan. The Joint Board, Pershing told the Secretaries, had reached the following conclusions with regard to the Philippines:

(1)   That the Islands were of great strategic value to the United
      States, for they provided the best available bases for military and

naval forces operating in defense of American interests in the Far East.

(2)   That their capture by Japan would seriously affect American prestige and make offensive operations in the Western Pacific extremely difficult.

(3)   That the recapture of the Islands would be a long and costly undertaking, requiring a far greater effort than timely measures for defense.

(4)   That national interests and military necessity required that the Philippines be made as strong as possible in peacetime.

With the Secretaries' approval, given three days later, work on Joint War Plan ORANGE moved forward rapidly. As a matter of fact, the planners had by this time already adopted the basic strategic concept to guide American forces in a war with Japan. Such a war, they foresaw, would be primarily naval in character. The United States, in their view, should take the offensive and engage in operations "directed toward the isolation and harassment of Japan." These objectives, they thought, could be achieved by gaining control of Japan's vital sea lanes and by undertaking offensive air and naval operations against her naval forces and economic life. If these measures alone did not bring Japan to her knees, then the planners would take "such further action as may be required to win the war." The major role in a war fought as the planners envisaged it would be played by the Navy. To the Army would fall the vital task of holding the base in Manila Bay until the arrival of the Fleet. Without it, the Fleet would be unable to operate in Far Eastern waters.

The concept of "an offensive war, primarily naval," was firmly embodied in the plan that was finally evolved. From it stemmed the emphasis placed on sea power and a naval base in the Philippines. The first concern of the United States in a war with Japan and the initial mission of the Army and Navy, declared the joint planners, would be to establish sea power in the Western Pacific "in strength superior to that of Japan." This, they recognized, would require a "main outlying base" in that region. Manila Bay, it was acknowledged, best met the requirements for such a base and its retention would be essential in the event of hostilities. Thus, the primary mission of the Philippine Department in the ORANGE plan was to hold Manila Bay.

Though the final approval of War Plan ORANGE in September 1924 gave the United States for the first time since the end of World War I a broad outline of operations and objectives in the event of war with Japan, the plan was really more a statement of hopes than a realistic appraisal of what could be done. To have carried out such a plan in 1925 was far beyond the capabilities of either service. The entire military establishment in the Philippines did not then number more than 15,000 men. The 50,000 men who, according to the plan, were to sail for the Philippines from the West Coast on the outbreak of war represented more than one-third of the total strength of the Army. Moreover, naval facilities in Manila Bay were entirely inadequate to support the Fleet. The station at Cavite along the south shore of the bay had been largely neglected by the Navy and the facilities at Olongapo in Subic Bay dated from the early years of the century. Neither was capable of providing more than minor repairs. Only at Pearl Harbor, 5,000 miles to the east, was there a base even partially able to service the major surface units of the Battle Fleet.

The advantages of distance and location that gave the Philippines their strategic importance were all on the side of the Japanese. Japan's southernmost naval bases were less than 1,500 miles from the Philippines, and Formosa was only half that distance away. An expeditionary force from Japan could reach Manila in three days; one mounted from Formosa or the Ryukyus could make the journey in a much shorter time. An American force, even assuming that it reached the Philippines in record time, would require several weeks for the journey. By that time, the Japanese flag might be waving over Manila and the U.S. Fleet, with its bunkers depleted, would be "forced to fight under the most disadvantageous conditions or to beat an ignominious retreat."

III

Between 1924 and 1938 the ORANGE plan was revised many times in response to military necessity, the mood of Congress, and changes in the international situation. And with each change the task of the planners became more difficult, as the gap between American commitment to the defense of the Philippines and the forces that the United States was willing to commit to their defense widened. By 1938 the dichotomy between national policy and military strategy in the Far East had made the planners' work an exercise in frustration.

The first revision of ORANGE came in October 1926 and was designed to correct ambiguities in the original plan and to clear up confusion in regard to timing and forces. This was done by designating M-day, the date on which a general mobilization would go into effect, as the starting point for the plan. On that day the varied activities required to implement the plan would begin, and from that day were measured the phases which divided the operations covered in the plan.

The 1926 plan clearly specified Hawaii as the point of assembly for troops and supplies. Convoys were to be formed there for the journey westward. But the assumption of the earlier plan that reinforcements could sail directly to the Philippines—a doubtful assumption—was dropped in the 1926 plan. The

Marshall, Caroline, and Mariana Islands, it was recognized, would have to be brought under American control first, and bases established in one or more of these island groups to guard the line of communication.

Not satisfied with these changes, the planners proposed additional revisions the following month, with the result that the Joint Board directed the preparation of an entirely new plan. A difference of opinion became apparent almost immediately as the planners searched for a strategic formula that would produce victory in a war with Japan. One group argued for a strategic offensive in the Western Pacific as the only way to exert sufficient pressure on Japan to win the war, and the other for a strategic defensive— that is, the retention of the bulk of America's naval strength east of Hawaii— as the preferable course.

The advocates of a defensive strategy hoped to gain victory over Japan by economic pressure and raids on Japanese commerce, but conceded that this strategy would expose the Philippines, Guam, and Samoa to attack and would probably cut off American trade in the Pacific. The strength of a defensive strategy, it was argued, lay in the fact that it would make the West Coast and Hawaii "impregnable against attack," would cause little interference in the economy of the United States, and "would still permit our government to employ the political and industrial power and the great wealth of the country in an attempt to cut off Japanese world markets to both export and import." Faced with this choice of strategies, the Joint Board elected the former and on 26 January 1928 directed the planners to prepare a plan based on the concept of a strategic offensive.

Within three months, the new plan was completed. Though it retained the original concept of a naval advance across the Pacific, it allowed more time to assemble reinforcements and paid more attention to securing the line of communication. Forces in the Philippines were assigned the primary mission of holding the entrance to Manila Bay (Bataan and Corregidor), and the secondary mission of holding the bay itself "as long as consistent with the successful accomplishment of the primary mission."

That there was even then little expectation that the Philippines could be held is evident in the Army's estimate of the enemy's capacities as compared with its own. Japan, it was noted, could raise and transport to the Philippines a force of 300,000 men in thirty days. Within seven days of an attack, it could have from 50,000 to 60,000 men off Luzon; within fifteen days, another 100,000. The Americans would have to meet this attack with the forces then present in the Philippines: 11,000 troops, of whom 7,000 were Filipinos, plus a native constabulary numbering about 6,000 men, and an air component consisting of nine bombers and eleven pursuit planes. So great a discrepancy made any hope for a successful defense mere self-delusion.

The best that could be expected under such circumstances was a delaying action that might buy enough time for the Fleet to arrive with reinforcements.

Another clue to the views of military and naval strategists can be found in their recommendations for instructions to the delegates to the Geneva Conference of 1927. Asserting that national security required freedom of action to develop naval bases and to defend the Hawaiian Islands and the Canal Zone, the Joint Board recommended that the delegates be instructed to refuse discussion of "any question of elimination or limitation of the permanent fortifications, base development, or mobile defense in these areas."

This recommendation was the prelude to a consideration of the role of Hawaii and Panama in Pacific strategy, a review called forth by the Japanese proposals to extend the *status quo* arrangement of 1922 to both places. This proposal, the Joint Board thought, revealed "a distinctly hostile attitude," for "the advantage to be obtained by a nation proposing such restriction would exist only during a war against the United States." Any agreement extending the *status quo* to Panama, declared the Joint Board, would weaken the United States, limit the use of naval forces, and perhaps eliminate the Canal Zone altogether as a factor in national security. Unless the Navy was assured free passage through the Canal in wartime, the United States would have to maintain a Pacific and an Atlantic Fleet. It was vital, therefore, asserted the Joint Board, that no agreement be made limiting U.S. defense of the Panama Canal Zone. As a matter of fact, the Board declared, American defenses of the Canal were inadequate, and the Army and Navy were even then engaged in strengthening fortifications there.

The Joint Board viewed any limitation on the fortification of Hawaii with equal alarm. The Hawaiian Islands, it pointed out, were vital to the defense of the West Coast and to the naval position of the United States in the Pacific. Failure to complete construction of the naval base and protected fleet anchorage at Pearl Harbor, on which $50,000,000 had already been spent, would so restrict the operations of the U.S. Fleet as to render it unable to perform its mission. Moreover, the Joint Board declared, Pearl Harbor was the only base in the Pacific free from the restrictions imposed by the Washington Conference. To limit construction there would leave the United States without a base capable of supporting the Battle Fleet. And on this Fleet rested responsibility for the defense of the Philippines and Guam and the protection of American interests in the Western Pacific.

The move to grant the Philippines their independence, which was finding increasing support in Congress in the early 1930's, complicated enormously the problems of Pacific strategy and precipitated a comprehensive review of the effect of such a step on America's position. It was the opinion of the Joint Board in April 1930 that the Philippine Islands should not be granted independence at that time; that if they were, the United States should withdraw entirely from the Islands, abandoning its bases and repudiating any obligation to guarantee the sovereignty of the Philippines. If it was decided instead to grant the Islands their independence at the end of a specified period of time, then, the Joint Board recommended, the United States should retain its bases in the Philippines until that date. It was probably on the basis of this recommendation that the Chief of the Army War Plans Division, in considering the possible reduction of expenditures on the Philippines garrison, stated that "the future policy which this country may adopt" narrowed down to a choice of (1) maintenance of the *status quo*, while allowing the Filipinos a progressively greater degree of self-government in domestic affairs; (2) complete independence; and (3) gradual independence after a specified period of time.

As the pressure for a decision on Philippines independence grew, the Army and Navy came out more strongly for the retention of the Islands. In 1931 the joint planners developed a full-scale study of the importance of the Philippines to the United States. Possession of the Islands, the planners held, was essential not only for military and naval operations in case of war, but also for "carrying out our national policies relating to Far Eastern affairs and . . . our obligation to the world to act as a stabilizing factor in it." This was a view that the Joint Board thoroughly endorsed, going so far as to assert that American possession of the Philippines was "an asset to the world generally, with the exception of Japan."

But the Joint Board could not escape the fact that possession of the Philippines was a mixed blessing. The Islands were an economic drain requiring the expenditure of millions of dollars. Investments had been disappointing and uncertainty about the future of the Islands was discouraging potential investors and retarding the development of the country. These evils, the Joint Board believed, would disappear at once if the United States made clear its determination to retain control of the Islands. Assured that their investments would be protected, American businessmen would quickly take advantage of the opportunities offered in the Philippines and convert the Islands into a valuable economic asset.

Despite these persuasive arguments, the pressure for granting the Philippines their independence mounted. In the face of this sentiment, the military and naval planners stubbornly insisted that the Islands should be held, advancing fresh arguments to support their view. Withdrawal, they warned, would force the United States to abandon the Open Door policy in China, and "unquestionably" require England to renew its old alliance with Japan to protect British interests in the Far East. Gloomily, the planners predicted that the United States would lose its trade in the Orient to the British as well as its influence in Asia if it withdrew from the Philippines and was left without a base in the Far East. The United States would be unable to enforce its treaty obligations in China and would ultimately have to relinquish control of the affairs of Asia and the Western Pacific to Japan and the European powers. Retention of the Philippines, though the Islands were inadequately defended and beyond supporting distance of the naval base in Hawaii, was, in the view of the planners, preferable to the abandonment of America's position and interests in the Far East. In the event of war in that part of the world, their possession would be an "indispensable" condition of success.

From the Philippines came a strong dissenting voice. To the officers stationed in the Islands, the idea that the weak garrison could hold out against a powerful Japanese attack until reinforcements arrived seemed nothing less than self-delusion. If the Islands' defenses could not be strengthened, they should be set free. "To carry out the present ORANGE plan with its provisions for the early dispatch of our fleet to Philippine waters," wrote General Embick, the commander of the Corregidor garrison, "would be literally an act of madness." Corregidor, he believed, could hold out for about one year, but possession of this fortress at the entrance to Manila Bay did not necessarily mean that the Fleet could use the naval base in the bay. The Japanese, he pointed out, could easily capture Manila from the land side and deny the use of the bay to U.S. naval forces. The best that could be hoped for in the event of war, therefore, was that the garrison might be safely evacuated, or, as the Corregidor commander put it, that "wise counsels would prevail."

The Philippine Department commander, Major General E. E. Booth, agreed with Embick and bolstered his position with additional arguments in a letter to Washington. Since Corregidor could not be used by the Fleet if the enemy controlled Manila, Booth wrote, the only purpose that would be served by a last-ditch defense of this small island was "to keep the American Flag flying." He recommended, therefore, with General Embick, that the United States arrange for the neutralization of the Philippine Islands, withdraw the forces stationed there and in China, and adopt the line Alaska-Oahu-Panama as the "strategic peacetime frontier in the Pacific." This course, General Booth believed, would remove the weaknesses "inherent in our present situation in the Far East," make unnecessary the maintenance in peacetime of "a vastly increased naval establishment," reduce the drain on the budget, and, in case of war, leave U.S. forces free to take the offensive at a moment and place of their own choosing.

Desirable as this solution to the Philippines dilemma might be from the point of view of military policy, the decision ultimately made, General Booth recognized, would be based as much on diplomatic and political considerations as on military grounds, "If," he wrote, "diplomatic considerations required the defense of the mouth of Manila Bay, and political considerations the maintenance of some forces on the mainland of the Philippine Islands, and at the same time economic conditions dictated a reduction in cost of the maintenance of these troops," then, said General Booth, he was prepared as a soldier to do his duty and submit a plan by which the defense of Corregidor could be maintained at less than the present cost. That it would serve any other purpose than to keep the flag flying, he was doubtful.

The Army planners in Washington, though sympathetic, did not agree with either General Booth or General Embick. They favored withdrawal, at the proper time, of American troops from North China but not from the Philippines. And though they called for a review of the ORANGE plan— because of the change in naval strength and the development of Japanese air power—they made it clear that they thought the plan sound. The field commander, they maintained, had stressed the concept of an offensive in the Western Pacific, but the plan did not require the immediate advance of the Fleet westward "unless the situation existing . . . justifies such action." Instead, the Fleet would advance step by step through the Mandates, taking such islands as it needed and constructing advance bases before moving on. It was just this course, the Army planners pointed out, that the Navy now favored.

To the Washington experts, the idea that the Philippines could be neutralized by agreement with other powers was completely unrealistic. They thought it "highly improbable of attainment," at least so long as the United States retained military and naval bases in the Islands. When the Philippines became fully independent, it might be possible to follow this course, provided that the United States withdrew all of its forces.

The Army planners in Washington dismissed also the fear that Japan would attack the United States in the near future. In their view, Japan was too dependent upon trade with the United States to risk a war that would place all her gains on the Asiatic mainland in jeopardy. "Only by the adoption on the part of the United States of a policy of armed intervention," they concluded, "would ORANGE be justified in bringing on a war."

The lack of support in Washington did not silence the dissenters. In March 1934, while the Tydings-McDuffie Act was being considered by Congress, they expressed their opposition to the existing plan once again. This time the new Philippine Department commander, Maj. Gen. Frank

Parker, joined with his naval colleague, Rear Adm. F. B. Upham, the Asiatic Fleet commander, to ask for a clarification of American policy in the Far East. In a joint letter to their respective chiefs in Washington, the two commanders asserted that they could not carry out their missions under the ORANGE plan with the forces assigned. "The tremendous strides made in the art of warfare since Manila Bay and Corregidor were selected as a base," they pointed out, "and the spectacular rise of Japan as a military power have nullified the supposed value of that base." In addition, aerial and gas warfare, the increase in the speed and power of surface ships, and other factors had combined to make the defense of Manila Bay futile with the forces available.

The time had come, the two commanders believed, to make known the national policy regarding defense of the Philippines. If the policy was to defend, whether the Islands were given their independence or not, then steps should be taken to increase naval and land forces, denounce the treaties prohibiting fortifications, and start construction immediately of a base adequate to maintain the Fleet. On the other hand, if national policy called for withdrawal from the Islands, then, said the two commanders, the rest of the world ought to be informed and all naval and military stores, ammunition, and equipment returned to the United States. Only such forces as would be needed to maintain order during the transition period should be retained in the Islands.

Clarification of national policy was outside the province of the Washington planners. All they could do was assert that the Philippines would be defended and that reinforcements would be forthcoming in the event of war. The Army planners opposed any reduction of military strength in the Islands, pending the final grant of independence in 1946, and recommended that fortifications there be maintained at maximum efficiency. In their view, the defenses of the Philippines were strong enough "to give reasonable assurance" that Manila Bay could be held if reinforcements were sent as planned in ORANGE. Whether they could or could not be so sent depended on the Navy. If the Fleet could not convoy the needed reinforcements to the Philippines and reach the Western Pacific in time to affect the outcome, then, said the Chief of the Army planners, the mission of the commanders in the Philippines should be modified.

The decision reached by the Joint Board in June settled none of the questions raised by the Army and Navy commanders in the Philippines. Assured that the Fleet could carry out its assignment and that the ORANGE plan was sound, the Board ruled against the field commanders and held that the mission as stated—to hold Manila Bay—would stand. But the Board did agree that the Philippines garrison and the Asiatic Fleet should be increased and the harbor and anti-aircraft defenses of Manila Bay strengthened.

In a separate communication to the Philippine Department comman-der, General MacArthur, then Chief of Staff and senior member of the Joint Board, explained the Washington decision more fully. Parker's mission, he told him, was to hold Manila Bay as long as possible with the military forces available at the outbreak of war, and to deny the enemy the use of the bay as a naval base in case the U.S. Fleet could not use it. MacArthur doubted that the additional forces recommended for the Philippines by the Joint Board would be supplied, but he wanted Parker to know that the War Department was aware of his situation and appreciated how limited were the means he had to carry out his assignment. "Responsibility for the use of available forces," he reminded the Philippine Department commander, "rests solely with you."

Though the Philippines commanders had been unable to secure a change in their mission as outlined in ORANGE, the plan itself was revised again in 1935. The impetus for this revision came from the Chief of Staff and was occasioned by the new mobilization plan of the War Department and its Four Army organization. These developments, MacArthur pointed out to the Joint Board in January of the year, required adjustments in ORANGE to bring the war plan into harmony with the new situation.

The review that followed the Board's approval for revision gave the Navy opportunity to propose its own changes in ORANGE. For the provision in the existing plan calling for immediate movement of the Fleet to the Western Pacific in the event of war, the Navy wished to substitute an advance in progressive stages through the mandated islands. During this advance, the Marshall and Caroline Islands were to be seized in turn, and in each of these island groups bases would be developed. In this way the Fleet's advance would be supported by a secure line of communication stretching across the Central Pacific and ultimately reaching the Philippines.

This concept, as well as the changes proposed by the Army, were accepted by the Joint Board and incorporated in the revised ORANGE plan approved in May 1935. The basic provisions of the old plan remained unchanged insofar as they applied to the defense of the Philippines, but by making the initial task of the Fleet the seizure of positions in the mandated islands, the new plan increased the length of time the Philippines garrison would have to hold Manila Bay. In view of the doubts already expressed about the ability of the garrison to hold the bay until the arrival of reinforcements, this change made the ORANGE plan even more unrealistic than before.

By the end of 1935 there was a growing conviction among Army planners that the Philippine Islands could not be held, despite the elaborate plans for their defense. The essential condition for success was the establish-ment of naval superiority in the Western Pacific, a condition many thought could not be met for at least one or two years after the outbreak of hostilities.

Japan had revealed its expansionist aims in Manchuria and in China, had placed a veil of secrecy over the mandated islands, withdrawn from the League of Nations, and renounced the agreements of 1922 and 1930 limiting naval armaments. These facts, combined with Japan's rapidly growing military and naval strength, were clear signs of impending crisis in the Far East. If that crisis came at a time when Hitler and Mussolini chose to test their new-found strength in Europe, the Philippine Islands might well prove a liability, draining off the forces needed to defend Hawaii, the Panama Canal, and the continental United States.

In recognition of the growing threat in Europe and the Far East, the Secretaries of the War and Navy Departments, at the end of November 1935, called upon the Joint Board to re-examine the military position of the United States in the Far East. At the same time, they asked the Secretary of State to designate a representative from his department to meet with the Board, in one of the earliest efforts to co-ordinate national policy with military strategy. How seriously the service secretaries regarded the danger may be judged by their note to Mr. Hull. "The cumulative effects of successive developments during the past two decades have so weakened our military position vis-à-vis Japan," they wrote, "that today our position in the Far East is one that may result not only in our being forced into war but into a war that would have to be fought under conditions that might preclude its successful prosecution."

The action of the War and Navy Secretaries set off another round of discussions over strategy that ended in one more revision of ORANGE. The case for the Army planners was summarized by General Embick, now chief of the War Plans Division. Referring to the Philippines, Embick pointed out the obvious but often overlooked fact that the creation of an inadequately defended base meant the assumption of "a military liability of incalculable magnitude." In a war with Japan, the Philippines would be of no use and would probably be lost soon after the opening of hostilities. The best the United States would be able to do would be to advance progressively through the mandated islands. In effect, Embick declared, this meant that the Navy would be unable to reinforce the Philippines in time to prevent the Japanese from taking the islands. Sound strategy, in his view, dictated the adoption by the United States of the line Alaska-Hawaii-Panama as its peacetime frontier. To do so would place the nation in an invulnerable position and leave its military and naval forces free to conduct operations "in a manner that will promise success instead of national disaster."

The Army's position, as outlined by General Embick, called for an early decision on the basic question of Pacific strategy. This was the view presented by the Army members of the Joint Planning Committee, but it was vigorously opposed by the Navy members. With equal logic they insisted that no decision should be made at that time, but only after a complete re-estimate of the situation in connection with War Plan ORANGE. In a sense, the naval planners were more limited in their outlook and interpreted their instructions more narrowly than the Army. The latter wished to review the military position of the United States in the light of present conditions, without reference to ORANGE, and then make their recommendations. To couple such a review with the ORANGE plan, they believed, would be equivalent to making national policy dependent upon the existing war plan, or, as they put it, giving to ORANGE "an undue and unsound influence upon national policy."

The outcome of this sharp division of opinion between the Army and Navy members of the Joint Planning Committee was a split report. The Navy planners recommended an immediate re-estimate of the situation as the basis for military planning. In support of this recommendation they presented a comprehensive review of Japanese and American policy in the Pacific and Far East. American national interests, the naval planners assumed, were those already announced—the Open Door policy in China, maintenance of the balance of power in Asia, and the defense of the Philippines. Japanese policy they held to be one of progressive expansion, having as its objective complete domination of the Far East. To weaken American forces in the Philippines or in China would only lower American prestige and encourage Japan to further aggression.

The Army planners, pressing for immediate decision on withdrawal of American forces from the Philippines—and China—when independence was granted, traced the military policy of the United States in some detail. Recalling that America's position in the Far East vis-à-vis Japan had never been a strong one, the planners pointed out that in the period after the acquisition of the Philippines, the United States had been able to exert its influence in that area without undue risk of war. But since World War I, America's position in the Islands had been growing steadily weaker as a result of many factors: the reduction of military forces in the Islands, the abandonment of plans to establish a first-class naval base there, the Washington Treaties, the decline of U.S. naval strength relative to that of Japan, and the present status of the Philippines as a semi-independent nation. And though the limitations imposed by the Washington Treaties would end on 31 December 1936, the planners thought it doubtful that the American people would willingly spend the huge sums required to strengthen the Philippines. This attitude was perfectly understandable if shortsighted, for under the terms of the Tyding-McDuffie Act the Philippine Commonwealth was to become an independent and sovereign nation in 1946 and would acquire possession of all fortifications and defensive installations built by the United States.

The separate reports and recommendations of the Army and Navy planners hardly provided the Joint Board with an agreed program for action. There was nothing left to do in the absence of agreement but to pass on to other matters on which the two services could agree. As constituted, there was little more that the Joint Board could accomplish, since it had no authority to compel either service to accept its decision, even if its members had been disposed to reach agreement where the planners could not.

Though the debate had failed to produce a plan, it had revealed sharply the contradictions between American policy and military strategy in the Far East. The Philippines were to be held—that was the American policy. But it was abundantly clear that the forces assigned to the task could not carry out this policy, that the Philippines garrison would not be able to hold out until such time as the Fleet arrived with reinforcements, variously estimated at from two to three years.

Though this unpleasant truth was never made explicit in any plans, it is significant that the Army's strategic plan for 1936, unlike its earlier plans, made no provision for reinforcements. The defense of the Islands, as outlined in this plan, would be conducted by the peacetime garrison, a force of about 10,000 men, plus the Philippine Army then being organized by the newly appointed Military Advisor to the Philippine Commonwealth, General MacArthur. The defenders, it was estimated, would be able to hold out for about six months; to build up the defense reserves for a longer period would require funds that Congress clearly had no intention of granting. In recognition of this fact, the War Department carefully defined its policy in the Philippines as one designed to maintain existing strengths and levels of supply and "in particular to provide adequate fortification for the Harbor Defenses in Manila Bay, but to go to no further expense for permanent improvements, unless thereby ultimate saving will result."

The Navy did not agree with the Army's pessimistic view of the Philippine defenses and apparently made its position clear in certain quarters. So evident was this difference that the press in the fall of 1936 was able to point specifically to the area of disagreement. The Army, the public was told, thought the Philippines too exposed and vulnerable to be defended and favored withdrawal. This view, it was reported, was opposed by the naval experts, who favored retention of a base in the Islands in order to support American policy in the Far East.

This version was correct so far as it went, but it did not go far enough. What the public was not told was that the Army would also favor a base in the Philippines if Congress would provide the funds to make such a base defensible in the event of war with Japan. What with inadequate forces and the Navy's admitted inability to break through with reinforcements in time, the Army garrison in the Philippines was a hostage to fortune.

IV

By late 1937 the international situation had taken a turn for the worse. Germany, Italy, and Japan had joined hands in the Anti-Comintern Pact and aggression was the order of the day in Europe and in Asia. It was at this time, after Japan's attack in North China and after the President's famous "quarantine" speech, that the Joint Board, at the instigation of Army Chief of Staff Malin Craig, directed its planners to re-examine the ORANGE plan. In its view, the existing plan was now "unsound in general" and "wholly inapplicable to present conditions." The planners were to develop a new plan which should provide, the Board specified, for an initial "position in readiness" along the West Coast and the strategic triangle formed by Alaska, Hawaii, and Panama. In addition, the planners were to make "exploratory studies and estimates" of the various courses of action to be followed after the position in readiness had been assumed.

In less than two weeks, the Joint Planning Committee reported its inability to reach an agreement. The Army members, reading their instructions literally, wanted to restrict themselves to the area specified by the Board and drew up a plan, defensive in nature, which would provide for the security of the continental United States and the Pacific Ocean as far west as Hawaii. A war plan, they reasoned, must take into account political and economic factors and it was impossible at this time to determine whether the United States would be willing to fight an unlimited war against Japan. With the European Axis clearly in mind, they pointed out that political considerations might require limited action and purely defensive operations in the Pacific. Moreover, the forces available at the outbreak of war would hardly be adequate for assuring the defense of vital areas in the Western hemisphere. To uncover these positions for an offensive in the Far Pacific, the Army planners declared, would be foolhardy indeed.

The Navy members of the Joint Planning Committee took the position that American strategy could not be limited to a purely defensive position in readiness, but should aim at the defeat of the enemy. If it failed to do that, it was not, in the view of the naval planners, a realistic guide for the services in time of war. The question of who the enemy might be in case of war in Europe and the Far East was not considered at this time.

Once war began, the Navy members argued, production could be quickly increased to provide the means required for both the security of the continental United States and offensive operations in the Pacific. While these forces were being assembled, the Navy was prepared to take the offensive beyond Hawaii into Japanese territory. Should the European Axis give aid to the enemy, the planners assumed that the United States' own allies would provide the assistance needed by the U.S. Fleet to maintain naval superiority over Japan and to permit the protection of American naval power in the Western Pacific. "The character, amount, and location of allied assistance," they hastened to add, "cannot be predicted."

The separate reports submitted by the Army and Navy members of the Joint Planning Committee put the choice between the opposing strategies squarely up to the Joint Board. The Board deferred decision by issuing a new directive to the planners on 7 December 1937. Suggested by the Chief of Naval Operations, Admiral William D. Leahy, this directive attempted to compromise the differing interpretations of the Army and Navy planners, but gave the edge to the latter. The new plan, the Board now specified, should have as its basic objective the defeat of Japan and should provide for "an initial temporary position in readiness" for the Pacific coast and the strategic triangle. This last, the Board further directed, was to be the Army's job; the Navy's task would consist of "offensive operations against ORANGE armed forces and the interruption of ORANGE vital sea communications." Finally, the planners were to recommend the forces and matériel which would be required by each of the services to accomplish its mission in the new plan.

Even under these revised instructions, the planners were unable to agree on the best way to protect American interests in the Pacific and Far East in the event of war with Japan. The Army planners, thinking possibly of the situation in Europe, wished to maintain a defensive position east of the 180th meridian—the outermost limits of the Hawaiian chain. Offensive operations to the west of that line, they believed, should be undertaken only "as the situation may permit and require" and then only with the specific authorization of the President. Naval operations alone, they asserted, could not ensure the defeat of Japan and ultimately the maximum efforts of the two services would be required. Throughout its version of the plan, the Army emphasized its mission of defending the United States and its possessions. Though it did not exclude the Philippines, neither did it provide for augmenting the forces there as it did for the possessions east of the 180th meridian. The defense of the Islands would have to be conducted by the forces already assigned, plus whatever additional troops were available locally.

The naval planners, still offensive-minded so far as the Pacific was concerned, emphasized in their version of the plan operations designed to bring about the defeat of Japan. Thus, they made the destruction of ORANGE forces the primary mission of joint and separate Army and Navy forces. Moreover, they did not place any limits on operations in the Western Pacific, merely repeating the time-honored formula that victory would be won by establishing "at the earliest practicable date, U.S. naval power in the western Pacific in strength superior to that of ORANGE and [by operating] offensively in that area." This preference for the offensive was clearly reflected in Admiral Leahy's testimony to the Senate Naval Affairs Committee the following February, when he asserted that "the only way that war, once begun, can be brought to a successful conclusion is by making the enemy want to stop fighting. . . . Prompt and effective injury to an enemy at a distance from our shores is the only correct strategy to be employed."

Faced with another split report, the Joint Board turned over the task of working out a compromise to General Embick and Admiral Richardson. These two, after a month of discussion, finally submitted on 18 February 1938 a new ORANGE plan. This plan embodied the essential point of each of the services, with the result that its provisions were sometimes less than clear. In return for the Army's removal of the proviso that operations west of the Hawaiian Islands would require Presidential authorization, the Navy took out its references to an offensive war, the destruction of the Japanese forces, and the early movement of the Fleet into the Western Pacific. The result was a broad statement of strategy calling for "military and economic pressure," increasing in severity until "the national objective," the defeat of Japan, was attained. Initial operations under this concept were to be primarily naval, but would be coupled with measures required to ensure the security of the continental United States, Alaska, Oahu, and Panama.

Though each of the services retreated from its original position, each won recognition of principles it held important. The Navy retained its concept of a progressive advance across the Pacific, but avoided commitment on the time required for such a move—an essential point in any plan for the defense of the Philippines. The Army, on its side, gained recognition of the primary importance of the strategic triangle formed by Alaska, Oahu, and Panama to the defense of the United States. The earlier provision for the defense of Manila Bay was retained, but the omission of any reference to the reinforcement of the Philippines garrison or to the length of time it would take the Fleet to advance across the Pacific was a tacit admission that the planners did not believe the position could be held.

A war with Japan, the ORANGE plan of 1938 assumed, would be preceded by a period of strained relations during which the United States would have time to prepare for mobilization. No formal declaration of war was expected; when war came, the planners expected it to come with a sudden surprise attack—an assumption that had been made in every ORANGE plan since the Russo-Japanese War. They thought, too, that American forces at the start of the war would be strong enough to permit naval operations west of Pearl Harbor, and that no assistance that Japan could receive—presumably from Germany and Italy—would materially affect the balance of naval power in the Pacific.

The ORANGE plan provided that, on the outbreak of a war with Japan, the United States would first assume a position in readiness to meet all emergencies that might arise—a point the Army planners had insisted upon. During this initial period, the Army and Navy would place priority on such measures as were required to defend the West Coast, the strategic triangle, and the coastal defenses of the United States and its overseas possessions. At the same time, the Navy would make preparations, in co-operation with the Army, to open the offensive as soon as possible.

The plan outlined also the specific measures that would have to be taken to support offensive operations. These included: (1) mobilization of Army forces, initially 750,000 men, excluding strategic reserves ready if needed to support the Navy; (2) mobilization of naval vessels and an increase in personnel strength of 320,000 (including Marines); (3) an increase in the strength of the Marine Corps to 35,000 men; (4) additional increases in all services at a later date if necessary; and (5) plans for the movement of troops to vital areas for their defense and to ports for overseas movement.

Having assumed a position in readiness and completed initial preparations, the military and naval forces of the United States would then be free to meet any unexpected situation that might develop, including, presumably, an attack in the Atlantic. If none occurred, the Navy could then proceed to take the offensive against Japan with operations directed initially against the mandated islands and extending progressively westward across the Pacific. These operations combined with economic pressure (blockade) would, it was believed, result in the defeat of Japan and a settlement that would assure the peace and safeguard American interests in the Far East.

The prospective loss of the Philippines base in 1946 and the abrogation of the treaty limitations on fortifications led after 1935 to a renewed interest in Guam. Pan-American Airways had in 1936 established a regular schedule via Wake and Guam, utilizing Navy facilities at both places. And in the fall of the year, $2,000,000 had been allocated for seaplane bases at Midway and Wake. But the question of fortifying the mid-Pacific base did not become acute until a board headed by Rear Adm. Arthur J. Hepburn submitted its report on naval bases in December 1938. The finding of the Board reflected clearly the naval strategy of the day. Guam, it declared, should be developed into a fully equipped fleet base with air and submarine facilities. Such a project, it reminded the Congress, had been proposed earlier, but had been put aside because of the Washington Treaties. Those treaties had now expired and there was no longer any restriction on the military fortification of Guam.

The advantages of establishing a strong base at Guam were enormous, in the view of the Board. For one thing, it would greatly simplify the task of defending the Philippine Islands. In the opinion of "the most authoritative sources," such a base would make the Islands practically immune from attack, would create "the most favorable conditions . . . for the prosecution of naval operations in the western Pacific," and would contribute greatly to the defense of Hawaii and the continental United States. By limiting hostile naval operations to the south, a fortified base at Guam would serve to protect the trade routes to the Netherlands Indies and greatly simplify naval problems, "should the fleet ever be called upon for operations in the Far East." And even if the United States withdrew entirely from the Western Pacific, the base at Guam, as Admiral Leahy pointed out, would have great value as a deterrent to any nation "contemplating a hostile move from that general area toward the Hawaiian Islands." But after a heated debate, Congress rejected the Board's recommendations for fear of offending Japan, with the result that Guam, lying exposed at the southern end of the Marianas, was left virtually undefended.

The failure to fortify Guam, like the refusal to strengthen the forces in the Philippines, reveals strikingly the dilemma of America's position in the Pacific and the Far East. National policy dictated the defense of an insular position which, in the opinion of the military planners, could not be held with existing forces. The ORANGE plan of 1938, with its compromise between an offensive and a defensive strategy, was merely a reflection of this contradiction between American interests and commitments in the Pacific. The nation would not abandon the Philippines, but neither could it grant to the Army and Navy funds that would ensure the Islands' defense. Nowhere in the country, even where feeling against Japanese aggression in Asia ran highest, was there firm support for military appropriations. Strong isolationist sentiment endorsed a Congressional economy which by 1938 had so reduced the effectiveness of the nation's armed forces as to make its outposts in the Pacific "a distinct and exceedingly grave liability." American policy had created a wide gap between objectives and means, and forced on its planners a compromise strategy and the virtual abandonment of Guam and the Philippines. Already there was a shift in sentiment, a recognition of the danger ahead, and a disposition to prepare the country's defenses, but the neglect of almost two decades could not be overcome in the three years of peace that remained.

JOHN W. MOUNTCASTLE

FROM BAYOU TO BEACHHEAD
The Marines and Mr. Higgins

"Amphibious landing," General Douglas MacArthur once suggested, "is the most powerful tool we have." Indeed, American skill at orchestrating the complex operations making up an amphibious assault landing was crucial to the success of the Pacific campaigns of World War II, and contributed significantly to the success of landings in Sicily, Italy, and, above all, Normandy. In 1950 General MacArthur outflanked the North Koreans with an amphibious landing at Inchon, using the techniques and equipment developed for World War II. Modern variations of the same techniques were used in 1981 when American forces landed in Grenada.

The foundation of this skill was laid during the 1920s and 1930s by a small group of U.S. marine officers who believed that amphibious assault landings were both possible and necessary under the conditions established by War Plan ORANGE. That plan, described and discussed in Louis Morton's article earlier in this collection, involved a naval sweep across the Pacific in the event of war with Japan. Although doubts existed that the navy could fight its way across the Pacific in time to relieve the garrison in the Philippines, planners did agree that any advance would require the seizing of bases along the way. Even if American forces were unopposed, the establishment of a base would require the transfer of men and equipment from ships to shore. That would involve the marines, traditionally used by the navy for landing parties as well as for shipboard police.

Almost all historical experience, however, suggested that landings on a hostile shore were likely to fail disastrously. Perhaps the most vivid, and recent, example of such a failure had been the British and Australian–New Zealand landings at Gallipoli,

Turkey, in 1915. Even though the troops got ashore, they were pinned to shallow beachheads for months, suffering immense casualties before being withdrawn. The marine officers who studied the problems of amphibious assault landings, however, were more optimistic. They believed that shore defenses could be overcome with proper advance planning and the right coordination between the landing force and its supporting fleet combat units.

One of the early marine supporters of amphibious operations was Major Earl H. Ellis, variously described as brilliant and an alcoholic. Ellis was convinced of the Japanese threat in the Pacific, and in 1920 he eagerly began studying the problems involved in landing forces on Pacific islands. By 1921 he had written Operation Plan 712, which outlined the problems of amphibious assault landings and proposed solutions to those problems. Ellis himself died while visiting the Japanese-held Palau Islands in 1923, and his death under these circumstances (described as "sinister" or "mysterious" by many sources, but also described by others as resulting from his heavy consumption of alcohol) made Ellis a martyr. Beginning in 1922 the marines began to practice the techniques outlined by Ellis through exercises in the Caribbean. By 1924, during the first large-scale landing exercises, they also experimented for the first time with specialized landing vessels. These exercises confirmed the difficulties of amphibious assault landings, and marine planners spent the next several years refining their ideas.

The marines' concern was, in fact, two-fold. There was a clear need to seize Pacific island bases under War Plan ORANGE, and techniques for moving men and equipment ashore to do that did need to be developed. But the Marine Corps was under attack by the early 1930s. As part of the struggle over limited military budgets during the interwar years, army officials argued that the marines should give up their aviation squadrons and relinquish to the army their traditional role as an expeditionary force. Confronted by this threat, the marines convinced the navy, and through it the joint board of army and navy senior officers, to recommend preserving the Marine Corps for the purpose of seizing and holding overseas naval bases. The development of a doctrine for amphibious assault landings thus became the primary mission of the marines, and the basic reason for retaining it as an independent organization.

Although development of amphibious doctrine, which continued in the 1930s with renewed vigor, justified the continued existence of the Marine Corps, it did not immediately solve all technical or administrative problems. Particularly lacking were the means of carrying out such a doctrine, including the specialized landing craft needed to transport the marines from their ships to a potentially hostile shore.

In the following essay Marine Major John W. Mountcastle describes the efforts of the marines to persuade the navy to adopt the landing craft designed by Andrew Higgins. Although ultimately the "Higgins" boat would become the basis for a long, specialized landing craft, Mountcastle makes clear that adoption of Higgins's design, submitted unsolicited to the Navy Bureau of Construction and Repair with the encouragement of some marine officers, was not an easy process. Despite the pressing need for a landing craft that could help transform the marine doctrine of amphibious assault into a reality, the navy bureaucracy moved slowly. Even after adopting the basic Higgins design, Mountcastle points out, the Bureau of Ships initially resisted his other landing craft, including what would become the standard Landing Craft, Mechanized (or LCM) for ferrying tanks and other heavy equipment ashore.

As Major Mountcastle argues, the story of the Higgins boat illustrates many of the difficulties supporters of a new idea face in confronting the inertia of an entrenched bureaucracy. Considering that the navy was, officially, as eager as the marines to see amphibious assault become an effective technique, the resistance of the navy's own bureaus to Higgins's design becomes even more remarkable. Yet, it is a situation with parallels. Even today, entrenched design bureaus within the services resist the adoption of weapons or equipment designed outside the narrow confines of existing bureaucratic channels. As Major Mountcastle suggests, the success or failure of strategic plans may hinge on such seemingly small matters as the design of a landing craft and bureaucratic unwillingness to accept a novel solution to a problem which comes from outside.

However, there is more to the tale Mountcastle tells than just the story of how a stubborn, far-sighted inventor and a handful of gallant, resourceful marines overcame the bureaucracy. The struggle over the Higgins boat illustrates the problems of intra- and interservice wrangling that exist in nearly all large organizations. Entrenched groups may see change as threatening, or new ideas coming from the outside as indicators of a failure within their own organization. In such cases, the refusal to accept new ideas or new inventions is a way of retaining control. On the other hand, not all new ideas are good ones. Accepting all new things, just because they are new, suggests a lack of insight, or an inability to really see what is important and what is not. Readers must ask themselves how a balance between competing imperatives can be maintained. Can such disputes be avoided, or are they a natural, and inevitable, by-product of large organizations trying to grapple with important issues?

It is also interesting to compare the marines' development of a doctrine of amphibious assault with the Air Corps' development of a doctrine of strategic bombardment, outlined by Eugene Emme in an essay earlier in this collection. In both cases, the development of doctrine served legitimate military needs, while helping each organization preserve institutional independence. And, in both cases doctrine preceded the existence of the proper tool to carry it out. Readers should ask themselves, What functions are served when a service develops a doctrine? How much of doctrinal development is based on the real military need, and how much on the need to protect the existence or mission of the service in question? Where is the line between legitimate need and the defense of bureaucratic "turf"? In today's military environment, as services, and organizations within services, struggle over tighter budgets and confront more persistent questioning of their missions and roles, such questions are as important as they were when Andrew Higgins first confronted the stubborn officials of the Bureau of Ships.

World War II was, in the truest sense, a global conflict. In order to defeat its enemies, the United States sent armed forces across two oceans, several seas and the English Channel. History records the success with which this nation projected its military power abroad by seizing hostile shores through the use of amphibious assaults.

The far-flung American amphibious forces, while certainly worthy of high praise, would have accomplished much less without the foresight and determination of a few Marines and a civilian boat builder, Andrew J. Higgins. But for these forward-looking men, the United States would not have had many of the specialized landing craft needed to conduct seaborne invasions in Europe and throughout the Pacific.

This account records the struggle of Higgins and his Marine allies against the Navy bureaucracy in the period just before, and during, World War II. While this article addresses a problem that faced military leaders 40 years ago, modern planners may recognize many similarities in today's environment. Although short of manpower and strapped for funds, modern leaders must resist the tendency to rely on comfortable, outdated concepts. As history has shown, the inventor of a "better mousetrap" may be patiently waiting just outside the office door.

The years between World Wars I and II found the United States concerned mainly with domestic problems. That part of the US Navy which had survived the limitations of the Washington Naval Treaty and drastic cuts imposed by a budget-minded Congress had to content itself with showing the flag and planning for the next war. The halls of the Navy Department echoed the arguments between battleship admirals and those supporting the new aircraft carriers.

In an out-of-the-way corner of the Navy headquarters, a small group of Navy and Marine Corps officers was concerned with an entirely different question: landing operations. If the authors of War Plan *Orange* were to be believed, the United States might someday go to war with Japan. How would the island bases so critical to operations in the Pacific expanses be secured? An assault from the sea was the only answer. The force charged with the conduct of seaborne assault was the US Marine Corps.

Although the Marines had been given the mission of assaulting enemy strongholds from the sea, the Marine Corps was hardly capable of conducting such a mission. Following World War I, the swollen Marine Corps was quickly reduced in strength to a headquarters force, small shipboard detachments and garrisons in far-off China.

The restrictions to mission accomplishment resulting from puny appropriations were nowhere more evident than in landing operations carried out in the Caribbean. On several occasions during the 1920s, the Marines seized coastal ports being held by revolutionary elements. The hard-bitten leathernecks had to endure the taunts of American sailors, as well as bullets, while bobbing around in antiquated whaleboats and bailing furiously lest they sink before reaching the shore.

Marine requests for an improved landing craft capable of carrying troops from ship to shore were generally shunted around the Navy Bureau of Ships (BUSHIPS) until they died of old age. Any talk of amphibious assaults brought to mind the British debacle at Gallipoli in 1915 which was still a fresh memory of World War I. The Marine requests were in competition with those of the fleet. At BUSHIPS, the fleet came first—always.

By the mid-1930s, however, the Navy began to consider the possibility of landing troops on a hostile shore when Japanese forces invaded China. While campaigning in northeast China, the Japanese made excellent use of a flat-bottomed landing barge fitted with a bow ramp. The ramps, when lowered, permitted the assault troops on board to disembark quickly onto a beach or river bank.

American intelligence reports indicated that the Japanese were developing new amphibious tactics as well as equipment. Clearly, the Japanese were more experienced in matters of ship-to-shore movement than the Americans, having developed not only landing barges but troopships and cargo ships specifically equipped to support seaborne assaults.

While reports of Japanese actions flowed into the naval intelligence staff, Navy and Marine officers pored over plans associated with an embryonic organization that had been conceived in 1933. Known as the Fleet Marine Force, this planned organization was to become an integral part of the Atlantic Fleet. A regimental-sized Marine force transported aboard Navy ships was to provide the chief of naval operations a force in being that could be employed as an assault unit. The Marines were tasked with the mission of developing techniques and doctrine for seaborne assault of fortified coasts and the subsequent garrisoning of the territory seized by amphibious assault.

Faced with this mandate, the commandant of the Marine Corps School at Quantico, Virginia, instructed an outspoken critic of Navy landing equipment, Colonel Holland M. Smith, to report to Quantico for orders. Smith (known as "Howlin' Mad") was appointed as chairman of a committee which would, within a year, provide the Marine Corps with a doctrinal proposal for landing operations. So avidly did Smith's group of visionaries pursue this course that, by mid-1934, they had completed the *Tentative Landing Manual*.

This manual was quickly given Marine Corps approval and was subsequently accepted by the Joint Board of the Army and Navy. With only minor changes, the manual served as the amphibious warfare "bible" for US forces during World War II.

During the final stages of preparation of the *Tentative Landing Manual,* Colonel Smith began badgering the Marine Corps Equipment Board (MCEB) for prototypes of the fast, seaworthy craft he envisioned as necessary for modern assaults. The MCEB was able to offer only small ships' boats and a motley collection of rumrunners' boats captured during Prohibition. Colonel Smith, while thanking the Coast Guard for the use of the confiscated boats, said, "They may have been good for running booze, but these boats were worthless as assault craft."

With a manual in hand, but lacking the means to practice the doctrine they preached, the Marines were very receptive when a Louisiana boat builder, Andrew J. Higgins, arrived at Quantico with a boat of his own design called the *Eureka.* Higgins had traveled to Virginia at his own expense in hopes of interesting the Marines in this boat, originally designed for use by fur trappers and oil prospectors in the bayous of Louisiana.

With a shallow draft, rounded bow and protected propeller, the *Eureka* was well-suited for amphibious assaults. Loaded with 16 troops, the 26-foot-long boat could make 12 knots and could surmount moderate surf with little difficulty. The MCEB and Colonel Smith's study group tested the *Eureka* in the Chesapeake Bay and found it to their liking. Unfortunately for Higgins and the Marine Corps, no money was available in 1934 to purchase any of these craft.

A disappointed Higgins returned to Louisiana, but not before establishing a lasting friendship with Colonel Smith. The Marine persuaded Higgins to incorporate several suggested improvements in the *Eureka* and to build a prototype of the improved model. By 1937, Smith had convinced the Navy to appropriate sufficient funds for the purchase of a *Eureka.* The new boat, incorporating the suggestions made by Colonel Smith and the MCEB, was scheduled for intensive tests during the Fleet Landing Exercise 3 (FLEX 3) to be held in the summer of 1937.

The *Eureka* model which was tested during the summer exercises at San Clemente, California, in June 1937 and, again in 1938 and 1939, was unanimously applauded by the Marines involved in the landing exercises. The *Eureka*'s performance far outshone several landing craft of BUSHIPS design. One Marine report completed after FLEX 5 in 1939 stated:

> The Higgins boat gave the best performance under all conditions. It has more speed, more maneuverability, handles easier, and lands troops higher on the beach. It also has greater power in backing off the beach; not once was the boat observed having difficulty in retracting.

The only major shortcoming in the Higgins boat noted by the Marines was its small size. At 26 feet in length, the *Eureka* could only carry about 16 troops.

The Marines, anxious to get as many troops ashore as possible in a short period of time, would have preferred that the boat be 36 feet long. A troop capacity of 25 to 30 armed men was the desired payload.

The questions surrounding the boat's dimensions would not be solved at San Clemente, however. The Navy, not the Marines, dictated the specifications for landing craft design. BUSHIPS officers would have to be convinced of the value of a larger Higgins boat before any further improvements could be made.

When Smith and Higgins approached the Navy Department with the suggestion that the *Eureka* be redesigned in a longer version, the two men were met with an outright refusal to consider a longer landing craft. BUSHIPS officers insisted that all landing craft be less than 30 feet in length.

The Navy position was based on the fact that all warships and transports in the fleet were equipped with boat davits which could handle craft no more than 30 feet long. The Marines, naturally enough, were far more concerned with developing a landing craft that could best support the Marines' assault mission. The question of boat length was discussed for two more years, with no decision being reached.

Finally, in early 1939, the Navy and Higgins solved the problem of boat dimensions. During a very stormy session at the Navy Department, Andrew Higgins lost patience with the bureaucratic dogma being spouted by BUSHIPS staff officers. Slamming his blueprints for a 36-foot *Eureka* on the table, he exclaimed, "To hell with designing a boat to fit the davits! Why don't you design davits to fit a proper sized boat?!"

Backed up by the Marine representatives at the conference, Higgins won the argument. The Navy relented and agreed to fund the construction of 10 Higgins boats in the new 36-foot size. With his government contract in hand, Andrew Higgins returned to Louisiana to build a "proper sized boat" for the fleet landing exercises scheduled to be held in 1940 in the Caribbean. Fortunately for the Marines, Higgins' persistence had paid off.

In September 1939, Europe was again at war. While Hitler pushed his forces into Poland, the Navy Department in Washington began to function with a greater sense of urgency in areas that had received only moderate attention before the war started. BUSHIPS responded with alacrity to the increased tempo and soon had inspectors prowling about the Higgins boatyard in Louisiana. Andrew Higgins was polite but to the point when dealing with the naval officers. They could observe the construction of *Eureka* boats as long as they did not attempt to interfere with the process. Marine officers, sent by Holland Smith to work closely with Higgins, were always welcome.

While Higgins was building the longer *Eureka*, the Navy was building several similar craft that incorporated some of the features of the *Eureka*. The Navy tested numerous landing craft during landing exercises on Culebra Island off Puerto Rico in 1940. Again in 1941, the *Eureka* was pitted against BUSHIPS designs. In every test conducted during 1940 and 1941, the Higgins design proved superior to any other.

British officers who had observed the landing exercises of 1940 were so impressed by the *Eureka* that they ordered 136 for immediate delivery. By 1941, *Eurekas* were carrying British commandos on raids across the English Channel to the French coast.

As good as the Higgins boat was, it still needed to be improved. The MCEB urged Higgins to design a lightly armored ramp to replace the rounded spoonbill bow of the *Eureka*. The lack of a ramp necessitated a jump of 4 feet when disembarking over the bow. Troops leaping from the *Eureka* often landed in the surf, thereby subjecting weapons and equipment to a dousing with corrosive salt water. A ramp which could be lowered would allow troops to race directly onto the beach or into shallow water.

Higgins agreed to make the modification. By cutting off the bow of the *Eureka*, the overall length of the craft was reduced to 35.7 feet, too slight a difference to cause problems with the Navy's new davits. The redesigned craft with a squared-off bow was just as seaworthy as its forerunner.

The improved Higgins boat surpassed all other assault craft used in the landing exercises held during August 1941 at New River, North Carolina. (Yes, BUSHIPS was *still* building prototypes of their own design!) The Navy, recognizing the superiority of the Higgins boat, accepted it as the standard ramp landing craft and designated it the landing craft, vehicle, personnel (LCVP) (see Table 1).

With an infantry assault boat accepted, Andrew Higgins turned his full attention to a new project that his firm had been working on for several months: an assault craft for tanks. The Marines had requested in 1937 that the Navy provide a tank lighter that would enable the Marine assault troops to take tanks ashore with the early waves during a seaborne assault.

The Navy BUSHIPS, with characteristic speed, had spent four years designing and testing tank lighters. All of the design prototypes tested by the Marines in 1940 and 1941 had failed miserably. By June 1941, the MCEB was so vociferous in its complaints that Admiral Stark, chief of naval operations, directed that Andrew Higgins be given a chance to design a tank lighter.

Notified on 22 June 1941 that the Navy wanted him to design an assault vehicle capable of ferrying tanks ashore, Higgins immediately set to work. His first step was to declare that he would consult only with Marine Corps representatives on the project; BUSHIPS personnel were not needed or desired. The Navy acceded, and work began at a feverish pace in the Higgins boatyard.

By sheer coincidence, Higgins had a vessel in his yard that could be utilized with minor changes. A flat-bottomed, shallow-draft steel boat designed for use on the upper Amazon River, the vessel would fill the bill with a new bow design. Within 24 hours, Higgins had redrawn the plans for the nearly finished Amazon

TABLE 1   *Landing Craft, Vehicle, Personnel (LCVP)*

Length:	35.7 feet
Beam:	10.5 feet
Displacement:	20,600 pounds
Speed:	8 knots (full)
Propulsion:	One 225-horsepower diesel engine, single propeller
Endurance:	110 nautical miles (full load)
Draft: (forward)	2 feet 2 inches
Draft: (aft)	3 feet 5 inches
Capacity:	8,100 pounds or 36 combat troops
Crew:	Three enlisted

The LCVP was the most numerous landing craft in the amphibious force during World War II. It can beach through 4-foot surf.

boat, and work was already started as workmen cut the bow from the boat. A new bow with a drop-ramp similar to the LCVP was fabricated and welded into place.

On 25 June, work was completed, and Higgins gave the new tank lighter its first test. According to the Marine observers in the Higgins yard, the craft was nearly perfect. In less than three days, Andrew Higgins and his crew had surpassed the efforts of BUSHIPS that had spanned four years of design and trials.

The Higgins tank lighter was tested at New River in August 1941 and was loudly hailed by the Marines who at last had a craft that would assure them of tank support during assaults upon enemy shorelines. The Navy soon accepted the Higgins lighter as its standard tank lighter and labeled it the landing craft, mechanized (LCM). The LCM, which was 56 feet long and 14 feet wide, was capable of carrying 60 troops or an M4 medium tank. Higgins' amazing effort had produced a product that landed tanks during every major amphibious assault of World War II and the Korean conflict (see Table 2).

The Japanese attack on Pearl Harbor found the United States woefully unprepared to conduct amphibious landings. Although the LCVP and LCM had been accepted, these craft were just beginning to arrive at Marine training bases when the United States declared war. As work began on the design of many types of specialized landing craft, American military leaders wrestled with the problems of supplying the Army, Navy and Marines with the thousands of landing craft needed to carry out Allied strategy. As he had done in design problems, Andrew Higgins threw himself wholeheartedly into the mass construction of landing craft.

TABLE 2   *Landing Craft, Mechanized,* Mark VI (LCM6)

Length and beam:	56.1 by 14 feet
Draft: (forward)	3 feet
Draft: (aft)	4 feet
Displacement:	124,000 pounds
Capacity: *LCM6*	68,000 pounds or 80 combat troops
Propulsion:	Two 225-horsepower diesel engines, twin propellers
Speed:	9 knots (full load)
Endurance:	160 nautical miles (light)
	130 nautical miles (loaded)
Crew:	Five enlisted

The *Mark III (LCM3)* is the same as the *LCM6* except it is 6 feet shorter and has a capacity of 60,000 pounds or 60 combat troops. The *LCM3* and *LCM6* were the most commonly used craft in ship-to-shore movements during World War II. They can beach through 6-foot surf and are used to land medium-weight vehicles, equipment and personnel on the beach in an operation.

The Higgins boatyard doubled, tripled, then expanded beyond prewar imagination during 1942 as government purchase orders flooded in. Of course, the vast numbers of landing craft required could not be produced by a single builder. Higgins and his employees cooperated fully with the various services and ensured that other contractors were supplied with plans and technical advisers so that landing craft could be produced in the shortest possible time.

Andrew Higgins' service to the Marine Corps was acknowledged in a letter from his friend, Major General Holland M. Smith. This testament, from a man who was to achieve greatness as an amphibious commander in the Pacific, said in part:

> We look upon your equipment as a part of our [Fleet Marine] Force: quite as essential as tanks and guns and ammunition. I want to say that I never lose an opportunity to tell people in high latitudes that we have the best damn boats in the world, but only half enough.

As American war plans crystallized, the need for landing craft in un-dreamed-of numbers became evident. Sufficient craft to support the Allied invasion of North Africa in November 1942 were provided only because President Roosevelt demanded that the construction of landing craft be given priority over many other types of vessels.

Crews, too, were in short supply. Three men were needed for the LCVP (coxswain, engineer and gunner), and the numbers increased with the size of the craft. The Navy at first balked at the thought of investing such a great amount of manpower in small-boat training.

When it seemed that the plans for the North African invasion might be threatened by a lack of boat crews, Army Chief of Staff George C. Marshall threatened to train his own crews and create his version of a "small-craft navy." Admiral E. J. King found this prospect less than pleasing and gave priority to training Navy and Coast Guard boat crews during 1942 and 1943.

By early 1944, the vast industrial might of the United States had largely overcome the country's shortage in war materiel, to include the dearth of landing craft. Incorporating the designing genius of Andrew Higgins, small boatyards, factories and large shipyards all over the United States produced a giant fleet of landing craft for the United States and its Allies. These boats ranged in size from small rubber dinghies used by commandos to large seagoing landing ship, tanks, that could transport over 200 troops across oceans and deliver their passengers and cargo upon a distant shore.

When viewed in the whole context of the giant struggle that was World War II, the development of landing craft may seem a relatively minor matter. If, however, one realizes how utterly essential these unglamorous boats were to the prosecution of Allied strategy, the true value of landing craft is readily apparent. North Africa, Sicily, Italy and France were all assaulted from the sea. In the Pacific, amphibious assault was the only means of conquering the island empire of the Japanese.

Without the genius and determination of a civilian boat builder and the support of his Marine comrades, the successful record achieved by American forces may have been far different. If Allied successes in amphibious operations can attest to the value of landing craft, so, too, can failures in amphibious warfare.

In this vein, historians still ponder this question: What might have transpired if Nazi Germany had possessed a large fleet of landing craft in 1940? Could the embattled British have withstood a large and effectively executed cross-channel assault after the fall of France? Hitler's dreams of victory faded as he realized that his plans for Operation *Sea Lion* could never be. No landing craft meant no invasion.

If history is to serve mankind, lessons of the past must not be forgotten. In this sense, modern military leaders should remember the example set by Andrew Higgins in his fight for recognition. Today, stodgy, tradition-bound concepts are too often accepted as gospel simply because they exist. We must be aware that fertile, inquiring minds abound in areas outside the defense bureaucracy. To ignore this fact is to deny our past history.

The military forces of the United States continue to search for technological improvements. We will succeed in our quest only if we exploit to the fullest offerings of the modern-day counterparts of Andrew Higgins. The thinkers, the doers, the dreamers are all around us. They are the American people.

ROBERT ROSS SMITH

LUZON VERSUS FORMOSA

J *ust as the interaction of logistics and personality affected the decision for Operation Overlord in the European theater, so also did these factors affect the decisions in the Pacific theater. There, however, the personalities were almost all American, since the Pacific was basically an American-dominated theater. In fact, it was two theaters, the Pacific Ocean Areas, commanded by Admiral of the Fleet Chester W. Nimitz, and the Southwest Pacific Area, commanded by General of the Army Douglas MacArthur.*

The creation of the two theaters was a consequence of inter-service rivalries. MacArthur, a former army chief of staff and the senior officer on active duty in World War II, could hardly be denied a major command. The navy could hardly allow a soldier to command its forces in a theater composed mostly of water. The exact boundaries of the two theaters were contentious. The navy wanted part of the action early in the war and insisted that New Zealand and the Solomon Islands fall under Nimitz's control, while MacArthur retained Australia, the Netherlands East Indies (Indonesia), and the Philippines. Thus both services were able to participate in the initial 1942 offensives, on Guadalcanal (the navy), and on eastern New Guinea (the army).

In 1943 Allied forces in the Pacific began a two-pronged advance across the Pacific, one commanded by MacArthur along the northern coast of New Guinea toward the Philippines, and the other commanded by Nimitz across the Central Pacific islands toward the Japanese colony of Formosa (now Taiwan). Strategic commentators then and today debate the efficacy of the dual offensive. It defied the military principles of concentration of mass and of unity of command. Movement along the New Guinea coast allowed MacArthur to bypass and isolate Japanese strong points and to conserve manpower. In addition, MacArthur could effectively integrate Army Air Force assets in support of his operations that were not useful to Nimitz. The central Pacific drive by the navy involved implementation of a variant of War Plan ORANGE and a series of decisive encounters between the Pacific Fleet and the Imperial Japanese Navy. Nimitz's operations required a series of island invasions that ring large in American military annals—Tarawa, Kwajalein, Palau, Saipan, and Iwo Jima. They were more costly in American lives than MacArthur's campaigns.

At times the two-pronged advance had a deleterious effect on American operations. Dr. Ronald H. Spector, the former chief of the Naval Historical Center, notes that the Bougainville attack by Admiral William Halsey in late 1943 required him to risk carriers in a raid against land-based aircraft at the Japanese strongpoint on Rabaul. Halsey's success was based more on good fortune than good planning since most of the ships he needed for a margin of safety were being hoarded by Nimitz for the central Pacific drive. On the other hand, MacArthur's most astute biographer, Dr. D. Clayton James, concludes that while the "lack of unity of command in the Pacific and of a single axis of advance produced some liabilities in prosecuting the war against Japan, . . . the coordination by theater commands along the dual lines of advance sometimes brought about a degree of teamwork and mutual support that was effective and impressive."

Once they secured a western Pacific stronghold, strategists had to develop a plan for the final assault on the Japanese homeland. For the navy and the Army Air Forces, Formosa seemed the better objective from which to both interdict the Japanese lines of communication and to bombard the Japanese home islands. Led by General MacArthur, most army officers insisted upon the Philippines route and the seizure of Luzon, including the Philippine capital of Manila.

Since both MacArthur and Nimitz agreed that a central Philippines base had to be established, the argument favoring bypassing the whole archipelago died aborning. Moreover, MacArthur's insistence upon the political necessity of reclaiming the islands had strong adherents in Washington. Pacific theater planners began focusing their attention on Okinawa rather than Formosa as an objective for the planned invasion of Japan. Moreover, by early autumn 1944 the fortunes of war began favoring a rapid advance toward Luzon, and that constant limiting factor in military operations—logistics—began to raise its head. The small number of available service troops for a Formosa invasion as compared to the support from loyal Filipinos became an increasingly important element reinforcing a Luzon decision. In the end, only Admiral Ernest J. King, Chief of Naval Operations, held out for the Formosa operation.

Robert Ross Smith, who served as an historian on MacArthur's staff during this period, provides a detailed account of the decision-making process. Was MacArthur or King closer to the Clausewitzian dictum that "war is policy by another means"? Did MacArthur forget this during his controversy with President Harry S. Truman in 1951?

One of the thorniest problems of strategic planning for the war against Japan was to decide whether the principal objective of drives that had brought the Allies into the western Pacific should be Luzon or Formosa. The decision was made by the U.S. Joint Chiefs of Staff, since the Pacific was an American area of strategic responsibility. They made it after long debate and careful study of the views of the commanders in the Central and Southwest Pacific theaters. Among the considerations that determined their choice when they finally made it, logistical factors played the major role, but here, as in other connections, they had to take into account the commitments and progress of the Allies in other theaters, and particularly in Europe. It was in this sense a decision in global strategy.

THE STRATEGIC BACKGROUND

Pacific Strategy   In January 1945, after more than three years of war, United States forces returned to Luzon Island in the Philippines, where in 1942 American troops had suffered a historic defeat. The loss of the Philippines in May of that year, after the disaster that befell the U.S. Pacific Fleet at Pearl Harbor, had rendered obsolete the inoperable American prewar plans for action in the Pacific in the event of war with Japan. By the late spring of 1943 the U.S. Joint Chiefs of Staff (who, by agreement of the U.S.-British Combined Chiefs of Staff, were responsible for the conduct of the war in the Pacific) had developed a new strategic plan for the defeat of Japan. The plan was neither sacrosanct nor immutable—it was not intended to be—but its underlying concepts governed the planning and execution of operations in the Pacific during a year and a half of debate over the relative priority of Luzon and Formosa as primary objectives of an Allied drive into the western Pacific.

The plan was premised upon the concept that the Allies might very well find it necessary to invade Japan in order to end the war in the Pacific. The Joint Chiefs of Staff foresaw that intensive aerial bombardment of the Japanese home islands would be prerequisite to invasion, and that such bombardment would have to be co-ordinated with combined air, surface, and submarine operations aimed at cutting Japan's overwater lines of communication to the rich territories she had seized in the Netherlands Indies and southeastern Asia. The Joint Chiefs believed that the Allies could best undertake the necessary bombardment of Japan from airfields in eastern China. They decided that to secure and develop adequate air bases in China, Allied forces would have to seize at least one major port on the south China coast. The Allies would require such a port to replace the poor overland and air routes from India and Burma as the principal means of moving men and matériel into China.

To secure a port on the China coast, and simultaneously to cut Japan's line of communication to the south, the Allies would have to gain control of the South China Sea. Gaining this control, the Joint Chiefs realized, would in turn involve the seizure and development of large air, naval, and logistical bases in the strategic triangle formed by the south China coast, Formosa, and Luzon. But before they could safely move into this triangle, the Joint Chiefs decided, the Allies would have to secure air bases in the southern or central Philippines from which to neutralize Japanese air power on Luzon. The Allies might also need staging bases in the southern and central Philippines from which to mount amphibious attacks against Luzon, Formosa, and the China coast.

In accordance with these 1943 plans, Allied forces in the Pacific had struck westward toward the strategic triangle along two axes of advance. Air, ground, and naval forces of the Southwest Pacific Area, under General Douglas MacArthur, had driven up the north coast of New Guinea to Morotai Island, lying between the northwestern tip of New Guinea and Mindanao, south-ernmost large island of the Philippine Archipelago. Simultaneously, Admiral Chester W. Nimitz, commander of the Pacific Ocean Areas, had directed the forces of the Central Pacific Area in a drive through the Gilberts, Marshalls, and Marianas to the Palau Islands, some 500 miles east of Mindanao.

The Importance of Formosa   Studying various plans for Allied entry into the strategic triangle, the Joint Chiefs and their subordinate advisory committees concluded that Formosa constituted the most important single objective in the target area. The island possessed so many obvious advantages and was located in such a strategically important position that most planners in Washington be-lieved the Allies would have to seize it no matter what other operations they conducted in the western Pacific. Until they seized Formosa, the Allies would be unable to establish and secure an overwater supply route to China. Formosa, therefore, seemed a necessary steppingstone to the China coast. Moreover, Allied air and naval forces could sever the Japanese lines of communication to the south much more effectively from Formosa than from either Luzon or the south China coast alone. Furthermore, from fields in northern Formosa, the Army Air Forces' new B–29's could carry heavier bomb loads against Japan than from more distant Luzon.

Many planners considered Formosa such a valuable strategic prize that they devoted considerable attention to the possibility of bypassing all the Philippines in favor of a direct descent upon Formosa. Discussion of this proposal waxed and waned in Washington during much of 1943 and 1944 despite the fact that the strategic outline plan for the defeat of Japan called for the seizure of bases in the southern or central Philippines before going on into the Luzon–Formosa–China coast triangle. Such discussions found the War and Navy Departments internally divided. Admiral Ernest J. King, Chief of Naval Operations and Navy member of the Joint Chiefs of Staff, was a leading advocate of plans to bypass the Philippines. On the other hand, Admiral Nimitz and other ranking naval commanders in the Pacific favored at least reoccupying the southern or central Philippines before striking on toward Formosa. These officers believed it would be impossible to secure the Allied line of communications to Formosa until Allied land-based aircraft from southern Philippine bases had neutralized Japanese air power on Luzon.

General George C. Marshall, Chief of Staff and Army member of the Joint Chiefs, played a relatively inactive part in the debate until late 1944, but at one time at least seemed inclined toward bypassing both the Philippines *and* Formosa in favor of a direct invasion of Kyushu in southern Japan. Some officers high in Army councils, including Lt. Gen. Joseph T. McNarney, Deputy Chief of Staff, strongly advocated bypassing the Philippines on the way to Formosa. General Henry H. Arnold, Army Air Forces member of the Joint Chiefs, also appears to have maintained through much of 1943 and 1944 that it might prove desirable to bypass the Philippines. Other Army planners, including those of the chief logistician, Lt. Gen. Brehon B. Somervell, commander of the Army Service Forces, favored taking the entire Philippine Archipelago before making any move toward Formosa or the China coast. In the field, General MacArthur stood adamant against bypassing any part of the Philippines, a stand in which he had the support of most other ranking Army officers in the Pacific.

In March 1944 the Joint Chiefs had directed MacArthur to be ready to move into the southern Philippines before the end of the year and to make plans to invade Luzon during February 1945. Simultaneously, they had ordered Nimitz to prepare plans for an assault against Formosa in February 1945. These directives, which left in abeyance the relative priority of Luzon and Formosa, ostensibly settled the question of re-entry into the Philippines, but in mid-June the Joint Chiefs of Staff reopened the question of bypassing the archipelago.

Developments in the Pacific, Asia, and Europe between mid-March and mid-June 1944 tended to support those planners who wanted to bypass the Philippines. The U.S. army had acquired new intelligence indicating that the Japanese were rapidly reinforcing their bastions throughout the western Pacific, including Formosa. Thus, the longer the Allies delayed an attack on Formosa, the more the operation would ultimately cost. Army planners suggested that the Allies might be able to reach Formosa during November 1944 if the Joint Chiefs immediately decided to bypass the Philippines. Moreover, the Joint Chiefs were beginning to fear an imminent collapse of Chinese resistance—some planners felt that the only way to avert such an eventuality would be the early seizure of Formosa and a port on the China coast without undertaking intermediary operations in the Philippines. The Joint Chiefs were probably also stimulated by the success of the invasion of Normandy in early June and by the impending invasion of the Marianas in the Central Pacific, set for 15 June. At any rate, on 13 June, seeking ways and means to accelerate the pace of operations in the Pacific, and feeling that the time might be ripe for acceleration, the Joint Chiefs asked Admiral Nimitz and General MacArthur to consider the possibilities of bypassing all objectives already selected in the western Pacific, including both the Philippines and Formosa.

Neither Nimitz nor MacArthur gave the Joint Chiefs any encouragement. Both declared that the next major step in the Pacific after the advance to the Palaus–Morotai line would have to be the seizure of air bases in the southern or central Philippines. The Joint Chiefs' subordinate committees, examining the theater commanders' replies and undertaking new studies of their own, re-affirmed the concept that the Allies would have to move into the central or southern Philippines before advancing to either Formosa or Luzon. Like Mac-Arthur and Nimitz, the advisory bodies saw no possibility of a direct jump to Japan. The Joint Chiefs of Staff, apparently with some reluctance, agreed.

Meeting with President Franklin D. Roosevelt in a conference at Pearl Harbor in late July 1944, both MacArthur and Nimitz again emphasized that MacArthur's forces would have to be firmly established in the southern or central Philippines before any advance to either Formosa or Luzon could take place—on this point almost everyone was agreed. MacArthur then argued persuasively that it was both necessary and proper to take Luzon before going on to Formosa, while Nimitz expounded a plan for striking straight across the western Pacific to Formosa, bypassing Luzon. Apparently, no decisions on strategy were reached at the Pearl Harbor conferences. The Formosa versus Luzon debate continued without let-up at the highest planning levels for over two months, and even the question of bypassing the Philippines entirely in favor of a direct move on Formosa again came up for serious discussion. The net result of the debate through July 1944 was reaffirmation of the decision to strike into the southern or central Philippines before advancing to either Formosa or Luzon. The Joint Chiefs still had to decide whether to seize Luzon or Formosa, or both, before executing any other major attacks against Japan.

THE DEBATE OVER LUZON

The Views Presented   General MacArthur was a most vigorous adherent of the view that the Allies would have to secure Luzon before moving any farther toward Japan. Contrary to the views held by the Joint Chiefs of Staff, MacArthur believed that Luzon was a more valuable strategic prize than Formosa. He declared that the Allies would need to reoccupy the entire Philippine Archipel-ago before they could completely sever Japan's lines of communication to the south. MacArthur also believed that an invasion of Formosa would prove unduly hazardous unless he provided air and logistical support from Luzon. Finally, he suggested, if the Allies took Luzon first they could then bypass Formosa and strike for targets farther north, thus hastening the end of the war. The Luzon-first course of action, he averred, would be the cheaper in terms of time, men, and money.

In addition, MacArthur considered that bypassing part of the Philippines would have the "sinister implication" of imposing a food blockade upon unoccupied portions of the archipelago. (His meaning here is not clear, inasmuch as his own plans called for seizing a foothold in southeastern Mindanao, jumping thence to Leyte in the east-central Philippines, and then going on to Luzon, initially bypassing the bulk of Mindanao, the Sulu Archipelago, and most of the Visayan Islands.) MacArthur had a more cogent argument, and one that was bound to have some influence upon planning in Washington. The reoccupation of the entire Philippine Archipelago as quickly and early as possible, was, MacArthur said, a national obligation and political necessity. To bypass any or all the islands, he declared, would destroy American honor and prestige throughout the Far East, if not in the rest of the world as well.

Just as General MacArthur was the most vigorous proponent of Luzon, so Admiral King was the most persistent advocate of the Formosa-first strategy. King believed that the seizure of Luzon before Formosa could only delay the execution of more decisive operations to the north. He also argued that the capture of Formosa first would greatly facilitate the subsequent occupation of Luzon. Moreover, King pointed out, the Allies could not secure and maintain a foothold on the China coast until they had seized Formosa. Finally, he suggested, if the Allies should bypass Formosa, then the principal objective in the western Pacific should be Japan, itself, not Luzon.

MacArthur believed that the plans to bypass Luzon were purely Navy-inspired. Actually, the War and Navy Departments were as internally split during the Luzon versus Formosa debate as they had been earlier over the question of bypassing all the Philippines. For example, at least until mid-September 1944 General Marshall favored the Formosa-first strategy and like Admiral King had expressed the opinion that Japan itself, rather than Luzon, should be considered the substitute for Formosa. Most Army members of the Joint Chiefs' subordinate committees held similar views, and until September consistently pressed for an early decision in favor of Formosa. Army Air Forces planners, during the summer of 1944, expressed their interest in Formosa as a site for B–29 bases.

Admiral Nimitz, the ranking naval officer in the Pacific, went on record until late September as favoring Formosa first. However, there are indications that his views were not enthusiastically shared by his staff, and there are grounds to believe that Nimitz grew steadily more lukewarm toward the idea of seizing Formosa. Nimitz had been at variance with Admiral King on the question of bypassing the entire Philippine Archipelago, and it is possible that his support of the Formosa-first strategy stemmed at least in part from deference to King's judgment. A hint of Nimitz' attitude is apparent in the fact that his staff was preparing plans to seize Okinawa, as a substitute for Formosa, well before such an operation gained serious consideration among high-level planners in Washington.

The next ranking naval officer in the Pacific, Admiral William F. Halsey, commander of the Third Fleet (and until 15 June 1944 commander of the South Pacific Area as well), steadfastly opposed the Formosa-first plan. He wanted to go to Luzon and bypass Formosa in favor of seizing Okinawa. In this connection Halsey relates a classic story concerning a discussion between his chief of staff, Vice Adm. Robert B. Carney, and Admiral King. King, propounding his Formosa plan to Carney, who was arguing in favor of Luzon, asked, "Do you want to make a London out of Manila?" Carney's reply was: "No sir, I want to make an England out of Luzon."

Most of the other senior Army and Navy officers on duty in the Pacific also favored the Luzon-first strategy and advocated bypassing Formosa. Lt. Gen. Robert C. Richardson, commanding U.S. Army Forces, Pacific Ocean Areas, strongly advised against Formosa. So, too, did MacArthur's air commander, Lt. Gen. George C. Kenney, and the Southwest Pacific Area's naval commander, Vice Adm. Thomas C. Kinkaid. But among the Joint Chiefs of Staff during the summer and early fall of 1944 only Admiral William D. Leahy, the President's Chief of Staff, favored going to Luzon instead of Formosa, and this stand represented a reversal of Leahy's earlier thinking on the subject.

It is noteworthy that, with the possible exception of Nimitz, the ranking Army and Navy commanders in the Pacific—the men responsible for executing or supporting the operation—were opposed to the seizure of Formosa. In general, they favored a program calling for the capture of Luzon and a subsequent jump to Okinawa or Japan. In the face of this opinion of commanders on the spot, the consensus of most high-ranking Army and Navy planners in Washington—with Leahy and General Somervell as outstanding exceptions—was that the Formosa-first course of action was strategically the sounder and, therefore, the most desirable course for the Allies to follow in the western Pacific.

The Washington planners, however, had to give careful consideration to many factors other than ideal strategy. Study of these factors brought the Luzon versus Formosa debate to a climax in late September 1944.

Tactical and Logistical Problems   Perhaps the most influential event helping to precipitate the climax was a drastic change in the target date for the initial invasion of the Philippines. Until mid-September 1944, General MacArthur's plans had called for the first entry into the Philippines to take place in southeastern Mindanao on 15 November, while the major assault into the archipelago would occur at Leyte on 20 December. On 15 September, with the approval of the Joint Chiefs of Staff, MacArthur canceled preliminary Mindanao operations in favor of a direct jump from the Palaus–Morotai line to Leyte on 20 October.

Soon after this change of schedule, MacArthur informed the Joint Chiefs that he could push on from Leyte to Luzon on 20 December, two months earlier than the date currently under consideration for an attack on either Luzon or Formosa. This new plan, MacArthur suggested, would permit the Allies to execute the Formosa operation on the date already selected, but, he went on, the prior seizure of Luzon would render unnecessary the occupation of Formosa.

MacArthur's new schedule contained much to recommend it to the Joint Chiefs of Staff. His proposed sequence of operations—Leyte on 20 October, Luzon on 20 December, and Formosa, possibly, on 20 February 1945—would permit the Allies to maintain steady pressure against the Japanese. Should the Allies drop Luzon out of the sequence, the Japanese would have ample time to realign their defenses during the interval between the Leyte and Formosa operations. Moreover, dropping out Luzon could in no way accelerate the advance to Formosa—logistical problems would make it impossible for the Allies to mount an invasion of Formosa under any circumstances before late February 1945.

While MacArthur's proposals were gaining some favor in Washington, especially among Army planners, Nimitz' proposals for advancing to Formosa and the south China coast were losing ground. Plans developed in Washington had long called for the seizure of all Formosa, after which amphibious forces would strike on westward to secure a port on the mainland. But Nimitz' latest plans provided for simultaneous assaults on southern Formosa and in the Amoy area of the China coast. Nimitz proposed to occupy the bulk of Formosa only if such a step proved necessary and feasible after he had established a firm bridgehead at Amoy.

Army planners quickly decided that Nimitz' new plans possessed major drawbacks. The Japanese would hardly allow Allied forces to sit unmolested in southern Formosa. Instead, the Japanese would mount strong counterattacks from northern Formosa with troops already on the island and with reinforcements staged in from China. Occupying and defending one beachhead on southern Formosa and another at Amoy would involve problems far different from those the Allies had encountered previously in the Pacific. So far during the war, the Japanese had usually been hard put to move air and ground reinforcements against the island perimeters Allied amphibious task forces had seized. In the southern Formosa–Amoy area, on the other hand, the Allies would not have the protection of distance from major Japanese bases they had enjoyed in earlier campaigns. The Allies did not have sufficient aircraft in the Pacific to keep neutralized all existing Japanese airfields within range of southern Formosa and Amoy. In addition, experience in the Pacific had demonstrated that Allied air and naval forces could not be expected to forestall all Japanese efforts to move strong reinforcements across the narrow strait between China and Formosa.

Having considered these factors, Army planners swung to the opinion that a southern Formosa–Amoy operation would be impractical. They believed that it would inevitably lead to protracted, costly campaigns to secure all Formosa and large areas of the adjacent China mainland as well. Major ground campaigns of such scope could only delay progress toward Japan and would prove an unacceptable drain upon Allied manpower resources.

Further study of manpower needed for the southern Formosa–Amoy operation revealed additional difficulties. Army intelligence estimates of Japanese strength in Formosa–Amoy region, for example, were far higher than those Nimitz' staff had produced. Army planners therefore believed that the southern Formosa–Amoy campaign would require many more combat units than Nimitz was planning to employ. Furthermore, according to various estimates made during September, Nimitz would lack from 77,000 to 200,000 of the service troops needed for the campaign he proposed.

Planners studied a number of suggestions for securing the necessary service forces. One thought, originating with the Navy, which was seeking ways to accelerate the Formosa target date, proposed taking service units from the Southwest Pacific area. But MacArthur's command was already short of service troops. To remove any from his area might jeopardize the success of the Leyte operation and would certainly immobilize his forces in the central Philippines until long after Nimitz had secured the southern Formosa–Amoy region. Although the southern Formosa–Amoy and Luzon operations would each require about the same number of U.S. combat troops in the assault phase, MacArthur could count upon hundreds of thousands of loyal Filipinos to augment both his service and his combat strength. No similar source of friendly manpower would be available on Formosa.

By mid-September 1944 so few service units were available in the United States that the only way Army planners could see to solve the service troop shortage for Nimitz' proposed operation was to await redeployment

from Europe. Army planners and the Joint Logistic Committee both estimated that Nimitz could launch the southern Formosa–Amoy campaign even
as early as 1 March 1945 only if the war in Europe ended by 1 November
1944, thereby permitting timely redeployment of service units to the Pacific.
And even if the Allies could effect such redeployment from Europe, logistical
planners still felt that Nimitz would be unable to move against Formosa by 1
March 1945 unless the Joint Chiefs of Staff immediately decided to cancel the
Luzon operation, thus providing for an early and unbroken build-up of the
resources required to execute Nimitz' campaign. On the other hand, the
logistical experts were convinced that MacArthur could move to Luzon
before the end of 1944 regardless of developments in Europe. Army planners,
not as optimistic as they had been a few months earlier about an early end to
the war in Europe, pointed out that it would be unsound to schedule the
southern Formosa–Amoy operation on the presumption of a German collapse
by 1 November 1944. Events were to prove this argument sound.

Army planners saw other combined logistical-tactical disadvantages in
Nimitz' plan. They believed, for instance, that the campaign would tie down
so many troops, ships, landing craft, and planes that an invasion of Luzon,
assuming Formosa came first, could not take place until November 1945. By
the same token any other major step toward Japan, such as the seizure of
Okinawa, would be equally delayed. A hiatus of this length would be unacceptable for tactical reasons alone. In addition, the Luzon-first course, it
appeared, would be far safer logistically than the southern Formosa–Amoy
undertaking. As Army Service Forces planners pointed out, the Allied lines
of communication to Luzon would be shorter and easier to protect than those
to Formosa. The logisticians predicted that the Allies would find it especially
difficult to safeguard the lines of communication to Formosa if Luzon remained in Japanese hands.

Other aspects of the logistical problems attained disturbing overtones.
Admiral Leahy, for example, believed that although the Formosa-first course
of action might ultimately hasten the end of the war in the Pacific, capturing
Luzon and bypassing Formosa would prove far cheaper in terms of lives and
other resources. By mid-September he, as well as most Army planners, was
favoring what promised to be the longer course at the lesser cost. General
MacArthur, meanwhile, expressed the opinion that the Formosa-first
strategy would cost not only more lives but also more time. He was prepared
to guarantee to the Joint Chiefs that he could secure the most strategically
important area of Luzon—the Central Plains–Manila Bay region—within
four to six weeks after initial landings on the island.

General Marshall also began to show misgivings about the cost of the
southern Formosa–Amoy operation vis-à-vis Luzon, although he remained

convinced that the Formosa-first course was strategically the more desirable. Admiral Nimitz expressed no strong opinion on the relative cost of the two campaigns, but, "backing" into the problem, stated that the occupation of Luzon after Formosa need not delay the pace of the war in the Pacific. If Formosa came first, Nimitz pointed out, MacArthur's task on Luzon would be considerably eased and, presumably, less costly. Admiral King, however, declared himself convinced that the Formosa-first course would save time and, therefore, reduce casualties over the long run. By late September 1944 King alone among the upper-level planners seems to have retained a strong conviction along these lines.

While the discussions over tactical and logistical problems continued in Washington, the Allied position in China had been steadily deteriorating. In mid-September General Joseph W. Stilwell, commanding U.S. Army forces in China, Burma, and India, and Allied Chief of Staff to Generalissimo Chiang Kai-shek, reported to the Joint Chiefs that Japanese offensives in eastern and southeastern China were overrunning the last air bases from which the China-based U.S. Fourteenth Air Force could effectively support invasions of either Luzon or Formosa. Chiang's armies were unable to either hold or recapture the air bases.

This news had an obvious impact upon the thinking of both the ground and the air planners in Washington. The Army Air Forces had intended to expand its airfields in eastern China as staging bases for B–29's flying against targets in Japan, Korea, Manchuria, and Formosa, and to base on these fields much of the tactical bombardment preceding the actual invasion of Japan. The east China fields now appeared irretrievably lost, and the Allies could not afford to expend the manpower necessary to retake and hold them. The need for seizure and development of a port on the China coast was therefore deprived of much of its urgency since the Allies had needed such a port primarily to open a good supply route into China for the development of air bases. By the same token, one of the principal reasons for seizing Formosa—to secure a steppingstone to the China coast—became much less compelling.

This line of thinking forced naval planners to reconsider the southern Formosa–Amoy plan. To most Navy planners a move to Formosa without the concomitant seizure of a mainland port would prove unsound, because Formosa lacked the anchorages and ports required for the large fleet and logistical bases the Allies needed in the western Pacific. Inevitably the question arose: If it was no longer feasible or desirable to seize and develop a port on the south China coast, was it feasible or desirable to occupy any part of Formosa? Since early September 1944 Army planners had been answering that question with an emphatic "no."

The loss of existing and potential air base sites in eastern China, with the limitations inherent in Nimitz' plans to occupy only southern Formosa, weighed heavily with Army Air Forces planners. There was no question but that B–29's could operate more effectively against Japan from northern Formosa than they could from northern Luzon, the Mariana Islands, or western China, but the big bombers could accomplish little more from southern Formosa than they could from the other base areas. Indeed, Saipan and Tinian in the Marianas lay closer to Tokyo than Nimitz' proposed base area in southern Formosa, and the two islands of the Marianas were secure from Japanese air attack. Even northern Luzon, some 200 miles farther from Tokyo than southern Formosa, had some advantages over southern Formosa—it had more room for B–29 fields and was safer from air attack. Finally, assuming that Nimitz could meet the most optimistic target date for the invasion of southern Formosa—1 March 1945—B–29's could not begin operations from that island until the late spring or early summer. The Army Air Forces was already planning to initiate B–29 operations from the Marianas before the end of 1944. In brief, by mid-September, the Army Air Forces had lost interest in Formosa and had begun to see eye to eye with other Army elements on the disadvantages and drawbacks of the southern Formosa–Amoy scheme.

An obvious political consideration may have had a bearing on the ultimate decision in the Luzon versus Formosa debate. General MacArthur's argument that it would be disastrous to United States prestige to bypass any part of the Philippines could not be dismissed. Perhaps more important, Admiral Leahy took the same point of view. By virtue of his intimate contact with President Roosevelt, it must be presumed that his colleagues of the Joint Chiefs of Staff gave Leahy's opinion careful consideration.

Decision   Whatever the political implication involved, the Formosa versus Luzon question was decided primarily upon its military merits. By the end of September 1944 almost all the military considerations—especially the closely interrelated logistical problems concerning troops and timing—had weighted the scales heavily in favor of seizing Luzon, bypassing Formosa, forgetting about a port on the China coast, and jumping on to Okinawa. Admiral King was the only member of the Joint Chiefs of Staff, if not the only prominent military figure as well, who still maintained a strong stand in favor of bypassing Luzon and executing the southern Formosa–Amoy operation.

Realizing that the military and political factors had undermined his position, King took a new, negative tack in the debate by raising objections to the Luzon operation per se. He argued that the Luzon campaign as MacArthur had planned it would tie up all the Pacific Fleet's fast carrier task forces for at least six weeks for the purposes of protecting the Luzon beachhead and Luzon-bound convoys and neutralizing Japanese air power on both Luzon and Formosa. To pin down the carriers for so long would be unsound, King averred, and he therefore declared MacArthur's plan unacceptable to the U.S. Navy.

Alerted by his deputy chief of Staff (Maj. Gen. Richard J. Marshall, then in Washington on official business), General MacArthur was able to provide Army planners with ammunition to counter King's last-ditch arguments. MacArthur informed the Joint Chiefs that his only requirement for carriers after the initial assault on Luzon would be for a small group of escort carriers to remain off the island for a few days to provide support for ground operations until his engineers could ready a field for land-based planes at the invasion beaches. MacArthur continued by pointing out that only the first assault convoys would be routed through dangerous waters north of Luzon and consequently require protection from the fast carrier task forces. Resupply and reinforcement convoys would come through the central Philippines under an umbrella of land-based aircraft from Mindoro Island, south of Luzon, and would require no carrier-based air cover. Thus, MacArthur declared he would have no long-term requirement for the fast carrier task forces, which he could quickly release so that Nimitz could employ them elsewhere. MacArthur concluded with the counterargument that the fast carriers would be tied down to a specific area much longer during the proposed southern Formosa–Amoy operation, especially if Luzon remained in Japanese hands, than would be the case for the Luzon invasion.

This exchange took much of the wind out of King's sails. Next, Admiral Nimitz withdrew whatever support he was still giving the Formosa plan. He had concluded that sufficient troops could not be made available for him to execute the southern Formosa–Amoy campaign within the foreseeable future. Accordingly, at the end of September, he threw the weight of his opinion behind the Luzon operation, proposing that plans to seize Formosa be at least temporarily dropped. Simultaneously, Nimitz presented for Admiral King's consideration a planned series of operations designed to maintain steady pressure against the Japanese and carry Allied forces speedily on toward Japan: MacArthur's forces would initiate the Luzon campaign on 20 December 1944; Central Pacific forces would move against Iwo Jima, in the Volcano Islands some 650 miles south of Tokyo, late in January 1945; and the Central Pacific would next attack Okinawa, 850 miles southwest of Tokyo, and other targets in the Ryukyu Islands, beginning on 1 March 1945.

King accepted Nimitz' recommendations, with one last reservation. King felt that the hazards involved in routing the Luzon assault convoys into the waters between Luzon and Formosa were so great that approval for such action should come directly from the Joint Chiefs of Staff. He raised similar objections to plans for having the Pacific Fleet's fast carrier task forces operate in the same restricted waters. The other three members of the Joint Chiefs of

Staff, however, agreed to leave the decision on these problems up to Nimitz and MacArthur, a settlement that King finally accepted.

After King's eleventh-hour change of position, the Joint Chiefs were able to attain the unanimity that their major strategic decisions required. On 3 October 1944 they directed General MacArthur to launch the invasion of Luzon on or about 20 December and instructed Admiral Nimitz to execute the Iwo Jima and Okinawa operations on the dates he had proposed. Nimitz would provide naval cover and support, including fast and escort carriers, for the invasion of Luzon; MacArthur would provide Nimitz with as much air support as he could from Luzon for the attack on Okinawa. The two commanders would co-ordinate their plans with those of B–29 units in the Pacific and India and with the plans of General Stilwell and the Fourteenth Air Force in China. *

The Joint Chiefs of Staff did not formally cancel the Formosa operation. Instead, they left in abeyance a final decision on the seizure of that island, but thereafter the occupation of Formosa as an operation of World War II never came up for serious consideration at the higher levels of Washington planning councils.

The Joint Chiefs had not reached their decision to take Luzon, bypass Formosa, and, in effect, substitute Okinawa for Formosa, either lightly or easily. From the beginning of the Luzon versus Formosa debate they had believed the seizure of Formosa and a port on the south China coast—bypassing Luzon—to be the best strategy the Allies could follow in the western Pacific. In the end, however, the Joint Chiefs had had to face the fact that the Allies could not assemble the resources required to execute that strategy, at least until after the end of the war in Europe. They could not seriously consider delaying the progress of the war in the Pacific until Germany collapsed. In the last analysis then, logistical considerations alone would have forced the Joint Chiefs to the decision they reached in favor of Luzon, although other military realities, and possibly political factors as well, had some influence upon the outcome of strategic planning for operations in the western Pacific.

For the Allied forces of the Pacific theaters, the Joint Chiefs' directive of 3 October 1944 ended months of uncertainty. The die was cast. Luzon would be taken; Formosa would be bypassed. United States forces would recapture the entire Philippines Archipelago in a consecutive series of advances, just as General MacArthur had been planning ever since he had left Corregidor in March 1942.

---

* The B–29's operated under the direct control of the JCS, with General Arnold acting as the JCS executive agent.

W A Y N E P. H U G H E S

FLEET TACTICS
A Weaponry Revolution

By almost any measure, the way the U.S. Navy fought World War II in the Pacific was different than prewar planners anticipated. Although many of the broad themes of the naval campaigns were outlined in plans like War Plan ORANGE, American naval officers had to develop entirely new tactical concepts as the war progressed. Technology, much of it untried, altered everything, and did so in ways few officers foresaw.

To a large extent, the force structure and weaponry of the navy when the United States entered World War II was shaped by interwar policies of reduced expenditures, isolationism, and disarmament under a series of international treaties beginning in 1922. The Washington Naval Treaties, signed by all major naval powers, led to a halt of American battleship construction and a limitation in cruiser tonnage and gun size, and forced suspension of plans to fortify Pacific bases. Although the Japanese in 1936 declared their intent to build beyond established treaty limits, the United States did not renew naval construction on a large scale until 1938–39. As early as 1922, however, the navy was interested in the potential of naval aviation. The Washington Naval Treaties did not create any major limitations on the construction of carriers; indeed, those treaties, as several historians have observed, encouraged naval air power. Both the United States and Japan took advantage of this. Even though the Japanese had slightly more carriers than the United States when war broke out (ten versus seven), American carriers were larger on average, and carried more aircraft.

As described in Louis Morton's essay, War Plan ORANGE formed the basis for naval planning for a Pacific war with Japan. Both the Japanese and American naval *staffs anticipated a major surface fleet confrontation as the culmination of this war, but neither navy ignored the possibility that naval air power might play an important, and perhaps decisive, role. Fleet exercises during the 1920s and 1930s, in fact, made American naval officers acutely aware of the need to secure and keep control of the air over the fleet. They also recognized that air power was essentially an offensive weapon; aircraft acting in passive defense of the fleet were likely to be defeated, and the best role for aviation was to strike the enemy at a distance before his aircraft could strike the American fleet. However, in the absence of any real experience with carrier aviation in war, naval planners had to work with a series of theoretical models in the midst of ongoing technological changes to both aircraft and anti-aircraft armament.*

Technological change, and the way military institutions adapt to it, is the theme of several of the essays in this collection. Several deal with the bureaucratic imperatives involved in adjusting to new ideas and weapons, others deal with the difficulties of fitting new weapons into existing doctrinal or tactical frameworks, while a few also examine the psychological or sociological factors that help or hinder adaptation to new technologies. The following article by retired Navy Captain Wayne P. Hughes, excerpted from his book Fleet Tactics, *examines the way the American navy was forced to adjust its tactical practices in World War II as a result of technological change. Although he is primarily concerned with the way naval officers adjusted their tactical thinking, he also makes a critical point about the nature of technological innovation: technology rarely, if ever, changes in isolation. Surrounding the introduction of any new technology are a host of related changes that often alter the entire physical and emotional context in which the new technology will be used. Effective tactical thought must consider the totality of change, not just the single item of technology under consideration. Radar, for example, not only provided a means of identifying an enemy at long range, it fundamentally altered the way naval units would be positioned relative to each other at sea, and, in altered form, fundamentally altered the effectiveness of anti-aircraft gunnery. In doing so, it forced naval officers to totally, and continually, rethink their tactical practices.*

One way Captain Hughes illustrates his points is through mathematical models, a form of analysis basic to the carrying out of what is now called operations analysis. In the absence of real experience with new, untried weapons or tactics, operations analysis and modeling may be the only means we have of assessing how things might work. But as Captain Hughes indicates, mathematical models force analysts to make a series of assumptions about a host of variables, including weapon effectiveness, the effects of weather and fatigue, and the probable actions of the enemy. Each assumption the analyst makes, either to simplify the model or because data is simply unavailable, increases the chance the entire model will be utterly wrong. Of course, some form of what we call operations analysis has existed for centuries. By the late nineteenth century military planners routinely used models of one sort or another to predict battle outcomes under different conditions. Today, with a rapidly changing technological environment and most of our doctrines and weapons untested by actual use, we rely even more upon mathematical models and operations analysis as a guide to developing tactical and strategic doctrines. In this regard, it is instructive to reexamine the assumptions that underlay the tactical thought of both the Japanese and American navies at the beginning of World War II and see how many of those assumptions were in fact validated by events.

Habits of mind and action are difficult to change, and, as Captain Hughes argues, tactical doctrines are deliberately inculcated habits which should control the actions of soldiers, sailors, and airmen in combat. During World War II naval officers, indeed all commanders in all services, had to rethink their tactical doctrines and quickly learn new habits, overriding patterns that may have been years in the making. This was not an easy thing to do, and not all commanders succeeded. Readers might look back at John Mahon's essay on Civil War infantry tactics for a glimpse of a similar pattern of tactical adjustment. What similarities existed between the situations? What differences? One can also look at the essays by Edward Eckert on Civil War generalship and Edward M. Coffman on World War I commanders to see if there are any predictable indicators of how well or badly a commander will adapt to changing conditions. Effective command and effective tactics demand that technological change be accompanied by changes in habits of thought and doctrine. For military leaders the failure to respond appropriately to change will be costly indeed.

SURPRISE OR UPHEAVAL?

The phenomenal shift in tactics during World War II took nearly everyone by surprise. Even those who professed to have foreseen the tactical revolution—the air power zealots—foretold too much too soon. Pearl Harbor and the Battle of the Coral Sea were the culmination of events that had been building through the peacetime 1920s and 1930s. As we discuss the tactics of carrier warfare it is worth remembering that everyone was learning on the job. One only needs to read Bernard Brodie's 1942 edition of A Layman's Guide to Naval Strategy to appreciate the turmoil in many minds three years after fighting broke out.

The estimable Brodie need have had no cause for chagrin. An ex post facto reading of naval operations off the northern European coast and in the Mediterranean leads not to the conclusion that the ascendancy of air power should have been obvious but to an appreciation of how close the competition between gun and airplane really was. For instance, in 1940 two German battleships caught the British carrier HMS Glorious in the open sea and sank it. By 1944 U.S. Fleet antiair-warfare (AAW) defenses were so impregnable that Japan had to abandon bombing attacks and resort to kamikaze missions. Land-based horizontal-bomber attacks against warships—one of the B-17's original missions—were not effective. The torpedo bomber, while scoring successes, came to be a kind of unintentional kamikaze. In the end only the dive-bomber spelled the difference. As usual, vision played its part in the rise of naval air power, but it was the pragmatic tactician and technologist arm in arm who worked out the details.

The "battleship admirals" were not as important as they have been thought. For one thing, aerial bombing tests in the early 1920s against the old *Indiana, New Jersey,* and *Virginia,* and the new but uncompleted *Washington,* along with Billy Mitchell's rigged attacks on the *Ostfriesland,* proved not so much that heavy bombs could sink warships but that the aircraft of the day would have great difficulty sinking a moving, defended, buttoned-up warship. For another, the 1920s were a time when crucial decisions about development were being forcefully supported by the navy. Between 1922 and 1925 naval aviation's budget held steady at 14.5 million dollars while the navy budget as a whole shrank twenty-five percent. From 1923 to 1929 the naval air arm increased by 6,750 men, while navy manning overall decreased by 1,500—and this is excluding the crews of the manpower-intensive *Lexington* and *Saratoga.*

In an astonishing sleight of hand, carrier tonnage was allowed among the five major signatories of the Washington Disarmament Treaty of 1921—the United States, Great Britain, Japan, France, and Italy—at levels of 135, 135, 81, 60, and 60 thousand tons respectively, at a time when "no naval power . . . possessed a single ship that could be applied against the allowed carrier tonnage. All carriers in service or building were to be classified as experimental and therefore did not count. . . . Drastic as were its reductions in capital ships, the conference clearly determined that there would be no statutory interference with the development of aircraft carriers." From 1921 to 1935, the treaty years, there could be as much as but not more than about one-third as much carrier as battleship tonnage. Both Japan and the United States built every ton allowed for carriers. The disarmament treaty and those that followed were not a constraint on but an incentive for air power.

William Sims, Bradley Fiske, William Moffett, Ernest King, Joseph Reeves, and Thomas Hart were among the American surface officers who appreciated very early the importance of naval air and encouraged aviators like Henry Mustin, Kenneth Whiting, John Towers, and Marc Mitscher to hasten its development. The United States led the way, eyeing the broad Pacific, followed closely by Japan. Britain's naval air arm, backward in some ways, would prove to be the best in the Mediterranean. Still, no naval power could predict the dominance of naval aircraft. Technology which lay like a sleeping giant between the wars was prodded awake in 1939 by combat. Even then the issue was in doubt. Consider one of Charles Allen's perceptive illustrations of the connection between technology and tactics:

> In the delicate balance of interactions it is noteworthy that the
> greatest swing factor in the battleship versus carrier issue may have

been the actual performance of the newly introduced technology of radar. If it had proven more effective in directing heavy AA guns [or if, as others have said, the proximity fuze had come along a few years sooner], the effectiveness of tactical strike aircraft might have been largely neutralized. If it had been markedly less effective for early warning and fighter direction, carrier vulnerability might have been too great to bear. In either case, the fleet would have been dramatically different in 1945.

That aircraft would have *some* vital role was foreseen by all the powers. Aircraft were essential as scouts and, not to be overlooked, acted as spotters for gunfire in those days before radar. They were useful enough that the battle force deplored the possibility of losing its air cover. But if carriers were positioned too closely to the battle line, they would be exposed to attack. As early as 1930, commander, Aircraft Squadrons, Scouting Fleet, wrote, "Opposing carriers within a strategical area are like blindfolded men armed with daggers in a ring. There is apt to be sudden destruction to one or both." In developing their interwar plans, inferior navies—the Japanese when fighting the United States, and the United States when fighting the British—expected to use aircraft to soften up and slow the enemy battle line. Whether air power should be land or sea based was debated everywhere, but the need to command the air space over the fleet was acknowledged by all but the least perceptive, and fighter aircraft were seen as key players in this. By the 1930s U.S. and Japanese carrier aviators knew their own potency and used every infrequent opportunity to experiment. The Japanese navy already practiced leading with carrier strikes; and for insight into what U.S. naval officers thought was the paramount threat, one has only to consider the intensity with which naval intelligence tried—and failed—to track not Japanese battleships but Japanese carriers just before the raid on Pearl Harbor.

But how would battles be fought and what would the tactics be? These were questions hardly answered in 1941, even after two years of fighting in the North Sea, the Atlantic, and the Mediterranean.

This situation is in striking contrast with that prior to World War I. Then technological advances had been assimilated and fleet tactics set in place. At the onset of World War II technology was in ferment and tactics had not yet caught up with their potential. The visions of those who thought aircraft would sweep the oceans clean of surface warships were so patently premature that they helped fuel the passions of the conservatives, who clung doggedly to the supremacy of the line of battleships. In large measure the fleet tactics anticipated for World War II echoed those for the previous war, except that aircraft, the new mad dogs of their day, would fight each other overhead. This was the situation in all navies. Tacticians had to adapt in the midst of the war so extensively that by the end of it no major category of warship except minecraft was employed in the U.S. Navy tactically for the purpose for which it had been built. The striking and supporting roles of battleships and aircraft carriers were reversed; heavy cruisers, designed in part for fleet scouting, did nearly everything but that; light cruisers designed as destroyer leaders became AAW escorts for carriers; destroyers conceived for defending the van and rear of the battle line against torpedo attacks from other destroyers were adapted to function as ASW and AAW escorts; and submarines designed for forward reconnaissance and attacks on warships were diverted also to attack merchant ships and the sea lines of communication. By the end of World War II the upheaval of tactics, hastened by technology, was complete. Along the way tactical problems had to be solved.

In the fleet exercises of 1929 the *Saratoga* made a night run around the defending fleet and conducted a successful air strike against the Panama Canal. The attack is celebrated as the symbolic arrival of carrier aviation as a force to be reckoned with. But with it came double-edged ramifications. After launching the strike, the *Saratoga* was found and "sunk" not once but three times—by surface ships, a submarine, and aircraft from the *Lexington.* As it turned out, the center of concern in World War II was the vulnerability to naval aircraft of warships of every description, foremost among which was the carrier of the aircraft itself.

FIVE NEW TACTICAL PROBLEMS

Among the many tactical problems facing U.S. and Japanese naval commanders in the Pacific, five were prominent. Being interrelated, they were the more difficult to resolve.

1. *The tactical formation.* Thanks to prewar experimentation, the advantages of the circular formation for the defense of a carrier were understood by both U.S. and Japanese naval aviators. For the United States, the many-faceted radar made station-keeping easy. Offensively the formation could be maneuvered by simultaneous turns to maintain unity during flight operations under radio silence. Defensively a circle was best because it guarded against enemy aircraft seeing a gap in the screen of escorts and exploiting it. The question was whether each carrier should have its own screen to maximize its flexibility or whether two or three carriers should be surrounded by a single, stronger ring of escorts. Protection against submarines was also a consideration. A "bent line" screen would do better for that purpose, but it was generally incompatible with carrier operations; speed, then, was the carriers' best security against torpedoes from slow-moving submerged diesel submarines, along with a policy to avoid steaming through the same waters repeatedly.

The effectiveness of air offense and defense was the issue. The Japanese established separate carrier formations at the outset and changed only when forced to by a shortage of escorts. In the U.S. Navy the issue was less clearcut: the battle between senior aviators began to peak after the Battle of the Eastern Solomons, when one commanding officer added a new wrinkle by contending that the *Saratoga* had escaped attack and survived because of her ten- or fifteen-mile separation from the *Enterprise*, which was heavily damaged. Was it not better to lose one carrier and save the other than to lose two carriers to a concentrated attack? Which should take precedence, passive defense through physical separation with concomitant flexibility for air operations, or better AAW defense through compact defense?

2. *Dispersal or massing?* The range of attack aircraft opened up the possibility of concentrating offensively from two or more carrier formations that were physically separated by hundreds of miles. In practice, the need for radio silence hampered—perhaps spoiled—this possibility, and the United States never entertained it. American tacticians argued over separate formations but they kept the formations close enough that the fighter air defense—the combat air patrol (CAP)—could protect the entire carrier force. For the U.S. Navy, concentration and massing were synonymous.

The Japanese had a penchant for dividing their carriers, and they have been much criticized for it. E. B. Potter, for one, takes Vice Admiral Takeo Takagi to task for hoping with his approach in the Battle of the Coral Sea to "catch the American carriers in a sort of pincer movement." Later in 1942 Yamamoto's plan for the Eastern Solomons battle placed the light carrier *Ryujo* in front of the two big carriers as a decoy. She was sunk, and the Japanese have been condemned for dividing their forces. As explanation for complicated Japanese dispositions, U.S. critics have called Japan "sneaky" and pointed to her history of surprise attack. No doubt surprise attack—an effort to attack effectively first—was the basis of Japanese planning, but why divide carriers? At the Coral Sea the main striking fleet took advantage of a weather front and approached from a direction toward which land-based U.S. aircraft could not search and carrier aircraft were less likely to search. A pincer movement is an absurdity for someone as astute and familiar with carrier air power as Yamamoto. Should we not seek a better explanation for these strange Japanese dispositions? The answer is yes, and the explanation derives from Japanese faith in the dominance of successful air strikes.

3. *Offensive vs. defensive firepower.* Though the tactical commander must fight with the forces at his disposal, he has choices. He can emphasize fighter escort for his strikes, or he can emphasize his fighter CAP. He can add fighters for defense to his flight decks and carry fewer bombers and torpedo aircraft, or vice versa. He can use most of his scout bombers for scouting, or he can take calculated risks in scouting and husband them for a stronger attack. He can integrate his battleships in the carrier screen for AAW defense, as the U.S. Navy did in the Pacific, or he can keep his battleships separate for offensive

follow-up attack, as the Japanese did. These decisions hang much on the estimate of the power of the offense. Clark G. Reynolds, like many commentators, is impatient with Raymond Spruance for failing to use his carriers more offensively in 1944. Were not the enemy carriers Japan's threat and America's objective? Spruance was the best U.S. naval tactician in World War II. Then why didn't he act as the Japanese had, leaving a small force to cover the amphibious assault force and using his fast carriers to go after the Japanese carriers and hit them first?

4. *Daytime vs. nighttime tactics.* Carriers dominated the daylight hours but were sitting ducks for gunfire at night. Detaching before darkness, a battleship or heavy cruiser formation could travel two hundred nautical miles at night, a distance engraved in every tactical commander's mind. Since air strikes were mounted at ranges of around two hundred nautical miles, a carrier force could not be closed unless it pursued a crippled and presumably retreating enemy. Because of the damage to the U.S. battle line at Pearl Harbor, there would not need to be a command decision in 1942 about whether to send gunships against gunships halfway between two opposing carrier forces two hundred nautical miles apart. (Such a night action was a real possibility at the Battle of the Coral Sea, a remote possibility at the Battle of the Marianas. Of course, under rather different circumstances it occurred in the Battle for Leyte Gulf.) But the Japanese, who were the aggressors in 1942, three times sent their surface ships carrier hunting. The U.S. tactical problem in 1942 was whether to pursue after dark and risk an encounter with Japanese gunships or stand clear and let the enemy warships or invasion force steam safely away. In 1944 the problem was whether to employ the fast battleships as a unit for offensive action in the Japanese fashion or keep them with the carriers for defense. What was the basis for tactical decision?

5. *Dual objectives.* According to typical American prewar tactical planning, the U.S. battle fleet steaming west to relieve Guam and the Philippines would be met by the Japanese battle fleet and a great decisive action would occur. It is true that as logistical considerations intruded, the simple tactical paradigm was complicated by the need for bases and the fleet train. But guarding the train or an invasion force was not yet a thing that fleet tacticians worried much about.

The airplane changed that. Until there was a threat of invasion by the navy on the strategic offensive, a weaker battle fleet on the defensive could not be induced to fight. But an invasion force had the responsibility of protecting amphibious assault ships, and with aircraft in the offing this presented new and complicated problems. Aircraft had to cover the transports as well as attack the enemy. In all six of the Pacific carrier battles the attacker had a primary or secondary mission to attack and destroy the enemy fleet. In each instance an amphibious operation was involved. Obviously the attacker did not want to expose his transports. This dual objective was inescapable for the Japanese in 1942 and for the Americans in 1944. Tactical plans and decisions also had to deal with the new problem that strategic offensive brought: how to dispose forces while protecting transports. In the era of aircraft, tactical commanders had to solve the unprecedented problem of enemy attack from a long range.

A TACTICAL MODEL OF CARRIER WARFARE

The five major issues of Pacific carrier tactics can be illuminated in the context of a simple model, which will also promote understanding of the model of modern missile warfare to be discussed later. The model of carrier warfare compares with the Lanchester-Fiske model of gunnery in several ways. Fiske envisaged a mutual exchange of salvos that would erode the residual strengths of both sides simultaneously. His purpose was to show the cumulative effectiveness of superior firepower, the dominance of a small advantage if the advantage could be exploited with coherent maneuvers, and the disproportionately scanty damage the inferior force would inflict, no matter how well it was handled tactically. Gun range was a matter of indifference to Fiske because both sides faced the same range. He felt free to disregard for purposes of illustration the possibility that one side could outrange another and maintain an advantage that was in any way consequential. In effect, the pace of the battle would accelerate as the range closed, but the final ratio of losses would not change. His model took into account the "staying power"—warship survivability—that accorded with the assessments of his day: a modern battleship would be reduced to impotence in about twenty minutes by unopposed big guns within effective range.

The gunfire model of simultaneous erosive attrition does not work for the World War II carrier offensive force. That force is best represented as one large pulse of firepower unleashed upon the arrival of the air wing at the target. If, as was common, the second carrier force also located the first and launched its strike, simultaneous pulses of firepower would be delivered from both fleets. If the second carrier fleet did not find the first in time, it would have to accept the first blow. By then it would probably have located the first force and, if there were any attack capacity remaining, it would strike back.

To calculate damage from an air attack it is necessary to figure the defender's counterforce as the combination both of active defense (fighters and AAW strength) and passive defense (formation maneuverability and carrier survivability). In the Pacific, effective carrier-based air attack ranges were comparable, 200 to 250 nautical miles, and neither side could outrange the enemy's carrier aircraft. So in carrier battles, the crucial ingredients were *scouting effectiveness* and *net striking power*. Scouting effectiveness came from many sources: raw search capability, including organic and land-based air reconnaissance; submarine pickets; intelligence of every kind; all enemy efforts to evade detection; and, not to be overlooked, the planning skill of the commander and his staff. Net striking power was made up of raw numbers of attacking bombers and fighter escorts, reduced by the active and passive defenses and the relative quality of material and personnel on both sides.

For our purposes now, scouting effectiveness will be determined simply by asking who attacked first or whether the attacks were simultaneous. As for striking effectiveness—damage inflicted—the crucial question is the value of a carrier air wing's strike capacity. Of course there is much room to examine tradeoffs in practice between attack aircraft used for scouting or attacking and fighters used for escort or CAP. These were problems air staffs had to deal with. I need not introduce them in detail here.

For the moment I will assume (not unreasonably, as we will see) that in 1942 one air wing could on balance sink or inflict crippling damage on one carrier and that cumulative striking power was linear: two carriers were about twice as effective as one and so could sink or cripple two. A very rudimentary table of outcomes after the first strike can be constructed for three cases: (1) the equal or superior force A attacks first; (2) the inferior force B attacks first; or (3) A and B attack together.

TABLE 4.1   First Strike Survivors (A/B)*

	Initial Number of Carriers (A/B)				
	2/2	4/3	3/2	2/1	3/1
(1) A strikes first	2/0	4/0	3/0	2/0	3/0
(2) B strikes first	0/2	1/3	1/2	1/1	2/1
(3) A and B strike simultaneously	0/0	1/0	1/0	1/0	2/0

*It is immaterial here whether the nonsurvivors are sunk or out of action. But later we will take survivors to mean carriers with operational flight decks and viable air wings.

If we allow the survivors of the initially superior but surprised force A to counterattack, the final outcome is:

Initial force (A/B)	2/2	4/3	3/2	2/1	3/1
Survivors (A/B)	0/2	1/2	1/1	1/0	2/0

It may be inferred from reading the views of naval aviators at the time that they believed a carrier air wing would sink more than one enemy carrier on the average. It is pretty clear that U.S. aviators thought the thirty-six dive-bombers and eighteen torpedo bombers that comprised an air wing at the outset of the war would sink or put out of action (achieve a "firepower kill" on) several carriers with one cohesive strike. They estimated that the enemy could do the same. They were obsessed with the need to get at the enemy first, and we need not accept their optimism to see the enormous advantage of striking first.

The picture gets interesting when the results for B, the inferior force, are perused. If both sides attack together B cannot win, but compared with its performance in the Fiske model of continuous fire B does well—the enemy, while winning, can suffer severely. Even more instructive are the numbers when B successfully strikes first. Unlike B in Fiske's continuous-fire model, here B can be outnumbered 1:2 and establish the basis of future equality if he can attack and withdraw safely. He can be outnumbered 2:3 and establish the same after-action equality even if A is able to counterattack after absorbing the first blow. Evident as all this may be, to note it is crucial, since it is the basis for understanding much about the five interrelated tactical issues introduced above.

Before proceeding we should roughly calibrate attacker effectiveness by reviewing the four carrier battles of 1942 and then comparing them with the Battle of the Marianas, fought in June 1944.

For 1942 (not later) we will assume that:

— The carrier-air-wing effectiveness of every carrier on either side was equivalent.
— The defensive features of every carrier and its escorts on either side were equivalent.
— Japanese carriers physically separated should be counted. Deliberately or inadvertently they served as decoys and absorbed U.S. attention and air assets.

I indicate who attacked the enemy main force first. To compute theoretical results I show the results of all attacks, including diversionary actions, in the proper sequence. Although they do not enter into the calculations, initial and surviving carrier *aircraft* strengths are also shown.

The Coral Sea, May 1942   On 7 May the U.S. force (the *Lexington* and the *Yorktown*) sent a major strike against the little Japanese force covering the invasion force (the small carrier *Shoho*) and sank the carrier. On 8 May the U.S. force and the Japanese striking force (the *Shokaku* and the *Zuikaku*) struck simultaneously. The *Lexington* was sunk; the *Yorktown* suffered minor damage. The Japanese *Shokaku* suffered heavy damage; the *Zuikaku*, not found by U.S. aircraft, survived undamaged.

Theoretical Survivors

	After 7 May	After 8 May
A Japan	2	0
B United States	2	0

Battle Synopsis

	Initial forces		Actual survivors	
	CV	Aircraft	CV	Aircraft
A Japan	2½	146	1	66
B United States	2	143	1	77

Notes:

— The small Japanese carrier *Shoho* is counted as one-half.
— The *Yorktown*, though damaged, is counted as surviving. She fought at Midway.
— The *Shokaku* suffered heavy damage and is not counted as a survivor.
— This battle was marred tactically by very poor scouting on both sides.

Midway, June 1942   The U.S. force (the *Yorktown*, *Hornet*, and *Enterprise*) successfully surprised the Japanese striking force (the *Kaga*, *Akagi*, *Soryu*, and *Hiryu*) on 4 June. Most of the circumstances are well known, but many have not noted that the island of Midway served in effect as a highly significant decoy. After the successful U.S. surprise attack, the Japanese counterattacked, and then the surviving U.S. force reattacked.

Theoretical Survivors

	After U.S. attack	After Japanese counterattack	After U.S. reattack
A Japan	1	1	0
B United States	3	2	2

Battle Synopsis

	Initial forces		Actual survivors	
	CV	Aircraft	CV	Aircraft
A Japan	4	272	0	0
B United States	3	233	2	126

The Eastern Solomons, August 1942   On 24 August the U.S. force (the *Enterprise* and the *Saratoga*) attacked the small carrier *Ryujo* with its three escorts, which were exposed in front of the Japanese striking force. The *Ryujo* was sunk. The Americans having taken the bait, the Japanese striking force (the *Shokaku* and the *Zuikaku*) surprised the U.S. force. The Japanese striking force was never pinpointed by the United States for a counterattack.

Theoretical Survivors

	After U.S. attack	After Japanese attack
A Japan	2	2
B United States	2	0

Battle Synopsis

	Initial forces		Actual survivors	
	CV	Aircraft	CV	Aircraft
A Japan	2½	168	2	107
B United States	2	174	1	157

Notes:

— The *Ryujo* with her thirty-seven aircraft is counted as one-half.
— The *Enterprise* was heavily damaged and is not counted as a survivor.
— Though surprised and unable to find and counterattack the Japanese, the United States had fifty-three fighters in the air, warned by air-search radar.

— U.S. aircraft losses were light because the *Enterprise*'s aircraft were able to land at Henderson Field, Guadalcanal.
— The ascendancy of the attacker is starting to wane. Although the survival of the U.S. carriers under surprise attack can be explained by many details of battle training and leadership, a trend has emerged that reflects the increasing capabilities of U.S. defenses.

The Santa Cruz Islands, October 1942   On 26 October the U.S. force (the *Hornet* and the restored *Enterprise*) and the Japanese striking force (the *Shokaku, Zuikaku,* and small *Zuiho*) struck each other simultaneously. The small *Junyo* (fifty-five aircraft), although detached in a support unit covering reinforcements for Guadalcanal, was also able to attack the American carriers. The *Hornet* was sunk and the *Shokaku* and the *Zuiho* were heavily damaged.

Theoretical Survivors

	After 26 Oct
A Japan	1
B United States	0

Battle Synopsis

	Initial factors		Actual survivors	
	CV	Aircraft	CV	Aircraft
A Japan	3	212	1½	112
B United States	2	171	1	97

Notes:

— Two small Japanese carriers are counted as one-half each.
— The *Enterprise* suffered three bomb hits but was able to recover the *Hornet*'s and her own aircraft. She is counted as a survivor.
— The continuing terrible aircraft attrition—one hundred and seventy-four aircraft respectively for the Japanese and U.S. air wings—and the greater than theoretical survival rate for carriers

indicate strengthened defenses. This is the battle in which the
South Dakota is credited with twenty-six aircraft kills.

After the Battle of the Santa Cruz Islands both sides were reduced to a
single operational carrier. The air wings on both sides had suffered grievously.
In 1943 both sides husbanded their new and repaired carriers while the
Solomons campaign continued to rage. The Japanese, however, were too
quick in employing their naval aircraft from airfields in the Solomons and
Rabaul, and they suffered accordingly. Unavoidable as the Japanese commitment probably was, the loss of naval aviators established the basis for the air
disaster that overtook them in 1944.
   Meanwhile, the U.S. carrier navy sorted out its air tactics, added AAW
ships and AAW weapons, and built up its fast carrier task force to fifteen
carriers (more than double the number at the war's onset). The Japanese
succeeded only in building their carrier force back to nine (they had had ten
carriers in January 1942). Qualitatively the Japanese were even more out-
matched.

The Philippine Sea, June 1944   On 19 June Admiral Jisaburo Ozawa's fleet,
built around all nine of Japan's carriers, attacked the U.S. fleet of fifteen
carriers from four hundred nautical miles away. His plan was for Japanese
aircraft to attack from beyond the range of U.S. aircraft and then continue on
and land at Guam. Admiral Spruance could not simultaneously stay close to
Saipan, where he was supporting the amphibious assault, and reach the
Japanese. He chose to stay near the beach and concede the initiative of first
attack to the Japanese. Their air attack was crushed. That evening Spruance
allowed Marc Mitscher to attack at very long range—nearly three hundred
nautical miles—with 216 aircraft. Meanwhile U.S. submarines sank two
large carriers. The U.S. air attack, in part because of the long range, succeeded only in sinking the small *Hiyo* and heavily damaging the *Zuikaku*. In
this attack the United States suffered the only significant aircraft losses of the
battle; they were mostly operational, occurring on the long return flight at
night.

Theoretical Survivors

	After Japanese strikes	*After U.S. sub attack*	*After U.S. counterattacks*
A Japan	9	7	4
B United States	6	6	6

Battle Synopsis

	Initial forces		Actual survivors	
	CV	Aircraft	CV	Aircraft
A Japan	9	450	5	34
B United States	15	704	15	575

Notes:

— Mitscher's evening attack with 216 aircraft is the equivalent of three carrier deckloads. According to our rule of thumb, they should have sunk or incapacitated three carriers. In fact they knocked out two.

— Not all the carriers were large carriers. But putting the carriers in tables without distinguishing them does no violence to the comparisons and displays more familiar numbers.

— Of the 129 U.S. aircraft lost, Mitscher's late-evening counterattack accounts for 100.

— In addition to overwhelming Japanese carrier aircraft losses, there were a few losses among scout planes aboard Japanese battleships and cruisers, and many more losses among Japanese planes based at Guam.

The Battle of the Philippine Sea was no longer a battle of scouting and attack. The defense had overtaken the offense. Years later, in a rare public statement, Spruance said he would have preferred to move away from the beach and attack, but his mission was to defend the beachhead. Through either wisdom or inadvertence, his defensive tactics worked. Ozawa's plan hinged on combining sea- and land-based air. By waiting near Saipan for the Japanese fleet, Spruance was able to destroy the land-based air threat, achieving numerical superiority for the carrier battle. Ozawa's shuttle tactics were foredoomed, because U.S. fighters pounced on most of the Japanese aircraft at or en route to Guam. By staying nearby, Spruance continued to totally dominate the Mariana Islands' airfields. By waiting for the Japanese, the U.S. fleet could devote all fighters to CAP. And *two-thirds* of Spruance's aircraft, 470 of them in fifteen carriers, were fighters. The U.S. had more fighters than the Japanese had carrier aircraft.

The slaughter of Japanese aircraft was due to a combination of U.S. defensive strength and the inferiority of Japan's pilots. How much the result should be attributed to one factor or the other matters little. Either was sufficient to guarantee an American victory as long as the U.S. Fleet maintained effective tactical concentration, which had become so much a Spruance trademark that even Ozawa expected it.

Had the year been 1942, Spruance should have gone after the Japanese fleet. Then offense dominated defense, and the first strike could have been expected to be an effective one. Three-quarters of a U.S. air wing comprised attack aircraft. But in 1944 circumstances were different. The concentrated U.S. carrier battle fleet had great potential to defend itself effectively. To strengthen its defense, the proportion of fighters in the air wings had been increased from twenty-five to sixty-five percent. The Japanese carriers decks, however, were still heavy with attack aircraft: two-thirds were dive-bombers and torpedo bombers. We must surmise that until the Battle of the Marianas the Imperial Navy clung to the misplaced hope of surprise and a forlorn faith in the offensive. After that battle and until the end of the war Japanese carriers were impotent, used only as decoys at the Battle for Leyte Gulf.

Many more fighters escorted a strike in 1944. What had been a battle to sink carriers in 1942 had become a battle to destroy aircraft. From June 1944 on, battles were between Japanese land-based aircraft and American carrier aircraft.

There is not a thoroughgoing appreciation of this shift of emphasis among naval critics. Certainly on the written record even Spruance grasped the shift only instinctively and Halsey saw it not at all. And Nimitz, disappointed at the failure of Spruance to sink ships because his mission was to guard the beach, revised priorities at Leyte Gulf and made the destruction of the Japanese fleet Halsey's primary mission. For his part, Halsey was overly eager to be thrown into that briar patch. In the Battle for Leyte Gulf he ran north, after carriers that had been planted by the Japanese to draw him away from the main action around the Leyte beachhead.

RESOLUTION OF TACTICAL PROBLEMS

What insight do these rough and ready comparisons yield with regard to the five main tactical problems?

1. *The tactical formation.* The first problem was whether to give each carrier its own screen or to put two or more carriers inside a common screen of escorts. The Japanese used single-carrier formations at Coral Sea. But at Midway they were forced by a scarcity of escorts to double up (in 1942 Yamamoto still believed that carriers would protect battleships, not the converse). By 1944 the Japanese doubled up because too many cruisers and destroyers had been sunk. By 1944 the question was decided for the United

States by numbers of a different kind. For cohesive control, the fifteen and more fast carriers had to be combined in groups of three and four.

All of which begs the question. The wisest conclusion is probably that in 1942 single-carrier screens were best because defenses were poor, aircraft could be launched and landed more efficiently when carriers had their own screens, and attacking first was the object. Single carriers separated by even as few as ten or twenty miles might escape attack, as the carriers *Zuikaku* in the Coral Sea and *Saratoga* in the eastern Solomons did. (At the Coral Sea the *Lexington* and the *Yorktown* were formed by Frank Jack Fletcher to receive the Japanese air attack of 8 May inside a single screen of twelve cruisers and destroyers. They separated during thirty-knot evasive maneuvering into separately screened task groups.) But by 1944 something in offensive efficiency could be given up to exploit the withering defenses of the tight AAW circle. U.S. formations enclosed three or four carriers, and the entire disposition was kept close enough so that the whole fleet could be protected by a massed CAP. The decision to put two or more carriers in one formation depended on the effectiveness of the defense.

2. *Dispersal or massing?* The second tactical question was whether to divide the forces to the extent that mutual support was lost or significantly weakened. In 1942 the problem lay with the Japanese commanders, who were required to cover an invasion or reinforcement in all four of the big carrier battles. Their motives were mixed, for the Japanese also sought to draw out and defeat the U.S. Fleet. Admiral Nimitz, appreciating his inferiority, was not going to risk his fleet unless forced to do so. Each of the four battles had its own peculiar circumstances, but based on Yamamoto's otherwise incomprehensible manner of spreading his forces and, in at least one specific instance (the eastern Solomons), of baiting a trap, there seems to be only one conclusion: as a leading exponent of naval aviation Yamamoto must have believed, as American and Japanese naval aviators did, that a successful surprise attack by two big carrier air wings would destroy more than an equal number of the opposition. One carrier, it was thought, could sink two or three carriers clustered together, and therefore massing two or three units against one risked three units and gained nothing. If this was Yamamoto's rationale, then he was thrice confounded. Code breaking gave the United States too much strategic intelligence. Air search radar gave too much tactical early warning. And, from the evidence, it can be said that the destructive power of a carrier air wing was not sufficient to justify the anticipation of a two-for-one effectiveness potential.

We are left with two inferences: first, that concentration of *offensive* firepower sufficient to win at one blow is always desirable and can in principle be had with modern long-range aircraft or missiles without physically massing; and second, that the decision to mass rests on the potential to enhance defense or to coordinate a concentrated first attack. If massing fails on either count, dispersal may be better than massing. But before one jumps too readily to the conclusion that, since modern missiles now possess a many-for-one offensive punch, stealth and dispersal are appropriate, some thoughtful analysis of the scouting process is in order.

3. *Offensive vs. defensive firepower.* As for the third tactical problem, whether to optimize the formation for offense or defense, the solution in World War II may be inferred from the solutions to the first two problems. As the war progressed, the U.S. Navy strengthened carrier defenses. First, fighter numbers were increased at the expense of bomber numbers. Second, AAW batteries were steadily added, the *Atlanta*-class AAW cruisers entered service, and, starting with the Battle of the Eastern Solomons, fast battleships were integrated into carrier screens. Third, the damage control of warships was emphasized and improved. Thus defensive considerations came to dominate and the destruction of aircraft became, all too subtly, more significant than the destruction of carriers.

4. *Daytime vs. nighttime tactics.* The fourth tactical problem was the dominance of the gunship at night. As early as the Battle of the Coral Sea the Japanese tried a night air attack. But it was surface night action that they continually sought. In three of the four 1942 carrier battles, the Japanese detached gunships to find U.S. carriers. Owing to American prudence or luck, the Japanese never succeeded in forcing an engagement. Judging from the 1942 night battles in the Solomons, it is well that they failed. Later, when the U.S. Navy went over to the offensive, it set up an ingenious task organization that permitted fast battleships to be detached from their carrier screening role and to form a battle line for surface action. That guns still dominated after dark is clearly seen in the final, climactic action in the Battle for Leyte Gulf. That huge battle is best thought of as a final and desperate Japanese effort to bring gunships within range of their targets. The last and very effective line of American defense was surface warship guns.

5. *Dual objectives.* Fifth and last, there was the sticky tactical problem of split objectives for the attacker. In 1944, when the U.S. fleet swept across the Pacific from Pearl Harbor to the Philippines in just twelve months, it was so strong that it could accompany the landing force and dare the Japanese to come out. It had a 2:1 numerical advantage in carriers, decisive in itself, and an advantage greater still when the quality of pilots and screening ships is factored in. Moreover, it was no longer necessary to attack first. Mass and unity of action were the keys to effective application of force. Battle victory was not the issue. The issue was simply how to accomplish the objective with minimum losses and in minimum time.

In 1942 the Japanese tactical problem was not so simple. Strategic imperatives drove Yamamoto's tactics. Why were the Japanese caught at the Battle of the Coral Sea with a striking force of merely two carriers? It was because Yamamoto was in a hurry. His carriers were all busy. In just four months he had spread Japanese outposts like tentacles of an octopus out to the south, where his oil supply lay; to the southwest, so he could seize Singapore and safeguard the East Indies to the west; and to the southeast, so he could seize Rabaul and safeguard the Indies to the east. He had already secured his line of communications to the East Indies by taking the Philippines and Guam in December and January. He had eliminated Wake Island as a threat and he wanted Midway. Unlike the United States, he always envisioned supplementing sea-based air with land-based air.

Yamamoto proceeded unchecked until the Battle of the Coral Sea. Then he paid a price, though a modest one, for overconfidence. His alternative was to concentrate the Imperial Fleet's entire carrier striking power of ten carriers, which would have resulted in a glacial move southward that would have been inexorable but too slow. After all, the United States had seven big carriers flying as many aircraft as his, and soon they would be coming.

Still, while Yamamoto consolidated his network of air bases, he wanted—nay, needed—to entice the U.S. fleet into battle. In 1942 he could only do that with an invasion threat, the same way the United States planned to draw out the Japanese fleet in 1944. The Battle of the Coral Sea illustrates his priorities. The April operation was intended for the establishment of outposts at Tulagi and Port Moresby to screen Rabaul and threaten the U.S. link to Australia. Yet when the two U.S. carriers appeared and fought back, Yamamoto blasted Vice Admiral Shigeyoshi Inouye, who was in tactical command, not for pulling back the invasion force headed for Port Moresby but for pulling back from pursuing the surviving carrier. He ordered the *Zuikaku* to go plunging fruitlessly in pursuit of Fletcher in the *Yorktown.* At this stage of the war American naval leaders were no wiser than Yamamoto. The U.S. Navy had two carriers tied up in the Doolittle Raid against Tokyo, which is why the *Lexington* and the *Yorktown* were all that was available (the *Saratoga* had been crippled by torpedoes from a submarine).

Yamamoto split his carriers for the Midway operation because he was in a hurry and his motives were mixed. With two geographical objectives, Midway and Kiska/Attu, he had to cover two invasion forces. But the Kiska/Attu force was being used as a diversion, the Midway invasion force to draw out the U.S. Fleet. Yamamoto wanted the carrier striking force ahead of the invasion force. That was well and good, but he still thought of the battleships as final arbiters, there to mop up and too precious to expose until command of the air space was settled. He need not and should not have squandered effort in the Aleutian sideshow, which drew away two small carriers. It was right, however, not to wait for the repair of his damaged carriers. By all reasonable estimates there could have been at most two carriers plus Midway's aircraft facing him. If he had waited thirty days more, the *Yorktown*'s wounds would have been healed, the *Saratoga* would have joined up, and in another thirty days the *Wasp* would have arrived from the Atlantic.

History has been too eager to second-guess Yamamoto's decisions. He lost at Midway for all the following reasons:

— The U.S. Navy had strategic intelligence.
— Vice Admiral Chuichi Nagumo had no air search radar.
— Japanese scouting was mediocre. Nagumo launched a feeble air reconnaissance and the Japanese were beyond help from land-based air reconnaissance, a rare thing for them. And Yamamoto's subs arrived too late on picket stations.
— Spruance was skillful tactically.
— The American air wings were brave.
— The American air wings were lucky.

Take away any of these six conditions and it is more than likely the Japanese would have destroyed the American fleet and captured Midway. If good luck influences battle results, then results are not a perfect indicator of planning soundness. Historians must not evaluate the tactician's acumen solely on the outcome of the battle.

Still, the Battle of the Coral Sea was Yamamoto's clue that it was time to proceed more carefully—to make sure his operational plan was designed to achieve its objective. At the Battle of Midway the foremost objective was, or should have been, to draw the American fleet into a battle it would have to come out and fight. To split off two small carriers for the Aleutians operation was a mistake. The strategy to extend the Japanese defensive perimeter had stretched tactical capabilities too thin. It was time for tactics to counsel strategy, and tactics said that the Japanese navy had too many objectives.

Though we are not likely to see the Pacific war over island air bases reproduced, we can anticipate the recurring tactical problem a commander with superiority faces against an enemy who knows his inferiority and declines battle. When an attack on a land target is the way of drawing out an inferior enemy, it is too easy during planning to let the land attack become the end itself and to forget that the attack is but the means to a greater end, in this instance, of destroying the enemy's seagoing forces.

SUMMARY

In World War II aircraft became the chief naval weapon during daylight hours because of their effective range and their (not limitless) integral capacity for scouting, guidance to their target, and coordination. Not just any type of aircraft could do the job, and considering the combat loss rates, not just any pilots.

The polarized overestimates and underestimates of air strike effectiveness against warships that were made before the war led to unexpected tactical results during the war. Combat leaders, who by then had hard evidence that aircraft were effective against ships in daylight, had to learn the limits of the effectiveness—which we have deduced was never more than about one carrier sunk per air wing attack—and change their tactics accordingly.

Meanwhile the balance that favored air offense at the outset shifted back in favor of ship defense as the war progressed, and that also had to be appreciated for its tactical significance. It boiled down to a central tactical issue. If one carrier could sink two or three in an effective attack against any defense, there was no point in massing two or three carriers, which might be located together and sunk. If, however, it took two or more carriers (or repeated carrier strikes) to sink one, the *concentration* of enough striking force was essential (but it was only necessary to *mass* force if separate carrier task forces could not be coordinated by means of C^2). As the war progressed, a third case came to dominate in which the defensive firepower of two or more carriers operating in proximity could be massed to great effect. Concentration of force for offensive action became an automatic side benefit and the problem of coordinating separated forces disappeared. It was defensive considerations that drove the decision to mass and eliminated the need for stealth, deception, and divided forces.

The Japanese had to attack effectively first. A simultaneous exchange of attacks with similar losses to both sides would ruin them in the long run because they could not afford to exchange carriers one for one. They had to attempt stealth, deception, and (probably) divided forces as a calculated risk. They gambled, likely even believed, that one carrier could sink two. Even though wrong, this was a good gamble at the beginning of 1942. As early as late 1942 it was a very bad gamble.

We have discussed many reasons for the resurgence of defense. AAW guns alone could have been enough to cause it, but the final and decisive factors responsible for the success of American defense were things the Japanese could not possibly fold into their early planning, namely, radar and cryptanalysis. Except in the Battle of Britain, nowhere was radar more quickly put to decisive use than in the Pacific carrier battles. Cryptanalysis for its part almost eliminated the chance of the Japanese achieving surprise. Stealth and deception were foredoomed. Under the circumstances the Japanese might as well have massed and taken their chances, especially in 1942 when they had numerical superiority and qualitative equality. By 1944 nothing they could do mattered. The Japanese would have less and less to show for their efforts, whether they were expended against a conservative enemy like Spruance off the Marianas or a rash enemy like Halsey at Leyte Gulf. U.S. defensive strength ensured that the American fleet would survive long enough to counterattack, and U.S. offensive advantage ensured that the Japanese would perish.

R O N A L D   L E W I N

MASSACRE OF THE MARUS

Certainly one of the most forgotten dimensions of strategy is military intelligence. The capacity to know with a reasonable degree of certitude what the enemy is doing and to keep the enemy from knowing what friendly forces are doing can provide an enormous advantage to one side in a conflict. Nowhere has this been better illustrated than in the ability of the Allies to decipher German and Japanese diplomatic and operational messages during the Second World War. Many instances can illustrate this theme, but none greater than the importance of intercepting Japanese naval messages that led to the U.S. submarine massacre of the Japanese merchant marine—the Marus.

Early in the war the Poles assisted the British in breaking thousands of encrypted German signals, which led to invaluable intelligence information known as the Ultra secret. This contributed significantly to a number of Allied victories, particularly in North Africa and in the antisubmarine campaign in the North Atlantic. The American decipherment of Japanese codes began in the 1920s and remained one of the best kept and most important secrets of the Pacific War.

It all began when, under the leadership of Captain Andrew Long, the Office of Naval Intelligence's counterespionage agents broke into a Japanese office in New York City and secured a photograph of the Imperial Navy's fleet code. From this the navy began in the 1920s to develop a system to intercept and decode Japanese signal traffic. This capacity to break naval and military codes might be called Ultra-J, that is, decrypted intelligence data derived from Japanese sources, as contrasted with Ultra-G, which came from German sources. In addition to this intelligence, there was what was

413

known as Magic intelligence, that is, information derived from breaking Japanese diplomatic signals. Some of the most important of this information involved message traffic from the Japanese ambassador in Berlin to Tokyo, which provided detailed data on current German policy matters.

Ultra-J intercepts were a key factor in providing Admiral Chester Nimitz information necessary for him to take the calculated risk of moving all available carrier battle groups to the defense of Midway in June 1942. The result was the greatest naval victory in American history and a decisive turning point in the Pacific War. Central to this success were the activities of Commander Joseph Rochefort's Fleet Radio Unit, Pacific, in Hawaii, known mostly by its acronym—FRUPac. One observer of these cryptanalysts later commented: "Had I not witnessed it, I never would have believed that any group of men was capable of such sustained mental effort under such constant pressure for such a length of time." Commander Rochefort's intelligence estimates were of such a quality that he soon became Admiral Nimitz's confidant. Also critical was the Code and Signal Section in Washington known as Op-20-G, headed by Commander L. F. Safford. The navy signal intelligence unit at Belconnen in Australia, commanded by Commander Rudolph J. Fabian, was another critical source of information.

But intelligence alone was not enough to assure victory, and sometimes the data failed to yield the correct conclusion. Nowhere is this more evident than in the events surrounding the opening of World War II for the Americans. All intelligence suggested a Japanese attack, but the preponderance leaned so strongly toward the Philippines and the Netherlands East Indies (which received the brunt of the Japanese attack) that the limited evidence pointing toward Hawaii was discounted. The Americans knew an attack was coming, but their surprise was where it first hit—Pearl Harbor.

But nowhere was the naval intelligence more effective than in the operations against the Japanese merchant marine. The late British military historian Ronald Lewin, author of Ultra Goes to War and The American Magic, was one of the foremost students of World War II military intelligence activities. He exhibited an exceptional comprehension of the difficulties encountered in decrypting the German and Japanese codes as well as of the human interrelationships that affect all policy decisions. Lewin had no desire to engage in polemics. He constantly searched for truth in a subject often covered with veils of secrecy and cloaks of innuendo.

Following on the exertions of the cryptanalysts was the daring of the submarine crews who acted on the conclusions reached from the decipherment of the Japanese codes. Ultra could not fight the enemy, only the submariners could. Because some of them knew the source of the information that placed them in the right place at the right time, their capture constituted a potentially critical loss to the American cause. No one paid a greater price than Captain John P. Cromwell of the submarine Sculpin, which in November 1942 was forced to the surface by depth charges and sunk by gunfire. Because he feared revealing his knowledge of the link between message intercepts and submarine operations, Captain Cromwell refused to abandon ship along with the 42 members of his crew. For his self-sacrifice, Captain Cromwell received the Medal of Honor because he "chose to die to protect the Ultra secret." It is to such brave men as this that Lewin pays tribute with his list of submarine vessels and their victories at the end of this selection.

The success of the submariners was extraordinary. Once all the defects of the Mark-14 torpedo had been corrected by September 1943, the silent service became a most deadly weapon. Utilizing a hundred subs from Hawaii and another forty from Australia, this force, which comprised less than two percent of naval personnel, accounted for 55 percent of Japanese losses at sea. They sank 1,300 Japanese vessels including a battleship, eight aircraft carriers, and eleven cruisers. The cost of such success was high—over 22 percent of the crews never returned, the highest casualty rate for any service in World War II.

The steady development of the torpedo together with the gradual improvement in the size, motive power and speed of submarine craft of the near future will result in a most dangerous offensive weapon.
   Lieutenant Chester Nimitz, U.S. Naval Institute
   Proceedings, 1912

There were nights when nearly every American submarine on patrol in the central Pacific was working on the basis of information derived from cryptanalysis.
   Captain W. J. Holmes, Double-Edged Secrets

The first Japanese ship was sunk by an American submarine a week or so after Pearl Harbor: the last, a coast-defense vessel, was sunk in the Sea of Japan on August 14, 1945, the day before the end of hostilities. During operations which thus spanned the whole of the Pacific war many of the enemy's fighting ships were destroyed by submarines, sometimes dramatically and often with important results. And yet, paradoxically, it is their obliteration of Japan's merchant navy which had the most decisive consequences. Through the sinking of the marus— as the merchant and transport ships were called—Japan gradually bled to death. The process started with occasional attacks on individual targets. It ended in a massacre.

Admiral Chester Nimitz, the Neptune of the Pacific, was an old sub-mariner by trade and therefore supremely equipped to supervise this aspect of the many-sided war game played out in his theater. Long before 1914 he had been an instructor in the First Submarine Flotilla and commanded pioneer craft with evocative names like *Plunger, Snapper* and *Narwhal*. During the First World War he served as Chief of Staff to the Commander of the U.S. Atlantic Submarine Fleet. So the man who, after Pearl Harbor, became Commander in Chief, Pacific Fleet and Pacific Ocean Area, was the appropriate Supremo for an onslaught which signally succeeded where the German U-boats failed—in an absolute elimination of the enemy's merchant shipping. Like the Germans, the Americans owed their astonishing (and largely unrecognized) success to the accurate guidance of their signal intelligence, but whereas the German Navy's cryptanalysts lost their grip on the Allied convoy codes in the middle of 1943 and never recovered their dominance, the men at FRUPac, Belconnen and OP-20-G continued to supply the American submarine fleet with critically accurate information right up to the end. So the young lieutenant's prophecy of 1912 was justified, for Admiral Nimitz increasingly wielded "a most dangerous offensive weapon."

But not at first. By the end of 1942, it is true, Japan had lost about one million tons of merchant shipping from all causes, American submarines having accounted for 142 *marus*. (By 1945 ten times that number would be sunk.) It is true, also, that though the Japanese command had anticipated a loss of about 800,000 tons in the first year of the war, actual sinkings were already more than could be endured. Indeed, the decision to evacuate Guadalcanal early in 1943 flowed directly from high-level and impassioned conferences in Tokyo at which the bitter fact had to be swallowed that the 300,000 extra tons of shipping required to service further aggressive action in the Solomons did not exist. Nevertheless, these truths should not be allowed to conceal the reality. For many reasons, as will be seen, American submarines were not yet achieving their full potential.

It is often forgotten, however, that of all the main belligerents America had the shortest war. The British and the Germans fought from start to finish. The Japanese had been in a state of war since the thirties, and their swift succession of victories from December 1941 onward owed much to their previous battle experience, their training and their readiness for action. Before Pearl Harbor even the Russians had soldiered their way through half a year of disasters. In their role of Johnny-come-lately the Americans had to move fast—and, indeed, their achievement in the Pacific as in Europe was due to an astonishing speed of adaptation, of developing new techniques, organizing mass production, creating vast forces and, above all, learning. For Chester Nimitz the question was, how soon would new skills and new technologies enable his submarine fleet to respond, as lethally as the Germans in the Atlantic, to the test and challenge of the Pacific war?

The first need was for improved intelligence. For most of 1942, as has been seen, the important JN25 code was largely unreadable and, in any case, the signals in this high-level system tended to refer to the movements of warships: breaking of the special "*maru* code" used by the Japanese for routing freighters, tankers, etc., only occurred later in the war. Moreover, the submarine service was not, as yet, considered secure as a recipient of Ultra intelligence. Jasper Holmes, who took over from Layton as the clandestine link between the Combat Intelligence Unit on Hawaii and the Pacific Submarine Command, has described how he would convey information at this time: "I went directly to the chief of staff of ComSubPac and delivered it orally. I did not tell him how the information was obtained, but he must have guessed. We kept no records. If I had a position in latitude and longitude, I wrote the figures in ink on the palm of my hand, and scrubbed my hands after I had delivered the message." War, however, is a serious business, not likely to be won by compelling grown men to behave like schoolboys. Until an adult system was evolved for servicing the submarines with Ultra, their potential would inevitably be limited.

And, unfortunately, "moral fiber" and professional competence do not seem to have characterized every submarine commander in those early months. There are too many well-documented instances of a captain cracking under the tensions of a war patrol in distant enemy waters. At Midway, moreover, as Clay Blair puts it in his admirable *Silent Victory*, "the role played by U.S. submarines was one of confusion and error"; after the battle, heads rolled and, rightly or wrongly, several submarine commanders were rapidly transferred to staff appointments or otherwise removed from the scene of action. During the opening phase of both world wars most of the armed services, both American and British, had to hack out the dead wood: in this the U.S. submarine force was not exceptional.

Indeed, the situation is reminiscent of an earlier war. By an odd coincidence, it was in 1942 that Douglas Southall Freeman published his magisterial *Lee's Lieutenants: A Study in Command*. In his foreword Freeman wrote: "If the recountal of the change of officers in the first fifteen months of the war in Virginia seems discouraging, the events that followed the reorganization of July, 1862, are assurance that where the supreme command is capable, fair-minded and diligent, the search for competent executive officers is not in vain. The Lee and the 'Stonewall' Jackson of this war will emerge." *Mutatis mutandis*, this was now the challenge for the U.S. submarine service.

Yet it is difficult to be precise about the relative failure of the submariners during the operations of 1942, and surely it would be unjust to lay the whole burden on those young men who commanded the craft at sea. For not only were they inadequately supplied with intelligence about the enemy, and compelled to conduct their patrols according to peacetime tactical doctrines which war soon showed to be incorrect: they had not even got the right weapon with which to hit a hostile ship when one was observed through the periscope and all the complicated calculations for obtaining a strike appeared to have been carried out immaculately.

It is an extraordinary fact that the three great nations of the West who took so much pride in their technology, Germany, Great Britain and the United States, should all have entered the Second World War with stocks of torpedoes which functioned imperfectly, whereas the Japanese, long thought to be mere imitators of the "developed" West, possessed from the start a type of torpedo which was pre-eminent in range, in speed and in reliability. The technical deficiencies of the British and German weapons demand a complex explanation; here it is sufficient to say that the reasons for malfunction were identified and overcome with tolerable speed. In the Americans' case, however, what was blindingly obvious was allowed to persist for far too long. The background to this tragic delay is ugly and inexcusable.

The standard U.S. torpedo, the Mark 14, had two major defects. They were indicated in a letter to a senior officer on Admiral King's staff, written by Admiral Lockwood after he had arrived in Australia to take command of the submarines working out of Fremantle and sought to discover why the craft operating in Asiatic waters had met with so little success.

> The boys here have had a tough row to hoe in the last four months. Why they didn't get more enemy ships is a highly controversial point but my reading of all war diaries thus far submitted has convinced me that among the causes are: (a) bad choice of stations in that most likely invasion points were not covered soon enough nor heavily enough, (b) *bad torpedo performance, in that they evidently ran much too deep and had numerous prematures . . .* , (c) buck fever—firing with ship swinging when he thought it was on a steady course; set up for one target and firing at a totally different one, (d) lack of or misunderstanding of aggressiveness; many evaded destroyers in the belief that they should save torpedoes for convoy following; one said he thought a sub should never "pick a fight with a destroyer."

But another, Coe of *Skipjack,* laid it on the line when he observed in his patrol report that "to make a round trip of 8,500 miles into enemy waters, to gain attack position undetected within 800 yards of enemy ships only to find that the torpedoes run deep and over half the time will fail to explode, seems to me to be an undesirable manner of gaining information which might be gained any morning within a few miles of a torpedo station in the presence of comparatively few hazards."

The trouble was that it took too long for that morning to dawn. The torpedoes were the product and responsibility of the Bureau of Ordnance, and in spite of accumulating evidence to the contrary the Bureau of Ordnance continued to maintain that they were just fine. Yet the prescribed setting made the torpedoes run too deep, and the magnetic exploder at the torpedo's tip could not be relied on to detonate the warhead at the right, critical moment. Bitter experience made these defects familiar in the submarine fleet, but captains who set their torpedoes to run closer to the surface—and then fiddled their afteraction reports—tended to receive short shrift if their "insubordination" was discovered. In many an attack, moreover, skippers who followed the rule book thought that they had sunk their prey only to learn on return to harbor—often as a result of Ultra intercepts—that the ship had got away unharmed. One way and another, the early operations of the U.S. Navy's submarines were bedeviled. It was a situation that could not, and of course did not, last.

It is self-evident, from the submarines' ultimate and decisive success, that competent commanders emerged in abundance; that effective tactics were evolved; and that in spite of bureaucratic obscurantism (and some pigheaded professionals) torpedoes were at last produced capable of ensuring a kill if the captain did his job and the submarine was in the right place to attack a target. But the remarkable achievement of signal intelligence in guiding craft to that right place, over and over again, is less immediately obvious although, without that guidance, the record would be very different.

It was early in 1943 that the necessary and fundamental change occurred in the application of Ultra to submarine warfare in the Pacific: a change which altered the tentative and almost amateur practices of 1942 into a system which, as it matured, can be fairly compared with the control of the Atlantic U-boats by the German U-boat Command (based on the cryptanalytical achievements of the B-Dienst), or with the deadly use of Ultra by the British in, for example, the interdiction of Axis transport shipping in the Mediterranean. Several convergent reasons account for this critical development.

Although the American submarine force had not yet reached its full potential, Japanese losses were already such that a decision had to be taken running counter to Japanese naval doctrine—which had always tended to despise the notion of convoys and the necessary diversion, for their protection, of warships whose "honorable" function was always visualized as aggressive. But a convoy system was now reluctantly introduced: and to organize convoys meant a network of radio signals assigning routes, issuing instructions to the escort and the port of destination—not to speak of any ports of call *en voyage*—arranging for air cover and so on. However, the code used for this purpose—the *maru* code—was also broken in early 1943: apparently, according to Captain Holmes, by FRUPac. The submarine war thus entered a new dimension.

One of the reasons for caution in applying Ultra operationally to the submarines in 1942 had been the fact that the intelligence coming to hand (chiefly about Japanese warships) had been acquired from the main Japanese naval code, and there was a great and natural hesitancy about compromising a source of such wide and profound importance. But less reserve was reasonably felt about intelligence from the *maru* code: a compromise here, after all, would have been extremely inconvenient but not disastrous. As a result, the primitive arrangements which had existed in 1942 for applying Sigint operationally were put on a rational basis—the foundation for an ever-expanding system whose sophistication and efficiency moved steadily forward until 1945.

The intimate relationship now established between JICPOA's Combat Intelligence Unit and the Operations Officer of ComSubPac have been vividly described in *Double-Edged Secrets*. So close a connection was obviously not possible for the commander of the SWPA submarine force working from its bases in Australia. Still, it is evident, from the activities of the Australian craft, that the dissemination of Ultra intelligence bore fruit—even though the confidential report on the submarine service produced in December 1945 must have been overcalling its hand when it declared that "during the war submarine operational authorities were in constant communication by a direct telephone line with the United States Naval Communication Intelligence Organization"! But time and again we find the Australian-based submarines, even though they were on patrol at an immense distance from the Antipodes, striking with lethal assurance against targets whose precise location had been conveyed to them by radioed instructions derived from Ultra intelligence. Steadily and irreversibly, the net closed round the *marus*.

The terrible significance for Japan of the cumulative but remorseless erosion of her merchant navy can be illustrated by a single, striking statistic. From Midway onward, in the great fleet actions of the Solomons campaign and elsewhere, her fighting fleet had suffered shattering losses while the material strength of the U.S.A.—as Admiral Yamamoto had long ago predicted—was turning out new warships as if from the General Motors production line. And yet by 1944, of all the steel allocated in Japan for shipbuilding only one-sixth of the total was being diverted to reinforcements for the fleet: all the rest was absorbed in the effort to keep a merchant navy—above all, a tanker service—in being.

As one reads the Ultra information about Japanese convoys—whether in particular signals or, as it so often appears, in the Magic Summaries—there is one recurrent and salient feature. With a regularity which might seem common-place unless one remained alert to its priceless significance, the intelligence concerning a convoy presents not simply the number of ships, and often their names and individual cargoes, and the character of the escort, but also the route it is to take and *the noon position for some or all the days of its voyage*. Neither the German B-Dienst, in its accurate reporting of the Allied Atlantic convoys, nor the British service of Ultra, in its coverage of enemy shipping, supplied such precise and regular intelligence—certainly not on the scale that the breaking of the *maru* code made available in the Pacific.

Moreover, the area of that ocean, compared with the little inland sea of the Mediterranean or even the wide swathe of the Atlantic routinely used by convoys, is gargantuan, and the variety of islands and channels offers endless scope for alternative routing. To ensure a high rate of effective strikes against the Japanese convoys without the sure guidance of signal intelligence would there-fore have involved an astronomical number of submarines to supply constant standing patrols. Even air reconnaissance, on the most lavish scale, could not have brought much alleviation. Ultra, and particularly its provision of "noon positions," offered immense economies. Instead of having to keep huge numbers of submarines at sea to patrol all possible routes (even if they had been available) the staffs in Hawaii and Australia, knowing a convoy's route and noon positions, had merely to direct one or more craft to a specific point—and there was the target. If life was not always like this—since the imponderables of sea warfare are manifold—the pattern recurred in so many operations that it may be considered to be roughly characteristic.*

As Clay Blair found when writing *Silent Victory*, the captains' war diaries and patrol reports, which provided him with a rich variety of action stories and human drama, rarely—and then only incidentally—reflect the inner truth of many a successful engagement. And the reason is simple: to maintain security, any reference to Ultra in such reports was rigorously forbidden. Admiral King stamped on the practice before it took root, as this COMINCH circular of May 18, 1943, indicates. SUPER SECRET X ULTRA X WAR DIARIES OF SUBMARINES BASING WEST AUSTRALIA FOR MONTHS NOVEMBER DECEMBER JANUARY CON-TAIN NUMEROUS REFERENCES COMMUNICATION INTELLIGENCE X ALL MEN-TION THIS SOURCE MUST BE ELIMINATED FROM ORIGINAL AND ALL COPIES OF PAST AND FUTURE DIARIES. On July 13 ComSubPac in Hawaii reiterated the warning to the captains under his command. NEITHER ACTUALLY NOR BY IMPLI-CATION SHOULD REFERENCE BE MADE TO ULTRA MESSAGES SENT BY THIS COMMAND X SAME RULE APPLIES FOR WRITING UP PATROL REPORTS.

By a curious paradox, indeed, Ultra—as has already been pointed out—served on occasion as a corrective to the sincere but overoptimistic claims made by submarine commanders on their return from patrol. There is, as it happens, a

---

* By the end of 1943, when 435 *marus* had already been sunk, there were only 73 submarines operating in the Central Pacific and less than 30 from Australia. The arithmetic is self-explanatory.

classic example for which all the evidence is available, and though the target in question was a warship rather than a *maru*, the case illustrates so many aspects of the Ultra story—and is inherently so dramatic—that it is worth describing in full detail.

Early in June 1943 the submarines *Trigger* and *Salmon* were on patrol within the Japanese Inland Sea, where, by good luck, the enemy carrier force was engaged in training exercises. At 0815 on June 9 an urgent OP OP OP, or highest priority signal, went out from ComSubPac.

> ANOTHER HOT ULTRA COMSUBPAC SERIAL 27 X LARGEST AND
> NEWEST NIP CARRIER WITH TWO DESTROYERS DEPARTS
> YOKOSUKA AT 5 HOURS GCT 10 JUNE AND CRUISES AT 22 KNOTS
> ON COURSE 155 DEGREES UNTIL REACHING 33-55 NORTH 140 EAST
> WHERE THEY REDUCE SPEED TO 18 KNOTS AND CHANGE COURSE
> TO 230 DEGREES X SALMON AND TRIGGER INTERCEPT IF POSSIBLE
> AND WATCH OUT FOR EACH OTHER X WE HAVE ADDITIONAL
> DOPE ON THIS CARRIER FOR THE BOYS NEAR TRUK WHICH WE
> HOPE WE WON'T NEED SO LET US KNOW IF YOU GET HIM X . . .

And so it was that on the night of the 10th the aircraft carrier *Hiyo*, with a flank guard of a destroyer on each bow, came zigzagging down Tokyo Bay at 20 knots or so, the crisscrossing enabling Roy Benson in *Trigger* to work in to a range of 1,200 yards. He then fired a spread of six torpedoes—and dived deep and fast as a destroyer moved in for the kill.

We have his log. "Sighted what was reported as smoke on horizon. On the next observation it showed itself as the island of a huge aircraft carrier. She was totally unlike any other Japanese aircraft carrier seen: looked most like the U.S.S. *Saratoga* . . . 1955. Fired 6 bow torpedoes . . . went deep and stood by heading for the carrier. The target's screws had slowed and then stopped. 2013. Crackling and popping sound in the direction of the recent target. These were clearly audible through the hull." *Trigger* returned to Pearl Harbor on June 22 "elated in the conviction that she was the first submarine to sink a Japanese aircraft carrier."

But during her evasive actions she must have missed a signal from Com-SubPac to *Salmon* and *Trigger* transmitted almost immediately after the operation. It read:

> COMSUBPAC SENDS ULTRA TO SALMON OR TRIGGER X
> CONGRATULATIONS TO WHICHEVER OF YOU DID THE BEAUTIFUL
> JOB X BOTH NOTE THAT ABOUT HALF THE NIP NAVY IS NOW
> ENGAGED IN TRYING TO TOW THE BIG FLAT TOP BACK TO

YOKOSUKA FROM APPROXIMATE VICINITY 34-14 NORTH 139-52
EAST X IF EITHER OF YOU ARE IN POSITION TO DO SO THERE
MIGHT STILL BE TIME TO FINISH HER OFF X SHE IS UNABLE
NAVIGATE BY HERSELF.

What in fact happened was an old, old story. Four of *Trigger's* torpedoes had exploded prematurely. But one had indeed struck home, in *Hiyo's* boiler room. She was towed back to Yokosuka and reached dry dock with her decks awash: a temporary respite, since she would be sunk in June 1944 during the Battle of the Philippine Sea. But the significant fact is that all the Japanese signals relating to her recovery were being read in Hawaii—including a sad instruction: "For the time being, mail addressed to this ship will be sent to Yokosuka Post Office."

There was a sense in which the quality and accuracy of Ultra intelligence were sometimes more noteworthy than the ability of the submarine command to apply it in action. But things were on the mend. In *Undersea Victory* Captain Holmes summarized the general situation on New Year's Day, 1944, and noted that: "All U.S. submarines had dependable radar. An answer to their torpedo exploder difficulties had at last been found. A new explosive greatly increased the destructive effect of torpedo warheads. The electric torpedo was in service." Moreover, although Japan had started the war with 6,000,000 tons of transport shipping, a figure which even then was dangerously low considering the vast spread of her commitments, by the beginning of 1944 that figure had been reduced by no less than a million tons in spite of all the output of Japanese shipyards. The balance sheet was certainly not unfavorable: particularly since, during the two years after Pearl Harbor, the United States had only lost 25 submarines as against 47 Japanese.

By the spring of 1944, indeed, a tone of despair is beginning to enter the enemy's signals. The Japanese Army Supplement to the Magic Far Eastern Summary for March 6, for example, reproduces an Army signal from Manila to Tokyo of March 1 which could hardly have been transmitted a few months earlier. "While returning to Japan," it stated, "a convoy of six tankers was attacked by enemy submarines on February 20 in the waters NW of the Philippines and five tankers were sunk. . . . *The present situation is such that the majority of tankers returning to Japan are being lost.*" And, significantly, an intercept of May 9 from Shipping Headquarters in Tokyo to Manila ascribed these losses to the difficulty of preventing espionage in Manila harbor!

Perhaps the most striking example of how the submarine force, guided by Ultra, was now capable of dealing clinically with a convoy of Japanese transports, and thus not only reducing the enemy's *maru* fleet but also having a direct effect on the land battle, is the case of the "Take" convoy (known to the

Americans as Bamboo No. 1). Its function was to ferry from Shanghai to New Guinea the 32nd and 35th divisions as reinforcements to stem MacArthur's advance. On April 17 an escorted group of nine vessels (under the command of an admiral) started on its long voyage by way of Manila. In view of what was to happen, there was a certain irony in the fact that at the time of the Coral Sea action Admiral Kajioka, the convoy commander, was to have led the invasion force into Port Moresby.

For Bamboo No. 1 was doomed. In the habitual way, Ultra had identified its route and noon positions. Moreover, the wretched Kajioka had been furnished with an ancient coal-burning minelayer, the *Shirataka,* as his flagship, so that when the submarine *Jack* met the convoy north of Luzon its presence was announced by clouds of filthy smoke. Down went the freighter *Yoshida Maru,* taking with her a complete infantry regiment.

After a call at Manila the convoy moved on, only to be caught again in the Celebes Sea by the submarine *Gurnard.* At least three more ships were sunk and others damaged—the Magic Far Eastern Summary for August 1 recorded the precise details from Ultra intercepts. After desperate rescue operations had scraped the survivors together, Tokyo refused to risk any further convoying, and the broken remnants of two infantry divisions were ignominiously ferried to New Guinea by devious routes in landing barges. Here was a supreme example of how immaculate Sigint immaculately applied in action could produce a decisive result.

No wonder: for the accuracy of intelligence was now extraordinary. In the Magic Far Eastern Summary for August 18, 1944, details are given of a captured document known as "the X List." Issued by the Japanese Navy as "A List of Ship Names for Communication Security at Sea," it contained the radio call signs for all vessels listed as well as the name, speed and tonnage. It was a basic list of shipping registered up to July 1, 1943, updated by ten supplements to February 25, 1944. The impressive fact is this: of the 1,720 *marus* of 1,000 gross tons or over which had been identified by American intelligence (over half from Ultra) only 13 did not fit with "the X List."

It was this quality of precise Sigint which made possible a further and increasingly lethal development in American tactics—the use of the "wolf pack" technique. Only a brief reminder of the great wilderness of the Pacific is necessary to make it clear that without very specific locations of targets it would have been impossible to muster killer groups of submarines concentrated at the right place and at the right time. But Ultra made this feasible. As more submarines and trained crews became available, therefore, the Americans essayed—at first tentatively—a technique which the German U-boats had applied so murderously in the Atlantic battle under that great exponent of the art, Admiral Doenitz.

Not even the most ardent aficionado of the U.S. Navy would probably claim that the Americans ever reached an equivalent mastery. The German wolf pack was like a highly tuned machine, massive in its impact but flexible, adaptable and beautifully integrated. It was some time before the Americans even worked out a satisfactory method for controlling a submarine group: should it be by a supervising officer at sea, or should instructions be issued from ashore? Nevertheless—in their usual persistent way—by experiment, failure and fresh endeavor the means were evolved so that, in the end, we have instances of successful assaults not merely by a single pack but by several attacking an important target in sequence. Without Ultra, sophisticated operations of this character would have been no more practicable than, without the Sigint supplied to U-boat Command by B-Dienst, would it have been possible to orchestrate the maneuvers of those voracious Atlantic wolf packs.

Inevitably, the result of improved tactics and increasing strength was a one-way process. Between January and April 1944 U.S. submarines sank 179 ships of some 799,000 gross tons: between May and the end of August a further 219 ships had gone to the bottom, and their ton reckoning had passed the million mark. By the end of 1944 imports of oil, the vital essence of war, had almost entirely ceased and domestic stocks in Japan, as high as 43,000,000 barrels at the end of 1941, sank to less than 4,000,000 by March 1945.

"Until late in the war," Craven and Cate observe in the final volume of their history of the Army Air Forces, "and for the whole of the war, the submarine was the chief killer, but it was ably seconded and made more effective by Navy, AAF, and Marine planes." This generous (though accurate) apportioning of the various contributions in the attack on Japanese shipping is, of course, a salutary reminder that other agencies were at work. With their range and their flexibility the air forces could seek targets beyond the reach of the submarines and then, as the throttling encirclement of Japan grew tighter and tighter, concentrated air strikes could be mounted from the neighboring islands on such shipping lanes as still remained open (fewer and fewer, since by the spring of 1945, 35 out of 47 regular convoy routes had been abandoned). This very diminution of viable seaways, plus the narrowing of the ring around the home islands of Japan, also provided the U.S. Air Force with opportunities that were fully grasped for sealing off harbors and infesting shipping routes with airborne mines. As abundant targets for submarines disappeared from the high seas and operations became more difficult and dangerous in the constricted waters still available to the enemy, air power—virtually unimpeded—was able to take over.

And yet, while this is true, the central fact is undeniable: until the fall of 1944 over 70 percent of Japan's shipping losses can be attributed to the U.S. submarines, apart from their incidental successes thereafter. When surrender came, the *marus* were mainly a memory and—thanks in large measure to Ultra—no major merchant fleet in history had been so mercilessly savaged.

It seems appropriate, therefore, to end this chapter with a kind of roll of honor: a list of the sinkings of Japanese merchant ships attributed to individual submarines by the Joint Army-Navy Assessment Committee which reported in 1947. The list is rigorously restricted to vessels under the headings Cargo, Passenger-Cargo, Transport and Tanker: it excludes warships large or small. It also excludes all sinkings assessed as "by combinations including U.S. submarines." As this book is not a technical history of submarine warfare the list has not been checked against later appraisals, and no doubt in this case or that the relevant figure should be larger or smaller. But as it stands, it provides a broad but graphic demonstration of the way things went, in a conflict during which the submarines of the United States accounted for some 4,780,000 tons of Japanese merchant shipping.

Attributions

Albacore 2:	Burrfish 1:	Grampus 1:	Herring 5:
Amberjack 2:	Bumper 1:	Grayback 10:	Hoe 2:
Angler 2:	Cabezon 1:	Grayling 5:	Icefish 2:
Apogon 1:	Cabrilla 6:	Greenling 13:	Jack 14:
Barbel 5:	Capelin 1:	Grenadier 1:	Jallao 1:
Barbero 3:	Cavalla 1:	Grouper 4:	Kete 3:
Bashaw 3:	Cero 5:	Growler 6:	Kingfish 12:
Batfish 2:	Cobia 3:	Guardfish 16:	Lagarto 2:
Baya 2:	Cod 4:	Guavina 5:	Lapon 11:
Becuna 1:	Crevalle 7:	Gudgeon 10:	Mingo 1:
Bergall 2:	Croaker 4:	Guitarro 6:	Muskellunge 1:
Billfish 3:	Dace 5:	Gunnel 4:	Narwhal 6:
Blackfish 1:	Darter 1:	Gurnard 10:	Nautilus 5:
Blackfin 1:	Drum 14:	Haddo 5:	Paddle 4:
Blenny 6:	Finback 11:	Haddock 8:	Pampanito 5:
Bluefish 8:	Flasher 15:	Hake 6:	Parch 6:
Bluegill 8:	Flier 1:	Halibut 10:	Pargo 5:
Boarfish 1:	Flying Fish 15:	Hammerhead 9:	Permit 3:
Bonefish 11:	Gablian 1:	Harder 9:	Peto 7:
Bowfin 15:	Gar 8:	Hardhead 3:	Pickerel 2:
Bream 1:	Gato 8:	Hawkhill 1:	Picuda 9:

Pike 1:	*U.S.S. S-36,* 1:	*Seahorse* 17:	*Sunfish* 14:
Pintado 5:	*S-31,* 1:	*Seal* 7:	*Swordfish* 9:
Pipefish 1:	*S-35,* 1:	*Sealion II,* 8:	*Tambar* 10:
Piranha 2:	*S-37,* 1	*Searaven* 3:	*Tang* 24:
Plunger 11:	*S-38,* 2:	*Seawolf* 15:	*Tarpon* 2:
Pogy 11:	*S-39,* 1:	*Segundo* 2:	*Tautog* 19:
Pollack 7:	*S-41,* 1:	*Sennet* 5:	*Tench* 4:
Pomfret 4:	*Sailfish* 6:	*Shad* 2:	*Threadfin* 1:
Pompano 5:	*Salmon* 2:	*Shark* 4:	*Thresher* 16:
Pompon 3:	*Sandlance* 8:	*Silversides* 21:	*Tinosa* 16:
Porpoise 3:	*Sargo* 7:	*Skate* 7:	*Tirante* 6:
Puffer 6:	*Saury* 5:	*Skipjack* 4:	*Torsk* 1:
Queenfish 6:	*Sawfish* 3:	*Snapper* 2:	*Trepang* 7:
Rasher 16:	*Scabbardfish* 1:	*Snook* 16:	*Trigger* 14:
Raton 10:	*Scamp* 3:	*Spadefish* 17:	*Triton* 8:
Ray 9:	*Scorpion* 3:	*Spearfish* 4:	*Trout* 8:
Redfin 5:	*Sculpin* 3:	*Spot* 1:	*Tullibee* 2:
Redfish 4:	*Sea Devil* 6:	*Steelhead* 2:	*Tuna* 4:
Rock 1:	*Sea Dog* 8:	*Sterlet* 4:	*Tunny* 4:
Ronquil 2:	*Sea Robin* 5:	*Stingray* 3:	*Wahoo* 20:
Runner 2:	*Seadragon* 9:	*Sturgeon* 8:	*Whale* 8:

SEARCH FOR COLD WAR STRATEGY

GEORGE H. QUESTER

THE IMPACT OF STRATEGIC
AIR WARFARE

No problem has so bedeviled American military analysts since the First World War as the utility and morality of aerial bombardment as a weapon of warfare. There can be little doubt that Allied air power was a critical element in the victories in Europe and the Pacific. By the end of 1943, army, navy, and marine aviation efforts had achieved control over the tactical battlefields. Hitler's air defense fighter force was destroyed by the spring of 1944 and about the same time the Japanese lost the battle for air supremacy. These tactical victories allowed virtually unrestricted strategic bombardment.

In Europe, the greatest U.S. Strategic Air Forces impact came in its offensive against German oil production. By the spring of 1944, German war efforts were severely curtailed by a lack of petroleum products and, as the war wore on, the situation became increasingly more difficult. The effect of the transportation campaign was less conclusive, but was greatest late in the conflict. But by the spring of 1945, the German transportation system was paralyzed. Operations against military equipment manufacturing facilities were much less successful, and some, such as the attempt to destroy German ball bearing plants, were outright failures. Some target possibilities were not exploited as they might have been, for instance electric power stations, explosive plants, chemical plants, and synthetic rubber and gasoline facilities. The prewar theory that aerial bombardment would destroy civilian morale proved illusory. Despite placing some twenty-five million people subject to the terror of bombing raids, killing perhaps 305,000 Germans, and seriously injuring another 780,000, German morale did not break.

431

Strategic bombardment may have been more decisive against Japan. In this theater the air forces possessed a longer-range, higher-flying, heavier bomb capacity aircraft in the B-29. The Japanese lacked the anti-aircraft artillery and fighter aircraft to defend the home islands the way the Germans had defended the Fatherland. Yet the losses sustained by Brigadier General Haywood S. Hansell and later Major General Curtis LeMay's XXI Bomber Command based in the Marianas Islands still were high and bombing accuracy was low. Much of their problem was the result of mechanical failure, not enemy air defenses. Many would argue that the U.S. increasingly reverted to terror bombing of Japan rather than concentrating on military targets.

Political science Professor George Quester of Cornell University examines not only the issues of operational success and failure, but also the morality of strategic bombardment. His conclusions contradict popular belief regarding the attitudes of U.S. policymakers from the Second World War through the Vietnam War. The key to understanding many of the morality arguments lies in the definition of critical terms. "Counterforce" or "countercapability" targets are enemy military installations and industrial facilities. "Countervalue" targets are enemy urban and political assets that may have little immediate military value, but their destruction can ruin an enemy's morale and capacity to control its forces and populace. Often counterforce targets are located in urban centers and the distinction becomes blurred.

While avoiding the issue of nuclear weapon targeting, Professor Quester notes that even the most wanton bombing by the United States (against Japan in 1945) did require justification as destruction of alleged military targets. Every effort was made to avoid artistic, intellectual, and religious centers in the Japanese home islands. From the beginning of strategic bombardment in the combined bomber offensive against Germany, 1942–45, political authorities constrained the employment of bombers. They required aviators to concentrate on counterforce targets rather than countervalue targets. In Japan, conventional bombardment did hit civilian residential areas, under the guise of attacking small home-based machine shops. It is doubtful if this demoralized the Japanese people, but it did contribute (along with the defeat of the Imperial Japanese Navy and the blockade of the import-dependent home islands described in the articles by Hughes and Lewin) to the government's decision to surrender.

Target selection remains a critical problem for military planners to this day. While Professor Quester avoids discussing counterforce versus countervalue targeting in potential thermonuclear warfare, he articulates the dilemmas of conventional strategic bombing operations in Korea and Vietnam. To this day the American public deplores wanton bombardment of urban areas with little regard for civilian casualties. Moreover, U.S. political leaders in limited conflicts like Korea and Vietnam are constrained by apprehensions of escalation and doubts about effectiveness, in addition to moral compunctions. We may never know just how much the threats of wholesale bombardment of North Korea (possibly using atomic weapons) and the 1972 bombing of Hanoi contributed to the respective governments' decisions to sign an armistice. Or for that *matter, did the raid over Tripoli and Benghazi in 1986 cause Libya (and maybe Syria and Iran) to reduce their support of terrorist activities against Europeans and Americans?*

In the end, Professor Quester introduces a new moral dilemma. During the 1970s and 1980s, precision-guided munitions entered the military inventory along with much smaller explosive capacity individually targeted nuclear warheads for intercontinental ballistic missiles. The greater precision of these weapons significantly reduces the potential for incidental damage to civilian targets that is part of conventional and nuclear counterforce attacks. Does this make aerial bombardment a more moral use of force? Is there not an irony that the very incapacity of early nuclear weapons to make a precise discrimination between counterforce and countervalue targets created a mutual balance of terror leading to the avoidance of superpower conflict in the last half of the twentieth century? Does the acquisition of more accurate weapons that can reduce civilian casualties make major conflict a viable alternative in the future? As we have seen before in the readings in this volume, technological innovation presents new possibilities and new dilemmas to the modern strategist.

Major American participation in the Vietnam war ended in almost the same way as it began, with the use of air power to strike at targets in North Vietnam. Since 1965, and perhaps since 1945, the United States has thus become typecast as addicted to the threats and use of bomber aircraft. Does this show a peculiarly American infatuation with capital-intensive methods and technological gimmicks? If so, does it also demonstrate a particular callousness and brutality among Americans, whereby we harness technology to inflict suffering on the inhabitants of North Vietnamese cities, or Dresden, or Hiroshima? Or have Americans instead tried to harness the technology of the bomber airplane to what they expected to be a moral war, in which "military targets" were hit while "civilian targets" were spared? In the end could it be that Americans have hypocritically been deceiving themselves, expecting to fight air wars with morality and discrimination, while actually relying on substantial brutality?

This paper will thus be examining two separate questions simultaneously. What has shaped American attitudes on the effectiveness of bombing? And what indeed has been the effectiveness of bombing?

To turn to the first question: many commentators assume that Americans have tended to be optimistic about what aerial bombardment can accomplish. The opposite will be argued here, for much of the account will show how Americans have been biased by culture and analytical style *against* the aerial bombardment tool. This has been especially true wherever bombing could be used in ways that would hurt civilians, i.e., could be used to intimidate an enemy, rather than to disable his armed forces.

To move to the second question: the same commentators may conclude that aerial bombardment has rarely, if ever, been effective. Yet the evidence on this "objective" point is also mixed, for there are some interesting cases where bombing apparently had some truly valuable military and political effects.

The following discussion will thus trace the evolution of American attitudes before, during, and after World War II. It will, for the same periods, try to strike a balance about where and when bombings were in fact effective.

THE HERITAGE OF AMERICAN MORAL ATTITUDES

It is remarkable that American official policy has so long disapproved of countercivilian uses of the bomber airplane, not only for most of the years between the world wars but also well into World War II. The residue of such American moral feelings about waging aerial war indeed may account for some of the confusion in governmental explanation of bombing in Vietnam, and perhaps for much of what seems hypocritical or irrational.

The years after World War I saw a great enthusiasm expressed in Great Britain for "knockout blows" by strategic air warfare, especially among such RAF officers as Air Marshal Trenchard, who planned to defeat Germany by a countercity air attack, if the war had not already ended by 1919. Nothing similar developed in the United States. American air officers *were* enthusiastic about the strategic potential of the bomber, but Air Corps field manuals were careful to stress techniques of precision bombing that might cripple the enemy by destroying specific factories while sparing residential areas even a few blocks away. Thus, in 1926,

> In the World War the Germans bombed London and Paris, while the dream of all the Allies was to bomb Berlin. Whether such bombing actually accomplishes its avowed purpose—to weaken the morale of the hostile nation and thus hasten the end of hostilities— is doubtful in some cases. The reactions may be in exactly the opposite direction.

And, in 1938,

> It is possible that a moral collapse brought about by disturbances in this close-knit web may be sufficient to force an enemy to surrender but the real target is industry itself, not national morale.

Why did the United States adopt such relatively high-minded attitudes? Perhaps it was already a technological fixation, this time with the vastly over-

TABLE 1   *Bombing of Civilians, April 15, 1938*

	Yes	No
5a. "Do you think all nations should agree not to bomb civilians in cities during wartime?"	91%	9%
By Sex: Men	89	11
Women	94	6

	Yes	No
5b. "Should the United States call a conference of all nations to make such an agreement?"	61%	39%
By Sex: Men	58	42
Women	65	35

SOURCE: Gallup polls of April 2–7, 1938, cited in *The Gallup Poll*, ed. George Gallup (New York: Random House, 1972), p. 97.

rated "superaccurate" Norden bombsight. A more cynical observer might have concluded that Americans in the 1920s and 1930s felt that they had more to lose than to gain in any legitimation of brutal air attack. How else could any foreign power ever menace Pittsburgh or Denver or St. Louis, except by flying over the U.S. Navy and Army? Obviously it made sense for the United States, like Japan, to demand that aerial bombardment in any future war be constricted to only the more explicitly military targets.

In larger part, however, such attitudes also reflected the general holier-than-thou attitude of most Americans toward other states in the international system, a naïveté early exemplified by Woodrow Wilson in his internationalist activist role and then retained by the isolationists later. In this view, other states were power-mad and brutal and selfish; Americans, military officers included, saw themselves instead as peace-loving and selfless, fighting wars only in self-defense, and then fighting only in ways which respected civilian lives.

The nature of American public attitudes is illustrated by a Gallup poll taken in April 1938, as war began to seem imminent in Europe, asking Americans to express their attitudes on the use of countervalue bombing as a weapon in any future war (see Table 1).

As World War II broke out in Europe in 1939, one of the earliest American "interventions" came when President Roosevelt made a statement urging all belligerents to limit their air forces to bombing strictly military targets. The British and French governments signaled their acceptance of this appeal on September 2; the German government, on September 18.

This is not the place to discuss at any length where the blame should be directed for the subsequent escalation in bombings during World War II. Contrary to conventional recollections of the war, at first there was indeed a prolonged period of mutual restraint when the Luftwaffe and the RAF did not bomb each other's civilian targets. Conventional wisdom then normally charges Hitler with deliberately escalating to all-out bombing of Britain during the Blitz, presumably as part of an attempt to force the British to surrender. Let us note only that this author is convinced that the crucial sequence of escalation to population bombing can be attributed in great part to the British, for Winston Churchill may indeed have deliberately launched such bombing raids during the Battle of Britain to bait Hitler into wasting the potential of his Air Force.

If Americans generally concluded that Hitler had struck the first blow in countercivilian air warfare, knowledgeable Americans nonetheless were not so ready to approve of the way that the RAF was "retaliating." Even during the joint British-American bombing campaigns against German cities, from 1942 to 1945, U.S. Army Air Force officers often congratulated themselves that American methods were more humane than those of the RAF. The RAF's Bomber Command consistently attacked at night, when it would lose fewer planes to Luftwaffe interceptors (and also would be able to carry larger bombloads, since less defensive machine-gun armament would be needed against such interceptors). Yet precision bombing by night was impossible, and the RAF target simply became working-class residential sectors in an "area-bombing" assault.

The USAAF, in contrast, flew by day, carrying lighter bombloads and attempting to drop the bombs more precisely on specific factories, railway yards, and oil refineries. The distinction was obviously not based solely on moral considerations. The low-bombload B-17 and B-24 in the U.S. arsenal had originally been designed in part to intercept and bomb enemy battleships on the Atlantic, when U.S. isolationism would not have tolerated any other scenario for military planning purposes. An air force fights a war with whatever tools it has; the presence of B-17s in the inventory may thus have dictated strategy in 1944 as much as the B-52 would in 1972. Yet, to complete the circle, the kind of U.S. bomber available reflected earlier rejections, largely on moral grounds, of city bombing.

Such a "debate" about alternative bombing strategies of course overlooks the question of whether any form of strategic bombing was wise. Bombers were not a total advantage for the RAF or the USAAF; the steel and manpower involved might have produced important results for the ground forces of 1944, or at least for close tactical air support for those forces.

The American endorsements of "careful counterindustry bombing" in World War II thus closely resemble what we have come to see as the prerequisites for limited war today. Care must always be taken not to kill hostages; if the other fellow's cities and populations are hurt, he will lose his reason for sparing our cities and population.

Yet the exact motivation for American behavior in World War II departs significantly from this model, for Hitler never could bomb American cities in reprisal. There has indeed been much comment on the Roosevelt administration's commitment to "total war" and "unconditional surrender," as part of a zealous American commitment to war, once the traumatic decision had been made to enter it; there has been a similar extensive analysis of how uncomfortable the American people seemed to be with the rules of "limited war" in Korea in 1950. The reluctance to admit to bombing cities from 1941 to 1945 thus did not stem directly from any sophisticated understanding of the mutual-restraint model of limited war; indeed, the British were much more conscious of and attuned to this model than were Americans. Rather, the American desire for a sense of restraint stemmed from a straightforward "respect for law" or morality, a feeling that winning wars by aiming at civilians was contrary to the traditions of civilization, and therefore wrong.

In part, this distinction accounts for the heavy emphasis on "intent" in explications of bombing policy in all the cases we are examining here. Christian theology stresses intent heavily, unlike other religions which place more stress on the rightfulness or wrongfulness of the act committed, whatever the intention. If one kills civilians as an accidental by-product of having aimed at a factory or a fortress, therefore, one's conscience is thus considerably relieved; one can even privately relish the "bonus destruction" achieved—destruction all the more welcome because it was not intended.

The mutual limitation of warfare is, of course, generally not so easy when the motives of one side are complicated. A side whose civilians were suffering as an "inadvertent" consequence of the American air raids might feel that it no longer had reason to hold back its own destructive bomber forces. As mentioned, the absence of serious German and Japanese retaliatory capabilities kept this peculiarity of American motivation from making much difference in World War II. If American strategy has been based only on "limited-war" theory, there would have been no need to limit *that* war; limits make nonmoral sense only when the other side has destructive capabilities of its own.

The element of moral feeling thus in some ways prepared the U.S. for the limited-war experience of Korea and Vietnam; but in other ways it greatly confused the logical preparation.

BOMBING EFFECTIVENESS IN WORLD WAR II

Much has been made of the postwar findings of the *U.S. Strategic Bombing Survey,* which studied the impacts of bombing campaigns in Germany and Japan. The study of Germany in 1945 began even before the war in the Pacific was over. Many analogies to the Vietnam bombing have been drawn from the study in recent years. For example, it has been contended that bombing has always been ineffective. The study was an impressive piece of work, drawing in men from whom much would be heard later: George Ball, John Kenneth

Galbraith, and Paul Nitze were among the directors. Yet the volumes of the study are hardly consistent or coherent in their conclusions. This is not surprising, since the staffs of the *Survey* comprised hundreds of civilian analysts and hundreds of military officers. Studies of particular targets are at times difficult to reconcile with the conclusions of the summary volumes. The summary volumes for the European theater are not really consistent with those for the Pacific. It is quite dangerous for anyone, even a former director of the USSBS, to be too quick in stating generally that "the *Strategic Bombing Survey* proved" this or that.

In analyzing the U.S. precision bombardment in Europe, the summary concluded that such bombing had not been effective in crippling German military *capability*—but only because the correct target had been identified too late. If the offensive had shifted to oil earlier, instead of striking at ball bearings, the German Army might indeed have ground to a halt. As it was, the oil offensive was begun in summer 1944; the German Army and Air Force would have run out of gas by approximately June 1945, presumably having been defeated by air power. They were, of course, defeated by ground power of the American, British, and Russian armies before then, surrendering on May 7, 1945.

The same *Survey* volume was more generally critical of the British bombing effort, at least in "countercapability" terms, noting that the area-bombing raids never really inhibited German war production by producing demoralization or absenteeism in the labor supply. Indeed, the available pool of factory labor sometimes increased a few weeks after a heavy raid on a city, since the proprietors of nearby delicatessens and bakeries which had been leveled now had to find employment.

Before belittling the countercapability accomplishment of the Allied bombings too much, however, we must generally acknowledge that there was a great deal of slack in German war industry during much of World War II. Hitler had simply not imposed an austerity on the German economy comparable to what Winston Churchill had imposed on Britain. In part, this probably reflected Hitler's fears that an austerity comparable to that of World War I might cause the German people to want to surrender again. In part, it also reflected the corrupt accommodations that had been reached between German capitalists and the Nazi regime, which often allowed the industrialists to do things in their accustomed ways.

Albert Speer is quite rightly respected as an extraordinary technocrat, having succeeded in raising the German output of munitions month after month through 1943 and 1944 despite the Allied bombings. Yet his major contribution came precisely in taking the redundancy and slack out of the German manufacturing arrangements; if he had not, his impressive record would not have been possible. If there had been no bombings, German war production might have gone up far more spectacularly in 1943 and 1944.

The British area-bombing campaign may simply have been intended to weaken war production by tiring out and demoralizing the labor force. Or the British planners may have hoped to inspire opposition to the war in the German people or government by a brutal bombing policy which the RAF could not advertise explicitly, but admitted often enough.

Hitler would not surrender merely to end the Allied bombings. Since no German popular revolt ever showed signs of materializing, it is common to write off this entire British effort as a misguided failure. Yet such a conclusion, voiced in a number of the *Bombing Survey* volumes, might be premature, for officers of the German Army did, after all, attempt to assassinate Adolf Hitler; the German cities' being destroyed day after day could only have furthered these officers' conviction that the Nazi regime and the war should be terminated as early as possible.

The average German frontline soldier (like the average civilian) was kept immobilized politically throughout the war, and indeed showed no signs of approving the attempt on Hitler's life. Yet we have evidence that the Nazi authorities devoted considerable effort to keeping detailed news of the air raids from reaching the front lines, for fear that this immobilization might not otherwise be maintained.

It is thus especially interesting to note that the U.S. Army Air Force's response to the preliminary findings of the USSBS in Europe was to shift its B-29 campaign against Japan to emulate the British area-bombing attack. The B-29 was a bigger airplane, perhaps capable of carrying enough tonnage to make an area assault meaningful (especially if defensive armament could be stripped off as unnecessary when missions were to be flown at night). If U.S. precision bombings had not found exactly the right industrial target over Europe, General LeMay, in command of the 20th Air Force, concluded that a campaign of bombing residential areas might force the Japanese government—or people—to surrender.

Americans may generally worship technology, but the shift to night bombing was clearly a step backward. The B-29s were stripped of a defensive machine-gun system which had just been developed as an enormous improvement over that of the B-17. Precise bomb aiming was to be abandoned for a crude blunderbuss approach. Everything expendable was stripped from these expensive new planes to increase the bombload they could carry. LeMay's decision in the field thus in effect converted his bombers from 1945 to 1942 models, the equivalent of the high-payload bombers the RAF had used over Germany.

Yet American morality still had to be appeased with the argument that many Japanese homes were housing small machine shops that contributed to war production. If incendiary raids were to burn down entire residential neighborhoods, this action could be rationalized as consistent with international law and American morality, as long as "military-industrial" objectives were always the target. Privately, U.S. Army Air Force planners in Washington now noted that a choice might have to be made between industrial targets and the Japanese population as a target; their suggestion to LeMay's headquarters was that he press the attack on population.

The 20th Air Force had thus shifted to area bombing in its assault on Japan before the atomic bombs were dropped on Hiroshima and Nagasaki. The criticism is often made that the atomic bombings were unnecessary, since Japan may already have been on the verge of surrendering. Yet such an argument begs the question of what was causing the Japanese government to be so close to making peace. The two major factors here were the naval blockade of the home islands and the conventional bombings already under way, bombings which on occasion had done more civilian damage than the Hiroshima and Nagasaki bombs.

It is interesting to note how the Survey volume for Japan concludes that it had been wise to try to bomb Japan into wanting to surrender:

> With the benefit of hindsight, it appears that the twin objectives of surrender without invasion and reduction of Japan's capacity and will to resist an invasion, should the first not succeed, called for basically the same type of attack. Japan had been critically wounded by military defeats, destruction of the bulk of her merchant fleet, and almost complete blockade. The proper target, after an initial attack on aircraft engine plants, either to bring overwhelming pressure on her to surrender, or to reduce her capability of resisting invasion, was the basic economic and social fabric of the country. Disruption of her railroad and transportation system by daylight attacks, coupled with destruction of her cities by night and bad weather attacks, would have applied maximum pressure in support of either aim.

There was, of course, no way that so powerful an explosive as the A-bomb could be dropped "discriminately" on a city. Yet the United States, in the use of even this weapon, put forward "military" arguments for the target choice. Hiroshima *was* an unusually military city, the home base for a number of army units, and a place that had been virtually off limits to foreigners in the late 1930s. Nagasaki was an important industrial city.

One wonders why exactly there should have been this kind of rationalization at the final stage of the bloodletting. There was no mutual-restraint bargaining under way by which Japan was supposed to consider this as only a limited war. Just as surely, neutral opinion could no longer have been a consideration; were we worried about hostility from the Swedes, Swiss, or Portuguese? Those who expected that Japan would never surrender wanted the Japanese Army to be "militarily disabled." Yet the statements about "military targeting" also stemmed in the end from an internal morality in the United States, a morality whose considerations were not yet shelved at the onset of the nuclear age.

"LIMITED WAR" AND "CONVENTIONAL BOMBING"

If the American bombing of Japan, conventional as well as nuclear, was wanton, American morality still necessitated that it be defined otherwise. This illusion about "military targets" has persisted well after 1945, even with regard to nuclear World War III scenarios. It has been only very recently that any American spokesmen could admit publicly that H-bombs would be directed at Moscow in retaliation for a Soviet strike merely to make the Soviet leadership regret its aggression. For a long time, the Strategic Air Command maintained that its nuclear arsenal would be directed at Soviet industry and arsenals to cripple the Red Army's advance on Europe. Millions of Soviet citizens would have been killed under either rubric, of course; so the real purpose of deterrence was accomplished. Yet SAC had to pretend that deterrence was almost a by-product, as the U.S. Air Force would fight by the rules of 1938.

Perhaps moral restraints will be meaningless or counterproductive today for any war fought totally with H-bombs carried by missiles. Yet the distinction between military and civilian targets can still be relevant to the fighting of conventional limited wars, and American moral restraints here were reinforced once the USSR had acquired the atomic bomb. A restraint on all-out and explicit terror bombing might now be required to keep any future war limited, to keep the Russian Air Force from being drawn in as part of an escalation to World War III. The German and Japanese air forces had retained little capacity for retaliation in 1945, but massive retaliation after 1949 could be a two-way street.

American bombing campaigns in the Korean War were thus constrained by President Truman, despite pleas from his Air Force leaders that air raids should be directed to imposing expense and hardship on the Communists, with a view to reducing their willingness and ability to fight. When it seemed from time to time that the Communist side had ceased to be serious about negotiating a truce, a very limited dispensation was given the Air Force to conduct countervalue raids, as with the attack on the Suiho power plants in June 1952—the plant, incidentally, supplied electrical power to Manchuria as well as to North Korea—or the raids on irrigation dams at Toksan and

Chasan in May 1953. Yet even such raids had always to be labelable within the rubric of attacks on military targets:

> Whenever possible, attacks will be scheduled against targets of military significance so situated that their destruction will have a deleterious effect upon the morale of the civilian population actively engaged in the logistic support of the enemy forces.

Much of the same reasoning explains the constrained, gradual, and measured introduction of bombing raids over North Vietnam. American moral aversion to needless civilian destruction played a role. Fear of public outcry in the United States or in foreign countries also played a role. But a most important consideration was that neither Communist China nor the USSR be drawn into active participation in the war, with all the risks of further escalation this would entail. It may well be that bombings mild enough to avoid such escalation would never be severe enough to force Hanoi to stop infiltrating South Vietnam.

American goals in bombing North Vietnam from 1965 to 1968 were often stated in terms of three objectives. For example, Secretary McNamara testified to the Stennis Committee in August 1967:

> Our primary objective was to reduce the flow and/or to increase the cost of the continued infiltration of men and supplies from North to South Vietnam.
>
> It was also anticipated that these air operations would raise the morale of the South Vietnamese people who, at the time the bombing started, were under severe military pressure.
>
> Finally, we hoped to make clear to the North Vietnamese leadership that so long as they continued their aggression against the South they would have to pay a price in the North.

In reality, these three objectives may collapse into the first and the third; unless one attaches enormous significance to any South Vietnamese higher morale derived from simple sadism or revenge, such morale logically would stem from the expectation that Hanoi's ability or will to infiltrate was being impaired by the air attacks.

The countercapability theme over North Vietnam was thus typically phrased in terms of interdiction, of interfering with the movement of supplies to the South. While this was initially intended simply to mask the more brutal intention of the offensive, after a time it became a way to inhibit advocates of more severe bombings within the American decision process. As Secretary McNamara lost confidence in the countervalue aspects of the bombings, he found it very helpful that the interdiction euphemism had been employed all along; much of his lobbying in 1967 for a bombing halt north of the 20th parallel could thus be couched simply in terms of taking seriously the public statements of American policy, i.e., that the air strikes were intended to be countercapability.

Interdiction should not be totally belittled, for it surely hampered somewhat the movement of supplies south, even if the military returns per ton of bombs delivered could never approach the results achieved in World War II. Since North Vietnam had so little industry, an interdiction approach made more sense than any serious pursuit of industry as a target. Yet a real commitment to interdiction as the goal would probably have shifted the bombing farther south long before Lyndon Johnson's decision not to seek reelection in 1968. The bombing campaign had in truth been intended as a countervalue campaign, if necessarily disguised behind countercapability interdiction euphemisms. When Nixon sent bombers into the Hanoi and Haiphong areas again in 1972, it was with the same intention.

The bombings per se were costly for the U.S. in airplanes shot down and pilots killed or captured, as well as in resources expended to keep the Air Force flying. The bombings furthermore came to be attached symbolically to the level of American ground-force commitment within South Vietnam. Each small escalation of air activity by the U.S. had come as advance warning of an additional ground-force deployment; a halt in the bombing conversely was to be seen as a sign that peace might be negotiated and the ground forces brought home. If there had been no ground-force presence, the American public might have been more patiently tolerant of a protracted air assault on North Vietnam; such patience perhaps might have forced Hanoi to reassess its priorities. As it was, Hanoi had reason for hope unavailable to the Japanese in 1945—that demonstrations on the campuses and city streets of the United States would keep the bombings from continuing indefinitely.

Richard Nixon was able to resume the bombing of North Vietnam in April 1972, and again in December, and to conduct it in a considerably more brutal—that is, more comprehensive—manner than Lyndon Johnson had. The American public may have tolerated this precisely because Nixon had withdrawn enough of the American ground forces from South Vietnam so that bombing could really seem a substitute for ground commitment, rather than a sign that the ground commitment was going to increase. Nixon could also renew the bombings because he had significantly bettered U.S. relations with Communist China and the Soviet Union, in part exploiting the differences between the two Communist powers; this at least served to reassure him that World War III would not result from mining Haiphong or the B-52 bombings within previously exempted North Vietnamese cities.

The last round of U.S. air attacks on North Vietnam again had the major purpose of being painful, of hurting civilian life as well as reducing military capability. To avoid a total affront to the moral feelings of Americans or others, however, some pretense, as always, had to be made that pain was less the goal than was the military incapacitation of North Vietnam. As a result, the air attacks were less deadly and brutal than if no such obfuscation had been needed. Bombs fell on dwellings as an unavoidable consequence of attacks on warehouses and arsenals, and on dikes as a by-product of attacks on antiaircraft guns. Surely this was pretense, but just as surely it reduced the civilian casualties per ton of bombs from what they would have been if the U.S. had not been constrained to make the pretense. Since Hanoi and Haiphong are densely populated, the North Vietnamese regime's casualty figures of 1,318 deaths from the American B-52 bombing raids suggests that the raids could indeed have been more wanton. In a similar bit of pretense over Japan in 1945, entire residential areas were burned to the ground allegedly as a by-product of the destruction of small machine shops located within them, but that bombing produced 100,000 deaths in a single night in Tokyo.

Perhaps the low casualty figures instead testify to the civil defense preparations of the Hanoi regime, without which the B-52 attacks would have appeared much more "indiscriminate." It is also possible, of course, that Hanoi was concealing and understating the bomb casualties to avoid suggesting a crack in its determination; if so, Hanoi and Washington were parties to a curious de facto conspiracy for concealing the U.S. Air Force's brutality.

The final B-52 bombings of Hanoi were launched and terminated almost too quickly for American opinion to be fairly sampled. A phenomenon noticed in polling is that people often oppose a policy until the government adopts it, then back it while it remains policy, and then heave a sigh of relief that the policy has been terminated after the government drops it. Some such factor may explain some of the disapproval of the last round of bombing expressed in a poll of January 1973.

Yet responses to various suggested statements about the bombing still tend to support a number of the themes that have been stressed here. A great majority of Americans found it important to accept their government's assurances that "places where people live in Hanoi" were not being deliberately bombed. At the same time, many were persuaded that "inhuman and immoral" damage was being inflicted.

TABLE 2   *Bombing of Hanoi, 1972*

"Did you approve or disapprove of the heavy bombing of North Vietnam by U.S. planes which took place at the end of this past year?"

Approve	37%
Disapprove	51
Not sure	12

"Let me read you some statements people have made about the Vietnam situation. For each, tell me if you tend to agree or disagree.

	Agree	Disagree	Not Sure
Pro-Bombing			
What we did in bombing Hanoi was no worse than what the Communists have done in the Vietnam war.	71%	16%	13%
President Nixon is experienced in dealing with the Communists and knew the bombings would bring North Vietnam back to negotiating.	53	30	17
The only language Hanoi will listen to is force, such as bombing their cities.	48	33	19
President Nixon was not taking a big risk in bombing Hanoi, because he knew Russia and China would stay out of it.	46	31	23
Anti-Bombing			
We lost many American lives and big B-52s unnecessarily in the recent bombing raids.	55	30	15
It was inhuman and immoral for the U.S. to have bombed Hanoi's civilian centers the way we did.	46	37	17
The bombings were wrong, because we lost the support and respect of allies and friends around the world.	36	49	15
I believe the claims that we deliberately bombed hospitals and places where people live in Hanoi, besides military targets.	17	67	16

SOURCE: The Harris Survey, January 1973. © 1973, *Chicago Tribune.*

NOTE: National adult sample of 1,472.

GUERRILLA WAR AND AERIAL BOMBARDMENTS: THE ANALOGIES OF ASSESSING IMPACT

There are many analogies that could be drawn between the methods of guerrilla warfare and the methods of countervalue aerial bombardment. Each technique works entirely to disrupt normal functions and to destroy, without for the moment trying to "hold a line," a line behind which normal functions would be maintained. A bomb placed on railroad tracks in South Vietnam by a Viet Cong agent serves almost identical purposes as a bomb placed on railroad tracks in North Vietnam by an airplane of the U.S. Air Force.

Each technique pays a great deal of lip service, and places a small amount of effort, behind its "counterforce" aspect, i.e., dynamiting troop trains. But each achieves a great deal of its purpose by more "countervalue" techniques, i.e., making life unpleasant for the enemy rather than disabling his military capability. Each then seeks in effect to "torture, not kill."

The similarities between the two forms of warfare then extend to the analyses of impact. Just as in the case of air attacks, one can speculate about whether IRA bombings in London steel the British public and government to be even more resistant to making concessions in Northern Ireland, or whether they instead cause Englishmen to want to get out. Perhaps they enhance resolve, but perhaps they eat away at it. Just as in the instance of air attack, it would be foolish for a British prime minister to admit the fading of resolve any earlier than he had to, for to be candid would serve only to encourage and accelerate the IRA's offensive. Some guerrilla campaigns succeed; others fail. The same must probably be the fair-minded conclusion about air attacks.

There is one aspect, however, on which supporters of guerrilla war would be most vehement in rejecting parallels to aerial bombing campaigns. Maoist and other theorists of guerrilla war often contend that success at such tactics proves the support of the masses of the people who feed, shelter, and hide the guerrillas between raids. In effect, they portray guerrilla war as a sort of plebiscite, a direct means of implementing political democracy. Critics of such theories contend that a majority of mass support is quite often not a prerequisite to guerrilla success, that a fraction of supporters as small as 10% might suffice. Who, for example, believes that the IRA speaks for the majority in Northern Ireland, given that Protestants number more than half the total population?

The comparison nonetheless makes air war look a little less legitimate, for no popular support at all is required for such attacks to be conducted. When U.S. air attacks against North Vietnam were launched explicitly as reprisals for the Hanoi-supported guerrilla operations in South Vietnam, at least a few outside viewers were troubled by the apparent asymmetry. The Viet Cong had at any rate proved *something* by operating successfully in the South (reasonable men might differ about what). In contrast, the precedent of U.S. air attacks could be extended anywhere—to Bulgaria after an insurrection in Greece, etc.

Does aerial bombardment thus never serve the purposes of the country using it? Would that it were so, for then air raids might rarely if ever be made. Liberals like to have their goods and bads together. If one disapproves of bombing per se on moral grounds, one would also be gratified to discover that enemy capabilities are never crippled, that an enemy's will to fight is never impaired by bombardment.

It is dangerous to contend that capabilities have never been crippled. The bombings of the two Axis countries in World War II did hamper weapons production and reduce the enemy's ability to fight the war.

It is much easier to criticize any projection from Germany or Japan as an industrial target to North Vietnam. There has not been that much vulnerable industry or supplies in Vietnam to attack; even when the bomb tonnages dropped on the North became some multiple of what was dropped on Germany, far less "crippling" of Hanoi's military capability could have been produced. Much of the necessary manufactured goods for the North Vietnamese Army were at all times being produced in China and the USSR, which of course were not bombed.

Yet all of this may not be so relevant as critics of the war have continually assumed. Those responsible for the American bombings of North Vietnam should be charged with the same duplicity as those responsible for the 1945 raids against Japan, which were officially explained by stressing their countercapability while they were actually often conducted largely as countervalue. If this betrays deceit, it should nonetheless indicate less stupidity in U.S. policy decisions than the statements of American planners taken at face value.

McNamara's critics may have been taken in by his propaganda, which was phrased to satisfy the American morality of 1926 and 1938 about bombing. But do we know that McNamara and his associates were not themselves taken in by such propaganda, leading them to take interdiction and specific military targeting seriously, rather than merely using them as a cover for brutality? Perhaps Americans through the history of air war have been destined all along to overrate the precision of technology, as well as the possibility of wartime morality. When the JCS proposed air raids which would have been more damaging to civilian life in North Vietnam, the civilian leadership in the Pentagon and White House proposed interdiction, rather than no air raids at all. Was this merely a necessary tactical ploy within the U.S. decision process, or does it illustrate some fixation with the bomber that all Americans may share?

Yet if the most honest intention of the bombing was normally to impose hardship on Hanoi and thus to deter any further support for the insurgents in the South, this is still where the bulk of any evaluation and criticism of American decisions and American syndromes would have to be directed. And here the critics may have a less than airtight case.

Is it really so, historically, that no one can ever be bombed into surrendering, i.e., into terminating military operations even when its forces are capable of fighting on? The Japanese surrender in World War II (far more of a surrender than Hanoi had ever been asked to make) was indeed produced in important part by air attack, very possibly by the conventional B-29 attacks on Japanese cities, or, if not, more certainly by the final atomic bomb attacks. There is, similarly, reason to believe that the Italian Army's coup against Mussolini and its subsequent switching of sides in World War II was accelerated by fear of Allied air attacks on Italian cities. Hitler would never have surrendered to spare German cities from bombardment, but he would have made many more minor concessions in exchange for a bombing halt. The Army officers who tried to kill Hitler, moreover, would certainly have offered an armistice and withdrawal in exchange for an end to the air raids.

Being bombed is decidedly unpleasant, and even the most ruthless dictators must have some sympathy for the populations who suffer it; even dictators prefer buildings to rubble. Perhaps such leaders have had little reason to fear that the population would rebel. The secret police of Hamburg or Haiphong surely could keep such rebellion under control by timely arrests of potential ringleaders or the most vocal grumblers; no wonder, then, that the experience of being bombed only "stiffened the resistance" of city dwellers. Yet the political leader in question must reckon at least with the unhappiness of his military officers, or of the remainder of the political elite—the Italian Army coup or the July 20 plot against Hitler demonstrate this necessity. If any part of the Communist party leadership in Hanoi had a particular aversion to being bombed, Pham Van Dong could not ignore that totally.

Ernest May assembled an interesting collection of materials and analysis on the issue of whether bombing had ever achieved any political effect in the past, with a view to whether it could be expected to have achieved such an effect in Vietnam. May's empirical conclusion was quite interesting: bombing could not be expected to weaken the resolve of an incumbent in office (and indeed might steel such resolve), but bombing could sometimes embolden others to drive the incumbent from office and thus bring in a new team who genuinely feared further bombing and was ready to make concessions to avoid it.

TABLE 3   *Bombing of North Vietnam, 1968*

16. "Some people say that a halt in bombing will improve our chances in Vietnam for meaningful peace talks. Others say that our chances are better if the bombing is continued. With which group are you more inclined to agree?"

Continue	70%
Halt	15
No Opinion	15

17. "How do you think the war in Vietnam will end—in an all out victory for the United States and the South Vietnamese, in a compromise peace settlement, or in a defeat for the United States and the South Vietnamese?"

Victory	20%
Compromise	61
Defeat	5
No Opinion	14

SOURCE: Gallup polls of February 1–6, 1968, cited in Gallup, *Gallup Poll*, p. 2106.

Even if May's conclusion had proved to be quite accurate, it would not have ruled out some success for the U.S. air campaigns against Hanoi; our knowledge of the leadership succession patterns in North Vietnam, or indeed in many of the Communist countries, is hardly so perfect that we could dismiss the chances of a palace coup. Moreover, May's distinction between incumbents and nonincumbents may stretch political reality a little too much, for many political coups consist of some of the leaders conspiring to oust the rest. Italy's response to bombing thus consisted of the ouster of Mussolini, engineered in part by individuals who already held a great deal of power. Japan's response to being bombed in 1944 was to oust Tojo, but few would deny that some very powerful elements of the incumbent establishment remained just as powerful afterward.

Even incumbents, therefore, sometimes seem to be weakened in their resolve by the prospect of seeing their cities destroyed and their people hurt. If they are clever—and most incumbents get to be incumbents by being politically clever—they will hide any weakening of their resolve as long as they can. But it may not be concealable indefinitely.

A large fraction of the American public was certainly not unaware of this kind of logic as the bombing campaigns against North Vietnam were going on. A set of poll questions from February 1968 (when American enthusiasm for the war was in marked decline) shows fairly clearly that many Americans saw themselves to be in a contest of resolve with the North Vietnamese, and that the disutility imposed on Hanoi by the bombings was thought related to achieving a more favorable outcome in that contest of resolve (see Table 3).

On Establishing the "Lesson of Vietnam"

Is it true that Hanoi's willingness to fight on increased day by day as the F-4 and B-52 raids continued, or was it unaffected by such raids? If North Vietnamese spokesmen claim the first, can such claims be taken at anything like face value? One thing is certain: if the Hanoi leaders had contemplated giving up their southern goals in 1968 or 1972 to escape bombing in the north, it would have been very foolish to let hints of this leak out until they had decided to surrender. The strategic psychology of a bombing campaign is parallel to that of a labor dispute. If the employer is thinking of capitulating to labor's demands to end a strike, he may still want to wait a week or two to see if the union will give up first; during that time, it would be very foolhardy for the employer even to hint that he is thinking of giving in.

In retrospect, we know that the 1965–68 bombings amounted to a limited and constrained venture in bombing for the sake of inflicting pain—a venture that failed in those terms. By contrast, the 1972–73 bombings were significantly less constrained, and very possibly had some tangible impact on the Hanoi regime's intentions. The 1945 bombings of Japan were hardly constrained at all, and were quite effective in persuading the Japanese leaders to surrender. The bombings of North Korea in 1952, as mentioned, were a more limited venture in terror bombing whose impact is hard to evaluate. In the Korean War, and in the first round of Vietnam bombings, the U.S. Air Force and Joint Chiefs of Staff indeed had advocated a more extensive bombing campaign to impose greater hardships on the Communist leaders; these recommendations were rejected, because of the threats of escalation and not because bombing "merely stiffens a people's resistance."

Those who doubt that Hanoi was in any way intimidated by the bombings will, of course, persist in their indictment that American bombing was foolish in all respects, in real as well as pretended motives. This leads us into what may be a prolonged debate about who gave up the most in the 1973 Vietnam truce, and about what happened thereafter. Did Hanoi make significant concessions in October 1972, compared with its demands in 1969 or 1971? Did Hanoi confirm such concessions in January 1973, after the next round of bombings of the North, when it might have been trying to back out of the October concessions? If the truce involved any surrender of position by the Communist leadership, an aversion to being bombed is very probably a part of the explanation. There is no law in history that populations and governments always stiffen their resistance while their residences and public buildings are being reduced to rubble. Again, would that it were so.

South Vietnam fell to the forces commanded from Hanoi in spring 1975. At the end, the offensive involved a substantial use of tanks and artillery, producing campaigns much more reminiscent of the Korean War in

1950 than the prolonged guerrilla campaigns of the Vietnamese war. Would such an open campaign have been launched if the U.S. administration had not been specifically forbidden, by congressional act, from reintroducing any form of American military force into the battle, including the B-52s which had bombed the North? Would such a ban have been imposed if Congress had not been emboldened by the domestic crisis evolving after the opening of the Watergate case?

It would seem that the answers should be negative on both counts. Some part of the resistance to future U.S. air operations against North Vietnam stemmed from the widely stated assumptions that these operations could not have any meaningful effects; yet the fact remains that Hanoi never dared commit itself to so open a southern assault until the risk of the air raids had been removed. Some Americans may have had fewer doubts about the effectiveness of the air threat for maintaining the stalemate, but had developed a major ambivalence or moral concern about whether the stalemate in South Vietnam (in which great numbers of people were still losing their lives each week) was something that should be maintained. However few welcomed the Communist victory in the South, many welcomed the end of the fighting.

Yet the upshot may well be that the threat of B-52 attack had at least been effective enough to maintain the fighting, in the sense of deterring Hanoi's move to total victory. The threat of conventional air attack had not sufficed to force a Communist surrender, but for the moment it did preclude a Communist victory. Bombing may not have "failed," in terms of the goals of those who had ordered the bombing.

AERIAL BOMBARDMENT: THE BROADER QUESTION OF AMERICAN INTERVENTIONISM

Is the United States therefore to be judged excessively technology-bound, and in what way? A fixation with technology could encourage brutality at a distance, via bombloads dropped from B-52s, in lieu of the bayonet charge of the infantryman. But a parallel fixation could lead or mislead Americans into imagining that they were waging careful and clean bombardment campaigns, counting on the Norden bombsight in 1942 and sophisticated radar guidance or "smart bombs" in 1972, to impose military damage while limiting civilian damage. Perhaps the American instinct either way is to make "full use" of whatever technology is at hand, the B-17 or the B-52, with inhumane consequences possibly alternating with the more humane.

Yet we have made a prima facie case here that aerial bombardment sometimes produces the political results governments desire; it may even have done so in Vietnam. If one disapproved of Johnson's or Nixon's judgment on the legitimacy of various factions in Vietnam, this would not by itself indict the air campaigns they launched as mindless technological tinkering.

To change the question slightly: what role has the option of aerial bombardment played in shaping the extent of American military commitments and foreign policy in general? Can it be that expectations of positive effects from air warfare have produced exaggerated expectations more generally about the utility of military force, about how much American power and influence can be projected into other countries and other continents?

The American discussion of air power options in the 1930s plainly shows an awareness of these issues. In a way, the bomber seemed clearly to be an offensive weapon, a weapon which would have most utility when extended into someone else's air space, poised over someone else's cities or military bases. We thus see a memorandum for the Army chief of staff in 1936 condemning plans for procurement of a long-range bomber, precisely because it would be a weapon of intervention or aggression at a time when the foreign policy of the United States called for isolation and self-limitation in foreign policy goals.

> The subject airplane is distinctly an airplane of aggression. It can bomb points in Europe and South America and return without refueling. It has no place in the armament of a nation which has a National Policy of good will and Military Policy of protection, not aggression.

American foreign policy would, of course, shift its emphasis soon enough, as the menace of Hitler made isolation seem impossible or dangerous. As a logical corollary to all of this, the extension of military power suggested by the aerial bomber thus ceased to be a liability or an embarrassment; rather, it became an asset for making the power potential of the United States tangible on the continent of Europe. We thus find President Roosevelt suddenly expressing considerable enthusiasm about such weapons, in decisions which were to prove altogether gratifying to the advocates of an expanded Air Force.

> To the surprise, I think, of particularly everyone in the room except Harry Hopkins and myself, and to my own delight, the President came straight out for air power. Air planes—now—and lots of them! At that time, the War Department was handling the entire expansion for the ground *and* air forces, but F.D.R. was not satisfied with their submitted report. A new regiment of field artillery, or new barracks at an Army post in Wyoming, or new

machine tools in an ordnance arsenal, he said sharply, would not scare Hitler one blankety-blank-blank bit! What he wanted was airplanes!

Some may see analogies between the American "interventionism" that drew us into war with Hitler and the "interventionism" that drew the country into the Vietnam war. Others, of course, indignantly deny any parallel between the two. So far as discussions of aerial strategy are concerned, the 1930s are also not lacking for discussions of air power potential for suppressing insurrections in more economically underdeveloped areas, i.e., in moves intended to preserve European empires against the "national liberation movements" of the time. The Royal Air Force, quite consistent with its well-developed belief in the "knock-out punch" power of aerial bombardment in general, developed and practiced a theory of "air control" as a means of suppressing insurrections in Iraq and British Somaliland, a technique then borrowed by the Royal South African Air Force for use against rebels in Southwest Africa. "Air control" came very close to being an explicitly countervalue or countercivilian technique, calling for the aerial bombard-ment of the villages from which the rebels had come, whether or not the village inhabitants actively in rebellion were known to be back in the village at the time.

In the British view, such techniques would deter rebellion. They would, moreover, do so more cheaply and effectively than if a ground army had to march and fight its way to the village to make retaliation more directly. Air power could thus maintain and extend more of an empire than armies could, establishing police authority and law and order where they had not existed before. The technique was comparable to the shellings of coastal cities in "gunboat diplomacy," but it could now be extended inland. All this, of course, is reminiscent of the sea and air power mixture so relished by Americans as the means of maintaining a position in Asia.

Sometimes the theories of impact propounded here have not been based on any straightforward rational motivation, i.e., "they will not want to attack any more because we have made the price too high." Rather, the motivation has been based on a metapsychological theory that the vision of aerial attack will be so awesome as to be directly incapacitating, a blow in an exchange of machismo, where the more backward side, lacking an air force, simply loses its nerve. Such were occasionally the expectations of the RAF in its colonial operations. Such have sometimes been the expectations expressed by Israelis in explaining their air attacks on "refugee" camps in Jordan or Lebanon. The simple prospect of hostile overflight, inflicting "sonic booms" on Beirut or Damascus, could have an effect by this calculus, even when no material damage at all is being inflicted.

In the 1930s, the United States also experimented with the use of air power in counterinsurgency situations; the Marine Corps allegedly perfected dive-bombing techniques while chasing Sandino in Nicaragua. Yet the American emphasis on "accuracy" again comes to light here, as accuracy is precisely what dive-bombing was to become touted for. Presumably the planes were scoring direct hits on concentrations of Sandino's mounted guerrillas, rather than bombing Nicaraguan villages.

There is, then, a link between the American faith in air power and the enthusiasm for overseas commitments. We have already mentioned the unsettled question of whether the American public might not have tolerated a forward deployment limited to air power continuously into the future, but for the decline in Nixon's domestic political position. If the Guam Doctrine had any concrete meaning at all, it was simply that U.S. air and naval power would combine with the Asian ground forces of regimes friendly to the United States to repulse or deter an adversary's attacks.

Vietnam is presumably not the only theater in which the threat of American air raids has been used to discourage Communist attacks. The protection of South Korea ever since 1950 has seemed to depend on a blend of American commitments, in part the threat of American ground forces' fighting another conventional war, augmented by the prospect of major conventional aerial bombardments of targets around North Korea and also by a latent threat of escalation to the use of tactical nuclear weapons.

One observation seems safe. If Americans lose their faith in air power, they will therefore lose a substantial portion of their commitment to protecting such outlying areas. Vietnam is lost, but what of Korea and Thailand and Iran and Yugoslavia? Some would welcome the end of lingering American military commitments in these areas, while others would not. After the experience of Vietnam, however, relatively few Americans would want to base such commitments primarily on ground-force deployment; any statement that "bombing doesn't work" more typically amounts to a shorthand for "America shouldn't get involved there."

Pinpoint Accuracy: Déjà Vu

It is somewhat paradoxical that the very end of the Vietnam war may have launched new enthusiasm in the American military establishment for more precise (and therefore once again promising more effectiveness) air warfare techniques. The final bombardments of Hanoi and Haiphong brought into use the various "smart-bomb" devices which a handful of Air Force officers had been developing throughout the previous decade, despite the opposition or lack of interest of their superiors.

Normally designated remote-piloted vehicles (RPV), these devices' slow development is now cited as a classic example of the parochial venality of the professional military. The Air Force is commanded by pilots who continue to have pilots' career interests at heart; therefore, deliberately or otherwise, they held back weapons which might ultimately have threatened to put human pilots out of business. Even the RPV title appears to be a euphemism, minted by the backers of such devices to try to reduce pilots' opposition; in candor, the new weapons might better be labeled unpiloted vehicles.

Having wasted enormous numbers of dollars and lives in trying to hit specific North Vietnamese targets by more traditional methods, the United States belatedly applied the "smart-bomb" techniques with incredible accuracy. Thus it seems possible to repeat the air offensives of the 1960s in the future with lower costs and greater results. Since the polls show that the losses of bomber aircraft and aircrews rank high among the American public's objections to bombing, this would provide administrations with an important counter to such concerns.

But the "smart-bombs" go beyond considerations of aircrew safety, because their promise of pinpoint accuracy reopens all the discussions of morality and opportunity which have been traced. As during the final bombings of Hanoi, but now even more so, one can tell oneself and one's critics that a superb counterforce bombing campaign is being waged. Specific bridges or factories are being hit, while hospitals and residential areas are being spared. If implemented seriously, of course, this would mean that the "bonus destruction" of such bombings would indeed be reduced. Perhaps an enemy's war economy and war *capability* could at last truly be crippled, while punishment of civilians is, at the same time, really avoided.

Yet the same pinpoint accuracies would open other avenues. The increased accuracy of such guidance systems could enable us to apply suffering in very measured doses, destroying a particular cultural monument or a particular electric power plant that supports a residential area without hitting the residences themselves. Aerial bombardment, like guerrilla war and some other contests of politics, can be a means of "torturing, not killing," of trying to apply enough disutility to dissuade and deter, while not applying so much that additional escalation or outside-world condemnation would occur. Accuracy may thus be put to varying uses in the future, just as the promised accuracy has in the past.

There is further a risk that expectations of increased accuracy will affect nuclear and conventional warfare systems alike, perhaps causing strategic analysis to deemphasize the distinction between them. The improved versions of the RPV may after a time come to resemble the improved versions of the cruise-missile now being sought as an augmentation of the strategic nuclear deterrent force. The phrase "precision-guided missiles" (PGM) is already being applied to improvements in the guidance system and terminal accuracy of weapons all across the spectrum. When this is combined with renewed speculation about new nuclear warheads with extremely small explosive yields and/or very small amounts of radioactive fallout, the risk that we may lose an important arms control distinction becomes greater.

As noted, such extremes of accuracy could clearly be destabilizing if developed for the strategic nuclear weapons themselves. A failure to maintain the line between conventional and nuclear tactical weapons would, moreover, erase a most valuable firebreak of limited war, a firebreak which has been respected ever since Hiroshima and Nagasaki.

Happily, the odds are that the strategic nuclear forces will never come to seem preemptively vulnerable, if only because the fraction that are deployed on board submarines will not be preemptable, however accurate missiles become. It also remains likely that nuclear weapons will not be put to "tactical use" in any repetitions of the Vietnam war. Yet the B-52s with conventional explosives may indeed come into use again, perhaps this time with all the greater accuracies described.

SOME CONCLUSIONS

A central argument of this paper is all too aptly illustrated by the familiarity of the discussion that will emerge about superaccurate weapons, the PGMs. Once again, advocates of the use of such weapons will try to avert moral condemnation by claiming that no immoral damage is being done, since no nonmilitary targets are being bombed. Once again, the critics of bombardment will see this as confirmation of their own view that there could never have been a justification for bombing such nonmilitary targets. Once again, the bombers that "intended to" avoid hitting painful targets may rejoice in the "inadvertent bonus" of having done such damage anyway—not because they are sadistic, but because they know there is a nontrivial possibility that imposing such pain will dissuade the opponent, even when the opponent's capabilities cannot be reduced.

Thus the debate will again not call a spade a spade, but will consist of euphemisms on the one side, and of misleading evaluations on the other side that purport to take such euphemisms as serious statements of administration purpose. This may all, of course, be only the irreducible flow of static in the communications system, but it remains static nonetheless.

Almost every reader will find strategic bombing morally unattractive. If the conclusion could once and for all be reached that bombing was ineffective, even for the goals of the generals directing such bombings, what good news it would be! Yet it is dangerous to decide that only good means are effective for political ends, just as it is dangerous to lie to oneself in any other way.

There have been cases where bombing was effective in reducing an opponent's military *capability*, either by interdiction or by industrial bombing. There have been other instances where such efforts have clearly been a waste of resources, for no interdiction or crippling of industry was possible.

Yet to wage or evaluate a bombing campaign in this day and age with a view only to such military impact would be foolish, for the possibility surely remains that an enemy leadership can be dissuaded from fighting even before it loses its ability to fight. Who has ever possessed an air force capable of extensive morale bombing or terror bombing without exploiting at least some of this capability?

If two or more air forces possess such a capability, a mutual deterrence may be established by which wars can be kept limited, by which civilian destruction can be held down. The world's morality disapproves of terror bombing, moreover; most states would have to pretend that their intention was to bomb military capability rather than to be brutal. But, as noted, American morality has disapproved of such bombing even more than the rest of the world; and U.S. policy has been affected by this.

HARRY L. COLES

STRATEGIC STUDIES SINCE 1945
The Era of Overthink

T he end of World War II marks the beginning of a transformation of the American
military tradition. Throughout its national history the United States maintained a small
national military, especially a small army, and relied on its ocean barriers and friendly
neighbors (at least after the War of 1812 and the Mexican War) to provide a breathing
space for the mobilization of its large manpower and industrial base on a war footing.
This worked most successfully in the two world wars. But the situation changed. The
United States and the Soviet Union engaged in a "cold war" in Europe and Asia, a war
of increased tensions that were exacerbated, from the American standpoint, by Soviet
failures to allow free governments in the occupied nations of Eastern Europe. The coup
against a freely elected democratic government in Czechoslovakia, the Berlin blockade,
and the overthrow of the Chinese Nationalist regime contributed to profound anticom-
munist consensus in the American body politic. This led to a policy of "containment" of
Soviet expansionism embodied most importantly in the formation of the North Atlantic
Treaty Organization (NATO) and in the decision to defend South Korea in 1950.

Containment required military outlays far in excess of anything the republic
previously had been willing to assume. During the late 1940s containment was achieved
through reliance on the air force and the monopoly the United States had in nuclear
weaponry. Security could easily be maintained with limited funding by relying on the
ultimate weapon. The emergence of the newly created Department of the Air Force and
its favored position in the halls of Congress and the body politic was deeply resented by
the navy, which had constituted the strategic defense of the nation since the days of

459

William McKinley. Hoping to find a strategic role in the age of nuclear weaponry, the navy sought to build a supercarrier that would carry aircraft capable of delivering nuclear bombloads. The ensuing 1949 "revolt of the admirals" against the cancellation of the supercarrier by a secretary of defense constituted a strategic crisis of major proportions inside the defense community. This event may well have been the first major demonstration that control of strategic policy was gradually slipping from the hands of the military leadership. The air force relied considerably on civilian advisors to justify its position.

Nothing has so dominated western strategic thought since the Second World War as the emergence of civilian centers for strategic study. War is not only too important to be left to the generals and admirals, it is also too important to be left to the politicians. From their offices across the continent—from Santa Monica, California, to Cambridge, Massachusetts—the defense intellectuals became advisors to both the Department of Defense and presidents and would-be presidents. Among the more important of these have been Bernard Brodie and Albert Wohlstetter of the Rand Corporation, Herman Kahn of the Hudson Institute, and William Kaufmann and Henry Kissinger of Harvard University.

Historian Harry Coles, professor emeritus at Ohio State University, roundly criticizes these scholars on two grounds. First, they usually ignore historical precedents, believing instead that the nuclear era so changed the nature of human conflict as to negate the usefulness of previous experience. Second, these "oversubsidized and over-cultivated" men so over-intellectualized their subject that they divorced their technology-based, social science rhetoric from the real world. During the John F. Kennedy administration these military intellectuals, advocating a doctrine of flexible response, assumed a mastery over national strategic policy. This mastery fell apart in the Vietnam War era.

Not only did the doctrine of limited war inherent in both Korea and Vietnam become discredited (see, for instance, George Herring's article), but also the unity of the defense intellectuals regarding nuclear policy became threatened in the face of the argument over counterforce versus countervalue targeting policy (see George Quester's article). As one might expect given his academic orientation, Professor Coles concludes with an appeal for greater emphasis on historical precedent in strategic analysis. But today one may not be as optimistic about the future as Professor Coles was in 1973 when this article was a speech given to the army's Command and General Staff College. The debates between the civilian strategists have gone public with politicians of one stripe accusing their opponents of being soft-on-communism liberal weaklings and those on the other side accusing their opposites of being warmongering, spend-us-into-bankruptcy militarists.

Despite Professor Coles's warnings, the defense intellectual establishment grew and prospered, especially in the halcyon days of the Ronald Reagan administration. A series of such "think tanks" grew up at major universities and around Washington, D.C.'s interstate highway loop. Critics derisively called the latter "beltway bandits" *because they saw them as intellectual stooges for the Pentagon. Is this criticism justified? Do we need such groups to provide a counterweight to Defense Department and defense industry proponents of favorite weapons systems? In recent years have they been as disrespectful of history as Professor Coles contends? Are they as necessary in what many feel is the post-cold war era of the 1990s?*

There is one sense in which my subtitle is a contradiction in terms. Just as one cannot be too healthy, too sane or too good, one cannot think too much or too well. What I wish to suggest by the term "overthink" is that strategic studies since 1945 have been oversubsidized and overcultivated. By the early 1960s, the military intellectuals assumed that a mastery over a new vocabulary meant a mastery over situations in the real world.

In order to make my point a little clearer, I might say that, if strategic studies since World War II have suffered from overthink, the period of the 1920s and 30s suffered from the opposite malady—underthink. The intellectual history of these two decades was deeply affected first by the reaction and disillusionment following World War I and then by the Depression. Quincy Wright's monumental work entitled *A Study of War*, begun in 1926, had its origin, I would guess, in the revulsion toward war characteristic of the era. The underlying assumption of this two-volume work seems to be that war is a social disease that should be dissected in all its manifestations with the hope of finding a cure.

Edward Meade Earle's *Makers of Modern Strategy*, on the other hand, had its origin in growing apprehension over the threat of another world war. It is interesting to note that, in this survey of modern strategic thought published in 1943, the only American to rate a chapter all to himself was Alfred Thayer Mahan. Other Americans were discussed briefly, but Alexander Hamilton, Billy Mitchell and De Seversky rated only parts of chapters. I venture to say that any compilation of *Makers of Modern Strategy Since 1945* would be dominated (though not monopolized) by Americans.

The reasons for the vast increase of American interest in strategy are not far to seek. They can be traced back to World War II and the technological explosion that followed, for the Soviet Union victory in World War II meant the end of a career as a second-class citizen in the international community. The last external barriers were removed, and the revolution was poised to move into another phase. The Soviets felt that there must be tangible evidence of victory, and this meant satellite states and defensible frontiers.

The United States, on the other hand, emerged a satiated power neither needing nor wanting territorial acquisitions. US postwar goals were indefinite and very difficult to obtain. President Franklin Delano Roosevelt and every president following him regarded the two world wars as unmitigated catastrophes, the repetition of which must be avoided at all costs. The ever-increasing destructiveness and skyrocketing costs of weapons added an urgency to deter war and prevent escalation.

The problems of power, survival and security are so vast that the Armed Services, the quasi-governmental agencies, the foundations and research centers in higher education have subsidized strategic studies on a scale unknown to history. Most of the literature clusters around deterrence, general war, limited war, civil defense, disarmament, counterinsurgency and flexible response. Obviously, these topics are interrelated, but, in a brief article, I could not hope to cover all these topics. Hence, I have decided to concentrate on deterrence.

The prominent place that deterrence occupies in recent strategic thought is quite in contrast to classical strategy. True, military men since the dawn of the modern era have maintained that the best way to prevent war is to prepare for it. Diplomats have liked the comfortable feeling that large, alert military forces give them in dealing with recalcitrants. The literature of international relations has much to say about power and diplomacy.

In the classical writers, there is considerable discussion about maneuver, deception, cover plans and other devices designed to lessen or to avoid altogether the necessity for fighting. Mahan actually uses the word "deterrence," and he introduces the refined concept that, with proper weapons, properly placed, an inferior power can effectively deter a superior one. By and large, however, the classical strategists addressed themselves not to the problem of deterring or preventing wars, but, rather, how to marshal one's resources so as to survive and ultimately to win.

A charge often made against military men and military writers is that they fail adequately to take into account the effect of weapons developments. There may be some truth to this charge as far as the distant past is concerned, but it can hardly be said that the atomic bomb failed to have an impact. In the theorizing about deterrence, the period from about 1945 to 1955 might be described as "Two Scorpions in a Bottle"—a metaphor coined by J. Robert Oppenheimer. One of the first books in the new field was *The Absolute Weapon,* a collection of essays edited by Bernard Brodie in 1946. The new doctrine of deterrence was boldly proclaimed:

> Thus far the chief purpose of our military establishment has been to win wars. From now on its chief purpose must be to avert them.

A corollary assumption was that all wars—certainly all wars between major powers—would escalate. P. M. S. Blackett, a Nobel prize-winning physicist with wartime experience in military operations research, wrote:

If it is in fact true, as most current opinion holds, that strategic air power has abolished global war, then an urgent problem for the West is to assess how little effort must be put into keeping global war abolished.

When Walter Millis brought out his excellent book, *Arms and Men*, in 1956, he proclaimed that:

The advent of the nuclear arsenals has at least seemed to render most of the military history of the Second World War as outdated and inapplicable as the history of the War with Mexico.

Both publicly and privately, Millis continued to maintain that military history had no relevance in an age of nuclear weapons.

The strategists writing soon after the war may have made mistakes, but they cannot be faulted with failure to recognize the impact of the new weapon. What they did fail to recognize was that the technological race had only begun and that they would have to run hard to stay even with developments. Brodie's "absolute" weapon, like all absolute weapons before it, was soon replaced by something even deadlier. The atomic bombs used at Hiroshima and Nagasaki had an explosive power of 20 kilotons—or an equivalent of 20,000 tons of TNT. The H-bomb, exploded on 7 November 1952, had an explosive power of 5 megatons or five million tons of TNT.

The further development of nuclear bombs, the growing awareness of the effects of radioactive fallout, Dulles' doctrine of massive retaliation enunciated in 1954, and the development of tactical nuclear weapons produced an outpouring of books, pamphlets and articles on strategy in the late 1950s. These centered around the themes of graduated deterrence, second-strike capability and the oceanic system.

The exact origin of any idea is difficult to trace, but I believe Rear Admiral Sir Anthony Buzzard, Director of British Naval Intelligence in the 1950s, was one of the principal authors, certainly one of the chief propagators of graduated deterrence. Sir Basil Liddell Hart held views very similar to Sir Anthony's, and graduated deterrence became the subject of a cross-Atlantic collaboration. Sir Anthony corresponded with Colonel Richard Leghorn, William Kaufmann and others in the United States.

In a letter to the Manchester *Guardian*, Sir Anthony asked:

Why not start by announcing our future intention of pursuing the moral principle of never using more force than necessary? To this end we might declare a distinction between the tactical and strategic use of nuclear weapons.

Tactical use, we might say, we consider as confined to atomic weapons and as excluding even these from targets in centers of population.

Strategic use we might declare as including hydrogen weapons and any nuclear attack on targets in centers of population.

Next, without being too specific, we might state generally that we would reserve strategic use unless the aggressor resorted to it. By this method we would be gradually modifying our present policy of 'massive retaliation' to one which has been aptly named 'graduated deterrence'—that of limiting all wars (in weapons, targets, area and time) to the minimum force necessary to deter and repel aggression, and return to negotiation at the earliest opportunity, without seeking total victory of unconditional surrender.

These basic ideas were later enlarged and refined by Sir Anthony in articles and books.

In 1957, two massive and influential books by Americans attempted to deal with this same problem of reducing war to something less than nuclear holocaust. The bulk of Robert E. Osgood's *Limited War: The Challenge to American Strategy* dealt with traditional American attitudes toward war. The basic failure, according to Osgood, was the penchant for making every war a moral crusade rather than a means to political ends as Clausewitz had advocated. The same theme with variations was played in Henry Kissinger's *Nuclear Weapons and Foreign Policy* appearing in the same year. Kissinger proclaimed:

The notion that war and peace, military and political goals, were separate and opposite had become so commonplace in our strategy doctrine by the end of World War II that the most powerful nation in the world found itself hamstrung by its inability to adjust its political aims to the risks of the nuclear period.

The best means of taking advantage of the economic and technological superiority of the United States was to adopt a policy of limited nuclear war. In a book that is generally difficult reading, Kissinger manages to achieve something like eloquence on the supposed advantages of tactical nuclear weapons. Kissinger's message was exactly what the Army and Navy people, starved by Eisenhower's "new look," wanted to hear. For the first and, possibly, the only time in American history, a book on strategy became a best seller.

Despite the shift toward graduated deterrence and limited war, the general idea of two scorpions in a bottle pervaded until a major revision in deterrence theory was brought about by Albert Wohlstetter in 1959. Completely shattering the assumption of a balance of terror, Wohlstetter concluded that, if the Soviets struck first with a surprise attack, US air bases would be obliterated and the planes would never leave the ground.

In other words, the strategists and publicists who had assumed not only nuclear plenty but a capacity for overkill were dead wrong. The implication of Wohlstetter's study was that the US deterrent was no deterrent at all. In fact, our vulnerability limited us to a first-strike capability. Therefore—and this was the most sobering implication of all—the state of US defenses gave the Soviets good reason to surprise our forces. In short, we were inviting attack.

Wohlstetter maintained that a deterrent force exists only if it is capable of inflicting reprisals. He then laid down six conditions of a second-strike capability: a stable, "steady-state" peacetime operation within feasible budgets; the ability to survive enemy attacks; to make and communicate the decision to retaliate; to reach enemy territory with fuel enough to complete the assigned missions; to penetrate enemy active defenses; and to destroy the target in spite of any "passive" civil defense in the form of dispersal or protective construction or evacuation of the target itself. The United States possessed none of the six at that time.

Originally a Rand study, Wohlstetter's article entitled "The Delicate Balance of Terror" was published in the January 1959 issue of *Foreign Affairs*. Though Kissinger's book probably enjoyed more commercial success, Wohlstetter's article probably had more influence on policy. Coming soon after the launching of *Sputnik*, followed by the first Soviet intercontinental ballistic missiles, there is little doubt that Wohlstetter's studies had an immediate and far-reaching influence not only on Air Force policy, but in theoretical studies as well.

Besides dispelling the myth that merely possessing nuclear weapons creates deterrence, Wohlstetter also planted another idea that took firm root in all strategic thinking after his famous article: the concept that strong retaliatory forces make for stability. In 1959, Oskar Morgenstern published *The Question of National Defense* in which he states that:

> In view of modern technology of speedy weapons delivery from any point on earth to any other, it is in the interest of the United States for Russia to have an invulnerable retaliatory force and vice versa.

This proposition, Morgenstern assured his readers, was capable of ". . . rigorous proof. The argument is complicated and difficult; it makes use of notions of mathematical theory of games of strategy."

You will recall that, after Hiroshima and Nagasaki, the strategists were convinced that the absolute weapon had been produced. With *Polaris* on the horizon, Morgenstern was convinced that the answer to stability was to be found in the "Oceanic System: The Invulnerable Force." He maintained that:

> Holding our main retaliatory force at sea makes the greatest immediate contributions to the defense of the country; it protects the force proper and it frees the country thereby from direct and indirect effects of a possible attack on this force itself.

For various reasons, Morgenstern's deterrent did not turn out to be the cure-all he envisaged.

Oddly enough, one of the most influential documents affecting strategy is a report few people have seen. The famous Gaither Report, made in the late 1950s, dealt with the inadequacies of the Eisenhower-Dulles defense policies, and it was never made public. Yet the Gaither Report influenced several studies which are in the public domain, including Kissinger's second important book, *The Necessity for Choice*, published in 1960. Kissinger acknowledged that:

> Some years ago this author advocated a nuclear strategy. . . . The need for forces capable of fighting limited nuclear war remains. However, several developments have caused a shift in the view about the relative emphasis to be given conventional forces as against nuclear forces. These are: (1) the disagreement within our military establishment and within the alliance about the nature of limited nuclear war; (2) the growth of the Soviet nuclear stockpile and the increased significance of long-range missiles; (3) the impact of arms control negotiation.

The vastly increased destructiveness and the improved delivery systems had raised the stakes in any confrontation so high that strategists now began to wonder out loud whether nuclear threats would be believed. The word "credibility" came into extensive use in deterrence theory, and Kissinger, in his new book, emphasized the psychological aspects of strategy—the role of will as well as capacity. "Deterrence requires a combination of power, the will to use it, and the assessment of these by the potential aggressor," he maintained.

Reflecting much of the discussion that had been generated by the Gaither Report, Kissinger accepted the existence of a missile gap and embraced the new gospel of limited war. With regard to the missile gap, he not only accepted its existence as a fact, but also asserted that "from 1961 until at least the end of 1964 the Soviet Union will possess more missiles than the United States." Emphasizing the need for capabilities other than missiles, he maintained that:

> Limited war is not a solution for all contemporary problems. It is not a substitute for constructive policy. It does offer the possibility—not the certainty—of avoiding catastrophe. A strategy based on it enhances deterrence. If deterrence fails, it provides another opportunity for both sides to prevent a catastrophe.

The ideas contained in Kissinger's *Necessity for Choice* and in Maxwell Taylor's *Uncertain Trumpet* were the harbingers of the new Kennedy-McNamara strategy of flexible response. You will recall that Kennedy, in addition to his slogan of "getting this country going again," fought his campaign partly on the charge of a missile gap and partly on the charge that cutting back the military had left the President with no choice between submitting to blackmail and pushing the button for nuclear holocaust.

Soon after the election and the appointment of Robert McNamara as Secretary of Defense, the new strategy of flexible response began to emerge. It was an amalgam: It promised something for everybody. Flexible response meant more and better missiles on land and sea; stronger conventional forces; special forces that could fight in mountains, swamps or rice paddies; a high degree of mobility for land, sea and air forces; civil defense (everyone his own fallout shelter); collective security; and arms control—all with the object of increasing the options open to the President in his conduct of foreign and military affairs.

Thoroughly convinced that massive retaliation had restricted the Executive's initiative, the new administration laid particular emphasis on unconventional warfare. Roscoe Drummond reported that:

> The decision to expand our capability in unconventional warfare stems in part from two White House conferences with the Joint Chiefs of Staff. In these discussions President Kennedy himself raised the question of increasing the Army's ability to deter, and if necessary, to assist in waging unconventional warfare by unconventional means. It developed that the Army Chief of Staff had already prepared the directive expanding the Special Warfare Training at Fort Bragg.

One might pause briefly to sniff the sweet odor of deterrence in this context. Obviously, by this time, all arms of the service conceived it to be their first duty to deter war and, if deterrence failed, to fight to victory. The phrases roll lightly off the tongue. One cannot help wondering what these people conceived to be the easiest, deterring war or achieving victory if deterrence failed.

Drummond went on to explain that the new capability (in these halcyon days there seems to have been only minor if any distinction between a capability, a plan or a hope) meant that the:

> . . . newly independent and sometimes insecure regimes, whether in Laos, Viet Nam or Indonesia or Africa fighting to survive against disorder and subversion, will not have to ask America for an atomic bomb or a Sherman tank when they really need on-the-spot training in guerrilla and counter-guerrilla warfare from multilingual American commandos who can show them how to build a bomb with bamboo stick.

The Navy, too, was prepared to deter aggression in whatever form it might present itself. Admiral Arleigh Burke, Chief of Naval Operations, announced that the Soviet Union was the "sponsor, instigator, and supporter of aggression by proxy." He assured the Congress that the Seventh Fleet in the Pacific was on the alert and ready to act in support of US policy in Laos.

Expectations mounted steadily. Jack Raymond reported in *The New York Times* that the Army was circulating a paper on the desirability of turning the guerrilla warfare coin over. The Army felt "we must find a way to overthrow a Communist regime even short of limited war." This was to be done by training and equipping some of the hundreds of thousands of nationals who had escaped from Communist domination. These refugees were to be trained to become special forces capable of overthrowing Communist regimes in Eastern Europe and Latin America. The Bay of Pigs was not far away.

From Bad Toelz, C. L. Sulzberger of *The New York Times* reported that, for three weeks, the 10th Special Forces Group stationed in this Bavarian spa had been training in guerrilla and counterguerrilla warfare. This airborne unit called itself "the President's own" in a manner reminiscent of the English Queen's "own" Royal regiments.

If there were serious doubts about the new capabilities among American newsmen, commentators and intellectuals, I have failed to find them. The British expressed slight—but only slight—skepticism. A reporter for the London *Times* informed his readers that President Kennedy was known to be fond of James Bond. The President and his advisers were also credited with having read Mao Tse-tung, T. E. Lawrence and Che Guevara. This varied diet had persuaded the New Frontiersmen that unconventional warfare and subversion must be used as instruments of high policy:

> The new hero is not a commando trained to precede conventional armies or carry out quick acts of sabotage, but a soldier expected to join in, and win the military-political battles being fought in exotic countries such as South Vietnam.

Notably absent from all these plans was any reference to the ideological nature of the contest. The *Times* article concluded that:

> The review may lead to a better understanding of political guerrilla warfare, but the chances are not bright.

The administration was careful all along to emphasize that a capability for unconventional warfare did not mean that the nuclear deterrent would be neglected. The defense intellectuals came into their own in the early 1960s. Theory became ever more highly refined, and deterrence was variously categorized as active, passive, offensive, defensive, direct, indirect, total, relative, absolute, finite, positive, negative, deterrence of supremacy, types 1, 2, and 3 and so on. We lack the space—and I certainly lack the will—to explore the meaning and implications of all these terms.

However, in order to follow the McNamara strategy, it is perhaps worthwhile to try to grasp the difference between counterforce and finite deterrence. Counterforce aimed at the elimination of the opposing military establishment, while finite deterrence aimed at the enemy's warmaking potential and civilian population. The Air Force espoused counterforce while the Navy claimed that finite deterrence was sufficient.

Some strategists seemed to regard counterforce as extreme and unnecessary. In 1960, for example, Kissinger maintained that:

> The effort to develop such a counterforce capability would impose staggering force requirements on us, draining off all other military capabilities. . . . A counterforce strategy designed to win a victory *after* we concede the first blow is an illusion.

Yet, soon after McNamara became Secretary of Defense, counterforce was linked with a new "save our cities" idea. As explained by the new Secretary, counterforce seemed the most logical and humane plan after all. In a famous speech at Ann Arbor, 16 June 1962, McNamara stated that:

The United States has come to the conclusion that the objective should be the destruction of the enemy's military forces, not his civilian population. . . . In other words we are giving a possible opponent the strongest possible incentive to refrain from striking our own cities.

I must be frank. I have never understood "save the cities" strategy. In the first place, surely we would not undertake an attack on the enemy's forces unless we thought we could destroy all or most of them. What, then, would he have left to strike back with? Secondly, why should an enemy be so grateful for the destruction of his military forces that he reciprocates by sparing our people who live in cities?

Apparently, the masters of the Kremlin were as perplexed as I am. They simply used the Ann Arbor speech as evidence of the aggressive and hostile tendencies of capitalism. There was a gradual retreat from counterforce, a retreat hastened by the activities of the Soviets in hardening their missile sites and in building missile-launching submarines. On 18 November 1963, Mc-Namara stated that:

. . . the damage which the Soviets could inflict on us and our allies, no matter what we do to limit it remains extremely high . . . the same situation confronts the Soviet leaders, in a way that is even more confining. In fact, enormous increases in the Soviet budget would be required for them to achieve any significant degree of damaging-limiting capability.

In other words, the Soviet Union would not undertake an antiballistic-missile system because of the cost. By 1966, counterforce seems to have been dropped altogether from the McNamara strategy. He said:

It is clear that our strategic offensive forces are far more than adequate to inflict unacceptable damage on the Soviet Union, even after absorbing a well-coordinated Soviet first strike against these forces.

In fact, the year 1966 is a kind of watershed in the McNamara strategy. Up to this time, McNamara seemed to have had great confidence in the various levels of power he had created and a conviction that he had mastered all the subtleties of deterrence. After 1966, instead of ever more ingenious statements about how the United States would meet differing challenges, McNamara's utterances take on a ritualistic monotone. Time and again, he states that the strategic air forces consisting of 1700 ballistic missiles and 700 bombers are sufficient to inflict "unacceptable damage" on the Soviet Union. I do not believe that he ever explained how he determined what the Soviets would consider unacceptable damage.

Ironically enough, about the time official policy reached a point of self-doubt and uncertainty, the defense intellectuals seem to have reached new heights of mastery of their subject. In 1965–66, a spate of books appeared. Urs Schwarz, a Swiss newspaper editor, published *American Strategy: A New Perspective* with an admiring preface by Henry Kissinger. Schwarz had paid a visit to this country and was hospitably received by the defense intellectuals and the foundations. All doors were opened to him, and he liked what he saw inside. He wrote:

> The growth of politico-military thought in the United States reflects the capacity of the human mind to adjust to new developments and to dominate them.

The vast gains of the human mind were also reflected in institutions, for the United States had created:

> . . . a national defense establishment in the modern sense, directed toward the use of all the nation's resources for the mastery of the infinitely complex problems confronting it.

Thomas C. Schelling in *Arms and Influence* (1966) seemed convinced that the application of military power to political ends had reached something of an exact science. A Harvard-based economist who had pioneered in the application of mathematics and game theory to military strategy, Schelling made a distinction between deterrence (to prevent by fear) and "compellence" (to force by hurting). It will take no special powers of divination for you to guess that what was being done in Vietnam came under the rubric of compellence, which Schelling said was:

> . . . the direct exercise of the power to hurt, applied as coercive pressure, intended to create for the enemy the prospect of cumulative losses that were more than the local war was worth, more unattractive than concession, compromise or limited capitulation.

To one reading books and articles on strategy in the mid-1960s, a comfortable and alluring prospect opens up. For every international ill, there is available, one is assured, a medicine in the exact dosage. Even Bernard Brodie, for whose work generally I have the highest regard, and who was one of the few military intellectuals to take issue with the McNamara strategy of flexible response, was quite convinced that deterrence would work:

> Unless we are dealing with utter madmen, there is no conceivable reason in any necessary show down with the Soviet Union why appropriate manipulation of force or threats of force, certainly coordinated with more positive diplomatic manoeuvre, cannot bring about deterrence.

This conviction of intellectual mastery was shared by at least some European strategists. General d'Armée André Beaufre, in his book *Deterrence and Strategy* (1966), wrote:

> The deterrent manoeuvre must, therefore, combine in judiciously measured quantities the apocalyptic threat, the checks and the military risks with moral or political inhibitions; it can thus weave the various levels into a close-knit network of measured and carefully confirmed threats, together with security safeguards, all of which will combine to paralyze the enemy while at the same time preserving our freedom of action.

Apparently, even experience in the real world could not shake this faith in intellectual mastery. General Maxwell Taylor served as Chief of Staff under Kennedy and later as ambassador to the Republic of Vietnam, yet, as late as 1968, he wrote:

> Military force in its various configurations provides a means by which the leaders of government may bend the will and influence the conduct of adversaries in conformity with the requirements of national interest as interpreted at a given time and place.

Please note that General Taylor is not advocating conducting one's own foreign and military policy in accordance with national interest (a goal difficult enough in itself), but proposes through military force to fashion the conduct of adversaries so that they serve *our* national interests.

Since about 1968, there have been many sober second thoughts. At the 10th Annual Conference of The International Institute for Strategic Studies (London), Urs Schwarz, Bernard Brodie, Raymond Aron and others expressed grave misgivings. Schwarz, who only a few years before had expressed such admiration of the power of the United States, now doubted the uses to which that power was being put. "Intervention has had its day, . . . it has ceased to be a rational and useful weapon," he concluded.

Bernard Brodie felt that the experience in Vietnam had highlighted the limitations of the new strategy. While conceding that systems analysis had been useful at tactical levels, he pointed out that it had no applicability at higher levels of policy.

> What should have been supplementary talent tended in fact to become preemptive of the field of strategic study. Under the seven critical years of the regime of Mr. McNamara, something like the effect I am describing took place in the United States. . . . If pride goeth before a fall, members of the American strategic fraternity have had both their pride and their fall.

Raymond Aron spoke from a different point of view, but the burden of his message was remarkably similar to Brodie's:

> One should hardly be surprised that today more than ever before the analysis of the present situation and the suggested courses of action should take into account actual situations in their historical context.
>
> When the question turns to Vietnam, or the use of force or escalation, the analyst who wishes to be the Prince's counselor . . . has to step down from hypothetical plan of models and schemes and get to know in their totality the elements which make up a situation and in terms of which the statesman will have to make his decision. Does make-believe tell us more about the reality of a situation and the development of a crisis than does historical and sociological analysis?

What may we conclude about strategic studies since World War II? First of all, I think we must recognize that, whatever its limitations, a true renaissance of strategic thought has occurred. Cursory though this review has been, I hope I have conveyed some idea of the quantity, variety and sophistication of the literature.

I venture to say that more books and articles have been produced since 1945 than in all the years previous. How much of this vast outpouring will find a permanent place in military history is difficult to say, but my impression is that the new strategy is far more remarkable for its quantity than its quality. I think any historian who examines these works *in extenso* will agree that there is a certain amount of fruitless elaboration, tiresome repetition and, in some cases, just plain padding.

A second characteristic of the new strategy is what might be called the primacy of technology. The scientists and engineers have called the tunes, and the strategists have danced. The ever-shifting technological foundation has inevitably produced a shaky superstructure. Until the technological environment becomes stabilized, we are unlikely to have profound analyses on the order of Clausewitz.

The new strategists were quite right, of course, in trying to come to grips with the new technology. If strategic studies were to be of any relevance, the doctrine of the use of nuclear weapons which are qualitatively different from those labeled classic or conventional had to be integrated into strategic thinking. But some of the new strategists were so determined to see what was different that they failed to see what was the same.

A good example is that brilliant and original historian, Walter Millis. Although he had spent a large portion of his life writing military history, Millis proclaimed that everything written before Hiroshima was simply worthless. One is forced to wonder about this matter of relevance. The wars in Korea and Vietnam were fought with conventional weapons, and conventional wisdom might have been applied with happier results. Deterrence theory was irrelevant, and limited war theories seem mainly to have misled the politicians as to the feasibility of their enterprises.

We must, of course, give credit where credit is due. During the 1950s, the military intellectuals effectively pointed out the limitations of massive retaliation doctrine proclaimed by John Foster Dulles. But this was an easy victory. Massive retaliation never rested on a firm foundation of either practicability or credibility. Furthermore, the Soviets aided and abetted the military intellectuals first by simply ignoring threats of massive retaliation and later by equaling and then surpassing the United States in nuclear capabilities.

A more impressive accomplishment of the new strategists was the discrediting of the idea of two scorpions in a bottle. Making use of systems analysis and other new methods, the strategists demolished the idea that mere possession of nuclear weapons guaranteed stability. The complicated requirements of effective deterrence were set forth with convincing logic.

When Kennedy became President, the military intellectuals achieved something like total victory. Gone was the missile gap. Gone was massive retaliation, and in its place was flexible response which claimed to have an exact and appropriate answer to all challenges, large and small. Again "overthink."

It is obvious from what I have said that historians have contributed little to the new strategy. Nearly all the writers have made some use of history, but few have had history as their main interest.

I confess that, when I began my study some years ago, I expected to discover a new social science called national security policy. I had some vague idea that a new discipline had emerged based on systems analysis, model building and game theory. According to some of the best authorities, these occult sciences have been useful in problem solving on the tactical and technical levels. Some of these same people have a suspicion, however, that the analysts may have influenced our political leaders to underestimate the importance of psychological, moral and political elements that vary with every historical situation.

The war in Vietnam has had a sobering effect, and the era of "over-think" is, I suspect, largely past. For the foreseeable future, the main interests of both the academic community and the public generally are apt to lie in those areas where strategy and the larger questions of public policy merge. There are precisely the areas where the historian has been, and can be, most useful.

In predicting a larger role for the historian, I hope I am not yielding to a disciplinary bias. I have already quoted Bernard Brodie, a political scientist, and Raymond Aron, a sociologist, as favoring greater attention to historical particularity. Recently, Herman Kahn deplored the lack of history in our general educational system, and he found it disturbing that so many people in the elaboration of their ideas were opposed, or at least uninterested, in any reality testing. In any case, the intellectual climate of the 1970s is vastly different from the period we have surveyed in this article, and that difference is apt to widen as the decade unfolds.

GEORGE C. HERRING

AMERICAN STRATEGY
IN VIETNAM
The Postwar Debate

Not since the Mexican War has debate over the use of military force to further national objectives so divided the nation as did the American involvement in southeast Asia, 1965–75. Hawks, doves, and counterinsurgency advocates argue over topics ranging from "we could have won with more," to "we could have won with a different strategy," to "we could not have won in this environment," to "we never should have been there in the first place." The problem of strategy is closely linked to American national purposes in this conflict. We sought to secure the right of self-determination for the peoples of South Vietnam. In this effort American leaders saw national interests served; stopping aggression here would stop it elsewhere (the Munich syndrome) and maintaining an independent South Vietnam would contribute to the balance of ideological power in southeast Asia (the equilibrium thesis). These attitudes colored the perceptions of how to conduct the war itself. One group sought victory through application of traditional American concepts of firepower and maneuver (in this case, through massive application of artillery and aerial bombardment combined with exceptional mobility supplied by the helicopter). In other words, they adhered to the type of warfare described in Russell Weigley's article. The other camp envisioned a counterinsurgency war with emphasis on winning the "hearts and minds" of the Vietnamese people. They advocated using a combination of economic and security assistance efforts designed to secure the countryside from the control of the guerrillas—the Vietcong.

Central to the American strategy is the think tank concept of "escalation." The idea was that one could gradually increase the level of pressure and pain upon the enemy so that they would eventually give up the effort as too costly. This led to the greatest American weakness in this conflict—misperceptions about the capacities and determination of the North Vietnamese. We did not escalate the conflict fast enough nor hard enough to compel the enemy to alter their ultimate objective, which was reunification of North and South Vietnam. Could we have done so? That is an unanswerable question.

George Herring, professor of history at the University of Kentucky and author of the popular America's Longest War: The United States and Vietnam (1979), traces the postwar debate over the failure to achieve the national objective in a review of writings of major participants and analysts. There emerged three basic positions in the postwar debate: the hawkish position, the counterinsurgency school, and the no-win war argument. Each of these arguments has weaknesses. Most observers conclude that the central contribution to American failure was a lack of a coherent strategy.

Two of the more perceptive military commentators on the Vietnam War appeared too late to be considered in Professor Herring's critique. In On Strategy: A Critical Analysis of the Vietnam War (1982), army colonel Harry G. Summers, Jr., took a different tack from any of Herring's three categories. He claimed the American failure resulted from a misplaced objective. Too much effort was devoted to the counterinsurgency war and not enough to preparing the South Vietnamese for the real war—the conventional juggernaut that led to Hanoi's victory in 1975. Although the Americans were successful in logistics and tactics, Colonel Summers found that the U.S. defense establishment failed to insure that those skills were "applied in pursuit of a sound strategy." In The 25-Year War: America's Military Role in Vietnam (1984), General Bruce Palmer, Jr., placed the principal blame for the Vietnam debacle on the failure of senior military leaders to present to the civilian leadership their disagreements with the administration's reliance on a military solution to the Indochina problem. Army Chief of Staff Harold K. Johnson later admitted that his greatest failure was an unwillingness to demand mobilization of the reserve components as a necessary component in the increased involvement that developed in 1965. Despite fundamental disagreements over war strategy, General Johnson refused to resign in 1967 to protest the stopping of the bombing in North Vietnam. The joint chiefs' lack of strategic conception reflected both a military disinclination toward strategic analysis and a "can-do" attitude regardless of misgivings.

All of this reflects, as Harry Coles noted in a previous article, the lack of military contribution to the evolution of American military strategic planning in the post–World War II era. As we suggest in the following article by General Flint, could one of the consequences of General MacArthur's dismissal be that military leaders avoided becoming active contributors in the evolving debate over national strategic policy? If so, did the senior military officials consequently find themselves engaged in operations with which they had been little involved during strategic conception?

To the surprise of many observers, the traumatic climax of the Vietnam War in 1975 did not provoke a great national debate on what had gone wrong. Quite the contrary, the first postwar years were marked by a conspicuous silence on the subject, almost as though the war had not happened. In the past few years, there have been sporadic and sometimes heated mini-debates. Vietnam lurked just beneath the surface of discussions of foreign and defense policies during the 1980 presidential campaign, although it came out into the open only once—in Ronald Reagan's "noble war" speech. More recently, it assumed a prominent role in the brief debate over the Reagan administration's decision to send military aid and advisers to El Salvador. In neither case, however, did the discussions really grapple with the fundamental issues posed by the war, and they disappeared from the public forum almost as quickly and mysteriously as they had emerged. Apparently, for many Americans, the Vietnam experience is still too painful to relive, too politically sensitive to dwell upon, or too unique to offer any useful lessons.

Although it has not captured the attention of the media or the public, a debate has nevertheless occurred, in the memoirs of participants, in government agencies, in private think tanks, and among scholars in the universities. This debate has already exerted subtle influence on our foreign and defense policies. In the event of some major external crisis in the near or even distant future, it may exert greater and more noticeable influence. It is therefore worthwhile, even though the war is not far behind us, to examine critically the positions being assumed and to evaluate the lessons being proclaimed. This essay will focus on the strategic dimension of the debate, the fundamental question of why the United States failed to achieve its objectives, although this issue cannot, of course, be entirely separated from the related problem of the causes and wisdom of American involvement.

It should be noted at the outset that the positions assumed in the current debate have not moved far beyond those advanced during the war itself. They have simply been documented, filled out in detail, and given the longer range perspective that the end of the war and the passage of time permits. For the sake of clarity, I have broken down the massive literature on Vietnam into three schools of thought, although inevitably there is some overlap among them and some nuances are lost.

THE HAWKS

First is what might be called the hawk point of view, since it parallels closely the arguments advanced by those labelled hawks in the debate of the 1960s. This view has been developed with considerable passion in the published memoirs of

General William Westmoreland and Admiral U. S. Grant Sharp. It is perhaps best stated in *Summons of the Trumpet,* a military history of the war covering the period 1961 to 1975 and written by Dave Richard Palmer, a U.S. Army officer who served in Vietnam. It is by no means the exclusive argument of military figures, however, nor is it accepted by all military figures who write on the war. In general, it is endorsed by the more conservative elements in American politics, and if the statements of President Reagan and Secretary of State Alexander Haig can be taken at face value, it now represents the official point of view.

The argument of the hawks, simply stated, is that the United States failed in Vietnam because it did not use its military power to best advantage. Responsibility for this failure rests primarily with the civilian leadership, particularly President Lyndon B. Johnson and Secretary of Defense Robert McNamara, who developed and imposed the ill-considered strategy of gradual response and hemmed in the military with so many restrictions that it could not do the job it was assigned.

Advocates of this point of view share a number of implicit assumptions. They do not all agree on the wisdom of the American commitment in Vietnam. Some commentators, President Reagan included, have argued that it was an altruistic attempt on the part of the United States to help a small country defend itself against a totalitarian neighbor bent on conquest. Some see it as having been necessary to forestall the advance of Communism across Asia and to maintain the credibility of America's global commitments. Others, however, regard it as an example of reckless overcommitment. Westmoreland himself, in retrospect, is sharply critical of the United States for "getting blindly committed in such a remote area." All agree, nevertheless, that the commitment, once made, should have been kept, no matter what level of force was required to do the job. The hawks, by and large, share an implicit faith in the ability of military power to achieve the stated ends of American policy. Their commentary on the war is almost exclusively military—it focusses on the use, or misuse, of military instruments and concerns itself scarcely at all with such problems as pacification and the political situation in South Vietnam.

Westmoreland, Sharp, and Palmer are especially critical of the conduct of the air war against North Vietnam. Sharp indicts the civilians in Washington, particularly McNamara and his "whiz kids," for ignoring "sound, time-vindicated principles of military strategy" in their direction of the air war. Instead of striking North Vietnam with immediate, devastating blows that could have crippled its capacity to wage war in the South, they compelled the Air Force and Navy to "peck away at seemingly random targets," always under "severe restrictions," nullifying America's "immensely superior firepower and technology" and producing a "strategy of defeat." Palmer generally agrees that however good gradualism in the use of air power may have seemed in theory, it was a disaster in practice. It left the initiative to the North Vietnamese and gave them time to adjust to the bombing. "Escalation was a built-in hazard," he adds, "and the point past which the foe would not dare step might very well turn out to be further than Washington would be willing to carry the conflict." Palmer is even more critical of the "overcentralized direction and skin-tight control exercised by Washington. Policy makers on the Potomac seemed to do everything but actually fly the aircraft," he complains. As a result, the United States did not hit the most important targets in North Vietnam and those hit were not struck decisively. The numerous bombing pauses initiated by Johnson for purely political purposes further mitigated the effects of American air power. Despite the restrictions, Palmer concludes, the bombing had significantly weakened North Vietnam's warmaking capacity by 1968, but just when it was beginning to take a toll it was curtailed for the sake of meaningless gestures from Hanoi.

Hawk writers agree, with few qualifications, that if American air power had been used as the Joint Chiefs of Staff advocated—a sharp, knockout blow—it could have decisively affected the outcome of the war. They point to Linebacker I and II, implemented by the Nixon administration in the Summer and late Fall of 1972, to suggest what it might have accomplished, arguing that these bombing campaigns forced North Vietnam to the conference table for serious negotiations and eventually led to a satisfactory agreement.

The hawk writers also defend Westmoreland's conduct of the ground war in South Vietnam. Westmoreland himself contends that once North Vietnam had committed significant numbers of regular troops to the war, he had no option but to adopt what came to be called the search and destroy strategy. South Vietnam could not be stabilized or Hanoi forced to negotiate until the North Vietnamese main forces had been eliminated. Palmer more or less agrees. He concedes that a strategy of attrition was no strategy at all, but he goes on to argue that Westmoreland was placed in an impossible position by his civilian superiors. His mission was imprecisely defined, and he was given only the vaguest notion what resources would be available to him. He was absolutely forbidden from pursuing the enemy into his sanctuaries in Laos, Cambodia, and across the demilitarized zone, squandering the initiative and violating every basic principle of warfare. As a consequence, Westmoreland had no choice but to wage a war of attrition in South Vietnam, a clear sign, Palmer concludes, that the United States was "strategically bankrupt" in Vietnam.

As with the air war, however, Palmer argues that Westmoreland's strategy could have worked if the United States had continued to prosecute the war vigorously. The heavy losses inflicted by U.S. search and destroy operations in 1966 and 1967 forced Hanoi to alter its strategy, culminating in the Tet

Offensive of 1968, which turned out to be an unmitigated disaster for North Vietnam and created opportunities for a knockout blow by the United States. This opportunity was not seized, of course, and the hawk writers generally blame a timid civilian leadership and an irresponsible media. Ignoring massive evidence to the contrary, a panicky and perhaps spiteful media overreacted to the initial battles of Tet, portraying a disastrous enemy defeat as a dramatic enemy victory, creating widespread public disillusionment at home, and forcing a harried and irresolute Johnson to reject Westmoreland's plan for a major counteroffensive and seek a negotiated settlement. "It was like two boxers in a ring," Westmoreland concludes, "one having the other on the ropes, close to a knockout, when the apparent winner's second inexplicably throws in the towel."

In a variation on the same theme, many writers of this persuasion go on to argue that once again, in the years 1973–1975, the United States snatched defeat from the jaws of victory. Through the timely and decisive use of military power in 1972, the Nixon administration secured a peace settlement that Westmoreland had described as "defective in many ways but theoretically workable." But a vengeful Congress, pandering to public weariness of Vietnam, denied Nixon the means to uphold the agreement and ruthlessly slashed American military aid to South Vietnam, crippling the morale of an ally of more than 20 years and encouraging North Vietnam to launch the last offensive. "Congress, in effect, handed South Vietnam over to Hanoi," Senator John Tower has recently observed, initiating a drastic decline in America's global position which if not arrested could eventually prove disastrous.

Hawk writers generally concur on the lessons to be learned from Vietnam. Alarmed by America's presumed weakness in the face of the Soviet menace, they call for a vigorous defense of the nation's global interests and an increase in military power commensurate with that task. Vietnam underscores, in their view, not the limitations on the use of force in the modern world, but the urgency of using military power decisively. Terming American handling of the conflict a "shameful national blunder," Westmoreland stresses that henceforth the nation should not engage in war unless it has a clear idea why it is fighting and is prepared to see the war through to a successful conclusion. "When there is a threat of war," he adds, "our military leaders deserve a stronger voice in policy-making. When our political leaders commit us to war, the military should be given the strongest voice." Once committed, he goes on to say, the nation should heed an old Oriental saying: "It takes the full strength of a tiger to kill a rabbit." In other words, the United States must use "timely and appropriate force" to end the conflict. Finally, when "our national reputation and men's lives are at stake, the news media must show a more convincing sense of responsibility then it did during the Vietnam war."

THE COUNTERINSURGENCY SCHOOL

A second school of thought, similar to the hawks in some ways but drastically different in others, might be loosely labelled the counterinsurgency school. These writers by and large accept the validity and importance of the American commitment in Vietnam. They generally agree with the hawks that the war could and should have been won, and they too feel that American strategy was badly flawed. They place more blame, however, on the military than on the civilians for the strategic failure; their fundamental conclusion being that the United States, and particularly American military leaders, attempted to fight a conventional war in a revolutionary war setting, thereby ensuring ultimate failure. Had the United States adapted its strategy to the type of conflict it was engaged in, the war could have been won.

Like the hawk position, this interpretation is by no means new. It was pressed relentlessly during the war by such critics of American strategy as the British counterinsurgency expert, Sir Robert Thompson, U.S. Army officer John Vann, Ambassadors Henry Cabot Lodge and Robert Komer, the old Vietnam hand, Edward Lansdale, and journalist David Halberstam. Although it is somewhat muted, this view also pervades the *Pentagon Papers,* and it was promoted during the war by the civilian Pentagon officials who helped engineer McNamara's conversion and who influenced Clark Clifford to undertake a full-scale review of American strategy after Tet.

The most articulate postwar advocate of the counterinsurgency point of view is Guenter Lewy, Professor of Political Science at the University of Massachusetts, whose *America in Vietnam* (1978) set off a storm of protest. Characterized by one reviewer as the "first salvo in the refighting of the Vietnam War," Lewy's book drew particularly heavy fire from former doves for its vigorous defense of the United States against charges of war crimes and atrocities, and was dismissed by some angry critics as a "whitewash." While defending American conduct of the war in legal and moral terms, Lewy harshly indicts the United States for its strategic failure, and his book contains a detailed and systematic critique of the way the war was fought.

Lewy waffles a bit on the fundamental question of the necessity of American intervention. He concedes that American policy makers may have exaggerated the importance of Vietnam in the early stages of involvement. Like Henry Kissinger (and many of the hawks), however, he eventually concludes that the longstanding commitment in Vietnam established a vital interest that had to be upheld. The basic mistake was not intervention but fighting the war in a manner that made failure likely if not inevitable.

Lewy concurs with the hawks that the air war against North Vietnam was ineffective, but there the similarity ends. He categorically rejects the argument that the Rolling Thunder campaign caused North Vietnam insurmountable problems. Certainly it caused some economic disruption and manpower dislocation, but it did not significantly affect North Vietnam's ability to maintain essential services in the North or to infiltrate men and supplies into the South. Nor did it appreciably weaken Hanoi's will. "On the contrary," he concludes, "the bombing appeared to have engendered a psychological climate of common danger which aided the government in winning support for its demands of stern sacrifices and facilitated other measures of control." Like contemporary critics of the bombing, particularly the Pentagon civilians, Lewy also concludes that the costs far exceeded any gains, noting that they were not restricted to dollar costs, which were high, but must also be calculated in terms of diminished American prestige abroad and increased opposition to the war at home.

Lewy flatly rejects the view that a more intensive bombing campaign could have produced the desired results without incurring unacceptable risks. To have forced North Vietnam to stop fighting, he argues, would have required, at a minimum, cutting off all imports from the Soviet Union and China. Before the advent of the "smart bomb," he contends, the United States probably lacked the technical capacity to do this. More important, fear of Chinese intervention precluded the sort of air campaign the military advocated. Lewy concedes that Johnson's fears of Chinese intervention may have been exaggerated. But there was no way to know at what point they might have intervened, he adds, and Johnson would have been foolish to take undue risks in this regard.

In any case, the "sharp blow" air war promoted by the military probably would not have stopped North Vietnam from sending men and supplies to the South or forced it to sue for peace. This argument rests on an exaggerated notion of the capabilities of strategic airpower, one persuasively challenged by the results of the strategic bombing surveys conducted after World War II. Lewy dismisses out of hand the hawk argument that Linebacker I and II were decisive strategically. The bombing campaign of the Summer of 1972 may have contributed to North Vietnam's decision to negotiate later in the year, and the so-called "Christmas bombing" may have facilitated the signing of the 1973 cease-fire. In order to consider these results as "conclusive proof of the decisiveness of air power," he argues, "one would have to be convinced that North Vietnam, in signing the Paris agreements, put itself at a serious disadvantage, and the evidence for this assumption is lacking." The cease-fire terms did not significantly hamper North Vietnam in the next stage of the war. By no stretch of the imagination can they be regarded as an American victory, moreover, since Nixon yielded vital points he had steadfastly refused to concede in 1969. There were no major targets left in North Vietnam in 1972 short of obliteration of the country, and yet Hanoi had not been compelled to withdraw its troops from the

South and it seems clear that no continuation of the bombing at any level could have achieved this end. That the bombing did not "bring final victory is no reflection on the true importance of air power," Lewy concludes, "only a refutation of the illusions of air power enthusiasts."

Lewy is equally critical of Westmoreland's search and destroy strategy. It represented, he says, the "traditional attack mission of the infantry," but since the "setting of a counterinsurgency war in the environment of Vietnam posed anything but traditional problems, the results of this conventional way of thinking and acting were to prove a great disappointment." Search and destroy contained numerous flaws. It drastically underestimated the ability of the enemy to match or even exceed U.S. escalation. It diverted attention and resources away from pacification, which, in Lewy's view, was the indispensable ingredient for success in Vietnam. As carried out by American forces under Westmoreland and Abrams, it was counterproductive. The destruction of the countryside, the creation of millions of refugees, the inflation that stemmed from the American buildup, all further weakened the already fragile economic, political, and social system of South Vietnam. Moreover, the results attained were no more than ephemeral. Large numbers of enemy troops were killed, but they were quickly replaced. Enemy forces were driven out of their strongholds in South Vietnam, but once American units went on to fight somewhere else, they returned. Lewy flatly rejects the argument that the sanctuaries enjoyed by North Vietnam were crucial to the American failure. In the final analysis, he argues, the war had to be won in South Vietnam if American goals were to be attained. Military action in Laos and Cambodia and across the demilitarized zone might have hampered North Vietnam's supply network, but it would not have ensured the attainment of American goals, and it might have complicated their achievement and raised the costs much higher.

Lewy assigns primary blame for the strategic debacle of Vietnam to the military, charging them with a singular lack of imagination and a rigid adherence to traditions and doctrine which had little relevance in Vietnam. Borrowing an argument earlier advanced by Robert Komer and developed in greater detail by Robert Gallucci, he emphasizes the importance of tradition, professionalism, and organizational pressures in shaping military strategy. "The military," he says, "like all bureaucracies encountering a new situation for which they were not prepared and in which they did not know what to do, did what they knew to do. That happened to be the inappropriate thing." Indeed, he argues, even after it was obvious that the strategy was not working and even after changes had been ordered by the civilian leadership in 1968, things continued much as before, the changes actually effected by Abrams being little more than superficial. The rigid attitude of the military, and particularly the army, he concludes, is best summed up by the senior officer who stated: "I'll be damned if I permit the United States

Army, its institutions, its doctrine, and its traditions to be destroyed just to win this lousy war."

Lewy is not uncritical of the civilian leadership. In contrast to the hawks, however, he argues that they exercised too little control, providing no clearcut strategic guidelines to commanders in the field. Moreover, Johnson failed to offer to a confused and uncertain nation a convincing rationale for the war. It would have been better, Lewy argues, if the President had asked for a declaration of war in 1965 to ensure the popular backing he needed. He also blames the media for its one-sided publicity which contributed decisively to the growing war-weariness at home. His study is essentially an analysis of the military conduct of the war, however, and the emphasis is on the strategic failure.

Was there an alternative? Echoing Thompson, Komer, Lansdale, and others, Lewy suggests that with a proper strategy the United States could have prevailed in Vietnam. In lieu of Westmoreland's war of attrition, he argues, the United States might have implemented a strategy of population security better attuned to the realities of the type of war being fought in Vietnam. Such a strategy would have been based on established principles of counterinsurgency warfare, instead of conventional war doctrine. It might have followed the Civic Action program developed by the Army's Special Forces. The Vietnamization program initiated in the aftermath of Tet might have been developed much earlier, although along different lines, the South Vietnamese being trained and equipped for counterinsurgency rather than conventional war. These essential methods could have been joined, at some critical juncture, by a campaign of intense military pressures against North Vietnam. The United States might have assumed greater responsibility for the government of South Vietnam, perhaps even taking on the role of the "good colonialist" who manages affairs temporarily until native leaders can be prepared to take over. "While one cannot be sure that these different strategies, singly or in combination, would necessarily have brought about a different outcome," he concludes rather cautiously, "neither can one take their failure for granted."

In reaching this qualifiedly upbeat conclusion, Lewy is trying to make a larger and more important point. He expresses grave concern that an overreaction to failure in Vietnam may have crippling consequences for American foreign policy and hence for world stability. His arguments are designed at least in part to combat such a trend. Had the war been conducted differently, he argues, it could have been successfully ended, and this must be kept in mind in addressing future international crises. The United States "cannot and should not be the world's policeman, but, it can be argued, the U.S. has a moral obligation to support nations in their endeavor to remain independent when we, and we alone, possess the means to do so." The fundamental lesson of Vietnam is not indiscriminately to avoid all similar situations in the future, but to adapt our methods to the conflicts in which we become engaged.

AMERICANS AND LIMITED WAR

A third school of thought takes direct issue with both the hawks and the counterinsurgents. This group concludes that neither the unrestricted use of American military power nor the application of counterinsurgency techniques would likely have produced a more satisfactory outcome. On the contrary, they argue, conditions in Vietnam itself, our own historical experience, and our estimation of the importance of Vietnam as opposed to other perceived interests, virtually guaranteed that we would not achieve our objectives at a cost we regarded as acceptable. The emphasis here is *not* on an alleged failure of strategy or will, but on the intractable nature of the problem itself. Vietnam is regarded not primarily as a cause of America's present impotence, but rather as a symptom of its general decline from the position of world preeminence it enjoyed briefly after World War II, the result of broad historical forces beyond its control.

Like the other points of view, this argument is not new. It was advanced at the time not only by liberal doves but also by conservative intellectuals such as Hans Morgenthau who in the early stages of involvement warned that Vietnam might not be susceptible to American power and influence. Similarly, those who now endorse this position represent diverse political persuasions. Included in the ranks are many former doves, most of them liberals, who view intervention as misguided or worse. But one of the most sophisticated recent statements has been made by Robert E. Osgood, a distinguished Johns Hopkins political scientist. Osgood was one of the most important academic theorists on the subject of limited war in the 1950s, and his recent book, *Limited War Revisited,* although brief, is one of the more significant contributions to the postwar debate on Vietnam.

Those who share this point of view accept, without major qualification, Lewy's argument that the sort of escalation proposed by hawks at the time and in retrospect would not have produced the desired results. Osgood concedes that Johnson's fear of Chinese intervention may have been exaggerated. "But probably the greatest constraint," he adds, "and the basic reason for gradualism, was simply the tacit assumption that U.S. interest in the war did not warrant even a small risk of widening the war politically, or indeed, of enlarging it in any way beyond the minimum measures that seemed to be necessary to avoid defeat." In any event, he argues, it is unlikely that even massive escalation would have dampened Hanoi's fanatical commitment to achieve its goals. Nor would it have stopped the guerrilla warfare in the South or enabled the South Vietnamese government to "overcome the political weaknesses that enabled such a war to continue."

For similar reasons, however, Osgood and others emphatically reject Lewy's contention that an imaginative program of counterinsurgency, even if adopted early and applied systematically, would have produced favorable results.

They concur with Sir Robert Thompson that the United States did not really commit itself to pacification until it was too late, but the major problem, they contend, was not the lack of commitment or the methods used. Rather, it was inherent in the conditions in Vietnam and was probably beyond the control of the United States. South Vietnam was not a real nation in the sense that we understand the word, and it lacked most of the basic ingredients for nationhood. It came into being almost inadvertently, an accident of history, with a little push from Ngo Dinh Diem and John Foster Dulles. It was, Osgood stresses, "a fractured society with no experience in self-government and no unifying traditions or sense of nationality, governed by urban elites remote from the village and peasantry, dependent on an incompetent civil service and an untrustworthy army." A "nation" such as this was peculiarly vulnerable to insurgency. From the outset, moreover, it faced a disciplined and determined adversary, with an ideology adapted to Vietnamese political culture, skilled in the methods of revolutionary warfare perfected in the ten year struggle with France, and fanatically committed to its goals. Writers of this persuasion thus conclude that the sources of American failure resided in conditions in Vietnam itself—a fragmented, weak ally, with an ineffectual client government and a tightly organized and determined enemy.

Many postwar writers question whether there was a satisfactory solution to this problem. To have corrected the deficiencies in South Vietnamese society would have required drastic—indeed revolutionary—change. "But the very forces on which we relied and which we maintained in power," the Harvard political scientist Stanley Hoffmann observes, "were the least capable of such a feat." Other groups to whom the United States might have turned were suspect on one ground or another, and in any event, to undercut the very regime we were supporting in time of war was unthinkable. The United States could not have effected the necessary change without assuming direct responsibility for running the country. But the "good colonialist" role, as Lewy calls it, ran against the American grain, and the vast cultural gap which separated us from our ally and the profound antiforeignism of the Vietnamese would have made such a role difficult if not impossible.

Osgood and others single out additional flaws in the argument that counterinsurgency techniques would have produced a different outcome. The United States was not prepared by temperament or recent experience to conduct such a war—that is precisely the reason it fought as it did. To have waged an effective counterinsurgency war would also have required a long-term American commitment, substantial military forces, most likely heavy casualties, and there is nothing to suggest that the American public would have been more willing to support this kind of war than the one that was actually waged between 1965 and 1973.

By neglecting "local circumstances" and concluding that "small Vietnam was manageable by us," Hoffman concludes, the United States snared itself in a cruel trap. "The goal, a 'free' South Vietnam, could only be reached, if at all, through means that were either repugnant or unlikely to work. For a successful outcome would have required either the physical annihilation of North Vietnam, obliterated from the air or occupied on the ground, or else the establishment of a genuine South Vietnamese nation." Limited involvement could not ensure victory; massive involvement was unacceptable. Never really coming to grips with its dilemma, or perhaps even fully comprehending it, the United States "merely held back the tide at a terrifying human cost." Paraphrasing a statement made by Elliot Richardson shortly after the fall of Saigon in 1975, Hoffman concludes with more than a touch of sarcasm that "surely the same result could have been achieved sooner at less cost."

The conclusion that Vietnam was not susceptible to our will is not an easy one to accept. It runs counter to the American temper, the can-do spirit, which, however frayed in the aftermath of Vietnam, still lurks deep in the national consciousness. It is scarcely a comforting conclusion in the complex, extraordinarily confusing, and frequently hostile, world we face today. It is nevertheless one Osgood and Hoffmann suggest that we must learn to live with.

THE LESSONS AND THE FUTURE

Like the hawks and counterinsurgents, those who regard Vietnam as a classic, no-win situation have attempted to derive lessons from the American experience there. But they differ sharply in the lessons they have found.

Some have concluded that Vietnam was a unique situation, so unique that virtually nothing can or should be drawn from it in terms of guidelines for future policy decisions. They take quite literally James Thomson's tongue-in-cheek observation of some years ago that the "central lesson" to be learned is that we should never again "take on the job of trying to defeat a nationalist anti-colonial movement under indigenous communist control in former French Indochina," a lesson Thomson redundantly added, "of less than universal relevance." Vietnam, some say, was a fluke, an abberation, and our foreign policy should not be redesigned on the basis of its alleged lessons. We should continue where we left off in the mid-1960s, playing much the same role as guardians of world order. It seems entirely possible in the light of recent events in Iran and Afghanistan that this view may gain considerable popular acceptance.

Others have gone very near to the opposite extreme. In his provocative critique of lessons learned thus far, Earl Ravenal sees Vietnam not as unique but as all too typical of the problems the United States is likely to encounter if it attempts to maintain in the troubled world of the 1980s the policies it pursued in the 1950s and 1960s. He accordingly proposes what can only be described as a neo-isolationist alternative. The United States should strive for the maximum economic self-sufficiency. It should liquidate as quickly as possible the many commitments left over from the Cold War. It must take drastic measures, he concludes, to adjust to a world that for the foreseeable future will be fragmented, unstable, and unfriendly, to what he calls a "second best order of things."

Concluding that neither of these extreme alternatives is feasible or desirable, Hoffmann and Osgood seek ground between the two. Hoffmann emphasizes that in the pluralistic, fragmented world of the 1980s, the United States cannot realistically expect to defend its interests through economic and military superiority. He therefore advocates shifting the focus of American policy from maintaining primacy to promoting new forms of world order. In addition to developing a central balance of power with the Soviet Union and contributing to regional balances based largely on local forces, the nation should assist in the creation of viable rules of international conduct and effective multilateral institutions that can assist in the resolution of conflicts and promote a more stable, secure, and mutually beneficial international environment. Such an order, he cautions, cannot be American imposed or based on American values. It will by no means ensure that the United States will have its way in the world. Quite the contrary, it is likely to mean sacrifice of some of the advantages we have taken for granted. In the long run, however, it may offer the best hope for survival.

At least partly on the basis of the Vietnam experience, Hoffmann advocates sharp breaks from past practices in meeting the dual challenges posed by the Soviet Union and Third World nationalism. He concedes that conflict with the Soviet Union will be an integral feature of world politics for the forseeable future, and that checking Soviet advances is indispensable to the larger concept of world order. Third World nationalism, he adds, will likely remain hostile to the United States. The challenge to American policy is to separate the two as much as possible. In dealing with Third World nationalism, the United States should pursue a policy of "non-collision," refraining from intervention in the domestic affairs of these nations and avoiding any sort of conflict that might fan the latent anti-Americanism and give the Soviets opportunities to exploit. Should Communists threaten to take power in these countries, the United States must exercise discrimination, asking whether their success would significantly add to Soviet power or diminish that of the United States, and examining carefully the costs of maintaining the status quo. As long as local Communists retain some degree of independence, the United States should pursue a policy of "prophylactic accommodation," using every available means to disconnect the local situation from the central balance of power and to encourage diversity. Military intervention can be justified, if at all, only in cases where the Soviets directly threaten the central balance or where their clients threaten regional balances.

Osgood's approach is more conservative. Less optimistic than Hoffmann about the prospects for a new world order and more concerned with the immediate threat posed by the drastic increase in Soviet military power, he concludes that a policy of containment in some form is both "necessary and unavoidable." Such a policy, he quickly adds, must avoid the excesses and overcommitment of the past. It cannot, as before, be an "all-encompassing rationale." Rather, it must form "one component of a complex global equilibrium." Those applying the policy, particularly when making crucial decisions on possible military intervention, must heed the lessons of Vietnam, however murky these remain.

Osgood suggests a few modest lessons to serve as guideposts. He cautions, first, that any lessons drawn must remain "highly contingent," since in any future situation the circumstances are bound to be different. Such lessons can only be applied to a similar conflict, moreover, "a large-scale protracted local war in the Third World at a place of minor national interest." The obvious lesson of Vietnam is that the United States should not intervene unless the war can be won quickly or the Soviet Union would exploit American non-intervention in a way detrimental to its vital interests. It is equally apparent, however, that these factors will be difficult to weigh at the point of intervention. "Considering the variety of conditions that might characterize such a war," Osgood concludes, "one can prudently generalize only to the extent of saying that henceforth U.S. interests . . . must not be assessed only in terms of a general commitment to stopping the expansion of Communism or defeating Communist aggression." The intrinsic importance of the country involved must be considered, as well as the possible impact of its loss on the balance of power with the Soviet Union. "This lesson at least puts a greater burden of justification on the advocates of intervention."

Evaluating the prospects of eventual success or failure poses even more difficult problems. It is very difficult to determine, before it is too late, the possibilities of a friendly government saving itself with outside support. Vietnam does suggest, Osgood stresses, that "if indirect assistance is not sufficient, the direct participation of foreign troops is not likely to succeed either and could make the situation worse." Under most circumstances, moreover, direct participation is likely to lead to a protracted war that may well become unpopular at home. Rapid and intense escalation, since it will probably enlarge the war, may not avoid this result. The lessons that may be derived from Vietnam, Osgood concludes, are "so qualified that they can be no more than cautionary items on a very long agenda of relevant considerations. At best these lessons serve as antidotes, if we need any, to the grand simplifications and ingenious strategems of the Kennedy era."

CONCLUSION

The debate on Vietnam, thus far muted and beneath the surface, seems no closer to resolution today than it was during the war. At this point, there is no consensus among the elites or the mass public. Most of the questions raised cannot be answered definitively—we cannot know what would have happened if we had done things differently—and they will undoubtedly remain controversial. Although these questions go to the heart of some of the major foreign policy issues we confront today, in time, as a result of circumstances that cannot be foreseen, the debate may pass quietly away and become the exclusive preserve of historians. Or it may explode into the public forum once again and become part of another great debate on American foreign policy. It is instructive, in this regard, to recall that the perceived lessons of World War I had their greatest impact on American foreign policy in the 1930s and that the perceived lessons of World War II were central to our commitments in Vietnam in the 1960s. The only thing that can be predicted with certainty is that the debate on one of the most traumatic and convulsive episodes in American history will continue in some form.

CONFLICTS OF CONTAINMENT AND CONTINGENCY

ROY K. FLINT

THE RELIEF OF MACARTHUR

*F*ew events have more polarized American public opinion than President Harry S. Truman's relief of General of the Army Douglas MacArthur in 1951. In the aftermath of the worst defeat in American military history, the Chinese Communist offensive against the United Nations forces in North Korea, President Harry S. Truman fired General MacArthur as commander of American and United Nations forces in the Far East. But that defeat was not the cause of MacArthur's relief. Rather, it was his increasing insubordination to directions from Washington. MacArthur acted increasingly like an "American Caesar" who crossed his Rubicon when he undertook to engage in diplomatic negotiations with the Chinese. For President Truman this was the last straw. But there can be little doubt that the administration's maladroit handling of the affair contributed to public discontent and made MacArthur a more important and more popular figure than he might otherwise have been.

Those who heard MacArthur's "old soldiers never die, they just fade away" conclusion to a dramatic farewell address to Congress following the event will never forget it. MacArthur appealed to fundamental American values—"there is no substitute for victory." The country was frustrated with a no-win war. It ran against a tradition of eventual victory that John Shy, in the last article in this collection, finds to be a cornerstone of the American military tradition.

The president was not without his supporters. Truman had a tradition of military subordination to the civilian authority on his side, as well as the Joint Chiefs of Staff who feared the Korean War was a Soviet ruse to draw America away from defending the more critical European theater. To counter the image of General MacArthur as representing a unified front of military opinion, the administration sent to a congressional committee investigating the MacArthur sacking an array of distinguished officers backing the president's decision. It was a classic confrontation between a general and a president. As in the case of the relief of General George McClellan in the Civil War, the president won. But it was not without its costs. Politically the Democratic party was saddled with the image of getting the country into wars—Woodrow Wilson in World War I, Franklin Roosevelt in World War II, and now Truman in Korea. Moreover, the stalemate in Korea caused many to label Truman and the Democrats as soft on communism. Undoubtedly it contributed to the Democrats' loss of the White House to Dwight Eisenhower in 1952.

Brigadier General Roy K. Flint was an infantry company commander in Korea and a battalion commander in Vietnam. After receiving his doctorate from Duke University, he began a career with the United States Military Academy's history department. Recently he became dean of the USMA Academic Board. In this excerpt from a West Point military history textbook, he provides a balanced treatment of the emotional Truman-MacArthur controversy.

General Flint avoids making conclusions about this event. Did it cause the American military leaders to avoid political issues? Did it lead them to refrain from telling the political leadership in the 1960s of their misgivings about the involvement in Vietnam? In 1967, Joint Chiefs of Staff Chairman General Earl Wheeler and the service chiefs were on the verge of resignation over policy decisions made relative to that conflict. But in the final analysis, they decided against it. And, did MacArthur's case allow strategic thought to fall into the hands of the civilian defense strategic community, which did not bear the burden of the political or military decisions, as described in Harry Coles's earlier article? Was, as some commentators have suggested, one of the greatest tragedies of Vietnam that no senior commanders resigned over a war whose tactical decisions were often run from the White House? In other words, did the MacArthur relief excessively subordinate professional military decisions to the whims of the defense intellectuals and political leaders without the best advice of military leaders?

Like the protagonist in a classical tragedy, MacArthur hastened his own ruin as the consequence of a defect in character that was responsible for both his greatness and his downfall. His tragic flaw was arrogance and overbearing pride.

From the beginning of the war, MacArthur had relied upon his reputation and strong personality to achieve his ends. Still the national hero, his hauteur was accepted as a natural trait of a great old soldier. In fact, one could argue that without his arrogant treatment of friends and enemies alike, he would never have been able to accumulate the forces he used so boldly to surprise the North Koreans at Inchon. On a more mundane level, the trait caused nothing but trouble. Even before the intervention of the Chinese, the general and the President had clashed over American policy regarding Taiwan. Early in the war, MacArthur had made an ill-advised visit to Chiang Kai-shek to discuss their mutual interests in East Asia. A public statement issued by Chiang hinted at secret agreements between the two, and cast MacArthur more in the light of an independent sovereign than an American general. Truman was irritated, but inclined to overlook the indiscretion. Later, in a letter to the Veterans of Foreign Wars, MacArthur stressed the strategic importance of Taiwan and called for continued American control over the island. Just as the United States might profitably use Taiwan as a base against China, so too would it be a formidable threat to the United States in the Pacific if controlled by the Chinese.

Because the United States position on Taiwan in Congress and the UN was to deny any territorial ambitions or special relationship with Chiang's domain, Truman directed MacArthur to withdraw the letter before it became public. Although MacArthur protested innocence of any overt attempt to embarrass the administration, Truman was indignant, and considered relieving MacArthur as early as August 26, 1950. Thereafter, MacArthur confined his criticism—primarily concerning restrictions on his use of combat power—to private official channels between himself and the JCS. Nevertheless, he created great concern in Washington and allied capitals when he lifted the restraining line on nonAsian troops in October. Similarly, he startled his superiors when he proposed bombing the Yalu River bridges in November. But these disagreements had been worked out quietly. More serious was MacArthur's erratic fluctuation of moods in response to evidence of Chinese intervention in November; his alternating optimism and pessimism began to undermine confidence in his military judgment. Still, all criticism had been kept private, and it was only after the Chinese intervened that he decided to take his case to the public.

With his historical position threatened by the defeat of the UN Command in North Korea, MacArthur spoke sharply in his own defense. Early in December, he complained to the press that the restrictions placed upon him were "without precedent in military history." President Truman smoldered, as by inference his administration had been blamed for the defeat along the Ch'ongch'on River. For the second time, the President considered relieving MacArthur. More public criticism in the first week of December caused the President to issue an Executive order to his Cabinet chiefs requiring government officials to clear all public statements concerning foreign policy with the Department of State and those concerning military affairs with the Department of Defense. Clearly, the order was aimed at MacArthur. The general once again resorted to official channels to communicate his views about his government's policy. As discussed earlier, he proposed retaliatory measures against China and repeated them frequently, but always properly, through the JCS. Then, on

February 13, 1951, he told the press that unless he was permitted to attack the Chinese in their sanctuary, he could not hope to move north of the 38th Parallel in strength. Again, on March 7, he reminded the nation that a new strategy for war against the Chinese—presumably, his—had yet to be formulated. Both of these statements were in violation of the President's Executive order of December 6.

The crisis reached its peak in mid-March. Encouraged by Ridgway's offensive, the administration decided to renew its efforts for negotiation in hopes that the Chinese might now be more receptive to a truce. The President's advisers reasoned that since the CCF and North Koreans had been driven north of the 38th Parallel, the objective of UN operations—that is, the ejection of the aggressors from South Korea—had been achieved. Further, unification of the peninsula should and could be accomplished without further fighting. Placing the prestige of the President behind the proposal, Truman's staff drafted a message to the Chinese Government, offering to negotiate a settlement of the war. On March 20, the JCS forwarded the general contents of the President's message to MacArthur, making it clear that further coordination with allies in the UN was necessary before it could be put in final form. At the same time, they asked him to comment on what latitude he needed in his directive to insure successful operations in North Korea and the continued security of forces. MacArthur replied that the restrictions placed on his forces prevented him from mounting large-scale operations in North Korea leading to occupation, and that, therefore, his current directives were adequate. Then, to the shock of the President and his advisers, on March 24 MacArthur issued his own "ultimatum" to the enemy, kicking the pins from under the President's initiative. Brimming with new-found confidence, the general claimed that the recent success of UN military forces revealed the CCF to be overrated in all aspects of combat power, except numerical strength. Despite the restrictions placed on UN military activities and the advantages accruing to the enemy, the Chinese were incapable of achieving their goal of unifying the peninsula under Communist rule. Ignoring the intention of the President to invite negotiations, MacArthur went on to say, "I stand ready at any time to confer in the field with the Commander-in-Chief of the enemy . . ." to find a way to achieve the goals of the UN without further fighting.

President Truman was furious. Not only had MacArthur pre-empted Presidential prerogatives and once again criticized the policy of the United States, but he had also frightened UN members, who now wondered just who was directing the American war effort. The least of MacArthur's sins was violation of the December 6 directive on public statements. Technically, MacArthur had stayed within his authority as Commander-in-Chief, UN Command. He had not seen the full text of the President's message, and had clearly dealt with military matters only in his own announcement. Nonetheless, he had acted at cross-purposes with both his President and the UN. Truman interpreted this to be a direct challenge to his authority as Commander-in-Chief. He could no longer tolerate what he saw as insubordination.

As it turned out, the chain of events that ultimately led to MacArthur's relief was already underway. On March 20, MacArthur had written to Joseph W. Martin, the minority (Republican) leader of the House of Representatives, expressing his views on American foreign policy. In that letter, which was a response to Martin's request for comments, MacArthur repeated his belief that Asia was as important as Europe, and that the war in Korea should be pressed to victory. On April 5, close on the heels of the negotiations incident, Martin released the contents of MacArthur's letter. The next day, Truman started the process through which MacArthur would be relieved from command on April 11.

From a historical point of view, the drama of this incident obscured crucial problems endemic to the Korean situation in which the President and MacArthur found themselves involved. MacArthur's relief shocked the American people, for he represented traditions and widely held attitudes about the meaning of victory. His disagreement with Truman's policy of seeking a settlement short of enemy capitulation was shared by many Americans. Although short-lived, the clamor on his behalf amounted to a sizable political uprising, enjoyed and encouraged by the President's political opposition. Pressing their advantage, Republican Congressmen forced a senatorial investigation of the facts behind the incident. During May and June, lengthy hearings, which, for the most part, were open to public scrutiny, enabled MacArthur's advocates to vie with administration spokesmen in a political struggle over the history and future of American foreign policy. As the contending arguments were aired, and after the emotionalism surrounding the general's return to the United States died down, a consensus emerged among Americans that generally supported Truman's actions. Thus, in the end, the President won widespread support for his views that America's real interests lay with her European and NATO allies, and that the fighting in Korea should be contained and ended as quickly as possible to avoid a widening of the war. Nevertheless, agreement with Truman's overall view did not imply support for the implementation of his policies. Throughout the last two years of the war, frustrated critics decried the difficult negotiations, and condemned the wasteful and seemingly meaningless war of attrition fought along the line of contact in Korea. Eventually, disenchantment with protracted war became the major political issue in the Presidential election of 1952, and played a large part in the victory of Dwight D. Eisenhower.

Less conspicuous, but perhaps more important to the military profession than the political effects of MacArthur's relief, was the impact on the American system of command. First, the traditional supremacy of civilian authority over military command was affirmed. Even though partisan Republican support for MacArthur grew hysterical at times, few seriously doubted that the facts in the case warranted the relief of a general who challenged a constitutional principle. It is possible to argue, at least in theory, that MacArthur's loyalty was to the Constitution, rather than to the political administration that was temporarily running the government. MacArthur considered it his duty to speak out on issues that he thought were vital to the security of his country. If he was stifled, who then would warn the country of danger? Nevertheless, MacArthur's oath of office demanded that he obey the legal orders of his superiors. This he repeatedly failed to do when he defied the Executive order of December 6 requiring the clearance of public statements by senior government officials.

For failing seriously to consider consolidation short of the border, the nation's senior military leaders must take responsibility. The Department of Defense and the Joint Chiefs of Staff, relatively new organizations trying to localize the first potentially dangerous war in the nuclear age, were at first prudently cautious. Overburdened by their responsibilities, however, they too easily abandoned their wary approach. The Joint Chiefs, conservative in their response to the Inchon plan and then overbold in their assessment of the risks to be incurred by crossing the 38th Parallel, failed to see their inconsistency, and permitted their error to be built into the President's decision to cross. Moreover, after the spectacular success at Inchon they were only too willing to give the victorious MacArthur wide latitude in winding up the whole Korean affair as they concentrated their attention on the rearmament of the United States and the reinforcement of NATO. As a consequence, the Joint Chiefs saw the drive into North Korea through the eyes of MacArthur. Too late, they realized that the military situation was not as he had portrayed it.

But what were they to do? The Joint Chiefs, as well as the President and his top civilian advisers, were grappling with an entirely new experience. Never before had the direction of battle contained such far-reaching implications as it did in Korea in the nuclear age. In World War II, decentralization of authority and responsibility to unified military commanders was found to be the only effective way to direct the efforts of air, sea, and ground forces. Under these conditions, MacArthur and the other theater commanders worked effectively. The Joint Chiefs themselves had been a part of that system and fully endorsed it, for they knew no other way. But once the Soviet Union's possession of the air-delivered nuclear weapon made strategic nuclear attack against United States territory a real possibility, there was an urgent need to coordinate closely the policies of the President, the Joint Chiefs, and the theater commander. Failing this, an ill-advised decision in a local war might easily spark a global conflict. Although the President and his advisers understood this, they had not as yet explored alternative systems for controlling their field commanders, and were unwilling to risk the consequences of tampering with tradition. As Truman said: "You pick your man, you've got to back him up." In the end, it took MacArthur's challenge to the constitutional authority of the President to force a change in the American system of command.

Finally, the greater dilemma involved strategic direction of the war. What had been missing all along was close coordination between battlefield goals and worldwide coalition goals. Having assumed the leadership in both areas, the President and his advisers had allowed the battlefield objective, which was to unify Korea by force, to coexist with the broader strategic goal of avoiding a wider war, a goal that proved to be incompatible with unification. Either MacArthur should have been given the resources to unify Korea regardless of the risks, or he should have been stopped short of the Manchurian border in order to avoid a wider war. After directing MacArthur to cross into North Korea without the resources to defeat both the North Koreans and the Chinese, the administration found itself faced with the worst possible outcome: a divided Korea *and* a war with China. Clearly, the Truman administration was neither conceptually nor organizationally ready to fight a limited war. After the defeat in North Korea, the administration finally subordinated the freedom of action traditionally accorded the local commander to the demands of global strategy. Eventually, this priority led to the dismissal of MacArthur.

RICK ATKINSON

AMERICAN TACTICS
IN VIETNAM
The Riverine Force

T he military force the United States took into Vietnam in 1965 and 1966 was the finest ever fielded. It contained a highly professional officer and noncommissioned officer corps backed by enlisted ranks that received far more training than was provided any of our armed forces in earlier conflicts. It could have fought another World War II or Korean conflict with a verve and skill unmatched in previous history. Unfortunately this war was unlike any conflict American forces had previously faced in its political ramifications and tactical implications. It was, at least, different from anything American forces had faced since the long-forgotten guerrilla battles of the Philippine insurrection. The military confronted not merely a determined foe who fought both conventional and unconventional battles, but it also undertook the immense task of creating a government and a loyalty to it in the midst of war, inflation, ethnic and religious hostilities, and corruption. Even if the strategic tasks were too great or merely botched, the valor and suffering of the individual soldier was similar to that of all soldiers since colonial days. Nowhere did this become better known than among the infantrymen who bore the brunt of battle.

Combat operations in Vietnam have been described as "the company commander's war." The bulk of the fighting was done at small unit levels. Generals and colonels, sometimes even battalion commanders (lieutenant colonels), could do little to influence the where and when of a combat operation, as they had done in the world wars. It was the captains, lieutenants, sergeants, corporals, specialists, and privates who fought the

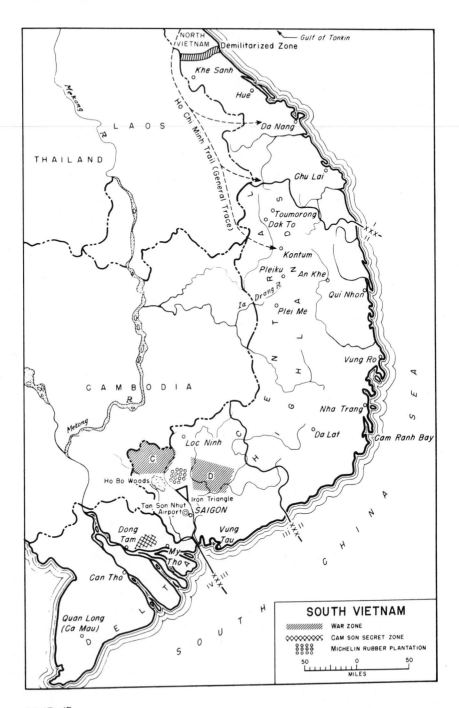

MAP 47

battles and who often looked to those in higher headquarters as being in the "echelons above reason."

In Vietnam Americans sought to exploit that in which they excelled—technology. The greatest symbol of that technology was the ubiquitous helicopter. The U.S. Army saw Vietnam as an opportunity to vindicate its new airmobile doctrine and began sending more helicopter units to reinforce the conventional infantry divisions arriving in Vietnam. Following the lead of the First Cavalry Division, virtually all divisions became airmobile. The UH-1 Huey and CH-47 Chinook became familiar sights in the Vietnamese sky. Among the new helicopters added to the arsenal were the AH-1 Huey Cobra (operational in 1967), which could be armed with antitank missiles, 7.62-mm machine guns, 40-mm grenade launchers, 70-mm rockets, or other armament. Important in many operations was the CH-54 Skycrane which lifted tanks, artillery, and bulldozers into remote positions. Eventually, the Americans lost 5,000 helicopters in Vietnam at a rate of one per 2,000 sorties.

While helicopter operations merited the most headlines, a novel approach to tactics occurred in the Mekong River delta south and west of Saigon. There the navy and the Second Brigade of the Ninth Infantry Division formed the Mobile Riverine Force. Living in naval barracks ships anchored in the river, the Second Brigade's troops went into battle aboard modified landing craft, known as armored troop carriers or ATCs, manned by navy crews. In combat, the infantry sometimes left the vessels and the navy crews manned the guns, acting as a blocking force or a heavy gun force in a maneuver. Also supporting the ATCs were monitors armed with 20-mm and 40-mm guns plus 81-mm mortars. The navy also built special command and communications boats which allowed effective control over movements in the difficult delta terrain. In front of each line of vessels, assault support patrol boats acted as minesweepers. Supporting all of this were army artillery mounted on barges, and the ever-present helicopters.

Beginning in 1967, the riverine campaign involved an integration of army and navy forces in a way unknown since the Civil War. The Mobile Riverine Force was uniquely tailored to meet the environment of the Mekong delta. It provided an ability to attack the Vietcong base areas that had placed at least a fourth of the delta's population under communist control. Although there was some disharmony between the navy flotilla and army brigade commanders regarding command and operational arrangements, there was a unique degree of cooperation between the two services throughout the experiment. Most of the efforts were concentrated against Long An and Dinh Tuong Provinces, key economic areas of the northern delta region. By 1968, the riverine force helped tip the balance in favor of the South Vietnamese and pushed the major Vietcong battalions operating in the area out of the most populous regions.

All this was not done without cost. Rick Atkinson, a reporter for the Washington Post, illustrates the platoon-level combat of such operations with the story of Lieutenant George Crocker of the Third Battalion, Forty-seventh Infantry Regiment, known to its members as the "Wolfhounds." Taken from Atkinson's provocative The

Long Gray Line, this excerpt is part of a much larger tracing by the author of the U.S. Military Academy's class of 1966. In this selection the reader will face the exuberance and tragedy of combat faced by Lieutenant Crocker and his men. The description of loss in the Mekong Delta of the lieutenant's West Point classmates Frank Rybicki, Denny Loftheim, and Fred Bertolino illustrates the trauma of combat upon its participants. What is particularly important is Lieutenant Crocker's gradual maturation under the strain of combat along with the growing cohesion of the platoon under his command. Readers will recall similar concepts in Robert Middlekauff's article on the Revolutionary War soldier. At the "sharp end," there are some essentially unchanging aspects of war.

The deployment of the 9th Division into the Mekong Delta in early 1967 marked the resumption of a kind of warfare—riverine combat—that the U.S. Army had last experienced more than a century earlier. American soldiers had once had considerable expertise in fighting a river war. During the Revolution, one of the principal strategic struggles was over control of the Hudson–Lake Champlain–St. Lawrence axis; West Point itself had first been fortified as part of the thrust-and-parry of that riverine conflict. In the War of 1812, the Americans mounted a river force, and in the grim Seminole War a mosquito fleet of 150 schooners, bateaux, and canoes had hunted Indians in the Florida sloughs, where a fourth of the U.S. Army's regulars subsequently died. With the exception of a foray up the Yangtze during the Boxer Rebellion, however, the Army had not fought extensively on rivers since Grant bisected the Confederacy by taking control of the Mississippi.

Now, more than a century later, riverine fighting was about to come back into fashion. The 9th Division was determined to control the Mekong, one of the world's greatest rivers. Flowing for twenty-five hundred miles from the Tibetan plateau, the Mekong split into four main fingers south of Saigon before emptying into the South China Sea. Command of the river and its myriad tributaries and canals was essential to wresting the delta away from the Viet Cong. But the French riverine experience was not heartening; in 1954 alone, at the end of their Indochina war, the French had lost more than a dozen boats to the Viet Minh. Some of those carcasses still sat in the Mekong mud as a reminder of things gone wrong.

In early 1964, the U.S. ambassador to Vietnam, Henry Cabot Lodge, had remarked, "I would not be surprised to see the Mekong Delta totally cleared of communist forces by the end of 1965." Instead, by the time the 9th Division arrived, the Viet Cong had more than eighty thousand troops in the region. The guerrillas were well supported by the local population—swimming like fish in the sea, in Mao's phrase—and they moved with elusive ease by sampan throughout the delta.

The American strategy aimed to clean out the Viet Cong infrastructure, freeing Route 4—the main road to Saigon—and the rest of the rice bowl from communist domination. If the delta, which had a population density comparable with that of Massachusetts, could be stabilized to produce enough food to feed South Vietnam, other parts of the nation could begin to industrialize. As a base for his riverine force, William Westmoreland picked a site on the northernmost of the four Mekong fingers, west of the town of My Tho. The camp was originally called Base Whiskey, but Westmoreland gave it a loftier name to fit his aspirations: Dong Tam. It meant "united hearts and minds."

George Crocker's first view of Dong Tam was disheartening. He had not expected Windsor Palace, but the camp was little more than a barren mudflat on the north bank of the river. The site was even less appealing than Beckwith's Field Seven had been; at least that had showed some semblance of human habitation. The only sign of life at Dong Tam, besides one pathetic mechanized company camped in the muck, was a large dredge, named the *New Jersey*. It sat in the middle of the river spewing fresh layers of mud on top of the old mud in an effort to build up the riverbank before the monsoon season. Now, with typical American vigor, the Army set out to transform Dong Tam into a thriving fortress. Shortly after he and his platoon arrived, George ordered the men to pitch their tents and begin building hootches from prefabrication kits, which came complete with blueprints, lumber, nails, and even hammers.

The thirty-five men in his platoon, which was part of the 3rd Battalion of the 47th Infantry Regiment, quickly discovered that soldiering in the delta was beset with problems. The mud and brackish water quickly ruined weapons that were not routinely disassembled, cleaned, and oiled. Every morning, George had his men remove the rounds in their rifle chambers, since they would often get damp overnight and cause the weapons to jam. Every three days, each magazine was emptied, and the dirty ammunition replaced with clean bullets. Once the river operations began, the platoon periodically rotated onto one of several World War II ships that had been converted into floating barracks. Offering clean sheets, hot showers, and air conditioning, the ships gave the men a chance to dry out and escape the fungi that thrived inside wet boots. Better still, the Navy returned their laundry clean and fragrant, unlike the *mama sans* at Dong Tam, who rinsed the fatigues in river water and left them smelling, oddly, like oatmeal.

On the day before a search-and-destroy sweep, the men cleaned their weapons and fueled the boats. In the evening, boat captains got briefings on the mission, steaming formations, radio codes, tidal currents, and the latest G2, or intelligence. Before dawn, George and his troops would stand on a pontoon pier, rummaging around in different-colored barrels for claymores, grenades, and smoke canisters. Then, with other platoons from the company, they climbed into eight or ten shallow-draught troop carriers. The boats, each sixty feet long, were protected with armor and a trellis of iron bars to deflect rocket-propelled grenades. Canvas awnings shielded the soldiers from the sun.

In the early morning light, the delta presented a lush palette of blues and greens. Water buffalo, ridden by scrawny peasant boys in conical straw hats, pulled crude plows across the paddies to prepare them for the green rice shoots that would be planted as the monsoon season neared. Like armored geese, the American boats puttered past in a V formation, often led by a minesweeper. Helicopters scouted ahead for enemy ambushes. Sometimes the river tributaries were only fifty to a hundred feet wide, clogged with fish traps or Viet Cong barricades. Banana and coconut groves lined the banks.

As they approached the landing site, the Americans would open up with "reconnaissance by fire," bombarding suspected Viet Cong positions on both sides of the water with a Monitor—a seventy-five-ton floating fortress—or artillery, which was towed on barges and anchored in the mud with sharp cleats. Later in the war, large flame-throwing boats called Zippos sometimes scorched the banks with thick tongues of fire. The infantrymen then splashed ashore and fanned out, always eyeing the dikes and tree lines across the rice paddies for signs of the enemy. Frequently, another U.S. force would be inserted by helicopter to block the Viet Cong escape routes. Sometimes the enemy stood fast to fight, but more typically the sweeps encountered only sporadic sniper fire or came up empty altogether.

Even so, there were constant reminders of death's ubiquity. The winnowing of the West Point class of '66, which began on the first day of Beast Barracks, had abated temporarily at graduation, only to resume in Vietnam in an infinitely more sinister form. As the war intensified, as ever more lieutenants were shuttled into combat, the manifest of KIAs grew steadily longer.

One of George's classmates who also served in the delta was a native of the Panama Canal Zone named Frank Rybicki, Jr. A man of irrepressible good cheer, Rybicki seemed perpetually happy, whether strumming his guitar, practicing his jitterbug, or simply talking to his friends. At West Point, as president of the Glee Club, he would write to the Miss America candidates from each state where the club was touring, soliciting dates. He adored John Kennedy and had studied on a desk blotter inscribed with the "ask not what your country can do for you" quotation. Rybicki's sister married his academy roommate, Terry Stull, who also joined the 9th as a platoon leader.

One day in late spring, two Viet Cong companies badly decimated Stull's platoon in a six-hour firefight. Rybicki's platoon was among those ordered to reinforce. "We're coming down to help you out," he told Stull on the phone. "About time we worked together again."

The platoon waded into the Rung Sat Special Zone, near the main shipping channel to Saigon. Also known as the Forest of Assassins, the Rung Sat was an ancient pirate haven, a 350-square-mile nightmare of mangrove trees and nipa palms. Shortly after arriving, Rybicki bogged down in the mud. Without flipping the safety on, he thrust the stock of his rifle to one of his men to pull him out. The soldier accidentally grabbed the trigger, and Rybicki fell dead in a burst of his own gunfire.

By chance, George happened to get word of the accident before Terry Stull did, and it fell to him to inform Stull that his brother-in-law had been killed. *Newsweek* magazine devoted an entire page to Rybicki's funeral at West Point, calling him "an integer in the unending statistics in an unending war," and noting that "he was the second to die in West Point's class of '66, the 101st academy graduate, one of 10,000 Americans lost in what has now become the fifth costliest war in U.S. history." Twenty years later, some of Frank Rybicki's classmates would recall his death with particular anguish; to them it seemed the ultimate metaphor of self-destruction in Vietnam.

In addition to conducting search-and-destroy sweeps on the Mekong, units from the 9th occasionally walked patrol duty near Dong Tam in an effort to thwart the Viet Cong mortar crews who frequently harassed the compound. One night, around the time of Rybicki's death, George had been out with his platoon for several hours on just such a defensive patrol when he heard a harsh whisper. "Sssst! Sir!"

One of his soldiers, flattened against the side of a dike, pointed across the rice paddy. George crawled to the crest of the levee and peered into the darkness. The perimeter of Dong Tam lay only a kilometer behind him to the east. Ahead, a hundred yards to the west, the next dike rose like a dark wall above the field. He saw nothing out of the ordinary and heard only the usual buzzing of countless insects.

He inched along the dike toward the soldier who had whispered. Taking the GI's sniper rifle, George hoisted the starlight scope to his right eye. The night instantly gave way to an eerie twilight. The scope sucked in all available moon- and starlight and painted the landscape with a pale green illumination, as if the world were covered with penicillin mold.

George saw him instantly. A solitary Viet Cong wearing his *ao baba*—the customary black pajamas—stood on the adjacent dike. George couldn't quite make out what the enemy soldier was doing. Sometimes, he knew, the VC liked to reverse the American claymores so that the blast would be directed back at the unwitting U.S. soldiers.

George watched for a while through the scope, the hunter stalking his prey. This was a rare opportunity to watch the enemy at work. But he didn't want the soldier to slip away in the paddy. Easy does it, he told himself. He steadied his breathing, drew a bead on the soldier's heart, and gently squeezed the trigger.

BAM! A single red tracer streaked across the paddy and struck the VC in the chest, knocking him over with a small *splat* sound that carried to the Americans.

Got you! George thought. Got you, you little son of a bitch! Adrenaline surged through him, again quickening his pulse and his breathing. The platoon crouched expectantly behind the dike, but no one returned the fire. The western front of Dong Tam remained quiet.

Back at the base, George exulted, replaying in his mind the red streak of the tracer and the dull noise as the round found its mark. As many of his classmates were also discovering, nothing in the world compared to the exhilaration of combat. Some soldiers never overcame their fear or their revulsion at the killing, but he could understand how others became adrenaline freaks. The world outside the combat zone—the peaceful world at home—seemed oddly tame by contrast, almost boring. Men, Homer had observed, grow tired of sleep, love, singing, and dancing sooner than of war. The enemy here was faceless and nameless—except for gook, dink, slope, or Charlie—and while George did not exactly hate him, killing him was not difficult. It was not difficult at all.

After but a few weeks in Vietnam, he was beginning to realize that war boiled down to a few irreducible truths. No longer did he see it as an adventure; war was brutal, often harrowing. No longer did he imagine that he was invincible; he knew death could claim him at any moment. And it was also true that the killing of the enemy was no longer cloaked in ideology or patriotism. George had heard little discussion in the war zone of the domino theory or just causes or checking the spread of godless communism. Killing was much more elemental, an accession of animal instincts and soldierly axioms: survival against a foe who was trying to kill you; revenge for comrades who had died; loyalty unto death to those who shared the fight; and a fierce determination to be better than the enemy. West Point did not—could not—teach these things; what the academy could teach, implicitly, was how to keep the killing within the warrior's code so that combat did not degenerate into blood lust, nor decent men warp into butchers.

In 1943, George Patton had written in his diary: "War is very simple, direct, and ruthless. It takes a simple, direct, and ruthless man to wage war." Combat required a certain implacability of the best. George Meade had been too much the genteel Philadelphian to crush the Confederates; it took U. S. Grant, that indifferent cadet and one-time Galena shopkeeper, to annihilate the rebellion, simply, directly, ruthlessly.

That requirement held true on Sicily and true at Spotsylvania Court House; now it was true in Vietnam. And Patton's dictum held true even for a young lieutenant in a place named United Hearts and Minds.

★ ★ ★ ★ ★

In early May, the brigade left Dong Tam and moved inland on a search-and-destroy operation. For three days the Americans tramped through the countryside looking for a fight without finding one. The troops discovered elaborate bunkers and even some new equipment. But the enemy always seemed to stay one step ahead.

On the afternoon of May 3, George was summoned by his company and battalion commanders. "We're going to pull the brigade out but leave a stay-behind ambush," the battalion commander told him. "You're it. Why don't you go up in the chopper now with the S3 and take a look around?"

Sitting in the Huey next to the battalion operations officer fifteen hundred feet above the ground, George saw many Americans but no Victor Charlie. He had few doubts, however, that the enemy was down there in force. Not far away was the hamlet of Ap Bac, now deserted, where in January 1963 the Army of the Republic of Vietnam (ARVN) and the Viet Cong had fought their first major battle. Three hundred and fifty lightly armed VC had humiliated an ARVN force four times its size and had shot down five U.S.-piloted helicopters. The senior American adviser on the scene, a legendary lieutenant colonel named John Paul Vann, had offered a candid assessment of ARVN combat prowess—"a miserable damn performance"—which made front-page headlines across the United States.

Now, four years later, the VC still maintained control. Long since abandoned to the war, the rice fields, dikes, and small banana plantations near Ap Bac had begun reverting to jungle. George, scanning the country-side, saw that an enemy division could hide down there without being detected. This is going to be interesting, he told himself.

Shortly after he returned to the camp, the brigade began to pull out. It took a long time to ferry more than two thousand troops back to Dong Tam in helicopters, and shadows had begun to stretch across the desolate paddies as the last Huey lifted into the sky. George and his platoon crouched in the elephant grass, straining to catch the fading beat of the rotors until even their imaginations could no longer pretend to hear it. They were alone—three dozen scared infantrymen left behind as bait.

George gestured to the platoon. "Okay," he whispered, "let's move out."

Holding their rifles high, they waded waist-deep into a swamp. Their objective was a small canal, perhaps thirty feet wide, about a mile away; from the air it had looked like a twisting black snake. The commander had suggested that they cut through an open area to reach the canal quickly, but George preferred the back door through the swamp. It was an old Ranger tactic: use the least expected route. By moving this way, the platoon would also be able to hear anyone who tried to follow.

As always in the tropics, night fell with the abruptness of a dropped curtain. After reaching a copse of small trees and grass near the canal, the men fanned out in a circle thirty yards in diameter. They couldn't dig in—the water table was only six or eight inches below the surface—so the soldiers scratched small battlements for cover. George helped site the two M-60 machine guns and camouflage the claymore mines along the canal bank. The claymores could be devastatingly effective at close range: weighing three pounds, each mine contained seven hundred steel peas packed into a paste of C-4 explosive. When triggered with a hand-held detonator, a "clacker," the C-4 spat the pellets for about fifty yards with the force of a shotgun blast.

As a final precaution, George raised the artillery firebase on the radio. A battery of 105mm howitzers, mounted on triangular platforms, had been flown into the middle of a rice paddy six miles away. Before the brigade flew back to Dong Tam, George had been assigned an artillery forward observer— a nervous young lieutenant—and one of his sergeants. Using the grids on his map, the FO now called in several rounds, which soon exploded nearby. By registering the proper deflection and elevation, the battery would be able to respond instantly with fire on potential approach routes to the platoon's perimeter.

There was always a chance, George knew, that the rounds would alert the enemy to the platoon's presence. But random explosions were common in Vietnam; something was always blowing up somewhere in the middle of the night. In Beast Barracks, new cadets had been required to memorize a saw that seemed particularly apt now: "A calculated risk is a known risk for the sake of a real gain. A risk for the sake of a risk is a fool's choice." Registering the artillery was a calculated risk.

Once in place, the platoon remained utterly quiet. That was good, George thought, very good. In four months these men had been transformed into a fine combat team. Lieutenant Crocker had been insistent—at times even harshly demanding—that they religiously follow the precepts of Ranger training. He was convinced that all of [Major Charles] Beckwith's tricks picked up from the British in Malaya—minimizing noise and light, avoiding smelly insect repellent, stressing guile and subterfuge—saved lives. Several soldiers in the platoon had been wounded, but no one had been killed yet. That was something to be proud of.

George's own flirtation with death, however, had not abated. The near misses he began having during his first week with the Wolfhounds had continued with the 9th. On one occasion, a sniper had wounded two American soldiers in the head and George moved up to the perimeter. He assigned each remaining man five trees to watch. See if you can spot any movement, he ordered, and we'll call in some artillery. Suddenly, another shot rang out and the branch a few inches above his helmet fell to the ground as neatly as if snipped with hedge shears.

Not long after that the platoon was deployed on Thoi San Island near Dong Tam. George's platoon sergeant was a savvy career NCO named Diaz, who had been an outstanding instructor at the Army's jungle school in Panama. As they were patrolling across the island, Diaz grabbed George's arm. "Nobody move!" he yelled. "Don't step!" He pointed at the ground. "Look, sir. The banana leaf, but no banana tree." Carefully lifting the leaf, Diaz revealed an undetonated Air Force cluster bomb that had been converted into a booby trap.

When, soon after, the platoon again drew night patrol duty outside Dong Tam, George set out in his usual spot, fourth in the column. But when the men began to slow down and bunch too closely, he moved up front to see why. As he climbed onto a dike next to the point man, a Chinese antipersonnel mine exploded. Shrapnel and barbed wire blew back between his legs, severely wounding the soldier who had taken his place in the file. The fireball flung George into the air and knocked the rifle from his hands. Dazed and temporarily deaf, he called for a helicopter to evacuate the wounded. Then he ordered the platoon back a thousand meters while he and Diaz crouched in the weeds for an hour, vainly hoping to ambush whoever had placed the mine.

Each close call took its toll. The stress, the rush of adrenaline, the inevitable reliving of the episode at night as he tried to sleep, all wore him down. He felt fatigued, as though he had been treading water for a long time. His exuberance ebbed a little with each incident. Always calm, at times he now found himself jumpy and distracted when the platoon prepared for yet another air assault or river sweep.

The drone of a plane interrupted his thoughts. An old C-47 Gooney Bird on a psyops—psychological operation—mission flew past. A steady stream of Vietnamese blared from loudspeakers on the plane's belly, urging the VC to surrender. *You must give up, soldiers. Death will be your only reward if you continue this futile struggle.*

Suddenly, on every side of the platoon, the jungle erupted in a roar of gunfire. Hundreds of enemy soldiers fired their rifles furiously at the plane. Then the .50-calibers opened up, hosing the night sky with tracer rounds.

Still lying quietly in their hiding place, the men in the platoon gaped in disbelief. Tracers stitched green threads through the air. The Gooney Bird, apparently untouched, continued to babble for another minute before lumbering off to proselytize elsewhere. After a few final bursts, the night fell silent again.

George gestured to the men to remain motionless. He found the .50-calibers particularly disturbing. Division intelligence had estimated that only battalion-size VC units or larger were outfitted with the heavy machine guns. At least two or three .50s had been firing; perhaps more. Two or three battalions? Is that possible? he wondered. It would not take long for two or three battalions to overrun three dozen Americans.

Someone shook his arm and pointed at the canal. The black silhouettes of two sampans silently glided by. A moment later, in a crimson burst, several claymores on the canal bank detonated, raking the sampans with steel. A piece of hot plastic from a claymore casing struck George in the back of the neck; he flicked it away with his hand. The boats burned for a few moments before sinking; once again the silence returned.

Not a single soldier in the platoon had fired his rifle yet. George had stressed over and over the importance of not signaling their position at night with rifle fire. Explosions were anonymous, but the popping of an M-16 told the enemy that an American soldier was squeezing the trigger. So far, the men had been admirably disciplined, and that's what would keep them alive: discipline held an infantry unit together, allowing every man to draw strength from every other man. Good infantrymen had once been likened to dangerous vermin that were hard to brush from the seams of the soil.

The VC began to probe. Soon George heard them rooting off to the left. As the enemy moved closer, Diaz law sprawled on the ground nearby, clutching a pair of grenades. It sounded as though six or eight of them had closed to within a few yards of the platoon.

Out of the darkness, two enemy soldiers came running toward the perimeter, spraying the brush with their AK-47s. Diaz popped the handles from the grenades, let them "cook" in his hands for two seconds, and flipped them at the charging VC. Both grenades detonated in midair, brilliantly illuminating the scene as the soldiers jackknifed and fell dead. George ordered each man to pull the pin on a grenade. On his command, thirty grenades bounced in front of the perimeter and exploded in a spray of dirt and shrapnel.

Things began happening very quickly now. Two hundred yards away, a large enemy force, still uncertain of the platoon's precise location, rushed at what they mistakenly believed to be the American position. George crawled over to the artillery FO. "Let's get some fire on that bunch over there," he ordered.

There was no response. Petrified, the artillery lieutenant stared blankly. George grabbed him and jerked him upright.

"You get hold of yourself," he growled, his face inches from the FO's. "You get to it or get your sergeant over here to do it."

The FO nodded and raised the firebase on the radio. A minute later, 105mm rounds began raining on the enemy position with the familiar express train sound of incoming artillery. The Americans heard shrieks and moans as the VC retreated, leaving behind the dying.

Half an hour later, the enemy tried again. Once again they missed the platoon by several hundred yards; once again a curtain of artillery fell on the attack. By dawn, it appeared that the enemy had melted back into the jungle. George called the battalion on the radio. Howard Kirk, a classmate from '66, listened on the network back at camp. He thought George's voice sounded cool, controlled, yet frightened: "The sun's up. We killed a few last night. We're searching the dead now and we'll be ready for extraction shortly."

George crawled over to the canal to look at the sampans. A dead VC floated in the water. The force of the claymore had wrapped his leg bizarrely around his neck, like twine around a finger. Several other soldiers came over to tug on the edge of a sunken boat in a search for booty.

Diaz snapped his fingers twice and without uttering a word, jabbed his finger at the air. George turned his head. In a woodline 250 yards away, stretching as far as he could see in either direction, were the unmistakable signs of an impending attack. He caught glimpses of black and the glint of metal in the morning light. The Viet Cong made no effort to conceal themselves. George heard whoops and yells followed by the trill of whistles.

He turned back to Diaz. "I guess they found us."

The battalion commander was already in the air aboard his helicopter when George reached him on the radio.

"Sir, I've got a big ground attack about to start and I need some gunships. Right away."

Small-arms fire began slicing into the foliage above the platoon, sporadically at first and then in a heavy fusillade that shredded the leaves and branches. For the first time, the platoon returned fire with their M-16s and M-60s. The artillery lieutenant, having composed himself after George's tongue lashing the night before, called in coordinates to the artillery battery; within seconds the treeline erupted in fire and smoke.

That stalled the first charge. The Americans heard shouted commands as the VC tried to reorganize in the midst of the artillery barrage. For a few minutes, the enemy firing faltered, then resumed even more intensely. Hugging the ground as closely as he could, George spread a red panel to mark his position for the gunships. The gunships, he wondered; where are the gunships?

Thacka-thacka-thacka. As if on cue, a Huey swooped overhead.

"Hey, we're taking some fire," the pilot complained over the radio. "We see you, we see them."

George pressed the radio key. "You want me to throw some smoke?"

"No, don't do that. We've got you. I'm going to make a pass at them."

The gunship veered toward the woodline, raking the trees with machine guns and rockets before circling back.

"We make four or five of them hiding in a ditch right down beside you," the pilot radioed. "You want to go kill them, or do you want us to get them?"

George pressed the key. "Hell, let's not fool around. You get them."

Another ship came on station, followed by two others. A cacophony of gunfire, explosions, and rotor noise washed over the platoon. Enemy bullets had stripped the thicket in which they were hiding as clean as if it had been mowed with a scythe; leaves and small branches covered the ground. Between M-16 bursts, the men pressed their cheeks into the dirt in an effort to lower the crowns of their heads an extra inch.

The battalion commander came back on the radio. "We're getting you out of there. Be ready to extract back about three hundred meters in that open area we talked about."

"Yes, sir. We're ready."

George shouted above the din to Diaz and the squad leaders. "Get ready to go. That clearing over there, about three hundred meters. Ready—GO!"

Like sprinters coming out of their blocks, three dozen men exploded from the brake while the four gunships sprayed the treeline. Running as fast as he could, George passed a beautifully preserved old American M-1 rifle lying on the ground. He suppressed the urge to snatch it and kept sprinting. Several Hueys glided in just as the platoon reached the clearing; the men leaped inside and collapsed panting on the floor.

Once again, George felt the exhilaration of survival. What an immense sense of power there was in pressing a little microphone key and seeing the woods erupt in fire. As the ground fell away beneath the helicopter, he saw several more dead Viet Cong spread-eagled below, each body marking the green earth with a dark X.

After landing at Dong Tam, he counted heads and found everyone present and accounted for; the platoon had escaped without a single casualty. The brigade commander, Colonel Fulton, ordered the men into formation. Filthy and exhausted, they stood at attention as the colonel strolled down the line, awarding each a Bronze Star.

"How many did you kill, soldier?"

"I think I got two, sir."

"Good, good. How about you, soldier?"

"At least one, sir, maybe more."

"Good. Very good."

After the ceremony, George walked back to his tent on the southeast corner of the base. Fulton had given him a Bronze Star and also recommended that he receive a Silver Star for "conspicuous gallantry and intrepidity in action."

This small, anonymous firefight, George thought, offered further insights into men at war. However insignificant the battle had been within the larger conflict, it demonstrated, in microcosm, certain verities. The American military historian S. L. A. Marshall had written that most men in combat "are unwilling to take extraordinary risks and do not aspire to a hero's role, but they are equally unwilling they should be considered the least worthy among those present." What soldiers most desire, Marshall wrote, is the esteem of their comrades.

That seemed on target, but another of Marshall's conclusions from his study of American infantrymen in World War II did not track. He had estimated that only one soldier in four fired his weapon when closely engaged with the enemy; the majority, Marshall concluded, were paralyzed with fright or preoccupied with survival. George could not see that. It seemed to him that when told to fire, these men—all of them—had done so with exceptional discipline.

Something about courage was also clearer now. At West Point, the cadets—Cadet Crocker among them—had been full of bravado. They had joked about which hand they would prefer to lose in combat, blustering about how many enemy soldiers they planned to kill. But bravado was grounded in ignorance; true courage was possible only after one gained the visceral comprehension that death was the potential price of valor. The men in the platoon—Lieutenant Crocker among them—had been truly brave.

"Sir?"

Two of his squad leaders and two PFCs stood at the entrance to the tent. It was unusual to see them here. George had made a conscious effort to remain distant from the other soldiers. Any platoon leader could be a great friend to his men, but George believed that getting too close eroded the unit's effectiveness. The biggest temptation to overcome in combat, he had discovered, was the impulse to abandon everything and tend the wounded rather than continuing to fight with the platoon. In February, he had even summoned the squad leaders to make the point explicit. "Maybe it's best that we not get too friendly," he told them. "It might affect how we do business if I know I have to put you guys in body bags."

Now, he waved the four men in.

"Sir," one of the sergeants said, "we're a delegation from the platoon and we don't really know how to say it, but we want to just say thanks for being hard on us and making sure we didn't talk or smoke or whatever. We really appreciated that last night. We know that all the things you were trying to do are worth it."

George shook their hands. When they left, he sat on his bunk and smiled. These guys have learned, he thought; they're true soldiers. And that thirty-second speech was worth more than all the Silver Stars in the United States Army.

★ ★ ★ ★ ★

George rarely dwelt on the dead. Like getting too close to the troops, that was fraught with danger. By temperament, he was not given to philosophical ruminations on cruel fate. But the death of friends like Loftheim and Bertolino hit him hard, further sapping the boyish excitement he had once felt about the great adventure of combat. Occasionally, as when he heard that Loftheim had been killed, he sat on his bunk at Dong Tam, brooding. It seemed so unfair that such men should die. Why, he wondered, did war seem to single out the best? Why couldn't at least the very best of the best survive? When such fine soldiers died, he thought, their loss was a waste, a pointless, tragic waste.

Robert E. Lee had once mused that it was fortunate war was such a terrible thing because otherwise men would grow too fond of it. The deaths of men like Frank Rybicki and Denny Loftheim and Fred Bertolino served to guarantee that men like George Crocker would never grow too fond of war.

D A N I E L   P.   B O L G E R

AN ERA OF VIOLENT PEACE, 1975–1986

In 1971 a special presidential commission headed by former Secretary of Defense Thomas S. Gates reported that an all-volunteer military force was feasible and desirable for the postwar period. Some liberals opposed ending conscription because they feared the armed forces would become disproportionately poor and black and that the military needed the leavening influence of civilian soldiers. Some conservatives feared the loss of strategic flexibility if most young men had no military training. Nonetheless, President Richard Nixon endorsed the Gates Commission recommendations as did a Congress wanting to rid itself of the politically objectionable draft. Consequently, starting in 1973, after depending upon conscription for its manpower resources for most of the previous third of a century, the military had to rely on voluntary enlistments and reenlistments to meet its manpower requirements.

Initially the worst forebodings about the all-volunteer army came true. Indiscipline rates relative to absence without leave, desertion, and drug and alcohol abuse rose to peacetime highs. During the late 1970s, minorities (blacks and Hispanics) constituted over a third of all enlisted personnel in the army. The high school graduate percentage of enlistees dropped to just over half in 1980. Few soldiers enlisted or reenlisted in combat arms units, thereby reducing the essential fighting capacity of the army. There was considerable talk in the popular press about America's "hollow army."

Having to compete for talent in the marketplace meant a number of changes had to be made. Foremost was need for a dramatic increase in the pay of lower-ranking enlisted personnel. The annual salary cost per person tripled. Recruiting expenses rose

519

and recruiting techniques had to be modernized. Women represented an increasingly higher proportion of military strength, about eleven percent in 1990. Many commentators questioned the effect on readiness this situation created, while others sought to include women in combat units, from which they were excluded by law. Another problem was the growing proportion of minorities in an armed force officered by white, middle-class Americans. In the peacetime military, race relations became a touchy issue, duplicating the situation in American society at large and reflecting a rise in militancy among African Americans. A variety of minority affairs programs and sensitivity sessions assisted in the resolution of many issues, but there was no easy solution to achieving racial equality. Finally, drug problems plagued many in the barracks and aboard ship.

During the 1980s, the situation began to correct itself. The combination of reenlistment numbers and first-time enlistees exceeded manpower goals in 1981. So long as the military did not try to increase its size, it seemed capable of achieving its numerical goals. The emphasis then turned to quality. Recruiters were discouraged from enlisting non-high school graduates and the enlistment rate of graduates rose to 91 percent by 1986. Enhanced powers were given commanders to eliminate marginal soldiers, sailors, airmen, and marines from the service. Special bonuses were given for combat arms enlistments and reenlistments. Promotion boards received instructions to promote in those career fields where vacancies existed, thereby enhancing the promotion chances of combat arms enlisted men. By the mid-1980s, both the quality and skill qualification needs of the armed forces were better satisfied than a decade earlier. And, as the following selection illustrates, there were situations into which they could be employed.

Much of the emphasis in the military during the 1970s concerned the potential for mechanized and armored warfare in Central Europe or the Middle East and the importance of a maritime strategy against the Eurasian landmass. However, the rise in terrorism and hostage taking in those areas, the continued communist emphasis on wars of national liberation, and the potential for military involvement in volatile regions like Latin America or Africa caused military and political leaders of the 1980s to urge the military to be available for a variety of situations. Moreover, it was becoming increasingly apparent that moving heavy forces to critical areas in a timely fashion was outside the airlift or sealift capacity of the United States.

To meet such contingencies the armed forces moved to increase their light infantry and special operations capabilities. This desire for the capacity to fight anywhere, anytime, under any circumstance also led to increased emphasis on special and joint operations. Strong congressional interest in this area led to an increase in special operations units and training. Exactly what orientation—insurgency, counterinsurgency, combat, or advisory—the special operations forces should undertake continued to affect training and potential use for these highly skilled soldiers, sailors, marines, and airmen. Congress also pressed the armed forces to emphasize joint-, rather than *single-service assignments for those being promoted to high rank. Certainly the best example of what Congress wanted came with the Panamanian incursion of 1989.*

All this emphasis on contingency operations and joint assignments reflects a recognition that such activities were more likely to be the norm as the threat of a NATO–Warsaw Pact conflict in Central Europe and of large-scale involvement in containment wars like Korea and Vietnam appears increasingly remote. The 1975 Mayaguez rescue mission and 1983 Operation Urgent Fury to Grenada (both of which contained many military mistakes), the failure of Operation Eagle Claw (the 1980 Iranian rescue mission which ended in abortion and tragedy at the Desert One landing site), and the bombing of the marine barracks in Beirut in 1983, caused many commentators to criticize our military as bloated and ineffective. Army Major Daniel Bolger, until recently an instructor at West Point, reviews these criticisms by William Lind, Richard Gabriel, and Edward Luttwak in the summary chapter of his Americans at War: 1975–1986, An Era of Violent Peace.

Are the critics expecting too much? Do they forget the Clausewitzian dictum about "friction" in war? Is the military too much a bureaucracy and not a fighting force? Finally, is Major Bolger too apologetic for the modern failures of the American military?

> *Everything is very simple in war, but the simplest thing is difficult. These difficulties accumulate and produce a friction beyond the imagination of those who have not seen war. . . . Friction is the only conception which, in a fairly general way, corresponds to the distinction between real war and war on paper.*
>   Karl von Clausewitz, *On War*

> *When things went wrong at the Pentagon, really wrong, you'd always hear some bright guy in a business suit complaining that a country able to land a man on the moon should be able to carry out any operations on earth: raid Hanoi, drop into Tehran, whatever. I always pointed out to these smart alecks that as I recalled, the moon didn't hide, move around under its own steam, or shoot back.*
>   Col. John R. Boyd, USAF (retired)

The seven major U.S. expeditions since the evacuation of Saigon resulted in five successes and two failures. Armed interventions exacted a price. American casualties in these actions totaled 712, with 337 dead, missing, or died of wounds. More than two-thirds of those killed fell in a single searing second in Beirut. To put these losses in perspective, in Vietnam the 1st Cavalry Division

(Airmobile) suffered 334 dead and 736 wounded in its first major engagement in the Ia Drang Valley during October and November of 1965. In Normandy, American assault units staging for Operation COBRA (24–25 July 1944) lost 757 men to misdirected "friendly" bombing. Of course, statistics are cold comfort to those who paid in blood.

What did the U.S. get for these efforts? Americans secured *Mayaguez* and its crew unhurt, brushed back a Libyan air challenge, rescued more than 600 students unharmed from the midst of a defended island, snatched brigands from midair over a dark sea, and blew holes in Colonel Gadhafi's terrorist schemes. All of these victories came far from American shores, in hostile skies, on disputed ground, and upon unfriendly waters. U.S. forces crushed their opposition in almost every instance in which combat occurred. In addition, American military prowess enforced national strategies in many other situations short of conflict. Far from being the hobbled giant portrayed in so many dire predictions of 1973–74, the United States reasserted its traditional role as keeper of the peace. Having recovered from the doldrums of the Vietnam era, capable armed forces once again gave the president the big stick needed to back up U.S. policy worldwide.

The dismal outcomes of EAGLE CLAW and the marine deployment in Beirut reflected individual, political, and organizational problems. Although U.S. citizens can be proud of troop performance, neither of these episodes offered comfort to American military leaders. The Defense Department's forthright insistence on learning what went wrong, and why, stands in marked contrast to the inordinate focus on "good news only, please" that led the country down the road to ruin in Indochina in the 1960s. Reviews of the failed expeditions were hard-nosed, uncompromising, and thorough. Evidently, the military paid attention. In consequence, the two defeats provided valuable, sobering lessons that were not lost on U.S. planners during later operations. For example, American special operations forces reorganized after Desert One played a major, and far more fruitful, role in the Grenada campaign. Similarly, U.S. troops in Honduras have avoided the marines' mistakes in Lebanon; they routinely guard strong defensive perimeters in order to frustrate local insurrectionaries. Finally, in a less celebrated case, determined naval aviators studied the mistakes of the bungled December 1983 strike near Beirut. The USN jet crews functioned far more effectively when they bombed Gadhafi's Libya in 1986. This willingness to admit errors and correct them bodes well for the future.

Amazingly, many self-appointed military experts have been highly critical of not only the defeats but the victories as well. Journalists have given much credence to such thinking, and in almost any piece on defense matters, one will encounter assertions of allegedly severe flaws in post-Vietnam actions. William

Lind wrote *America Can Win*, suggesting that recent battles were anything but successful. Richard Gabriel, a college professor and reserve army intelligence officer, penned the venomous *Military Incompetence*—the title summarizes Gabriel's assessment of America's armed forces. In *The Pentagon and the Art of War*, Edward Luttwak also complains that the U.S. military does not know how to fight. In each case, these authors recount the American expeditions after the second Indochina war, dissecting every miscue and accident and inventing or distorting more than a few events for good measure.

A bit of Luttwak will suffice to set the tone. The *Mayaguez* rescue was "clumsy," the Sidra air battle of 1981 a "most feeble" triumph, and Grenada supposedly featured "gross failures of planning and command." In his key diatribe, Luttwak echoes the other critics as he derides U.S. errors in URGENT FURY. He describes a version of Grenada in which "each engagement should have been swiftly victorious. It was not." Instead, "the Grenadian leaders and the Cubans were left undisturbed to organize resistance" from St. George's, in "the central part of the island." Luttwak judged most of the Cubans as "only construction workers" and found that "not more than 43 were professional soldiers," numbers derived from press reports based upon, of all things, Fidel Castro's somewhat suspect postinvasion protest speeches. Luttwak concludes: "The most disheartening aspect of the entire Grenada episode was the ease with which the performance of the armed forces was accepted as satisfactory, even praiseworthy." If the American military did as poorly on Grenada and in other expeditions as Luttwak, Lind, and Gabriel indicated, there would be cause for real alarm.

These men want drastic reforms in American military structure and practice, and look for anecdotal evidence that buttresses their ideas. Lind wants "maneuver warfare," rather than what he sees as an American dependence on material superiority and "attrition." Gabriel decries "managers in uniform," and Luttwak denigrates "interservice rivalry." They cite real and half-real problems since Vietnam to "prove" their cases. In Washington budget battles, this all may make some sense, and probably impresses civilian lawmakers and executives. But these vague prescriptions offer little for the professional soldier, even in the few cases where the reformers' descriptive case studies coincide with actual events. It is the military analog to sports writing—entertaining "inside" stories based vaguely on real occurrences and penned by "experts" who never played the game.

Lacking any significant military experience, these writers have seized upon what military theorist Karl von Clausewitz called "friction," that compendium of self-sustaining, nagging confusion peculiar to the danger, physical exertion, incomplete information, and other annoying situational pitfalls of warfare. Expeditions are dangerous by nature, small snippets cut from the likely canvas of full-scale war. Even among the most hardened professionals, nobody wants to die or be maimed. This is especially clear when one notes that most post-Vietnam actions featured troops new to combat. Consider the plight of the marines on Koh Tang as the sun went down, or Captain Kearney's frightening initiation at Calvigny. Only training, discipline, and forceful leadership can counter the effects of danger.

Physical exertion in combat cannot be neglected. War saps strength and spirit, and expeditions are no different for those involved. It was easy to say afterward that Grenada always looked like a short mission; the marines in Beirut were once told the same thing. Thirst, lack of sleep, and exposure to weather played a part on Grenada. But not all exertion occurs on the ground. Pilots exhausted by low-level flight over long distances do not always function at full efficiency, as seen in Iran, at Calvigny, and over Libya. Commanders must know when to call for that last full measure from their men; when leaders guess incorrectly and press beyond human capacities, mishaps, aborts, and even failures result.

Clausewitz warned that "a great part of the information in war is contradictory, a still greater part is false, and by far the greatest part is doubtful." Despite satellites, signal intercepts, infrared photography, and other modern wizardry, intelligence still turns out to be inadequate, especially on short-notice expeditionary missions. The marines found plenty of Khmers and no American merchant seamen on Koh Tang; JTF 120 had to scour Grenada to find the bulk of the young people they had been sent to rescue. All one can do is weigh the possibilities and bring enough extra fighting power, or units with a wide range of abilities, to exploit unforeseen surprises rather than be exploited by them.

Finally, there are what Clausewitz called "innumerable trifling circumstances." Since humans make war, they make errors. The more complex the operation, the more likely that parts will break down or go awry. Perceptions can prove false, as for the 24th MAU in Lebanon. Snarled and missed communications played major roles in the Desert One failure, the muddled December 1983 air raid on Syrian air defenses, and the hasty helicopter assault on Calvigny barracks. Finally, odd phenomena and unexpected elements enter the fray: dust clouds in Iran or uninvited carabinieri at Sigonella. Simple, shrewd plans, flexibly executed, can beat back some of these frustrations.

Friction is equivalent to Murphy's Law, and neglect of this factor risks a major disaster. It was fully present during the seven American combat actions after the Indochina war, and when the participants accommodated friction, victory followed. Unfortunately, by scrutinizing minor military operations through highly focused lenses, the critics fault any action that falls short of perfection. But as Clausewitz warned, military operations cannot be perfect—it is not in their nature. One cannot remedy friction.

That realization, in essence, is what is lacking in many critiques of U.S. performances in these small conflicts. There is a feeling that somehow, because these engagements involve only a fraction of American might against Third World opposition, they should be textbook affairs. Armchair generals are not satisfied with a quick victory or low casualties; it should be quicker, and casualties of any kind are unacceptable. For these experts, every weapon, every commander, and every unit should enjoy unsurpassed success, because they are participating in "easy" little squabbles. But for those men under fire, the dogfight over Sidra or the defense of the marines' Beirut perimeter were not insignificant skirmishes. And, of course, the local adversaries might well be like the Khmer Rouge on Koh Tang, and fail to recognize their evident inferiority with a handy capitulation in the face of U.S. power.

In sum, Clausewitz cautioned against overreliance on the views of inexperienced thinkers: "Action in war is movement in a resistant medium. Just as a man immersed in water is unable to perform with ease and regularity the simplest and most natural of movements, that of walking, so in war, with ordinary powers one cannot keep even the line of mediocrity. This is why the correct theorist is like a swimming master, who teaches on dry land movements which are required in water, which must appear ludicrous to those who forget about the water. This is also why theorists who have never plunged in themselves, or who cannot deduce any generalizations from their experience, are impractical and even absurd, because they teach only what everyone knows—how to walk." Winning in expeditionary combat, or any warfare, is never a walkover, especially for those involved.

★ ★ ★ ★ ★

Having considered expeditionary battles since Vietnam with allowances for the influences of friction, are there any conclusions to be drawn from the U.S. experience? In recent missions, air strikes and special operations were the most prevalent types of combat, followed by amphibious assaults and ground defensive operations. Mass, flexibility, and command keyed the victories.

Since even the United States has finite military resources, what sort of forces provide the mass and flexibility that allow for success by imaginative local commanders? Aircraft carrier battle groups, special operations forces, and marines exhibited a terrific amount of versatility, and proved useful in a majority of the situations. These are the muscles and sinews of American power projection.

The aircraft carrier battle group is often criticized as an overly expensive relic of the Pacific war of 1941–45, and commentators speculate on the short lives these leviathans might lead in a nuclear war. Barring Armageddon, the

Types of U.S. Expeditionary Combat Operations 1975–1986

Operation	Mayaguez	Iran	Sidra	Lebanon	Grenada	Achille Lauro	Libya
Air to air combat			X				
Air strike vs. ship	X						X
Air strike vs. ground	X			X	X		X
Close air support	X				X		
Naval surface combat							X
Naval gunfire support	X			X	X		
Amphibious sea assault					X		
Amphibious air assault*	X				X		
Airborne drop					X		
Helicopter raid		X			X		
Ground attack	X				X		
Ground defense	X			X	X		
Special operations	X	X		?	X	X	

*Assaults to gain a lodgement versus limited objective, short-duration helicopter raids.

carriers have been well suited for a variety of missions, including air strikes at sea or ashore, cover for amphibious landings, sea control, and even odd jobs like launching the Iran helicopter contingent or snatching terrorists from midair. The power concentrated in the flattop, its brood of planes, and its brace of escorting warships has many aspects, from the subtlety of electronic eaves-dropping to the screaming lances of Harpoon missiles or the mighty hammer of air bombardment. Not surprisingly, the Reagan administration has built up fourteen of these carrier battle groups, with provisions for a fifteenth. These floating airfields and their sea and air outriders constitute a principal American advantage in the global balance of power. U.S. naval intelligence indicates that the Soviets are finally about to commission their first aircraft carrier. But for now, the USN sets the standard for large-deck flight operations and ancillary combat capabilities. America's superbly trained carrier groups have been ready whenever called upon.

Whereas aircraft carriers have clearly contributed to American successes, special operations forces have a more ambiguous record, although their services are in equal or perhaps even greater demand. The USAF 1st Special Operations Wing has always performed well, with yeoman service in the Iran rescue attempt

U.S. Armed Forces Expeditionary Participation 1975–1986

Force	Mayaguez	Iran	Sidra	Lebanon	Grenada	Achille Lauro	Libya
USN							
Carriers	X	X	X	X	X	X	X
Surface	X	X	X	X	X	X	X
Amphibs				X	X		
USAF							
Tactical	X						X
Airlift	X	X		X	X	X	
Tankers	X	X			X		X
Recon	X	X			X	X	X
USMC							
Ground	X			X	X		
Air		X		X	X		
USA							
Ground				X	X		
Air	X				X		
Special Ops							
Delta		X			X	X	
ST-6					X	X	
1st SOW		X			X		
ALLIES				X	X	X	

and during URGENT FURY. Navy SEAL Team 6 accomplished most of its difficult tasks on Grenada. The army's 160th Aviation Battalion trains very hard, but it took a terrible beating over the Spice Island. As for America's highly trained premier hostage rescue unit, Delta still awaits its first publicly acknowledged triumph to balance the sad images of the Desert One debacle and the disheartening repulse at Richmond Hill prison. Although hardly glamorous and largely neglected, Green Berets in Lebanon and psychological operations units in Grenada performed valuable, unique tasks in support of the conventional missions in progress. In the shadow of the expeditionary conflicts, Green Beret advisory teams served with distinction throughout the Third World, and with notable promise in El Salvador, a Vietnam on the verge of being won. In sum, the U.S. special warfare troops have evidenced plenty of skill and combat potential in many efforts, but their few significant failures show that there is still room for improvement.

Planners agree that much is expected from these units, but so far, they have yet to pull off an American equivalent of Entebbe. Recognizing the myriad of possible threats, the Department of Defense, under strong congressional prodding, has taken major measures to strengthen national special warfare capabilities. New equipment coming on line includes improved USAF MH-53J Pave Low, Army MH-60X Blackhawk, and Army MH-47E Chinook long-range helicopters, new MC-130H Combat Talon II transports, and refurbished AC-130U Spectre gunships. By 1992, these modified models will be supplemented by the truly unique MV-22 Osprey, a propeller plane with a tilting wing to permit vertical takeoff and landing. Ospreys might make a future version of EAGLE CLAW more viable. All services have taken steps to attract, recognize, and retain high-quality special troopers and commanders; for example, the army has established a distinct special operations branch for the officers and men traditionally seconded from other arms of the service. Finally, the somewhat ad hoc JSOC has been replaced by the unified U.S. Special Operations Command, a major organization on par with such regional headquarters as PACOM and EUCOM.

Curiously, despite much ink spilled on the supposedly arcane nature of special warfare, the most effective American special efforts since Vietnam have been carried out by conventional forces or special warfare units working conventionally. These include the convoluted but victorious *Mayaguez* recovery, the Rangers' and marines' swift Grand Anse raid, and the brilliantly executed interception of the *Achille Lauro* hijackers. American defense officials acknowledge that their strategy for dealing with demanding special warfare contingencies includes both dedicated special operations elements and general purpose forces. Simpler, regularly exercised conventional actions offer a useful complement that can offset the innate riskiness of special missions; Grenada offers the best example of such a concept in practice.

Along with the carriers and special units, the U.S. Marine Corps played a role in those expeditions necessitating land combat. With their own armor, artillery, engineers, sealift, helilift, and service support, backed up by powerful naval task forces, USMC battalion landing teams can deal with many unexpected situations, from handling civilian evacuations to conducting outright invasions. Without the full BLT, as at Koh Tang Island, the marines lose some of their intrinsic flexibility and much of their combat power. Marines regularly point out that they do their best work as assault troops. But their varied capabilities and availability offshore from trouble spots make them likely actors in any crisis requiring a ground force. Only Grenada, however, featured a traditional "hit the beach" situation; the Koh Tang rescue attempt and the confusing Lebanon deployment stretched marine ingenuity to the limit and, in Beirut, beyond. Like the carrier battle groups, the marines exist to project power. They, too, represent a major U.S. edge in comparison to the USSR. Of all the marines and naval infantry in the world, almost half wear the globe and anchor of the USMC.

If any element of the armed forces could be said to have disappointed American hopes after Vietnam, it is that darling of Southeast Asia, the helicopter. Many proponents warned that these ungainly aircraft were not panaceas for tactical problems, and recent U.S. experiences have proven that with a vengeance. Yes, they could go straight down, hover, and lift straight up. But when damaged, helicopters enjoy all the aerodynamic stability of a chipped brick. Finicky, complicated, fatiguing to fly and fly in, and vulnerable to the most unsophisticated air defenses, choppers have shown a wide panoply of definite limitations. Koh Tang, the bleak journey to Desert One, Richmond Hill, and Calvigny might well be warnings. The days of direct helicopter air assaults may be numbered. Like horse cavalry in the American Civil War, they may have to eschew shock action in favor of reconnaissance, flank security, and utility roles, not to mention their important logistic and transport assignments behind the main battle area. The U.S. Army recently established a new aviation branch to direct the many initiatives of its vast rotary wing fleet, and these aviators and their marine and USAF special operations colleagues would do well to consider the sobering performance of helicopters under direct fire during post-Vietnam combat.

In the final analysis, the real reason for the overall record of American success since the fall of Saigon does not revolve around arms or organizations, but people. U.S. unit quality has been uniformly good, a marked contrast from the ragged, dispirited remnants of the later Vietnam era. The leaders, especially those at the lower and middle level, have made a difference. Their insistence on quality paid off in battle. Even the setbacks were normally the result of misjudgments, not incompetence and never malice. Brigadier General S. L. A. Marshall aptly described the ethos of the men who inspired America's post-Vietnam expeditionary forces: "In any situation of extreme pressure or moral exhaustion, where the men cannot otherwise be rallied and led forward, officers are expected to do the actual, physical act of leading, such as performing the first scout or point." Lieutenant Colonel Randall Austin on the smoking green hell of Koh Tang, Sgt. Maj. Don Linkey in the burning transport plane at Desert One, Comdr. Henry Kleeman rolling into action over the Gulf of Sidra, Lt. Dave Hough on the firing line in wild Beirut, Capt. Frank Kearney among the exploding inferno of Calvigny barracks, and Col. Sam Westbrook under the streaking SAMs of Tripoli—they and many like them took charge when the going got tough. In the final reckoning, wars are won by men, not weapons. Fortunately, the United States has the right sort of men.

HISTORICAL PERSPECTIVE

JOHN SHY

THE AMERICAN MILITARY EXPERIENCE
History and Learning

Without a doubt the most traumatic event in American military history was the Vietnam War. Even before its final unraveling, it was obvious that an estrangement between the military and American society had taken place. The war cost 57,000 American lives and probably a million Vietnamese, it wounded 300,000 Americans, and it contributed to the slaughter in the "killing fields" of Cambodia. Billions of U.S. dollars failed to buy military success and inflation and dissent at home brought the American public to a point where it determined to halt America's "endless support of an endless war."

Inside the American military a massive deterioration in morale arose. Lieutenant George Crocker's (in the Rick Atkinson article) West Point classmates of 1966 resigned in unprecedented numbers. Their dismay was symptomatic of a malaise that affected the whole of the American military, both officers and enlisted men. The decision to wage war without calling up the reserve components caused critical shortages in middle ranks of the noncommissioned officer corps—sergeants and chief petty officers. Too many inexperienced "Shake and Bake NCOs" led disgruntled troops. Officer candidate schools reduced standards to produce new, desperately needed lieutenants. After the war ended Congress terminated the draft, which was the major source of manpower for the army and the promoter of "voluntary" enlistments in the other services. In a desperate effort to maintain manpower levels, the military kept too many personnel who would otherwise have been discharged. Indiscipline rates soared. Racial tensions and drug use rose in the barracks. It was not until the end of the 1970s that these problems were corrected and the military reasserted its discipline and standards of excellence.

In the dismay over the tragedy of Vietnam and in fear over the reaction to that event by both the American people and the American military, Professor John Shy of the University of Michigan composed this essay as a speech to the Army War College. Although he subsequently admitted that his concluding paragraph may have been too pessimistic, his integration of social science learning theory into historical analysis remains one of the classic commentaries on the American military tradition.

Central to his thesis is that the violence and infrequency of war results in a learning pattern determined not by proximity in chronological time, but rather by priority in historical time. During the first of his three periods of the American military past—the "age of survival," from the seventeenth century until 1815—the country developed the three fundamental and remembered characteristics of this tradition: first, a definition of nationhood that integrated military prowess with a disdain for military professionals; second, a quest for absolute military security and domination of one's opponents; and third, "an extraordinary optimism about what . . . could be achieved by the exertion of American military force." Each of these concepts found reinforcement in subsequent American conflicts through 1945.

It was after the Second World War that this tradition underwent considerable challenge. The contempt for military professionalism was modified, as the insecurity of the era required large and expensive regular establishments. The possibility of achieving absolute security seemed thwarted not only by the rising threat of nuclear holocaust, but also from the inconclusive ends of the wars in Korea and Vietnam. Finally, the optimistic expectation of eventual victory despite early defeats came unglued as our quests for military solutions in Korea and Vietnam failed.

Some of that frustration may be seen in initial enthusiastic response to General MacArthur's return from Korea. Some may be seen in the current debate over a Strategic Defense Initiative ("Star Wars") and its appeal for an umbrella of protection from intercontinental ballistic missiles. More may be seen in popular press depictions of military personnel as rank-hungry careerists with little respect for public opinion. In 1970 Professor Shy feared use of a "stab-in-the-back" psychology by military personnel and their supporters against the press and politicians. Was he justified? Is he justified today? Are Professor Shy's three basic components of the American military tradition beginning to reassert themselves in the 1990s?

An old, yet compelling idea states that international behavior may be best understood in terms of national peculiarities. In other words, a nation's behavior toward the rest of the world cannot be adequately explained as a function of the universal factors of power and interest when its behavior is irrelevant or even detrimental to those factors. And, as the debate over American international behavior has grown increasingly bitter, this idea has moved toward the center of a controversy among those who can agree only in their unhappiness with American foreign and military policy.

Within the current welter of criticism and conflicting interpretations of American international behavior, one can discern at least three basic types of explanation. The *accidental* type of explanation is proffered by those who insist that what they dislike is essentially a product of bad leadership: misinformation, lack of understanding, and poor control of the pressures of time and high office have caused mistakes that might have been avoided. Radically opposed to the accidental explanation are various *structural* explanations: a "military-industrial complex," or something similar, is viewed as having debased the process of rational thought and choice, and to be dictating decisions and policies which are harmful to the true interests of the society as a whole. The structural explanation implies conflict, because it assumes that there are intelligent, responsible people who have been overcome by others whose self-interest and political strength are produced by a level of annual military expenditure far exceeding the gross national product of all but a few other nations. A more sophisticated version of the structural explanation emphasizes less the machinations of a coalition of selfish, willful magnates than their more widely diffused way of seeing the outside world. "The military metaphysic" was Wright Mills' term for this world view, which never fails to find a foreign danger that will justify subordinating all other considerations to an ever inadequate, ever more costly, and ever bolder system of "national security." Marxist and neo-Marxist analysis provides the chief but by no means the only form of structural explanation—witness Eisenhower's Farewell Address. Superficially similar to the concept of a military metaphysic is the *cultural* form of explanation, which attributes unfortunate international behavior to some characteristic of American culture: racism, or endemic violence, or aggressive and materialist ethnocentrism. The difference between structural and cultural modes of explanation is clear: one points to powerful interest groups within the society, while the other points to the whole society. Yet both agree in asserting the importance of characteristically American patterns of behavior, as against those explanations that see no more than avoidable error and the accidents of personal choice.

None of these explanations are especially new or American. The behavior of Russia, and, before that, Germany, has been debated in much the same categories. The aberrant personalities of Hitler and Stalin, Prussian militarism or Nazi ideology and Communist conflict doctrine, German megalomania and Russian paranoia—each is respectively a crude version of accidental, structural, and cultural explanation. The disasters of the twentieth century have made the idea that there are national patterns of international behavior as attractive to some as it is repulsive to others, but the imaginations of all of us seem to be gripped by the thought. In addition, both structural and cultural explanations of behavior have been maddeningly vague and one-sided. They are so obviously linked to moral judgment and political argument that one has little confidence in the use and selection of evidence. More serious is their habitual failure either to deal with alternative explanations or to set forth criteria for testing any explanation, which may be to say only that the entire question of national character is extremely complex and far from being satisfactorily answered. And yet even after all of its deficiencies have been admitted, the idea that there are national patterns of international behavior retains an impressive degree of plausibility. The evidence seems too strong for serious doubt. Fuzzy as the idea may be, its intrinsic importance and the probability that it contains some measure of vital truth make it worth pursuing further.

This essay does not attempt to answer the question of national character, nor does it claim to remove any of the main weaknesses in that concept. It is open to the charge of trying to solve an undemonstrated problem, because it begins with the premise that American international behavior has been and is sufficiently unusual to require some unusual kind of explanation. It seeks to place that behavior in a historical context more satisfying than those offered by available modes of explanation which emphasize social structure or national culture. In particular, it is concerned with the military dimension of American behavior, with thought and action involving war and the threat or use of force.

★ ★ ★ ★ ★

We need at the outset to recognize that there is something peculiar about *all* military activity, and that its peculiarities demand attention. Military activity, compared to other forms of human activity, and considered historically along the dimension of time, is unique in two respects: it is violent, and it is episodic. Violence continues to be an area of great ignorance, even of mystery, and its primal quality, the way it touches the very root of our existence, ensures that the use or contemplation of violence will trigger the most powerful emotions. The episodic or intermittent character of warfare has less obvious effects, but they are no less important. Intense, usually quite brief, periods of military activity are separated by long, sometimes very long, periods in which the activity itself is replaced by anticipation of the military future, and by recollection of the military past. The key process is memory. Operating, as it must, in a climate of strong feeling and considerable ignorance induced by the violent nature of war, memory becomes a strange and selective thing; but the brevity, intensity, and relative infrequence of war drastically reduce the chance for military memory to become more empirical, to learn from the feedback of trial and error as men do in more continuous, less exciting, and better understood forms of activity. Again and again, we find military memory, under the pressures of war, failing to adapt readily to the unanticipated or unprecedented results of action, and, instead, trying to hammer facts into the mold of preconceptions derived from the remembered military past. Trench warfare in 1917, strategic bombing in 1943, and search-and-destroy missions in 1967 are only the most notorious cases in point. Shattering defeat may indeed traumatically change thinking, but fear, ignorance, and belief seem all but to strangle the capability for more gradual kinds of adjustment. We are speaking here not simply of military technicians or theorists, but of whole societies.

When we consider war in this way—not as a set of military operations, an instrument of policy, or an agent of social change, but as a recurrent activity, always intense, sometimes traumatic, which closely touches national identity— then we may reasonably look for help to whatever theory deals with the recurrent behavior of human beings. The very words ("learn," "memory") used to describe the subject suggest a relevant theory: the branch of psychology that deals with learning.

Elementary concepts of learning, which have a strong experimental foundation, appear most immediately useful:

— That learning occurs more readily through repeated encounters with what the learner perceives to be similar situations;
— That the learner tends to remember only those features of a recurrent situation that in some way dictate or control his "successful" response; and
— That the pattern of successful responses is best learned when it is "reinforced" by the experience of subsequent encounters.

Less self-evidently, learning theory teaches us that a certain lapse of time between encounters may actually strengthen learning in comparison with the results of a more nearly continuous set of encounters. Still more surprisingly, learning, in the sense of the tendency to repeat a pattern of responses, is further strengthened by "partial reward" or "intermittent reinforcement," which means that if the response is sometimes unsuccessful the learner will learn not to be discouraged by an occasional setback, and so will tend all the more to respond in the patterned way that he has previously learned. A corollary of the concept of intermittent reinforcement would seem to be that the learner-actor is made less sensitive to the "irrelevant" features of each situation, even to anomalous features which might otherwise suggest to him that the situation is essentially different from those about which he has previously learned. Finally, there are two experimentally derived hypotheses that appear useful for our purposes: One states that *infrequent* situations tend to be perceived in terms of a very small number of "preferred cues"; the other states that *complex* situations tend to be studied by the technique called "successive scanning." The two hypotheses converge when they are applied to situations that are both infrequent *and* complex; The use of "preferred cues" means reducing complexity to a few "key" features, while "successive scanning" means selecting information by a relatively clumsy method that leads to relatively simplistic conclusions; in terms of results, the one process sounds very much like the other.

The relevance, or at least the suggestiveness, of this body of theoretical insight for the historical study of war should be obvious. Wars are recurrent, remembered, similar, separated by intervals of time, various in form and outcome, relatively infrequent in the life of an individual or a generation, and highly complex. That the behavior associated with war is often "traditional," insensitive to nuance, inflexible, compulsive, and simplistic hardly needs demonstration. One may object, however, to the intrusion of theory by asking what historical insight it offers that might not be attained as easily and more safely from a direct study of historical data and a normal exercise of historical imagination. A preliminary answer to the question is that the use of learning theory in the study of the military history of American society reverses a frequent, but rarely articulated, common-sense approach to the analysis of contemporary military affairs. This approach rests on the working assumption that the current significance of an event decreases directly with its distance in time from the present: the more remote, the less likely it is to be important. Thus, all events before 1945 or 1940 may be relegated to an introductory "background," and those before 1900 or 1890 may be ignored. Learning theory invites us to challenge this common-sense approach by considering the possibility that the explanatory importance of events should be reckoned not by *proximity*, but by *priority* in historical time.

Learning theory, applied to the military history of a whole society, obviously entails assumptions and biases of its own. One is that a society and a person are not crucially dissimilar, and that individual and collective perception, memory, and behavior may be treated as comparable. Another is that time will be measured less in days or years than in decades and centuries, and action less in terms of the differences and conflicts that divide society than in terms of the shared attitudes that unite it. By thus measuring long-run continuity and broad consensus, rather than change or internal conflict, we are regarding American society as in some sense a living organism whose behavior reveals coherence and consistency, and which can be said to learn from and remember its military past. We are saying, in effect, that the emotional stress of combat, the enduring mysteries of violence, and the intermittent character of war create a situation not unlike that created by a psychologist in his laboratory when he examines perception and action, under conditions of ignorance and stress, by means of intermittent encounters. Using this conception of military history, we raise questions about the American military experience—about what patterns are evident in that experience, about how that experience has been perceived, and about how discrete episodes appear to be related in time. Instead of assuming that nothing prior to the steam engine or the machine gun or the atomic bomb or America's rise to world power is relevant to what happened subsequently, we assume that a remembered past has always more or less constricted both action in the present and thinking about the future.

★ ★ ★ ★ ★

Let us begin by dividing almost four centuries of military experience into smaller units of time, according to major changes in the historical situation. The seventeenth and eighteenth centuries appear as the first natural unit: they represent not merely "colonial background," but a formative period of quite serious military troubles which gave rise to considerable anxiety and led to ways of thinking about war, and of acting in war, that set British North America clearly apart from Europe. To call these first centuries an age of survival may seem hyperbolic, but military "survival," at least in a political if not a physical sense, was an important question for American society even to the end of the War of 1812. The second natural period, a golden age, or "age of free security" as Woodward has called it, was the nineteenth century. There were of course wars and rumors of war in the nineteenth century, and it is possible to argue that the Civil War is the most important single episode in American history. But it is unreasonable to argue, as has recently been tried, that the nineteenth century was almost as full of real and perceived military perils and problems as is our own time. The truth is that for about a century after 1815 American society enjoyed, and was conscious of enjoying, a remarkable freedom from external military threat.

Exactly when the age of free security ended is a complex question, and the answer depends very much on our perspective. Woodward selects 1945; other historians would point to 1898. But the emerging tendencies of the third age, our own age, are clear enough. To call the twentieth century an age of power and insecurity sounds like a textbook cliché, but such a label is an accurate and useful characterization. On the one hand, by the turn of the century there was a growing sense of insecurity, of new threats perceived although the specific dangers could not, and even now cannot, be clearly defined. On the other hand, as American society itself grew in numbers and wealth, there was a growing accumulation of potential military power, with no apparent economic or demographic limits on how much military power it might be possible to accumulate. The limits of American power were thus not seen to be intrinsic, as they were in France, for example, but rather were to be set by the political process, which presumably would establish them on the basis of some strategic calculation. But without clearly defined dangers, such calculations could not be made, at least not convincingly, and any politically established level of military power inevitably seemed arbitrary. These, then, are the principal features of American military experience since the end of the nineteenth century: military insecurity without a clear definition of danger, and military power without any apparent limits—the two constantly interacting to produce a kind of military indeterminacy, and giving a name to our own age of power and insecurity.

With the basic outline of American military experience established, we can now turn to the most important relationships and patterns within this general framework.

★ ★ ★ ★ ★

The first English colonies were planted in an extraordinarily violent and ideologically polarized period of Western history. It is an obvious point, but one that American historians for some reason have frequently ignored. They have tended instead to treat colonization as a successful flight from European violence and insecurity, as indeed it was seen by many colonists themselves; but to view colonization in that way hardly reduces the historical significance of this particular aspect of the environment in which the colonies originated. The early history of any seventeenth-century colony, even as late as the settlement of Pennsylvania and South Carolina, reveals that these were dangerous times, with violent people and tough leaders who felt the dangers keenly and were ready to use violence themselves. The frightfulness of the Thirty Years War, which coincided with the settlement of Virginia and Massachusetts, had been prefigured in late Elizabethan Ireland, and Irish pacification and early American colonization were closely related in method, problems, and personnel. We should remember, for example, that, while Sir Humphrey Gilbert allegedly prayed aloud when his ship foundered on his last voyage to the New World, he was much better known to contemporaries for the way he had lined the path to his tent with the severed heads of Irish peasants. Gilbert and his numerous English successors knew very well that their ventures in the Western Hemisphere were semi-military, semi-piratical intrusions on the established empire of Spain and the antecedent colonial claims of France. The likelihood of violent consequences was never far from their minds.

The irony is that during most of the seventeenth century these European threats failed to materialize. Instead, the chief threat came from those on whom considerable hopes had been centered. Conversion of Indians to Christianity stood higher among the priorities of early English colonizers, even in Virginia, than is usually recognized, and serious (though ultimately futile) efforts were devoted to that end. But the normal pattern of Anglo-Indian relations became one not of Christian conversion and worship, but of uneasy truce, punctuated by incredibly barbaric warfare, often followed by migration or subjugation. From about 1650 to about 1750, when European states were moving toward forms of military organization, techniques of fighting, goals of foreign policy, and a generally accepted code of military and diplomatic behavior that eliminated or mitigated the worst effects of warfare on society, the English colonists in North America found themselves reenacting on a small scale the horrors of Irish pacification and the Thirty Years War.

There is no need to exaggerate either the frequency of Indian warfare or the vulnerability of colonial society to it, but the difference between American and European military experience in this period is unmistakable and extremely important. The colonies did not have the means to create a hard military shell, composed of specialists, that could protect the soft center of society, composed of the great mass of people, nor would such a shell have been effective against Indian tactics. The colonies, as they became more heavily and densely populated, soon acquired a high military potential, much greater than that of even the strongest Indian tribes, but they never had more than a fairly low capacity for effective self-defense. The distinction between potential strength and defensive capacity is crucial. Moreover, the fighting strength of the colonies was mobilized in wartime only at the price of considerable social disruption caused by the militia system—a general, unspecialized obligation for military service. With great strength but weak defenses, the colonies experienced warfare less in terms of protection, of somehow insulating society against external violence (as was increasingly true of European warfare), than in terms of retribution, of retaliating against violence already committed.

The consequences of this situation would surely have been much less severe if, at the time when hostile Indians were losing their own capacity to do really serious harm to the English settlements, a long period of war between England and France, usually joined by Spain, had not begun. Both sides used Indian auxiliaries against the other, but the English were far more numerous; as a result, the relative weakness of the thinly populated neighboring French and Spanish settlements, plus the costliness and inefficiency of regular troops transported to the Western Hemisphere, forced the French and Spanish to depend heavily on Indian allies, and thus on the forms of Indian warfare. The effect was to perpetuate, and in some areas of English settlement even to intensify, the quality of the seventeenth-century military experience. This effect was further reinforced because these new dangers could be perceived in terms of anti-Catholicism, just at a time when religious antagonism was no longer a major factor in European diplomacy and warfare.

These European wars in America, like the purely Indian wars before them, puzzled and frustrated the English colonists. Invariably war originated in Europe, beyond their reach and even their understanding. Its causes had nothing to do with anything that had happened or been done in the colonies, or so it seemed, but every European war meant inevitable and often horrible death and suffering in the Western Hemisphere. Schemes of neutralization were tried but soon broke down. The delicate territorial adjustments of European diplomacy had no meaning in a wilderness where boundaries were seldom known (even when they could be established) and never respected, just as the elaborate defensive arrangements of forts and lines that suited the Low Countries or the Po Valley were almost completely ineffective where spaces were vast and armies ill-trained and numerically small.

Strong but highly vulnerable, angered and frightened by repeated and ruthless attack, bewildered by the causes of war, disrupted by its effects, and powerless to prevent it, articulate English colonists by the end of the seventeenth century were making extreme proposals for the solution of their military problem. Nothing would do, they wrote, but the complete elimination of French and Spanish power from North America; anything less, it was claimed by those who purported to speak for America, was worse than useless, because it would create a false sense of security. Of course these were fantastic demands by European standards; territorial exchanges and adjustments followed every eighteenth-century war, but the actual conquest and retention of large spaces was too costly militarily and too dangerous diplomatically. When the fortress of Bergen-op-Zoom—a place few colonists could have found on a map—fell to the French in 1747, it became necessary to give Cape Breton Island back to France after Massachusetts had seized it in 1745. These were the rules of the game, but the Americans wanted to change them. Even the Anglicized, judicious, and irenic Benjamin Franklin is found in 1760 reiterating what was by then the classic American demand for a definitive military solution. After recounting the atrocities of the French and Indian wars, he called for the "extirpation" of the French in Canada because of their manifold wickedness. He was writing for the public, to be sure, but there is no evidence to suggest that he did not sincerely believe every word that he wrote.

Several things may be said about this typically American belief that nothing less than a complete solution was required to solve the problem of American military security: One is that it seems a not unreasonable response to difficult military circumstances; another is that it was grossly unrealistic in terms of normal eighteenth-century international relations; a third is that in three great wars, from 1760 to 1815, it was almost completely realized. Precisely how and why an understandable but unrealistic belief which gave rise to a set of fantastic demands was translated into concrete reality is an interesting story; but more important here is the fact of realization itself.

Considered together, from the American point of view, the Seven Years War (1755–63), the Revolutionary War (1775–83), and the War of 1812 reveal a remarkable pattern. In each the very existence of American society was seen to be at stake; invasion and early defeats brought hopes in each of these wars to low ebb. But early setbacks were followed by military recovery, perseverance, and ultimate victory. And the magnitude of victory was the most remarkable and important similarity of all. In 1763, following British naval success so great as to be politically and diplomatically embarrassing, all French and Spanish power on the North American continent east of the Mississippi was actually "extirpated." The British government paid for these extraordinary military and diplomatic results when, twenty years later, isolated by its own success, it was forced by a hostile France, an unfriendly Europe, and rebellious Americans to give to the new United States most of what had been previously won. And thirty years later the United States, caught squarely between Napoleonic France and its strongest enemy, emerged from an unwanted war with a virtual (and within a few years obvious) guarantee that the threat of European military intervention in American affairs was finally at an end.

More might be said about the specific impressions created in the American mind by these great wars. Here it is enough to recognize their impact in a general way. Each war had a rhythm of defeat, despair, endurance, and victory. Each repetition of that rhythm reinforced the impression first made by the Seven Years War. Seen altogether and in conjunction with the earlier colonial experience, these wars repeated on a grand historical scale their own internal rhythmic structure: from the frequent little disasters and occasional despair of colonies that had been beset for a century by ruthless Indians and apparently "implacable" Catholics, to the recovery, total victory, and unique security of a free, successful, and republican nation.

★ ★ ★ ★ ★

The military experience of those first two centuries was described earlier as formative, and that description seems to be true in a quite literal way. American society entered its age of free security with certain military attitudes which had already been implanted and powerfully reinforced: (1) a deep respect for the kind of military prowess that had become so closely bound up with the very definition of American nationhood, a respect tinged with contempt for military professionalism which was viewed as unnecessary, ineffectual, and thus somehow un-American; (2) a concept of military security that was expressed not in relative but in absolute terms (the society knew both extremes: what had seemed to be total military insecurity, and what now looked like total military security—though opposite, the two were perceptually linked); and, (3) an extraordinary optimism about what, when necessary, could be achieved by the exertion of American military force, as the three wars demonstrated beyond all doubt.

Little happened in the nineteenth century to call any of these attitudes into question, and much to reinforce them still further. In particular, the belief that military security was an absolute value, like chastity or grace, and that

American society had been granted it, presumably deserved it, and ought to be able to keep it, was verified simply by the passage of time without the appearance of any perceptible threat. Foreign relations ceased to attract the popular and political attention that they had received for so long. American diplomacy became increasingly free-wheeling, even careless and bombastic, but the occasional confrontations with a European Power—with Spain over Florida after the War of 1812, with all the Powers over Latin American independence and recognition in the 1820s, with France over unpaid American claims in the 1830s, with Britain over Oregon in the 1840s, again with France over Mexico in the 1860s, with Germany over Samoa in the 1880s, with Britain and Germany over Venezuela at the end of the century—always ended in what looked very much like a Great Power back-down. And in fact no Great Power could find that its interests were served by pushing disagreement with the inept, unpredictable, but very numerous Americans to the point of war.

The several wars actually fought by the United States during the nineteenth century can be divided into two categories: the Civil War, and all the others. The others—the Mexican War, the Spanish-American War, and the many small wars against various Indian tribes—are a disparate group, but they have essential features in common. The causes of each could be traced back to atrocious behavior by the enemy: the usual murders and mutilation connected with every Indian War, the massacres of the Alamo and Goliad by the Mexicans, and the brutal pacification policies of the Spanish in Cuba. Enemy atrocities were by no means the only or even the main cause of these wars, and in all of them Americans themselves flagrantly broke the rules of civilized warfare—the Illinois militia in the Black Hawk War, Texans at San Jacinto, and the U.S. Army during the Philippine insurrection committed some major atrocities of their own. But the main point is that it was very easy for Americans to explain and justify the outbreak of war in terms of the criminal conduct of an inhuman, perhaps degenerate, foe. And once Americans had been attacked and killed, whether they were a few Western farmers or fur traders, a detachment of soldiers on the Rio Grande, or sailors on a battleship in Havana harbor, other arguments about the causes and the objectives of war came to seem irrelevant.

Each of these nineteenth-century wars also ended in a similar way, with an important extension of American territory and control. A defeated Indian tribe could mean the opening of a future state to American settlement; the Mexican War secured an enormous southwestern territory for the United States; and the war with Spain brought in its wake Hawaii, the Philippines, and new bases in the Pacific and Caribbean. These gains were not the avowed war aims of the United States, nor even the conscious objectives of most war leaders; rather, they seemed, under the circumstances, to be the natural rewards of superior virtue and military skill.

Perhaps the most important similarity of these wars is that in every one the enemy was very weak and easily beaten. There were, obviously, military difficulties: the old Duke of Wellington believed—with some reason—that Winfield Scott would be defeated before he could get his army to Mexico City; the Seminoles in Florida fought tenaciously, and, of course, the Sioux defeated General Custer in 1876; and Colonel Theodore Roosevelt thought that the American military situation was desperate during the siege of Santiago. But in the end the United States always managed to achieve an overwhelming victory at a fairly small cost. Nothing happened in any of these wars to shake American optimism about the ability of the society to use military force successfully, and a great deal happened to strengthen further that already well established attitude.

The Civil War is obviously a quite different case. As the bloodiest war in American history, and as unmistakable evidence of failure in American society, we might expect the Civil War to have disrupted or rearranged the evident patterns of American military experience. The curious fact is that it did not have this effect, and the important question is, why not? We have already noted that the key to understanding the deeper effects of the other wars of the nineteenth century is the weakness of the enemy. There is a comparable key to understanding the Civil War; that key is *symmetry*. Both sides were American, and both went to war with a characteristic American optimism about its outcome. Both had to start from scratch and improvise huge war machines, so neither had any immediate military advantage over the other in the beginning. Both sides had been schooled in the same ways of looking at war and both drew their military cadres from the same source, so there was little sense that a tradition was being tested by a new, external standard. Although the human damage done to American society by the Civil War was comparable to that done to European society by World War I, the fact that it was a civil war protected Americans against many of its potentially traumatic effects. A long, bloody stalemate might logically have shattered optimistic ideas about the use of armed force, but with Americans on both sides it was possible to regard the Civil War as a military anomaly— an exceptional case that proved nothing. The only mistake seen in retrospect was that of underestimating the fighting qualities of other Americans. The concept of "intermittent reinforcement," which explains how perversely the mind may read lessons into a single unhappy experience, helps us to understand why the Civil War may have even strengthened an older, seemingly inappropriate pattern of perception and response.

Because the South lost the war, some historians have argued that the experience of military defeat changed that region in fundamental ways, setting it apart from the rest of American society and producing much of its odd behavior over the next hundred years. If their argument is sound, we

would have to modify our own argument that the Civil War was a symmetri-
cal experience in which the military resultant was close to zero. But those
who stress the peculiar impact of defeat on the South may not have grasped
the nature of Southern "defeat."

When the Confederacy gave up, its main armies had been destroyed, its
people were tired, and its resources depleted. Continued military resistance,
however, was possible and was seriously considered at the time. There were
historical precedents for such resistance in the American Revolution and the
Spanish opposition to Napoleon, and later it would become common for wars
of national independence to be carried on with few resources and without
conventional military means. The defeat of regular armies does not, in itself,
explain capitulation when manpower, basic weapons, and the will to resist
are still present, as they were in 1865. The vast spaces, rural economy, and
poor transportation system of the South were ideal factors for an effective
large-scale resistance movement along guerrilla lines, and it seems reasonable
to believe that the South could have been made virtually indigestible for a
Federal army which was not much larger and had far less mobility and
firepower than the American force presently in South Vietnam. Whether a
resistance movement would have drawn clandestine support, from blockade
running and through the trans-Mississippi area, is of course problematical,
but here again other historical examples indicate that the small increment of
outside help needed to keep a guerrilla war alive could have been found.
Jefferson Davis had said in his inaugural address that no sacrifice would be too
great to secure Southern independence, but Southern leaders decided instead
to give up in 1865.

By quitting when they did, Southerners were able to believe that they
had fought as long as they could, which was true by strictly conventional
standards. Defeat was thus honorable. But they saved more than honor; they
saved the basic elements—with the exception of slavery itself—of the Southern social, that is to say racial, order. The social order could not possibly have
survived the guerrilla warfare which a continued resistance movement would
have required. Too many Negroes, a large part of the "people" on which
guerrillas must depend, had already voted with their feet. By saving honor
and preserving the social order, Southerners could claim that they had won a
moral, if not a military, victory. And historians, from Buck to McKitrick,
have explained how the Federal government and the people of the North,
both deliberately and unwittingly, did not effectively refute the Southern
claim to moral victory, but even sustained it, virtually conspiring with the
South to prove that no one—no white man at least—had really lost the Civil
War, and to demonstrate that both sides, as Americans, should take the
brave deeds and great men of the war as their own. The national cult of

Robert E. Lee is only the most obvious case in point. The conspiracy survived until it died amidst the mawkish sentimentality of the Civil War Centennial, appropriately killed by the Civil Rights Movement. Before the conspiracy died, however, it had successfully drawn most of the psychological sting of defeat, although Southerners have often found it useful to play the role of a defeated and oppressed people, in part because so many Northerners have been such a sympathetic audience. For our purpose in describing the quality of the American military experience, we can simply note that the Civil War did surprisingly little to change basic American patterns of thought and action.

★ ★ ★ ★ ★

At this point, before entering the twentieth century, we should pause to reconsider the approach we have been taking to the American military past. There can hardly be any question that, whenever Americans before the end of the nineteenth century thought about questions of war or military force, their perception of those questions was strongly affected by certain peculiar attitudes and beliefs that, through the conditioning effect of long historical experience, had become almost reflexive. A dichotomous idea of national security, an unthinking optimism about the natural American aptitude for warfare, and an ambivalent attitude toward those Americans who specialized in the use of force, all have had consequences in the twentieth century, and it is easy enough to speculate about what those consequences have been. But it is difficult to continue the discussion beyond 1900 in quite the way that we have carried it on so far. Before 1900, military history is a rather amorphous and often peripheral aspect of American society. Only sporadically, even in the colonial period, were military problems of central, explicit concern, while military institutions hardly existed apart from the inherent military strength of the whole society. But by 1900 this situation was changing. The problem of military security, in one form or another, began—very slowly at first—to move toward the center of politics; and military institutions—again almost imperceptibly—began to play an expanded social role. All public issues came to be touched by the growing consciousness of military problems, until at last a conservative President, a former general, could warn the nation of the peril of a garrison state. Accordingly, as it becomes more difficult to isolate military experience, our analysis must become more complex.

On the very general level on which we have been operating so far, we can say that, regarded in military terms, American involvement in both World Wars certainly further reinforced historically implanted attitudes and beliefs. Delayed entry in both wars, followed by fairly uninterrupted progress toward victory, made it possible in each case for Americans to overlook the extent to which France, Britain, and Russia had worn down German strength, and instead to believe that the United States had really won the war. Even at the tactical level, American self-confidence was confirmed. General John Pershing's naive demand for a return to open-field tactics could be realized only under the special conditions of 1918, while the success of the Normandy landings in 1944 seemed to prove that the British had been unduly timid in their long argument with Americans about the feasibility of a cross-channel attack. In other respects, the historic American outlook helps to explain what otherwise might be hard to understand. Only a fundamental self-confidence in the ability to fight, combined with a Manichaean idea of security, made it natural to wait so long, to be so peace-loving, before intervening in these World Wars, and then to intervene so massively on every front. Although Woodrow Wilson had earlier—and accurately— proclaimed peace without victory as the only satisfactory outcome for the United States, he responded to an essentially limited attack—submarine warfare—in a way that made a stalemate peace impossible, and thus guaranteed overwhelming Allied victory. Franklin D. Roosevelt and his advisers had agreed in 1940 that Germany was the principal threat to American security, but virtually nothing was done to avert war with Japan, nor, once it had begun, was its prosecution kept strictly subordinate to European strategy. Even the remarkable position of American military leaders in both wars, with strong political support but with little effective political guidance, reflects the ambivalent position of the military profession in American society.

By looking at twentieth-century American military experience in this way, we have simply extended an approach that seeks to define a broad consensus on military questions, an image of war which helps to explain the military behavior of the society as a whole. It does not emphasize technical military theories, which are international and not merely American in scope, and which actively interest only a small fraction of the society. We do know that American military leaders, from George Washington to William Sherman, were more responsive than is generally realized to European modes of military thought. Yet we are able to subordinate such technical military ideas to broader and cruder forms of thought because, prior to about 1890, technical military thinking never played more than a secondary role. But by the end of the nineteenth century, when the rate of change in the technology of warfare had, in a few decades, become perhaps as great as it is today, military theory assumed an importance, even in American society, that requires us to treat it as a primary and independent variable.

If we focus on these technical ideas in the period since 1890, particularly on those that have become fully articulated and clearly differentiated systems of military thought (which may be called doctrines), we encounter an interesting fact: Of about a half-dozen doctrines which have informed Western military behavior in the twentieth century, three of them reached their most complete development in the United States.

The doctrines, to describe them in their own technical terms, are those of Sea Power, Strategic Air Attack, and Limited War or, as it came to be known, Flexible Response. The doctrine of sea power as it was developed by Alfred T. Mahan stated that by offensive action a concentrated battle fleet could effectively deny the use of the sea to inferior naval forces and could pierce the coastal defense of any hostile power. The doctrine of strategic air attack, not an American invention but adopted and enthusiastically implemented by the United States, asserted that the hard military shell around the soft center of a modern industrial society could be outflanked from the air, with the result that the capacity of such a society to wage war could be quickly and completely destroyed. The doctrine of flexible response, a product of the great debate over military policy in the 1950s and a military reality only in the last decade, states that violence in any form can most effectively be dealt with by equivalent violence.

These technical doctrines have guided both thought and action on much broader issues involving war because they have had a responsive audience outside the narrow circle of military technicians. Theodore Roosevelt, Brooks Adams, and many other American intellectuals found Mahan's ideas exciting and persuasive.* Strategic air doctrine was worked out at Maxwell Field, but it was also actively promoted in the popular press, and its wide appeal was reflected, for example, in the columns of the *New Republic*, in the isolationist attack on Roosevelt by Charles Lindbergh, and in Roosevelt's own first decisions on strategy in 1938 and 1940. Flexible response is a product less of the Pentagon than of American universities, and it could never have been realized without first capturing the imagination of the Kennedy Administration.

Equally important is the fact that each doctrine emerged from a crisis within the military profession. More than military professionals in other societies, American career officers have always felt a special need to justify

---

* In addition to the three doctrines discussed below, the others may be described as the doctrines of the Short Total War (exemplified in pre-1914 war planning, which stressed the offensive power of mass armies and the fragility of modern industrial society), Blitzkrieg (which in both its German and Japanese forms stressed lightning thrusts for limited ends, to be followed by consolidation and defense of *faits accomplis*), and *Guerre révolutionnaire* (usually involving guerrilla warfare but always combining political and military action, directed at the masses, for either revolutionary or counterrevolutionary ends). Others that might be considered, although they never achieved the same state of definition or acceptance, were doctrines of Material Attrition (Western Front in World War I, and German and American use of submarine blockade) and Psychological Attrition (Sir Basil Liddell Hart's concept of the Indirect Approach). Still others, like American amphibious doctrine, never reached the level of uniting political and military aspects of warfare.

their very existence. But there were truly critical periods for the Navy in the 1880s, for the new Air Corps in the 1920s, and for the Army in the decade after 1945. In these times of professional crisis, when it seemed as if a particular military service might almost wither away in the absence of any clear need for what it could do best, the doctrines of sea power, strategic air attack, and flexible response each carried considerable justificatory power on behalf of the service so threatened. Under the circumstances peculiar both to American society and to the particular crisis, it is not surprising that each doctrine was adopted and promoted with a zeal that blinded its proponents to alternative possibilities and to its inherent shortcomings.

Each doctrine can also be associated with an epoch of American foreign policy: sea power with imperialism and active intervention, especially in the Caribbean but also in the Far East; strategic air attack with isolationism not only in the inter-war period but also in the sector of post-war strategy that depended solely on the threat to retaliate massively; and flexible response with global containment of Communist-supported revolution. The connections between technical doctrine and broad patterns of foreign policy are not all immediately obvious, and, especially in the case of the relationship between air power doctrine and isolationism, it is necessary to go beyond the apparent contradictions in order to see the underlying positive connections. But, in every case, military doctrine and foreign policy have been mutually and dynamically reinforcing.

This brings us to the last point about these doctrines: Do they reveal, when considered sequentially, some kind of fundamental shift during the twentieth century, or since 1945, in the characteristic American outlook on war, some new lessons from new experience? A positive answer might seem obviously in order, because in substance each doctrine differs markedly from the others, and each was developed in bitter opposition to what had preceded it. Sea power doctrine was a critique of traditional defensive notions of American security in the same way that strategic air doctrine exploited the revealed weaknesses of sea power, and "limited-war" thinking grew out of the logical and practical deficiencies of thermonuclear retaliation. Moreover, all seem to break with a more distant past in their emphasis on offensive military action, and the flexible-response doctrine explicitly repudiates what were taken to be traditional American ideas about the all-or-nothing use of force.

Even when all of the above is conceded, the elements of continuity are still most impressive: New ideas were absorbed and reshaped by old, deeply imbedded modes of thinking about war. Certainly the curious historical position of the military profession in American society helps to account for the passionate, often obsessive, espousal of these doctrines by segments of the military elite. But the doctrines have also had great political and even social resonance. They have not only underpinned foreign policy; at times they have themselves created foreign policy, as in 1964–65, when the existence of military force and a doctrine for its employment seemed to move into a vacuum of informed and constructive political thinking. This resonance is fully explained only when we see how each doctrine has rested upon, and drawn upon for emotional sustenance, the characteristic attitudes and beliefs that were implanted, transmitted, and reinforced by almost four centuries of American military experience. Each doctrine incorporates within it something like what we have called an absolute or dichotomous conception of security. The United States is secure, or it is not; it is threatened, or it is not. None of the doctrines, even flexible response, really allows for differences in the degree or quality of the threat. Both sea and air doctrine argue that effective military action must be total, and that anything less is worse than useless. The doctrine of flexible response, while stating that force should be carefully proportioned to the military strength of the threatening force, implies that *all* unfriendly force endangers American security and so deserves forceful confrontation; it explicitly rejects the inherently passive posture of merely theatening to retaliate. All three doctrines also incorporate an extremely optimistic view of the skill with which American society can use force; in all three, there is a promise that, if the doctrine is followed, military success will be surgically swift and effective.

What has happened in the twentieth century is that, amidst rapid military and social change and unprecedented kinds of military experience, American society has been able to find—unconsciously, of course—the intellectual and psychological means to preserve much of an older response to military problems, and to preserve within that response much of its primitive force.

★ ★ ★ ★ ★

Throughout this essay, historical data have been ordered to fit the presumption that a society learns about war in much the same way that a rat learns to find food in a laboratory maze, or a child learns to cope with strange animals. As noted in the beginning, there are difficulties with such an approach. One, clearly, is evidential. Has anything been demonstrated beyond reasonable doubt? The answer is No. Once the theory is invoked, the data fall into place and the patterns become visible, but the relationship of act-thought-act remains unproved in any specific case, and is not easily reduced to a hypothetical statement which the historian can test by his usual methods. A second, theoretical difficulty follows closely on the first: May not military activity within American or any society be explained by other than prior military experience? The answer, surely, is Yes. Domestic political crisis, economic interest, child-rearing practices, the behavior of the enemy—any or all might indeed be part of complete explanation in a given case. The weakness here lies with the theory, which isolates the learner from the total context of his life. A third difficulty, mentioned earlier, is in the peril of equating an entire society with a biological individual; we have not been applying theory in any strict sense, but have simply been using a theoretical analogy.

Even faced with these unresolved difficulties, we can conclude that, in the future, those who seek to explain American governmental or popular behavior on issues involving war and the military must ask more seriously than they have before to what extent they are dealing with learned responses which operate beneath the level of full consciousness. The general national perception of the ethics and uses of war, and of the status and character of the military, is not the only important factor to be considered in understanding behavior in a particular war or positions taken on a question of military policy; but this perception is clearly a major factor, especially in American society with its unique pattern of military experience. Yet this perception is consistently ignored, partly because the time-frame of military studies is usually too short to take most sequential relationships into account, partly because the very notion of learned perception and response has seemed unusably vague.

Beyond its relevance to American society, the hypothesis that national military behavior is in a real sense learned behavior should have value for the study of any modern nation, or perhaps of any society. Certainly the constantly reinforcing pattern of American military experience has been extraordinary, just as the relationship between popular sentiment and governmental action has been exceptionally close throughout American history. Yet less democratic societies, with more varied military experiences, must also have learned to perceive military situations and to respond to them in ways that differentiate one society from another. Merely to ascribe significantly different patterns or styles of military behavior to differences in objective conditions—to size, wealth, geography, vulnerability, etc.—is to beg the difficult question of why nations often wage war in "strange" ways. We ask why governments collapse under military pressure, or capitulate, or run inordinate, even suicidal risks; why societies are militarily aggressive or apathetic, resist or yield under assault; why one, and not another, of several equally "rational" choices is selected. Definitive answers are probably beyond our power, but surely an approximation of truth must take into account the deep, primitive understanding of what war means in the life history of the tribe.

A last word is prompted by the admission that we have been using not a theory but an analogy. This admission gives us the freedom to look for other theoretical analogies in considering the present and future implications of our picture of the American military past. The nation appears to have reached a stage where its military learning is no longer appropriate, and so we wonder about the process of un-learning. Learning theory treats the so-called "extinction" of learning, but the theoretical discussion does not fit either the data or our impressions as well as before; extinction of learning appears in the literature as a relatively tame and straightforward process compared to what we know about the convulsions of American society during the last five years. Our own historical analysis suggests that something more profound than "rat-finds-cheese" occurred in the course of several centuries of national military experience. The facts alone—that no other nation, not even Wilhelmine Germany, has had its official origin (Revolutionary War) and constitutional preservation (Civil War) so clearly linked to warfare, or has acquired such overwhelming military power after seeming so vulnerable— indicate that Freud and Erikson speak more directly to our current situation than do Pavlov and his successors.

If warfare is as tightly bound up with American national identity as the body of this essay argues, then we will need theories of personality, and not merely of learning, to help us understand the present and even anticipate the future. What we find is a suggestion that our current condition is pathological, and that a considerable disruption of national personality is inevitable. The first symptoms appeared during the Korean War. Even if military failure can be acknowledged, the crisis will be displaced onto other objects, and the costs to the organism will still be very high. Already there are signs that the military profession, and not just an occasional General Edwin Walker or Curtis Lemay, is losing touch with its ambivalent but satisfying role, a role which was largely self-policed. For the first time, American soldiers may be as despised as they have liked to claim to be when they were not. Disappointment and disgust with failures, as much as moral and political disapproval of wrong policies, have provided the emotional fuel for antiwar action. Even the outrage of the young indicates how far they were taught to expect a smoother, cleaner American military performance, and how little prepared they were to face the prospect of military failure; their expectations and standards for judging international behavior are as inordinately high as those of a John Foster Dulles or a Lyndon B. Johnson. For the first time, very large numbers of ordinary Americans as well as their leaders are deeply ashamed of their national identity, but see no effective remedy. Many of them no doubt have moments when they think that they and the nation will ride it out, that the

Ten Years' War is only a bad dream which will soon be over and forgotten, that the social and psychic damage can be limited, and that other issues, other dangers are really more urgent. Perhaps so; all gloomy prediction is mere speculation. Nothing, however, in the historical record gives much support to their modest optimism. On the contrary, the American military past, if I have interpreted it correctly, warns us that the effects of confessed failure are likely to be protracted, unpredictable, and severe.